Dear Professor,

We want to take a moment to introduce you to our new Introductory Criminology textbook.

If you're like us, you're usually interested in new titles that come across your desk and you'll jump straight to the table of contents. If you've already done so with our text, you've probably noticed we are taking an exciting new approach in applied learning. Most books—perhaps some you have used—split chapters into theories and then crime types, which often presents a struggle for students to connect the two. So we have integrated street crimes into the theory chapters to offer students a much more applied approach to learning Criminology, while still offering the high level of coverage found in traditional textbooks. This text also emphasizes the theoretical perspectives respected by modern criminologists, including developmental/life course-criminology, biosocial theory, and feminist theory. On the crimes side, it's important to include modern crimes—such as cybercrime, hate crime, white-collar crime, terrorism, and identity theft—so those are in there, too.

We also wanted to include various examples of high-profile crimes/criminals, and apply the theories discussed in each chapter. We include discussion of notorious serial killers, as well as recent individuals who were spree killers or mass murderers such as Christopher Dorner (who stalked and killed law enforcement officers and their family members in Southern California in 2013) and James Holmes (who killed many people at a movie theatre at the opening of a Batman movie in Colorado). Our goal is to address these recent crimes, as well as to apply criminological theories for understanding why these individuals engaged in such acts. This is why the subtitle of our book, "Why Do They Do It?" is so appropriate and needed in considering this book to be used in an introductory course for criminology.

Finally, we felt it was very important to include cross-cultural comparisons of rates of various crimes around the world. Thus, we included a comparative section in each chapter of the book, which examines how rates of specific crimes vary from one jurisdiction to another. Most of these entries focus on noting the regions or countries that have the highest rates in recent years, especially as compared to rates in the United States.

Don't forget to review the Interactive eBook and online website, which offer you and your students the opportunity to go beyond the pages of the text and explore the world of criminology through media in the form of links to video clips, audio clips, journal articles, and so on.

We hope you find our applied and interactive approach to Criminology useful in your course.

All the best,

Pamela Schram and Stephen Tibbetts

A fresh approach to Criminology

> ## THE BIGGEST PROBLEM IS THAT CURRENT TEXTBOOKS DON'T INTEGRATE THEORY WITH CRIME.

—Michael Hollingsworth, Old Dominion University

86%

of instructors surveyed* are open to a textbook that integrates established crime theories and research with traditional street-level crimes so students see the theory application in context.

*SAGE Marketing Survey, February 2013

▼ Applying Theory to Crime features are found throughout the book to help students relate concepts they learn to real-life crimes and scenarios.

APPLYING THEORY TO CRIME: *AGGRAVATED ASSAULT*

Assault, especially aggravated assault is a very serious crime in terms of FBI/UCR standards, and is categorized as an Index crime. After all, an aggravated assault is typically considered an unsuccessful murder, in the sense that it typically involves an inherent intent to do major harm, such as involving a weapon or intending major bodily injury. This leads us to the FBI/UCR definition of aggravated assault as being: "the unlawful attack by one person upon another for the purpose of inflicting severe or aggravated bodily injury on another." According to recent reports by the FBI, there are approximately 850,000 aggravated assaults each year in modern years. The NCVS reported close to twice this amount in recent years, but that is consistent with differences in methodology and accounting for the "dark figure" as discussed in previous chapters. Reports of such assaults were highest in urban areas, which is not surpris-

ing because that is where the rates of homicides are highest. Some reviews have noted that aggravated assault occurs most often during the summer months, when people (including offenders) are out-and-about.

One significant difference about most aggravated assaults versus homicides is that the largest proportion of the former includes blunt objects, such as baseball bats, sticks, etc., as opposed to firearms, which is probably why the victim did not die in the attack. Like most other Index crimes, assault has shown a dramatic decrease in rates over the last two decades. Although most of the time there is a living victim, the clearance rate of aggravated assault is often close to or less than 50% for most years. This is likely due to victims not wanting to contribute to the investigation because usually it is a family member, good friend, or other associate that attacked them. Also,

it may be a gang member or person in the community that they fear retaliation from. Regardless of the reasons, aggravated assault is not typically reported when it happens, and even when it does, the offender is typically not formally prosecuted.

Relating back to our Case Study at the beginning of this chapter, Faith was charged with aggravated assault because she used a weapon, albeit one found on the street, to beat up a drug "customer." Although it wasn't premeditated, the use of this "weapon" seemed to exhibit an intentional infliction of bodily harm on the woman, so it does fit the definition of aggravated assault. That is why Faith was charged with this crime. Still, it is subjective, so if it went to trial, which it did not in her case, a jury would have to decide if such severe bodily harm was intended, as opposed to simply getting her money or drugs back, or self-defense.

Sources: Schmalleger, F. (2009). Criminology Today. Upper Saddle River, NJ: Pearson.; Ibid., p. 60.; Ibid., pp. 60-61.

> "*I like the increased emphasis on the biosocial, psychological, and life-course theories in the current textbook. This is a clear strength over the competitors and makes the learning of these leading criminological theories easier for the undergraduates.*"
>
> —Henriikka Weir
> **University of Texas, Dallas**

> "*I really like how the authors integrate the various street crimes with the theories, which is not normally how Criminology texts are written.*"
>
> —Christopher Davis
> **Campbell University - Buies Creek**

TAKE A LOOK

Features and tools designed for classroom engagement:

Applying Theory to Crime features help students integrate the concepts they learn with real-life street crimes and scenarios.

Why Do They Do It? high profile cases give students an opportunity to critically analyze some of the most high profile cases they hear about in the news.

Chapter-opening vignettes present real-life cases that tie directly to the concepts learned in the chapter. These cases are revisited throughout the chapter as students learn additional theories and concepts.

Chapter-opening Learning Objectives help prepare students to focus on concepts they will learn throughout the chapter.

Helpful **end-of-chapter** pedagogical features include **theory comparisons** and **policy implications**.

> *"The opening vignettes would be the most beneficial for my students. I try to look through books the way my students do, and these really caught my eye."*
>
> —Bruce Johnson
> **Houston Community College**

> *"I predict that the opening case studies will be most beneficial to my students because the case studies link theory to real-life behavior and profiles."*
>
> —Tim Goddard
> **Florida International University**

> *"Of the boxed features, I thought the high profile cases would be the most beneficial since students may already have some familiarity with the cases and they relate theory to real-life examples."*
>
> —Douglas Weiss
> **University of Maryland**

The tools you need

Instructors can access the password-protected **Instructor Teaching Site** at **www.sagepub.com/schram**, which contains:

- Test Bank in Word and with Respondus test-generation capabilities

- PowerPoint and illustrative materials

- Original video of author Stephen Tibbetts and lecturer/ex-offender Jose Rivera

- Video links to related content

- Audio resources, including author podcasts

- Lecture notes

- Sample syllabi annotated with suggested digital resources

- Class activities and case studies

- Select SAGE Journal Articles for each chapter with critical thinking questions

Students can maximize their learning experience by accessing the free, open-access **Student Study Site** at **www.sagepub.com/schram**, which contains:

- Mobile-friendly eFlashcards

- Mobile-friendly web quizzes

- Chapter outlines

- Original video of author Stephen Tibbetts and lecturer/ex-offender Jose Rivera

- Video links to related content

- Audio resources, including author podcasts

- Web resources

- City and State Crime Rankings

- Select SAGE Journal Articles for each chapter with critical thinking questions

introduction to criminology

Los Angeles | London | New Delhi
Singapore | Washington DC

I dedicate this book to my two wonderful, older brothers,
Doug and Jeff. I appreciate your help when I got stuck!

—Pam Schram

I dedicate this book to my best friend and loving wife, Kim. I appreciate your support
so much. You have truly made my life rich in happiness.

—Steve Tibbetts

introduction to
criminology

WHY DO THEY DO IT?

pamela j. schram
CALIFORNIA STATE UNIVERSITY, SAN BERNARDINO

stephen g. tibbetts
CALIFORNIA STATE UNIVERSITY, SAN BERNARDINO

Los Angeles | London | New Delhi
Singapore | Washington DC

Los Angeles | London | New Delhi
Singapore | Washington DC

FOR INFORMATION:

SAGE Publications, Inc.
2455 Teller Road
Thousand Oaks, California 91320
E-mail: order@sagepub.com

SAGE Publications Ltd.
1 Oliver's Yard
55 City Road
London, EC1Y 1SP
United Kingdom

SAGE Publications India Pvt. Ltd.
B 1/I 1 Mohan Cooperative Industrial Area
Mathura Road, New Delhi 110 044
India

SAGE Publications Asia-Pacific Pte. Ltd.
3 Church Street
#10-04 Samsung Hub
Singapore 049483

Acquisitions Editor: Jerry Westby
Associate Editor: Theresa Accomazzo
Editorial Assistant: MaryAnn Vail
Production Editor: Libby Larson
Copy Editor: Megan Granger
Typesetter: C&M Digitals (P) Ltd
Proofreader: Scott Oney
Indexer: Maria Sosnowski
Cover Designer: Scott Van Atta
Marketing Manager: Terra Schultz

Printed in Canada

Library of Congress Cataloging-in-Publication Data

Schram, Pamela J.
Introduction to criminology: why do they do it? /
Pamela J. Schram, California State University, San Bernardino,
Stephen G. Tibbetts, California State University, San Bernardino.

pages cm

ISBN 978-1-4129-9085-1 (pbk.)
ISBN 978-1-4522-5648-1 (web pdf) 1.

Criminology. I. Tibbetts, Stephen G. II. Title.

HV6025.S38 2013

364—dc23   2013016896

This book is printed on acid-free paper.

13 14 15 16 17 10 9 8 7 6 5 4 3 2 1

CONTENTS

CHAPTER 1. INTRODUCTION TO CRIMINOLOGY 1

CHAPTER 2. CLASSICAL SCHOOL OF CRIMINOLOGICAL THOUGHT 32

CHAPTER 3. CONTEMPORARY CLASSICAL AND DETERRENCE RESEARCH 60

CHAPTER 4. EARLY POSITIVISM: BIOLOGICAL THEORIES OF CRIME 82

CHAPTER 5. MODERN BIOSOCIAL PERSPECTIVES OF CRIMINAL BEHAVIOR 108

CHAPTER 6. PSYCHOLOGICAL/ TRAIT THEORIES OF CRIME 136

CHAPTER 7. SOCIAL STRUCTURE THEORIES OF CRIME I: EARLY DEVELOPMENT AND STRAIN MODELS OF CRIME 162

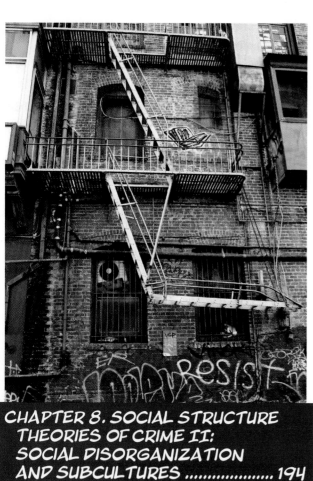

CHAPTER 8. SOCIAL STRUCTURE THEORIES OF CRIME II: SOCIAL DISORGANIZATION AND SUBCULTURES 194

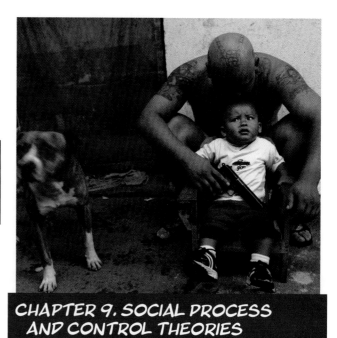

CHAPTER 9. SOCIAL PROCESS AND CONTROL THEORIES OF CRIME 214

CHAPTER 10. LABELING
THEORY AND CONFLICT/
MARXIST/RADICAL
THEORIES OF CRIME.................. 252

CHAPTER 11. FEMINIST THEORIES OF CRIME................. 284

CHAPTER 12. DEVELOPMENTAL/ LIFE-COURSE PERSPECTIVES OF CRIMINALITY 314

CHAPTER 13. WHITE-COLLAR CRIME, ORGANIZED CRIME, AND CYBERCRIME 336

CHAPTER 14. HATE CRIMES, TERRORISM, AND HOMELAND SECURITY 378

CHAPTER 15. DRUGS AND CRIME 416

Preface

If you are considering a career in any aspect of criminal justice, and want to know more about the motivations and socio-psychological make-up of serious offenders, then this book is meant for you! *Introduction to Criminology: Why Do They Do It?* places a primary emphasis on applying the dominant theories in the existing criminological literature for why people commit crimes, and we also examine in detail many recent true (as well as many hypothetical) examples of serious crimes, and demonstrate theoretical applications for why they offended in those particular cases. While other textbooks do a decent job in discussing both the basic theories, as well as exploring the various types of crime, our book is distinctively unique in that it integrates various street (FBI Part I-Index) crimes within each chapter, and applies theories that are appropriate in explaining such criminal activity. This is extremely important because most instructors never get to the latter typology chapters in a given semester or term. So our approach is to incorporate them into the theoretical chapters in which they apply directly to the theories that are being presented in the sections that they are most appropriate.

The emphasis on specific examples and true crime stories, such as notable serial killers and other recent crime stories, as well as utilizing established theoretical models to explain their offenses in each chapter, is another primary distinction of this book from that of most other criminology textbooks. Obviously, this book is meant to be used as a textbook in an introductory course in criminology, but due to the emphasis on applied theoretical explanations, this book is highly appropriate for higher-level undergraduate and graduate courses in criminological theory, as well as a reference for any person working in the field of criminal justice. This integration of true crimes (and some hypothetical examples) in this text occurs on both a general level, such as our Applying Crime to Theory section in each chapter, as well as more specific cases – the High Profile Crime sections—in each section, which often involve notable cases of serial killers, mass murderers, or other notorious example of offender/offending.

The subtitle of our book, "Why Do They Do It?" is the running theme in this book. Our goal in writing this book was to apply established theories of crime, which are often seen as abstract and hypothetical, to actual examples that have occurred, as well as to hypothetical examples that are quite likely to occur. To this end, we explore the various reasons of offending or the " why they do it" [the subtitle for this book] for various cases, from the first documented serial killers in the US—the Harpe Brothers in the late-1700s—to the most recent killers, such as California cop-killer/spree-killer Christopher Dorner and Newtown, Connecticut, mass-shooter Adam Lanza, both occurring in 2013. Importantly, theories will be applied throughout these discussions of the actual crimes. We shall see that some of the theories that applied to the earliest crimes also seem to apply to the most modern crimes as well.

Additionally, our textbook is unique from others because it does not include separate chapters on violent or property crimes, because we have worked those into each chapter, and applied them to the theories explored in those chapters. We strongly believe that by integrating discussions of such serious crimes—all of the FBI Index offenses of murder, rape, robbery, aggravated assault, burglary, motor vehicle theft, larceny, and arson, as well as other non-Index crimes such as simple assault and driving under the influence—into the theoretical chapters is the best approach toward explaining why individuals commit such offenses. And the flip side is good as well; by discussing the offenses with the theories, this also provides an example of how to apply theories toward explaining criminal behavior. Again, this goes back to our theme of "Why Do They Do It?" Our integration of such specific offenses into the chapters that discuss relevant theories in explaining them is the best way to approach such material and demonstrates our goal: apply the appropriate theories for the specific crime.

Additionally, our book is distinguished from other textbooks in that we don't have an overwhelming amount of boxes and special sections that diverge from the text material. Rather, we narrowed down the special sections into three basic categories, largely based on the goal of this text, which are mostly dedicated to applying criminological theory to actual offenses, or true cases. We also added a special section in each chapter regarding international comparison of certain offenses (comparative criminology), with an emphasis on how various rates of such crimes differ across the world, especially as compared to the United States. The offenses we compare range widely, from homicide to human trafficking to the correlations of beer consumption and assaults (Ireland was a high outlier!, see page 71). We felt this was important for readers to see how the US compares to other nations in terms of various criminal offenses. So our goal is for readers to understand the ever-growing global nature of criminality, and where the United States is positioned regarding various rates and trends in illegal behavior.

This text is also unique from all of the others by providing a separate chapter on feminist criminology. Given that over half of our citizens are female, and there has been a recent increase in females committing certain crimes (e.g., simple assault), this is an important addition to the study of crime. Furthermore, while males are still universally responsible for the vast majority of violent acts—murder, robbery, aggravated assault—in all societies, if we can understand why females commit so much less violence, then maybe this will have significant implications for reducing male violence. So this separate chapter is vitally important for not only understanding female offenders, but also has implications for male criminals as well.

Another unique aspect of this book is that we devoted separate chapters on the developmental/life-course perspective, as well as modern biosocial approaches regarding propensities to commit crime. These two frameworks/perspectives have become some of the most accepted and valid frameworks on understanding why individuals engage in criminal behavior, but most other criminology textbooks do not examine these topics as closely as we do. A recent study that surveyed key criminologists in the field showed that the developmental/life-course perspective ranked as the second most accepted perspective in explaining chronic offending (and biosocial perspective ranked #6, out of 24+ theories), yet most other textbooks have only a small portion or shallow coverage of this perspective. This developmental/life-course perspective, as well as the biosocial perspective, currently is the "cutting-edge" of the field right now, and our chapters on those frameworks highlights the importance of these theoretical models, as well as the recent empirical studies that have been done in those areas of study.

Our text does follow a somewhat traditional format in that it presents theories chronologically from the Classical School to the Positive School of Criminology, discussing all of the established theories in the areas of social structure, social process, and conflict theories as they became popular over time. However, we place much emphasis on examining why certain theories became popular at certain times, which is often due more to politics and societal trends than what empirical studies showed regarding the empirical validity of the given theory. These political and societal trends are vital in every aspect of our lives, and criminological theory is no different. So we tried to work that principle into the text throughout each chapter, showing how crime and theorizing about it is just one manifestation about society at that time period.

Finally, our special typology chapters, located in the last three chapters of the book, are dedicated to more contemporary topics, such as cybercrime, hate crimes, terrorism, white-collar/corporate crimes, drug-related offenses, as well as several others that do not fit into the FBI Index crimes. We have done our best to provide the most current research on these topics, and we hope that readers will gain far more insight on these topics. Furthermore, we believe that our coverage of these modern forms of offending are the most vital in understanding the current state of criminal offending occurring in our society.

Our book also provides an ancillary package with numerous resources to support instructors and students.

INSTRUCTOR TEACHING SITE

A password-protected site, available at **www.sagepub.com/schram,** features resources that have been designed to help instructors plan and teach their courses. These resources include an extensive test bank, chapter-specific PowerPoint presentations, lecture notes, sample syllabi for semester and quarter courses, class activities, web resources, and links to the video, audio, city and state rankings, author podcasts, and SAGE journal and reference articles featured in the margins of the text.

STUDENT STUDY SITE

An open-access student study site is available at **www.sagepub.com/schram.** This site provides access to the video, audio, city and state rankings, author podcasts, and SAGE journal and reference articles featured in the margins of the text as well as several study tools including eFlashcards, web quizzes, web resources and chapter outlines.

INTERACTIVE EBOOK

Introduction to Criminology: Why Do They Do It? is also available as an Interactive eBook, which can be packaged free with the book or purchased separately. The interactive eBook features highlighting, note taking, and search functions and offers links to video, audio, city and state rankings, author podcasts, and SAGE journal and reference articles.

Overall, we really hope you appreciate our unique approach to studying criminology, and hope you believe that after reading this book that you will have a better understanding of why offenders do what they do.

Pamela J. Schram, PhD
Stephen G. Tibbetts, PhD
California State University, San Bernardino

Acknowledgments

We would first like to thank Executive Editor Jerry Westby. It was Jerry's idea for us to write this book, and he has "gone to bat" for us numerous times regarding various unique things about this text, such as integrating the violent and property street crimes into the theoretical chapters, rather than just having separate chapters on these topics at the end of the book that instructors often don't get time to cover in a single term, as well as including separate chapters on feminist and developmental/life-course perspectives. This is a rather unorthodox approach, compared to other introduction to criminology textbooks, but Jerry was fully supportive, even at the outset. So we offer him the highest level of respect for his support in backing us on our rather deviant way of approaching this material.

We would also like to thank the staff at SAGE publications, for doing such a great job at putting the book together, which includes checking all of the mistakes we made in drafts of the chapters, as well as so many other things that go into producing this book. We specifically want to thank Associate Editor Theresa Accomazzo for all of her help in getting the drafts of the chapters in order to be sent to the copyeditor, and for giving advice on how to make the book far more polished than it was in its original draft. We also want to thank our copyeditor, Megan Granger, who has gone to great lengths to make us sound much better than we are. She did a fantastic job, and it was a pleasure working with her. Also, we would like give a special thanks to Digital Content Editor Rachael Leblond, who was invaluable in finding the various links to videos and other sources that were vital in the e-text version of the text. Overall, we give the greatest thanks to all of the Sage staff that worked on this book!

Pamela Schram would like to acknowledge some very special people who had an influence on her life prior to her college years. First and foremost, she would like to thank her ninth grade English teacher, Mr. Joe Devlin. She remembers her first day of English class. Mr. Devlin said, "I can't learn you. First, that is poor English, and second, that is not how it works. I can teach you, but the learning part is on you." Obviously, this has "stuck" with her; it has been over 30 years and she still remembers his "opening" lecture. Later, he was Pam's Latin teacher; Pam continued to take Latin and she was the only student for Latin III. Mr. Devlin would stay after school to conduct this class. As you can imagine, this was not a popular after school activity. But, it taught Pam an important lesson as to how a truly dedicated teacher cares about his students.

Pam would also like to acknowledge Mrs. Frank. She was her second grade teacher. Mrs. Frank was one of those teachers who would incorporate learning with fun things, especially arts and crafts. Mrs. Frank encouraged Pam to write, especially short stories. These were the times when students learned cursive writing on paper with the various lines for lower and upper case. Pam still has some of those short stories written on the "special writing paper. " It brings back many fond memories as well as an appreciation for another special teacher who touched her life.

Pam would finally like to give a special thanks to her organ teacher, Mrs. Cessna. (As you can tell, Pam wasn't considered popular in school.) Mrs. Cessna was one of the most patient teachers Pam has ever had in terms of continuously giving her encouraging words. It may have also helped that Mrs. Cessna had some hearing difficulties. When most of her friends were taking piano, she decided to try organ lessons. She obviously endured some ridicule, especially from her brothers. Their words of encouragement were something like, "Well, with those lessons you can one day play at the Detroit Tiger stadium."

As Pam has gotten older, she has realized the numerous people that have touched her life in so many special ways. One of those special people is her co-author Steve Tibbetts. Steve is an extremely intelligent and well-respected criminologist in the field. He is also a wonderful friend with those important words of encouragement, usually with a sense of humor. He has been very patient and understanding with her not just when writing this book but during his years at CSUSB. Through his friendship, he has helped her to be a better person.

Stephen Tibbetts would like to thank some of the various individuals who helped him complete this book. First, he would like to thank some of the professors he had while earning his undergraduate degree in criminal justice at the University of Florida, who first exposed him to the study of crime and inspired him to become a criminologist. These professors include Ron Akers, Donna Bishop, and Lonn Lanza-Kaduce. He would also like to thank several professors who were key influences in his studies during his graduate studies at University of Maryland, such as Denise Gottfredson, Colin Loftin, David McDowell, Lawrence Sherman, and Charles Wellford. A special thanks goes to Raymond Paternoster, who was his mentor during his graduate studies at Maryland, and provided the best advice and support that any mentor could have given.

Tibbetts would also like to mention the support and influence that work with Alex Piquero, and his wife, Nicole Piquero, had on his career. He was lucky enough to share an office with Alex early on in graduate school, and the work that they did together early on in his career was key in inspiring him to do more work on biosocial and life-course criminology, which are both important portions of this book. Tibbetts' collaboration with Nicole Piquero on the issues of white-collar crime was also important, and has led to more recent studies in this often neglected topic of illegal behavior. He would also like to acknowledge several colleagues who have been important in his research in more recent years, such as John Paul Wright at University of Cincinnati, Nichole H. Rafter at Northeastern University, Chris L. Gibson at University of Florida, Kevin Beaver at Florida State University, and Cesar Rebellon at University of New Hampshire.

Tibbetts would also like to include a special acknowledgment to Jose Rivera, who has contributed much to this book in terms of both video and written sections. Jose has gone above-and-beyond in trying to contribute to the information provided in this book, given his experience as a former incarcerated inmate for over 9 years in various prisons in Southern California. He has shown that such inmates can excel after they have been incarcerated, not only by earning his Master's degree in Communication Studies, but by becoming a fantastic educator, which was proven when he was awarded the Graduate Teaching Assistant of the Year Award by his college at California State University, San Bernardino, in 2012. Jose also recently was a recipient of the President Obama's Presidential Volunteer Service Award in 2012 for his work in programs that promote educational opportunities for Latinos.

Finally, but most important, Tibbetts would especially like to thank his co-author on this book, Pamela Schram, for providing him with the inspiration, motivation, and collaboration for completing this project. Without Pam's constant support and advice, his work on this book could not have materialized. So he gives the highest acknowledgement to Pam; she will always be his most trusted *consigliere*.

Pam and Steve would like to thank the reviewers of the initial proposal for their advice and critiques. They would also like to express their sincere appreciation to their colleagues who reviewed the text and gave them invaluable feedback:

Kevin Beaver, Florida State University—Tallahassee

Doris Chu, Arkansas State University—Jonesboro

Christopher Davis, Campbell University—Buies Creek

Melissa Deller, University of Wisconsin-Whitewater

Daniel Dexheimer, San Jose State University

Tina Freiburger, University of Wisconsin-Milwaukee

Chris L. Gibson, University of Florida

Jennifer Grimes, Indiana State University—Terre Haute

W. Bruce Johnson, Houston Community College / Northeast College

Michael A Long, Oklahoma State University

Scott Maggard, Old Dominion University—Norfolk

PJ McGann, University Of Michigan—Ann Arbor

Anna Netterville, University of Louisiana at Monroe

Angela Overton, Old Dominion University—Norfolk

Allison Payne, Villanova University—Villanova

Lacey Rohledef, University of Cincinnati

Anne Strouth, North Central State College—Mansfield

Patricia Warren, Florida State University—Tallahassee

Henriikka Weir, University Of Texas At Dallas—Richardson

Douglas Weiss, University of Maryland

Shonda Whetstone, Blinn College

About the Authors

Pamela J. Schram has published articles on such topics as violent female offenders, female juvenile gang and non-gang members, as well as issues pertaining to women in prison, such as stereotypes about mothers in prison and vocational programming. She has co-authored three books on women in prison, theory and practice in feminist criminology, and a juvenile delinquency text. She is currently interested in issues pertaining to elderly prisoners. Dr. Schram has been involved in various research projects that have primarily focused on evaluating treatment effectiveness such as juvenile diversion options and programs for at-risk youths as well as programs for women in prison. Dr. Schram received her Ph.D. from Michigan State University. She is a professor in the Department of Criminal Justice. She is currently the Associate Dean of the College of Social and Behavior Sciences at California State University, San Bernardino.

Stephen G. Tibbetts is a professor in the Department of Criminal Justice at California State University, San Bernardino (CSUSB). He earned his undergraduate degree in criminology and law (with high honors) from the University of Florida, and his masters and doctorate degrees from the University of Maryland. For more than a decade, he worked as a sworn officer of the court (juvenile) in both Washington County, Tennessee, and San Bernardino County, California, providing recommendations for disposing numerous juvenile court cases. He has published more than 40 scholarly publications in scientific journals (including *Criminology, Justice Quarterly, Journal of Research in Crime and Delinquency, Journal of Criminal Justice*, and *Criminal Justice and Behavior*), as well as eight books, all examining various topics regarding criminal offending and policies to reduce such behavior. One of these books, *American Youth Gangs at the Millennium*, was given a Choice award by the American Library Association as an Outstanding Academic Title. Tibbetts received a Golden Apple award from the Mayor of San Bernardino for being chosen as the Outstanding Professor at the CSUSB campus in 2010. One of his recent books, *Criminals in the Making: Criminality Across the Life Course* (Sage, 2008), was recently lauded by *The Chronicle of Higher Education* as one of the key scholarly publications in advancing the study of biosocial criminology.

CHAPTER 1

Introduction to Criminology

INTRODUCTION

When introducing students to criminology, it is essential to stress how various concepts and principles of theoretical development are woven into our understanding of crime, as well as policy. This chapter begins with a brief discussion of such concepts as *crime, criminal, deviant, criminology, criminal justice,* and *consensus* and *conflict perspectives of crime.* The following section presents readers with a general summary of the different stages of the adult criminal justice system as well as the juvenile justice system. Next, this chapter provides students with an overview of how and on what we base our understanding of crime and criminal patterns. Specifically, this section covers various approaches to measuring crime; we stress the importance of criminological theory and empirical testing, and how such scientific endeavors help advance the knowledge and understanding of criminal offending. The concluding section illustrates how criminology informs policies and programs. Unfortunately, there are instances when policies lack evidence and are not founded on criminological theory and rigorous research but are more of a "knee-jerk" reaction.

KEY CONCEPTS TO UNDERSTANDING CRIMINOLOGY

WHAT IS A CRIME?

There are various definitions of **crime**. Many scholars have disagreed as to what should be considered a crime. For instance, if one takes a legalistic approach, then crime is that which violates the law. But should one consider if certain actions cause serious harm? If governments violate the basic human rights of their citizens, are they engaging in criminal behavior?[1] As illustrated by these questions, the issue with defining crime from a legalistic approach is that one jurisdiction may designate an action as a crime while another does not recognize such an action as a crime. Some acts, such as murder, are against the law in most countries as well as in all jurisdictions of the United States. These are referred to as acts of *mala in se*, meaning the act is "inherently and essentially evil, that is immoral in its nature and injurious in its consequence, without any regard to the fact of its being noticed or punished by the law of the state."[2]

Other crimes are known as acts of *mala prohibita*, which means "a wrong prohibited; an act which is not inherently immoral, but becomes so because its commission is expressly forbidden by positive law."[3] For instance, prostitution is illegal in most jurisdictions in the United States. However, prostitution is legal, and licensed, in most counties of Nevada. The same can be said about gambling and drug possession or use.

This text focuses on both *mala in se* and *mala prohibita* offenses, as well as other acts of **deviance**. Deviant acts are not necessarily against the law but are considered atypical and may be deemed immoral rather than illegal. For example, in Nevada in the 1990s, a young man watched his friend (who was later criminally prosecuted) kill a young girl in a casino

LEARNING OBJECTIVES

As students are reading this chapter, they should consider the following topics:

- **Describe the various definitions of crime. Distinguish between criminal behavior and deviant behavior.**

- **Distinguish between criminology and criminal justice.**

- **When reviewing the various theoretical perspectives in this text, consider whether that theory would be considered from a consensus or conflict perspective of crime.**

- **List and describe the three general components of the criminal justice system.**

- **Identify some of the key distinguishing features of the juvenile justice system compared with the adult criminal justice system.**

- **Describe some of the various approaches to measuring crime.**

- **Identify the criteria that characterize a good theory.**

CASE STUDY

MARY MORGAN

Mary Morgan was a teenager who worked in the kitchen of a wealthy family. It was assumed that the father of her baby also worked in the kitchen. After complaining of feeling ill, Mary returned to her room. Later that day, the cook went into her room. He claimed that Mary had given birth to a newborn daughter. The infant was found under the mattress with her head almost severed, along with the knife presumed to be the murder weapon. Subsequently, Mary went to trial and was convicted; she received the death penalty.

Unfortunately, this case may sound similar to other cases we read about in the newspapers or hear about on the news, cases of teenage mothers who kill their newborn infants, such as the 14-year-old Florida girl who strangled her infant son and placed his body in a shoe box. The case of Mary Morgan, however, occurred in 1804. Mary was 16 years old; she worked as a kitchen maid for the Wilkins family in Maesllwch Castle near Glasbury (Wales); Walter Wilkins was a local member of Parliament.

Mary was imprisoned for 7 months prior to her trial. Given the horrific conditions of an early 19th century jail, Mary would have no protection against abuses inflicted on her by prison staff. In fact, when she arrived in court in April of 1805, she appeared battered, malnourished, and seriously ill. A huge crowd gathered for her public execution. On April 13, 1805, she was hanged and buried in what was then deemed unconsecrated ground near St. Andrew's Churchyard, near Presteigne.

Some have challenged whether Mary Morgan did kill her infant daughter. Some maintain that Walter Wilkins (junior), the son of the local member of Parliament, was the father of the newborn. The younger Walter Wilkins was engaged to the daughter of a socially prominent family. Thus, if he was the father of Mary's child and this was revealed, his aspirations of social advancement would be ruined.

Another theory is that Judge Hardinge could have been the father of Mary's baby and possibly involved in the infant's death. Judge Hardinge presided over Mary's trial and condemned her to death. The judge apparently was a family friend of the Wilkins's and stayed at the Maesllwch Castle on numerous occasions. An interesting note is that Judge Hardinge frequently visited Mary's grave and wrote poems about her.[4]

It is essential to realize that criminal behavior does not occur in a vacuum; criminal activity is not *outside* of society; rather, it is a part of society. Various aspects of society, such as social class and gender, intersect with criminal behavior. The case of Mary Morgan illustrates these intersections. She was a female adolescent from a marginalized social position; thus, some would argue that she was more vulnerable than someone in a more advantaged social position.

> CRIMINAL ACTIVITY IS NOT OUTSIDE OF SOCIETY; RATHER, IT IS A PART OF SOCIETY.

bathroom. He never told anyone of the murder. While most people would consider this highly immoral, at that time, Nevada state laws did not require people who witnessed a killing to report it to authorities. This act was deviant, because most would consider it immoral; it was not criminal, because it was not against the laws of that jurisdiction. It is essential to note that as a result of this event, Nevada made withholding such information a criminal act.

Other acts of deviance are not necessarily seen as immoral but are considered strange and violate social norms, such as purposely belching at a formal dinner. These types of deviant acts are relevant even if not considered criminal under the legal definition, for individuals engaging in these types of activities reveal a disposition toward antisocial behavior often linked to criminal behavior. Further, some acts are moving from being deemed deviant to being declared illegal, such as using a cell phone while driving or smoking cigarettes in public. Many jurisdictions are moving to have these behaviors made illegal and have been quite successful, especially in New York and California.

While most *mala in se* activities are also considered highly deviant, this is not necessarily the case for *mala prohibita* acts. For instance, speeding on a highway (a *mala prohibita* act) is not deviant, because many people engage in this act. Thus, while this is illegal, it is not considered deviant. This book presents theories for all these types of activities, even those that do not violate the law.[5]

WHAT IS CRIMINOLOGY AND CRIMINAL JUSTICE?

The term **criminology** was first coined by the Italian law professor Raffaele Garafalo in 1885 (in Italian, *criminologia*). In 1887, French anthropologist Paul Topinard used it for the first time in French (*criminologie*).[6] In 1934, American criminologist Edwin Sutherland defined criminology as

> the body of knowledge regarding crime as a social phenomenon. It includes within its scope the process of making laws, of breaking laws, and of reacting toward the breaking of laws. . . . The objective of criminology is the development of a body of general and verified principles and of other types of knowledge regarding this process of law, crime, and treatment or prevention.[7]

Criminology is the scientific study of crime, especially why people engage in criminal behavior. While other textbooks may provide a more complex definition of crime, the word *scientific* distinguishes our definition from other perspectives and examinations of crime.[8] Philosophical and legal examinations of crime are based on logic and deductive reasoning—for example, by developing what makes logical sense. Journalists play a key role in examining crime by exploring what is happening in criminal justice and revealing injustices as well as new forms of crime. However, the philosophical, legal, and journalistic perspectives of crime are not scientific, because they do not involve the use of scientific method.

Criminal justice often refers to the various criminal justice agencies and institutions (e.g., police, courts, and corrections) that are interrelated and work together toward common goals. Interestingly, many scholars who referred to criminal justice as a system did so only as a way to collectively refer to those agencies and organizations, rather than to imply they were interrelated.[9] Some individuals argue that the term *criminal justice system* is an oxymoron. For instance, Joanne Belknap noted that she preferred to use the term *crime processing, criminal processing,* and *criminal legal system,* given that "the processing of victims and offenders [is] anything but 'just.'"[10]

VIDEO

Deviance

REFERENCE ARTICLE

Deviance

crime: there are various definitions of crime. From a legalistic approach, crime is that which violates the law.

mala in se: acts that are considered inherently evil

mala prohibita: acts that are considered crimes primarily because they have been declared bad by the legal codes in that jurisdiction

deviance: behaviors that are not normal; includes many illegal acts, as well as activities that are not necessarily criminal but are unusual and often violate social norms

criminology: the scientific study of crime and the reasons why people engage (or don't engage) in criminal behavior

criminal justice: criminal justice often refers to the various criminal justice agencies and institutions (e.g., police, courts, and corrections) that were interrelated

This photo of a woman texting while driving illustrates the dangers involved with this type of behavior.

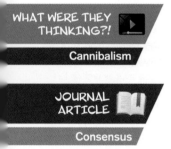

WHAT WERE THEY THINKING?!

Cannibalism

JOURNAL ARTICLE

Consensus

. . . .

consensus perspective: theories that assume virtually everyone is in agreement on the laws and therefore assume no conflict in attitudes regarding the laws and rules of society

CONSENSUS AND CONFLICT PERSPECTIVES OF CRIME

A **consensus perspective** of crime views the formal system of laws, as well as the enforcement of those laws, as incorporating societal norms for which there is a broad normative consensus.[11] The consensus perspective developed from the writings of late 19th and early 20th century sociologists such as Durkheim, Weber, Ross, and Sumner.[12] This perspective assumes that individuals, for the most part, agree on what is right and wrong, as well as on how those norms have been implemented into laws and how those laws are enforced. Thus, people obey laws not for fear of punishment but, rather, because they have internalized societal norms and values and perceive these laws as appropriate to observe rather than disobey.[13] The consensus perspective was more dominant during the early part of the 1900s. Since the 1950s, however, no major theorist has considered this to be the best perspective of law. Further, "to the extent that assumptions or hypotheses about consensus theory are still given credence in current theories of law, they are most apt to be found in 'mutualist' models."[14]

Around the 1950s, the **conflict perspective** was challenging the consensus approach.[15] The conflict perspective maintains that there is conflict between various societal groups with different interests. This conflict is often resolved when the group in power achieves control.

Several criminologists, such as Richard Quinney, William Chambliss, and Austin Turk, maintained that criminological theory has placed too much emphasis on explaining criminal behavior; rather, theory needs to shift this focus toward explaining criminal law.

The emphasis should not be on understanding the causes of criminal behavior but on understanding the process by which certain behaviors and individuals are formally designated as criminal. From this perspective, one would ask different questions. For instance, instead of asking, "Why do some people commit crimes while others do not?" one would ask, "Why are some behaviors defined as criminal while others are not?" Asking these types of questions raises the issue of whether the formulation and enforcement of laws serve the interests of those in a more powerful position in society.[16]

CRIMINAL JUSTICE SYSTEM

According to the 1967 President's Commission on Law Enforcement and Administration of Justice,

> any criminal justice system is an apparatus society uses to enforce the standards of conduct necessary to protect individuals and the community. It operates by apprehending, prosecuting, convicting, and sentencing those members of the community who violate the basic rules of group existence.[17]

This general purpose of the criminal justice system can be further simplified into three goals: to control crime, to prevent crime, and to provide and maintain justice. The structure and organization of the criminal justice system has evolved in an effort to meet these goals. The structure and organization is often presented as three components: law enforcement, courts, and corrections.[18]

LAW ENFORCEMENT

Law enforcement includes various organizational levels (i.e., federal, state, and local). One of the key features distinguishing federal law enforcement agencies from others is that they were often established to enforce specific statutes. Thus, their units are highly specialized and often associated with specialized training and resources.[19] Federal law enforcement agencies include the Federal Bureau of Investigation (FBI), the Drug Enforcement Administration (DEA), the U.S. Secret Service, the U.S. Marshals Service, and the Bureau of Alcohol, Tobacco, Firearms, and Explosives (ATF). Further, almost all federal agencies, including the Postal Service and the Forest Service, have some police power. In a later chapter, we discuss how the federal agencies were reorganized and restructured to establish the Department of Homeland Security. In 2002, President George W. Bush created this department in an effort to protect and defend the United States from terrorist threats.[20]

The earliest form of state police agency to emerge in the United States was the Texas Rangers, founded by Stephen Austin in 1823 to protect settlers. By 1925, formal state police departments existed throughout most of the country. While some organizational variations exist among the different states, two models generally characterize the structure of these state police departments.

The first model can be designated as **state police**. States such as Michigan, New York, Pennsylvania, Delaware, Vermont, and Arkansas have a state police structure. These agencies have general police powers and enforce state laws, as well as performing routine patrols and traffic regulation. Further, they have additional functions such as specialized units to investigate major crimes, intelligence units, drug trafficking units, juvenile units, and crime laboratories. The second model can be designated as **highway patrol**. States such as California, Ohio, Georgia, Florida, and the Carolinas have a highway patrol model. For these agencies, the primary focus is to enforce the laws that govern the operation of motor vehicles on public roads and highways. In some instances, this also includes not just enforcing traffic laws but investigating crimes that occur in specific locations or under certain circumstances, such as on state highways or state property.[21]

Agencies on the local level are divided into counties and municipalities. The primary law enforcement office for most counties is that of county sheriff. In most instances, the sheriff is an elected position. The majority of local police officers are employed by municipalities. Most of these agencies comprise fewer than 10 officers. Local police agencies are responsible for the "nuts and bolts" of law enforcement responsibilities. For instance, they investigate most crimes and engage in crime prevention activities such as patrol duties. Further, these officers are often responsible for providing social services such as responding to incidents of domestic violence and child abuse.[22]

LEARNING CHECK 1.1

Crime that is evil in itself is referred to as _____. Acts that are not necessarily against the law but are considered atypical and may be considered more immoral than illegal are _____ acts. Criminology is distinguished from other perspectives of crime, such as journalistic, philosophical, or legal perspectives, because it involves the use of _____.

Answers located at www.sagepub.com/schram

🔊)) AUDIO

DEA

---

criminology: the scientific study of crime and the reasons why people engage (or don't engage) in criminal behavior

conflict perspective or conflict theory: criminal behavior theories that assume most people disagree on what the law should be and that law is used as a tool by those in power to keep down other groups

state police: agencies with general police powers to enforce state laws as well as to investigate major crimes; they may have intelligence units, drug trafficking units, juvenile units, and crime laboratories

highway patrol: one type of model characterizing statewide police departments. The primary focus is to enforce the laws that govern the operation of motor vehicles on public roads and highways

Various law enforcement agencies, including the DEA, confiscating marijuana plants

VIDEO ▶

Courts

limited jurisdiction: the authority of a court to hear and decide cases within an area of the law or a geographic territory

probation: probation is essentially an *arrangement* between the sentencing authorities and the offender requiring the offender to comply with certain terms for a specified amount of time

jail: jails are often designated for individuals convicted of a minor crime, and to house individuals awaiting trial

COURTS

The United States does not have just one judicial system. Rather, the judicial system is quite complex. In fact, there are 52 different systems, one for each state, the District of Columbia, and the federal government. Given this complexity, however, one can characterize the United States as having a *dual court system*. This dual court system consists of separate, yet interrelated systems: the federal courts and the state courts. While there are variations among the states in terms of judicial structure, usually a state court system consists of different levels or tiers, such as lower courts, trial courts, appellate courts, and the state's highest court. The federal court system is a three-tiered model: U.S. district courts (i.e., trial courts) and other specialized courts, U.S. courts of appeals, and the U.S. Supreme Court (see Figure 1.1).[23]

Before any case can be brought to a court, that court must have *jurisdiction* over those individuals involved in the case. Jurisdiction is the authority of a court to hear and decide cases within an area of the law (i.e., subject matter such as serious felonies, civil cases, or misdemeanors) or a geographic territory.[24] Essentially, jurisdiction is categorized as limited, general, or appellate:

*Courts of **limited jurisdiction.*** These are also designated as lower courts. They do not have power that extends to the overall administration of justice; thus, they do not try felony cases and do not have appellate authority.

Courts of general jurisdiction. These are also designated as major trial courts. They have the power and authority to try and decide any case, including appeals from a lower court.

Courts of appellate jurisdiction. These are also designated as appeals courts. They are limited in their jurisdiction decisions on matters of appeal from lower courts and trial courts.[25]

Every court, including the U.S. Supreme Court, is limited in terms of jurisdiction.

CORRECTIONS

After an offender is convicted and sentenced, he or she is processed in the corrections system. An offender can be placed on probation, incarcerated, or transferred to some type of community-based corrections facility. **Probation** is essentially an *arrangement* between the sentencing authorities and the offender. While under supervision, the offender must comply with certain terms for a specified amount of time to return to the community. These terms are often referred to as conditions of probation.[26] Examples of *general conditions* include the offenders regularly reporting to their supervising officer, obeying the laws, submitting to searches, and not being in possession of firearms or using drugs. *Specific conditions* can also be imposed, such as participating in methadone maintenance, urine testing, house arrest, vocational training, or psychological or psychiatric treatment.[27] There are also variations to probation. For instance, a judge can combine probation with incarceration, such as *shock incarceration*. This involves sentencing the offender to spend a certain amount of time each week, oftentimes over the weekend, in some type of institution like a jail; during the remaining time period, the offender is on probation.

Some offenders are required to serve their sentences in a corrections facility. One type of corrections facility is **jail**. Jails are often designated for individuals convicted

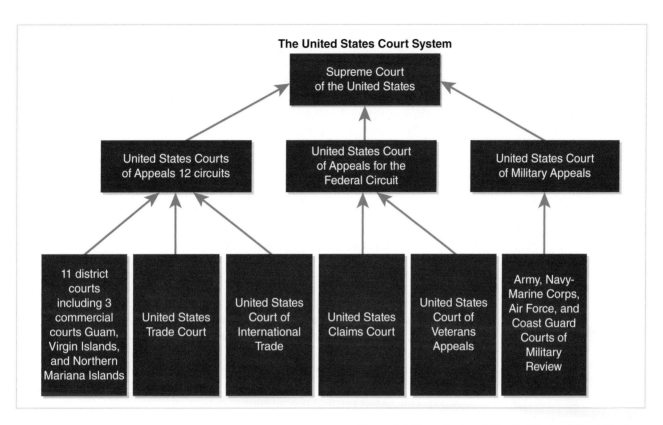

The United States Court System

Figure 1.1 Organizational Chart of Federal Court System
Source: http://usinfo.org/enus/government/branches/8994.html

of minor crimes. Jails are also used to house individuals awaiting trial; these people have not been convicted but are incarcerated for various reasons, such as preventative detention. Another type of corrections facility is **prison.** Those sentenced to prison are often convicted of more serious crimes with longer sentences. There are different types of prisons, based on security concerns, such as supermax, maximum, medium, and minimum security. Generally, counties and municipalities operate jails, while prisons are operated by federal and state governments.[28]

Given the rising jail and prison populations, there has been increased use of alternatives to traditional incarceration. For instance, examples of residential sanctions include halfway houses as well as work and study release. Examples of nonresidential sanctions include house arrest, electronic monitoring, and day reporting centers.[29]

JUVENILE JUSTICE SYSTEM

Prior to the establishment of the juvenile justice system, children were treated the same as adults in terms of criminal processing. Children were considered as "imperfect" adults or "adults in miniature." They were held to the same standards of behavior as adults. The American colonists brought with them the common law doctrine from England, which held that juveniles 7 years or older could be treated the same as adult offenders. Thus, they were incarcerated with adults and could also receive similarly harsh punishments, including the death penalty. It should be noted, however, that youths rarely received such harsh and severe punishments.[30] Beginning in the early 1800s, many recognized the need for a separate system for juveniles.[31] For instance, Johann Heinrich Pestalozzi, a Swiss educator, maintained that children are distinct from adults, both physically and psychologically.

))) AUDIO

Corrections

prison: generally for those convicted of more serious crimes with longer sentences, who may be housed in a supermax, maximum, medium, or minimum security prison, based on security concerns

While there is some disagreement in accrediting the establishment of the first juvenile court, most acknowledge that the first comprehensive juvenile court system was initiated in 1899 in Cook County, Illinois. An essential component to understanding the juvenile justice system is the concept of *parens patriae*. This Latin term literally means "the parent of the country." This philosophical perspective recognizes that the state has both the right and obligation to intervene on behalf of and to protect its citizens who have some impairment or impediment such as mental incompetence or, in the case of juveniles, immaturity. The primary objective of processing juveniles was to determine what was in the best interest of the child. This resulted in the proceedings resembling more of a civil case than a criminal case. The implication of this approach was that the juvenile's basic constitutional rights were not recognized; these rights included the right to the confrontation and cross-examination of the witnesses, the right to protection against self in crimination, and compliance regarding the rules of evidence. Another distinctive feature separating the juvenile justice system and the adult criminal justice system is the use of different terms for similar procedures in each system (see Table 1.1).

During the 1960s, there was a dramatic increase in juvenile crime. The existing juvenile justice system came under severe criticism, including questions concerning the informal procedures of the juvenile courts. Eventually, numerous U.S. Supreme Court decisions challenged these procedures, and some maintained these decisions would radically change the nature of processing juveniles. For instance, in the case *In re Gault* (1967), the U.S. Supreme Court ruled that a juvenile is entitled to certain due process protections constitutionally guaranteed to adults, such as a right to notice of the charges, right to counsel, right to confront and cross-examine witnesses, and right against self-incrimination. The case *In re Winship* (1970) decided that the standard of proof in juvenile delinquency proceedings is proof beyond a reasonable doubt. The first U.S. Supreme Court case to address juvenile court procedures was *Kent v. United States* (1966). The court ruled that juveniles who are facing a waiver to adult court are entitled to some essential due process rights.

Although the major impetus for establishing the juvenile justice system was to emphasize rehabilitation, since the 1980s, there has been an emerging trend toward a more punitive approach to juveniles. This changing trend is due to various converging developments, such as broadening due process protections of adults to include juveniles, the resurgence of retribution, and societal changes in perceptions about children's responsibility and accountability.[32] Another aspect to this more punitive trend is in reference to transfer provisions—waiving a juvenile offender from the juvenile justice system to the adult criminal justice system. The reasons for waivers have often been that the juvenile justice system cannot provide the needed treatment or protect the community from the offender. In reality, however, the reason for waivers is an immediate increase in the severity of response to the juvenile.[33]

Some states have had transfer provisions since the 1920s; other states have had such provisions since the 1940s.[34] Transfer provisions can be categorized into three types: judicial waiver, concurrent jurisdiction, and statutory exclusion.

Judicial waiver: The juvenile court judge has the authority to waive juvenile court jurisdiction and transfer the case to criminal court. States may use terms other than *judicial waiver*. Some call the process *certification, remand,* or *bind over* for criminal prosecution. Others *transfer* or *decline* rather than waive jurisdiction.

An offender wearing an electronic monitoring device

CRIME IN THE NEWS

Juveniles

parens patriae: a philosophical perspective that recognizes that the state has both the right and obligation to intervene on behalf of its citizens due to some impairment or impediment, or age and immaturity

judicial waiver: the authority to waive juvenile court jurisdiction and transfer the case to criminal court

JUVENILE JUSTICE SYSTEM TERM	CRIMINAL JUSTICE SYSTEM TERM
Adjudication – Decision by a juvenile court judge that the juvenile committed the delinquent act	Conviction
Adjudication hearing – A hearing to determine whether there is evidence beyond a reasonable doubt to support the allegations against the juvenile	Trial
Aftercare – Supervision of a juvenile after release from an institution	Parole
Commitment – Decision by a juvenile court judge to send the adjudicated juvenile to an institution	Sentence to prison
Delinquent act – A behavior committed by a juvenile that would have been a crime if committed by an adult	Crime
Delinquent – A juvenile who has been adjudicated of a delinquent act in juvenile court	Criminal
Detention center – A facility designed for short-term secure confinement of a juvenile prior to court disposition or execution of a court order	Jail
Disposition – The sanction imposed on a juvenile who has been adjudicated in juvenile court	Sentence
Disposition hearing – A hearing held after a juvenile has been adjudicated to determine what sanction should be imposed on the juvenile	Sentencing hearing
Institution – A facility designed for long-term secure confinement of a juvenile after adjudication (also referred to as a training school)	Prison
Petition – A document that states the allegations against a juvenile and requests a juvenile court	Indictment to adjudicate the juvenile
Taken into custody – The action on the part of a police officer to obtain custody of a juvenile accused of committing a delinquent act	Arrest

Table1.1 Comparing Juvenile and Criminal Justice System Terms

Taylor, R. W., Fritsch, E. J., & Caeti, T. J. (2002). *Juvenile justice: Policies, programs, and practices.* New York: Glencoe McGraw-Hill, p. 11.

Concurrent jurisdiction: Original jurisdiction for certain cases is shared by both criminal and juvenile courts, and the prosecutor has discretion to file such cases in either court. Transfer under concurrent jurisdiction provisions is also known as *prosecutorial waiver, prosecutor discretion,* or *direct file.*

Statutory exclusion: State statute excludes certain juvenile offenders from juvenile court jurisdiction. Under statutory exclusion provisions, cases originate in criminal rather than juvenile court. Statutory exclusion is also known as *legislative exclusion.*[35]

While all states have some type of provision that allows some juveniles to be tried in adult criminal court, 34 states have what is termed the "once an adult, always an adult" provision. Under this provision, juveniles who have been tried and convicted as adults *must* be prosecuted in criminal court for any subsequent offenses.

concurrent jurisdiction: original jurisdiction for certain cases is shared by both criminal and juvenile courts; the prosecutor has discretion to file such cases in either court

statutory exclusion: excludes certain juvenile offenders from juvenile court jurisdiction; cases originate in criminal rather than juvenile court

INTRODUCTION TO COMPARATIVE CRIMINOLOGY

REFERENCE ARTICLE

Juveniles

JOURNAL ARTICLE

Comparative Criminology

Another area of criminological research is the study of the nature and extent of crime and criminal justice systems across societies. This is an expanding area of research given the complexities associated with crime, prevention, and detection in a high-tech, global environment.[36] There are various definitions for the term **comparative criminology**, with some more comprehensive in scope than others. Hardie-Bick, Sheptycki, and Wardak noted that comparative criminology should address questions such as the following:

- Why do some societies have lower crime rates?

- What are the differences and similarities in crime definition and control across social and cultural frontiers?

- How do theoretical models relating to crime translate across cultures?[37]

LEARNING CHECK 1.2

Law enforcement agencies on the state level that have general police powers as well as additional functions, such as investigating major crimes, are designated as the _____ model; law enforcement agencies on the state level whose primary focus is to enforce laws concerning public roads and highways are designated as the _____ model. Every court, including the U.S. Supreme Court, is limited in terms of _____. Recognizing that the state has both the right and an obligation to protect juveniles is referred to as _____.

Answers located at www.sagepub.com/schram

The comparative perspective is not a relatively new approach. In 1889, E. B. Taylor outlined the benefits of such an approach during his presentation to the Royal Anthropological Institute of Great Britain. But it was not until the mid-1950s that researchers outside anthropological studies incorporated a more comparative approach in their research, such as sociology, psychology, and political science. Criminologists also began to incorporate this perspective in the late 1960s and early 1970s. While this approach has been relatively slow, a growing body of research incorporates this perspective.[38]

The study of comparative criminology is no longer considered an option but, rather, a necessity:[39]

In our global village, crime problems are no longer a domestic concern. Many types of crime have international dimensions, and trends in crime and justice in different countries are increasingly interdependent. The international nature of markets for drugs, sexual services, and illicit firearms is generally recognized. Less well understood is the international nature of many other criminal markets such as that for stolen cars with an estimated half million stolen cars transported from developed to less developed countries annually. More and more criminal groups operate internationally through loose networks of partners in crime.[40]

As mentioned previously, although there is an increased appreciation for the study of comparative criminology, there are limitations regarding the availability of international statistics on crime and criminal justice. In recent years, there have been increasing efforts to enhance international statistics on global social issues such as diseases, infant mortality, and the consumption of illegal drugs. However, efforts to collect information on crime are limited. One explanation for the relative paucity of data on this global issue is that some governments do not want to be exposed to data that may reveal their countries in a negative light. Scholars are working to break this politically inspired *conspiracy of silence*.[41]

comparative criminology: the study of crime across various cultures to identify similarities and differences in crime patterns

This text will include a series of boxes that compare the United States with foreign nations in terms of various aspects of criminology and criminal justice. Nearly every chapter in this textbook will include a comparative criminology box, and each will focus on a single type of serious crime; for example, the comparative criminology box in this chapter examines relative rates of motor vehicle theft. It is important to be aware of and understand where the United States stands in relative terms of crime rates, which enlightens us on how cultural and socioeconomic factors influence such relative rates. The same can be said of comparing various regions/states/cities across the United States, which some of the comparative boxes will also examine.

Most of the statistics in the various comparative criminology boxes of this book were obtained from a recently published book, *The World of Crime,* written by Jan Van Dijk, which is one of the best compilations of international crime statistics in that it synthesizes and reports on a variety of measures using both police reports and victimization surveys from a multitude of sources.

MEASURING CRIME

Measuring crime is necessary for various reasons.[42] Some of these reasons include describing crime, explaining why crime occurs, and evaluating programs and policies. It is important to legislators, as well as concerned citizens, that crime statistics are available to describe, or gauge, criminal activity that can influence community well-being. Measuring crime is also needed for risk assessment of different social groups, including their potential for becoming offenders or victims. Another purpose of measuring crime is explanation. Identifying causes requires that differences in crime rates can be related to differences in people and their situations. Counting crime is also used to evaluate and justify programs and policies that try to address criminal activity (e.g., rehabilitation, incapacitation, deterrence).

This section examines various data collection methods used to enhance our understanding of criminal behaviors and patterns. The first portion describes various statistics collected by law enforcement agencies. The next portion provides an overview of the National Crime Victimization Survey. We then present a few examples of self-report surveys. The last portion summarizes additional approaches used to collect crime data, such as the National Youth Gang Survey and spatial analyses of crime.

CRIME DATA FROM LAW ENFORCEMENT AGENCIES

Law enforcement agencies throughout the United States gather a number of crime statistics. In this section, we look at five methods used to accomplish this. They are the Uniform Crime Reports, the Supplementary Homicide Reports, the National Incident-Based Reporting System, Hate Crime Statistics, and the Law Enforcement Officers Killed and Assaulted Statistics.

UNIFORM CRIME REPORTS. During the 1927 meeting of the International Chiefs of Police, efforts were made to collect crime statistics in a consistent and uniform manner.[43] As a result, seven main classifications of crime were selected to assess fluctuations in crime rates. These classifications were later identified as Part I crimes. In 1960, these Part I crimes were termed the Crime Index. Part I crimes were those crimes most likely to be reported to the police, including murder, rape, robbery, aggravated assault, larceny, burglary, and motor vehicle theft. Information was collected on additional categories of crimes, ranging from sex offenses to parking violations; these are designated as Part II crimes (see Table 1.2).

The primary objective of the **Uniform Crime Reports (UCR)** is to generate a consistent (or reliable) set of crime statistics that can be used in law enforcement administration,

Uniform Crime Reports (UCR): an annual report published by the FBI in the DOJ, which is meant to estimate most of the major street crimes in the United States

Offenses	
Part I Offenses	
Part I offense classifications include (in this particular order):	
1. Criminal Homicide	5. Burglary
2. Forcible Rape	6. Larceny-theft (except motor vehicle theft)
3. Robbery	7. Motor Vehicle Theft
4. Aggravated Assault	8. Arson
Part II Offenses	
Part II offenses encompass all other reportable classifications outside those defined as Part I. Law enforcement agencies report to the FBI only arrest data involving the Part II crimes:	
9. Other Assaults	20. Offenses Against the Family and Children
10. Forgery and Counterfeiting	21. Driving Under the Influence
11. Fraud	22. Liquor Laws
12. Embezzlement	23. Drunkenness
13. Stolen Property: Buying, Receiving, Processing	24. Disorderly Conduct
14. Vandalism	25. Vagrancy
15. Weapons: Carrying, Possessing, etc.	26. All Other Offenses
16. Prostitution and Commercialized Vice	27. Suspicion
17. Sex Offenses	28. Curfew and Loitering Laws–(Persons under 18)
18. Drug Abuse Violations	29. Runaways–(Persons under 18)
19. Gambling	

Table 1.2 Part I and Part II Offenses

Source: Federal Bureau of Investigations. (2004). *UCR: Uniform Crime Reporting Handbook.* Washington, DC: U.S. Department of Justice, p. 8.

operation, and management. Over the years, however, the UCR has become one of the country's foremost indicators of crime. The UCR has provided information on fluctuations in the level of crime for criminologists, sociologists, legislators, municipal planners, and the media—information that has subsequently been used for both research and planning purposes (see Figure 1.2).[44]

In 2004, the FBI discontinued use of what was referred to as the Crime Index. The Crime Index was often used to detect overall changes in crime across the country:

> The Crime Index and the Modified Crime Index were not true indicators of the degrees of criminality because they were always driven upward by the offense with the highest number, typically larceny-theft. The sheer volume of those offenses overshadowed more serious but less frequently committed offenses, creating a bias against a jurisdiction with a high number of larceny-thefts but a low number of other serious crimes such as murder and forcible rape.[45]

As mentioned previously, the UCR Program classifies offenses into two groups: Part I and Part II crimes. In October 1978, by congressional mandate, arson was included as a Part I crime. Compared with other index crimes, however, arson is less likely to be reported to the police; arsons are often classified as "fires of suspicious origin."[46]

2010 CRIME CLOCK STATISTICS

A Violent Crime occurred every	25.3 seconds
One Murder every	35.6 minutes
One Forcible Rape every	6.2 minutes
One Robbery every	1.4 minutes
One Aggravated Assault every	40.5 seconds
A Property Crime occurred every	3.5 seconds
One Burglary every	14.6 seconds
One Larceny-theft every	5.1 seconds
One Motor Vehicle Theft every	42.8 seconds

Figure 1.2 2010 FBI Crime Clock

As early as 1931, there were criticisms concerning the UCR, and some of these still apply to the current UCR.[47] Even with these criticisms, more than 17,000 law enforcement agencies voluntarily submit their crime data to the FBI, and the UCR continues to be a major source of information pertaining to crime in the United States.[48] Below is a brief overview of the criticisms and limitations concerning the UCR:

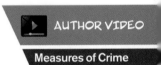

AUTHOR VIDEO

Measures of Crime

1. Some crimes do not come to the attention of those responsible for collecting this information. In reference to the UCR, this pertains to law enforcement agencies. European criminologists named these *unknown* crimes *the dark figure of crime*.[49]

2. The UCR concentrates on conventional street crime (e.g., assaults, robbery) but does not adequately include other serious types of offenses such as corporate crime.[50] This is illustrated by the priority given to the investigation and prosecution of such crimes within the federal government, including the collection of crime statistics.[51]

3. Crime statistics, such as the UCR, can be used for political purposes. Some argue that official crime statistics are a social construction.[52] In this vein, these statistics are perceived as an *objective reality* for program and policy purposes.[53] When these claims are stated and supported by powerful groups, this can influence public perceptions, which can then result in policy changes.

4. Some law enforcement agencies may submit incomplete or delinquent reports. These incomplete or delinquent reports can result from budgetary restrictions and changes in personnel experienced in preparing UCR data, for example.[54]

5. Problems with the collection of UCR data can also occur because of clerical and data processing errors. Based on his experience as a senior analyst in the New York Division of Criminal Justice Services, Henry Brownstein described how accuracy can be compromised due to clerical error.[55]

6. Changes in the legal code can influence subsequent crime reports and make later comparisons difficult. Thus, when a previously acceptable behavior is later criminalized or when a classification is altered (e.g., from misdemeanor to felony, or the reverse), this will likely result in a change in reported crimes.[56] For instance, some have argued that there are increasing efforts to *criminalize homelessness*. Some cities have implemented laws that make it illegal to sleep, eat, or sit in public spaces.[57]

SUPPLEMENTARY HOMICIDE REPORTS. Homicides are less likely to be underreported compared with other crimes counted in the UCR. Homicides are also more likely to result in an arrest or to be cleared compared with other offenses. Finally, compared with other offenses such as forcible rape, robbery, and aggravated assault, homicide offenses are more likely to include details about the incident, such as information about victims and/or offenders.[58] Thus, in the 1960s, the FBI developed the Supplementary Homicide Reports (SHR).[59] Since 1976, these data have been archived at the National Archive of Criminal Justice Data, which is maintained by the University of Michigan's Inter-university Consortium for Political and Social Research.[60]

The SHR collects additional information pertaining to the homicide incident, including details of the murder victim and offender, their relationship to one another, the weapon used, and the circumstances in each criminal homicide.[61] The SHR has been key in developing policy related to homicide, especially since these data include not only the number of homicides but also factors associated with these crimes (e.g., characteristics of the victims and offenders).[62] The SHR has also been used to enhance our understanding of patterns and trends pertaining to homicides, including exploring sibling homicide, or siblicide;[63] comparing and understanding lethal violence in Finland and the United States;[64] examining the relationship between race, the death penalty, and homicide;[65] and suggested improvements to the SHR for collecting data on workplace homicides.[66] The SHR can also be considered the forerunner to the National Incident-Based Reporting System (NIBRS), since it provided additional information about specific incidents.[67]

NATIONAL INCIDENT-BASED REPORTING SYSTEM. Initially, the UCR was considered primarily a tool for law enforcement agencies. By the 1980s, it was evident that these data were being used by other entities involved with social planning and policy. Thus, there was a need to collect more detailed information on these data. The FBI, the Department of Justice Statistics (the agency responsible for funding criminal justice information projects), and other agencies and individuals from various disciplines were involved with setting in place the changes needed to update the program for collecting crime data.[68] By the end of the 1980s, NIBRS was operational.[69]

NIBRS uses an incident-based reporting system; the UCR Program uses a summary reporting system (i.e., counts). NIBRS includes a greater degree of detail in reporting. The unit of analysis for the UCR is the reporting agency. For NIBRS data, however, there are six possible "units of analysis" or segments pertaining to the crime incident: administrative, offense, property, victim, offender, and arrestee. Within each segment, various kinds of information are collected on each incident. As a result of providing more "detailed, accurate, and meaningful data than those produced by the traditional UCR Program,"[70] NIBRS data have also been used to enhance criminological research. Examples of studies using NIBRS include evaluating factors associated with current culture of violence theories;[71] predicting survival among elderly victims of violence;[72] comparing characteristics of assaults motivated by bias with other types of assault;[73] studying the prevalence and nature of violent offending by females;[74] examining the relationship between illegal gun availability and violent crime;[75] and exploring explanations of female–female aggression.[76]

HATE CRIME DATA. On April 23, 1990, the president signed into law the Hate Crime Statistics Act. This was due to an increasing concern about these types of offenses.[77] As part of the UCR Program, the attorney general is required to develop guidelines and collect data about crimes that manifest evidence of prejudice based on race, religion, sexual orientation, or ethnicity, including, where appropriate, the crimes of murder and nonnegligent manslaughter; forcible rape; aggravated assault, simple assault, and intimidation; arson; and destruction, damage, or vandalism of property.[78] The Violent Crime Control and Law Enforcement Act of 1994 amended the original act to include crimes based on both physical and mental disabilities, which should also be viewed as hate crimes.[79]

CITY CRIME RANKINGS

Murder in 2011

To develop procedures for collecting national hate crime data, many emphasized avoiding assignment of any new data-reporting responsibilities to those law enforcement agencies participating in the UCR Program. Thus, the collection of hate crime data provides additional information on traditional UCR collection. If a traditional offense has been motivated by the offender's bias, the reporting agency is to complete the Hate Crime Incident Report. This form collects information on the location, victim type (e.g., individual, business), number of offenders, race of offender(s), and bias motivation. The various categories of bias motivation include race, ethnicity/national origin, religion, sexual orientation, and disability.

LAW ENFORCEMENT OFFICERS KILLED AND ASSAULTED STATISTICS. The FBI also collects data on the number of law enforcement officers killed and assaulted in the United States each year. This is important information that has been used for several reasons, including for estimates of the risk involved in police work and analyses of what influences assaults against and killings of police officers. The UCR Program began gathering these data in 1972.[80] The Law Enforcement Officers Killed and Assaulted (LEOKA) is a supplementary data collection program of the UCR. LEOKA collects from participating agencies data on officer line-of-duty deaths and assaults. Information obtained from these data assists agencies in developing policies to enhance officer safety.

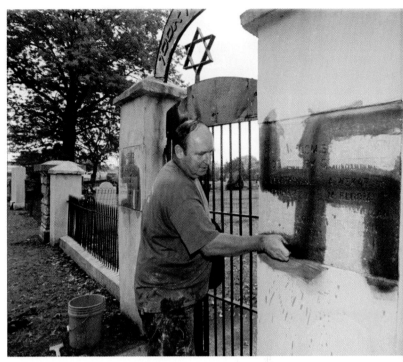

A man trying to remove a swastika from the entrance to a Jewish cemetery

Participating law enforcement agencies are required to report on officers who are killed or assaulted and meet the following criteria: (1) working in an official capacity, (2) having full arrest powers, (3) wearing a badge (ordinarily), (4) carrying a firearm (ordinarily), and (5) being paid from governmental funds allocated for payment of sworn law enforcement representatives. These officers are usually employed by local, county, state, tribal, or federal entities and working in occupations such as municipal or county police, constables, state police, highway patrol officers, sheriffs and deputies, marshals, and special agents. Officers usually not included are those involved with protective, prosecutorial, or confinement activities, such as federal judges, U.S. attorneys, probation officers, corrections officers, jailers, and prison officials.[81]

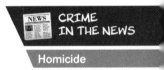

CRIME IN THE NEWS

Homicide

The UCR Program includes a special form used to collect information on those incidents involving line-of-duty felonious or accidental killing of an officer or assault of an officer. In reference to officer assaults, the UCR emphasizes that reporting agencies must count all assaults. Even those incidents that involve more than verbal abuse or minor resistance to an arrest but do not result in the officer being injured need to be reported.[82]

CRIME DATA FROM VICTIMS OF CRIME: THE NATIONAL CRIME VICTIMIZATION SURVEY

While Canada and some European countries have surveyed individuals regarding their experiences of being victims of crimes, the United States has the longest and most extensive background with such surveys. Unofficial measures of crime, such as the National Crime Victimization Survey (NCVS), further broaden our understanding of crime with information from official measures of crime (e.g., the UCR).

National Crime Victimization Survey (NCVS): a primary measure of crime in the United States; collected by the DOJ and the Census Bureau, based on interviews with victims of crime

The primary purpose of these data is to provide additional insight into what was referred to at the beginning of this chapter as the *dark figure* of crime (e.g., crimes unreported to law enforcement). Some of the reasons why victims failed to report these crimes to law enforcement include the following: (1) The victim believed nothing could be done about the incident; (2) the victim felt that the crime incident was not important enough to report to the police; (3) the victim perceived the incident to be too private or personal; and (4) the victim thought that the police would not want to be inconvenienced with the crime incident.[83] The NCVS is also intended to (1) identify portions of the population at risk of victimization, (2) estimate multiple victimization rates, (3) provide data needed to evaluate crime prevention programs, and (4) allow for comparisons of patterns, amounts, and locations of crime with the UCR.[84]

Any individual living in the United States and 12 years of age or older is eligible for participation in the NCVS.[85] The households are selected by using scientific sampling methods.[86] The NCVS collects data on individuals who have been the victims of crimes, whether or not these crimes were reported to law enforcement. The NCVS estimates the proportion of the various crime types reported to law enforcement; it also provides information as to why victims reported, or did not report, these crimes to law enforcement.[87] The NCVS provides various information including data about the victims (e.g., age, sex, race, ethnicity, marital status, income, and educational level), the offenders (e.g., sex, race, approximate age, and victim–offender relationship), and the crimes (e.g., time and place of occurrence, use of weapons, nature of injury, and economic consequences). The victims are also asked about their experiences with the criminal justice system, if they used any self-protective measures, and possible substance abuse by offenders.[88]

Because the NCVS was developed to complement the UCR, both data collection programs are similar in some respects. They both collect data on the same types of serious crimes: rape, robbery, aggravated assault, burglary, theft, and motor vehicle theft. The definitions of rape, robbery, theft, and motor vehicle theft are practically the same for both programs. However, the UCR measures rape as a crime against women *only*, while the NCVS measures rape as a crime against both sexes.

There are some meaningful differences between the UCR and the NCVS. First, each program was developed to serve different purposes. The UCR's primary purpose was to provide reliable criminal justice data for law enforcement administration, operation, and management. The purpose of the NCVS was to collect information that was previously unavailable on crime (e.g., crimes unreported to the police), victims, and offenders.

Second, while both programs collect information on overlapping types of crimes, these types of crimes are not necessarily identical. As mentioned previously, the NCVS collects data on crimes that were both reported and unreported to law enforcement. The UCR collects information on homicides, arson, commercial crimes, and crimes against children under the age of 12, whereas the NCVS does not collect these data. The UCR does not include sexual assaults and simple assaults.

Third, the UCR and NCVS programs use different methods to collect crime data. Thus, for some crimes, they use different definitions. For instance, the UCR defines burglary as the unlawful entry or attempted entry of a structure to commit a felony or theft. Since the NCVS surveys individuals and it is difficult for victims to ascertain offender motives, burglary is defined as the entry or attempted entry of a residence by a person who had no right to be in that residence.

Fourth, the two programs used different bases to calculate rates for certain crimes. For property crimes (e.g., burglary, theft, and motor vehicle theft), the UCR calculates rates for these crimes using a per-capita rate of 100,000 persons. The NCVS calculates rates for these crimes using a 1,000-per-household rate. If the number of households does not grow at the same rate each year, compared with the population, trend data for property crimes rates for these two programs may not be comparable.

Fifth, since the UCR and NCVS implement different sampling procedures, there may be variations in estimates of crime. Estimates from the NCVS are obtained from interviews; thus, these data are susceptible to a margin of error. The NCVS uses rigorous statistical methods to calculate confidence intervals around all survey estimates. Trend data in the NCVS reports are listed as genuine only if there is at least a 90% certainty that the measured changes are not due to sampling variation. The UCR data are based on actual counts of those crimes reported by law enforcement agencies. There are instances when UCR data are estimated for nonparticipating jurisdictions or for those jurisdictions reporting only partial data.[89]

SELF-REPORT SURVEYS

JOURNAL ARTICLE

Measuring Crime

Generally, surveys address four broad classes of questions: (1) the prevalence of attitudes, beliefs, and behaviors; (2) changes in these attitudes, beliefs, and behaviors over time; (3) differences between groups of people in their attitudes, beliefs, and behaviors; and (4) causal propositions about these attitudes, beliefs, and behaviors.[90] Self-report surveys collect data by asking respondents to provide information about themselves, usually as to whether they have engaged in certain forms of illegal behavior. Self-report information can be collected either through written questionnaires or through in-person interviews.

While no nationwide surveys are implemented to collect self-report surveys of all types of crime, various types of self-report surveys have been implemented to collect data on specific types of behavior. In addition to focusing on certain types of behavior, these surveys sometimes focus on certain groups (e.g., juveniles). Three self-report surveys are discussed below: Monitoring the Future, the National Household Survey on Drug Abuse, and the National Youth Survey.

MONITORING THE FUTURE. Substance abuse by adolescents continues to be an issue not only because it is itself illegal and can pose a health risk but also because it may be linked to other types of criminal activity. In 1975, the National Institute on Drug Abuse sponsored the annual self-report survey *Monitoring the Future: A Continuing Study of Lifestyles and Values of Youth*. It is sometimes referred to as Monitoring the Future (MTF). The MTF collects information to measure patterns of substance and alcohol use among youths. While the survey initially sampled just 12th-grade students, 8th- and 10th-grade students were also included in the annual survey in 1981.

Currently, the MTF survey of 12th-grade students contains about 1,400 variables. The survey measures use of drugs such as tobacco, alcohol, marijuana, hashish, LSD, hallucinogens, amphetamines, Ritalin, Quaaludes, barbiturates, cocaine, crack cocaine, GHB (gamma hydroxy butyrate), and heroin.[91] The MTF also collects information on students' attitudes and beliefs about drugs, drug availability, and social meanings of drug use. In addition to measuring issues about substance and alcohol use, the survey asks students about their attitudes on topics such as education, work and leisure, sex roles and family, population concerns (overpopulation and birth control), conservation, religion, politics, interpersonal relationships, race relations, and happiness.[92] One limitation to the MTF research design is that it does not survey those youth who drop out of high school. This is a problem because certain behaviors, such as illegal drug use, are higher than average among this group of individuals; however, it would be difficult to survey them.[93]

NATIONAL HOUSEHOLD SURVEY ON DRUG ABUSE. Since 1971, the National Household Survey on Drug Abuse (NHSDA) has been used to collect information annually on the use of illegal drugs by individuals in the United States. The NHSDA is currently sponsored by the Substance Abuse and Mental Health Services Administration, Department of Health and Human Services; the data collection is conducted by the Research Triangle Institute.[94] The NHSDA is one of the largest surveys of drug use ever conducted in the United States.

The NHSDA is administered through face-to-face interviews with individuals at their place of residence. The NHSDA samples individuals 12 years of age and older who are residents of households (e.g., shelters, rooming/boarding houses, college dormitories, migratory workers' camps, halfway houses) and civilians living on military bases. It does not sample individuals who are homeless people not living in shelters, active military personnel, and institutionalized individuals (e.g., prisoners, nursing home patients).[95]

Over the years, there have been some changes to how NHSDA data are collected. First, prior to 1999, NHSDA was solely a national design rather than a state-based sampling plan. In 1999, the NHSDA modified its sampling procedure in an effort to develop a 5-year sample design that would provide estimates for all 50 states and the District of Columbia from 1999 to 2003.[96] Second, prior to 1999, the questionnaire was conducted as a paper-and-pencil interview that lasted about an hour. Starting in 1999, the NHSDA data collection procedure has been conducted by a computer-assisted interview technique that consists of a computer-assisted personal interview and an audio computer-assisted self-interview.[97]

NATIONAL YOUTH SURVEY. A major shortcoming of earlier juvenile delinquency research was that it concentrated on those youths who were already in the juvenile justice system. (This will be discussed in later chapters in reference to developing theories based on these data.) One reason why these data were used for such studies was that their records (e.g., police, juvenile hall) were easily accessible to researchers. The problem was that this research focused only on those juveniles who were formally processed in the system. Usually, these juveniles came from disadvantaged backgrounds and were more likely to come to the attention of the system, whereas juveniles from middle- or upper-class backgrounds were more likely to be diverted from the system.[98]

Implementing self-report surveys is one approach to addressing problems associated with studying only those juveniles formally in the system. In 1977, researchers at the University of Colorado implemented the National Youth Survey (NYS) with an initial sample of 1,725 male and female juveniles born between 1959 and 1965. Each respondent, along with his or her parents/legal guardians, was asked about various events and behaviors that occurred the previous year. These juveniles were subsequently interviewed each year from 1976 to 1980. Each interview phase is referred as a "wave." Thus, the first five waves of the NYS were between 1976 and 1980.[99] Wave 6 covered a 3-year period from 1981 to 1983; Wave 7 covered the 3-year period from 1984 to 1986; Waves 8 and 9 occurred between 1987 and 1994.[100]

The NYS includes items that measure a respondent's involvement in criminal activity. It measures more than 40 offenses that represent the full range of offenses reported in the UCR. The NYS also includes measuring respondents' attitudes on issues such as level of community involvement, educational aspirations, employment skills, pregnancy, abortion, neighborhood problems, and the use of drugs and/or alcohol.[101] The NYS responses can be sorted into three general categories: (1) self-reports of delinquency; (2) parental appraisals of their children; and (3) the youths' internal appraisals of themselves from their parents', friends', and teachers' perspectives.[102]

When comparing data collected only on those youths who came to the attention of the criminal justice system (i.e., official statistics) and self-report studies, the researchers cautioned that "to abandon either self-report or official statistics in favor of the other is 'rather shortsighted; to systematically ignore the findings of either is dangerous, particularly when the two measures provide apparently contradictory findings.'"[103] Instead, they emphasized that to obtain a full understanding of delinquent behavior, one should use *both* self-report surveys and official record research.

ADDITIONAL APPROACHES TO COLLECTING CRIME DATA

In this section, additional approaches to collecting crime data are briefly covered. It is important for those involved in the criminal justice field to realize that there are various types of data collection programs other than the UCR and NCVS. These additional data collection efforts are usually for a more specific purpose or target a more specific population. In this section, the National Youth Gang Survey and Spatial Analyses of Crime are reviewed.

NATIONAL YOUTH GANG SURVEY. In recent years, there has been an increasing number of gangs and gang-related crime. However, there was no single source of uniform data that could be used to compare patterns, changes, and trends over time.[104] In response to this growing concern, the Office of Juvenile Justice and Delinquency Prevention and the Institute for Intergovernmental Research established the National Youth Gang Center (NYGC). One of NYGC's primary tasks was to implement periodic national surveys to collect data on problems associated with youth gangs. The first National Youth Gang Survey was conducted in 1995. For this initial survey, NYGC wanted to collect basic information concerning the gang problem in different jurisdictions. The survey was mailed to 4,120 police and sheriff's departments across the United States.[105] About 83% of the participating agencies responded to the survey.[106]

While the 1995 survey was the most comprehensive national gang survey up to that time and provided useful baseline data, the sampling procedure was not adequately representative of the United States. The sample for the 1996 National Youth Gang Survey was more representative of the country. Subsequent annual surveys were administered to the same respondents in an effort to provide comparative and trend analyses.[107]

For the 2010 survey, of the 2,544 survey recipients, 2,158 (85%) responded to the survey. The sample consisted of two groups: (1) all police departments in cities with more than 50,000 residents (i.e., larger cities) and all suburban county police and sheriff's departments (collectively referred to as "larger areas"), and (2) a random sample of police departments in cities with populations between 2,500 and 50,000 and rural county sheriff's departments (collectively referred to as "small areas").[108]

Obtain a better understanding of delinquent behavior, researchers should incorporate both self-report surveys and official data.

SPATIAL ANALYSES OF CRIME. Spatial analyses of crime focus on crime *places*. This interest in crime places "spans theory from the perspective of understanding the etiology of crime, and practice from the perspective of developing effective criminal justice interventions to reduce crime."[109] Thus, rather than attempting to understand crime from an individual perspective, spatial analysis also incorporates where and when crimes occur. This perspective can then assist in efforts to reduce future criminal activity (see Figure 1.3).

Figure 1.3 Example of Crime Mapping

Source: http://en.wikipedia.org/wiki/File:DChomicides.jpg; http://creativecommons.org/licenses/by-sa/2.5/.

Mapping crimes can provide such information as location, distance, direction, and pattern. Location is considered the most important piece of information. Understanding where crimes have occurred or what crimes may occur in the future is essential, especially when considering how to allocate police personnel and community resources. Distance is also a crucial element. For instance, distance can answer such questions as, "How far did the victim live from the place where she was attacked?" Direction is most helpful when considered along with distance. Usually, direction is referred to in a broader context, in statements such as, "Serial robberies are moving southeast" or "The east side is becoming a high-crime area." Finally, pattern is what crime analysts attempt to develop when using place-based crime data. Patterns are usually designated as random, uniform, clustered, or dispersed.[110]

Attempting to understand crime through location is not new. Law enforcement agencies have considered crime location to be an important component of crime control. In fact, the use of maps can be traced as far back as 1900 by the New York City Police Department.[111] Police departments would place pins on those maps to represent crimes that occurred in various locations. Criminologists have also explored whether there is a relationship between criminal activity and location. These criminologists attempt to understand crime with what are called social ecological theories.[112] These criminologists examine how ecological conditions such as housing standards, poverty, and transient populations influence criminal activity.

Since the 1990s, there have been major advances in the methods available for analyzing place-based crime data. These advances are primarily due to technological improvements, especially with computer capabilities. In addition to these computer capabilities, there have been major contributions with geographic information systems (GIS). GIS is a system not only made up of hardware but also incorporating computer software and data

CRIME IN THE NEWS

Crime Mapping

APPLYING THEORY TO CRIME: *MOTOR VEHICLE THEFT*

Considered one of the eight Part I or Index offenses, motor vehicle theft is defined by the FBI's UCR Program as "the theft or attempted theft of a motor vehicle. . . . A motor vehicle is a self-propelled vehicle that runs on land surfaces and not on rails."[113] Examples of motor vehicles include sport utility vehicles, automobiles, trucks, buses, motorcycles, motor scooters, all-terrain vehicles, and snowmobiles. They do not, however, include farm equipment, bulldozers, airplanes, construction equipment, or watercraft. In 2011, about 715,373 motor vehicle thefts were reported in the United States. In that time, more than $4.3 billion was lost as a result of motor vehicle thefts; the average dollar loss per stolen vehicle was $6,089.

Almost 74% of all motor vehicle thefts were automobiles. According to the National Insurance Crime Bureau (NICB), the Honda Civic (1995) is stolen more often than any other car in the United States. This is followed by the Honda Accord (1991), Toyota Camry (1989), Ford F-150 (1997), Chevrolet C/K 1500 (1994), Acura Integra (1994), Dodge Ram Pickup (2004), Nissan Sentra (1994), Toyota Pickup (1988), and Toyota Corolla (2007). Note that the year in parentheses is the model year most often stolen.[114] Further, the NICB noted that one should also consider vehicle theft fraud. In the past, vehicle thieves were focused on stealing cars and trucks the "old-fashioned way" such as by forced entry and circumventing ignitions. Today, there are new scams for stealing vehicles that involve fraud:

- Owner give-ups: The vehicle owner lies about the theft of the vehicle and then orchestrates its destruction to collect insurance money. He or she claims the vehicle was stolen, but then it is found burned or heavily damaged in a secluded area, submerged in a lake, or in extreme cases, buried underground.

- 30-day specials: Owners whose vehicles need extensive repairs sometimes perpetrate the 30-day special scam. They will report the vehicle stolen and hide it for 30 days—just long enough for the insurance company to settle the claim. Once the claim is paid, the vehicle is often found abandoned.

- Export fraud: After securing a bank loan for a new vehicle, an owner obtains an insurance policy for it. The owner reports the vehicle stolen to a U.S. law enforcement agency but, in reality, has illegally shipped it overseas to be sold on the black market. The owner then collects on the insurance policy, as well as any illegal profits earned through overseas conspirators who sell the vehicle.

- Phantom vehicles: An individual creates a phony title or registration to secure insurance on a nonexistent vehicle. The insured then reports the vehicle stolen before filing a fraudulent insurance claim. Oftentimes, antique or luxury vehicles are used in this scam, since these valuable vehicles produce larger insurance settlements.[115]

One interesting approach to addressing the problem of motor vehicle thefts, which has been popularized by the media, is the use of *bait cars*. The Los Angeles Police Department defines use of a bait car as "an undercover operation where [they] bring in a plain motor vehicle and load it with desirable goods (iPod, GPS, cigarettes, etc.) and hope someone breaks into the car as [they] are watching."[116] On June 25, 2012, police in Albuquerque, New Mexico, were quite surprised when one of their bait cars was stolen by an 11-year-old boy. This boy wanted to take the car for a joy ride; on

the way, he also decided to pick up two of his 10-year-old friends. A video camera had been placed in the bait car. In the video, the boy can be heard bragging to his friends about his driving skills. For instance, while turning up the radio to enjoy the music as he drives, the boy says, "I'm a good driver, huh?" During their joy ride, apparently one of the boys spotted a police officer; one of the boys said, "Quiet," while the other said, "Slow down."[117]

After reading about this youth, one might ask, "Why would he do that?" Some of you might consider that his 10-year-old peers somehow influenced his behavior, especially since it seems he wanted them to be a part of his criminal adventure. Others may argue that these boys lacked some form of adult supervision resulting from a dysfunctional family environment. Another possible explanation is that these boys lacked self-control, that they are thrill seekers who knew this was wrong, especially given their reaction when spotting the police. When we read about this type of behavior in a newspaper or hear about it on the news and ask, "Why would someone do that?" we are trying to find some kind of explanation. This is what theory attempts to do but in a more rigorous, scientific manner. Throughout this text, as we discuss various theories, we attempt to apply key points of those theories to either a real or hypothetical situation in boxes labeled "Applying Theories to Crime." For each of these special boxes, we begin with a brief discussion of a particular crime, such as motor vehicle theft, robbery, or murder. Subsequently, we apply the relevant theory or theories in that chapter to that particular crime. With this approach, you will obtain general information about particular offenses, especially the Part I offenses in the UCR, as well as applying key features of various theories to those crimes.

that are later used to analyze and describe information (e.g., crime). This information is then linked to spatial location. Further, law enforcement agencies continue to enhance the computerization of police records management systems as well as computer-aided dispatch systems (i.e., citizen calls to police).

VIDEO ▶

Motor Vehicle Theft

WHAT THESE CRIME MEASURES REVEAL ABOUT THE DISTRIBUTION OF OFFENDERS AND VICTIMS

Data collection programs, such as the UCR and NCVS, provide comparable data that allow researchers as well as policymakers to examine crime patterns and trends on different factors over varying time periods. For instance, annually the FBI submits the *Crime in the United States* report based on the data collected through the UCR Program. The *2011 Crime in the United States* report estimated a 3.8% decrease in violent crimes from 2010. When comparing 5- and 10-year patterns, the 2011 violent crime total was 15.4% below the 2007 level; the 2011 violent crime total was 15.5% below the 2002 level. For information collected on the type of weapon involved, firearms were used in 67.7% of murders, 41.3% of robberies, and 21.2% of aggravated assaults.

In terms of property crimes, according to the *2011 Crime in the United States* report, there were about 9,063,173 property crime offenses in the country that year. This was a 0.5% decrease when compared with 2010 and an 8.3% decrease compared with 2007. Larceny-theft accounted for 68.0% of all property crimes, followed by burglary (24.1%) and motor vehicle theft (7.9%).

When examining information on offenders, 69.2% of all individuals arrested were white, 28.4% were black, and the remaining 2.4% were of other races. Almost three quarters of individuals arrested were male (74.1%). The largest number of arrests was for drug abuse violations, larceny-theft, and driving under the influence.[118]

When comparing patterns of victimization not reported to the police, the following are some key findings:

- The percentage of violent and property crimes that went unreported to police declined from 1994 to 2010. During this period, victims most often did not report violent victimizations to the police because they dealt with the crime in another way (e.g., reporting it to another official or handling it privately). Among unreported violent victimizations, the percentage of victims who believed the police would not or could not help increased, from 10% in 1994 to 20% in 2010.

- From 2006 to 2010, about 3 in 10 crimes involving a weapon and an injury went unreported to police. The most often cited reason (42%) for not reporting was fear of retaliation or of getting the offender in trouble. This fear was also the most common reason (46%) victims did not report intimate partner violence to the police. Crimes perpetrated by someone the victim knew well, such as a neighbor, coworker, or teacher (62%), or by a casual acquaintance (60%) were more likely to go unreported than were crimes committed by a stranger (51%).

- Serious violent crime (defined as rape or sexual assault, robbery, or aggravated assault) was less likely to go unreported to the police in 2010 than in 1994. The percentage of unreported serious violent victimizations declined from 50% in 1994 to 42% in 2010.[119]

STATE CRIME RANKINGS

Motor Vehicle Thefts in 2011

CRIMINOLOGICAL THEORY

Respected scientific theories in all fields of study, whether chemistry, physics, or criminology, tend to have the same characteristics. This is further illustrated by the scientific review process (i.e., blind peer review by experts) used in all fields to

COMPARATIVE CRIMINOLOGY: *MOTOR VEHICLE THEFT*

Ranking Regions/ Countries on Rates of Motor Vehicle Theft

The key measure of prevalence of motor vehicle theft in the world is the International Crime Victimization Survey (ICVS), which is a data bank that collects and standardizes police reports from more than 70 countries around the world. This measure has been conducted since 1987 and does have some weaknesses, but it is currently the best international measure of most crimes for such cross-national comparisons.

The ICVS has collected many years' worth of data on motor vehicle theft. Van Dijk synthesized the data from ICVS regarding car theft from the years 1996 to 2005.[120] Some regions have very high numbers of stolen vehicles, but to make a fair comparison across regions, rates of ownership should be accounted for. As seen in Figure 1.4, the countries with by far the highest percentages of car owners in urban areas that had been victimized by car theft were in the continent of Africa. A relatively distant second highest ranking was countries in the region of Latin America/Caribbean.

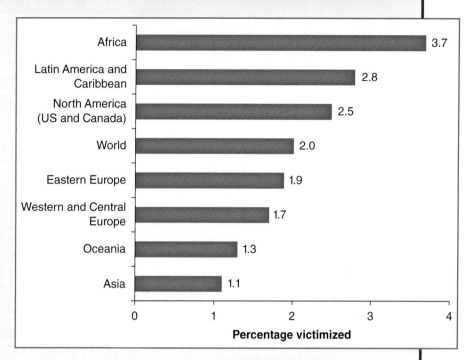

Figure 1.4 Percentages of Car Owners in Urban Areas Victimized by Car Theft or Joyriding During the Past 12 Months

Source: ICVS. 1996–2005.

To be more specific, we can examine the ranking of the countries in terms of their rates of vehicle theft. As can be seen in Table 1.3, ICVS data show that Papua New Guinea had by far the highest rate (at 9.8% of car owners victimized each year), followed by Mozambique (7.5%) and then South Africa, Swaziland, and Brazil rounding out the Top 5. It is notable that the United States did not rank in the worst 15 countries for motor vehicle theft.

FIFTEEN COUNTRIES WITH THE HIGHEST RATES					
1 Papua New Guinea*	9.8	6 Tanzania*	5.7	11 Colombia	3.5
2 Mozambique	7.5	7 Tunisia*	4.6	12 Albania	3.5
3 South Africa	7.1	8 Argentina	3.9	13 Ireland	3.2
4 Swaziland	6.3	9 Italy	3.7	14 Zambia	3.2
5 Brazil	6.0	10 Czech Republic	3.5	15 Slovak Republic	3.0
FIFTEEN COUNTRIES WITH MEDIUM-HIGH RATES					
18 Unites States	2.7	34 United Kingdom	2.0	49 Norway	1.2
19 Mexico	2.6	35 New Zealand	1.9	50 Belgium	1.1
20 Portugal	2.6	36 Latvia	1.9	51 Iceland	1.1
26 Belarus	2.2	42 Peru	1.5	55 Netherlands	1.0
27 Ukraine	2.2	48 Zimbabwe	1.2	56 Canada	1.0

...CONTINUED

FIFTEEN COUNTRIES WITH THE LOWEST RATES					
58 India	0.9	63 Germany	0.6	68 Switzerland	0.3
59 Slovenia	0.8	64 China	0.6	69 France	0.3
60 Indonesia	0.8	65 Austria	0.5	70 Japan	0.2
61 Austria	0.8	66 Macedonia, FYR	0.5	71 Romania	0.2
62 Hungary	0.6	67 Korea, Rep.	0.4	72 Hong Kong, China	0.0

Table1.3 World Ranking of Countries According to Victimization of Car Owners in Urban Areas by Theft of a Car in the Course of One Year, Rank Number, and Percentage of Victims per Year

Sources: ICVS, 1992, 1996–2005, latest survey available.

*Countries with data from ICVS, 1992.

It is not too surprising that motor vehicle theft tends to be higher (when accounting for rates of ownership) in some of the most deprived nations in the world, such as Africa and various Latin American/Caribbean countries. After all, in such extreme poverty, many individuals are driven to commit such crimes to survive. However, the results from the ICVS also reveal that vehicle theft actually happens quite a bit in many regions of the world (North America being ranked third), so motor vehicle theft is alive and well throughout virtually all societies.

Regarding relative rates of vehicle theft in the United States, FBI data for 2010 show that the city with the highest rate is Richmond, California, followed by Detroit and then Newark, New Jersey (see Table 1.4). Everett, Washington, and St. Louis, Missouri, round out the Top 5. It is notable that the state of California had nine cities in the Top 20 for highest rates of motor vehicle theft in that year, which is consistent with most recent years.[121]

RANK AND CITY	RATE	RANK AND CITY	RATE	RANK AND CITY	RATE
1 Richmond, CA	1,542.9	18 San Bernardino, CA	863.9	35 Stockton, CA	698.9
2 Detroit, MI	1,401.1	19 South Gate, CA	856.7	36 Hayward, CA	696.8
3 Newark, NJ	1,291.1	20 Sacramento, CA	845.3	37 Baltimore, MD	689.0
4 St. Louis, MO	1,200.3	21 Salt Lake City, UT	837.1	38 Yakima, WA	687.6
5 Everett, WA	1,149.0	22 Cleveland, OH	822.2	39 New Orleans, LA	676.4
6 Oakland, CA	1,133.4	23 New Haven, CT	811.3	40 Miami Beach, FL	675.1
7 Vallejo, CA	1,030.1	24 Washington, DC	808.3	41 Chicago, IL	673.3
8 Tacoma, WA	1,020.1	25 Pomona, CA	806.3	42 Hartford, CT	666.3
9 Spokane, WA	988.3	26 Reading, PA	805.0	43 Camden, NJ	656.3
10 Antioch, CA	940.0	27 Kansas City, KS	784.8	44 Baldwin Park, CA	656.1
11 Atlanta, GA	940.0	28 Compton, CA	760.3	45 Kansas City, MO	656.1
12 Fresno, CA	939.3	29 San Leandro, CA	754.6	46 El Monte, CA	653.9
13 Kent, WA	910.6	30 Bakersfield, CA	736.2	47 Tucson, AZ	651.3
14 Elizabeth, NJ	905.2	31 St. Paul, MN	730.2	48 Providence, RI	651.1
15 Jackson, MS	892.9	32 Milwaukee, WI	714.1	49 Gresham, OR	650.5
16 Downey, CA	867.4	33 Macon, GA	701.3	50 Hammond, IN	648.2
17 Federal Way, WA	865.4	34 Modesto, CA	699.4		

Table1.4 Motor Vehicle Theft Rate in 2010
National Rate = 238.8 Motor Vehicle Thefts per 100,000 Population

Source: FBI. "Crime in the United States 2010."

assess which studies and theoretical frameworks are of high quality. The criteria that characterize a good theory in chemistry are the same ones used to assess what makes a good criminological theory. These characteristics include parsimony, scope, logical consistency, testability, empirical validity, and policy implications.[122] Each of these characteristics is examined in the next section. (It should be noted that this discussion and the examples provided for the characteristics are taken from Akers & Sellers, 2004.)[123]

CHARACTERISTICS OF GOOD THEORIES

Parsimony is attained by explaining a phenomenon, such as criminal activity, in the simplest way possible. Other characteristics being equal, the simpler a theory, the better. The challenge with criminal behavior is that it is highly complex; however, some criminologists have attempted to explain this complex phenomenon using rather simplistic approaches. For instance, the theory of low self-control maintains that one personality factor— low self-control—is responsible for all criminal activity. As will be discussed in a later chapter, the originators of this theory, Michael Gottfredson and Travis Hirschi, contend that every act of crime and deviance is caused by this same factor: low self-control.[124] A simple theory is better than a more complex one. Given the complex nature of criminal behavior, however, it is likely that a simple explanation, such as identifying one factor to explain all types of criminal and deviant behavior, will not be adequate.

Scope is the trait that indicates how much of a given phenomenon the theory attempts to explain. Other traits being equal, the larger the scope, the better the theory. To some extent, this is related to parsimony in the sense that some theories, such as the theory of low self-control, seek to explain all crimes and all deviant acts. Thus, the theory of low self-control has a very wide scope. As we will discuss later, other theories of crime may attempt to explain only property crime, such as some versions of strain theory or drug use. However, the wider the scope of what a theory can explain, the better the theory.

Logical consistency is the extent to which a theory makes sense in terms of its concepts and propositions. Sometimes it is easier to illustrate this point with an example. Some theories do not make sense simply because of the face value of their propositions. For instance, Cesare Lombroso maintained that the most serious offenders are *born criminals;* they are biological throwbacks to an earlier stage of evolutionary development and can be identified by their physical features.[125] Lombroso, who is discussed later in this book, maintained that tattoos were one of the physical features that distinguished these born criminals. This does not make sense, or lacks logical consistency, because tattoos are not biological physical features (i.e., no baby has been born with a tattoo).

How would Lombroso classify this person?

Parsimony: a characteristic of a good theory, meaning that it explains a certain phenomenon, such as criminal behavior, with the fewest possible propositions or concepts

LEARNING CHECK 1.4

When a theory can explain a phenomenon using a simplistic approach, this is considered _____. When a theory attempts to explain all crimes and all deviant acts, this theory is broad in _____. Empirical validity is the extent to which a theoretical model is supported by _____.

Answers located at www.sagepub.com/schram

PERSONAL PERSPECTIVE

Background

scope: refers to the range of criminal behavior that a theory attempts to explain

logical consistency: the extent to which concepts and propositions of a theoretical model make sense in terms of face value and consistency with what is readily known about crime rates and trends

testability: the extent to which a theoretical model can be empirically or scientifically tested through observation and empirical research

empirical validity: refers to the extent to which a theoretical model is supported by scientific research

Testability is the extent to which a theory can be empirically and scientifically tested. Some theories simply cannot be tested. A good example of such a theory is Freud's theory of the psyche, discussed in more detail later in this book. Freud described three domains of the psyche—the conscious ego, the subconscious id, and the superego. None of these domains, however, can be observed or tested.[126] While some theories can be quite influential without being testable (e.g., Freud's theory), a theoretical model that is untestable and unobservable is at a considerable disadvantage. Fortunately, most established criminological theories can be examined through empirical testing.

Empirical validity is the extent to which a theoretical model is supported by scientific research. This is closely associated with the previous characteristic of testability. While almost all accepted modern criminological theories are testable, this does not mean they are equal in terms of empirical validity.

For instance, deterrence theory proposed in part that offenders will not repeat their crimes if they have been caught and given severe legal punishment. If research finds that this is true for only a small minority of offenders or that punished offenders are only slightly less likely to repeat crimes than are unpunished offenders, then the theory has some, but not much, empirical validity.[127]

Thus, questions of empirical validity include these: "What degree of empirical support does the theory have?" "Do the findings of research provide weak or strong support?" "Does the preponderance of evidence support or undermine the theory?"[128]

THREE REQUIREMENTS FOR DETERMINING CAUSALITY

Various criteria are involved in determining whether a certain variable causes another variable to change—in other words, causality. For this discussion, we will be referring to the commonly used scientific notation of a predictor variable—called X—as causing an explanatory variable—called Y. These variables are often referred to as an independent or predictor variable (X) and a dependent or explanatory variable (Y). These criteria are used for all scientific disciplines, whether chemistry, physics, biology, or criminology. The three criteria required to determine causality are temporal ordering, covariation or correlation, and accounting for spuriousness.

Temporal ordering requires that the predictor variable (X) precede the explanatory variable (Y) if one is attempting to determine that X causes Y. Although this issue of time order appears to be quite obvious, there are instances when this criterion is violated in criminological theories. For instance, a recent scientific debate has focused on whether delinquency is an outcome variable (Y) caused by associations with delinquent peers and associates (X) or whether delinquency (X) causes associations with delinquent peers and associates (Y), which then leads to more delinquent behavior. This is an example of temporal ordering, or "which came first, the chicken or the egg?" Research has revealed that both processes often occur, meaning that delinquency and associations with delinquent peers are likely to be both predictor and explanatory variables.

Correlation or covariation is the extent to which a change in the predictor (X) is associated with a change in the explanatory variable (Y). For instance, an increase in unemployment

WHY DO THEY DO IT?

JERRY SANDUSKY

In 1969, Gerald "Jerry" Sandusky was hired by Pennsylvania State University (PSU) to serve as an assistant coach. He remained at PSU until his retirement in 1999. On June 22, 2012, Sandusky was convicted of sexually assaulting 10 boys. All these children were from disadvantaged homes. Specifically, he was convicted on 45 of the 48 counts against him, including involuntary deviate sexual intercourse, indecent assault, criminal intent to commit indecent assault, unlawful contact with minors, corruption of minors, and endangering the welfare of children. He was sentenced to 30 to 60 years in prison.

One of the most disturbing aspects of this case is that Sandusky's sexual abuse of children had come to the attention of some administrators at PSU prior to his arrest in 2011. On July 12, 2012, Louis Freeh and his law firm compiled an independent report concerning the facts and circumstances of PSU's actions regarding the child abuse committed by Sandusky. In his press release, Freeh stated the following:

> Our most saddening and sobering finding is the total disregard for the safety and welfare of Sandusky's child victims by the most senior leaders at Penn State. The most powerful men at Penn State failed to take any steps for 14 years to protect the children who Sandusky victimized.[129]

One particular incident that clearly demonstrated this lack of safety and welfare occurred on February 9, 2001. Mike McQueary, then a graduate assistant, walked in on Sandusky anally raping a 10-year-old boy. The following day, McQueary reported the incident to Joe Paterno (former football coach, now deceased). Freeh's press release noted the reasons for these "most senior leaders" neither taking action to identify the victims nor reporting Sandusky to the police or to child welfare:

- Through counsel, Tim Curley (former director of athletics) and Gary Schultz (former vice president) stated that the "humane" thing to do was carefully and responsibly to assess the best way to handle vague but troubling allegations.

- Paterno said, "I didn't know exactly how to handle it and I was afraid to do something that might jeopardize what the university procedure was. So I backed away and turned it over to some other people, people I thought would have a little more expertise than I did. It didn't work out that way."

- Graham Spanier (former university president) told the Special Investigative Counsel that no one ever told him the February 2001 incident in the shower involved the sexual abuse of a child but only "horsing around." He further stated that he never asked what Sandusky's "horsing around" entailed.

Sandusky's sexual abuse of young boys, along with PSU high-level administrators' lack of proper action, continues to have repercussions. For instance, the victims of Sandusky's abuse could sue PSU for millions of dollars. Also, the National Collegiate Athletic Association could impose the "death penalty" on PSU's football program. More important, like other victims of sexual abuse, those victimized by Sandusky will have to face many challenges throughout their lifetimes, such as trust issues, feeling responsible, negative sense of self and self-esteem, anxiety and fear, depression, posttraumatic stress disorder, sexualized behavior, aggression, substance abuse, suicidal behavior, and criminal activity.[130]

This case has had many individuals asking, "How do people respond to individuals who commit crimes but have not been 'caught,' especially those crimes involving the abuse of children?" Further, some may question the importance placed on college sports. Others may consider the power differential between these high-level administrators and the young boys from disadvantaged homes.

In this text, we will be presenting what some may consider "high-profile" crimes. These are crimes that have received a great deal of media attention due to those individuals involved and/or the horrendous nature of the offense. In some instances, such as the Sandusky case, these types of crimes go beyond the question, "Why did he do it?"

(X) is likely to lead to a rise in crime rates (Y). This would indicate a positive association, because both increased. Similarly, an increase in employment (X) is likely to lead to a decrease in crime rates (Y). This would be a negative, or inverse, association, because as one decreases, the other increases. The criterion of covariance is not met when a change in X does not produce any change in Y. Thus, if a significant change in X does not lead to a significant change in Y, this criterion is not met.

It is essential to stress, however, that correlation alone does not mean that X causes Y. For example, ice cream sales (X) tend to be highly associated with crime rates (Y). This does not mean that ice cream sales cause higher crime rates. Instead, other factors, such as warm weather, lead to an increase in both sales of ice cream and the number of people who are outdoors in public areas, which could lead to greater opportunities and tendencies to engage in criminal activity. This example leads to the final criterion for determining causality.

Considering for **spuriousness** is a complicated way of saying, to determine that X causes Y, other factors (typically called Z factors) that could be causing the observed association must be accounted for before one can be sure that X is actually causing Y. In other words, these other Z factors may account for the observed association between X and Y. What often happens is that a third factor (Z) causes two events to occur together in time and place. Referring back to Lombroso, tattoos may have predicted criminality at the time he wrote. However, Lombroso did not account for an important Z factor—namely, associates or friends who also had tattoos. This Z factor caused the simultaneous occurrence of both other factors.

Would this be considered a *disorganized* neighborhood?

AUDIO

Sexual Assault

temporal ordering: the criterion for determining causality; requires that the predictor variable (X) precedes the explanatory variable (Y) in time

correlation or covariation: a criterion of causality that requires a change in a predictor variable (X) to be consistently associated with some change in the explanatory variable (Y)

Researchers in criminology are fairly good at determining the first two criteria of causality—temporal ordering and covariance or correlation. Most scientists can perform classical experiments that randomly assign participants either to receive or not to receive the experimental manipulation to examine the effect on outcomes. The problem for criminologists, however, is that the factors that appear to be important (according to police officers, parole agents, or corrections officers) are family variables, personality traits, employment variables, intelligence, and other similar characteristics that cannot be experimentally manipulated to control for possible Z factors. Thus, as criminologists, we may never be able to meet all the criteria for causality. Rather, we are often restricted to building a case for the factors we think are causing crime by amassing as much support as we can regarding temporal ordering and covariance or correlation, and perhaps accounting for other factors in advanced statistical models. Ultimately, social science, particularly criminology, is a difficult field in terms of establishing causality, and as we shall see, empirical validity of various criminological theories is hindered by such issues.

THEORY INFORMS POLICIES AND PROGRAMS

An essential aspect of a good theory is that it can help inform and guide policies that attempt to reduce crime. After all, a criminological theory is truly useful in the real world only if it helps reduce criminal offending. For instance, referring to the 11-year-old boy in Albuquerque who took the bait car for a joy ride, if one maintains that the reason he engaged in this criminal behavior was a lack of adult supervision, suggested policies and programs might be directed toward some type of after-school program. Many theories have been used as the basis of such changes in policy.

All major criminological theories have implications for, and have indeed been utilized in, criminal justice policy and practice. Every therapy method, treatment program, prison regimen, police policy, or criminal justice practice is based, either explicitly or implicitly, on some explanation of human nature in general or criminal behavior in particular.[131] In each chapter, we will present examples of how the theories of crime discussed have guided policy making.

One theoretical perspective we will be discussing is differential association. A central tenet of this theory is the influence of close peer groups or other role models. The major implication of this theory is to replace negative, antisocial role models with more positive, prosocial role models. The influence of this position is reflected in the conditions of probation or parole; offenders are required to stay away from convicted felons. Programs that bring juveniles together for positive purposes and positive interaction with others will face obstacles because "the lure of 'the streets' and of the friends they have grown up with remains a powerful countervailing force regarding rehabilitation."[132]

Another theory perspective we will be presenting focuses on social structure. If individuals live in an environment that is considered *disorganized*, such as one characterized by high unemployment and transiency, this could be deemed the *root cause* of crime. The challenge with implementing policies and programs with this perspective is that it does not necessarily focus on the individual but, rather, the community. Clifford Shaw argued that rather than treating individual offenders, one needs to focus on the community. Subsequently, he developed the Chicago Area Project. Shaw, along with his staff, organized various programs aimed at establishing or enhancing a sense of community with neighborhoods. He also obtained the assistance and cooperation of schools, churches, recreational clubs, trade unions, and businesses.[133]

spuriousness: when other factors (often referred to as Z factors) are actually causing two variables (X and Y) to occur at the same time; it may appear as if X causes Y, when in fact they are both being caused by other Z factor(s)

CONCLUSION

The purpose of this chapter was twofold. First, we wanted to provide students with a general understanding of different aspects related to the field. We started with key concepts to understanding criminology, such as *crime, criminal, deviant,* and *victim.* We explored the difference between *criminology* and *criminal justice,* as well as *consensus* and *conflict perspectives of crime.* Next, we provided a broad overview of the major components of the criminal justice system: law enforcement, courts, and corrections. When discussing the juvenile justice system, we attempted to provide readers with some fundamental differences between the adult criminal justice system and the juvenile justice system. Finally, we presented various approaches to measuring crime, such as crime data from law enforcement agencies, from victims of crime, and from self-report surveys. How we measure crime is an essential aspect of criminological theory.

The second purpose of this chapter was to introduce students to criminological theory by initially discussing what criteria are considered when assessing whether a theory is deemed *good.* We also briefly discussed the three requirements to show that a given factor causes changes in another factor. We ended this chapter with a comment about how theory should inform policies and programs. It is essential to stress that theory is not to be thought of as some *abstract* or *out-of-touch* scientific endeavor. Rather, theory has an important purpose in terms of developing policies and programs. As Ronald Akers noted,

> The question, then, is not whether policy can be or should be based on theory—it already is guided by theory—but rather, how well is policy guided by theory and how good is the theory on which the policy is predicated?[134]

While students are learning and critiquing the various theories presented in this text, it is essential that they ask that question *continually!*

KEY TERMS

comparative criminology

concurrent jurisdiction

conflict perspective

consensus perspective

correlation or covariation

crime

criminal justice

criminology

deviance

empirical validity

highway patrol

jail

judicial waiver

limited jurisdiction

logical consistency

mala prohibita

mala in se

National Crime Victimization Survey (NCVS)

parens patriae

parsimony

prison

probation

scope

spuriousness

state police

statutory exclusion

temporary ordering

testability

Uniform Crime Reports (UCR)

STUDENT STUDY SITE

Visit the student study site at **www.sagepub.com/schram** to access links to the video, audio, city and state rankings, author podcasts, and SAGE journal and reference articles featured in this chapter, as well as additional study tools, including eFlashcards, web quizzes, web resources, and chapter outlines.

DISCUSSION QUESTIONS

1. How does criminology differ from other perspectives of crime?

2. Should criminologists emphasize only crimes made illegal by law, or should they also study acts that are deviant but not illegal? Explain why you feel this way.

3. Do you think the juvenile justice system procedures, as well as its philosophy, have changed since its inception in 1899? Why?

4. Would you consider the term *criminal justice system* an oxymoron? Explain your answer.

5. Which of the measures of crime do you think is the best estimate of crime in the United States? Why? Also, which measure is the best to use for determining associations between crime and personality traits? Why?

6. What characteristics of a good theory do you find most important? What are least important? Make sure to explain why you feel that way.

WEB RESOURCES

FBI's UCR

http://www.fbi.gov/about-us/cjis/ucr/ucr/

NCVS

http://bjs.ojp.usdoj.gov/index.cfm?ty=dcdetail&iid=245

Overview of the criminal justice system

http://bjs.ojp.usdoj.gov/content/justsys.cfm/

CHAPTER 2

Classical School of Criminological Thought

INTRODUCTION

A 2009 report from the Death Penalty Information Center, citing a study based on FBI data and other national reports, showed that states with the death penalty have consistently higher murder rates than states without the death penalty.[1] The report highlighted the fact that if the death penalty were acting as a deterrent, the gap between these two groups of states would be expected to converge, or at least lessen over time. But that has not been the case. In fact, this disparity in murder rates has actually grown over the past two decades, with states allowing the death penalty having a 42% higher murder rate (as of 2007) compared with states that do not—up from only 4% in 1990.

Thus, it appears that in terms of **deterrence theory**, at least when it comes to the death penalty, such potential punishment is not an effective deterrent. This chapter deals with the various issues and factors that go into offenders' decision making about committing crime. While many would likely anticipate that potential murderers in states with the death penalty would be deterred from committing such offenses, this is clearly not the case, given the findings of the study discussed above. This type of deterrence, or rather the lack thereof, regarding the death penalty and related issues makes up a key portion of this chapter.

This chapter examines explanations of criminal conduct that emphasize individuals' ability to make decisions based on the potential consequences of their behavior. The natural capability of human beings to make decisions based on expected costs and benefits was acknowledged during the **Age of Enlightenment** in the 17th and 18th centuries. This understanding of human capability led to what is considered the first rational theory of criminal activity— namely, deterrence theory. Of any other perspective to date, deterrence theory has had the most profound impact on justice systems in our nation. Furthermore, it is easy to see examples in contemporary life of offenders engaging in such rational decision making, and a number of variations of this theoretical model have been developed that focus on the reasoning processes of people considering criminal acts.

Such theories of human rationality stand in stark contrast to the theories perpetuated for most of human civilization, up to the Age of Enlightenment— theories that focused on religious or supernatural causes of crime. Additionally, the **Classical School** theories of crime are distinguished from the other theories we examine in future chapters by their emphasis on free will and rational decision making, which modern theories of crime tend to ignore. Specifically, the theoretical perspectives discussed in this chapter all focus on the human ability to choose one's own behavior and destiny, whereas paradigms popular before the Enlightenment and in contemporary times tend to emphasize the influence of external factors on individual choice. Therefore, the Classical School is perhaps the paradigm best suited for analysis of what types of calculations go on in someone's head before committing a crime.

LEARNING OBJECTIVES

While reading this chapter, readers should consider the following questions:

- During most of the history of human civilization, what were the primary types of "theories" explaining why individuals committed violent and other deviant acts?

- How did the Age of Enlightenment drastically alter the theories for how and why individuals commit crimes? What propositions/ assumptions were presented during that period that led to this transition in theories about crime?

- How did Cesare Beccaria's book in 1764 drastically influence various criminal justice systems throughout the world? What types of concepts or propositions were recommended in his book?

- What did Jeremy Bentham contribute to this movement toward the Classical School of criminological thought?

- What did the Neoclassical School of criminology contribute to the propositions of the Classical School that led most of the Western world (including the United States) to embrace this model as the major paradigm for the criminal justice system?

DEBORAH JEANE PALFREY

Deborah Jeane Palfrey, known as the "D.C. Madam," was brought up on charges of racketeering and money laundering related to running a prostitution ring in Washington, D.C., and surrounding suburbs of Maryland and Virginia. The clientele of this prostitution ring included some notable politicians, such as state senators and other elected officials. Palfrey faced a maximum of 55 years in prison but likely would have received far less time had she not committed suicide before her sentencing. Her body was found in a storage facility at her mother's home in Tarpon Springs, Florida.

News reports revealed that she had served time before (for prostitution). Author Dan Moldea told *TIME* magazine that she contacted him for a book he was working on and told him "she had done time once before . . . and it damned near killed her. She said there was enormous stress—it made her sick, she couldn't take it, and she wasn't going to let that happen again."[2] The situation could have been worsened by the heightened media attention this case received; while most prostitution cases are handled by local or state courts, this one was handled by federal courts because it concerned Washington, D.C.

It is quite likely that the impending maximum prison sentence led her to take her own life, given what she had said to Moldea. This shows the type of deterrent effect that jail/prison can have on an individual—in this case, possibly leading her to choose death over serving time. Ironically, Palfrey had commented to the press, after the suicide of a former employee in her prostitution network—Brandy Britton, who hanged herself before going to trial—"I guess I'm made of something that Brandy Britton wasn't made of."[3] It seems that Palfrey had the same concerns as Britton, and she ended up contradicting her bold statement when she ended her own life.

This case study provides an example of the profound effects legal sanctions can have on individuals. Legal sanctions are not meant to inspire offenders to end their lives, but this case does illustrate the potential deterrent effects of facing punishment from the legal system. We can see this on a smaller scale when a speeding driver's heart rate increases at the sight of a highway patrol or other police vehicle (which studies show happens to most drivers). Even though this offense would result in only a fine, it is a good example of deterrence in our everyday lives. We will revisit the Palfrey

Deborah Jeane Palfrey, known as the "D.C. Madam," committed suicide in jail before being sentenced. Her case reveals the potentially powerful effects of formal sanctions on individuals' decision making.

case in the conclusion of this chapter, after you have had a chance to review some of the theoretical propositions and concepts that make up deterrence theory.

On a related note, a special report from the U.S. Department of Justice, Bureau of Justice Statistics, concludes that the suicide rate has been far higher among jail inmates than among prison inmates (see Table 2.1).[4] Specifically, suicides in jails have tended over the past few decades to occur 300% (or 3 times) more often than among prison inmates.

A likely reason for this phenomenon is that many persons arrested and/or awaiting trial (which is generally the status of those in jail) have more to lose, such as in their relationships with family, friends, and employers, than do the typical chronic offenders that end up in prison. Specifically, many of the individuals picked up for prostitution and other relatively minor, albeit embarrassing, offenses are of the middle- and upper-class mentality and, thus, are ill-equipped to face the real-world consequences of their arrest. The good news is, this same Department of Justice report showed that suicides in both jails and prisons have decreased during the past few decades, likely due to better policies in correctional settings regarding persons considered at "high risk" for suicide.

> "SHE HAD DONE TIME ONCE BEFORE . . . AND IT DAMNED NEAR KILLED HER. SHE SAID THERE WAS ENORMOUS STRESS—IT MADE HER SICK, SHE COULDN'T TAKE IT, AND SHE WASN'T GOING TO LET THAT HAPPEN AGAIN."

The aspects of Classical School theory presented in this chapter vary in many ways, most notably in what they propose as the primary constructs and processes by which individuals determine whether or not to commit a crime. For example, some Classical School theories emphasize only the potential negative consequences of criminal actions, whereas others focus on the possible benefits. Still others concentrate on the opportunities and circumstances that predispose one to engage in criminal activity. Regardless of their differences, all the theories examined in this chapter emphasize a common theme: Individuals commit crimes because they identify certain situations and actions as beneficial due to a perceived lack of punishment and a perceived likelihood of profits, such as money or peer status. In other words, the potential offender weighs out the possible costs and pleasures of committing a given act and then behaves in a rational way based on the conclusions of that analysis.

The most important distinction of these Classical School theories, as opposed to those discussed in future chapters, is that they emphasize individual decision making regardless of any extraneous influences on a person's free will, such as the economy or bonding with society. Although many outside factors may influence an individual's ability to rationally consider offending situations—and many of the theories in this chapter deal with such influences—primary responsibility rests on the individual to take all influences into account when deciding whether to engage in criminal behavior. Given this emphasis on individual responsibility, it is not surprising that Classical School theories are used as the basis for U.S. policies on punishment for criminal activity. After all, in the conservative "get-tough" movement that has existed since the mid-1970s, the Classical School theories are highly compatible and consistent with such a perspective because they focus on individual responsibility. Thus, the Classical School still retains the highest influence in terms of policy and pragmatic punishment in the United States, as well as throughout the Western world.

As you will see, the Classical School theoretical paradigm was presented as early as the mid-1700s, and it is still the dominant model of offending behavior in criminal justice systems. The Classical School paradigm remains the most popular theoretical framework among U.S. legislators and society, and throughout the world. Although the Classical School theories have remained dominant in most Western societies, the scientific and academic circles have somewhat dismissed many of the claims of this perspective. For reasons we explore in this chapter, the assumptions and primary propositions of the Classical School theories have been neglected by most recent theoretical models of criminology, which is likely premature given the impact this perspective has had on understanding human nature, as well as its profound influence on most criminal justice systems, especially in the United States.

PRE-CLASSICAL PERSPECTIVES OF CRIME AND PUNISHMENT

For the vast majority of human civilization's history, people believed that criminal activity was caused by either supernatural or religious factors. Some primitive societies believed that crime increased during major thunderstorms or draughts. Most primitive cultures believed that when people engaged in behavior that violated the rules of the tribe or clan, the devil or evil spirits were making them do it.[5] For example, in many societies at that time, if a person had committed a criminal act, it was common to perform an exorcism or primitive surgery, such as breaking open the offender's skull to release the demons thought to be lodged there. Of course, this almost always resulted in the death of the accused, but it was seen as a liberating experience for the defendant.

CRIME IN THE NEWS

Death Penalty Information Center

AUTHOR PODCAST

The Classical School

AUDIO

D.C. Madam Case

deterrence theory: theory of crime associated with the Classical School; proposes that individuals will make rational decisions regarding their behavior

Age of Enlightenment: a period of the late 17th century to 18th century in which philosophers and scholars began to emphasize the rights of individuals in society

Classical School: model of crime that assumes crime occurs after a rational individual mentally weighs the potential good and bad consequences of crime and then makes a decision about whether to engage in a given behavior

	LOCAL JAIL INMATE DEATHS				STATE PRISON INMATE DEATHS		
CAUSE	2000	2001	2002	2000–02 (%)	2001	2002	2001–02 (%)
All causes	912	953	978	100	2,878	2,946	100
Illness	462	432	459	47.6	2,304	2,379	80.4
AIDS	60	59	50	5.9	270	245	8.8
Suicide	289	315	314	32.3	169	168	5.8
Homicide	17	22	20	2.1	39	48	1.5
Accident	25	35	35	3.3	23	31	0.9
Intoxication	37	58	54	5.2	35	37	1.2
Other/unknown	22	32	46	3.6	38	38	1.3

State prison, local jail suicide rates have fallen sharply since the 1980s

Suicides per 100,000 inmates

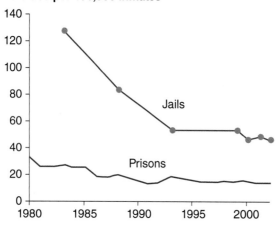

- In 2002 the suicide rate in local jails (47 per 100,000 inmates) was over 3 times the rate in state prisons (14 per 100,000 inmates).

- The suicide rate in the nation's 50 largest jail systems (29 per 100,000 inmates) was half that of other jails (57 per 100,000).

- Violent offenders in both local jails (92 per 100,000) and state prisons (19 per 100,000) had suicide rates more than twice as high as those of nonviolent offenders (31 and 9 per 100,000, respectively).

Homicide rates in state prisons dropped 93% from 1980 to 2002

Homicides per 100,000 inmates

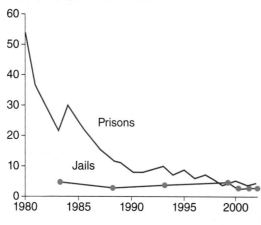

- Homicide rates were similar in local jails (3 per 100,000) and state prisons (4 per 100,000).

- 67% of homicide victims in state prisons had served at least 2 years; 37% had served at least 5 years.

- Violent offenders were the victims of most state prison homicides (61%), and their jail homicide rate (5 per 100,000) was over twice that of nonviolent offenders (2 per 100,000).

Table 2.1 Suicide and Homicides in State Prisons and Local Jails

Source: Mumola, C. J. (2005, August). *Suicide and homicide in state prisons and local jails*. Washington, DC: U.S. Department of Justice, Office of Justice Programs. Retrieved from http://bjs.ojp.usdoj.gov/content/pub/pdf/shsplj.pdf

Exorcism was just one form of dealing with criminal behavior, but it epitomizes the nature of primitive cultures' understanding of what causes crime. However, as the movie *The Exorcist* showed, the Catholic Church, among other religious institutions, still uses exorcism in extreme cases. Exorcisms are performed in the 21st century by representatives of a number of religions, including Catholicism, "to get the devil out." For instance, in June 2005, a Romanian monk and four nuns acknowledged engaging in an exorcism that led to the death of a 23-year-old woman. During the procedure, the woman was chained to a cross, had a towel stuffed in her mouth, and was deprived of food for 3 days.[6] When the monk and nuns were asked to explain why they did this, they were defiant and said they were trying to take the devils out of the woman. Although they were prosecuted by Romanian authorities, many governments around the world still believe in and condone such practices and may not have prosecuted in this case.

One of the most common supernatural beliefs of primitive cultures was that the moon, in its fullest state, was a trigger for criminal activity. Then, as now, there was much truth to that theory. But in primitive times, this influence was believed to be caused by higher powers, such as the "destructive influence" of the moon itself. Modern studies have shown that this connection between the full moon and crime is primarily due to a Classical School theoretical model: There are simply more opportunities to commit crime when the moon is full. Specifically, there is more light during the full-moon phase, which means more people on the streets and more opportunity for crime. Also, nighttime is well established as a higher-risk period for adult crime, such as sexual assault.

Some of the primitive theories of crime had some validity in determining when crime was more likely to occur; however, virtually none of the primitive theories accurately predicted who would commit the offenses. During the Middle Ages and before, nearly all individuals were part of the lower classes and only a subsection of that group engaged in offending against the normative society. So, for most of human civilization, there was close to no rational theoretical understanding for why certain individuals violated the laws of society.

Thus, for most of human civilization's history, people believed that crime was caused by supernatural or religious factors, leading to theories of crime such as "the devil made me do it." There were many variations on this perspective, such as crime caused by the full moon or excessive thunder. Due to the assumption that evil spirits were driving the motivations for criminal activity, punishments for criminal acts—especially for those deemed particularly offensive to the norms of a given society—were often quite inhumane by modern standards.

For example, during the Middle Ages (Dark Ages), common punishments included beheading, torturing, burning alive at the stake, drowning, stoning (still used by many Islamic courts in portions of Africa and the Middle East), and quartering (in which the limbs of a convicted criminal are tied to four horses and then the horses are made to run in opposite directions, ripping limbs from torso). These punishments seem harsh by contemporary standards, but given the context of the times, they were fairly standard and widely accepted.[7]

Theories for most of human civilization placed the earth at the center of the universe. This shows how inaccurate theories can be when they don't explain the causes of a given phenomenon.

Although many would find primitive forms of punishment and execution quite barbaric, many societies still practice some of them. Recent examples can be seen among Islamic court systems (as well as in other religious/ethnic cultures), which are often allowed to carry out executions and other forms of corporal punishment. For instance, a number of offenders were flogged (i.e., whipped) for what is considered a relatively minor crime—or no crime at all—in most of the United States: gambling. Gambling was the most serious offense committed by the 15 individuals in Aceh, Indonesia (a highly conservative Muslim region of that country) who were publicly caned outside a mosque.[8]

It is interesting to note that a relatively recent Gallup Poll addressing the practice of caning (i.e., publicly whipping) convicted individuals revealed support for the practice from most of the American public. More extreme forms of corporal punishment, particularly the methods of public execution carried out by many religious courts and countries—such as stoning, in which persons are buried up to the waist and local citizens throw small stones (but not large stones, as those lead to death too quickly)—are drawn out and painful compared with modern forms of punishment in the United States. In most of the Western world, such brutal forms of punishment and execution were done away with in the 1700s due to the impact of the Age of Enlightenment.

THE AGE OF ENLIGHTENMENT

In the midst of these extremely draconian times of the mid-1600s, Thomas Hobbes, in his book *Leviathan* (1651), proposed a rational theory for why people are motivated to form democratic states of governance.[9] Hobbes proclaimed that people are rational, so they will logically organize a sound system of governance to create rules that will help alleviate the constant fear of offense by others. It is interesting that the very emotion (fear) that motivates individuals to cooperate in the formation of government is the same emotion that inspires these individuals to obey the laws of the government created—because they fear the punishment imposed for breaking the rules.

Hobbes clearly stated that until citizens in such societies received a certain degree of respect from their governing bodies, as well as from their justice systems, they would never fully buy in to the authority of government or the system of justice. Hobbes proposed a number of extraordinary ideas that came to define the Age of Enlightenment. He suggested a drastic paradigm shift with this new idea of social structure, which had extreme implications for justice systems throughout the world.

Specifically, Hobbes declared that human beings are rational beings who choose their destiny by creating a society. Hobbes further proposed that individuals in such societies democratically create rules of conduct that all members of society must follow. These rules that all citizens decide on become laws, and the result of not following these laws is a punishment determined by the democratically instituted government. It is clear from Hobbes's statements that the government, as instructed by the citizens, not only has the authority to punish individuals who violate the rules of the society but, more important, is bound by duty to punish such individuals. If such an authority fails to fulfill this duty, it can quickly result in a breakdown in the social order.

The arrangement of citizens agreeing to abide by the rules or laws set forth by a given society in return for protection is commonly referred to as the **social contract**. Hobbes introduced this idea, but it was emphasized by all the other Enlightenment theorists after him, such as Rousseau, Locke, Voltaire, and Montesquieu, and it embodies their underlying philosophies. Although all the Enlightenment philosophers had significant differences of belief, the one belief they had in common was that in the social contract. This idea that people invest in the laws of their society in exchange for the guarantee that

social contract: an Enlightenment ideal or assumption that stipulates an unspecified arrangement among citizens in which they promise the state or government not to commit offenses against other citizens, and in turn, they gain protection from being violated by other citizens they will be protected from others who violate those laws is universal across all the Enlightenment philosophers.

Another shared belief among Enlightenment philosophers was that each individual should have a say in the government, especially in the justice system. Virtually all the Enlightenment philosophers also emphasized fairness in determining who was guilty, as well as the appropriate punishments or sentences for misconduct. During the time in which they wrote, Enlightenment philosophers saw individuals who stole a loaf of bread to feed their families receive death sentences, while upper-class individuals who had stolen large sums of money or even committed murder were pardoned. This not only goes against common sense but also violates the social contract. After all, if citizens observe certain persons being excused from punishment for violation of the law, their belief in the social contract will break down. This same standard can be applied to modern times. For example, when Los Angeles police officers who were filmed beating a suspect were acquitted of criminal charges, a massive riot erupted among members of the community. This is a good example of the social contract breaking down, largely due to the realization that the government failed to punish members of the community (significantly, police officers) who had violated the rules.

Perhaps the most relevant concept the Enlightenment philosophers highlighted, as mentioned above, was the idea that human beings are rational and therefore have free will. The philosophers of this age focused on the ability of individuals to consider the consequences of their actions, and the philosophers assumed that people freely choose how to behave, especially in regard to criminal activity. We shall see that this was an extremely important part of Enlightenment philosophy, which the Father of Criminal Justice assumed in his formulation of what is considered to be the first bona fide theory for why people commit crime.

AUDIO

Social Contract

THE CLASSICAL SCHOOL OF CRIMINOLOGY

The foundation of the Classical School of criminological theorizing can be traced to the Enlightenment philosophers discussed above, but the more specific and well-known origin of the Classical School is considered to be the 1764 publication of *On Crimes and Punishments*, written by Italian scholar Cesare Bonesana, Marchese di Beccaria (1738–1794), commonly known as Cesare Beccaria. He wrote this book at the age of 26 and published it anonymously, but after its almost instant popularity, he came forward as the author. Because of this significant work, most experts consider Beccaria not only the Father of Criminal Justice and the Father of the Classical School of Criminology but, perhaps most important, the Father of Deterrence Theory. All this will be explained in the following sections, in which we comprehensively survey the ideas and impact of Beccaria and the Classical School.

Cesare Beccaria (1738–1794), considered the Father of Criminal Justice, Father of Deterrence Theory, and Father of the Classical School of Criminology, due to the influence of his *On Crimes and Punishments* (1764)

INFLUENCES ON BECCARIA AND HIS WRITINGS

As discussed previously in this chapter, the Enlightenment philosophers profoundly impacted the social and political climate of the late 1600s and 1700s. Growing up in this time, Beccaria was a child of the Enlightenment; as such, he was highly influenced by the concepts and propositions introduced by these great thinkers. The Enlightenment philosophy is readily evident in Beccaria's writing, and he incorporates many of these philosophers' assumptions into his work. As a student of law, Beccaria had a solid background for determining what was rational in legal policy, as well as what was not. But his loyalty to the Enlightenment ideal is ever present throughout his work.

Specifically, Beccaria emphasized the social contract and incorporated the idea that citizens give up certain rights in exchange for protection from the state or government. He also claimed that actions or punishments carried out by the government that violate the overall sense of unity will not be accepted by the populace, largely due to the requirement that the social contract be a fair deal. Beccaria stated that laws are compacts of free individuals in a society. Additionally, he appealed to the ideal of the greatest happiness shared by the greatest number, otherwise known as **utilitarianism**. This, too, was a focus of the Enlightenment philosophers. Finally, the importance of free will and individual choice is key to his propositions and theorizing. Although these points are the main assumptions of his reforms and ideas on motives for committing crimes, taken directly from Enlightenment theorists, we shall see in the following sections that Enlightenment philosophy is present in virtually all his propositions, most clearly shown in his directly citing Hobbes, Montesquieu, and others in his work.[10]

BECCARIA'S PROPOSED REFORMS AND IDEAS OF JUSTICE

Beccaria wrote at a time when authoritarian governments ruled the justice system, which was actually quite unjust. For example, back then, it was not uncommon for a person who stole food for his or her family to be imprisoned for life. A good example of this is the story of *Les Misérables,* in which the protagonist, Jean Valjean, receives a lengthy prison sentence after stealing a loaf of bread for his starving loved ones. On the other hand, a person at that time who had committed several murders could be excused by the judge if that person was from a prominent family.

As Beccaria claimed, "The true measure of crimes is namely the harm done to society"[11] (i.e., to the social contract). Thus, Beccaria was very clear that for a given act, a particular punishment should be administered as established by law, regardless of the contextual circumstances. (This point is the subject of much scrutiny later in this chapter.)

However, this principle did not take into account the offender's intent in committing the crime. In most modern justice systems, intent plays a key role in the charges and sentencing of defendants for many types of crimes. Most notably, the degrees of homicide in most jurisdictions of the United States include first-degree murder (which requires proof of planning or "malice aforethought"), second-degree murder (which typically involves no evidence of planning but, rather, is the spontaneous act of killing), and various degrees of manslaughter (which generally include some level of provocation on the part of the victim).

The degrees of homicide are just one example of the importance of intent—legally known as **mens rea** (literally, "guilty mind")—in most modern justice systems. Many types of offending are graded by degree of intent, as opposed to focusing on only the act itself—known legally as **actus reus** (literally, "guilty act"). Beccaria's propositions focus on only the actus reus, because he claimed that an act against society was harmful regardless

utilitarianism: a philosophical concept that relates to the idea of the greatest good for the greatest number

mens rea: concept regarding whether offenders actually knew what they were doing and meant to do it

actus reus: in legal terms, whether the offender actually engaged in a given criminal act of the intent, or mens rea. Despite his recommendation, most societies factor in the offender's intent in criminal activity. Still, this proposal that "a given act should be given equal punishment" certainly seemed to represent a significant improvement over the arbitrary punishments doled out by the regimes and justice systems of the 1700s.

Another sweeping reform Beccaria proposed was to do away with certain practices common in justice systems at the time. For example, he proposed that secret accusations not be allowed; rather, witnesses should be publically confronted and cross-examined. Although some modern countries still accept and use secret accusations, as well as disallowing the cross-examination of so-called witnesses, Beccaria set the standard for most modern systems of justice in guaranteeing such rights to defendants in the United States and most other Western societies.

Formal, public processing and trial of criminal defendants (rather than secret accusations and closed courtrooms) is a key part of Beccaria's proposed reforms of justice systems, as well as of deterrence theory.

Additionally, Beccaria claimed that torture should not be used against defendants. Although some countries, such as Israel and Mexico, explicitly allow use of torture for eliciting information and confessions, most countries now abstain from the practice. However, former U.S. Attorney General Alberto Gonzalez (the highest law enforcement rank in the country) wrote a memo stating that torture of terrorist suspects by the U.S. military is condoned. Despite this relatively recent change in U.S. philosophy regarding torture, the United States has traditionally agreed with Beccaria, who claimed that any information or oaths obtained under torture were relatively worthless. And our country apparently still agrees with Beccaria, at least in terms of domestic criminal defendants. Beccaria's belief in the worthlessness of torture is further expressed in this statement: "It is useless to reveal the author of a crime that lies deeply buried in darkness."[12]

Beccaria believed that this use of torture was one of the worst aspects of the criminal justice systems of his time and a manifestation of the truly barbaric acts common in feudal times in the Middle Ages (or "Dark Ages"). Beccaria expressed his doubt about the relevance of any information obtained via torture, a doubt best represented in this statement: "The impression of pain may become so great that, filling the entire sensory capacity of the tortured person, it leaves him free only to choose what for the moment is the shortest way of escape from pain."[13]

Beccaria addresses the possible policy implications of using torture in stating that, "of two men, equally innocent or equally guilty, the strong and courageous will be acquitted, the weak and timid condemned."[14]

Beccaria also asserted that defendants should be tried by fellow citizens or peers, not only by judges. As he stated, "I consider an excellent law that which assigns popular jurors, taken by lot, to assist the chief judge . . . that each man ought to be judged by his peers."[15] Beccaria clearly felt that the responsibility for determining the facts of a case should be placed in the hands of more than one person (such as a judge). Related to prior discussions in this chapter, Beccaria's feelings on this subject were likely driven by his Enlightenment beliefs on democratic philosophy, in which citizens should have a voice and serve in judging the facts, and in making ultimate justice decisions, in criminal cases. This proposition is representative of Beccaria's overall philosophy toward fairness and democratic process, which all the Enlightenment philosophers shared.

Although the United States typically uses torture methods only in times of war, such as in the recent war against terrorism, many countries still commonly use this practice against citizens accused of criminal activity.

CRIME IN THE NEWS

Russian Convictions

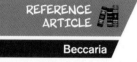

REFERENCE ARTICLE

Beccaria

As with other reforms discussed in this section, the right of all U.S. citizens to trial by a jury of their peers is often taken for granted. It may surprise some readers to know that many modern developed countries have not provided this right. For example, Russia just recently held its first jury trials since Vladimir Lenin banished the practice 85 years ago. During Lenin's rule, the "bench-trials" of the old system produced almost a 100% conviction rate (99.6%, to be exact). This means that virtually every person convicted of a crime in Russia was found guilty, whether or not they were actually guilty. Given the relatively high percentage of persons found innocent of crimes (such as murder) in the United States—not to mention the numerous persons in our country recently released from death row after DNA analysis proved them not guilty—it is frightening to think of how many individuals were falsely convicted and unjustly sentenced in Russia over the past century.

Another important aspect of Beccaria's reforms involves his emphasis on making the justice system, particularly the laws and decisions made in processing, more public and understandable. After all, this fits the Enlightenment assumption that individuals are rational and that if individuals know the consequences of their actions, they will act accordingly. Specifically, Beccaria stated, "When the number of those who can understand the sacred code of laws and hold it in their hands increases, the frequency of crimes will be found to decrease."[16] In Beccaria's time, the laws were often unknown to the populace. This was somewhat due to widespread illiteracy but perhaps more due to current laws not being publicly declared. Even when laws were posted, they were often printed in languages (e.g., Latin) that the citizens did not read or speak. So Beccaria stressed the need for society to ensure that citizens are educated on current laws, explaining that this alone will lead to a significant decrease in law violations.

Furthermore, Beccaria believed that the important stages and decision-making processes of any justice system should be public knowledge, rather than being held secretly or decided behind closed doors. As Beccaria stated, "Punishment . . . must be essentially public."[17] This statement has a highly democratic and Enlightenment feel to it, in the sense that citizens of a society have the right to know what vital judgments are being made. After all, in a democratic society, the citizens assign the government the profound responsibility of distributing punishment for crimes against the society. Citizens are entitled to know what decisions their government officials are making, particularly regarding justice. This provides not only knowledge and an understanding of what is going on but also a form of "checks and balances." Furthermore, the public nature of trials and punishments inherently produces a form of deterrence for those individuals who may be considering criminal activity, which is explored in the following sections of this chapter.

One of Beccaria's most profound and important proposed reforms is one of the least noted; in fact, it is largely ignored by every other review of his work. Specifically, Beccaria claimed to know the most certain way to reduce crime: "The surest but most difficult way to prevent crimes is by perfecting education."[18] Although he clearly expressed this as his primary recommendation for reducing crime, we know of no other review of his work that notes this hypothesis, which is amazing considering that most of the reviews are written for an educational audience. Furthermore, the importance placed on education makes sense given Beccaria's emphasis on knowledge of laws and consequences of criminal activity, as well as his focus on deterrence, which is explored in the following sections of this chapter.

BECCARIA'S IDEAS OF THE DEATH PENALTY

Another primary area of Beccaria's suggested reforms dealt with the use—and, in his day, abuse—of the death penalty. First, let it be said that Beccaria was against the use of capital punishment. (Interestingly, he was not against corporal punishment, which he explicitly stated was appropriate for violent offenders.) Perhaps this was due to the times in which he wrote, when a large number of people were put to death, often by harsh methods. Still, Beccaria provided several rational reasons for why he felt the death penalty was not an efficient and effective punishment.

First, Beccaria claimed that the use of capital punishment inherently violated the social contract:

> Is it conceivable that the least sacrifice of each person's liberty should include sacrifice of the greatest of all goods, life? . . . The punishment of death, therefore, is not a right, for I have demonstrated that it cannot be such.[19]

On a related note, the second reason for why Beccaria felt that the death penalty was an inappropriate form of punishment was that the government's endorsing the death of a citizen would provide a negative example for the rest of society. As Beccaria claimed, "The death penalty cannot be useful, because of the example of barbarity it gives men."[20] Although some studies show evidence that use of the death penalty in the United States deters crime,[21] most show no effect or even a positive correlation with homicide.[22] Researchers have called this increase of homicides after executions the **brutalization effect**, and a similar phenomenon can be seen at sporting events, such as boxing matches, hockey games, and soccer/football games, when violence breaks out among spectators. In recent years, there have even been notable incidents of fighting among spectators at youth sporting events.

To further complicate the possible contradictory effects of capital punishment, some analyses show that both deterrence and brutalization occur at the same time for different types of crime, depending on the level of planning or spontaneity of a given act. For example, one sophisticated analysis of homicide data from California examined the effects of a high-profile execution in 1992, largely because it was the first one in the state in 25 years.[23] As predicted, the authors of the study found that nonstranger felony-murders (which typically involve some planning) significantly decreased after the high-profile execution, whereas the level of argument-based stranger murders (typically more spontaneous) significantly increased during the same time period. Thus, the effects of both deterrence and brutalization were observed at the same time and in the same location following this execution.

Another primary reason why Beccaria was against the use of capital punishment was that he believed it was an ineffective deterrent. Specifically, he thought that a quick punishment, such as the death penalty, could not be an effective deterrent compared with a more drawn-out penalty. As Beccaria stated, "It is not the intensity of punishment that has the greatest effect on the human spirit, but its duration."[24] Many readers can likely relate to this type of argument even if they do not necessarily agree with it; the idea of spending the rest of one's life in a cell is a scary one for most people. And for many, such a concept

Fights among spectators at sporting events illustrate the type of "brutalization effect" Beccaria predicted in connection with the death penalty. Some individuals who see aggressive or violent acts are more likely to behave aggressively.

JOURNAL ARTICLE

Brutalization Effect

CRIME IN THE NEWS

Violent Crime

AUDIO

Death Penalty Debate

brutalization effect: the predicted tendency of homicides to increase after an execution, particularly after high-profile executions

LEARNING CHECK 2.2

1. Beccaria's seminal work, published in 1764, regarding criminal justice reforms was titled (translated from Italian)

   a. *The Criminal Man*

   b. *A General Theory of Crime*

   c. *On Crimes and Punishments*

   d. *Criminals in the Making*

2. According to the text, Beccaria proposed the use of the following in his book to make the criminal justice system more effective:

   a. Jury trials

   b. Secret/anonymous accusations

   c. Public trials

   d. All of the above

3. According to the text, Beccaria believed that the death penalty/capital punishment could be used as an effective deterrent if done correctly. True or false?

4. According to the text, Beccaria claimed that punishments should be based on which of the following?

   a. Actus reus

   b. Mens rea

Answers located at www.sagepub.com/schram

is more frightening than death, which supports Beccaria's idea that a more extended punishment may be a more effective deterrent than a short, albeit extremely severe, punishment such as execution.

BECCARIA'S CONCEPT OF DETERRENCE AND THE THREE KEY ELEMENTS OF PUNISHMENT

As noted previously in this chapter, Beccaria is widely considered the Father of Deterrence, and this is for good reason. After all, Beccaria was the first known scholar to write a work that summarized such extravagant ideas regarding the role of choice in human behavior, as opposed to the influence of fate or destiny. Prior to his work, the common wisdom on the issue of human destiny in criminal behavior was that it was controlled by the gods or God. At that time, governments and society generally believed that certain persons were born either good or bad. Beccaria, as a child of the Enlightenment, defied this belief by proclaiming that persons freely choose their destinies and, thus, whether or not to engage in criminal behavior.

Specifically, Beccaria claimed that three characteristics of punishment make a significant difference in whether an individual will commit a criminal act—in other words, they deter crime. These vital deterrent characteristics of punishment include celerity (swiftness), certainty, and severity.

SWIFTNESS OF PUNISHMENT. The first of these characteristics is celerity, which we will refer to as **swiftness of punishment**. Beccaria claimed that swiftness of punishment was important for two reasons. The first dealt with Beccaria's claim, consistent with his reforms discussed previously in this chapter, that some defendants were spending many years awaiting trial. Often, this was a longer incarceration than their alleged offenses would have warranted, even if the maximum penalty were imposed. As Beccaria stated, "The more promptly and the more closely punishment follows upon the commission of a crime, the more just and useful will it be."[25] Thus, Beccaria's first reason for recommending swiftness of punishment was that reformation of punishment was severely lacking in the time when he wrote.

The second reason Beccaria emphasized swift sentencing was related to the deterrence aspect of punishment. At the time when Beccaria wrote, some accused individuals would spend years in detention awaiting trial. A swift trial and punishment were important because, as Beccaria stated, "privation of liberty, being itself a punishment, should not precede the sentence."[26] Not only was this unjust in the sense that some of these defendants would not have been incarcerated for as long even if they received the maximum sentence for the charges against them; it also was detrimental in terms of deterrence, because the individual did not link the sanction with the violation. Specifically, Beccaria believed that persons build an association between the pains of punishment and their criminal acts. As Beccaria stated,

VIDEO

Deterrence

swiftness of punishment: assumption that the faster punishment occurs after a crime is committed, the more an individual will be deterred in the future

Promptness of punishments is more useful because when the length of time that passes between the punishment and the misdeed is less, so much the stronger and more lasting in the human mind is the association of these two ideas, crime and punishment . . . one as the cause, the other as the necessary inevitable effect.[27]

A parallel can be drawn with training animals or teaching children: You have to catch them in or soon after the act, or the punishment given does not matter because the offender does not know why he or she is being punished. Ultimately, Beccaria claimed that, for both reform and deterrent reasons, punishment should occur immediately after the act. Regarding the reform aspect, the defendant may spend a longer time in detention than the crime merits, and more important, the deterrent effect may be lost because the person will not relate the punishment with the negative act if punishment comes much later. Despite the commonsense aspects of swift punishment, this has not been examined by modern empirical research and is therefore the most neglected of the three elements of punishment Beccaria emphasized.

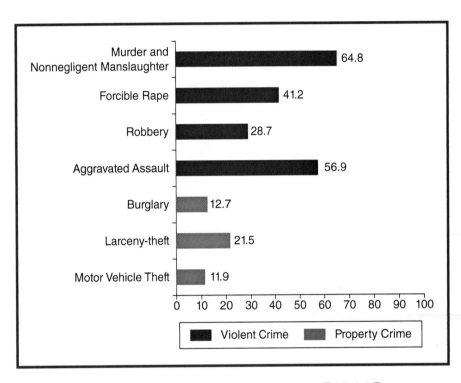

Table 2.2 Percentage of Crimes Cleared by Arrest or Exceptional Means, 2011

Source: FBI ."Crime in the United States 2010."

CERTAINTY OF PUNISHMENT. The second characteristic Beccaria felt was vital to the effectiveness of deterrence was **certainty of punishment**. Beccaria considered this the most important quality of punishment, which is evident in his statement, "Even the least of evils, when they are certain, always terrify men's minds."[28] It is obvious from this statement that Beccaria felt that certainty was the most important aspect of punishment—specifically, more important than severity and more important than swiftness/celerity by implication. He makes this clear when he says, "The certainty of punishment, even if it be moderate, will always make a stronger impression than the fear of another which is more terrible but combined with the hope of impunity."[29] As will be shown by scientific studies discussed later in this chapter, Beccaria was accurate in his assumption that perceived certainty or risk of punishment is the most important aspect of punishment.

It is interesting to note that the aspect of punishment Beccaria believed, and recent studies have shown (see below), to be most important in deterring crime—namely, certainty—is also the least likely to be enhanced in modern criminal justice policy. For example, over the past few decades, the rate of criminals being caught and/or arrested has not increased (see Table 2.2). Specifically, over the past few decades, law enforcement officials have been able to clear only about 21% of known felonies. Such clearance rates are based on the rate at which known suspects are apprehended for crimes reported to police. As shown in Table 2.2, law enforcement officials are no better at solving serious crimes known to police than they were in past decades, despite increased knowledge and resources for solving such crimes.

certainty of punishment: one of the key elements of deterrence; the assumption that when people commit a crime, they will perceive a high likelihood of being caught and punished

SEVERITY OF PUNISHMENT. The third characteristic Beccaria emphasized was **severity of punishment**. Specifically, Beccaria claimed that in order for a punishment to be effective, the set penalty must outweigh the potential benefits (e.g., financial payoff) of the given crime. However, this came with a caveat: This aspect of punishment was perhaps the most complicated of the three, primarily because while the punishment must exceed any benefits expected from the crime, Beccaria thought too much severity would lead to more crime. Specifically, Beccaria stated,

> For a punishment to attain its end, the evil which it inflicts has only to exceed the advantage derivable from the crime; in this excess of evil one should include the . . . loss of the good which the crime might have produced. All beyond this is superfluous and for that reason tyrannical.[30]

Beccaria makes clear in this statement that punishments should equal or outweigh any benefits of a crime if they are to deter individuals from considering engaging in such acts; however, he also explicitly states that any punishments that exceed the reasonable punishment for a given crime not only are inhumane but also may lead to further criminality.

A modern example of how punishments can be taken to an extreme, thereby causing more crime rather than deterring it, is shown by current "three-strikes-you're-out" laws. Such laws have become common in many states, such as California. In such jurisdictions, individuals can be sentenced to life imprisonment for committing a crime, even a nonviolent crime, that fits the state statutes' definition of a "serious felony" if it is their third offense. Such laws have been known to drive some relatively minor property offenders to wound or even kill people to avoid apprehension, knowing that they face life imprisonment if caught. The effectiveness of such "three-strikes" laws in reducing crime will be examined in a later chapter, but it is worthwhile to note here that a recent review of the impact of such laws across the nation shows them to be minimally effective; specifically, the authors analyzed the impact of three-strikes laws in virtually all large cities (188) in the 25 states with such laws and concluded that there was no significant reduction in crime rates due to the laws. Furthermore, the areas with three-strikes laws typically had higher homicide rates.[31]

Ultimately, Beccaria's philosophy on the three characteristics—swiftness, certainty, and severity—that make up a good punishment in terms of deterrence is still highly respected and adhered to in most Western criminal justice systems. Despite its contemporary flaws and caveats, perhaps no other traditional framework is followed as closely as Beccaria's—with only one exception, as we shall see in the coming sections.

BECCARIA'S CONCEPTUALIZATION OF SPECIFIC AND GENERAL DETERRENCE

Beyond the three characteristics of punishment Beccaria emphasized for improving the deterrent effect of punishment, he also developed the concepts of two identifiable forms of deterrence: **specific deterrence** and **general deterrence**. Although these two forms of deterrence tend to overlap in most sentences assigned by judges, they can be distinguished in terms of the intended target of the punishment. Sometimes the emphasis is clearly on one or the other, as Beccaria noted in his work.

Although Beccaria did not coin the terms *specific deterrence* and *general deterrence*, he makes the case that they are both important. Specifically, regarding punishment, Beccaria stated, "The purpose can only be to prevent the criminal from inflicting new injuries on its citizens and to deter others from similar acts."[32] The first portion of this statement, involving punishment preventing "the criminal" from reoffending, focuses on the defendant and only the defendant, regardless of any possible offending by others. Punishments that focus on the individual are considered *specific deterrence* (also referred to as

CRIME IN THE NEWS

Three-Strikes Law

JOURNAL ARTICLE

Deterrence

severity of punishment: the assumption that a given punishment must be serious enough to outweigh any potential benefits gained from a crime

specific deterrence: punishments given to an individual meant to prevent or deter that particular individual from committing crime in the future

general deterrence: punishments given to an individual meant to prevent or deter other potential offenders from engaging in such criminal activity in the future special or individual deterrence). This concept is appropriately labeled because the emphasis is on the specific individual who offended. On the other hand, the latter portion of Beccaria's quote above emphasizes the deterrence of "others," regardless of whether the individual criminal is deterred. Punishments that focus primarily on potential criminals, and not on the criminal in the present case, are referred to as *general deterrence.*

Readers are probably wondering how a punishment would not be inherently both a specific and a general deterrent. After all, in today's society, virtually all criminal punishments for individuals (i.e., specific deterrence) are decided in court, a public venue; so other people are made somewhat aware of the sanctions (i.e., general deterrence). However, at the time in which Beccaria wrote in the 18th century, much if not most sentencing was done behind closed doors and was unknown to the public, thereby having no power to deter potential offenders. Therefore, Beccaria saw much utility in letting the public know what punishments were handed out for given crimes. This fulfilled not only the goal of general deterrence, which was essentially scaring others away from committing criminal acts, but also his previously discussed reforms of assuring the public that fair and balanced justice was being administered.

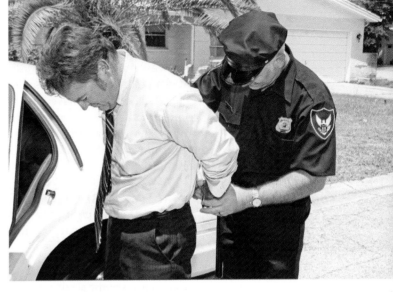

Public arrest is a formal sanction due to the embarrassment and trauma of going through the booking process, even if charges are later dismissed. Arrest is a form of both specific deterrence and general deterrence.

Despite the obvious overlap, there are some identifiable distinctions between specific and general deterrence in modern sentencing strategy. For example, some judges have chosen to hand down punishments that obligate defendants, as a condition of their probation/parole, to walk along the town's main streets wearing a sign that says something such as "Convicted Child Molester" or "Convicted Shoplifter." Other cities have implemented policies whereby pictures and identifying information of individuals arrested for prostitution or for soliciting prostitutes are printed in the paper or even displayed on billboards.

These punishment strategies are likely not much of a specific deterrent. After all, these individuals have now been labeled, so they may be psychologically encouraged to do what the public expects them to do (for more discussion and studies, see Chapter 10). So the specific deterrent effect may not be particularly strong in such cases. However, there is likely a strong general deterrent effect, which is what authorities are counting on in most of these cases. Specifically, they are expecting that many of the people who see these sign-laden individuals walking through the streets or publically displayed in pictures are going to be frightened away from criminal activity.

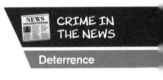

On the other hand, numerous diversion programs, particularly for juvenile, first-time, and minor offenders, seek to punish offenders without engaging them in public hearings or trials. The goal of such programs is to hold the individuals accountable and have them fulfill certain obligations without dragging them through the often-public government system. The goal in such cases is specific deterrence, without using the person as a "poster child" for the public, which thus negates any possibility of general deterrence.

So while most judges likely invoke both specific *and* general deterrence in many of the criminal sentences they hand down, in notable cases either specific or general deterrence is emphasized, sometimes exclusively. Ultimately, Beccaria seemed to emphasize general deterrence and overall crime prevention, suggested by this statement: "It is better to prevent crimes than to punish them. This is the ultimate end of every good legislation."[33] In other words, he claimed that it is better to deter potential offenders before they offend, rather than imposing sanctions after the fact. Beccaria's emphasis on prevention (rather than reaction) and general deterrence is also evident in his claim that education is likely the best way to reduce crime, as discussed previously in this chapter. After all, the more educated an individual is regarding the law and potential punishments, as well as public cases in which offenders have been punished, the less likely he or she will be to engage in criminal activity. As mentioned previously, Beccaria did not coin the terms *specific deterrence* and *general deterrence*; however, his explicit identification of the differential emphases in terms of punishment was a key element in his work and is still considered important today.

SUMMARY OF BECCARIA'S IDEAS AND INFLUENCE ON POLICY

Ultimately, Beccaria summarized his ideas on reforms and deterrence with this statement:

> In order for punishment not to be, in every instance, an act of violence of one or of many against a private citizen, it must be essentially public, prompt, necessary, the least possible in the given circumstances, proportionate to the crimes, dictated by the laws.[34]

Beccaria is saying here that the processing and punishment administered by justice systems must be known to the public that delegates to the state the authority to make such decisions. Furthermore, he claims that the punishment must be appropriately swift, certain (i.e., necessary), and severe, in keeping with his concept of deterrence. Finally, he again reiterates the need to standardize the punishments for given criminal acts, as opposed to arbitrary punishments imposed by a judge. These are just some of the many ideas Beccaria proposed, but he apparently saw them as being most important.

Although we, as U.S. citizens, take for granted the rights proposed by Beccaria and reviewed above, they were quite unique in the 18th century. In fact, the ideas Beccaria proposed were so revolutionary then that he published his book anonymously. He was worried the church would accuse him of blasphemy and the government would persecute him for his views.

Regarding the first worry, Beccaria was right; the Roman Catholic Church excommunicated him when the book's authorship became known. In fact, his book remained on the list of condemned works until relatively recently (the 1960s). On the other hand, the government officials of the time embraced his work. Not only did the Italian government endorse Beccaria's book; most European and other world officials, particularly dictators, embraced it as well. Specifically, Beccaria was invited to visit many countries' capitals, even those of the most authoritarian states at that time, to help reform their criminal justice systems. For example, Beccaria was invited to meet with Catherine the Great, empress of Russia during the late 1700s, to help revise and improve that country's justice system. Most historical records suggest that Beccaria was not an ideal diplomat or representative of his ideas, largely because he was not physically or socially equipped for such endeavors. However, his ideas were strong and stood on their own merit.

It is likely that the reason dictators and authoritarian governments liked his reformatory framework so much was that it explicitly named treason as the most serious crime. As Beccaria stated,

> The first class of crime, which are the gravest because most injurious, are those known as crimes of lese majeste [high treason]. . . . Every crime . . . injures society, but it is not every crime that aims at its immediate destruction.[35]

After all, treason was the criminal offense that most directly violated the government. To clarify, according to Enlightenment philosophy, not only are violations of law criminal acts against the direct victims, but such behaviors directly attack society as a whole by breaking the social contract. As Beccaria stated, the most heinous criminal acts are those that directly violate the social contract—treason and espionage. Therefore, it is not surprising that treason and similar offenses were considered the most serious crimes.

Thus, this is likely the reason why dictators of the time invited him to visit and presented him to the citizens as a "reformer" of their systems. These dictators likely saw a chance to pacify the revolutionary citizens, who the dictators could sense were about to overthrow their governments. In many of these cases, it was only a temporary solution. After all, the American Revolution occurred in the 1770s, the French Revolution in the 1780s, and other revolutions soon after this period.

We will see in later sections that governments that tried to apply Beccaria's ideas to the letter experienced problems, but most European (and American) societies that incorporated his ideas were more fair and democratic in their justice systems than those societies implementing any framework in existence prior to Beccaria. This is why he is, to this day, considered the Father of Criminal Justice.

LEARNING CHECK 2.3

1. According to the text, which element of deterrence did Beccaria believe was the most important in ensuring that individuals were deterred from committing crime?
   a. Swiftness of punishment
   b. Certainty of being caught
   c. Severity of punishment/sentences
   d. All were equally important

2. According to the text, Beccaria claimed which crime was the absolute worst offense?
   a. Murder
   b. Rape
   c. Robbery
   d. Treason

3. According to the text, Beccaria's book was well received by dictators around the world, even in those countries with more draconian criminal justice systems. True or false?

Answers located at www.sagepub.com/schram

IMPACT OF BECCARIA'S WORK ON OTHER THEORISTS

As discussed above, Beccaria's work had an immediate impact on the political and philosophical state of affairs in the late 18th century. In addition to being invited to help reform other countries' justice systems, his propositions and theoretical model of deterrence were incorporated into many countries' newly formed constitutions, most written after major revolutions. The most notable of these was the U.S. Constitution and Bill of Rights.

It is apparent that the many documents constructed before and during the time of the American Revolution in the late 1700s were heavily influenced by Beccaria and other Enlightenment philosophers. Specifically, the concept that our government is "of the people, by the people, and for the people" makes it clear that the Enlightenment idea of democracy and having a voice in the government is of utmost importance in the United States. Another clear example is the emphasis on due process and individual rights in the U.S. Bill of Rights. Specifically, the important concepts of right to trial by jury, right to confront and cross-examine witnesses, right to a speedy trial, and requirement that the public be informed of all decisions regarding their justice system (such as charges, pleas, trials, verdicts, sentences, etc.), as well as many other rights contained in our Constitution, are all products of Beccaria's work.

WHAT WERE THEY THINKING?!

Punishment

Beyond the incredible influence the Enlightenment and Beccaria had on individual rights in the United States via the Constitution and Bill of Rights, the impact of Beccaria's

Jeremy Bentham (1748–1832), one of the seminal theorists of the Classical and Neo-classical perspectives of criminology, insisted that his body be displayed at University College London. His preserved skeleton, with a wax head, sits there still.

VIDEO ▶

Utilitarianism

CRIME IN THE NEWS

Hedonistic Calculus

propositions on the working ideology of our justice system cannot be overstated. Specifically, the public nature of our justice system comes from Beccaria, as does the emphasis on deterrence. After all, our criminal justice system (as well as those of virtually all Western countries) uses the method of increasing the certainty and severity of punishment to reduce crime. This system of deterrence remains the dominant model in criminal justice, in which the goal is to deter potential and previous offenders from committing crime by enforcing punishment that will make them reconsider the next time they think about engaging in such activity. This model assumes a rational thinking human being, as described by Enlightenment philosophy, who can learn from past experiences or from seeing others punished for offenses that he or she is rationally thinking about committing. Thus, Beccaria's work has had a profound impact on the philosophy and workings of the justice systems in most countries throughout the world.

Beyond his influence in the workings of justice systems, Beccaria also had a large impact on further theorizing about human decision making related to criminal behavior. One of the more notable theorists inspired by Beccaria's ideas was Jeremy Bentham (1748–1832) of England, who has become a well-known Classical theorist in his own right, perhaps because he helped spread the Enlightenment/Beccarian philosophy to Britain. His influence in the development of Classical theorizing is debated, with a number of major texts not covering his writings at all.[36] Although he did not contribute a significant amount of theorizing beyond Beccaria's propositions regarding reform and deterrence, Bentham did further refine the ideas presented by previous theorists, and his legacy is well known.

One of Bentham's more important contributions was the concept of "hedonistic calculus," which was essentially the weighing of pleasure versus pain. This, of course, is strongly based on the Enlightenment/Beccarian concept of rational choice and utility. After all, if the expected pain outweighs the expected benefit of committing a given act, the rational individual is far less likely to do it. On the other hand, if the expected pleasure outweighs the expected pain, a rational person will likely engage in the act. Bentham listed a set of criteria that he thought would go into a rational individual's decision-making process. One analogy for this is a theoretical two-sided balance scale on which the pros and cons of crimes are weighed, with the individual then making a rational decision either to commit the crime or not.

Beyond the idea of hedonistic calculus, Bentham's contributions to the overall assumptions of Classical theorizing did not significantly revise the theoretical model. Perhaps the most important contribution he made to the Classical School was helping popularize the framework in Britain. Bentham became best known for his design of a prison structure, known as the "Panopticon," that was used in several countries, including the United States in early Pennsylvania penitentiaries. (This model used a type of wagon-wheel design, in which a post at the center allowed a 360-degree visual observation point for the various "spokes," or corridors, containing the inmate cells.) Thus, Beccaria remains the primary figure in the formation and articulation of the Classical School, and his conceptualization is the one that persisted for most of the late 18th and early 19th centuries.

WHY DO THEY DO IT?

THE HARPE BROTHERS

County, Kentucky. Wiley Harpe lived under an alias for a while to elude the local authorities but was captured, tried, and hanged in 1804.

So why did they do it? Aside from the psychological motivation to kidnap, rape, and kill so many people, the primary reason likely was because they could. This sounds crude and harsh, but there have always been evil people in the world. With no systematic formal justice system in the colonial period, especially in the frontier areas of Tennessee, Kentucky, and other pioneer regions in the 1700s, there was likely a sense of "do whatever you want." At that time, this was the Wild West of the colonies, and even if you violated local norms or rules, who was going to track you down and arrest you? After all, the first official law enforcement department did not form until the early 1800s in Texas (Texas Rangers, 1835), and the first municipal police force did not form until after that (Boston Police, 1838). Although some regions had a constable or similar officer who was supposed to enforce the rules or laws of that area, even such men were likely hesitant to go after two violent brothers who would likely attack anyone who came after them.

Without a certain formal policing authority, individuals can literally get away with murder. We have seen this happen in modern times when there is no stable law enforcement in place, such as in regions undergoing widespread chaos, whether it be Congo, Africa, or New Orleans, Louisiana, after Hurricane Katrina. The bottom line is that any time there is no formal, stable law enforcement authority in place, individuals can get away with any number of crimes, without facing sanctions or accountability. This is perhaps why New Orleans recently ranked as the top city in the United States for violent crime; formal structures were thrown into complete chaos after the flooding and resulting disarray from Hurricane Katrina. So it is for this reason—the lack of any stable law enforcement or criminal justice system—that the Harpe brothers were able to get away with as much as they did, until they were finally apprehended by more informal authorities, such as the revenge posse made up of nonsworn individuals and local constables that had limited authority at that time. But by the time they were stopped, they had for years been brutalizing many victims without facing any accountability or formal sanctions for their crimes.

The Harpe brothers, also known as the "Bloody Harpes," were likely the first notable serial killers in the United States and certainly the first sibling team of serial killers, if one marks our beginning as the colonial era. In the late 1700s, Micajah "Big" Harpe and Wiley "Little" Harpe were basically river pirates and highway robbers (in the traditional sense), who were active in various states in the Appalachian region of the Southeastern United States, including Tennessee, Kentucky, North Carolina, Mississippi, and Illinois. Despite the financial gains from their various crimes, they seemed more motivated by the act of kidnapping, raping, and killing. They were known to butcher all their enemies and their enemies' families, including infants. In one notable incident, Micajah Harpe bashed his own daughter's head against a tree because of her constant crying. It is claimed that this was the only crime for which he actually showed remorse when he confessed.

The brothers also took part in the kidnap and rape of several teenage girls in North Carolina, and pillaged (in every sense of the word) various farms. They later joined several different militias and Native American tribes, such as the renegade Creek and Chickamauga Cherokees (whom they had lived with at certain points), to attack frontier settlements and forts, such as Fort Nashborough (now Nashville, Tennessee). They were also known for kidnapping women and forcing them to become their wives. Given the time when they offended, little can be certain regarding the number of their victims or extent of their offenses, outside of the fact that historical records report they killed no fewer than 40 people and seemed to take great joy in doing so.

Regarding their demise, Micajah Harpe was killed by a revenge posse (after he killed a woman); he died after being shot and then attacked with a tomahawk. Legend has it his head was hung on a pole at a crossroads known as Harpe's Head or Harpe's Head Road in Webster

Sources: Musgrave, J. (1998, October 23). Frontier serial killers: The Harpes. *American Weekend*; Rothert, O. A. (1927). The Harpes, two outlaws in pioneer times. *Filson Club Historical Quarterly, 1*(4), 155–163.

THE NEOCLASSICAL SCHOOL OF CRIMINOLOGY

As discussed in prior sections, a number of governments, including the newly formed U.S. government, incorporated Beccaria's concepts and propositions in the development of their justice systems. However, the government that most strictly applied Beccaria's ideas—the French government after that country's revolution in the late 1780s—found that his concepts worked pretty well, with just one exception. Beccaria had claimed that every individual who committed a given act against the law should be punished in the same manner and to the same extent. Although equality in punishment sounds like a good philosophy, what the French quickly realized was that not everyone who commits a given act should be punished identically.

Specifically, the French system found that sentencing a first-time offender the same as a repeat offender did not make much sense, especially if the first-time offender was a juvenile. Furthermore, there were many cases in which malice did not appear to motivate the defendant's actions, such as when the defendant had limited mental capacity or committed a crime out of necessity. Perhaps most important, Beccaria's framework specifically dismisses the intent (i.e., mens rea) of criminal offenders and focuses only on the harm done to society by a given act (i.e., actus reus). French society—as well as most modern societies, including the United States—deviated from Beccaria's framework in considering the intent of offenders, often in a crucial way, such as in determining what types of charges should be filed against those accused of homicide (see the previous discussion on degrees of homicide in this chapter). Therefore, a new school of thought regarding the Classical/deterrence model developed, which became known as the **Neoclassical School** of criminology.

The only significant difference between the Neoclassical School and the Classical School is that the Neoclassical ("neo" means new) takes into account contextual circumstances of the individual or situation that allow for increases or decreases in the punishment. For example, would a society want to punish a 12-year-old, first-time shoplifter the same way as a 35-year-old, previous offender who shoplifted the same item? Additionally, does a society want to punish a mentally challenged, one-time car thief to the same extent as it would a normally functioning person who has been convicted of stealing more than a dozen cars? The answer to both is, probably not. At least that is what most modern criminal justice authorities, including those in the United States, have decided.

This was also the conclusion of French society, and although French authorities for some time fully embraced the idea of equal punishment for a given act against society (i.e., equal harm done to society, as Beccaria advised), they quickly realized that the system was neither fair nor effective in terms of deterrence. So they came to acknowledge that circumstantial factors play an important part in how malicious or guilty a defendant is. A number of contextual factors either alleviate or increase the level of malicious intent involved in engaging in criminal activity.

Thus, the French revised their laws to take into account both mitigating and aggravating circumstances. This Neoclassical concept became the standard in all Western societies' justice systems. Fortunately, the United States also follows this model and considers such contextual factors in virtually all decision making related to charges and sentences. For example, if a defendant is a juvenile, he or she is processed in a completely different system from the criminal court. Furthermore, first-time offenders are generally given the option of a diversion program or probation, as long as their offense is not serious.

Neoclassical School: assumes that aggravating and mitigating circumstances should be taken into account for purposes of sentencing and punishing an offender

APPLYING THEORY TO CRIME: *OTHER ASSAULTS (SIMPLE)*

The FBI's Uniform Crime Report Program defines "other assaults," or "simple assaults," as "assaults and attempted assaults where no weapon was used or no serious or aggravated injury resulted to the victim. Stalking, intimidation, coercion, and hazing are included."[37] In 2009, there were a total of 1,319,458 simple assaults. From 2000 to 2009, the number of simple assaults by males increased by 0.2%; for the same period, the number of simple assaults by females increased by 17.5%.[38]

Based on 2009 National Crime Victimization Survey data, the Bureau of Justice Statistics reported that there were 2,860,410 victims of simple assault, which means 11.3 simple assaults per 1,000 persons age 12 or older. Comparing this rate with the rate of simple assaults for 2000 (i.e., 17.8) reveals a significant decrease (36.8%). Men and women reported similar rates of victimization (11.3 and 11.2, respectively); however, when examining the relationships between victims and offenders, some interesting differences appear.

For the male victims of simple assault, 48% were nonstranger, 49% were stranger, and the remaining were "relationship unknown." Within the 48% nonstranger simple assaults, 6% involved intimate partners (i.e., current or former spouses, boyfriends, or girlfriends), 8% involved another relative, and 34% were between friends or acquaintances. For the female victims of simple assault, 70% were nonstranger, 28% were stranger, and the remaining were "relationship unknown." Within the 70% nonstranger simple assaults, 28% involved intimate partners, 10% involved another relative, and 33% were between friends or

acquaintances. When examining the rates of intimate partner violence by gender, 0.9 per 1,000 persons age 12 or older were male victims compared with 4.1 per 1,000 for female victims.[39]

It is essential to stress, however, that the scope and extent of domestic violence varies a great deal depending on the definition used to measure the incidence and prevalence of these assaults. Further, there is a general assumption that both official reports and self-reports understate the problem of domestic assault for a variety of reasons. For instance, a direct question pertaining to past victims or perpetrators of violence may not evoke a positive response. Some individuals may not remember or may not be willing to acknowledge or admit to illegal or inappropriate behavior.[40]

One area of study that has explored the application of deterrence theory is that of law enforcement responses to domestic violence. In the Minneapolis Domestic Violence Experiment, Sherman and Berk examined the effects of police responses in deterring domestic assaults.[41] Officers were randomly assigned to respond in one of the following manners: (a) separate the parties and order one of them to leave, (b) inform the parties of various alternatives (e.g., mediating disputes), or (c) arrest the abuser. The results revealed that 10% of those arrested, 19% of those advised of alternatives, and 24% of those ordered to leave subsequently engaged in further violence. Thus, Sherman and Berk concluded that arresting perpetrators of domestic violence has the strongest deterrent effect. Some researchers, however, noted methodological

shortcomings of the Minneapolis Domestic Violence Experiment. For instance, some officers involved in the experiment claimed to have prior knowledge of what type of action they were to take when responding to a domestic violence call. Thus, they would reclassify the offense in an effort to have it omitted from the study.[42]

The Minneapolis Domestic Violence Experiment had a tremendous policy impact:

> Within 1 year of the study's first publication, almost two thirds of major police departments had heard of the Minneapolis experiment, and three quarters of the departments correctly remembered its general conclusion that arrest was the preferable police response. Similarly, the number of police departments encouraging arrests for domestic violence tripled in 1 year from only 10% to 31%.[43]

It has also been suggested that the Minneapolis experiment was favorable among policymakers given the emerging support for deterrence theory. Due to the major policy impact of this experiment, the National Institute of Justice funded six experimental replications of the Minneapolis Domestic Violence Experiment; these have been collectively referred to as the "Replication Studies."[44] Essentially, these replications failed to confirm the earlier findings of the Minneapolis experiment. Buzawa and Buzawa contend that there may be a "middle ground." Specifically, deterrence may result for *some* offenders but not *all* offenders.[45]

(Continued)

APPLYING THEORY TO CRIME: (CONTINUED)

Police officers are a primary component of deterrence. Without the police, chaos might ensue, as seen during police strikes. However, studies show that concentrating officers in certain neighborhoods doesn't reduce crime in those areas.

To further highlight key aspects of deterrence theory, we apply this perspective to the crime of simple assault, specifically domestic violence. Doug and Emily have been living together for more than 3 years. They have a 2-year-old son and are expecting their second child in a few months. Throughout their relationship, Doug has become increasingly violent toward Emily. At first, he would shout at and belittle her; soon after, he was pushing and shoving her. Now, Doug has started to hit, slap, and kick Emily. One evening, the violence became so overwhelming, Emily called the police. Following department policy, the officers arrested Doug for simple assault. Doug was convicted and sentenced to probation and mandatory counseling.

Doug's arrest incorporates the concepts associated with deterrence theory. For instance, the certainty of punishment is supported by the departmental policy to make an arrest in such instances of domestic violence. The concept of swiftness is also evident, with Doug being arrested soon after Emily called the police. One may ask, however, whether the punishment of probation and counseling was too severe or not severe enough. Also, one might consider whether such punishment will deter Doug from assaulting Emily again.

CITY CRIME RANKINGS

Violent Crimes

STATE CRIME RANKINGS

Arrests for Violence

The Neoclassical School is an important caveat to the previously important Classical School. Still, the Neoclassical School assumes virtually all the other concepts and propositions of the Classical School. For example, the Neoclassical School also endorses the idea of the social contract, due process rights, and rational beings who are deterred by the certainty, swiftness, and severity of punishment. So with the exception of aggravating and mitigating circumstances in sentencing and punishment, the Neoclassical School is identical to the Classical School. And this Neoclassical School is the model used by all Western societies in their justice systems. Thus, this framework had and continues to have an extremely important influence around the world.

LOSS OF DOMINANCE OF CLASSICAL/ NEOCLASSICAL THEORY

For about 100 years after Beccaria wrote his book, the Classical/Neoclassical School was dominant in criminological theorizing. During this time, most governments, especially those in the Western world, shifted their justice frameworks toward the Neoclassical model. This has not changed, even in modern times. After all, virtually every society still uses the Neoclassical/Classical model as the framework for their systems of justice.

However, the Classical/Neoclassical framework lost dominance among academics and scientists in the 19th century, especially after Charles Darwin's publication of *The Origin of Species* in the 1860s, a book that introduced the concept of evolution and natural selection. This perspective shed new light on other influences of human behavior (e.g., genetics, psychological deficits) beyond that of free will and rational choice (covered in Chapters 4 and 5). Despite this shift in emphasis among academic and scientific circles, it remains true that the actual workings of the justice systems in most Western societies retained use of the Classical/Neoclassical model.

COMPARATIVE CRIMINOLOGY: *HOMICIDE RATES*

Ranking Countries by Rate of Prison Population and Homicide Rates

This box continues the book's theme of comparing the United States with foreign nations in terms of various aspects of criminology and criminal justice (see Comparative Criminology 1.1 in Chapter 1, which provides an introduction to this feature). In this section, we will examine the findings and conclusions from the eighth United Nations Crime Survey, specifically the portion dealing with rates of incarceration compared with rates of homicide in 89 countries. This comparison provides a recent analysis of the extent to which more severe sentences (as indicated by rate of incarceration) correlate with homicide rates in various countries. Readers should note that although most of the inmates in these countries were not convicted of murder, it is assumed that the countries that incarcerate the most offenders are also the most likely to be punitive in terms of a serious offense such as murder—an assumption supported by empirical research.

According to the research findings from the eighth United Nations Crime Survey, the trend is that the higher the ranking of countries in terms of prison population, the higher the homicide rates (see Figure 2.1). As can be seen in the figure, a higher prison population in a given country is strongly and positively associated with the homicide rate in that country. The estimated correlation for this association was significant, and the estimated coefficient was strong to moderate ($r = .48$). To clarify, the rate of incarceration is positively correlated with the occurrence of murder in most of the reporting countries, while the countries that reported the lowest incarceration

rates are also the most likely to report the lowest murder rates. For example, the rate of incarceration is highest (of the 89 countries) in the United States, and the rate of homicide is also high. Regarding other countries, the Russian Federation, South Africa, Swaziland, Estonia, Latvia, Panama, Belarus, and Ukraine also have high rates of incarceration, as well as high rates of homicide (see Figure 2.1).

On the other hand, a number of countries have low rates of incarceration and low rates of murder. Such countries include Japan, Iceland, Indonesia,

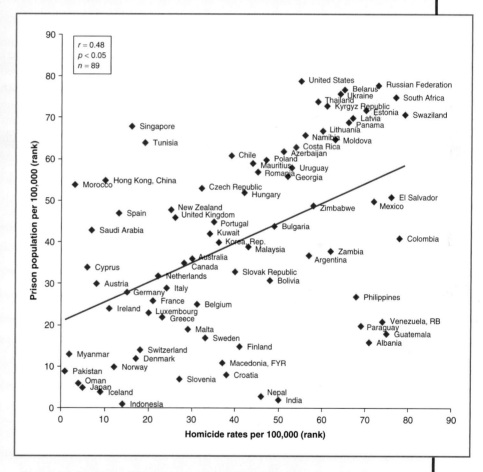

Figure 2.1 Ranking of Countries on Prison Population per 100,000 Population and on Homicide Rates per 100,000 Population

Sources: www.unodc.org; 8th UN Crime Survey; World Prison Population List (Seventh Edition), King's College, London, UK, 2007.

and Norway (see Figure 2.1). Again, countries that experience low levels of violence likely do not need to lock up such violent offenders; however, this analysis is done per capita, or by rate, so such comparisons are applicable. Of course, this observed association of countries that have the highest rates

COMPARATIVE CRIMINOLOGY: *HOMICIDE RATES*

of murder tending to have the most punitive sanctions could be spurious, in the sense that sanctions in these countries are so punitive because they have higher rates of violence. But the bottom line of this analysis is that despite more punitive sanctions in some countries (e.g., the United States, Russia), there appears to be no deterrent effect among individuals who commit murder. Perhaps this is due to the offenders not actually thinking about the sentences or penalties likely to result from the act of homicide, which will be explored more in the next section of this book.

Source: Van Dijk, J. (2008). *The world of crime.* Thousand Oaks, CA: Sage.

POLICY IMPLICATIONS

Even now, when authorities want to crack down on certain crimes such as drugs or gang activity, they focus on law enforcement and enhanced punishments to create more certainty and severity of being caught, respectively. So, although the Classical/Neoclassical perspective fell out of favor with researchers and academics over the past 150 years, it remains the primary model in terms of policy implications favored by most officials in the criminal justice system, legislators, and the general public. Many policies are based on deterrence theory: the premise that increasing punishment sanctions will deter crime. This is seen throughout the system of law enforcement, courts, and corrections.

This is interesting given the fact that Classical/deterrence theory has not been the dominant explanatory model among criminologists for decades. In fact, a recent poll of close to 400 criminologists in the nation ranked Classical theory as 22 out of 24 in terms of being the most valid explanation for serious and persistent offending.[46] Still, given the dominance of Classical/deterrence theory in most criminal justice policies, it is important to discuss the most common strategies.

For example, "three-strikes" laws have become prevalent in many states, as have police department gang units and injunctions (which condemn any observed loitering by or gathering of gang members in a specified region by listing members of established gangs). Furthermore, some states, such as California, have created gang enhancements in which juries decide whether the defendant is guilty of a given crime and also make a separate decision as to whether the person is a gang member. If a jury in California determines that the defendant is a gang member (usually with evidence provided by local police gang units), this automatically adds more time to any sentence assigned by the judge if the individual is convicted of the crime. However, some states are starting to reconsider this hard-line approach to locking up offenders for life for nonviolent felonies, such as in the case of Shane Taylor in California, who was sentenced to life under the "three-strikes" law after being convicted of two burglaries (a property crime, according to the FBI definition) and then possession of 0.14 grams of methamphemine.[47]

Also, the still-common use of the death penalty and programs such as "scared straight" are based heavily on the deterrence framework of the Classical/Neoclassical perspective, despite much evidence showing that neither tends to be effective in deterring individuals from committing crimes and both may have even led to more recidivism by the participants of such programs.[48] Furthermore, in terms of individuals' decision making when it comes to crime, formal deterrence elements such as law enforcement or possible severe sanctions for a given act tend to have little impact. This is because such a model assumes people are rational and think carefully before engaging in criminal behavior, whereas most research findings suggest that people often engage in behaviors they know to be irrational or that offenders tend to engage in behaviors without rational decision making, which criminologists often refer to as "bounded rationality." This means that individuals tend to be oblivious to many of the risks that may result from their behavior.[49] On the macro or group level, the same can be said for adding more officers to random street patrol in a given neighborhood or area, which shows negligible effects in crime reduction.[50] Rather, most deterrence effects and reductions of crime are more highly influenced by informal elements, such as families and communities having strong ties and "policing" their own neighborhoods, which we discuss in the next chapter.

These are just some examples of how the justice system in the United States, as well as most other Western systems, still relies primarily on deterrence of criminal activity through increased formal controls, such as law enforcement and enhanced sentencing, despite much evidence showing that these changes likely have little impact on individuals' decisions to engage in illegal behavior. The bottom line is that modern justice systems still base most of their ideology on the ability of individuals to be deterred by the certainty, severity, and swiftness of punishment—namely, the Classical/Neoclassical School of thought—despite the fact that this theoretical framework fell out of favor among scientists and philosophers in the mid- to late 1800s.

CONCLUSION

This chapter began with a discussion of the dominant perspectives throughout most of human civilization, which were supernatural- or religious-based theories. Once the Age of Enlightenment presented a more logical framework of individual decision making and rationality in the 18th century, the Classical School of criminological thought became dominant, largely due to the propositions in Beccaria's *On Crimes and Punishments* (1764). Along with many proposed reforms, his perspective focused on the assumption that individuals have free will and make a rational choice to commit a given offense after first considering the risk of getting caught and punished, a proposition that established the deterrence theory of reducing offender behavior. Thus, the goal was to deter individuals from engaging in criminal activities by increasing their likelihood of being caught and/or punished via formal sanctions.

We also started this chapter with a case study of Deborah Jeane Palfrey, the "D.C. Madam," who committed suicide before she could be sentenced for her crimes. Although this is an extreme example, it shows the pressing influence of incarceration on the human psyche. Ms. Palfrey killed herself when facing a prison sentence, and given that she had been incarcerated before, this shows the negative effects of such a sentence. This is proof that there is a lot to be said for the deterrent effect of formal sanctions, which is the keystone of the Classical School. Thus, there is still a case to be made for the deterrent effects of formal sanctions, such as incarceration, among many potential offenders in our society.

The Classical School as originally proposed by Beccaria included some elements that virtually all countries had problems implementing, which led to the Neoclassical perspective that allowed for consideration of contextual aspects in sentencing decisions. This improved Neoclassical framework became the dominant model for close to a century, until the late 19th century, but is still commonly used as the basis for most criminal justice systems in the Western world, especially in the United States. We will see in the next chapter that the concepts and propositions of the Classical/Neoclassical framework were recently expanded to develop a more logically valid and empirically supported theory of offending behavior.

SUMMARY OF THEORIES IN CHAPTER 2

THEORY	CONCEPTS	PROPONENTS	KEY PROPOSITIONS
Supernatural/religious/ metaphysical theories	Full moon Lightning God/gods	Various pre-Classical groups Most common belief among societies prior to Enlightenment period	Belief that crime is caused by Satan (i.e., "the devil made them do it") or exceptional phenomenon (e.g., full moon, thunderstorms)
Classical theory	Rationality Free will Social contract Deterrence theory Swiftness of punishment Certainty of punishment Severity of punishment	Cesare Beccaria Jeremy Bentham	Individuals have rational thought and decide to commit crime based on perceived risk of being caught/punished
Neoclassical perspective	Takes into account the contextual factors in a given crime in terms of punishment but assumes all other propositions of the Classical School (e.g., rationality, free will, deterrence)	No one key proponent, but this is the model all criminal justice systems in the Western world are based on (e.g., United States)	Same as Classical School but takes into account mitigating and aggravating factors when deciding the sentence for a given criminal activity

KEY TERMS

actus reus

Age of Enlightenment

brutalization effect

certainty of punishment

Classical School

deterrence theory

general deterrence

mens rea

Neoclassical School

severity of punishment

social contract

specific deterrence

swiftness of punishment

utilitarianism

STUDENT STUDY SITE

Visit the student study site at **www.sagepub.com/schram** to access links to the video, audio, city and state rankings, author podcasts, and SAGE journal and reference articles featured in this chapter, as well as additional study tools, including eFlashcards, web quizzes, web resources, and chapter outlines.

DISCUSSION QUESTIONS

1. How do pre-Enlightenment perspectives of crime differ from those in the Age of Enlightenment?

2. What Enlightenment philosophy do you feel was most important for criminal policy?

3. Can you think of modern examples of violations of Enlightenment philosophy?

4. What concept/proposition of Beccaria's reforms do you find least practical? Most practical?

5. Which of the three elements of deterrence do you find to be most important? Least important?

6. Do you agree with Beccaria's assessment of the death penalty? What portions of his reasoning do you most agree or disagree with?

7. Can you define and explain the differences between general and specific deterrence?

8. What modern-day applications and policies do you think were inspired or influenced by Beccaria and Bentham?

WEB RESOURCES

Demonic theories of crime

http://www.criminology.fsu.edu/crimtheory/week2.htm

http://www.salemweb.com/memorial/

Age of Enlightenment

http://history-world.org/age_of_enlightenment.htm

http://www.motivationalandinspirational.com/age-of-enlightenment.asp

Thomas Hobbes

http://www.philosophypages.com/hy/3x.htm

http://oregonstate.edu/instruct/phl302/philosophers/hobbes.html

Cesare Beccaria

http://www.constitution.org/cb/beccaria_bio.htm

http://www.criminology.fsu.edu/crimtheory/beccaria.htm

Deterrence

http://www.associatedcontent.com/article/32600/evolution_of_deterrence_crime_theory.html

http://www.deathpenaltyinfo.org/article.php?scid=12&did=167

Jeremy Bentham

http://www.utilitarianism.com/bentham.htm

http://www.ucl.ac.uk/Bentham-Project/who

Neoclassical School

http://www.answers.com/topic/neo-classical-school

CHAPTER 3

Contemporary Classical and Deterrence Research

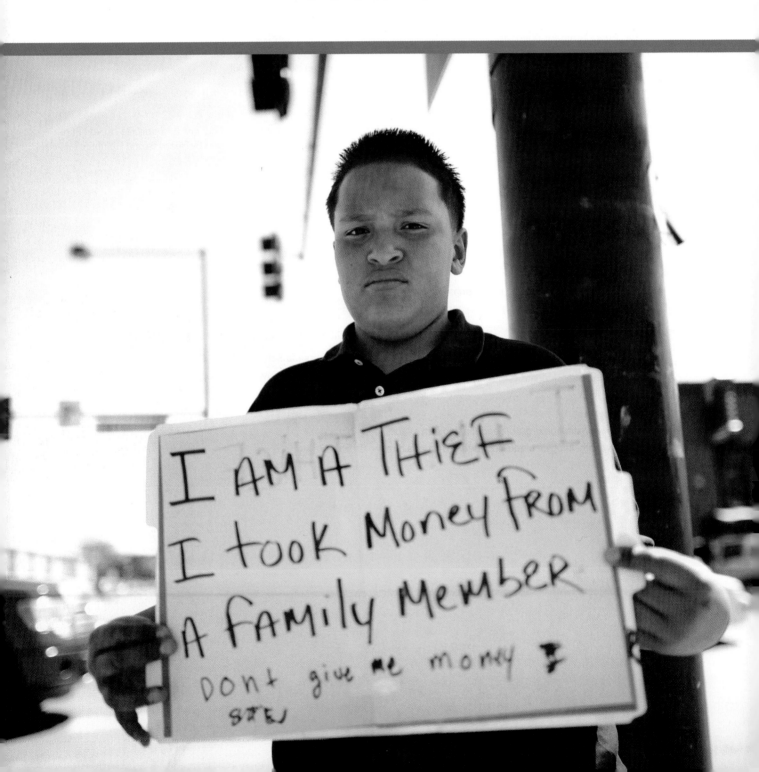

INTRODUCTION

On two separate days in August 2012, 13-year-old Brandon Mathison's mother forced him to wear a humiliating sign and walk along a busy intersection in Beaufort, South Carolina.[1] She made him do this because she had caught him smoking marijuana with his friends. The rather large placard he wore read, "Smoked pot, got caught! Don't I look cool? NOT!" on the front. On the back it read, "Learn from me, don't do drugs." This type of shaming strategy is an informal form of deterrence that stems from family, friends, and community, as opposed to the formal sanctions of law enforcement, courts, and jail or prison. And for most individuals in society, the informal controls are what actually deter and reduce our likelihood of engaging in criminal activity, because we don't want to risk losing our friends and jobs, and we care what our families and others think about us. The various theoretical models that emphasize such informal deterrent elements are examined in this chapter. But first, let's briefly review the previous chapter and see where we are headed in this one.

In the previous chapter, we examined the early history of the theorizing about crime, which included pre–Classical School perspectives (e.g., religious, supernatural explanations) as well as early Classical School theorizing during and just after the Age of Enlightenment. Early theorizing by Cesare Beccaria and others during the late 18th century remained dominant in terms of academics and, more important, policymakers for close to 100 years. But the Classical framework as a model for understanding crime fell out of favor among academics and researchers in the late 19th century.

While the Classical model never stopped being the favorite of policymakers, virtually all dominant theories presented by scientists of the past century have been premised on assumptions and propositions that go against such Classical concepts as deterrence, free will/choice, and rational decision making. However, Classical School concepts, assumptions, and propositions have experienced a "rebirth" in the past few decades. Furthermore, since the 1980s, several modern theoretical frameworks, such as rational choice, routine activities, and lifestyle perspectives, have given new life to the Classical perspective of criminological theorizing.

We will see that some of these more modern Classical School–based theories emphasize only the potential negative consequences of criminal actions, whereas other theories focus on the possible benefits. Still others concentrate on the opportunities and existing situations that predispose one to engage in criminal activity. Regardless of their differences, all the modern theoretical perspectives discussed in this chapter emphasize a common theme: Individuals commit crime because they identify certain situations and/or acts as beneficial due to the perceived low risk of punishment and perceived likelihood of profits, such as money or peer status. In other words, the potential offender weighs out the possible costs and pleasures of committing a given act and then behaves in a rational way based on this analysis of the situation.

LEARNING OBJECTIVES

As students read this chapter, they should consider the following questions:

- What are the various types of research performed from the 1960s to the present to determine whether perceptions of sanctions had a significant impact on individual decisions to commit crimes?

- What are the components of rational choice theory that were not included or emphasized by traditional Classical/deterrence theory in explaining criminal behavior?

- What are the three key elements of routine activities theory? Which of these three factors does the theory not explain very well? Which one do you think is most important?

- What types of individuals are most likely to be deterred? What types are least likely to be deterred? Do you see a paradox in these findings?

- What modern-day applications most apply Beccaria's principles?

- Which types of modern-day sanctions and policies apply to early Classical/deterrence theory? Do these applications seem to work according to empirical evaluations of such policies?

CASE STUDY

WAYNE

Wayne, raised in an upper-middle-class household in South Florida, was intelligent but also a risk taker, even at an early age. He was charismatic and made friends easily; even his teachers tended to like him, despite his sometimes deviant behavior. In high school, he engaged in many delinquent activities but nothing too serious. Although he had some encounters with police, it was usually for underage drinking or minor offenses, so he was never officially arrested. This is quite common, especially among teenage males.

This pattern took a more serious turn in college, when he was apprehended by police for a couple of incidents. However, these were also relatively minor, such as public intoxication, and even for these incidents, either charges were dismissed or he was never officially charged. But that is what it took to wake him up to the risks he was taking that could possibly jeopardize his future career. He wanted to be a lawyer, and he realized it would be difficult to get into law school, let alone be approved by the state bar association, if he had a criminal record. He was also potentially risking losing the respect of and strong bonds he had with family and friends.

So he realized around his junior year that he had to keep his nose clean and refocus his efforts on school, which he did. He eventually made the grades and test scores needed to gain entry into one of the top-tier law programs in the country, in Washington, D.C.—perhaps the best place to study law in our nation, given the opportunities and resources of that area. He did fantastically in law school and then moved back to Florida, where he became a respected and effective assistant district attorney. After a few years, he joined a private practice for a while, and within about 10 years he started his own law firm, where he has continued to be successful.

We shall see in this chapter that most individuals in society grow out of teenage tendencies to engage in delinquent or criminal behavior, largely due not to the fear of going to jail but, rather, the fear of losing positive aspects of their lives that they have worked hard for, such as bonds with friends and family and, often most important, a great career.

We will follow up on Wayne in the conclusion of this chapter as a reminder to apply some of the theoretical models and concepts toward explaining his change in behavior. These so-called informal elements of deterrence (e.g., family, friends, employers) are the ones that matter most for the vast majority of society—namely, the ones who have much to lose. And it is these types of considerations that the more traditional versions of Classical School/deterrence theory do not specify or take into account. Thus, the more modern versions of deterrence theory, such as rational choice theory, are far more robust and valid. But first, we will examine the rebirth of research in deterrence theory, which you shall see led to an evolution of theorizing and testing that resulted in the formation of these more fully specified explanations of criminal offending.

> THESE SO-CALLED INFORMAL ELEMENTS OF DETERRENCE (E.G., FAMILY, FRIENDS, EMPLOYERS) ARE THE ONES THAT MATTER MOST FOR THE VAST MAJORITY OF SOCIETY.

The most important distinction of these Classical School theories, as opposed to those discussed in future chapters, is that they emphasize individual decision making regardless of any extraneous influences on a person's free will, such as the economy or bonding with society. Although many outside factors may influence an individual's ability to rationally consider offending situations—and many of the theories in this chapter deal with such influences—the emphasis remains on the individual to consider all influences before making the decision to engage in or abstain from criminal behavior.

Given the focus on individual responsibility in modern times, it is not surprising that Classical School theories are still used as the basis for U.S. policies on punishment for criminal activity. After all, in the conservative "get tough" movement that has existed since the mid-1970s, the modern Classical School theories discussed in this chapter are highly compatible and consistent because they place responsibility on the individual. Thus, the Classical School still retains the highest influence in terms of policy and pragmatic punishment in the United States, as well as throughout all countries in the Western world. So the theories we examine in this chapter are the modern versions of the important assumptions, concepts, and propositions currently in use in virtually every system of justice in the Western world. Although most practitioners (even the judges who decide on sentences for a given illegal act) are likely not aware of these modern Classical theories of why individuals commit crimes (or do not), these modern perspectives represent the very types of concepts that all practitioners in our criminal justice system use to decide what is deserved or needed to reform an individual who has engaged in criminal activity.

REBIRTH OF DETERRENCE THEORY AND CONTEMPORARY RESEARCH

As discussed above, the Classical/Neoclassical framework fell out of favor among scientists and philosophers in the late 19th century, largely due to the introduction of Darwin's ideas on evolution and natural selection. However, virtually all Western criminal systems, particularly that of the United States, retained the Classical/Neoclassical framework for their models of justice. Despite the use of Beccaria's framework as the model for most justice systems, the ideology of his work was largely dismissed by academics and theorists after the presentation of Darwin's theory of evolution in the 1860s. Therefore, the Classical/Neoclassical model fell out of favor in terms of criminological theorizing for about 100 years. In the late 1960s and early 1970s, however, the Beccarian model of offending experienced a rebirth.

This rebirth was largely due to scientific reviews showing that the rehabilitation programs popular during the 1960s had virtually no impact in reducing recidivism among offenders, especially chronic offenders.[2] Specifically, Walter Bailey's review of 100 programs in the late 1960s showed that very few showed beneficial outcomes in reducing offenders' recidivism. Even more attention was given to Robert Martinson's review of such rehabilitative programs, which concluded that "nothing works." Although this conclusion was a bit overstated, it was true that virtually none of the rehab programs significantly reduced offending among participants. Therefore, criminologists returned to their "roots" in focusing more on Classical/deterrence principles.

In the late 1960s, several studies were published that used aggregate measures of crime and punishment and a deterrence model for explaining why individuals engage in criminal behavior.[3] These **aggregate studies** revealed a new interest in the deterrent aspects of criminal behavior and further supported the importance of certainty and

aggregate studies: collection of studies, generally on a particular topic

San Quentin State Prison. Incarceration in prison is a key element of formal deterrence.

A traditional electric chair. At one point in American history, electrocution was the primary method of execution but has since been largely replaced by lethal injection.

severity of punishment in deterring individuals from committing crime, particularly homicide. Specifically, evidence showed that increased risk or certainty of punishment was associated with less crime for most serious offenses. Plus, most offenders who are arrested once never get arrested again, which lends some basic support for deterrence.

Many of these studies used statistical formulas to measure the degree of certainty and severity of punishment in given jurisdictions. Specifically, the measures of certainty of punishment often were determined by creating a ratio of the crimes reported to police compared with the number of arrests in a given jurisdiction. Another employed measure of certainty of punishment was the percentage of arrests that resulted in convictions, or findings of guilt, in criminal cases. Although other similar measures were employed, most of the studies showed the same result—namely, that an examination of both measures indicated that the higher the likelihood of arrest given reports of crime, or the higher the conviction rate after arrest, the lower the crime rate in a given jurisdiction. On the other hand, the scientific evidence regarding measures of severity, which such studies generally indicated by the length of sentence for comparable crimes or a similar type of measure, did not show much impact on crime.

Additional aggregate studies examined the prevalence and influence of capital punishment and crime in given states.[4] The evidence largely showed that the states that had death penalty statutes also had higher murder rates than did non-death-penalty states. Furthermore, these studies showed that murderers in death penalty states who were not executed actually served less time than did murderers in non-death-penalty states. Thus, the evidence regarding increased sanctions, including capital punishment, was mixed. Still, a review by the National Academy of Sciences of the early deterrence studies concluded that there was more evidence for a deterrent effect than against it overall, although the Academy stated this in a tone that lacked confidence—perhaps cautious of what future studies would show.[5]

However, it was not long before critics noted that studies incorporating aggregate (i.e., macro-level) statistics are not adequate indicators or valid measures of the deterrence theory framework, largely because the model emphasizes the perceptions of individuals. After all, using aggregate/group statistics is flawed because different regions may have higher or lower crime rates than others, thereby creating bias in the level of ratios for certainty and/or severity of punishment. Further, the group measures produced by these studies provide virtually no information on the degree to which individuals in those regions perceive sanctions to be certain, severe, or swift. Therefore, the emphasis on the unit of analysis in deterrence research shifted from the aggregate level to a more individual level.

The following phase of deterrence research focused on individual perceptions of certainty and severity of sanctions, primarily drawn at one point ·in time—known as **cross-sectional studies**. A number of cross-sectional studies of individual perceptions of deterrence showed that perceptions of the risk or certainty of punishment were strongly associated with intentions to commit future crimes, but individual perceptions of severity of crimes were mixed. Furthermore, it was not clear whether perceptions were causing changes in behavior or whether behavior was causing changes in perception. This led to the next wave of research—longitudinal studies of individual perceptions and deterrence, which measured perceptions of risk and severity as well as behavior over time.[6]

One of the primary concepts revealed by longitudinal research was that behavior was influencing perceptions of the risk and severity of punishment more than perceptions were influencing behavior. This was referred to as the **experiential effect**, appropriately named because an individual's previous experience highly influences expectations regarding the chance of being caught and resulting penalties. A common example is people who drive under the influence of alcohol (or other substances).

Studies show that when asked the chances of getting caught driving under the influence, most people who have never driven drunk predict an unrealistically high likelihood of arrest. However, if you ask persons who have been arrested for driving drunk—even those arrested several times for this offense—they typically predict that the chance of being caught is low. The reason for this is that chronic drunk drivers have typically been driving under the influence for many years, mostly without being caught. After all, it is estimated that drunk drivers traverse more than 1 million miles before one drunk driver is arrested.[7] If anything, this is likely a conservative estimate. Thus, people who drive drunk—some doing so every day—are not likely to be deterred even when arrested more than once, largely because they have been driving drunk for years by that time. In fact, H. L. Ross—perhaps the most notable expert on the deterrence of drunk drivers—and his colleagues concluded that drunk drivers who "perceive a severe punishment if caught, but a near-zero chance of being caught, are being rational in ignoring the threat."[8] Even the most respected scholars in this area admit that sanctions against drunk driving are nowhere certain enough, even if they are growing in severity.

A similar phenomenon is seen among white-collar criminals. Some researchers have used the measure of being caught by authorities for violating government rules—often enforced by the Securities and Exchange Commission (SEC)—as an indication that the organizations in violation will be less likely to commit future offenses.[9] However, organizations in violation of established practices that have been caught once by authorities have likely been committing these offenses for years; so they are more likely to continue doing so in the future than are organizations that have never violated the rules. Like the conclusion made regarding drunk drivers, the certainty of punishment for white-collar violations is so low (and many would argue that the severity is also quite low) that it is rational for businesses and business professionals to take the risk.

It is interesting to note that of the many forms of criminal offending, white-collar crimes and drunk driving should be among the most likely to be deterred, due to their prevalence among citizens of the middle and upper socioeconomic classes. After all, if the extant research on deterrence has shown one thing, it is that individuals who have something

Police conducting a field test with a suspected drunk driver. Driving under the influence is a popular topic in deterrence research because it tends to range across social status and racial/ethnic groups.

Experiential Effect

cross-sectional studies: a form of research design model in which a collection of data is taken at one point in time (often in survey format)

experiential effect: extent to which previous experience affects individuals' perceptions of how severe criminal punishment will be when deciding whether or not to offend again to lose are the most likely to be deterred by sanctions. This makes sense because many unemployed, poor individuals will probably not be deterred by incarceration or other punishments, largely because they do not have much to lose. For some persons, particularly those of the lower class, minority populations, incarceration does not present a significant departure from the deprived lives they already lead.

The fact that official sanctions are limited in deterring individuals—many of whom have a lot to lose—from drunk driving and white-collar crime is not a good indication of effectiveness for deterrence-based policies. This becomes even more questionable when other populations are considered, particularly the offenders in most predatory street crimes (e.g., robbery, burglary), who typically have nothing to lose because they come from poverty-stricken areas and are often unemployed. One recent study that examined the influence of sanctions showed that arrests had little effect on perceptions of certainty, whereas offending corresponded with decreases in such perceptions.[10]

Some individuals do not consider incarceration much of a step down in life, given the three meals a day, shelter, and relative stability entailed. This epitomizes one of the most notable paradoxes of the discipline: The individuals we most want to deter are the least likely to be deterred, primarily because they have nothing to fear. Even going back to early Enlightenment thought, Thomas Hobbes claimed that fear was the tool used to enforce the social contract; however, persons who don't fear punishment cannot be effectively deterred. Thus, it remains true that the individuals we most need to deter (chronic offenders) are the least likely to be deterred by the threatened punishments of our society, because they have so little to lose.

Along these same lines, studies have consistently shown that official deterrence is highly ineffective against criminal acts that involve immediate payoff, young male offenders, higher risk, low emotional/moral inhibitions, low self-control, and impulsivity.[11] Thus, many factors affect the extent to which official sanctions can deter crime. However, even among the most "deterrable" offenders, official sanctions exhibit failings, particularly when individuals in the highly deterrable categories have experience in the criminal behavior because they are rarely caught.

Identification and understanding of the experiential effect had a profound influence on evidence regarding the impact of deterrence. After all, any estimation of the influence of perceived certainty or severity of punishment must control for previous behaviors and experiences with such behavior to account for an experiential effect. Identification of the experiential effect was the primary contribution of the longitudinal studies of deterrence, but such studies faced even further criticism.

Longitudinal studies of deterrence provided a significant improvement over the preceding cross-sectional studies. However, such longitudinal studies typically involved designs in which measures of perception of certainty and severity of punishment were collected up to a year apart, including long stretches between the time of the criminal offense and when offenders were asked their perceptions of punishment. After all, psychological studies have clearly established that perceptions of the likelihood and severity of sanctions vary significantly from day to day, let alone from month to month or year to year.[12] Therefore, in the late 1980s and early 1990s, a new wave of deterrence research evolved that asked study participants to estimate their immediate intent to commit a criminal act in a given situation, as well as asking their immediate perceptions of certainty and severity of punishment in the same situation. This wave of research was known as **scenario research**, or **vignettes**.[13]

Scenario research was created to deal with the limitations of the previous methodological strategies for studying the effects of deterrence on criminal offending. Specifically, the critics of longitudinal research argued that individuals' perceptions of the certainty

scenario research: studies that involve providing participants with specific hypothetical scenarios and then asking them what they would do in each situation

vignettes: short, descriptive sketches

and severity of punishment changed drastically from one time to another, especially in different situations. The scenario method dealt with this criticism directly by providing a specific, realistic (albeit hypothetical) situation in which a person engages in a criminal act. The participant in the study was then asked to estimate the chances that he or she would engage in such an activity under the given circumstances, as well as to respond to questions regarding the perceptions of risk of getting caught (i.e., certainty of punishment) and degree of severity of punishment expected.

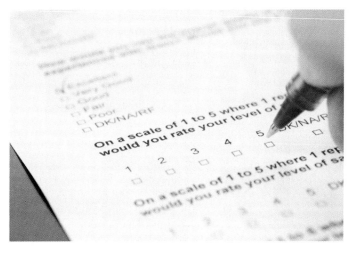

Another important and valuable aspect of scenario research was that it promoted a contemporaneous (i.e., instantaneous) response regarding perceptions of the risk and severity of possible sanctions. In comparison, previous studies (e.g., aggregate, cross-sectional, longitudinal) had always relied on either group rates or individual measures of perception across long stretches of time. As discussed previously, individuals' perceptions regarding risk and/or severity of punishment vary significantly by time and situation, but the scenario method eliminates such criticisms. Some argue that estimated likelihood of committing a crime given a hypothetical situation is not an accurate measure of what one would actually do. However, studies have shown an extremely high correlation between what one reports doing in a given scenario and what one would do in real life.[14] A recent review of criticisms of this method showed that one of the aspects where this research was lacking was in not allowing respondents to develop their own perceptions and costs associated with each offense.[15] Despite such criticisms, the scenario method appears to be the most accurate method we have to estimate the effects of individual perceptions on the likelihood of individuals engaging in a given criminal activity at a given time. This is something the previous waves of deterrence research—aggregate, cross-sectional, and longitudinal studies—could not estimate.

Ultimately, the studies using the scenario method showed that participants were more affected by perceptions of certainty and less so—albeit sometimes significantly—by perceptions of severity. This finding supported previous methods of estimating the effects of **formal/official deterrence** (see Figure 3.1), meaning the deterrent effects of law enforcement, courts, and corrections (i.e., prisons and probation or parole). So the overall conclusion regarding effects of official sanctions on individual decision making remained unaltered. However, one of the more interesting aspects of scenario research is that it helped solidify the importance of extralegal variables in deterring criminal behavior, which had been neglected by previous methods.

These extralegal variables, called **informal deterrence** factors, include any factors beyond the formal sanctions of police, courts, and corrections—such as employment, family, friends, and community. These studies helped show that such informal sanctions are what provide most of the deterrent effect for individuals considering criminal acts. These findings coincided with the advent of a new model of deterrence, which became commonly known as **rational choice theory**.

RATIONAL CHOICE THEORY

Rational choice theory is a perspective criminologists adapted from economists, who used it to explain a variety of individual decisions regarding different behaviors. This framework emphasizes all important factors that go into a person's decision to engage, or not engage, in a particular act. In terms of criminological research, the rational choice

The vast majority of findings on why people commit crimes are gained through self-report studies. Such studies explore factors (e.g., psychological, family life) that are not present in police reports or victimization studies.

PERSONAL PERSPECTIVE

Consequences

AUDIO

Deterrence

formal/official deterrence: deterrent effects of law enforcement, courts, and corrections

informal deterrence: factors like family, church, or friends that do not involve official aspects of criminal justice, such as police, courts, and corrections (e.g., prisons)

rational choice theory: a modern, Classical School–based framework for explaining crime that includes the traditional formal deterrence aspects and other informal factors that studies show consistently and strongly influence behavior

Formal Factors

Law enforcement

Courts

Prisons and corrections

Informal Factors

Family and friends

Employment

Community

Figure 3.1 Formal Deterrence Versus Informal Deterrence

VIDEO

Career Criminals

model emphasized official/formal forms of deterrence as well as the informal factors that influence individual decisions to engage in criminal behavior. This represented a profound advance in the understanding of human behavior. After all, as studies showed, most individuals are affected more by the influence of informal factors than by official/formal factors.

Although there were several previous attempts to apply the rational choice model to the understanding of criminal activity, the most significant work that brought rational choice theory into the mainstream of criminological research was Derek B. Cornish and Ronald V.

Clarke's (1986) *The Reasoning Criminal: Rational Choice Perspectives on Offending.*[16] Furthermore, around the same time, Jack Katz (1988) published his work *Seductions of Crime*, which for the first time emphasized the benefits (mostly the inherent physiological pleasure) of committing crime.[17] Before Katz's publication, virtually no attention had been paid to the benefits of offending, let alone the "fun" people can have when engaging in criminal behavior. A recent study showed that the publication of Cornish and Clarke's book, as well as the timing of other publications such as Katz's, led to an influx of criminological studies based on the rational choice model in the late 1980s to mid-1990s.[18]

These studies on rational choice showed that while official/formal sanctions tend to have some effect on individuals' decisions to commit crime, they almost always are relatively unimportant compared with extralegal/informal factors. Specifically, the effects of individual perceptions of how much shame or loss of self-esteem one would experience, even if no one else found out about the crime, was one of the most important variables in determining whether or not one would commit a crime.[19] Additional evidence indicated that females were more influenced by shame and moral beliefs when deciding to commit offenses than were males.[20] Recent studies have shown that levels of certain personality traits, especially low self-control and empathy, are likely the reason why males and females differ so much when it comes to engaging in criminal activity.[21] Finally, the influence of peers has a profound impact on individual perceptions of the pros and cons of offending—namely, by significantly decreasing the perceived risk of punishment when one sees friends getting away with crimes.[22]

Another area of rational choice research dealt with the influence of an individual's behavior on other individuals. A recent review and test of perceived social disapproval showed that this was one of the most important variables in decisions to commit crime.[23] In addition to self-sanctions, such as feelings of shame and embarrassment, the perception of how loved ones and friends, as well as employers, would react is perhaps the most important factor in a person's decision to engage in criminal activity. After all, these are the people we deal with every day, so it should not be too surprising that our perceptions of how they would react strongly affect how we choose to behave.

Perhaps the most important finding of rational choice research was that the expected benefits, particularly the pleasure gained from offending, was one of the most significant influences in decisions to offend. Many other conclusions have been reached regarding the effect of extralegal/informal factors on criminal offending, but the ultimate conclusion is that these informal deterrent variables typically hold more influence in individual decision making regarding deviant activity than do the official/formal deterrent factors emphasized by traditional Classical School models of behavior.

The rational choice model of criminal offending became the modern framework of deterrence. Even official authorities acknowledged the influence of extralegal/informal

---

LEARNING CHECK 3.1

1. According to the text, for which type of studies examining deterrence does the "experiential effect" pose the biggest threat of biased results?

   a. Longitudinal studies

   b. Aggregate studies

   c. Cross-sectional studies

2. According to the text, when looking at the results from the various waves of studies examining deterrence, which element of punishment has shown the most consistent deterrent effect?

   a. Perceived certainty of getting caught

   b. Perceived severity of the punishment/sentence

   c. Perceived swiftness of being punished

   d. They are all about equally important

3. According to the text, which type of studies by definition use data collected at one point in time?

   a. Longitudinal

   b. Aggregate

   c. Cross-sectional

Answers located at www.sagepub.com/schram

REFERENCE ARTICLE
Rational Choice Theory

JOURNAL ARTICLE
Shame and Rational Choice

CRIME IN THE NEWS
Shaming

APPLYING THEORY TO CRIME: DRIVING UNDER THE INFLUENCE

The Uniform Crime Reporting (UCR) program separates criminal offenses into two categories: Part I and Part II crimes. Part I offenses include criminal homicide, forcible rape, robbery, aggravated assault, burglary, larceny-theft, motor vehicle theft, and arson. Part II offenses include fraud, vandalism, gambling, and driving under the influence (DUI). The UCR defines DUI as "driving or operating a motor vehicle or common carrier while mentally or physically impaired as the result of consuming an alcoholic beverage or using a drug or narcotic."[24] According to the Insurance Institute for Highway Safety, all 50 states and the District of Columbia have laws defining what constitutes "drunk driving." These laws designate a blood alcohol concentration (BAC) at or above a certain level; currently, this level is 0.08% (i.e., 0.08 grams of alcohol per 100 milliliters of blood).[25]

The FBI reported a total of 1,112,384 DUI arrests in the United States in 2009, with a national rate of 463.8 arrests per 100,000. When examining these rates by region, the West reported the highest rate (552.2), followed by the Midwest (474.0), the South (449.9), and the Northeast (343.0). Overall, there was a 4.3% decrease in DUI arrests from 2000 to 2009. Specifically, for

those under 18 years of age there was a 36.3% decrease; for those 18 years of age or older, there was a 3.8% decrease.[26]

The Centers for Disease Control and Prevention reported that every day, almost 30 people in the United States die due to motor vehicle accidents involving an alcohol-impaired driver. The annual cost of alcohol-related accidents totals more than $51 billion. At all BAC levels, young people are at a higher risk of being involved in an alcohol-related accident, compared with older people. In 2010, more than 1 out of every 3 such fatalities involved someone between 21 and 24 years of age (34%), followed by those between 25 and 34 (30%) and those between 35 and 44 (25%).[27]

One of the suggestions to prevent death and injury due to impaired driving is to reduce the legal BAC limit to 0.05%.

Progress has been made during the past 25 years to reduce the numbers and proportions of fatally injured drivers with BACs at or above 0.08 percent. Since 1982 there has been a 37 percent decline in the number of passenger vehicle drivers killed in crashes who had BACs at

or above 0.08 percent. . . . In 2005 [Insurance Institute for Highway Safety] research estimated that 8,916 deaths would have been prevented if all drivers on the road had BACs lower than 0.08 percent.[28]

Another suggested prevention is to install ignition interlock devices in vehicles. This device is installed in the vehicle, usually in the glove compartment on the passenger's side. It is then wired to the engine's ignition system. In a vehicle with such a device installed, the driver has to blow about 1.5 liters of air into a handheld alcohol sensor unit. If his or her BAC is over a preset limit, the car will not start. While these preset limits vary by state, they are usually between 0.02% and 0.04%.[29] More than half of all states require *some* DUI offenders to install ignition interlock devices in their vehicles to drive during license suspension and/or a designated time period before receiving full relicensure.[30] For instance, in Florida, certain individuals convicted of DUI are required to install an ignition interlock device. The costs to the defendant include a $12 interlock fee, $75 for installation, $72.50 for monthly monitoring and calibration, and a $100 refundable deposit or $5 monthly insurance charge.[31]

WHAT WERE THEY THINKING?!

Shaming

routine activities theory: explanation of crime that assumes crime and victimization are highest in places where three factors come together in time and place: motivated offenders, suitable or attractive targets, and absence of a guardian

factors, which is seen in modern efforts to incorporate the family, employment, and community in rehabilitation efforts. Such efforts are highly consistent with the current state of understanding regarding the Classical School/rational choice framework—namely, that individuals are more deterred by the impact of their actions on the informal aspects of their lives than by the formal punishments they may face in committing illegal acts.

ROUTINE ACTIVITIES THEORY

Routine activities theory is another contemporary form of the Classical School framework in the sense that it assumes a rational, decision-making offender. The general model of routine activities theory was originally presented by Lawrence Cohen and Marcus Felson in 1979.[32] This theoretical framework emphasized the presence of three factors that come together in time and place to create a high likelihood of crime/victimization. These three factors are (1) motivated offender(s), (2) a suitable target, and (3) lack of

COMPARATIVE CRIMINOLOGY: *THREATS AND ASSAULTS*

Ranking Countries by Rate of Beer Consumption and Rate of Threats/Assaults

This box continues the book's theme of comparing the United States with foreign nations in terms of various aspects of criminology and criminal justice (see Comparative Criminology 1.1 in Chapter 1, which provides an introduction to this feature). In this section, we explore the association between rate of beer consumption and rate of violence—specifically, assaults and threats.

One of the modern versions of deterrence theory is rational choice theory. Rational choice theory assumes that individuals are rational and weigh the potential benefits against the potential costs of engaging in a criminal act. However, modern studies discussed in this chapter have shown that individuals often engage in activities, both legal and illegal, that are not rational. Many of these acts that appear quite irrational are committed by individuals who have been drinking alcohol. This fits a concept known in the field as "bounded rationality," in the sense that individuals are sometimes not thinking clearly or at the level of the average person—a situation to which alcohol often contributes.

As seen in Figure 3.2, there is a strong correlation ($r = .54$) between beer consumption in a given country and the corresponding rates of threats and assaults. For example, New Zealand, the United Kingdom, and Ireland have relatively high rates of beer consumption and threats and assaults. On the other hand, Italy, Japan, France, and Portugal tend to have relatively low levels of both beer consumption and threats and assaults. Therefore, it is clear that certain countries display far more beer consumption than do other countries and that this likely contributes to higher rates of violence in those countries. So the bottom line of this analysis is that most of the countries that exhibit high levels of beer consumption, which is very likely to "bound" individuals' rational thinking before committing illegal acts, tend to show far higher rates of violence as measured by threat and assault rates. This adds to the empirical evidence supporting the limitations of rational choice/deterrence theory, in the sense that individuals are not always rational, especially when they have consumed a good amount of beer.

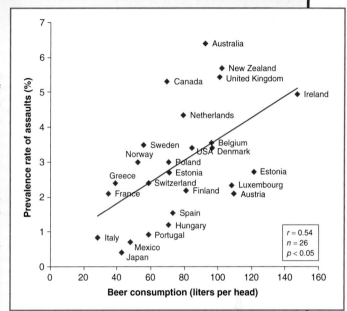

Figure 3.2 Rates of Victimization by Threats/Assault in 1996–2005 and Beer Consumption (Liters per Head) in Developed Countries (2004)

Sources: ICVS, 2005; World Drink Trends, 2004.

Excessive alcohol consumption has been strongly linked to criminal offending, especially violent crimes.

Sources: Van Dijk, J. (2008). *The world of crime.* Thousand Oaks, CA: Sage; World Advertising Research Center. (2004). *World drink trends 2004.* Henley-on-Thames, UK: Author.

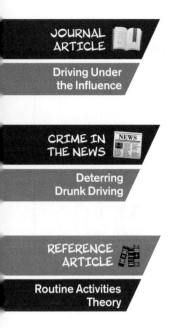

JOURNAL ARTICLE

Driving Under the Influence

CRIME IN THE NEWS

Deterring Drunk Driving

REFERENCE ARTICLE

Routine Activities Theory

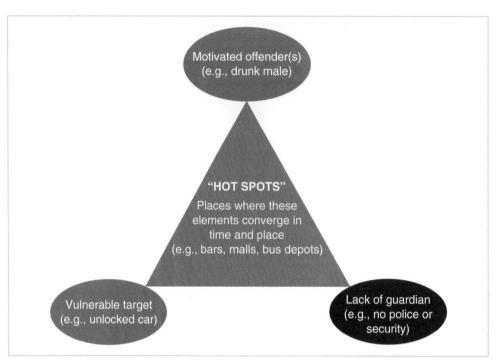

Figure 3.3 Routine Activities Theory

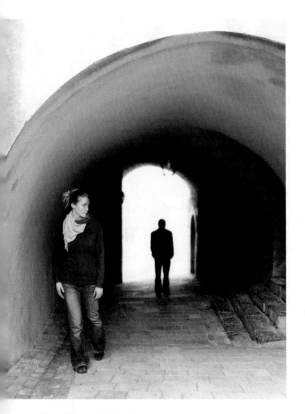

Routine activities theory focuses on the presence of suitable or vulnerable targets, such as a female walking alone in a secluded location.

guardianship (see Figure 3.3). Overall, the theory is appropriately named, in the sense that it assumes that most crime occurs in the daily "routine" of people who happen to see tempting opportunities to commit crime and seize them. Studies tend to support this idea, as opposed to the idea that most offenders tend to leave their homes knowing they are going to commit a crime; such offenders are called "hydraulic" and are relatively rare compared with the opportunistic type.

Regarding the first factor thought to increase the likelihood of criminal activity—a motivated offender—the theory of routine activities does not provide much insight. The model assumes that there are certain individuals who tend to be motivated, and leaves it at that. Fortunately, we have many other theories, as discussed previously in this chapter and in the remainder of the book, that can fill this notable absence. The strength of routine activities theory is in its elaboration on the other two characteristics of a crime-prone environment: suitable targets and lack of guardianship.

Suitable targets can include a variety of situations—for example, a house in the suburbs left vacant over summer vacation. After all, data clearly show that burglaries more than double in the summer, when most families are on vacation (see Figure 3.4). Other suitable targets include anything from an unlocked car to a lone female carrying a lot of cash or credit cards and/having purchased goods at a shopping mall, which is a common setting for victimization. Another likely location to be victimized is a bar or other place that serves alcohol, which has much to do with the fact that offenders have traditionally targeted drunk persons because they are less likely to be able to defend themselves—going back to rolling drunks for their wallets in the early part of the 20th century. This is only a short list of the many types of suitable targets available to motivated offenders in everyday life.

The third and final aspect of the routine activities model for increased likelihood of criminal activity is the lack of guardianship. Guardianship is often thought of as an on-duty police officer or security guard, which often is the case. However, there are many other forms of guardianship, such as a household dog, which studies demonstrate can be quite effective in home protection. Even a car or house alarm constitutes a form of guardianship. Furthermore, the presence of an adult, neighbor, or teacher can be quite effective in guarding an area against crime. Recent studies show that just increasing the lighting in an area can help prevent crime, with one study showing a 20% reduction in overall crime in areas randomly chosen to receive improved lighting, compared with control areas that did not.[33] Regardless of the type of guardianship, the absence of adequate guardianship sets the stage for crime; on the other hand, each step

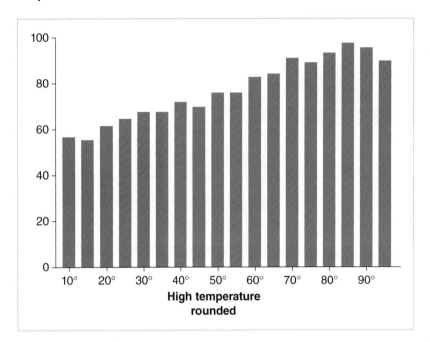

Violent crime in Columbus increases as the high temperature rises.

Average number of violent crimes in Columbus by a day's highest temperature:

taken toward protecting a place or person is likely to deter offenders from choosing that target over others. Locations that have a high convergence of motivated offenders, suitable targets, and lack of guardianship are typically referred to as "hot spots."

Perhaps the most supportive study of routine activities theory and "hot spots" was that analyzing 911 calls for service in Minneapolis, Minnesota.[34] This study examined all serious calls (as well as total calls) to police in a 1-year period. Of the top 10 locations police were called, half were bars or other places where alcohol was served (see Table 3.1). As mentioned above, establishments that serve alcohol are often targeted by motivated offenders because of a high proportion of suitable targets. Furthermore, many bars have low levels of guardianship in relation to the number of people served. Many readers of this book can likely relate to this situation. After all, most college towns and cities have certain drinking establishments known for being "hot spots" for crime.

Still, the Minneapolis study showed that a lot of other types of establishments made the top 10 or ranked high on the list. These included bus depots, convenience stores, rundown motels and hotels, downtown malls and strip malls, fast-food restaurants, and towing companies. The common theme across these locations and the bars was the convergence of the three aspects described by routine activities theory as being predictive of criminal activity. Specifically, these are places that attract motivated offenders, largely because they feature a lot of vulnerable targets or lack sufficient levels of security or guardianship. The routine activities framework has been applied in many contexts and places, many of them international.[35]

One of the many applications of routine activities theory is geographic profiling, which uses satellite positioning systems and is perhaps the most attractive and marketable aspect of criminological research in contemporary times. Essentially, such research applies global positioning systems (GPS) software to identify and plot the exact location of every crime in a given jurisdiction. Such information has been used to solve and/or predict various crimes; serial killers have been caught because victim locations were triangulated to reveal the most likely residence of the killer. Furthermore, such

Figure 3.4 Violent Crime and Temperature

Source: James Alan Fox, Heat Wave Has a Chilling Effect on Violent Crime, Boston.Com, July 6, 2010. http://boston.com/community/blogs/crime_punishment/2010/07/heat_wave_has_chilling_effect.html

VIDEO ▶

Hot Spots

RANK	DESCRIPTION	ROBBERIES, RAPES, AUTO THEFTS	ALL TYPES
1.	Intersection: bars, liquor, store, park	33	461
2.	Bus depot	28	343
3.	Intersection: homeless shelters, bars	27	549
4.	Downtown mall	27	445
5.	Intersection: adult bookstore, bars	27	431
6.	Bars	25	510
7.	Intersection: theater, mall, record store	25	458
8.	Hotel	23	240
9.	Convenience store	22	607
10.	Bar	21	219
11.	Intersection: drugstore, adult theater	18	513
12.	Intersection: restaurant, bar	15	445
13.	Apartment building	15	177
14.	Department store	15	449
15.	Intersection: Burger King, office bldg.	15	365
16.	Shopping mall	15	305
17.	Hotel	14	121
18.	Bar	14	244
19.	Towing company	14	113
20.	Movie theater	14	251
21.	Department store	14	810
22.	High-rise apartment building	14	479
23.	Intersection: drugstore, adult bookstore	13	290
24.	Convenience Store	13	113
25.	Intersection: high concentration of bars	13	206
26.	Parking lot	13	31
27.	Loring Park	13	212
28.	Restaurant	13	25
29.	Apartment building	12	142
30.	Restaurant	12	198
31.	Homeless shelter	12	379
32.	Detached house	11	190
33.	High-rise apartment building	11	125
34.	Apartment Building	10	233
35.	Intersection: high residential area	10	156

36.	High-rise apartment building	10	92
37.	Restaurant	10	122
38.	Intersection: apartments, gas stations	10	197
39.	Intersection: supermarket, liquor store	10	94
40.	Lake Harriet	10	171
41.	Bar	10	107
42.	Apartment building	10	142
	Totals	661	11,760

Table 3.1 Hot Spots in Minneapolis, December 15, 1985, to December 15, 1986, With 10 or More Predatory Crimes

Source: Sherman, L., Gartin, P., & Buerger, M. (1989). Hot spots of predatory crime: Routine activities and the criminology of place. *Criminology, 27,* 27–56.

GPS software has also been used to predict where certain chronic offenders or crews/gangs will strike next. In police departments that use geographical mapping software showing where crimes take place or 911 calls for service originate (i.e., "hot spots"), this technology helps policing authorities determine where they should concentrate their efforts, such as where to assign more officers.

Another theory strongly related to routine activities theory is that of the lifestyles perspective. The lifestyles theory claims that individuals increase their probability of becoming victims (as well as offenders) according to the type of lifestyle they choose. However, some recent reviews of the literature have noted the strong, perhaps even redundant, relationship between lifestyles theory and the more established routine activities theory.[36] To clarify, such reviews have noted that "deviant lifestyles bear more risk of victimization than do conforming ones."[37] For example, elderly persons are far less likely to be victimized, because they tend to stay indoors, especially at night. On the other hand, younger individuals (especially those in their teenage years and early 20s) are far more likely to be victimized, probably because they tend to go out late at night or hang out with other young persons, which significantly increases their probability of being victimized since this is the age-group most likely to offend. Still, the bottom line in terms of theorizing about lifestyles is that certain individuals tend

LEARNING CHECK 3.2

1. According to the text, which theorists first proposed the rational choice theory of criminal behavior?

   a. Clarke and Cornish

   b. Gottfredson and Hirschi

   c. Sampson and Laub

   d. Cohen and Felson

   e. Sykes and Matza

2. According to the text, which theorists first proposed the routine activities theory of crime?

   a. Clarke and Cornish

   b. Gottfredson and Hirschi

   c. Sampson and Laub

   d. Cohen and Felson

   e. Sykes and Matza

3. According to the text, what is NOT one of the elements of routine activities theory that create a likely crime opportunity when they converge in time and place?

   a. Motivated offender

   b. Suitable/attractive target

   c. Time of day/night

   d. Absence of guardianship

Answers located at www.sagepub.com/schram

to increase the likelihood of their own victimization by associating with the very individuals most likely to commit offenses (e.g., young males), hanging out in locales that tend to serve alcohol, or not taking adequate measures to protect themselves from being victimized. This is a perfect scenario for raising the risk of victimization, according to routine activities theory, which shows how lifestyles theory is simply an extension of routine activities theory; by itself, it offers no new revelations for why some individuals are victimized more than others.[38]

Teens can increase the likelihood of being victimized by staying out late at night, hanging with the wrong crowd, or taking part in drinking or risky behavior.

POLICY IMPLICATIONS

Numerous policy implications can be derived from the theories and scientific findings discussed in this chapter. In this section, we concentrate on some of the most important policies. The "broken windows" perspective—which shares many assumptions with routine activities and rational choice theories—emphasizes the need for police to crack down on minor offenses to reduce major crimes.[39] Although many cities (such as New York and Los Angeles) have claimed reductions in serious crime after applying this theory, crime was reduced by the same amount across most cities during the same time period (from the late 1990s to the mid-2000s).

Other policies that can be derived from theories in this section include the "three-strikes-you're-out" policy, which assumes that offenders will make a rational choice not to commit future offenses if they could go to prison for life after committing three; in such a case, the negatives would certainly outweigh any expected benefits of the third crime. For deterrence to be most effective, punishment must be swift, certain, and severe. Where does the three-strikes policy fit into this equation? The bottom line is that it is much more severe than it is swift or certain. Given Beccaria's theory and philosophy (see Chapter 2), this policy will probably not work because it is not certain or swift; however, it is severe, in the sense that a person can be sentenced to life for committing three felony offenses over time.

A controversial three-strikes law was passed by voter initiative in California, and other states have adopted similar laws. This law sends third-time felons to prison for the rest of their lives regardless of the nature of that third felony. California first requires convictions for two "strikeable" felonies—crimes such as murder, rape, aggravated assault, burglary, drug offenses, and so on. Then any third felony can trigger the life sentence. The cases of nonviolent offenders going to prison for life after stealing a piece of pizza or shoplifting DVDs, while rare, do occur.

The question we are concerned with here is, does the three-strikes policy work? As a specific deterrent, the answer is clearly yes; offenders who are imprisoned for life cannot commit more crimes on the street. In that regard, three strikes works well. Some people feel, however, that laws such as three strikes need to include a general deterrent effect to be considered successful, meaning that this law should deter everyone from engaging in

CRIME IN THE NEWS

Robbery

WHY DO THEY DO IT?

THE GREEN RIVER KILLER

Gary Leon Ridgway was convicted and sentenced in 2003 after many decades of acting as the Green River Killer; he had stabbed his first victim at age 16, in 1965. He confessed to killing 71 victims (although he was convicted of only 48), virtually all of them women. He appeared to live separate lives. In one aspect of his life in the Seattle area, he was the father of a son and husband to his third wife. The other side involved picking up women, mostly prostitutes and strippers, who were willing to engage in sexual activity with him in remote locations.

He claimed that he would hide or bury the bodies of the victims he really "liked" because he knew he would want to go back and have sex with them later, which he did on occasion. He would also place various objects, such as a fish, bottle, or sausage, at the crime scene to throw off authorities, because these objects didn't match the modus operandi they were expecting to help link the crimes together. So he did appear to plan his crimes, at least in terms of manipulating the crime scenes (whether the primary scene, where the killing took place, or the secondary scene, where the body was dumped).

He also notably said, "I would choke them . . . and I was really good at it." But when asked by an investigator in an official interview where he ranked on a scale of evil from 1 to 5, he said he was a 3. So there appears to be a

disconnect between the way he thinks and the way society at large thinks.

Ridgway was caught after DNA from crime scenes was matched to a saliva test he had taken years before, when authorities had suspected him but didn't have enough evidence to make an arrest. So he continued his killing spree for many years, until they finally obtained further evidence linking him to some of the murders. Ridgway is now serving 480 years in prison for 48 life sentences, due to a bargain that got him out of the death penalty.

But why did he do it? Obviously, he has some psychological issues. But he passed the psychological test to determine readiness to stand trial, so he was not ruled legally insane. Virtually all his victims easily fit within his lifestyle, as he traveled around in his truck and picked up women in essentially the same area where he worked and lived. He never went far out of his way. In fact, none of his victims seemed to come from outside of the Seattle area. And he would almost always dump or bury the bodies within a relatively limited radius in that region—hence his label, "the Green River Killer."

In one notable instance, he claimed that his son was with him in the truck when he picked up a woman. He had his son stay in the truck while he took the woman a distance away and killed her. But we know that he tended to pick up and kill these women as part of his daily routine, which included working at a truck-painting factory. Thus, this case applies to the routine activities theory and lifestyles perspective covered in this chapter. Also keep in mind that even at the time when he was apprehended for these murders, he had a relatively stable marriage, which is not atypical for serial killers. They often lead separate lives, and both lives can seem fairly routine despite extreme contradictions.

Sources: Jensen, J., & Case, J. (2011). *Green River Killer: A true detective story.* Milwaukie, Oregon: Dark Horse Books.

multiple crimes. So is three strikes a general deterrent? Unfortunately, there are no easy answers to this question, because laws vary from state to state, the laws are used at different rates across counties in a given state, and so forth. There is at least some consensus in the literature, however.

One study from California suggests that three strikes reduced crime,[40] but the remaining studies show that three strikes either has no effect on crime or actually *increases* crime.[41] How could three strikes increase crime? The authors of those studies attributed an increase in homicide, following three strikes, to the possibility that third-strikers have more incentive to kill victims and any witnesses to avoid apprehension. Although this

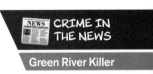

NEWS CRIME IN THE NEWS

Green River Killer

VIDEO

Broken Windows

AUDIO

Three-Strikes Law

AUTHOR PODCAST

Relating to Theories

argument is tentative, it may be true.[42] This is just one of the many policy implications that can be derived from this section. We expect that readers of this book will come up with many more, but it is vital that they examine the empirical literature in determining policies' usefulness in reducing criminal activity. Other policy implications regarding the theories and findings discussed in this chapter are discussed in the final section of this book.

In another strategy strongly based on the rational choice model, a number of judges have started using shaming penalties to deter offenders from recidivating. They have ordered everything from posting pictures of men arrested for soliciting prostitutes to forcing offenders to walk down their towns' main streets wearing signs that announce their crimes. These are just two examples of an increasing trend that emphasizes the informal or community factors required to deter crime effectively. Unfortunately, to date there have been virtually no empirical evaluations of the effectiveness of such shaming penalties, although studies of expected shame for committing an act consistently show a deterrent effect.[43]

CONCLUSION

This chapter reviewed the rebirth of deterrence studies in criminological literature. This reemphasis on deterrence was largely a response to the failure of most rehabilitation programs to lower recidivism in criminals. Specifically, the empirical evidence from studies in the late 1960s and early 1970s regarding various rehabilitation programs (often based on Positive School theories) showed that they were not effective in reducing recidivism, especially in chronic offenders. The first wave of research in this new focus on deterrence emphasized comparisons of jurisdictions (often various states in the United States) that tend to use more severe punishments than other jurisdictions. The subsequent waves of the rebirth of deterrence focused on longitudinal or panel studies that estimated how perceptions affect behavior, but this was quickly criticized by researchers who noted that the reverse was more likely: Behavior affected perceptions of being caught or punished. This led to the scenario methodology, in which individuals are asked their perceived likelihood of engaging in a specific situation at a given time, which is essentially where the current research on Classical/deterrence models remains.

We also examined more recent forms of Classical/deterrence theory, such as rational choice theory, which emphasizes the effects of informal sanctions (e.g., family, friends, employment) and benefits of offending (e.g., the "fun" of offending). We also discussed routine activities theory, which explains why victimization tends to occur far more often in certain locations (i.e., "hot spots") due to the convergence of three key elements in time and place—motivated offender(s), vulnerable target(s), and lack of guardianship—which create an attractive opportunity for crime as individuals go about their everyday activities. Another theory closely related to routine activities theory is the lifestyles perspective. The common element across all these perspectives is the underlying assumption that individuals are rational beings who have free will and thus choose their behavior based on assessments of a given situation, such as the possible risks versus the potential payoff. The bottom line of these various modern theories is that the perceptions and decisions made by individuals often put them at a much higher risk of engaging in criminal acts, as well as becoming victims of such crimes.

To follow up on the case study of Wayne at the beginning of this chapter, you should be able to see how his story relates well to some of the theories and concepts presented in this chapter—most notably, rational choice theory. Just to remind you, Wayne had engaged in some delinquent/criminal acts in high school and college; nothing violent, but he had come close to being arrested in high school and was apprehended and held by police for a couple of incidents in college (all charges were dropped or dismissed). But he realized that he had a lot to lose, such as all the work he had put toward getting good grades and completing the pre-law curriculum. Furthermore, he realized that he wanted to maintain strong bonds with his family and friends, not to mention relationships with future employers, and they would likely lose some level of respect for him if he continued to be caught for various offenses. So he completely changed his life trajectory by focusing on his studies, career, and family life.

This is a hypothetical (and some may say prototypical) scenario of what the more modern versions of deterrence, such as rational choice theory, offer in terms of explanations for individuals' decision making. But it is based on an actual case, according to the history of a good friend of one of the authors of this text. The point of this example is that each individual has the rationality and free will to examine the potential costs and benefits of his or her behavior and make decisions based on consideration of all major risks—both formal and informal sanctions—as well as the perceived benefits. This goes well beyond the traditional Classical version of deterrence, which focused only on formal sanctions, and provides a far more robust and valid model for explaining criminal behavior—or in Wayne's case, the decision *not* to engage in such behavior. The assumptions of this type of theorizing will be contradicted in the following chapters, which discuss theories that assume there is virtually no rationality or free will, let alone calculated decision making, involved in committing a crime.

SUMMARY OF THEORIES IN CHAPTER 3

THEORY	CONCEPTS	PROPONENTS	KEY PROPOSITIONS
Rational choice theory	Includes all traditional deterrence factors but adds • informal factors (e.g., family, friends, employers) • benefits of the crime (e.g., payoff and pleasure/thrill of offending)	Ronald V. Clarke and Derek B. Cornish	Assumes virtually all aspects of the traditional deterrence model but adds concepts that go into individuals' decisions to engage in criminal activity: The more a person believes his or her family, friends, and so forth will look down on the behavior, the more likely it is that he or she will be deterred. The more the expected pleasure or payoff of the crime, the less likely a person will be deterred.
Routine activities theory	Likely opportunity for victimization, given three concepts: • Motivated offender • Attractive/suitable target • Absence of guardianship	Lawrence Cohen and Marcus Felson	Victimization/crime is much more likely to occur when three elements converge in time and place (see concepts), typically as an individual is going about his or her daily activities, such as going to school or work or hanging out.
Lifestyles perspective	Risky lifestyles of offenders/victims	Various	Very similar propositions as routine activities theory but emphasizes the risky behavior (such as hanging out at seedy bars) of offenders, as opposed to victims.

KEY TERMS

aggregate studies	formal/official deterrence	rational choice theory	scenario research
cross-sectional studies	informal deterrence	routine activities theory	vignettes
experiential effect			

STUDENT STUDY SITE

Visit the student study site at **www.sagepub.com/schram** to access links to the video, audio, city and state rankings, author podcasts, and SAGE journal and reference articles featured in this chapter, as well as additional study tools, including eFlashcards, web quizzes, web resources, and chapter outlines.

DISCUSSION QUESTIONS

1. Do you think the deterrence model should have been rebirthed or left for dead? Explain why you feel this way.

2. Regarding the aggregate level of research in deterrence studies, do you find such studies valid? Explain why or why not.

3. In the comparison of longitudinal studies with vignette/scenario studies, which do you think offers the most valid method for examining individual perceptions regarding the costs and benefits of offending situations? Explain why you feel this way.

4. Can you relate to the experiential effect? If you can't, do you know someone who seems to resemble the behavior that results from this phenomenon? Make sure to articulate what the experiential effect is.

5. Regarding rational choice theory, would you rather be subject to formal sanctions if none of your family, friends, or employers found out that you engaged in shoplifting, or would you rather face the informal sanctions with no formal punishment (other than being arrested)? Explain your decision.

6. As a teenager, did you or family or friends get a "rush" out of doing things that were deviant or wrong? If so, did that feeling seem to outweigh any potential legal or informal consequences?

7. Regarding routine activities theory, which places, residences, or areas of your hometown do you feel fit this idea that certain places attract more crime than others (i.e., "hot spots")? Explain how you, friends, or others (including police) in your community deal with such areas. Does it work?

8. Regarding routine activities theory, which of the three elements of the theory do you feel is the most important to address in efforts to reduce crime in "hot spots"?

9. What types of lifestyle characteristics lead to the highest criminal/victimization rates? List at least five factors that lead to such propensities.

10. Find at least one study that uses mapping/geographical (GPS) data and report the conclusions of that study. Do the findings and conclusions fit the routine activities theoretical framework? Why or why not?

11. What types of policy strategies derived from rational choice and routine activities theories do you think would be most effective? Least effective?

WEB RESOURCES

Modern testing of deterrence

http://www.answers.com/topic/deterrence-legal
http://www.deathpenaltyinfo.org/reports

Rational choice theory

http://www.answers.com/topic/rational-choice-theory-criminology
http://www.umsl.edu/~keelr/200/ratchoc.html

Routine activities/lifestyles theory

http://www.popcenter.org/learning/pam/help/theory.cfm
http://www.slideshare.net/khadijahtgo/routine-activities-theory

Early Positivism
Biological Theories of Crime

INTRODUCTION

In the early 1940s, Charlie Follett was a teenage resident in California's Sonoma State Home, a placement facility for individuals deemed by the courts and other authorities as undesirable, with the common "medical" terms being feeble-minded or moron.[1] This meant he scored relatively low on an IQ test. One day, facility workers told him to lie down on an operating table, and without telling him what was about to happen, they began his vasectomy. He was one of more than 20,000 Californians—most of them female—to be forcibly sterilized by the state from the early 1900s to 1963. Sometimes they never learned of the procedure, and sometimes they were lied to (for example, told that they had an appendectomy or some other medical procedure). This procedure was performed throughout the nation (Virginia had the second highest number of such sterilizations, at about 8,300), with the support of the U.S. Supreme Court via the 1927 decision in Buck v. Bell. Although California Governor Gray Davis apologized much later, in 2003, no financial reparations were ever offered to the victims of this misguided policy. This is one of the ways early theories of criminality were abused in terms of policy, but we discuss many others in this chapter.

This chapter examines the early formulations of scientific criminological testing and theorizing, referred to as the **Positive School** of criminology. The emphasis on science in criminology started in the mid-1800s and provided a basis for what continues today. First, we examine why criminological theories became the topic of scientists at that time, and then we examine the early explanations of criminal behavior, as well as the many criticisms of such models, how they tested such theories, and especially the policy implications. We then discuss how Darwin's work inspired a giant change in how both academics and society viewed criminals.

We examine how the Father of Criminology developed his theory, as well as how IQ testing impacted the field and policies, as noted in the story above. We will also explore how these two models merged to form body type theory. Then we will discuss how such theories inspired future models of criminality, with an emphasis on how such traditional frameworks have contributed to modern-day applications and explanatory frameworks. But before we dive into the actual theories, let's discuss a case study that applies some of the theoretical concepts, propositions, and criticisms presented in this chapter.

EARLY BIOLOGICAL THEORIES OF BEHAVIOR

After many decades of dominance by the Classical School (see Chapter 2), academics and scientists were becoming aware that the deterrence framework was not explaining the distribution of crime. This restlessness led to new explanatory models of crime and behavior. Most of these perspectives focused on the fact that certain individuals or groups tend to offend more than others and that such "inferior" individuals should be controlled or even eliminated. This ideological framework fit a more general stance toward **eugenics**, which is the study of and policies related to improvement

CASE STUDY

JAVIER

Javier was born in an inner-city area in El Paso, Texas. Due to the lack of affordable prenatal and postnatal health care, his mother was largely on her own in taking steps to prevent developmental complications. She neglected to take any prenatal vitamins, and she did not have regular medical checkups to monitor the pregnancy. She gave birth prematurely, in the 34th week (the normal length of gestation is about 40 weeks). Everything seemed to go fine in the delivery, but as Javier grew he displayed many unusual physical features, including small, low-seated ears; a relatively large third toe and webbing between all his toes; a curved "pinky" finger; a cleft lip; and close-set eyes.

He had a relatively good home environment and a healthy diet, and he received constant attention and support from his mother and father. As he grew, he developed an athletic, muscular build. Even early on, his father noticed how athletic Javier was and signed him up for many local and school sports activities (e.g., soccer, football), where he excelled. However, his academic performance was problematic. In elementary and middle school, he performed better than average in math, but his verbal scores were low. Javier did well enough to advance to high school, where he became an outstanding linebacker on the school's football team.

Still, his verbal scores and grades were very low, and he became frustrated when writing papers and taking higher level essay exams in high school, which greatly reduced his grade point average. Javier realized that his chances for getting a college scholarship were low, and he began to hang out more with his best friends, also standouts on the team, who had said they could make some money burglarizing homes they knew were unoccupied. He participated in more than a dozen of these crimes before he was caught and arrested, which further harmed his chances of getting a college scholarship, especially since he was kicked off the football team.

However, because Javier got caught only once, he was placed on probation and successfully completed it. He realized he should not commit such crimes in the future and cleaned up his act. While he never received any scholarships, upon graduation from high school, he got a job offer from his father's friend to work at a local automotive factory, which paid double the hourly minimum wage. So he took the job, and after a few years his good performance earned him a promotion. Ultimately, Javier outgrew his offending behavior streak, got married, and had two children, and he is now living happily with his family in a modest but nice house that he owns.

We discuss Javier again at the end of this chapter, where we apply some of the key theoretical concepts and propositions that specifically pertain to his experience. We also discuss some of the criticisms of these theories that do not seem to fit Javier's situation.

> JAVIER REALIZED THAT HIS CHANCES FOR GETTING A COLLEGE SCHOLARSHIP WERE LOW, AND HE BEGAN TO HANG OUT MORE WITH HIS BEST FRIENDS, ALSO STANDOUTS ON THE TEAM, WHO HAD SAID THEY COULD MAKE SOME MONEY BURGLARIZING HOMES THEY KNEW WERE UNOCCUPIED.

of the human race via control over selective reproduction (policies that were explicitly mandated for certain groups, as we will see). Thus, the conclusion was that there must be notable variations across individuals (and groups) that can help determine those most at risk of offending.

So in the early to mid-1800s, several perspectives were offered regarding how to determine which individuals or groups are most likely to commit crime. Many of these theoretical frameworks were based on establishing a method for distinguishing the superior individuals and groups from the inferior individuals and groups. Such intentions were likely related to the increased use of slavery in the world during the 1800s, as well as imperialism's fight to suppress rebellions. For example, slavery was at its peak in the United States during this period, and many European countries had taken over colonies that they were trying to control for profit and domain.

Perhaps the first example of this theory was represented by craniometry. **Craniometry** is the belief that the size of the brain or skull represents the superiority or inferiority of certain individuals or ethnic/racial groups.[2] The reason the size of both the brain and the skull were considered is that a person's skull was believed to perfectly conform to the brain structure; thus, the size of the skull was thought to match the size of the brain. Although modern science has somewhat dismissed this assumption, there is a significant correlation between the size of the skull and the size of the brain. Still, even according to the assumptions of the craniometrists, it is unlikely that much can be gathered from measuring the overall mass of the brain, and certainly not the size of the skull.

The scientists who studied this model would measure the various sizes, or circumferences, of the skull if they were dealing with living subjects. If they were dealing with recently dead subjects, they would measure the weight or volume of the brain itself. When dealing with subjects who had died long before, the craniometrists would pour seeds into the skull and then measure the volume by pouring the seeds into a graduated cylinder. Later, when these scientists realized that seeds were not a valid measure of volume, they moved toward using buckshot or ball bearings.

Most studies by craniometrists showed that subjects of white, Western European descent tended to be far superior to other ethnic groups, in terms of larger circumference or volume in skull or brain size. Furthermore, the front portion of the brain (i.e., genu) was thought to be larger in the superior individuals and groups, and the hind portion of the brain/skull (i.e., splenium) was predicted to be larger in the lesser individuals and groups. Notably, these researchers typically knew to which ethnic/racial group the skulls/brains belonged before measuring them, making for an unethical and improper methodology of craniometry. Such biased measurements of brains and skulls continued throughout the 19th century and into the early 1900s.[3] These examinations were largely done with the intention of furthering the assumptions of eugenics, which aimed to prove under the banner of "science" that certain individuals and ethnic/racial groups were inferior to others.

This intent of noted craniometrists is supported by subsequent tests of some of these studies, conducted with the researchers not knowing which skulls/brains were from which ethnic/racial groups. These new studies showed only a small correlation between size of the skull/brain and certain behaviors or personality traits.[4] Furthermore, once some of the early "forefathers" of craniometry died, their brains showed average or below-average volume. The existing craniometrists then switched their postulates such that it was the more convoluted or complex structure of brains (those with more fissures and gyri than others) that distinguished superior brains from inferior ones (as suggested in the photo above).[5]

CRIME IN THE NEWS

Sterilization Cases

VIDEO

Eugenics

Craniometrists measured the size of brains and skulls and attempted to show that the larger the mass of the brain, the more superior the person or race.

Positive School: a perspective that assumes individuals have no free will to control their behavior

eugenics: the study of and policies related to the improvement of the human race via discriminary control over reproduction

craniometry: field of study that emphasized the belief that the size of the brain or skull reflected superiority or inferiority, with larger brains and skulls being considered superior

NUMBERING AND DEFINITION OF THE ORGANS.

1. **Amativeness**, Love between the sexes.
A. **Conjugality**, Matrimony—love of one. [etc.
2. **Parental Love**, Regard for offspring, pets,
3. **Friendship**, Adhesiveness—sociability.
4. **Inhabitiveness**, Love of home.
5. **Continuity**, One thing at a time.
E. **Vitativeness**, Love of life.
6. **Combativeness**, Resistance—defense.
7. **Destructiveness**, Executiveness—force.
8. **Alimentiveness**, Appetite—hunger.
9. **Acquisitiveness**, Accumulation.
10. **Secretiveness**, Policy—management.
11. **Cautiousness**, Prudence—provision.
12. **Approbativeness**, Ambition—display.
13. **Self-Esteem**, Self-respect—dignity.
14. **Firmness**, Decision—perseverance.
15. **Conscientiousness**, Justice, equity.
16. **Hope**, Expectation—enterprise.
17. **Spirituality**, Intuition—faith—credulity.
18. **Veneration**, Devotion—respect.
19. **Benevolence**, Kindness—goodness.

20. **Constructiveness**, Mechanical ingenuity
21. **Ideality**, Refinement—taste—purity.
B. **Sublimity**, Love of grandeur—infinitude.
22. **Imitation**, Copying—patterning.
23. **Mirthfulness**, Jocoseness—wit—fun.
24. **Individuality**, Observation.
25. **Form**, Recollection of shape.
26. **Size**, Measuring by the eye.
27. **Weight**, Balancing—climbing.
28. **Color**, Judgment of colors.
29. **Order**, Method—system—arrangement.
30. **Calculation**, Mental arithmetic.
31. **Locality**, Recollection of places.
32. **Eventuality**, Memory of facts.
33. **Time**, Cognizance of duration.
34. **Tune**, Sense of harmony and melody.
35. **Language**, Expression of ideas.
36. **Causality**, Applying causes to effect. [tion.
37. **Comparison**, Inductive reasoning—illustra-
C. **Human Nature**, Perception of motives.
D. **Agreeableness**, Pleasantness—suavity.

A prototypical mapping of the skull by phrenologists. This shows the various characteristics believed to be influenced by abnormalities in certain parts of the brain.

....

phrenology: the science of determining human dispositions based on distinctions (e.g., bumps) in the skull, which is believed to conform to the shape of the brain

However, this argument was even more tentative and vague than the former hypotheses of craniometrists and thus did not last long.

So craniometry did not last long, likely due to its noticeable lack of validity and the fact that Darwinian theory (not presented until the late 1800s) had not been presented or accepted at that time, so the model lacked a popular framework for basis. However, it is important to note that modern studies show that persons who have significantly larger brains do tend to score higher on intelligence tests.[6]

Despite the failure of craniometry to explain the difference between criminals and noncriminals, scientists were not ready to give up the assumption that this phenomenon could be explained by visual differences in the skull (or brain)—and they certainly weren't ready to give up the assumption that certain ethnic or racial groups were superior or inferior to others. Therefore, the experts of the time developed the perspective of phrenology. **Phrenology** is the science of determining human dispositions based on distinctions (e.g., bumps) in the skull, which are believed to conform to the shape of the brain (see photo on this page).[7] Readers should keep in mind that much of the theorizing of phrenologists was still targeted toward supporting the assumptions of eugenics and showing that certain individuals and groups were inferior or superior to others.

It is important to keep in mind that, like the craniometrists, phrenologists assumed that the shape of the skull conformed to the shape of the brain. Thus, a bump or other abnormality on the skull directly related to an abnormality in the brain. This assumption has been entirely refuted by modern scientific evidence, so it is not surprising that phrenology quickly fell out of favor in criminological thought. However, like its predecessor, phrenology did get some things right. Certain parts of the brain are indeed responsible for specific tasks.

For example, in the original phrenological map (*see photo above*), "destructiveness" was determined by the presence of abnormalities above the left ear. Modern scientific studies show that perhaps the most vital part of the brain in terms of criminality regarding trauma is that of the left temporal lobe, or the area above the left ear.[8] There are other indications that the phrenologists were right. After all, most readers are well aware of the fact that specific portions of the brain govern the operation of individualized activities in our bodies. For example, a particular portion of the brain governs the action of our hands, whereas other areas govern our arms, legs, and so forth. So the phrenologists weren't completely wrong, but the extent to which they relied on bumps on the skull to indicate who would be most disposed to criminal behavior was inaccurate.

After phrenology fell out of favor among scientists, researchers and society still did not want to depart from the assumption that certain individuals or ethnic groups were inferior to others. Therefore, another discipline, known as physiognomy, became popular in the mid-1800s. **Physiognomy** is the study of facial and other bodily aspects to indicate developmental problems, such as criminality. Not surprisingly, early physiognomy studies focused on contrasting various racial/ethnic groups to prove that certain groups or individuals were superior or inferior, as illustrated in Figure 4.1.[9]

Using modern understandings of science, it should be obvious from the illustrations above that physiognomy did not last long as a respected scientific perspective of criminality. At any time other than the late 1800s, the importance of observed facial and bodily features in determining criminality would not be highly accepted for long, if at all. However, the timing of this theory was on its side. Specifically, Darwin published his work *On the Origin of Species* in the late 1800s and made a huge impact on societal views regarding the rank order of ethnic groups.

Darwin's model outlined a vague framework that proposed humans had evolved from more primitive beings, and that the human species (as all others) developed with a number of adaptations preferred by natural selection. In other words, some species are selected by their ability to adapt to the environment, whereas others do not adapt so well and die off, or at least become inferior in terms of dominance. This assumption of Darwin's work, which was suddenly accepted widely by both society and scientists throughout the world, falsely led to an inclination to believe that certain ethnic/racial groups are inferior or superior.

Figure 4.1
Physiognomists attempted to show that criminals' facial profiles resembled those of animals, such as monkeys, apes, birds, and lions, implying they were a genetic "throwback" to an earlier, inferior stage of evolution.

Darwin was not a criminologist, so he is not considered the father or theorist of any major schools of thought. However, he did set the stage for what followed in criminological thought. Specifically, Darwin's theory laid the groundwork for what would become the first major scientific theory of crime—namely, Cesare Lombroso's theory of born criminals. Lombroso's theory also tied together the assumptions and propositions of the disciplines we have discussed in this section: craniometry, phrenology, and physiognomy.

LOMBROSO'S THEORY OF ATAVISM AND BORN CRIMINALS

Informed largely by Darwin's theory of natural selection, Lombroso (1835–1909) created what is widely considered the first attempt toward scientific theory in criminological thought. After all, most previous theorists were not scientists—Cesare Beccaria,

physiognomy: the study of facial and other bodily aspects to identify developmental problems, such as criminality

Charles Darwin (1809–1882) wrote *On the Origin of Species* (1859), which initially proposed the theory of evolution and set the stage for the dominance of the Positive School of criminology.

Cesare Lombroso (1836–1909) is considered the Father of Criminology and the Father of the Positive School for his contributions to the field in the late 19th century.

atavism: belief that certain characteristics or behaviors of a person are throwbacks to an earlier stage of evolutionary development

for example, was trained in law and never went out to test his propositions—or were not specifically concentrated on explaining levels of criminality, such as the craniometrists and phrenologists. However, Lombroso was trained in medical science and oriented toward documenting his observations and scientific methodology. Furthermore, timing was on his side in the sense that Darwin's theory was published 15 years prior to the publication of Lombroso's major work and had time to become immensely popular with both scientists and the public.

LOMBROSO'S THEORY OF CRIME

The first edition of Lombroso's *The Criminal Man* was published in 1876 and triggered an immediate response from most Western societies in both their ideas and policies related to crime and justice.[10] In this work, Lombroso outlined a theory of crime that brought together the pre-Darwinian theories of craniometry, phrenology, and physiognomy, discussed previously. Furthermore, Lombroso's theory was largely based on certain groups (and individuals) being "atavistic," and likely born to commit crime. **Atavism** means that a person or particular feature of an individual is a throwback to an earlier stage of evolutionary development. In other words, people who are serious criminals are manifestations of lower forms of humanity in terms of evolutionary progression. For example, Lombroso would likely suggest that chronic offenders are more similar to the earlier stages of humankind, such as the "missing link," than they are to modern humans.

Although Lombroso noted that there were other types of offenders, such as the mentally ill and "criminaloids," who committed minor offenses due to external or environmental circumstances, he specifically claimed that the "born criminals" were the ones who should be singled out in addressing crime. Specifically, Lombroso claimed that born criminals were the most serious and violent criminals in any society—those whom most criminologists now refer to as chronic offenders. Furthermore, Lombroso claimed that born criminals cannot deviate from their natural tendencies to be antisocial.

On the other hand, Lombroso claimed that despite the born criminal's inevitable tendency to commit crime, there was a way for societies to prevent or reduce these crimes—by identifying born criminals. According to Lombroso, the way for societies to identify born criminals, even early in life, is through stigmata. **Stigmata** are physical manifestations of the atavism of an individual, with such physical features indicating the prior evolutionary stages of development.

LOMBROSO'S LIST OF STIGMATA

According to Lombroso, the manifestation of more than five stigmata indicates that an individual is atavistic and thus a born criminal. Readers may be wondering what these stigmata are, given the importance of these criteria. This is a great question, the answers to which were constantly changing according to Lombroso's list of what constitutes stigmata. In the beginning, this list was largely based on Lombroso's work as a physician and included such things as large eyes and large ears. It is hard to specify what exact criteria were listed as stigmata because Lombroso changed this list as he went along (which can be argued is very poor science), even up until the last edition of his book well into the 1900s.

For the most part, stigmata consisted of facial and bodily features that deviated from the norm. In other words, abnormally small or large noses, abnormally small or large ears, abnormally small or large eyes, abnormally small or large jaws, or almost anything that went outside the "bell curve" of normal physical development in human beings. Beyond deviant physical features, Lombroso also threw in some extraphysiological features, such as tattoos and history of epilepsy (and other disorders) in the family.

Lombroso's documentation of some of the tattoos he saw on known criminal offenders included many tattoos that featured female names or some motto such as "born under an unlucky star" or "man of misfortune." Others were more intriguing, such as a tattoo on the penis of one offender that read "Entra Tutto," which means "it all goes in" or "it enters all."[11] Either translation is rather amusing. Although it is likely that these latter features are somewhat correlated to crime and delinquency, is it likely that they caused such antisocial behavior? Given Lombroso's model that persons are born criminal, it is quite unlikely that these factors are causally linked to criminality. After all, how many babies are born with tattoos? Regardless of the illogical nature of many of the stigmata, Lombroso professed that if a person had more than five of the physical features on his list, that person was indeed a born criminal and should be prevented from offending.

LEARNING CHECK 4.1

1. What term means the study of and policies related to the improvement of the human race via control of selective reproduction?
   a. Cytogenetics
   b. Ethnographics
   c. Racionology
   d. Eugenics
   e. Fascionics

2. What is the 19th century study of the size of the brain/skull, which posited that the bigger the brain, the more superior the person or race?
   a. Phrenology
   b. Physiognomy
   c. Craniometry
   d. Skullography
   e. Cerebrotology

3. What is the 19th century study of various bumps on or portions of the skull believed to reveal weaknesses in terms of certain cognitive or personality traits?
   a. Phrenology
   b. Physiognomy
   c. Craniometry
   d. Skullography
   e. Cerebrotology

Answers located at www.sagepub.com/schram

As a physician working for the Italian army, Lombroso examined the bodies of captured war criminals. According to Lombroso, he first realized the nature of the criminal when a particular war criminal was brought in for examination:

> This was not merely an idea, but a flash of inspiration. At the sight of that skull, I seemed to see all of a sudden, lighted up as a vast plain under a flaming sky, the problem of the nature of the criminal—an atavistic being who reproduces in his person the ferocious instincts of primitive humanity and the inferior animals. Thus were explained anatomically the enormous jaws, high cheek bones . . . solitary lines in the palms, extreme size of the orbits, handle-shaped ears found in criminals, savages and apes, insensibility to pain, extremely acute sight, tattooing, excessive idleness, love of orgies, and the irresponsible craving of evil for its own sake, the desire not only to extinguish life in the victim, but to mutilate the corpse, tear its flesh and drink its blood.[12]

While most laugh at his words now, at the time when he wrote this description it likely rang true to most readers, which is perhaps why his book was the dominant text in the

REFERENCE ARTICLE

The Criminal Man

VIDEO

Atavism

stigmata: the physical manifestations of atavism (biological inferiority), according to Lombroso

C. LOMBROSO — *L'homme criminel.*   PL. XLIX

RÉVOLUTIONNAIRES ET CRIMINELS POLITIQUES. — MATTOÏDES ET FOUS MORAUX.

Lombroso provided numerous profile images of criminals and claimed that his list of stigmata could identify a born criminal by facial features.

criminological field for many decades. In the description above, Lombroso incorporates many of the core principles of his theory—namely, the idea of criminals being atavistic, or biological evolutionary throwbacks, and the stigmata that became so important in his theoretical model. Furthermore, Lombroso's theory synthesized the themes of craniometry, phrenology, and physiognomy. This theory came just a decade after Darwin, when society was ready to accept such a perspective, which was not too far removed from the dominant perspective of the slavery period in this country. Perhaps this is why his theoretical framework became so popular.

A good example of the popular acceptance of Lombroso's "scientific" stigmata appears in Bram Stoker's *Dracula*, in which the physical appearance of the Count (Dracula) is based on "Lombrosian" traits, such as the high bridge of the thin nose, arched nostrils, massive eyebrows, and pointed ears. This reference makes sense given the time when the novel was published (the late 1800s), when Lombroso's theory was highly dominant in society and science. This is just one indication of this theory's importance among academics, scientists, philosophers, fiction writers, and criminal justice policy during that period. The theory became popular for other reasons as well.

Not only did Lombroso claim that he could identify born criminals by their stigmata; he also claimed that he could identify certain types of criminals. For example, he claimed that certain stigmata could be identified among groups of anarchists, burglars, murderers, shoplifters, and so forth. Of course, if most readers are confused by their failure to distinguish one kind of offender from another, that is fine; virtually no one can. Lombroso's stigmata as a way to distinguish certain individuals as born criminals, let alone to identify certain forms of criminals, are quite invalid by modern research standards. However, as mentioned above, Lombroso's theory became extremely popular throughout the developed Western world, and much of this popularity was due to good timing.

LOMBROSO AS THE FATHER OF CRIMINOLOGY AND THE FATHER OF THE POSITIVE SCHOOL

Lombroso's theory came a decade and a half after Darwin's work was published, so Darwin's views had already spread throughout the Western world. As mentioned previously,

AUTHOR VIDEO

Lombroso

Lombroso's model coincided with much of the Western world's views on slavery and deportation at that time. Because of this good timing and because he became known as the first individual to test his hypotheses through observation, Lombroso is widely considered the Father of Criminology. This title is not assigned out of respect for his theory (which has been largely rejected) or his methods (which are considered highly invalid by modern standards) but is deserved because he was the first person to gain recognition in testing his theoretical propositions. Furthermore, his theory coincided with political movements popular at that time—the Fascist and Nazi movements of the early 1900s.

Lombroso is also considered the Father of the Positive School of criminology, because he was the first to gain prominence in identifying factors beyond free will or free choice (i.e., Classical School) that were predicted to cause crime. Although previous theorists had presented perspectives that went beyond free will, such as craniometry and phrenology, Lombroso was the first to gain widespread attention due to the popularity of Darwin's perspective at that time. The pre-Darwinian frameworks had not gained much attention due to the lack of a theoretical perspective conducive to these models. Lombroso's perspective was timed well (just after Darwin's), and it gained almost immediate support in all developed countries at that time, which is the most likely reason for why Lombroso is considered the Father of the Positive School of criminology.

It is important to understand the assumptions of positivism, which most experts consider somewhat synonymous with the term *determinism*. **Determinism** is the idea that most human behavior is determined by factors beyond free will and free choice (i.e., the Classical School). In other words, determinism (i.e., the Positive School) assumes that human beings do not decide how they will act by rationally thinking through the costs and benefits of a given situation. Rather, the Positive School is based on the fundamental belief that factors outside of free will and choice—such as biological, psychological, and sociological variables—determine the choices we make regarding all types of behavior, especially decisions of whether or not to engage in criminal activity.

JOURNAL ARTICLE

Determinism

The majority of readers probably believe they have chosen their career paths, as well as most other aspects of their lives. However, scientific evidence shows otherwise. For example, although most people consider religion one of the most important aspects of their lives, studies show that far more than 90% of the world's population have chosen their religious affiliation (e.g., Baptist, Buddhist, Catholic, Judaism) based on the religious affiliation of their parents or caretakers. Therefore, it is clear that what most people consider an extremely important decision—namely, what to believe regarding a higher being or force—is almost completely determined by their environment. To clarify, almost no one sits down and goes through a list of descriptions of various religions to decide which fits best. Rather, in almost all cases, religious affiliation is determined by culture, which dismisses the factor of free will/free choice assumed by the Classical School. The same type of argument can be made regarding the clothes we wear, the food we prefer, and the activities we enjoy.

Another way to distinguish positivism and determinism is in the way scientists view human behavior, which can be understood using a chemistry analogy. Specifically, a chemist assumes that if a given element is subjected to certain temperatures, pressures, or mixtures with other elements, it will react in a predictable way. In a highly comparable way, a positivist assumes that when human beings are subjected to poverty, delinquent peers, low intelligence, or other factors, they will react in a predictable way. Therefore, there is virtually no difference between how a chemist feels about the behavior of particles and elements and how a positivistic scientist feels about human behavior.

determinism: the assumption that human behavior is caused by factors outside of free will and rational decision making

In Lombroso's case, the deterministic factor was the biological makeup of individuals. However, we shall see in the next several chapters that positivistic theories focus on a wide range of variables, from biology to psychology to social aspects. For example, many

WHY DO THEY DO IT?

DR. HAROLD SHIPMAN

Dr. Harold Shipman is one of the top three most prolific serial killers on official record in the Western world. He is known to have killed more than 250 of his patients. The only serial killers on record that exceed him are both from Colombia: Pedro Lopez, the "Monster of the Andes," believed to have killed 300 people, and Luis Garavito, "Le Bestia" or the beast, believed to have killed more than 400 people, including more than 100 children. However, Shipman could rank No. 1 if you break the list into categories of serial killers. After all, the others were predatory, hedonistic serial killers, but Dr. Shipman was an "Angel of Death." He was supposed to be helping his patients (indeed, he was paid to do so), but instead he killed them.

Shipman would typically inject his victims, almost always women, with lethal doses of diamorphine (i.e., heroin). It is believed he began killing patients in the late 1970s or early 1980s and continued until he was caught in the late 1990s. Investigators became suspicious when he was named in one of his victim's wills, which left him about 380,000 pounds. When it was discovered that he had forged this will, it triggered a much larger investigation.

However, the desire for money is not believed to be his main motive, because an investigation of the records revealed that this forged will was an isolated case; he had been killing his patients for years without any apparent monetary incentive.

Despite his consistent denials of guilt, in 2000 he was convicted and sentence to 15 consecutive life sentences, with recommendation of no release. Notably, he was the only doctor in British legal history to be found guilty of killing his patients. Dr. Shipman hanged himself in his cell at Wakefield Prison in West Yorkshire, England, on January 13, 2004.

So why did he do it? BBC News recently released a report examining why he may have done it but essentially gave up trying to understand his motive.

> He has never revealed anything about the extent of his murderous career, and probably never will. . . . The experience of killing was personal and private to him, and he is never going to give that up. . . . We are never going to know the truth.

The best guess is from some of those present when he was tried in Preston Crown Court. They claimed that he likely "enjoyed exercising the power over life and death."

This explanation probably doesn't seem satisfactory to most readers, but the truth is that many serial killers kill simply because they enjoy it. A large part of that enjoyment is the power–control factor they hold over their victims. Fortunately, there are not many doctors who feel this way. But doctors are people, too. And where you have people, you will have killers.

Although this high-profile case is not specifically linked to any theories presented in this chapter, it is presented here because the Father of Criminology, Lombroso, was also a medical doctor. In fact, it was during one of his criminal autopsies that he formulated his theoretical model.

Sources: BBC News. (2001, January 5). The secret world of Harold Shipman. Retrieved from http://news.bbc.co.uk/2/hi/uk_news/1102270.stm; Smith, J. D. (2004). *100 most infamous criminals.* New York: MetroBooks.

readers likely believe that bad parenting, poverty, and associating with delinquent peers are some of the most important factors in predicting criminality. If you believe that such variables significantly influence decisions to commit crime, then you are likely a positive theorist; you believe that crime is caused by factors above and beyond free choice or free will.

LOMBROSO'S POLICY IMPLICATIONS

Beyond the theoretical aspects of Lombroso's theory of criminality, it is important to realize that his perspective had profound consequences for policy as well. For example, Lombroso was called in to testify in numerous criminal processes and trials to determine the guilt or innocence of suspects. Under the banner of science (in much the same way we view DNA or fingerprint analysis now), Lombroso was called in to determine the guilt of certain persons in key criminal testimony, often during trial.[13] Lombroso even wrote about many of the trials or official identifications he made as an "expert" witness, which often included identifying which suspect (often out of many) had committed a crime. Lombroso based such judgments solely on the visual stigmata evident in the line of suspects.[14] In one such account of Lombroso's experiences as an expert witness, he noted:

> [One suspect] was, in fact, the most perfect type of the born criminal: enormous jaws, frontal sinuses, and zygomata, thin upper lip, huge incisors, unusually large head, tactile obtuseness with sensorial manicinism. . . . He was convicted.[15]

When Lombroso was not available for such "scientific" determinations of guilty persons, his colleagues or students (often referred to as "lieutenants") were often sent. Some of these students, such as Enrico Ferri and Raphael Garrofalo, became quite active in the Fascist regime of Italy in the early 1900s. This model of government, like the Nazi party in Germany, sought to remove the "inferior" groups from society. Thus, Lombroso's theory was timed well in terms of both societal and governmental ideologies. This was another reason why Lombroso gained such prominence throughout the Western world throughout the late 1800s and early 1900s.

Another policy implication that was implemented in some parts of the world was identifying young children on the basis of observed stigmata, which tend to manifest in the first 5 to 10 years of life. This led to tracking or isolating certain children based on such criteria, largely physiological features. Although many readers may consider such policies ridiculous, modern medicine has supported the identification, documentation, and importance of certain physical features as indications of high risk for developmental problems.

For example, modern medicine identifies a number of what are termed **minor physical anomalies** (MPAs) that indicate developmental problems. These MPAs include

- head circumference out of the normal range,
- malformed ears,
- low-set ears,
- excessively large gap between the first and second toes,
- webbing between toes or fingers,
- no earlobes,
- curved fifth finger,
- asymmetrical ears,
- furrowed tongue, and
- simian crease (see photo on next page).[16]

AUDIO

Shipman

VIDEO

Lombroso

WHAT WERE THEY THINKING?!

Murder

minor physical anomalies: physical features, such as asymmetrical or low-seated ears, which are believed to indicate developmental problems

LEARNING CHECK 4.2

1. Who is considered the Father of Criminology, as well as the Father of the Positive School of criminological thought?

   a. Beccaria

   b. Binet

   c. Lombroso

   d. Sheldon

   e. Hirschi

2. What did the Father of Criminology say was a way to identify the most dangerous, chronic criminals?

   a. Those with bad parents

   b. Those who were poor

   c. Those who had delinquent peers

   d. Those who had stigmata

   e. Those who had weak ties to conventional society

3. What does the Positive School of criminology assume that clearly distinguishes it from the Classical School of criminology?

   a. free will/free choice

   b. rational decision making in choosing behavior

   c. determinism

   d. hedonism

   e. utilitarianism

Answers located at www.sagepub.com/schram

Given the practice of correlating such visible physical aspects with developmental problems, including criminality, it is obvious that Lombroso's model of stigmata as predictors of antisocial problems has implications to the present day. Perhaps surprisingly, such implications are more accepted by modern medical science than they are in the criminological literature. Furthermore, some modern scientific studies have shown that being unattractive predicts criminal offending, which somewhat supports Lombroso's theory of crime.[17]

About three decades after Lombroso's original work was published, and after a long period of dominance during that time, criminologists began to question his theory of atavism and stigmata. Furthermore, it became clear that there was more involved in criminality than just the way people looked, such as psychological aspects of individuals. However, scientists and societies were not ready to depart from theories, such as Lombroso's, that assumed that certain people or groups of people were inferior to others, so they simply chose another factor to emphasize—intelligence, or IQ.

AFTER LOMBROSO: THE IQ-TESTING ERA

Despite the evidence presented against Lombroso, his theorizing remained dominant until the early 1900s, when criminologists realized that stigmata and the idea of a "born" criminal were not valid. However, even at that time, theorists and researchers were not ready to give up on the assumption that certain ethnic or racial groups were superior or inferior to others. Thus, a new theory emerged based on a more quantified measure originated by Alfred Binet in France. This new measure was IQ, which represents an individual's intelligence quotient. At that time, IQ was calculated as chronological age divided by mental age, which was then multiplied by 100—the average score being 100. This scale has changed enormously over time, but the bottom line is determining whether someone is above or below the base score of average (100).

Binet had good intentions in creating the concept of IQ scores in France, which he formulated to identify youth who were not performing up to par in educational skills. Binet was explicit in stating that IQ could be changed, which is why he proposed a score to identify slow learners

Simian crease

Normal palm creases

The simian crease is one of many minor physical anomalies recognized by modern medical science as being a manifestation of early developmental disorders.

so they could be trained to raise their IQs.[18] However, when Binet's work on developing the idea and methods of scoring IQs was brought to the United States, his basic assumptions and propositions were twisted. One of the most prominent individuals who utilized Binet's IQ test in the United States for purposes of deporting, incapacitating, sterilizing, and otherwise ridding society of low-IQ individuals was H. H. Goddard.

Goddard is generally considered the leading authority on the use and interpretation of IQ testing in the United States.[19] Goddard used the IQ test he adopted from Binet's model to examine immigrants coming into the United States. It is important to note that Goddard proposed quite different assumptions regarding intelligence or IQ than did Binet. To clarify, Goddard believed and claimed that IQ was static or innate, meaning that such levels could not be changed, even with training. The assumption of Goddard's perspective of intelligence was that it was passed from generation to generation, from parents to offspring.

Goddard is known for labeling this low IQ as **feeble-mindedness**, which actually became a technical, scientific term in the early 1900s referring to those who had significantly below-average levels of intelligence. Of course, being a scientist, Goddard specified certain levels of feeble-mindedness, which were ranked based on the degree to which the score was below average. In order from highest to lowest intelligence, the first group were the "morons," the second group were the "imbeciles," and the lowest group were the "idiots."

According to Goddard, from a eugenics point of view, the biggest threat to the progress of humanity was not the idiots. Rather, he believed the morons were the biggest threat to the genetic pool. In Goddard's words,

> The idiot is not our greatest problem. He is indeed loathsome. . . . Nevertheless, he lives his life and is done. He does not continue the race with a line of children like himself. . . . It is the moron type that makes for us our great problem.[20]

According to Goddard, of the three categories of feeble-mindedness, the morons are the group smart enough to slip through the cracks and reproduce, thus posing the biggest threat to humanity.

Goddard received many grants to fund his research, and he took his research team to Ellis Island in the early 1900s to identify the feeble-minded as they attempted to enter the United States. Much of his team was made up of women, who he believed were better at distinguishing the feeble-minded by sight:

> After a person has had considerable experience in this work, he almost gets a sense of what a feeble-minded person is so that he can tell one afar off. The people who are best at this work, and who I believe should do this work, are women. Women seem to have closer observation than men. It was quite impossible for others to see how . . . women could pick out the feeble-minded without the aid of the Binet test at all.[21]

Although Goddard never provided a good reason why, he insisted that women could pick out the feeble-minded better than men could, so he included them on his team of scientists stationed on Ellis Island.

Regarding policy implications of his work, Goddard was proud of the increase in the deportations of potential immigrants to the United States. For example, Goddard enthusiastically reported that deportations for the reason of mental deficiency increased by 350% in 1913 and 570% in 1914 from the average of the preceding 5 years.[22] However,

AUDIO
IQ Test

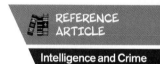
REFERENCE ARTICLE
Intelligence and Crime

feeble-mindedness: technical, scientific term in the early 1900s meaning those who had significantly below-average levels of intelligence

Aerial view of Ellis Island, where a large portion of immigrants were processed into the United States. Many of these immigrants were tested by Goddard and his research team for potentially being "feeble-minded."

over time Goddard realized that his policy recommendations of deportation, incarceration, and sterilization were not based on accurate science.

Specifically, after consistently validating his IQ test on immigrants and mental patients, Goddard finally tested his intelligence scale on a relatively representative cross-section of American citizens—namely, draftees for military service during World War I. The results showed that many of these recruits scored as feeble-minded (i.e., lower than a mental age of 12) on the given IQ test. Therefore, Goddard changed (lowered) the criteria of what determined a person's feeble-mindedness; specifically, the criteria changed from a mental age of 12 to a mental age of 8. Although this appears to be a clear admission that his scientific method was inaccurate, Goddard continued to profess his model of the feeble-minded for many years, and societies utilized his ideas.

Toward the end of his career, Goddard did admit that intelligence could be improved, despite his earlier assumptions that it was innate and static.[23] In fact, Goddard actually claimed that he had "gone over to the enemy."[24] However, despite Goddard's admission that his assumptions and testing were not determinant of individuals' intelligence, the snowball had been rolling for too long and had gathered too much strength to fight even the most notable theorist's admonishment of the perspective.

Specifically, the sterilization of individuals, mostly females, based on scores from intelligence tests continued in the United States. Often, the justification was based not on the intelligence scores of the person being sterilized but on the scores of that person's mother or father. After all, as Goddard had proclaimed, the "germ-plasm" that determined feeble-mindedness was passed on from one generation to the next, so it inevitably resulted in feeble-minded offspring as well. Thus, the U.S. government typically sterilized individuals—again, mostly women—based on their parents' IQ scores.

This issue came to the highest court in the 1920s. The case of *Buck v. Bell* made its way to the U.S. Supreme Court in 1927, and the court discussed the issue of sterilizing individuals who had scored, or whose parents had scored, as mentally deficient on intelligence scales. The majority opinion, written by one of the court's most respected jurists, Oliver Wendell Holmes, Jr., stated,

> We have seen more than once that the public welfare may call upon the best citizens for their lives. It would be strange if it could not call upon those who already sap the strength of the state for these lesser sacrifices. . . . Three generations of imbeciles are enough.[25]

Thus, the highest court in the United States upheld the use of sterilization for the purposes of limiting reproduction among individuals deemed feeble-minded by a test score that even the creator and administrator of the test admitted was not valid or accurate.

Due to this approval from the court, such sterilizations continued for many years, up to the 1970s. Governors of many states, such as North Carolina, Virginia, and California, have since delivered public apologies for these policy practices. For example, in 2002 the governor of California, Gray Davis, apologized for the state law passed almost a century before that resulted in the sterilization of about 19,000 women in California.

Although this aspect of U.S. history is often hidden from the public, it did occur and it is important to acknowledge this blot on our nation's history, especially since it occurred at a time when we were supposed to be fighting the Nazis' and other regimes' abuses of civil rights.

Ultimately, the sterilizations, deportations, and incarcerations based on IQ testing contributed to an embarrassing period in U.S. history. So for many decades, criminological researchers realized the atrocities that had been committed in the name of this theory, as well as the "Nazi" mentality of its assumptions, and IQ was not researched or discussed much in the literature. However, in the 1970s, an important study was published in which Travis Hirschi and Michael Hindelang examined the effect of intelligence on youths.[26] Hirschi and Hindelang found that even among youths in the same race and social class, intelligence has a significant effect on delinquency and criminality. This study, as well as others, showed that the IQs of delinquents or criminals are about 10 points lower than those of noncriminals.[27]

This study led to a rebirth in research regarding intelligence testing in criminological research. A number of recent studies have shown that certain types of intelligence are more important than others. Specifically, several studies have shown that a low verbal intelligence has the most significant impact in predicting delinquent and criminal behavior.[28]

Modern studies have shown a strong tie between low IQ, particularly verbal intelligence, and delinquency and criminality.

This tendency makes sense because verbal skills are important in virtually all aspects of life, from everyday interactions with significant others to filling out forms at work to dealing with people in the workplace, and so on. In contrast, most people do not have to display advanced math or quantitative skills in their jobs, or in day-to-day interactions, let alone spatial and other forms of intelligence that are more abstract. Thus, low verbal IQ is the type of intelligence that represents the most direct prediction of criminality, most likely due to the general need for such skills in routine daily activities. After all, persons who lack communication skills will likely find it hard to obtain or retain employment, or to deal with family and social problems.

This rebirth in studies of the link between intelligence and criminality seemed to reach a peak with the publication of Richard Herrnstein and Charles Murray's *The Bell Curve* in 1994.[29] Although this publication eschewed the terminology of *moron*, *imbecile*, and *idiot* in favor of relatively benign terms (e.g., *cognitively disadvantaged*), their argument was consistent with that of the feeble-mindedness researchers of the early 20th century. Specifically, Herrnstein and Murray argued that persons with low IQ scores are somewhat destined to be unsuccessful in school, become unemployed, produce illegitimate children, and commit crime. They also suggested that IQ or intelligence is primarily innate, or genetically determined, with little chance of improvement. These authors also noted that African Americans tend to score the lowest, whereas Asians and Jewish persons tend to score the highest. They provided results from social indicators that support their argument that these intelligence levels result in relative success in life in terms of group-level statistics.

APPLYING THEORY TO CRIME: *BURGLARY*

At the beginning of this chapter, we presented a case study of Javier. We will not repeat his history here, but as his major crime was burglary, we will discuss some facts about burglary.

The FBI (or Uniform Crime Reports) defines burglary as "the unlawful entry of a structure to commit a felony or theft" and classifies it as a serious Index Crime. Although burglaries are nonviolent by definition, they certainly pose much risk for becoming violent—for example, if the residents return while the burglary is taking place. Although some people may believe that burglary occurs only during the night, most police departments and certainly the FBI have moved beyond that common-law definition of this crime.

Despite a steady decrease in burglaries over the past decade, the FBI recorded more than 2 million burglaries in 2006. The vast majority of these burglaries involved some form of forced entry, and most were of home residences. Most burglaries occur during the hours of 6:00 a.m. and 6:00 p.m., when residents are most likely to be out. Still, even when victims do not encounter the burglar, the experience can be traumatic, given that victims know an offender has intruded into their home, often considered a place of refuge and security. In 2006, the average monetary/property loss of burglary per incident was about $1,834, but this loss was far less on average for residential victims compared with commercial and other nonresidential properties.

According to arrest reports, the vast majority (more than 80%) of burglary

offenders are male and a notable number (although not the majority) under 18. Notably, the likelihood of an offender being caught for burglary is extremely low, perhaps because of the categorization of burglary as a property crime, as well as the fact that there are no witnesses (unlike most violent crimes). This is reflected in the low national clearance rate/arrest rate for burglary, which was about 12% in 2006.

In an example of burglary's low priority with police, the San Diego Police Department wrote a press release in 1998 informing citizens that police would no longer investigate home burglaries. The department claimed that the low likelihood of catching anyone (i.e., the low clearance rate), as well as burglary's status as a nonviolent property crime, led them to decide they would rather spend their resources on more serious cases, or those they had a greater chance of solving. Although alarming, this reflects the opinion of many other police and sheriff departments throughout the country regarding incidents of burglary; specifically, most law enforcement officers find burglaries incredibly hard to solve, even when reported, because they typically involve no witnesses or hard evidence.

Burglary rates have decreased over the past decade, but this crime is still occurring in the millions each year.

In the case study at the beginning of this chapter, Javier realized he did not have much going for him in terms of education, so he decided to follow his friends in committing a number of burglaries. Javier was not a violent person, so he engaged in a property offense that he hoped would not result in violence. However, had he known the high potential for violence in a burglary—if, for instance, someone were sleeping in the back of the house or a homeowner returned unexpectedly—he may have thought twice.

Sources: Associated Press. (1999, July 28). San Diego police may stop routine home burglary investigations. *Lodi News-Sentinel*, p. 8; Federal Bureau of Investigation. (2010). *Crime in the United States, 2009*. Washington, DC: U.S. Department of Justice; Walsh, A., & Ellis, L. (2007). *Criminology*. Thousand Oaks, CA: Sage.

COMPARATIVE CRIMINOLOGY: *BURGLARY*

Ranking Regions/Countries as Most Likely for Burglary

This box continues the book's theme of comparing the United States with foreign nations in terms of various aspects in criminology and criminal justice (see Comparative Criminology 1.1 in Chapter 1, which provides an introduction to this feature). In this section, we examine the findings and conclusions of various studies of burglary, which involves attempted or actual breaking and entering for the purpose of stealing goods, money, and so forth. What distinguishes burglary from larceny is that burglary, by definition, involves trespassing on property where the offender has no permission to enter, whereas larceny does not include trespassing (e.g., shoplifting). Furthermore, burglary can be distinguished from robbery, which by definition involves a threat of or actual violence in taking someone's possessions, whereas burglary does not involve violence, according to FBI and most other definitions (Van Dijk, 2008, p. 54). The findings of recent studies regarding the prevalence of burglary across various regions and countries are enlightening in several ways.

The key measure of prevalence of burglary in the world is the International Crime Victimization Survey (ICVS), a databank that collects and standardizes police reports from more than 70 countries around the world. This measure has been conducted since 1987. It does have some weaknesses, but it is currently the best international measure of crime for such cross-national comparisons.

The ICVS has collected many years' worth of data on burglary. Van Dijk (2008) synthesized the ICVS data on burglary for the years 1996 to 2005. As seen in Figure 4.1, the countries with by far the highest percentages of households victimized by burglary in urban areas were countries in Africa. A distant second and third highest ranking were, respectively, countries in the region of Latin America/the Caribbean and Oceania (the islands near Southeast Asia and Australia).

It is not too surprising that burglary tends to be more common in some of the most deprived areas of the world, such as Africa and various Latin American/Caribbean countries. After all, in extreme poverty, many individuals are driven to commit such crimes to survive. However, the results from the ICVS reveal that burglary happens quite a bit in all regions of the world; so burglary is alive and well throughout virtually all societies, such as the US (see Table 4.1).

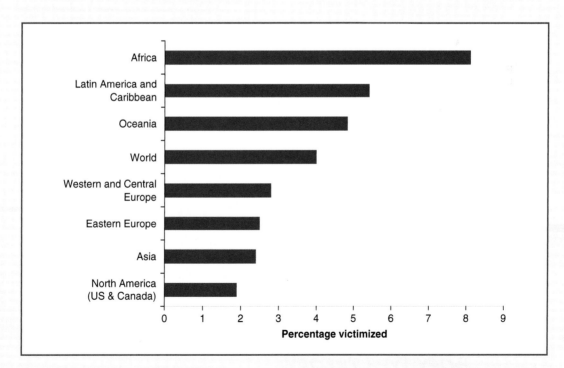

Figure 4.1 Percentages of the Public in Urban Areas Victimized by Household Burglary During the Past 12 Months, by World Region

Source: International Crime Victimization Surveys (ICVS) 1996–2005.

COMPARATIVE CRIMINOLOGY: *(CONTINUED)*

RANK AND CITY	RATE	RANK AND CITY	RATE	RANK AND CITY	RATE
1 Flint, MI	3,339.3	18 Detroit, MI	1,900.1	35 Syracuse, NY	1,595.2
2 Santa Fe, NM	3,129.2	19 St. Louis, MO	1,887.9	36 Pueblo, CO	1,565.5
3 Jackson, MS	2,766.5	20 Fayetteville, NC	1,886.1	37 Durham, NC	1,562.1
4 Macon, GA	2,396.6	21 Columbus, GA	1,871.3	38 Chattanooga, TN	1,560.4
5 Cleveland, OH	2,312.9	22 Springfield, IL	1,846.1	39 Stockton, CA	1,534.7
6 Toledo, OH	2,308.6	23 Tulsa, OK	1,816.4	40 Tuscaloosa, AL	1,529.8
7 Dayton, OH	2,219.0	24 Reading, PA	1,751.3	41 Fort Lauderdale, FL	1,526.0
8 Little Rock, AR	2,198.3	25 Oklahoma City, OK	1,731.4	42 Rockford, IL	1,520.7
9 South Bend, IN	2,127.0	26 Springfield, MA	1,723.8	43 Mobile, AL	1,517.8
10 Akron, OH	2,064.1	27 Yakima, WA	1,706.3	44 Dallas, TX	1,499.4
11 Columbus, OH	1,970.8	28 Rochester, NY	1,691.8	45 Atlanta, GA	1,494.2
12 Vallejo, CA	1,968.4	29 Killeen, TX	1,682.5	46 Kansas City, MO	1,474.4
13 Canton, OH	1,954.1	30 Tallahassee, FL	1,673.2	47 Beaumont, TX	1,472.2
14 Cincinnati, OH	1,952.7	31 Orlando, FL	1,671.4	48 Richmond, CA	1,470.4
15 Memphis, TN	1,943.7	32 Greensboro, NC	1,640.9	49 Knoxville, TN	1,467.5
16 Winston-Salem, NC	1,924.2	33 Buffalo, NY	1,620.3	50 St. Petersburg, FL	1,462.7
17 Lawton, OK	1,909.3	34 Montgomery, AL	1,607.6		

Table 4.1 Burglary Rate in 2010–U.S. Cities

Source: FBI "Crime in the US 2010".
Note: Rate out of 100,000 population

STATE CRIME RANKINGS

Burglaries

CITY CRIME RANKINGS

Burglary Rates

Their book inspired a public outcry, resulting in symposiums at major universities and other venues, during which the authors' postulates were largely condemned. As noted by other reviews of the impact of this work, some professors at public institutions were actually sued in court over their use of this book in their classes.[30] The book also received blistering reviews from other scientists.[31] However, none of these scientific critics have fully addressed the undisputed fact that African Americans consistently score low on intelligence tests and that Asians and Jewish people score high. Furthermore, none have adequately addressed the issue that even within these populations, low IQ scores (especially on verbal tests) predict criminality. For example, in samples of only African Americans, the group that scored lowest on verbal intelligence consistently committed more crime, and even among this population, the persons who scored low on IQ (especially the verbal portions) were more likely to become delinquent or criminal. So despite the harsh criticism of *The Bell Curve*, it is apparent that the authors' arguments carry some validity.

BODY TYPE THEORY: SHELDON'S MODEL OF SOMATOTYPING

Although numerous theories in the late 1800s and early 1900s were based on body types, such as Lombroso's theory and those of other criminal anthropologists, none of these perspectives had a more enduring impact than that of William Sheldon. In the mid-1940s, this new theoretical perspective merged the concepts of biology and psychology. Sheldon claimed that in the embryonic and fetal stages of development, there is an emphasis on the development of certain tissue layers.[32] According to Sheldon, these varying degrees of emphasis are largely due to heredity, which leads to the development of certain body types and temperaments or personalities. This theory, also known as **somatotyping**, became the best-known body type theory, for reasons we will discuss below.

According to Sheldon, all embryos must develop three distinct tissue layers, which are still acknowledged by perinatal medical researchers. The first layer of tissue is the **endoderm**, which is the inner layer of tissues and includes the internal organs, such as the stomach, large intestine, and small intestine. The middle layer of tissue, called the **mesoderm**, includes the muscles, bones, ligaments, and tendons. The **ectoderm** is the outer layer of tissue and includes the skin, capillaries, and much of the nervous system sensors.

Sheldon used these medical facts regarding the three tissue layers to propose that some individuals tend to emphasize certain tissue layers relative to others, typically due to inherited dispositions. In turn, Sheldon believed that such emphases led to certain body types, such that persons who had a focus on their endoderm in development would inevitably become **endomorphic**, or obese. In the same way, individuals who had an emphasis on the middle layer of tissue typically became **mesomorphic**, or of an athletic or muscular build. Finally, someone who had an emphasis on the third layer of tissue in embryonic development would end up having an **ectomorphic**, or thin, build (see Figure 4.2).

Sheldon and his research team would grade each subject on three dimensions, corresponding respectively to the body types described above. Each body type was measured on a scale of 1 to 7, with 7 being the highest. Obviously, no one could score a 0 for any body type, because we all need our internal organs, bone/muscular structure, and outer systems (e.g., skin, capillaries). As stated above, each somatotype always had the following order: endomorphy, mesomorphy, ectomorphy.

So the scores on a typical somatotype might be 3-6-2 (a similar example is seen in Figure 4.2), which would indicate that this person scored a 3 (a little below average) on endomorphy, a 6 (high) on mesomorphy, and a 2 (relatively low) on ectomorphy. According to Sheldon's theory, this hypothetical subject would be a likely candidate for criminality,

LEARNING CHECK 4.3

1. According to the text, which theorist invented IQ testing in France in the early 1900s?
   a. Lombroso
   b. Binet
   c. Goddard
   d. Sheldon
   e. Hirschi

2. According to the text, which theorist was one of the key proponents of IQ testing in the United States in the early 1900s and had his research team identify "feeble-minded" persons at Ellis Island, New York City?
   a. Lombroso
   b. Binet
   c. Goddard
   d. Sheldon
   e. Hirschi

3. According to the text, which level of "feeble-mindedness" was considered the highest level of the feeble-minded and the biggest threat to society?
   a. Moron
   b. Idiot
   c. Imbecile
   d. Stupid
   e. Retarded

4. According to the text, what U.S. Supreme Court case (decided in 1927) ruled it constitutional for individuals to be sterilized based on IQ scores?
   a. *Miranda v. Arizona*
   b. *Buck v. Bell*
   c. *Mapp v. Ohio*
   d. *McKeiver v. Pennsylvania*
   e. *Breed v. Jones*

Answers located at www.sagepub.com/schram

REFERENCE ARTICLE
Somatotypes

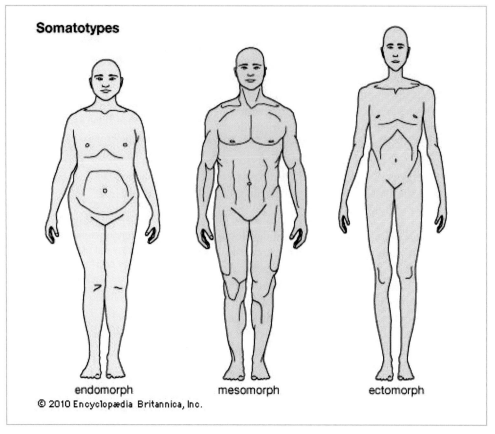

Somatotypes

endomorph   mesomorph   ectomorph

© 2010 Encyclopædia Britannica, Inc.

Figure 4.2 These three body types have been shown to have an influence on both temperament or personality and risk for criminality, with the mesomorph being at highest risk for delinquency or crime.

somatotyping: the area of study, primarily linked to William Sheldon, that links body type to risk for delinquent and criminal behavior. Also, as a methodology, it is a way of ranking body types based on three categories: *endomorphy*, *mesomorphy*, and *ectomorphy*

endoderm: medical term for the inner layer of tissue in our bodies

mesoderm: medical term for the middle layer of tissue in our bodies

ectoderm: medical term for the outer layer of tissue in our bodies

endomorphic: type of body shape associated with an emphasis on the inner layer of tissue (endoderm) during development

mesomorphic: type of body shape associated with an emphasis on the middle layer of tissue (mesoderm) during development

ectomorphic: type of body shape associated with an emphasis on the outer layer of tissue (ectoderm) during development

because he or she scored relatively high on the mesomorphy scale. In fact, the results from his data—as well as those from all studies that have examined the association of body types and delinquency and criminality—would support this prediction.

Perhaps most important, Sheldon proposed that these body types matched particular personality traits or temperaments. Specifically, Sheldon claimed that individuals who were endomorphic (obese) tended to be more jolly or lazy. The technical term for this temperament is **viscerotonic**. In contrast, persons who were mesomorphic (muscular) typically had a risk-taking and aggressive temperament, called **somatotonic**. Last, individuals who were ectomorphic (thin) tended to be introverted and shy, a personality type referred to as **cerebrotonic**. Obviously, it was the middle group, the mesomorphs, who had the greatest propensity for criminality, due to their risk-taking and aggressive dispositions.

Interestingly, many current and recent politicians were subjects in Sheldon's research. Specifically, most entering freshmen in Ivy League schools, especially Harvard, were asked to pose in the three positions for photos in Sheldon's studies. Many politicians who have been in the news in the past few years were participants in his studies. According to most sources, these subjects were told that posing naked in this way was for their own good (i.e., to check for medical conditions, such as scoliosis), when it was actually for Sheldon and his colleagues' research.[33]

Sheldon tested his theory using poor methodology. Specifically, he based his measures of individuals' body types on what he subjectively observed from three perspectives of each subject. He also had his trained staff view many of the photos and score these individuals in each body type category. Reliability among these scores was weak, meaning that the trained staff did not tend to agree with Sheldon or among themselves on the somatotype of each participant.

This is not surprising given the high level of variation in body types, and the fact that Sheldon and his colleagues did not employ the technology used today, such as caliper tests and submersion in water tanks, that provides virtually all the information needed. After all, many readers have probably radically altered their weight, and have gone from an ectomorphic or mesomorphic build to a more endomorphic form, or vice versa. Presented with the argument that individuals often alter their body types via diet and exercise, Sheldon's position was that he could tell what the "natural" body type of each individual was from the three pictures taken. This position is not a strong one, further confirmed by the poor interrater reliability shown among his staff. Therefore, Sheldon's methodology is questionable and raises concerns regarding the entire theoretical framework.

Despite the problematic issues of his methodology, Sheldon clearly showed that mesomorphs, or individuals who have muscular builds and tend to take risks, are more delinquent and criminal than are individuals of other body types/temperaments.[34] Furthermore, other researchers, even those who despised Sheldon's theory, found the same associations between mesomorphy and criminality, as well as related temperaments (i.e., somatotonia) and criminality.[35] Specifically, subsequent studies showed that mesomorphic boys were far more likely to have personality traits predictive of criminality, such as aggression, short temper, self-centeredness, and impulsivity.

Even recent theorists have noted the obvious link between an athletic, muscular build and the highly extroverted, aggressive personality often associated with that body type.[36] In fact, some recent theorists have gone so far as to claim that chronic offenders can be identified early in life by the shape of the muscles in their pelvic region. Specifically, these theorists claim that the most likely criminals (both male and female) can be identified by their "v-shaped" pelvic structure, as opposed to a "u-shaped" pelvic structure.[37] The v-shaped pelvis, in both males and females, is seen to be an indication of a relatively high level of androgens (male hormones, such as testosterone) in their system, which predisposes individuals to crime. On the other hand, a more u-shaped pelvis is indicative of relatively low levels of androgens and, therefore, a lower propensity for aggression and criminality. Using this logic, it may be true that the more hair on an individual's arms (whether male or female), the higher that person's likelihood of committing crime. However, no research exists to address this particular factor.

Regarding the use of body types/characteristics to explain crime, many of the hard-line sociologists who have attempted to examine or replicate Sheldon's results have not been able to refute the association between mesomorphs and delinquency and criminality or the association between mesomorphy and somatotonic temperament toward risk-taking or aggression.[38] Thus, the association between being muscular or athletically built and engaging in criminal activities is undisputed and assumed to be true. Still, sociologists have taken issue with determinations of what causes this association.

Whereas Sheldon claimed this association was due to inherited traits for a certain body type, sociologists claimed it was due to societal expectations for muscular male youth to engage in risk-taking and aggressive behavior. For example, if a young male has an athletic build, he will be expected to be aggressive and will be encouraged to join sports teams and engage in high-risk behavior. After all, who would be most desirable to gangs? More muscular, athletic individuals are assumed to be better at fighting and other acts that require a certain degree of physical strength and stamina.

viscerotonic: the type of temperament or personality associated with an endomorphic (obese) body type; these people tend to be jolly, lazy, and happy-go-lucky

somatotonic: type of temperament or personality associated with a mesomorphic (muscular) body type; these people tend to be risk-taking and aggressive

cerebrotonic: the type of temperament or personality associated with an ectomorphic (thin) body type; these people tend to be introverted and shy

LEARNING CHECK 4.4

1. According to the text, which theorist developed the most prominent theory on body types, known as somatotyping?
   a. Lombroso
   b. Binet
   c. Goddard
   d. Sheldon
   e. Hirschi

2. According to the text, which body type is a muscular/athletic build and the most likely among individuals who tend to be delinquent or criminal?
   a. Ectomorphic
   b. Endomorphic
   c. Mesomorphic
   d. Klectomorphic
   e. Candomorphic

3. According to the text, which type of personality is correlated with an ectomorphic body type?
   a. Jolly/happy-go-lucky
   b. Aggressive/extroverted
   c. Shy/introverted
   d. None of the above

Answers located at www.sagepub.com/schram

Ultimately, it is now established that mesomorphs are more likely to commit crime.[39] Furthermore, the personality traits linked to having an athletic or muscular build are dispositions toward risk-taking and aggressiveness, and few scientists dispute this correlation. No matter which theoretical model is adopted—whether it be that of the biopsychologists or the sociologists—the fact of the matter is that mesomorphs are indeed more likely to be risk-taking and aggressive and, thus, more likely to commit crime than individuals of other body types.

However, whether the explanation is biological or sociological is a question that shows the importance of theory in criminological research. After all, the link between mesomorphy and criminality is undisputed, but the explanation for why this link exists is still up for debate. Is it the biological influence or the sociological influence? The answer is up to readers, and we hope they will be able to make their own determination—if not now, then later, after we have discussed other theories of crime.

Our position is that the answer is likely both biology *and* social environment, which interact with each other. Thus, it is most likely that both "nature and nurture" are at play in this association between mesomorphy and crime. This would mean both Sheldon and some of his critics were correct. There is often a middle ground to be found in theorizing on criminality, but people don't often see theory as such. It is important to keep in mind that theories in criminology, as a science, are always subject to falsification and criticism and can always be improved. Therefore, our stance on the validity and influence of this theory, as well as others, should not be surprising.

CASE STUDY REVISITED: JAVIER

At the beginning of this chapter, we discussed the case of Javier, who had engaged in more than a dozen burglaries when he was in high school. As you may recall, Javier had numerous MPAs (minor physical anomalies) that became evident as he grew up, such as small, low-seated ears; a relatively large third toe and webbing between all his toes; a curved "pinky" finger; a cleft lip; and narrow-set eyes. All these characteristics are currently used by medical doctors and researchers as "red flags" or predictors of developmental problems that begin in the womb or during delivery. They are also key indicators or predictors of future criminality, especially when more than five are present in one individual.[40] These MPAs, as well as Javier's history of offending, to some extent support the propositions of early positivistic theorists, such as physiognomists and, later, Lombroso, who claimed that physical features predict criminality.

In addition, Javier's low verbal aptitude supports the early "feeble-mindedness" theory researchers, such as Goddard, and even more modern research that implicates verbal/

reading comprehension in predicting illegal behavior. In fact, modern studies show that verbal IQ scores have the greatest influence on criminality, which makes sense because we tend to use verbal and communication skills continuously, as opposed to mathematical skills, which are used more sporadically (and which Javier scored high in).

Finally, Javier developed an athletic, muscular physique. According to Sheldon, individuals (especially males) who are more muscular tend to be more likely to engage in criminal behavior. Whether it is due to an inherent aggressive or risk-taking temperament (as Sheldon claimed) or to being associated with or recruited by peers to engage in criminal activity (as more sociologically oriented theorists have claimed), Javier seemed to have both an aggressive personality (as an outstanding linebacker) and deviant peers (from his football team). Thus, Javier's experience seems to fit well with the body type perspective claiming that more muscular/athletic individuals will be more criminal on average.

However, you will also recall that Javier stopped his offending by the time he graduated high school. This defies virtually all the assumptions and propositions of the theories presented in this chapter. Specifically, all the theories assume that whether it be physical traits, IQ aptitude, or body type, individuals cannot change or reform from what they are destined to be. Javier's case study shows that, like many offenders, he actually did change the trajectory of his life and no longer offends. This happens more often than not and is perhaps the most important criticism of these theoretical perspectives. These early theories of the Positive School did not allow much room for the possibility of reform, because if a person has such physical anomalies, low IQ, or a certain body type, he or she is not likely to change much over time. Thus, these early theories do not hold much weight, in the sense that a vast majority of people who offend in their teenage or young adult years actually mature and stop committing crimes.

POLICY IMPLICATIONS

A variety of policy implications can be derived from the theories presented in this chapter. First, one could propose more thorough medical screening at birth and in early childhood, especially regarding MPAs such as Javier's in our hypothetical case study. The studies reviewed in this chapter implicate numerous MPAs in developmental problems (mostly originating in the womb). These MPAs are red flags signaling problems, especially in cognitive ability, which are likely to significantly impact criminal behavior.[41]

Other policy implications derived from the theories and findings of this chapter involve implementation of same-sex classes to allow for more focus on deficiencies shown to be specific to young boys or girls. For example, numerous school districts now have policies that prescribe same-sex math courses for female students. This same strategy might be considered for male students in English or literature courses, because males are biologically predisposed to have a lower aptitude in this area of study. Furthermore, far more screenings should be done regarding the IQ and aptitude levels of young children to identify which children require extra attention, because studies show that early intervention can make a big difference in improving IQ/aptitude.

A recent summary of the extant literature addressing what types of programs work best for reducing the long-term impact of early physiological risk factors for criminality noted the importance of diagnosing early head trauma and further concluded that the most consistently supported programs for at-risk children are those that involve weekly infant home visitations.[42] Another obvious policy implication derived from biosocial theory is mandatory health insurance for pregnant mothers and children, which is likely the most efficient way to reduce crime in the long term. Finally, all youth should be screened for abnormal levels of hormones, neurotransmitters, and toxins (especially lead).[43] These and other policy strategies are discussed in the last section of the book.

CONCLUSION

This chapter discussed the early formation of the Positive School of criminology, which was a giant departure from the Classical School paradigm. The Classical School assumes free will/choice in criminal behavior, whereas the Positive School assumes that free will is not involved at all. Rather, according to the Positive School, our behavior is determined by factors other than free will/choice, such as bad parenting, poverty, and low intelligence. We started this chapter by discussing the earliest positive perspectives, which included craniometry, phrenology, and physiognomy. Thus, the early formation of criminology was largely based on examinations of the skull and brain (e.g., craniometry) in the early 1800s. But these disciplines did not become popular then, because Darwin had not yet presented his theory of evolution. The post-Darwinian explanations of the late 19th century, on the other hand, became very popular, largely because society was ready to accept them.

Once Darwin's theory spread worldwide, the ground was more fertile for a theory of crime that claimed that certain individuals (or groups) were more likely to become criminals, which led to a eugenics movement among both scientists and society as a whole. By far the most notable of these theories are Lombroso's (the Father of Criminology), as well as Goddard's theory of feeble-mindedness and IQ testing. Early policy implications of these perspectives were also examined. These studies ultimately inspired far more focus on the influence of inheritance and genetics in predisposing certain individuals to criminal activity (which we also cover in the next chapter). This was supported by more recent studies on IQ testing and minor physical anomalies (MPAs) that show that individuals with low IQ scores and numerous MPAs do indeed engage in more criminal behavior than do their counterparts without MPAs.

Also, this chapter examined the connections between various body types, temperaments, and criminality, with recent research supporting a link between certain body types and criminal behavior. To some extent, these body type theories provide a bridge between the early emphasis on physical features (e.g., skull, stigmata, etc.) and the focus on psychological factors (e.g., temperament, personality). Thus, the body type theories appeared to advance the knowledge in criminological literature by emphasizing more than one dimension. Furthermore, most studies have supported the claim that body type actually does predict criminality, as well as the corresponding temperament or personality associated with certain body types most likely found among delinquents and criminals.

However, there are many criticisms of such early Positive School perspectives of crime. The next chapter sheds much more light on how valid these perspectives are, especially in terms of the empirical validity of the idea that biological or physiological factors influence criminality. Readers will likely be surprised by the results of these modern studies.

SUMMARY OF THEORIES IN CHAPTER 4

THEORIES	KEY PROPONENTS	FACTORS/CONCEPTS	KEY PROPOSITIONS
Craniometry	Various	Brain/skull size	Larger skull/brain, more superior
Phrenology	Various	Bumps on skull	Abnormalities on skull reveal deficiencies
Physiognomy	Various	Facial/bodily attributes	Certain facial or body features reveal inferiority
Atavism/ born criminal	Cesare Lombroso, Father of Criminology	Variety of stigmata identify "born criminals"	Stigmata reveal individuals likely to be born criminals
IQ testing/ feeble-mindedness	Alfred Binet, invented IQ; H. H. Goddard, used in United States	IQ identifies who is superior/ inferior	Low-IQ persons are likely criminals
Body type theories (we focused on the most well-known)	William Sheldon	Tissue-layer growth in embryonic stage leads to body type	Body type determines personality and behavior

KEY TERMS

atavism	ectomorphic	mesoderm	Positive School
cerebrotonic	endoderm	mesomorphic	somatotonic
craniometry	endomorphic	minor physical anomalies	somatotyping
determinism	eugenics	phrenology	stigmata
ectoderm	feeble-mindedness	physiognomy	viscerotonic

STUDENT STUDY SITE

Visit the student study site at **www.sagepub.com/schram** to access links to the video, audio, city and state rankings, author podcasts, and SAGE journal and reference articles featured in this chapter, as well as additional study tools, including eFlashcards, web quizzes, web resources, and chapter outlines.

DISCUSSION QUESTIONS

1. What characteristics distinguish the Positive School from the Classical School regarding criminal thought? Which of these schools do you lean toward in your own perspective of crime, and why?

2. Name and describe the various positivistic theories that existed in the early to mid-1800s (pre-Darwin), as well as the influence they had on later schools of thought regarding criminality. Do you see any validity in these approaches (because modern medical science does)? Why or why not?

3. What was the significant reason(s) these early positivistic theories did not gain much momentum in societal popularity? Does this lack of popularity relate to the neglect of biological perspectives of crime in modern times?

4. What portion of Lombroso's theory of criminality do you find least valid? Which do you find most valid?

5. Most readers have taken the equivalent of an IQ test (e.g., SAT or ACT). Do you believe that this score is a fair representation of your knowledge as compared with others? Why or why not? Do your feelings reflect the criticisms of experts regarding the use of IQ in identifying potential offenders, such as in the feeble-mindedness theory?

6. In light of the scientific findings that show verbal IQ to be a consistent predictor of criminality among virtually all populations or samples, can you provide evidence from your personal experience for why this occurs?

7. Regarding Sheldon's body type theory, what portion of this theory do you find most valid? What do you find least valid?

8. If you had to give yourself a somatotype (e.g., 3-6-2), what would it be? Explain your choice, and note whether this score would make you a likely criminal in Sheldon's model.

9. Provide a somatotype for five of your family members or best friends. Does each somatotype have any correlation with criminality according to Sheldon's predictions? Describe your findings.

10. Ultimately, do you believe some of the positive theoretical perspectives presented in this section are valid, or do you think they should be entirely dismissed in terms of understanding or predicting crime? State your case.

11. What types of policies would you implement, if you were in charge, given the theories and findings in this chapter?

WEB RESOURCES

Phrenology/craniometry

http://www.phrenology.org/index.html

http://skepdic.com/cranial.html

Cesare Lombroso

http://www.museocriminologico.it/lombroso_1_uk.htm

IQ testing/feeble-mindedness

http://www.vineland.org/history/trainingschool/history/
eugenics.htm

Body type theories/somatotyping

http://www.innerexplorations.com/psytext/shel.htm

http://www.teachpe.com/multi/somatotyping_eating_
disorders_performance.htm

CHAPTER 5

Modern Biosocial Perspectives of Criminal Behavior

INTRODUCTION

In 1996, a pair of identical twin sisters in Orange County, California, made headlines because, despite their remarkable similarities—both were co-valedictorians of their high school, and both had criminal records for stealing from family and friends—one of the pair conspired to kill the other when they were 22 years old.[1] Sunny and Gina Han, both originally from South Korea, were virtually identical in terms of looks, personality, and criminality. But at a certain point, one wanted the other dead. Gina hatched a plot with two teenage boys to kill her sister. Sunny was tied up, forced to sit in a bathtub, and threatened for a while. Sunny survived, and Gina was later convicted and sentenced to 26 years to life in prison; after that, an appellate court upheld her sentence. During her sentencing hearing, she infamously said through tears, "Sunny is my flesh and blood."[2]

This chapter examines the modern perspectives on the biological aspect of criminality by exploring modern factors and theories of biosocial positivism in the current criminological literature. First, we will go back in time and explore some of the early waves of studies that specifically examined the influence of biology versus environment (i.e., nature vs. nurture), which include studies of identical twins such as the pair in the story above, as well as family and adoption studies. We shall see that virtually all these studies support a more integrative approach of genetics/physiology via environment (i.e., nature via nurture). Then we will examine randomly occurring chromosomal mutations, as well as discussing which mutations seem most likely to predict criminality among individuals.

Next, we will discuss the influence of various hormones, such as testosterone, and level and activity of neurotransmitters (e.g., dopamine, serotonin) in how we behave in terms of criminality. Then we will discuss various parts of the brain that are most likely to show high correlation to criminality when traumatized or otherwise hindered in performance. In relation to brain trauma, we will then explore the extreme importance of the functioning of the central nervous system, in which the brain plays a vital part. We will also review the findings from various studies regarding the autonomic nervous system, which is vital in many aspects of our everyday lives—especially in making decisions related to illegal behavior.

Finally, we will discuss in this chapter the integration of both physiology and environment in what is called interaction effects, which modern studies show have the greatest impact on our behavior, whether in illegal activities or more conventional activities. But before we dive into the actual theories, let's discuss a case study that applies some of the theoretical concepts, propositions, and criticisms presented in this chapter.

NATURE VERSUS NURTURE: STUDIES EXAMINING THE INFLUENCE OF GENETICS AND ENVIRONMENT

In the early 1900s, researchers became highly interested in testing the influence of heredity versus environment to see which of these two components

LEARNING OBJECTIVES

As students are reading this chapter, they should consider the following questions:

- What are the various types of cytogenetic disorders, and which type(s) puts a person at highest risk for criminality? Why?

- What are the hormones that play a key role in individuals who tend to engage in chronic offending? Make sure to consider females as you read this chapter.

- How do neurotransmitters differ from hormones, and which of the former are the most often implicated in criminality? At high or low levels?

- Which regions of the brain do criminological studies implicate in both structural trauma and functioning disorders?

- How do the central nervous system and the autonomic nervous system differ, and how do both systems play an important part in individuals' decisions to engage in criminal activity or not?

CASE STUDY

FAITH AND HOPE

Two identical twin girls, Faith and Hope, were born to a poor, teenage, single mother from Chicago's South Side. Their mother smoked and drank heavily throughout the pregnancy—somewhat due to stress and frustration at the father of the babies, who was completely absent (both physically and financially), and also ignorance regarding the damage she was doing to the babies. When the twins were born, they both had relatively low diagnostic scores on breathing, responsiveness, color, and so forth (i.e., Apgar scores). Still, their mother wanted to do her best to raise the twins.

After only a month, their mother realized she could not handle the burden of two babies, so she gave Hope up for adoption. This realization came after their mother accidently dropped Faith on her head while changing the girls' diapers on a bathroom counter. Hope was adopted relatively quickly by an upper-middle-class family living in the affluent northwest side of Chicago. Their mother readily signed off on this adoption, because she knew Hope was going to a good environment. Faith stayed with her mother and grew up without knowing she had an identical twin.

Faith showed many problems in early development, with low scores and grades in virtually all topics in school. School-mandated medical checkups found that she had a significantly lower heartbeat than most children her age. Furthermore, in middle school—with her mother working two full-time, minimum-wage jobs to support them—Faith ate an unhealthy diet of fast food and gained far more weight than normal for her age. This led to her becoming obese by age 11, at which time she also entered puberty, largely due to high levels of fats and proteins in her system. Faith developed breasts and quickly caught the attention of teenage boys at school. Following her mother's guidance, she avoided these boys' advances until she was in high school. When she was a freshman, a junior asked her to the junior prom and she was so flattered and infatuated, she had sex with him in his car after the event.

Faith made him wear a condom, but as their relationship continued, she grew less cautious. She was pregnant by the end of her sophomore year. Once he found out, the father of the baby broke off all contact with Faith; so she explored other options to finance the cost of keeping the baby. She realized she would likely have to quit school and find a job, because her mother's two minimum-wage jobs were not bringing in enough. Faith began stealing small items from local department stores and selling them online or to people she met. Not only did this not raise enough money, but she was caught by local police and arrested. The charges were dismissed because this was her first offense.

One of Faith's friends told her that she could make more money in one day distributing drugs than in an entire week at a minimum-wage job, so she met with a local gangster and he put her to work. She quickly began making some money, but she also ended up taking some of the methamphetamine they were selling so she could stay awake for the calls from her "boss" and "customers" that came at all times of the night. At one point, she got into an altercation with a customer who tried to take the drugs without paying. Because Faith knew she would have to pay her boss if she didn't get the money for the meth, she hit the customer in the head with a tree branch. The customer then called the police. Faith was arrested and charged with aggravated assault. Once the police interviewed the customer, she dropped the charges because she realized she had much to lose in the eyes of the court. Still, being charged with aggravated assault weighed heavily on Faith, because she never saw herself as a violent person.

After a couple of months, Faith realized that her baby was in jeopardy and she had become addicted to methamphetamine. She aborted the child and then tried to go back to high school through a continuation program. She graduated and is currently living with a relatively steady boyfriend and one child in an apartment in Chicago. We will revisit Faith at the end of this chapter, as well as apply various theoretical concepts and propositions to her situation. We will also hear what happened to Hope, her twin sister.

> SHE QUICKLY BEGAN MAKING SOME MONEY, BUT SHE ALSO ENDED UP TAKING SOME OF THE METHAMPHETAMINE THEY WERE SELLING SO SHE COULD STAY AWAKE FOR THE CALLS FROM HER "BOSS" AND "CUSTOMERS" THAT CAME AT ALL TIMES OF THE NIGHT.

had the strongest effect on predicting criminality in people. This type of testing produced four waves of research: family studies, twin studies, adoption studies, and in recent years, studies of identical twins separated at birth. Each of these waves of research, some more than others, contributed knowledge to our understanding of how much criminality is inherited from our parents (or other ancestors) versus how much is due to cultural norms, such as family, community, and so forth. Ultimately, all have shown that the interaction between these two aspects—genetics and environment—is what causes crime among individuals and groups in society.

FAMILY STUDIES

The most notable **family studies** were done in the early 1900s by Richard L. Dugdale, in his work with the Jukes family, and by the previously discussed researcher H. H. Goddard, who studied the Kallikak family.[3] These studies were intended to test the proposition that criminality is more likely to be found in certain families, which would indicate that crime is inherited. Due to the similarity of the results from the two studies, we will focus here on Goddard's work with the Kallikak family.

Goddard's study of the Kallikak family showed that a high proportion of children from that family became criminals. Furthermore, Goddard claimed that many of the individuals (often children) from the Kallikak family actually looked like criminals, which fit Cesare Lombroso's theory of stigmata. In fact, Goddard had many members of this family photographed to back up these claims. However, follow-up investigations of Goddard's "research" show that many of these photographs were altered to make the subjects appear more sinister or evil—specifically by altering their facial features, most notably their eyes, to fit Lombroso's stigmata.[4]

Despite the despicable methodological problems with Goddard's data and subsequent conclusions, two important conclusions can be made from the family studies done in the early 1900s. The first is that criminality is indeed more common in some families; in fact, no study has ever shown otherwise. However, this tendency cannot be shown to be a product of heredity or genetics. After all, individuals from the same family are also products of a similar environment (often a bad one), so this conclusion of the family studies does little to advance knowledge regarding the relative influence of nature versus nurture in predicting criminality.

The second conclusion of family studies was more insightful and interesting. Specifically, the family studies showed that criminality in the mother (or head female caretaker) had a much stronger influence on future criminality of the children than did the father's criminality. This is likely due to two factors. The first is that the father is often absent while the children are being raised. But perhaps more important, it takes much more for a woman to transgress social norms and become a convicted offender, which indicates that the mother is highly antisocial and gives some (albeit limited) credence to the argument that criminality is inherited. Despite this conclusion, it should be apparent from the weaknesses in the methodology used in family studies that this finding

CRIME IN THE NEWS

Han Sisters

AUDIO

Nature vs. Nurture

The Hatfield clan poses in April 1897 at a logging camp in southern West Virginia. This family clan is part of the most infamous feud in American folklore, the long-running battle between the Hatfields and McCoys.

VIDEO

Kallikak Family

family studies: studies that examine the clustering of criminality in a given family

Members of the extended Kallikak family. Family studies such as Goddard's research on the Kallikak family were among the first attempts to examine the influence of genetics on deviant behavior.

VIDEO ▶

Twin Studies

twin studies: studies that examine the relative concordance rates for monozygotic versus dizygotic twins

monozygotic twins: twin pairs that come from a single egg (zygote) and thus share 100% of their genetic makeup

dizygotic twins: twin pairs that come from two separate eggs (zygotes) and thus share only 50% of the genetic makeup that can vary

concordance rates: rates at which twin pairs share either a trait (e.g., criminality) or the lack of the trait

did not hold much weight in the nature versus nurture debate. Thus, a new wave of research soon emerged that did a better job of measuring the influence of genetics versus environment—twin studies.

TWIN STUDIES

After family studies, the next wave of tests was called **twin studies**. These studies were specifically meant to determine, through examination of identical twin pairs versus fraternal twin pairs, the relative influence of nature and nurture on criminality. Identical twins are also known as **monozygotic twins** because they come from a single (hence "mono") egg (or zygote); they are typically referred to in scientific literature as MZ (monozygotic) twins. Such twins share 100% of their genotype, meaning they are identical in terms of genetic makeup. On the other hand, fraternal twins are typically referred to as **dizygotic twins** because they come from two (hence "di") separate eggs (or zygotes); they are known in the scientific literature as DZ (dizygotic) twins. DZ twins share 50% of the genes that can vary, which is the same amount that any siblings from the same two parents share. DZ twins can be of different gender and may look and behave quite differently, as many readers have probably observed.

It follows that the goal of the twin studies was to examine **concordance rates** of delinquency between MZ twin pairs versus DZ twin pairs. Concordance is a count based on whether two people (or a twin pair) share a certain trait (or lack of a certain trait); for our purposes, the trait is criminal offending. Regarding a count of concordance, if one twin is an offender, then we look to see if the other is also an offender. If he or she is, then there is concordance given the fact that the first twin is also a criminal offender. If neither of the twins are offenders, that also is concordant because they both lack the trait. However, if one twin is a criminal offender and the other is not, this is discordant because one has a trait that the other lacks.

Thus, the twin studies focused on comparing the concordance rates of MZ twin pairs versus those of DZ twin pairs, with the assumption that any significant difference in concordance could be attributed to the similarity of the genetic makeup of the MZ twins (100%) versus that of the DZ twins (50%). In other words, if genetics play a major role in determining the criminality of individuals, then MZ twins will be expected to have a significantly higher concordance rate for criminal offending than will DZ twins. After all, it is assumed that both the MZ twin pairs and DZ twin pairs compared in these studies were raised in the same relative environments, since they were raised in the same families at the same time.

The studies that have compared the concordance rates of MZ twins versus DZ twins clearly showed that MZ twins were far more similar in the trait of criminality than were DZ twins. Specifically, a number of studies were performed in the early and mid-1900s that examined the concordance rates between MZ and DZ twin pairs. These studies clearly showed that identical twins had far higher concordance rates than did fraternal (DZ) twins, with most studies showing twice as much or more concordance for MZ twins, even for serious criminality.[5]

However, these studies regarding comparisons between the twins were strongly criticized for reasons most readers see on an everyday basis. Specifically, identical twins, who look almost exactly alike, are typically dressed the same by their parents, as well as treated the same by the public. In other words, they are not only treated the same by society but are generally expected to behave the same. This can be observed in any large public space, such as the local shopping mall or a theme park. When you see identical twins, they are often dressed the same, treated the same, and expected to act the same. However, this is not true for fraternal twins, who often look very different and quite often are of different genders.

Twin studies are vital in building an understanding of the influence of genetics on criminal behavior.

This produced the foundation for criticisms of the twin studies, mainly that the higher rate of concordance among MZ twins could have been due to the extremely similar way they were treated, or expected to behave, by society. Another criticism of the early twin studies pertained to identification of twins as fraternal or identical, which was often determined by sight in the early tests.[6] Although these criticisms were seemingly valid, the most recent meta-analysis, which examined virtually all the twin studies conducted up to the 1990s, concluded that the twin studies showed evidence of a significant hereditary basis for criminality.[7] Still, the criticisms of such studies were valid, so researchers in the early to mid-1900s involved in the nature versus nurture debate attempted to address these criticisms by moving on to another methodological approach for examining this debate—adoption studies.

ADOPTION STUDIES

Due to the valid criticisms leveled at twin studies in determining the relative influence of nature (biology) or nurture (environment), researchers in this area moved on to **adoption studies** that examined the predictive influence of the biological parents of adopted children versus that of the adoptive parents who raised the children from infancy to adulthood. It is important to realize that in such studies, the adoptees were typically given up for adoption prior to 6 months of age, meaning that these children had relatively no interaction with their natural parents; rather, they were raised almost completely from infancy by the adoptive parents.

Although there have been many, perhaps the most notable of the adoption studies was done by Sarnoff Mednick and his colleagues, who examined male children born in Copenhagen between 1927 and 1941 and adopted early in life.[8] In this study, as well as in other similar analyses, the findings can be considered as a 2-by-2 matrix, containing four cells that

LEARNING CHECK 5.1

1. According to the text, family studies showed that the past criminality of which family member was the best predictor of whether or not others in the family would become criminals?

   a. Male siblings

   b. Grandfather

   c. Mother

   d. Father

   e. All the above

2. According to the text, which type of twins share 50% of their genotype?

   a. MZ twins

   b. DZ twins

   c. XZ twins

   d. ZZ twins

3. According to the text, studies have consistently shown that which type of twins have the highest concordance rates in terms of criminality (as well as virtually all other behaviors and traits)?

   a. MZ twins

   b. DZ twins

   c. XZ twins

   d. ZZ twins

Answers located at www.sagepub.com/schram

	ARE ADOPTIVE PARENTS CRIMINAL?	
	NO	YES
Are Biological Parents Criminal?		
No	13.5% (of 2,492)*	14.7% (of 204)
Yes	20.0% (of 1,226)	24.5% (of 143)

Figure 5.1 "Cross-Fostering" Analysis: Percentage of Adoptive Sons Who Have Been Convicted of Criminal Law Offenses

*Note: The numbers in parentheses are the numbers of cases in each cell, for a total sample of 4,065 adopted males.

Source: Adapted from Mednick, S. A., Gabrielli, W. F., & Hutchings, B. (1984). Genetic influences in criminal convictions: Evidence from an adoption cohort. *Science, 224,* 891–894. Also reported in Wilson, J. Q., & Herrnstein, R. J. (1985). *Crime and human nature.* New York: Simon & Schuster, p. 96.

represent adoptees in various circumstances in terms of the criminality of their biological and/or adoptive parents (see Figure 5.1).

As can be seen from the figure, the primary questions posed in such studies regarding each adoptee are whether the biological parents are criminal (yes or no) and whether the adoptive parents are criminal (yes or no). The final question is what percentage of youths in each of these four cells end up becoming criminal.

WHAT WERE THEY THINKING?!

Twin Studies

This study, as well as virtually all others that have examined adoptees in this light, found that the highest predictability for future criminality by far was for adopted youths whose biological parents and adoptive parents were *both* convicted criminals. On the other hand, the adopted children for whom *neither* set of parents was criminal were the least likely to become criminal. Although these results should be the highlight for the studies, the researchers did not portray the results in these terms. Readers should realize that these findings support the major contentions of the authors of this textbook, because they fully back up the "nature via nature" argument as opposed to the "nature versus nurture" argument; they support the idea that both biological *and* environmental factors contribute to the future criminality of youth.

adoption studies: studies that examine the criminality of adoptees as compared with the criminality of their biological and adoptive parents

selective placement: an argument that adoptees tend to be placed in households that resemble that of their biological parents; thus, adoptees from rich biological parents are placed in rich adoptive households

Unfortunately, the researchers who performed these studies focused on the other two groups (or cells) of youth—namely, only those who had either criminal biological parents or criminal adoptive parents. As can be seen in Figure 5.1, the adoption studies found that the adoptees who had only criminal biological parents had a much higher likelihood of becoming criminal compared with the youths who had only criminal adoptive parents. In other words, when the influence of biological versus adoptive parents was compared, the biological parents had far more influence on the youth's future criminality. This was used to support the genetic influence in predisposing one toward criminality; however, this methodology was subject to criticism.

Perhaps the most notable criticism of adoption studies was that adoption agencies typically incorporated a policy of **selective placement**. Selective placement is when adoptees are placed with adoptive families similar to their biological parents in terms of demographics and background. Such selective placement of adoptees could bias the results of the adoption studies. However, recent analyses that have examined the impact of such bias have concluded that even when accounting for the influence of selective placement, the ultimate findings of the adoption studies are still somewhat valid.[9] Specifically, the biological parents of adopted children likely have more influence on the children than do the adoptive parents who raise the child from infancy to adulthood. Still, the criticism of selective placement was strong enough to encourage a fourth wave of research in the "nature versus nurture" debate—studies on identical twins separated at birth.

TWINS SEPARATED AT BIRTH

The fourth, and final, wave of research that examined the relative influence of biological and environmental influences on individuals' criminality was **twins separated at birth studies**. Until recently, studies of identical twins separated at birth were virtually impossible because it was so difficult to find enough identical twins separated early in life. But since the early 1990s, such examinations have been possible. Readers should keep in mind that in many of the identical twin pairs studied in these investigations, the individuals did not know they had a twin. Furthermore, the environments in which they were raised were often extremely different, such as one twin being raised by a poor family in an urban environment while the other twin was raised by a middle- to upper-class family in a rural environment.

The studies on identical twins separated at birth—the most notable of these conducted at the University of Minnesota—found that the twin pairs often showed extremely similar tendencies for criminality, sometimes more than those seen in concordance rates for identical twins raised together.[10] This finding supported the profound influence of genetics and heredity, which is not surprising to most well-read scientists who now acknowledge the extreme importance of inheritance of physiological and psychological aspects regarding human behavior. Perhaps more surprising was why separated identical twins who never knew they had a twin, and who were often raised in extremely different circumstances, had just as similar or even more similar concordance rates than did identical twins raised together.

The leading theory for this phenomenon is that identical twins who are raised together go out of their way to deviate from their natural tendencies in an effort to form their own identity separate from that of their identical twin, with whom they have spent their entire life. As for criticisms of this methodology, no significant criticism has been presented. Thus, at this point, it is somewhat undisputed in the scientific literature that the studies of identical twins separated at birth have shown that genetics have a significant impact on human behavior, especially regarding criminal activity.

Ultimately, taking all the "nature versus nurture" methodological approaches and subsequent findings together, the best conclusion that can be made is that genetics and heredity both have a significant impact on criminality. After all, environment simply cannot account for all the consistent results from comparisons of identical twins and fraternal twins, nor for those of identical twins separated at birth, nor for those of adoptees with criminal biological parents versus those with noncriminal biological parents. Despite the taboo nature of and controversial response to the findings of such studies, it is quite clear that when nature and nurture are compared, biological factors, rather than

Some of the most advanced twin studies examine identical twins who were separated as infants, grew up in different environments, and yet often ended up sharing many personality traits and behavior patterns.

▶ **VIDEO**

Separated Twins

twins separated at birth studies: studies that examine the similarities between identical twins who were separated in infancy environmental factors, tend to have the most influence on the criminality of individuals. Still, the authors of this book hope that readers will emphasize the importance of the interaction between nature and nurture (better stated as nature *via* nurture). After all, we hope that we have shown quite convincingly through scientific study that the interplay between biology and the environment is what is most important in determining human behavior.

Perhaps in response to this "nature versus nurture" debate, a variety of new theoretical perspectives were offered in the mid- to late 1900s that merged biological and psychological factors in explaining criminality. Although leaning more toward the "nature" side of the debate, critics would use this same perspective to promote the "nurture" side; so this framework was useful in promoting the interaction between biological and sociological factors. One of the first of the various biosocial factors that will be examined is mutations of chromosomes (called cytogenetic abnormalities), which interact with environmental factors to increase the likelihood of criminality.

CYTOGENETIC STUDIES: THE XYY FACTOR

Beyond the body type theories, in the early 1900s another theory was proposed regarding biological conditions that predispose individuals toward crime: cytogenetic studies. **Cytogenetic studies** of crime focus on the genetic makeup of individuals, with a specific focus on abnormalities in their chromosomal makeup. Specifically, chromosomal abnormalities that occur randomly in the population are the primary focus of these types of studies. Many of the chromosomal mutations that have been studied (such as XYY) are typically not hereditary but, rather, are largely due to random mutations in chromosomal formation.

cytogenetic studies: studies of crime that focus on the genetic makeups of individuals, with a specific focus on abnormalities in chromosomal makeups

First, we should begin with the basics of chromosomal makeup, which is probably a review for most readers but may be necessary for some. The normal chromosomal makeup for women is XX, which represents an X from the mother and an X from the father. The normal chromosomal makeup for men is XY, which represents an X from the mother and a Y from the father. However, as in many species of animals, genetic mutations often occur in human beings. Consistent with evolutionary theory, virtually all possible variations of chromosomes have been found in the human population, such as XXY, XYY, and many others. We will focus our discussion on the chromosomal mutations that have been most strongly linked to criminality.

One of the first chromosomal mutations recognized as a predictor of criminal activity was that of XYY. In 1965, Patricia A. Jacobs and her colleagues presented the first major study showing that this mutation was far more common in a Scottish male population of mental patients than in the general population.[11] Specifically, in the general population, XYY occurs in about 1 of every 1,000 males.

The first major study that examined the influence of XYY sampled about 200 men in the mental hospital, which would have predicted (assuming general population occurrences) about 1 occurrence. However, the study found 13 individuals who were XYY, which suggested that individuals who have mental disorders are more likely to have XYY chromosomes than those who do not have mental disorders. In other words, males who have XYY are at least 13 times (or 1,300%) as likely to have behavioral disorders as are those without this chromosomal abnormality. Subsequent studies examining this association have not been able to dismiss the effect of XYY on criminality but have concluded that this mutation is more linked with property crime than with violent crime.[12]

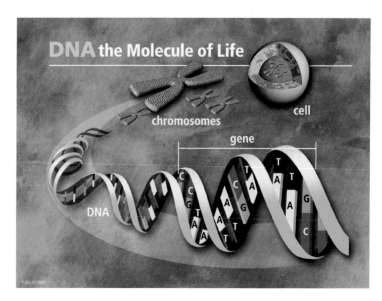

Studies consistently show that our genetics play an important role in how we think and behave.

However, even knowing this relationship, can this help in policies regarding crime? Probably not, considering that 90% of the male mental patients in the study discussed above were not XYY. Still, this study showed the importance of looking at chromosomal mutations as a predictor of criminal behavior.

Such mutations include numerous chromosomal abnormalities, such as the following:

- XYY—A male is given an extra Y chromosome, which makes him more "male-like." These individuals are often very tall but slow in terms of social and intelligence skills.

- XXY—Otherwise known as Klinefelter's syndrome, this mutation results in higher likelihood for homosexuality and other behaviors but is not typically linked to criminality.

- XXX—Otherwise known as triple X syndrome, this mutation is a form of chromosomal variation characterized by the presence of an extra X chromosome. The condition occurs only in females. Females with triple X syndrome have three X chromosomes instead of two, and this occurs about once in every 1,000 female births. Unlike most other chromosomal mutation conditions, there is typically no distinguishable difference between women with triple X syndrome and the rest of the female population. This mutation has not been consistently linked with criminality.

- XO—Commonly referred to as Turner's syndrome, this is a mutation in which females are missing an entire sex chromosome. This is typically accompanied by physical mutations (such as a webbed neck) but has not been consistently linked with criminal behavior.

One study examined the relative criminality and deviance of a group of individuals in each of these groups of chromosomal mutations (see Figure 5.2).[13] This study found that

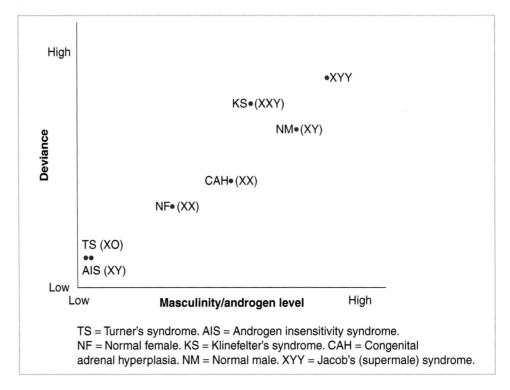

TS = Turner's syndrome. AIS = Androgen insensitivity syndrome.
NF = Normal female. KS = Klinefelter's syndrome. CAH = Congenital
adrenal hyperplasia. NM = Normal male. XYY = Jacob's (supermale) syndrome.

Figure 5.2 Hypothetical Scattergram Relating Masculinity/Androgen Level (Designated by Karyotype) to Deviance

Source: Tibbetts, S., & Hemmens, C. (2010). *Criminological Theory: Text/Reader.* Thousand Oaks, CA: SAGE Publications., p. 254.

the more the chromosomal mutation produced male hormones (androgens), the more likely the individuals were to commit crimes and deviant acts. On the other hand, the more the chromosomal mutation produced feminine hormones, the less likely the individuals were to commit criminal acts. Ultimately, all these variations in chromosomes show that there is a continuum of degrees of "femaleness" and "maleness" and that the more male-like the individual is in terms of chromosomes, the more likely he or she will be to engage in criminal behavior.

Ultimately, the cytogenetic studies showed that somewhat random abnormalities in an individual's genetic makeup can profoundly influence that person's level of criminality. Whether or not this can or should be used in policy related to crime is another matter, but the point is that genetics do indeed contribute to dispositions toward criminality. Furthermore, most of the associations seen in these chromosomal mutations directly address the influence of increased male hormones or androgens, which predict a high level of criminal traits. This leads to the next section, which discusses the effects of hormones on behavior.

AUTHOR VIDEO ▶

Neurotransmitters

HORMONES AND NEUROTRANSMITTERS: CHEMICALS THAT DETERMINE CRIMINAL BEHAVIOR

Various chemicals in the brain and the body determine how we think, perceive, and react to a range of stimuli. Hormones, such as testosterone and estrogen, carry chemical signals to the body as they are released from certain glands and structures. Some studies have shown that a relative excess of testosterone in the body is consistently linked to criminal

APPLYING THEORY TO CRIME: *AGGRAVATED ASSAULT*

Assault, especially aggravated assault, is a serious crime in terms of FBI/Uniform Crime Reports (UCR) standards, and is categorized as an Index crime. After all, an aggravated assault is typically considered an unsuccessful murder, in the sense that it usually involves an inherent intent to do serious harm, such as use of a weapon or infliction of major bodily injury. This leads us to the FBI/UCR definition of aggravated assault as being "the unlawful attack by one person upon another for the purpose of inflicting severe or aggravated bodily injury on another."

According to recent reports by the FBI, there are about 850,000 aggravated assaults each year. The National Crime Victimization Survey reported close to twice this amount in recent years, but that is consistent with differences in methodology and accounting for the "dark figure of crime," as discussed in previous chapters. Reports of such assaults were

highest in urban areas, which is not surprising since that is where homicide rates are highest. Some reviews have noted that aggravated assault occurs most often during the summer months, when people (including offenders) are more likely to be out and about.

One significant difference between most aggravated assaults and homicides is that the largest proportion of the former includes blunt objects, such as baseball bats, sticks, and so forth, as opposed to firearms, which is probably why the victims of aggravated assault do not die in the attack. Like most other Index crimes, assault rates have dramatically decreased over the past two decades. Although most of the time there is a living victim, the clearance rate of aggravated assault is close to or less than 50% for most years. This is likely due to victims not wanting to contribute to the investigation, because usually their attacker is a family member, good friend, or

other associate. Also, the attacker may be a gang member or person in the community from whom the victim fears retaliation. Regardless of the reasons, aggravated assault is not typically reported when it happens, and even when it is, the offender is typically not formally prosecuted.

Relating back to our case study at the beginning of this chapter, Faith was charged with aggravated assault because she used a weapon—a tree branch she picked up off the street—to hit a drug "customer." Although it wasn't premeditated, the use of this weapon seemed to exhibit an intent to inflict bodily harm, so it does fit the definition of aggravated assault. That is why Faith was charged with this crime. Still, intent is subjective, so if this case went to trial—which it did not—a jury would have to decide if such severe bodily harm was intended or if Faith was simply trying to retrieve her money or drugs, or if she was acting in self-defense.

Source: FBI. (2010). *Crime in the United States, 2009.* Washington, DC: U.S. Department of Justice.

or aggressive behavior, with most studies showing a moderate relationship.[14] This relationship is seen even in the early years of life.[15] On the other side of the coin, studies have also shown that hormonal changes in females can cause criminal behavior. Specifically, studies have shown that a high proportion of the women in prison for violent crimes committed those crimes during their premenstrual cycle, at which time women experience a high level of hormones that make them more "male-like," due to relatively low levels of estrogen compared with progesterone.[16]

If anyone doubts the impact of hormones on behavior, they should examine the scientific literature regarding performance on intelligence tests taken at different times of day. Virtually all individuals perform better on spatial and mathematical tests early in the day, when they have relatively high levels of testosterone and other male hormones in their bodies. On the other hand, virtually all individuals perform better on verbal tasks in the afternoon or evening, when they have relatively high levels of estrogen or other female hormones in their systems.[17] Furthermore, studies have shown that individuals given shots of androgens (male hormones) before math tests tend to do significantly better on spatial and mathematics tests than they would otherwise. Studies show the same is true for persons given shots of female hormones prior to verbal/reading tests.

It is important to realize that this process of differential levels of hormones begins very early in life, specifically in about the fifth week after conception. It is at that time that

COMPARATIVE CRIMINOLOGY: *ASSAULT*

Ranking Regions/Countries as Most Likely for Assault

This box continues the book's theme of comparing the United States with foreign nations in terms of various aspects in criminology and criminal justice (see Comparative Criminology 1.1 in Chapter 1, which provides an introduction to this feature). In this section, we will examine the findings and conclusions of various studies regarding assault, which is defined by the International Crime Victimization Survey (ICVS) as personal attacks or serious threats, without the purpose of stealing (Van Dijk, 2008, p. 78). The findings of recent studies regarding the prevalence of assault across various regions and countries of the world are enlightening in several ways.

The key measure of prevalence of assault in the world is the ICVS, a data bank that collects and standardizes police reports from more than 70 countries around the world. This measure has been conducted since 1987. It does have some weaknesses, but it is currently the best international measure of crime for such cross-national comparisons.

The ICVS has collected many years' worth of data on assault. Van Dijk (2008) synthesized the data from the ICVS regarding assault from the years 1996 to 2005. As seen in Figure 5.3, the countries with by far the highest percentages of persons victimized by assaults were those in Africa. Tied in a distant second and third were, respectively, countries in North America and Oceania (the islands near Southeast Asia and Australia).

It is not too surprising that assault tends to be more common in some of the most deprived nations in the world, such as Africa, given the studies that have linked poverty to violence. In such extreme poverty, many individuals appear to be frustrated and take out their stress on others. After all, similar results are seen for homicide rates across countries, with Southern Africa having by far the highest rates (see Chapter 9). However, the results from the ICVS reveal that assault happens frequently in all portions of the world; so assault is somewhat prevalent in virtually all societies, especially in inner-city, poor areas.

Source: Van Dijk, J. (2008). *The world of crime.* Thousand Oaks, CA: Sage.

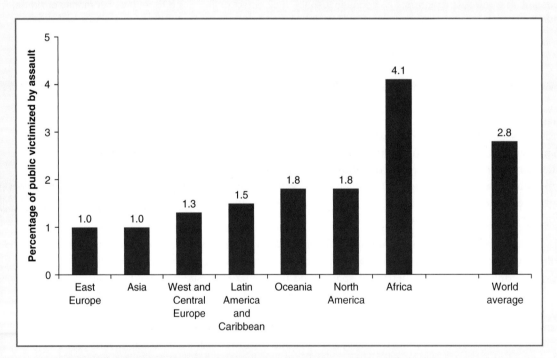

Figure 5.3 Percentages of the Public Victimized by Assaults in Urban Areas, by World Region

Source: International Crime Victimization Survey (ICVS), 1996–2005.

COMPARATIVE CRIMINOLOGY: *(CONTINUED)*

RANK AND CITY	RATE	RANK AND CITY	RATE	RANK AND CITY	RATE
1 Flint, MI	1,461.9	18 Trenton, NJ	801.9	35 Columbia, SC	667.4
2 Camden, NJ	1,288.6	19 Hartford, CT	781.7	36 Tulsa, OK	665.2
3 Detroit, MI	1,192.2	20 St. Petersburg, FL	774.8	37 Santa Maria, CA	665.1
4 St. Louis, MO	1,055.3	21 Lansing, MI	772.4	38 Oklahoma City, OK	664.1
5 Rockford, IL	1,053.9	22 Nashville, TN	771.6	39 Miami, FL	660.4
6 Little Rock, AR	987.4	23 Worcester, MA	742.1	40 Melbourne, FL	649.9
7 Memphis, TN	985.2	24 Orlando, FL	737.2	41 Atlanta, GA	634.7
8 Lowell, MA	920.8	25 Kansas City, MO	733.5	42 Rochester, NY	624.6
9 New Bedford, MA	910.6	26 Buffalo, NY	724.6	43 Syracuse, NY	609.8
10 New Haven, CT	890.6	27 Oakland, CA	718.0	44 Wichita, KS	605.8
11 Springfield, MA	880.0	28 Lawton, OK	711.8	45 Miami Gardens, FL	602.0
12 Fall River, MA	866.9	29 Lubbock, TX	689.9	46 Lynn, MA	593.0
13 Baltimore, MD	858.2	30 Redding, CA	683.7	47 Anchorage, AK	585.9
14 Springfield, IL	854.5	31 Richmond, CA	682.5	48 Odessa, TX	581.8
15 Compton, CA	851.8	32 Pueblo, CO	672.7	49 Davenport, IA	579.8
16 Stockton, CA	843.7	33 Albany, NY	669.8	50 Lafayette, LA	579.0
17 Brockton, MA	836.7	34 Tallahassee, FL	668.7		

Table 5.1 Aggravated Assault Rate in 2010 (rate out of 100,000)

Source: FBI "Crime in the United States." as reported by: O'Leary Morgan, K., Morgan, S., & Boba Santos, R. (2013). *City crime: Rankings 2011–2012*. Thousand Oaks, CA: CQ Press.

the Y chromosome of the male tells the developing fetus that it is a male and to stimulate production of higher levels of testosterone. So even during the first few months of gestation, the genes on the Y chromosome significantly alter the course of genital, and thus hormonal, development.[18]

Not only does this level of testosterone alter the genitals of the fetus/embryo through gestation, but the changes in the genital area later produce profound increases in testosterone in the teenage and early adult years. This not only produces physical differences but also huge personality and behavioral alterations.[19] High levels of testosterone and other androgens tend to "masculinize" the brain toward risk-taking behavior, while lower levels typically found in females tend to result in the default feminine model.[20] These high levels of testosterone result in numerous consequences, such as lowered sensitivity to pain, enhanced seeking of sensory stimulation, and a right-hemisphere shift of dominance in the brain, which has been linked to higher levels of spatial aptitude but lower levels of verbal reasoning and empathy. This has profound implications for criminal activity and has been found to be more likely in males than females.[21]

Ultimately, hormones have a profound effect on how individuals think and perceive their environment. It should be apparent that all criminal behavior, whether it is something we do or don't do, comes down to cognitive decisions in our 3-pound brain. So it should not

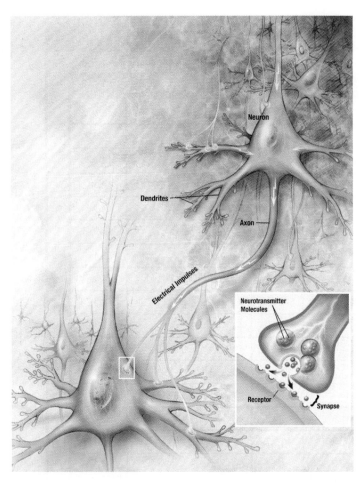

be surprising that hormones play a highly active role in this decision-making process. Although hormones are a key part of the criminal process, they probably are secondary in terms of levels of neurotransmitters, which we will now discuss.

Neurotransmitters are chemicals in the brain and body that help transmit electric signals from one neuron to another. They can be distinguished from hormones in the sense that hormones carry a signal that is not electric, whereas the signals neurotransmitters carry are indeed electric. Specifically, neurotransmitters are chemicals released when a neuron, which is the basic unit of our nervous system, wants to send an electric message to a neighboring neuron(s) (see photo this page). When a message is sent from somewhere in the brain or body, it requires that the neural pathways be told of this message, which inherently necessitates that neurotransmitters be activated in processing the signal. Specifically, in immediate time, this requires that healthy levels of various neurotransmitters be allowed to pass messages from one neuron to the next across gaps between neurons. These gaps between neurons are called synapses, and the passing of the electric message across these gaps is dependent on a multitude of neurotransmitters.

Although there are many types of neurotransmitters, the most studied in relation to criminal activity are dopamine and serotonin. **Dopamine** is the neurotransmitter most commonly linked to feeling good. For example, dopamine is the chemical that tells us when we are experiencing good sensations, such as delicious food, sex, and other pleasurable activities. Most illicit drugs elicit a pleasurable sensation through enhancing the level of dopamine in our systems. Specifically, cocaine and methamphetamine work to raise the level of dopamine in the body by telling the body to produce more dopamine or by inhibiting the enzymes that typically "mop up" the dopamine in our system after it is used.

Although a number of studies show that low levels of dopamine are linked to high rates of criminality, other studies show no association or even a positive link to criminal behavior.[22] However, it is likely that there is a curvilinear relationship between dopamine and criminal behavior, such that both extremely high and extremely low levels of dopamine are associated with deviance. Two of the most recent reviews of the literature on dopamine levels, by Wright, Tibbetts, and Daigle (2008) and Beaver (2008), have supported this curvilinear effect, as well as previous reviews such as Raine's (1993) archetypal review of the biological research up to the early 1990s.[23] Unfortunately, no conclusion can be drawn at this point about dopamine levels, due to the lack of scientific evidence regarding this chemical. However, there have been a number of more recent studies by Kevin Beaver and his colleagues regarding various receptor genes of the dopaminergic system that have been shown to be associated with criminological behaviors, especially given certain alleles on an individual's genotype.[24] Furthermore, such studies by Beaver and his colleagues have shown how receptor genes of the dopaminergic system interact with environmental factors, thus creating a biosocial effect.[25]

On the other hand, a clear conclusion can be reached about the other major neurotransmitter that has been implicated in criminal offending: serotonin. Specifically, studies have

Neurons are the basic cell in the functioning of our nervous system, and studies have shown that levels of neurotransmitters (the chemicals that transfer the electric message across neural paths) are consistently linked to criminal behavior.

neurotransmitters: nervous system chemicals in the brain and body that help transmit electric signals from one neuron to another

dopamine: a neurotransmitter that is largely responsible for good feelings in the brain; it is increased by many illicit drugs (e.g., cocaine) consistently shown that low levels of serotonin are linked with criminal offending.[26] **Serotonin** is important in virtually all information processing, whether it be learning, emotional processing, and the like; thus, it is vital in most aspects of interactions with the environment. Those who have low levels of serotonin are likely to have problems in everyday communication and life in general. Therefore, it is not surprising that low levels of serotonin are strongly linked to criminal activity.

BRAIN INJURIES

Another area of physiological problems associated with criminal activity is that of trauma to the brain. As mentioned before, the brain is responsible for virtually every criminal act an individual commits; so any problems related to this structure have profound implications regarding behavior, especially deviance and criminal activity.

Studies have consistently shown that damage to any part of the brain increases the risk of crime in the future. However, trauma to certain portions of the brain tends to have more serious consequences than trauma to other portions. Specifically, damage to the **frontal lobe** or **temporal lobe** (particularly on the left side) appears to have the most consistent associations with criminal offending.[27] These findings

LEARNING CHECK 5.3

1. According to the text, which type of cytogenetic mutation has been most linked to criminality?
   a. XXY
   b. XXX
   c. XYY
   d. XX

2. According to the text, which type of neurotransmitter, when in low levels, has been consistently linked by virtually all studies to criminality?
   a. Norepinephrine
   b. GABA
   c. Serotonin
   d. Dopamine
   e. None of the above

3. According to the text, which type of neurotransmitter is likely to have a curvilinear effect on criminality, meaning that both very high and very low levels have been linked to deviant, antisocial behavior?
   a. Norepinephrine
   b. GABA
   c. Serotonin
   d. Dopamine

Answers located at www.sagepub.com/schram

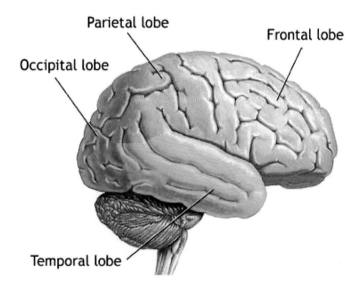

The four primary lobes of the brain, located in what is referred to as the cerebrum or cerebral cortex. Trauma to these lobes, especially the frontal and temporal lobes, has been consistently linked to criminality.

serotonin: a neurotransmitter that is key in information processing and most consistently linked to criminal behavior in its deficiency; low levels are linked to depression and other mental illnesses

frontal lobe: a region of the brain located in the frontal portion of the brain; most of the executive functions of the brain, such as problem solving, take place here

temporal lobe: the region of the brain responsible for a variety of functions and that is located right above many primary limbic structures that govern our emotional and memory functions

WHY DO THEY DO IT?

CHARLES WHITMAN

Charles Whitman, a mass murderer/sniper who killed 15 people and wounded 28 others from his perch in the main campus tower at University of Texas–Austin in 1966.

Charles Whitman's shooting spree is legendary and notorious for many reasons. He killed 15 people and injured 28 others from a landmark university tower at the University of Texas–Austin (the UT flagship campus). But what is almost more fascinating is his life story up until that fateful day.

Whitman was, by most accounts, a great person and a good soldier. He was one of the youngest Eagle Scouts ever to earn the honor. He graduated near the top of his class in high school and then went on to become a stellar member of the U.S. Marine Corps, earning the rating of sharpshooter. He used this skill when he went on his shooting rampage on August 1, 1966. It should be noted that the day before, he killed his wife and mother and left some letters (which will come up later). Then he planned out his attack on the university for the following day.

The day after Whitman killed his wife and mother, he proceeded to the main tower at UT–Austin, killed the receptionist, ascended the tower, and waited for classes to break; he then opened fire on the crowd of students. It is notable that he had taken with him a variety of materials that imply he was in it for the long haul. These items included toilet paper, spray deodorant, water canteens, gasoline, rope, and binoculars, as well as a variety of weapons, such as a machete, a hatchet, a .357 Magnum revolver, a 12-gauge sawed-off shotgun, two rifles (one with a telescopic sight), 700 rounds of ammunition, and other weapons.

Whitman was shooting people on the run and in places only a trained sharpshooter could hit. He shot a pregnant woman, who later gave birth to a still-born baby. He also shot a person crossing a street 500 yards away. This is the type of shot glorified in *Full Metal Jacket,* a Stanley Kubrick film that examined the Marine boot camps of the late 1960s. There is no doubt that Whitman was an expert sharpshooter and that the Marine Corps trained him well. Unfortunately, in this case his training was used against innocent targets. Whitman continued his mass killing for a couple of hours until several police officers were able to find a way through ground tunnels and then up to the top of the tower, where they shot and killed Whitman.

But why did he do it? The best guess we have, which directly relates to this chapter, began with one of his last letters. He wrote: "After my death, I wish an autopsy on me to be performed to see if there is any mental disorder." An autopsy was performed, and as Whitman sort of predicted, he did not simply have a mental disorder but a large brain tumor (about the size of a golf ball). As we examine how vulnerable our brain functioning can be to trauma, imagine the likely effects of a large tumor on thinking and processing skills.

Sources: Holmes, R. M., & Holmes, S. T. (2000). *Mass murders in the United States.* Upper Saddle River, NJ: Prentice Hall; Smith, J. D. (2003). *100 most infamous criminals.* New York: MetroBooks.

VIDEO ▶

Whitman

make sense, primarily because the frontal lobe (which includes the prefrontal cortex) is the area of the brain largely responsible for higher level problem solving and "executive" functioning.[28] Thus, the frontal lobe, and especially the left side of the frontal lobe, is the area that processes what we are thinking and is in charge of inhibiting us from doing what we are emotionally charged to do. After all, most of us have desires and emotional responses, but our (pre)frontal lobe, located just behind the forehead, inhibits us from acting on many of our natural instincts. Thus, any moral reasoning is reliant on this executive area of the brain because it is the region that considers long-term consequences of behavior.[29] Therefore, if there is damage to the frontal lobe, we will be far more inclined to act on our emotional urges without any logical inhibitions imputed from the frontal lobe region.

In a similar vein, the temporal lobe region is highly related to the memory and emotional structures of the brain. To clarify, the temporal lobe covers and communicates almost directly with certain structures of the brain's limbic system. Certain limbic structures largely govern our memories (hippocampus) and emotions (amygdala). Any damage to the temporal lobe, which is generally located above the ear, is likely to damage these structures or the effective communication of these structures with other portions of the brain. Therefore, it is understandable why trauma to the temporal region of the brain is linked to future criminality.

Recent studies of brain structure and activity—using the latest, most sophisticated brain-scanning techniques (the most current form of functional MRI)—have investigated the brain as it makes moral choices.[30] These studies have shown that certain regions of the brain tend to be more active in making moral decisions (e.g., the medial frontal gyrus, an area related to the emotional portion/system of the brain), versus more rational, calculated decisions (e.g., the prefrontal cortex, the decision-making portion of the brain). Of course, it depends on the situation, but when it comes to crime, it is likely that both portions of the brain play a part. The criminal acts an individual finds morally offensive will likely be governed by the emotional centers of the brain, such as the medial frontal gyrus, whereas the crimes he or she finds less morally offensive will be governed by the higher level, rational parts of the brain, such as the prefrontal cortex. It is likely that the latter instance is more about whether the individual can get away with the act, whereas the former is so deeply based in a personal moral code that the person likely wouldn't commit the act, even if he or she knew there was no chance of getting caught.[31] This is highly consistent with studies showing that moral beliefs typically trump any perceptions of getting caught for a given crime, no matter what the benefits or payout.[32] These types of brain activities, or lack thereof, are key in the next section we will discuss.

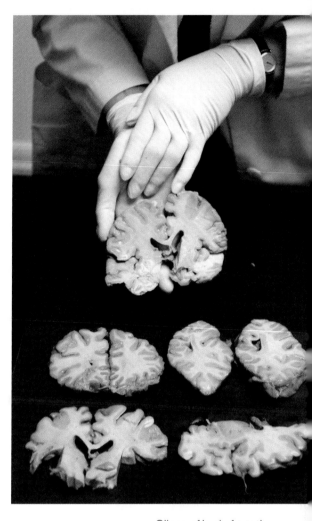

Slices of brain from the autopsy of John Wayne Gacy, a serial killer who murdered at least 33 teenage boys and young men

CENTRAL AND AUTONOMIC NERVOUS SYSTEM ACTIVITY

As has been mentioned in this chapter, the 3-pound mass that makes up our brain largely governs our decisions regarding whether to engage in criminal behavior. The brain is a key player in two different types of neurological systems that have been linked to criminal activity. The first we will discuss is the central nervous system, which encompasses our brain and spinal column and governs our voluntary motor activities.

The **central nervous system** (CNS) mostly consists of the brain and spinal column, which are largely responsible for what we as individuals choose to do, meaning our voluntary activities (see Figure 5.4). For example, that you are actually reading this sentence

REFERENCE ARTICLE

Brain Trauma

central nervous system: the portion of the nervous system that largely consists of the brain and spinal column and is responsible for our voluntary motor activities

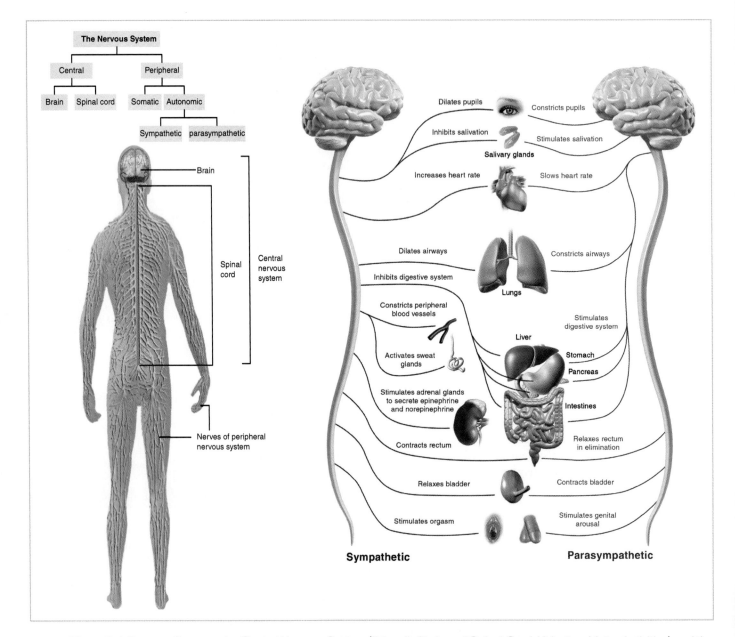

Figure 5.4 Contrast Between the Central Nervous System (Primarily Brain and Spinal Cord, Voluntary Motor Activities) and the Autonomic Nervous System (Fight-or-Flight Responses, Nonvoluntary Motor Activities)

means you are in control of this brain processing activity. Empirical studies of the influence of CNS functioning on criminality have traditionally focused on brain wave patterns, with most using electroencephalograms (EEGs). Although EEGs do not do a good job in describing which areas of the brain are active or inactive, they do reveal how much the brain as an entire organ is performing at certain times.

Specifically, studies have emphasized comparing brain wave patterns of known chronic offenders (i.e., psychopaths, repeat violent offenders) with those of "normal" persons (i.e., those who have never been charged with a crime).[33] These studies consistently show that the brain wave patterns of chronic offenders are abnormal compared with the normal population, with most studies showing slower brain wave patterns in psychopaths compared with normals.[34] Specifically, there are four types of brain wave patterns found in individuals. From slowest to fastest, they are delta, theta, alpha, and beta.[35] Delta waves are often seen when people sleep, whereas theta waves are typically observed in times of lower levels of wakefulness, such as drowsiness. Relatively, alpha waves (which tend to be divided into "slow alpha" and "fast alpha" wave patterns, as are beta waves) tend to be related to more relaxed wakefulness, and beta waves are observed with high levels of wakefulness, such as in times of extreme alertness and particularly in times of excited activity.

The studies that have compared brain wave patterns among chronic offenders and "normals" have shown significant differences. Psychopaths tend to have more activity in the theta (or sometimes "slow alpha") patterns, whereas normals tend to show more activity in the "fast alpha" or beta types of waves. These consistent findings reveal that the cortical arousal of chronic offenders tends to be significantly slower than that of persons who do not typically commit crimes. Thus, it is likely that chronic offenders generally do not have the mental functioning that would dispose them toward making accurate assessments about the consequences of criminal behavior. For a recent review of various forms of brain trauma, as well as the effects of such trauma on the functioning of the CNS, see Boots,[36] who concluded that regarding traumatic brain injury (TBI), "there is compelling evidence of a connection between TBI, antisocial behaviors, and mental health disorders that has been produced over the past two decades."[37] Consistent with these relatively low levels of cortical activity in the CNS are the findings of studies examining the autonomic nervous system.

VIDEO
Brain Injuries

The second area of the nervous system that involves the brain and has been most linked to criminal behavior is the **autonomic nervous system** (ANS), which is primarily responsible for involuntary motor activities, such as heart rate, dilation of pupils, electric conductivity in the skin, and so forth (see Figure 5.4). This is the type of physiological activity that can be measured by a polygraph machine, or lie-detector test. Polygraph measures capitalize on the inability of individuals to control these physiological responses to anxiety, which occur in most normal persons when they lie, especially regarding illegal behavior. However, such measures are not infallible, because the individuals who are most at risk of being serious, violent offenders are also the most likely to pass such tests even when they are lying (this will be further discussed below).

AUDIO
The Brain and Violence

Consistent with the findings regarding CNS arousal levels, studies have consistently shown that individuals who have a significantly low level of ANS functioning are far more likely to commit criminal acts.[38] For example, studies consistently show that chronic violent offenders tend to have much slower resting heartbeats than do normal persons, with a number of studies estimating this difference at 10 heartbeats per minute slower for offenders.[39] This is a highly significant gap that cannot be explained away by alternative theories, such as that offenders are less excited in laboratory tests. However, one recent review by Armstrong argued that the lower heart rate among serious violent criminals may not be causal but, rather, a spurious effect from a more limited ability to regulate emotions via brain functioning.[40] But even if this position is true, Armstrong admits that criminality still likely relates back to brain functioning, which is perhaps the most important component in ANS theory.

Furthermore, persons who have such low levels of ANS arousal tend to experience what is known in the psychological literature as "stimulus hunger." Stimulus hunger is a phenomenon in which individuals who have a low level of ANS arousal constantly seek out experiences and stimuli that are risky and often illegal. Most readers have probably known children who could never seem to get enough attention, with some even seeming to enjoy being spanked or receiving other forms of harsh punishment. In other words, individuals who have a low level of ANS arousal constantly seek out stimuli, to the point that they feel no anxiety from punishment (even corporal punishment) and thus do not adequately learn right from wrong through normal forms of discipline. This is perhaps one

autonomic nervous system: the portion of the nervous system that consists of our anxiety levels, such as the fight-or-flight response, as well as our involuntary motor activities (e.g., heart rate)

Child experiencing a temper tantrum, which can often happen among children who have a low-functioning autonomic nervous system

CRIME IN THE NEWS

ADHD and Behavior

of the reasons why children who are diagnosed with attention-deficit/hyperactivity disorder (ADHD) have a higher likelihood of becoming criminal than do their peers.

After all, persons who are accurately diagnosed with ADHD have a neurological abnormality; specifically, they have a significantly low level of ANS arousal. This is why doctors prescribe stimulants (e.g., Ritalin) for such youths. Although it may seem counterintuitive to prescribe a "hyperactive" person a stimulant, what the medication does is boost the individual's ANS functioning to a normal level of arousal. This enables such individuals to experience a healthy level of anxiety related to wrongdoing. Assuming that the medication is properly prescribed and at the correct dosage, such persons tend to become more attuned to the discipline they face if they violate the rules.

All readers of this book have likely encountered children who do not seem to fear punishment at all. In fact, some of them do not feel anxiety even when being physically punished (e.g., spanked). Such children are likely to have lower-than-average levels of ANS functioning and are also likely to become chronic offenders if this disorder is not addressed. This is largely due to their lack of response to discipline and inability to consider long-term consequences of risky behavior. After all, if human beings do not fear punishment or negative consequences, what will stop them from engaging in selfish, greedy behavior. So it is important to address this issue when it becomes evident that children and teenagers do not seem to be deterred by traditional forms of punishment. On the other hand, children will be children, and ADHD and other disorders have been overdiagnosed in recent years. So it is up to a well-trained physician to make such diagnoses regarding whether an individual has such a low level of ANS functioning that medication and/or therapy is required to curb deviant behavior.

Individuals with significantly low levels of ANS arousal are likely to pass lie-detector tests because they feel virtually no anxiety when they lie; so it is no surprise that many of these persons lie constantly. Thus, the very people that lie-detecting measures are meant to capture are the most likely to pass such tests, which is probably why these tests are typically not admissible in court. Only through medication and/or cognitive-behavioral therapy can such individuals develop the ability to consider the long-term consequences of their decisions.

It is notable that individuals with low levels of ANS functioning are not always destined to become chronic offenders. In fact, some evidence has shown that persons with low levels of ANS arousal often become successful corporate executives, decorated military soldiers, world-champion athletes, and high-level politicians. After all, most of these occupations require persons who seek out exciting, risky behavior, and others require the ability to lie constantly and convincingly. So there are many legal and productive outlets for the natural tendencies of individuals with low levels of ANS functioning. These individuals could perhaps be steered toward such occupations and opportunities when they present themselves. It is clearly a better option than committing antisocial acts.

Ultimately, abnormalities in the CNS and ANS systems are physiological aspects that contribute greatly to individuals' decisions regarding criminal activity, with the general conclusion that low levels of cortical arousal—in terms of both voluntary (CNS) and involuntary (ANS) activities—are clearly linked to a predisposition toward criminal activity. However, modern medical research and societal opportunities exist to help such individuals divert their tendencies toward more prosocial uses, often giving them an advantage in our competitive society.

BIOSOCIAL APPROACHES TOWARD EXPLAINING CRIMINAL BEHAVIOR

Perhaps the most important, and most recent, perspective on how criminality is formed is that of biosocial approaches toward explaining crime. Specifically, if any conclusion can be made regarding the previous theories and research in this chapter, it is that both genetics *and* environment influence behavior, particularly the interaction between the two. After all, even the most fundamental aspects of life can be explained by these two groups of factors.[41]

For example, we can predict with a great amount of accuracy how tall a person will be by looking at the individual's parents and other ancestors, because much of height is determined by a person's genotype. However, even for something as physiological as height, the environment plays a large role. As many readers will observe, individuals who are raised in poor, underdeveloped areas (e.g., Mexico, Asia) are shorter than U.S. citizens. However, individuals who descend from parents and relatives in these underdeveloped areas but are raised in the United States tend to be just as tall as (if not taller than) U.S. citizens. This is largely due to diet, which is an environmental factor.

In other words, genotype provides a certain range or "window" that determines the height of an individual, which is based on ancestral factors. But the extent to which an individual grows toward the maximum or minimum of that range is largely dependent on what occurs in the environment as he or she develops. This is why biologists make a distinction between genotype, which is directly due to genetics, and **phenotype**, which addresses the factors that are a manifestation of genetics interacting with the environment. Thus, diet influences height, as well as behavior, in human beings. The same type of biosocial effect is seen in connection with criminal behavior.

Over the past decade, a number of empirical investigations have examined the extent to which physiological variables interact with environmental variables, and the findings of these studies have shown consistent effects regarding criminality. Such studies have been more accurate than those that rely separately on either physiological/genetic variables or environmental factors. For example, findings from a cohort study in Philadelphia showed that individuals with a low birth weight were more likely to commit crime, primarily if they were raised in a lower income family or a family with a weak social structure.[42] To clarify, if a person had a low birth weight but was raised in a relatively high-income household or a strong family structure, then the person was not likely to become criminal.

LEARNING CHECK 5.4

1. According to the text, which area of the brain seems most important in terms of trauma when considering the likelihood of criminality?
   a. Occipital lobe
   b. Parietal lobe
   c. Frontal lobe
   d. Cerebellum

2. According to the text, which type of nervous system deals with the involuntary motor skills and is key in the "fight-or-flight" responses we have when in danger?
   a. Central nervous system
   b. Gastronomic nervous system
   c. Autonomic nervous system
   d. Cerebral nervous system

3. According to the text, many studies have consistently shown that individuals who have a _____ heart rate and brain waves are more likely to be criminals.
   a. Slower
   b. Faster

Answers located at www.sagepub.com/schram

---

phenotype: an observed manifestation of the interaction of genotypical traits with the environment, such as height

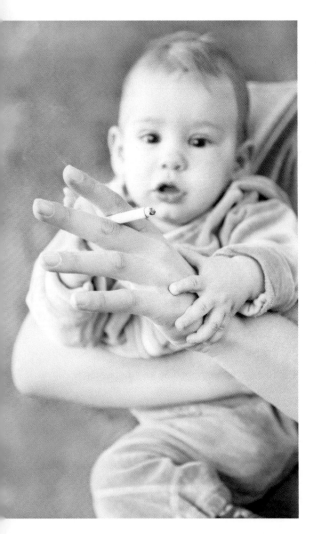

Exposure to second-hand smoke during infancy has been consistently linked to future criminal behavior.

Rather, it was the coupling of both a physiological deficiency (i.e., low birth weight) and an environmental deficit (i.e., weak family structure or low income) that had a profound effect on criminal behavior.

Consistent with these findings, other studies have shown that pre- and perinatal problems alone do not predict violence accurately. However, when perinatal problems were considered along with environmental deficits, such as weak family structure, this biosocial relationship predicted violent, but not property, crime.[43] Other studies have shown the effects on criminality of a biosocial interaction between the impact of physiological factors within the first minute of life, called Apgar scores, and environmental factors, such as exposure to cigarette smoke.[44] Additional studies have found that the interaction of maternal cigarette smoking and father's absence in the household, especially early in life, was associated with criminal behavior, which is one of the biggest predictors of chronic offending in the future.[45] One of the most revealing studies showed that although only 4% of a sample of 4,269 individuals had both birth complications and maternal rejection, this relatively small group of persons accounted for more than 18% of the total violent crimes committed by the whole sample.[46] So studies have clearly shown that the interaction of biological factors and environmental deficiencies is the most consistent predictor of criminality.

BEHAVIORAL GENETICS STUDIES

Another more modern approach to using identical twins to examine the influence of genetics and physiology on crime is the behavioral genetics approach, which estimates both the environmental and genetic influences on a given phenotype, such as criminal behavior.[47] These studies estimate heritability based on percentages derived from the variance of scores among identical versus fraternal twin pairs on a variety of characteristics and behaviors. This provides an approximate percentage of the influence in a given phenotype accounted for by genetic factors, shared environmental factors (i.e., the same across both twins in the pair, such as growing up in the same family), and nonshared environmental factors (i.e., accounting for different peer groups, significant events [e.g., employment, college education, arrests, etc.], and other nonshared environmental factors).[48]

The meta-analyses (a methodological tool used to summarize all the studies on a particular topic) of the 80-plus studies of behavioral genetics regarding criminality or antisocial behaviors consistently show that heritability/genetic factors explain about 50% of the variance in antisocial behavior.[49] It is notable that this conclusion is based on several meta-analyses, which examined studies that included thousands of twin pairs. One further insightful conclusion from these studies is that heritability estimates appear to fluctuate over the life course, with such estimates being very high during early childhood, relatively low during adolescence (during which time peer and environmental influences, and sometimes parents, are likely to have their greatest influence), and much stronger again in adulthood.[50] It should also be noted that while the heritability estimates show about half of the variation in antisocial behavior and criminality, environmental factors—such as peer, familial, or community influence—also explained about half of such variation across these many studies. This finding goes a long way toward supporting a "nature via nurture" perspective, as opposed to a "nature versus nurture" model—the latter of which was the dominant model for most of the history of criminological theorizing. As a recent summary in 2011 stated, the former perspective of biosocial interactions between physiology/genetics and environmental factors is the most accurate and current theoretical framework we have and can help us develop more fully specified models of criminality.[51]

DIET/NUTRITION

In addition, recent studies have shown that when incarcerated juveniles were assigned to diets with limited levels of simple carbohydrates (e.g., sugars), their reported violations during incarceration declined by almost half (45%).[52] Furthermore, other studies have reported that various food additives and dyes, such as those commonly found in processed foods, can also have a significant effect on criminal behavior. Thus, the old saying "You are what you eat" appears to have some scientific weight behind it, at least regarding criminal behavior.

TOXINS

Additional studies have found that high levels of certain toxins, particularly lead and manganese, can have a profound effect on behavior, including criminality. Recent studies have found a consistent, strong connection between criminal behavior and exposure to high levels of lead. Unfortunately, medical studies have also found many everyday objects that contain lead, such as the play jewelry many children wear. Also unfortunate is that children, as with virtually every toxin, are the most vulnerable to lead poisoning and the most likely to be exposed to it. Even more unfortunate is that the populations (e.g., poor, urban, etc.) most susceptible to biosocial interactions are also the most likely to be exposed to high levels of lead, largely due to old paint in their homes and other household products that contain dangerous toxins.[53] Exposure to toxins and nutritional problems are some of the best examples of the biosocial nature of criminality; specifically, the way our environments impact our physiology has the greatest impact on how we will behave, including our decisions regarding criminal behavior.

Cheap play jewelry has often been found to contain lead, a toxin that has been linked to criminality.

CASE STUDY REVISITED: FAITH (AND HOPE)

At the beginning of this chapter, we discussed the case of Faith and how she had engaged in a number of larcenies after she dropped out of high school, later participating in the distribution of methamphetamine and eventually becoming addicted to it. As you may recall, she started life in deprived circumstances, as a twin born to a poor, inner-city mother in Chicago. And after their mother dropped Faith on her head while changing their diapers, their mother gave up Faith's identical twin sister, Hope, for adoption.

That Faith suffered an early head trauma may have had a significant impact on her subsequent behavior. Studies reviewed in this chapter show that the brain, at only 3 pounds, is even smaller and more vulnerable in early life, especially in the first few months of infancy. It is likely that Faith's early head injury affected her grades in school, which

Many household paints contain lead, a toxin that has been linked to criminal behavior. Such tainted paint is more commonly found in older homes, especially inner-city, urban homes.

as you may recall were poor from even the earliest years of schooling. Such brain trauma, especially at an early age, is likely to impact the functioning of the CNS (central nervous system), which is key in governing one's voluntary motor skills.

During her elementary and middle school years, Faith was also found to have a very low heart rate, which is a key indicator of a low-functioning ANS (autonomic nervous system). Deficiencies in this ANS functioning are likely to have a vital impact on the discipline and development of individuals, because persons with low ANS functioning are far less likely to feel anxiety regarding punishment, as well as being more likely to engage in risk-taking behavior, such as illegal acts. Faith exhibited this type of behavior in suddenly quitting high school, committing acts of theft, and engaging in selling methamphetamine—not to mention using this drug.

All these behaviors were acted out without any consideration for future consequences or long-term plans, which is often the case in individuals who have a lower functioning ANS, as Faith appeared to have.

Faith was also raised by a single mother, who was largely absent because she had to work two jobs to make up for the father being physically and financially absent. This creates the prototypical interaction effect, whereby nurturing (or the environment) is weak and the nature (or physiological) portion is also weak. When an individual has weak support in terms of both nature and nurture, it creates a "perfect storm" of factors that increase that person's likelihood of becoming a criminal.

Another example of this nature via nurture effect was seen in Faith becoming obese, largely from her fast-food diet. This obesity led to early onset of puberty at age 11, which is a physiological factor. But this in turn led to the sociological factor of teenage males starting to seek her company, which increased the likelihood that she would engage in illegal behaviors (because teenage males have the highest rates of criminal offending in all societies). Thus, Faith's early menstruation (physiology) contributed to more attention from males (environment), which greatly increased her risk of criminality—thereby exemplifying the nature via nurture interaction.

Faith's identical twin sister, Hope, grew up fine in her upper-middle-class adoptive family. Although she, too, showed a relatively low heart rate in her medical checks and, like Faith, had problems with her grades early in school, she seemed to have a much easier time through high school and graduated on time. Hope did experiment with some drugs and alcohol, and she did find herself in one physical altercation with a classmate in her sophomore year (for which she was suspended from school for 2 days), but overall she did well in her teenage years and never earned a formal criminal record. She did not go to college but secured a job with the Chicago city government and is currently living in a small row house with a man and their child together. So Hope turned out to be in a similar situation as her identical twin sister, which supports the studies on identical twins reared apart. After all, both ended up taking drugs, engaging in violence, and so forth, but the social context for each was different. Ultimately, nature or biological factors tend to have an impact on behavior, often far more than the nurturing or environmental factors. All studies have been consistent in showing that. But the social environment always makes a large difference, especially in the way the same types of behaviors are handled (which will be discussed further in a later chapter).

POLICY IMPLICATIONS

Various policy implications have been introduced throughout this chapter, appropriate to the various biological or biosocial factors presented in each section. However, we feel that it is appropriate to emphasize one policy implication in particular—maternal/infant health care at all stages, including prenatal, postnatal, and first years of life. After reviewing all the extant research, as well as other experts' reviews of this literature, there is no doubt that providing adequate health care for expecting mothers, as well as extended care for infants in their first years of life, is absolutely the most cost-effective way for any society to reduce future criminality. If such maternal health care during pregnancy is not available, the risk of a multitude of birth and delivery complications rises.[54]

In fact, we know of very few respected researchers in medicine, psychology, or any other field who do not believe that this policy recommendation should be followed. For every dollar spent on such maternal/infant health care, studies show that not only will many dollars in criminal justice processing and prison time be saved but also many lives, due to the reduction in violence. There are many other policy implications, some discussed in this chapter, but we stand by maternal/infant health care in the perinatal stage as being the absolute No. 1 priority for any society in preventing biological or biosocial factors that influence future criminality.

CONCLUSION

This chapter has examined a large range of explanations for criminal behavior that place most of the blame on biological and/or psychological factors, which are typically intertwined. These types of explanations were primarily popular in the early years of the development of criminology as a science but have also been shown in recent years to be quite valid as significant factors in individual decisions to commit crime. Specifically, this chapter discussed the early studies that explored the relative influence of nature versus nurture, such as the early family studies, as well as the more robust subsequent wave of twin studies, adoption studies, and studies of identical twins raised apart. These studies revealed not only an answer to the nature versus nurture argument but also that "nature via nurture" should be emphasized when it comes to predicting criminality.

This chapter then examined the influence of hormones (e.g., testosterone) on human behavior, as well as the effect of variations in chromosomal mutations (e.g., XYY). Recent research has supported both of these theories in showing that persons with high levels of male androgens are far more likely to commit crime than are those who do not have high levels of these

hormones. The link between brain trauma and criminality was also discussed, with an emphasis on the consistent association between damage to the left and/or frontal parts of the brain, as well as trauma to special limbic structures involved in emotions and memory.

This chapter also examined theories regarding variations in levels of functioning of the CNS and the ANS, and all empirical studies have shown that low levels of functioning in these systems have links to criminality. Next, we explored the extent to which the interaction between physiological factors and environmental variables contributes to the most consistent prediction of criminal offending (hence, the importance of nature via nurture). Finally, we discussed how diet and nutrition, as well as exposure to dangerous toxins, furthered our understanding of how the environment interacts with physiology to predict future criminality. Ultimately, it is interesting that the very theories that were key in the early years of criminology as a science, such as brain structure/functioning and other early diagnostics from the first year(s) of life (e.g., Apgar scores), are now showing strong evidence of being a primary influence on criminal behavior.

SUMMARY OF THEORIES IN CHAPTER 5

THEORIES	KEY PROPONENTS	CONCEPTS/FACTORS	KEY PROPOSITIONS
Family studies	Richard L. Dugdale, H. H. Goddard	Criminality	Criminality runs in families
Twin studies	Various	Concordance for criminality	MZ twins have higher concordance than DZ twins
Adoption studies	Sarnoff Mednick and colleagues	Criminality among various adoptees	Adoptees with criminal biological parents, compared with criminal adoptive parents
MZ twins separated at birth	Various	Concordance rates of MZ twins raised apart	Criminality among MZ twins reared apart are similar
Cytogenetic studies	Patricia A. Jacobs	Chromosomal mutations	XYY individuals have more criminality
Hormonal theory	Various	Testosterone, estrogen levels	Higher levels of testosterone and lower levels of estrogen predict criminality
Neurotransmitters	Various	Dopamine, serotonin	Low levels of serotonin predict more criminality, whereas findings for other neurotransmitters are mixed
Brain injury	Various	Various lobes and brain structures	Trauma to certain portions of the brain (e.g., frontal lobe) and structures (e.g., limbic structures) predict criminality
Central nervous system functioning	Various	Brain wave patterns	Slower brain wave patterns predict criminality
Autonomic nervous system functioning	Various	Heart rate, sweating, and other indicators	Lower functioning predicts criminality
Biosocial interaction theory	Various	A variety of both physiological and developmental factors	Weak physiological factors interact with weak social and environmental factors to predict criminality

KEY TERMS

adoption studies	dizygotic twins	neurotransmitters	temporal lobe
autonomic nervous system	dopamine	phenotype	twin studies
central nervous system	family studies	selective placement	twins separated at birth studies
concordance rates	frontal lobe	serotonin	
cytogenetic studies	monozygotic twins		

STUDENT STUDY SITE

Visit the student study site at **www.sagepub.com/schram** to access links to the video, audio, city and state rankings, author podcasts, and SAGE journal and reference articles featured in this chapter, as well as additional study tools, including eFlashcards, web quizzes, web resources, and chapter outlines.

DISCUSSION QUESTIONS

1. Is there any validity to family studies in determining the role of genetics in criminal behavior? Why or why not?

2. Explain the rationale of studies that compare the concordance rates of identical twins and fraternal twins who are raised together. What do most of these studies show regarding the influence of genetics on criminal behavior? What are the criticisms of these studies?

3. Explain the rationale of studies that examine the biological and adoptive parents of adopted children. What do most of these studies show regarding the influence of genetics on criminal behavior? What are the criticisms of these studies?

4. What are the general findings in studies of identical twins separated at birth? What implications do these findings have for the importance of genetics or heritability regarding criminal behavior? Can you think of a criticism for such findings?

5. Explain what cytogenetic disorders are, and describe the related disorder that is most linked to criminal behavior. What characteristics of this type of disorder seem to be driving the higher propensity toward crime?

6. What types of hormones have been shown by scientific studies to be linked to criminal activity? Give specific examples that show this link to be true.

7. Explain what neurotransmitters are, and describe which neurotransmitters are key in predicting criminal offending. Provide support from previous scientific studies.

8. Which areas of the brain have shown the greatest vulnerability to trauma, regarding criminal offending? Does the lack of healthy functioning in these areas/lobes make sense? Why?

9. How do brain wave patterns differ among chronic, violent criminals versus normal people? Does this make sense in biosocial models of criminality?

10. How does the autonomic nervous system differ among chronic, violent criminals versus normal people? Does this make sense in biosocial models of criminality?

11. What types of policy implications would you support based on the information provided by empirical studies reviewed in this chapter?

WEB RESOURCES

Family/twin/adoption studies

http://www.criminology.fsu.edu/crimtheory/dugdale.htm

http://www.bookrags.com/research/twin-studies-wog/

Cytogenetic studies

http://bmjopen.bmj.com/content/2/1/e000650.full

https://en.wikipedia.org/wiki/Cytogenetics

Hormones and neurotransmitters

http://www.gender.org.uk/about/06encrn/63faggrs.htm

http://serendip.brynmawr.edu/biology/b103/f02/web1/kamlin.html

Autonomic/central nervous systems

http://www.crimetimes.org/

http://www.mentalhelp.net/poc/view_doc.php?type=doc&id=263

Brain trauma and crime

http://www.medicalnewstoday.com/articles/251798.php

http://www.crimetimes.org/

CHAPTER 6

Psychological/ Trait Theories of Crime

INTRODUCTION

Most sociological theories of crime focus on shared factors that influence offenders rather than factors that are unique to individuals:

> Individual difference variables are relegated to a minor, if not trivial, status in favor of influences that are thought to homogenize a collection of individuals into a population that is at risk for crime. At-risk populations are produced when social-cultural conditions combine to lower some groups' endorsement of legal norms and prohibitions.[1]

In contrast to sociological theories, psychological theories of crime focus on the influence of individuals' experiences or their emotional adjustment, as well as on their personality traits and types.[2]

This chapter highlights various psychological theories, beginning with early psychological perspectives such as the theories developed by Sigmund Freud, Hans Eysenck, Lawrence Kohlberg, and John Bowlby. The next portion of this chapter reviews what are considered more contemporary psychological theories of criminal behavior. This section begins with the controversial perspective concerning intelligence (e.g., IQ) and criminality. This section also discusses the theoretical perspective developed by James Q. Wilson and Richard J. Herrnstein. While these scholars never formally labeled their theory, one researcher suggested the name *operant-utilitarian theory of criminality*. Although Wilson and Herrnstein suggest that various factors influence criminal behavior, the most controversial aspect of their perspective was the biological factors, which include gender, low intelligence, impulsiveness, and body type. The following section explores research that has linked psychopathy with criminality. The last section in this chapter examines issues pertaining to mental illness and the criminal justice system. Specifically, we briefly discuss treatment, mental health courts, and the insanity defense.

EARLY PSYCHOLOGICAL THEORIZING REGARDING CRIMINAL BEHAVIOR

FREUD'S MODEL OF THE PSYCHE AND IMPLICATIONS FOR CRIMINAL BEHAVIOR

Sigmund Freud (1856–1939) originated psychoanalysis, which is founded on the perception of resistance used by individuals when therapists attempt to make them conscious of their unconscious.[3] The **psychoanalytic perspective** is both complex and extremely systematized. This discussion provides an overview of the general principles of psychoanalysis.

First, an individual's behavior is presumed to be due to the three aspects of his or her personality: the **id, ego**, and **superego**. The id is the source of instinctual drives; it contains everything that is present at birth.[4] Essentially, there are two types of instinctual drives: constructive and destructive. Constructive drives are usually sexual in nature. These drives make up the *libido*. Freud used the term *sex* in a broader context; thus, *sex* included

LEARNING OBJECTIVES

As students are reading this chapter, they should consider the following topics:

- Identify the general principles of psychoanalysis.

- Describe how psychoanalysis applies to criminal behavior.

- List and describe the three dimensions associated with Hans Eysenck's *theory of crime and personality*.

- Identify some of the key distinctions of the various stages of moral development.

- Describe some of the essential features of attachment theory.

- Identify some of the main issues concerning the debate over intelligence and criminality.

- Referring to James Q. Wilson and Richard J. Herrnstein, describe the three factors associated with street crime and human nature.

- List and describe the key features that distinguish a psychopath from other criminal offenders.

- Distinguish the M'Naghten rule, irresistible impulse test, Durham test, and American Law Institute's Model Penal Code.

CASE STUDY

ALBERT FISH

Albert Fish has been dubbed "America's boogeyman." From his physical appearance, many considered him a gentle, kind old man. Soon, it was revealed that this man was a serial killer, committing numerous depraved and unspeakable acts against children. Fish was brought to the attention of law enforcement after the 1928 kidnapping of a 12-year-old girl named Grace Budd. After befriending her parents, Fish told them that his niece was having a birthday party and asked if Grace would like to attend. Not suspicious of Fish's intentions, Mr. and Mrs. Budd gave their permission. Fish then escorted Grace to an isolated house in a northern suburb of New York City. He proceeded to strangle her and later mutilated her body and engaged in cannibalism.

The crime remained unsolved for 6 years. A New York City detective, William King, did not let up on the hunt for Grace's killer. He continued to question Fish during this time. Some contend that Fish would have gotten away with Grace's murder but was caught due to his arrogant and brazen behavior. In 1934, Fish sent a letter to Mrs. Budd, Grace's mother. The letter described, in gruesome detail, what he had done to Grace. Subsequently, King was able to link the letter to Fish.

While Fish was in custody, it soon became apparent that he was "a killer of unimaginable depravity, one who had spent his whole lifetime inflicting pain—on himself as well as others."[5] He considered the children he mutilated and murdered to be sacrificial offerings to the Lord. During his confession, Fish stated that he wanted to kill Edward Budd, but when he saw Edward's sister, Grace, he decided he wanted to kill her instead.[6] He later confessed to killing many children and molesting hundreds. Dr. Frederic Wertham, a New York City psychologist assigned to examine Fish, noted that he had engaged

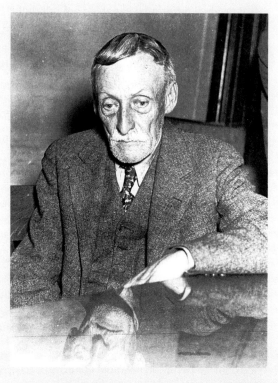

Albert Fish, nicknamed "America's boogeyman," was a notorious serial killer in the 1930s.

> IT SOON BECAME APPARENT THAT HE WAS "A KILLER OF UNIMAGINABLE DEPRAVITY, ONE WHO HAD SPENT HIS WHOLE LIFETIME INFLICTING PAIN—ON HIMSELF AS WELL AS OTHERS."

in "every sexual perversion known," as well as a few others that no one had heard of before that time.[7]

While the jurors at his trial acknowledged that Fish was insane, they maintained that he should be executed. Fish was executed in January of 1936 in Sing Sing Prison. He was 65 years old. It was reported that prior to his electrocution, Fish stated, "What a thrill it will be to die in the electric chair! It will be the supreme thrill—the only one I haven't tried."[8] How would you explain Fish's criminal behavior? Some would maintain that his behavior exceeds other types of murder because of the brutal, perverse nature of his crimes as well as the fact that he preyed on children.

those things, such as painting, that give people pleasure. The other type of instinctual drive is destructive. Destructive drives refer to such things as aggression, destruction, and death.[9]

The ego is the moderator between the demands of an instinct (i.e., the id), the *superego*, and reality. When discussing the relationship between the id and the ego, Freud noted that the ego characterizes what is referred to as reason and sanity, while the id refers to passions. Further, there are no conflicts in the id, whereas in the ego conflicts between impulses need to be resolved.[10] The superego is also designated as a conscience. This evolves during the course of an individual's development, during which he or she learns the restrictions, mores, and values of society.

Second, *anxiety*, *defense mechanisms*, and the *unconscious* are also key principles of the psychoanalytical perspective. In terms of *anxiety*, this is considered a warning of looming danger or a painful experience. This results in the individual attempting to correct the situation. In most instances, the ego can cope with this anxiety through rational measures. When this does not work, however, the ego uses irrational measures, such as rationalization. These are referred to as *ego-defense mechanisms*:[11]

> **Example:** A woman harassed by her boss at work initiates an argument with her husband. **Displacement Mechanism:** Discharging pent-up feelings, often of hostility, on objects less dangerous than those arousing the feelings.[12]

Freud maintained that large portions of the ego and superego can remain unconscious (see Figure 6.1). Further, it takes a great deal of effort for individuals to recognize their unconscious.[13] The unconscious can include disturbing memories, forbidden urges, and other experiences that have been repressed or pushed out of the conscious. While individuals may be unaware of their unconscious experiences, they continue to seek some form of expression, such as in fantasies and dreams. Until these unconscious experiences are brought to awareness, the individual could engage in irrational and destructive behavior.[14]

In reference to criminal behavior, Freud stated the following:

> I must work out an analogy between the criminal and the hysteric. In both we are concerned with a secret, with something hidden. . . . In the case of the criminal, it is a secret which he knows and hides from you, but in the case of the hysteric it is a secret hidden from him, a secret he himself does not know.[15]

One of the most well-known psychoanalysts to apply psychoanalysis to criminal behavior was August Aichhorn.[16] While most applications of psychoanalysis treated nervous disorders, he attempted to apply this method to uncover the unconscious motives of juveniles engaging in delinquent behavior. Aichhorn distinguished between *manifest* and *latent* delinquency. Delinquency is considered manifest when it results in antisocial behavior; latent delinquency is when the same state of mind exists but has not yet expressed itself through such behavior.[17]

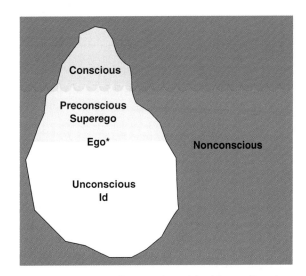

Figure 6.1 Freud's Conception of the Human Psyche (The Iceberg Metaphor)

*Note: Ego is free-floating in all three levels

psychoanalytic perspective: first, an individual's behavior is presumed to be due to the three aspects of his or her personality: the id, ego, and superego. *Anxiety, defense mechanisms,* and the *unconscious* are also key principles of the psychoanalytical perspective

id: a subconscious domain of the psyche, according to Freud, with which we are all born; it is responsible for our innate desires and drives (such as libido [sex drive]) and it battles the moral conscience of the superego

ego: the only conscious domain of the psyche; according to Freud, it functions to mediate the battle between id and superego

superego: a subconscious domain of the psyche, according to Freud; it is not part of our nature but must be developed through early social attachments

Since Aichhorn, there have been various adaptations of Freudian theory to understanding delinquency; some of these adaptations differ a great deal from the work of Freud and Aichhorn. For instance, Erik Erikson examined adolescents struggling to discover their own ego identity while negotiating, learning, and understanding social interactions, as well as developing a sense of morality and right and wrong.[18] David Abrahamsen maintained that criminal behavior is a symptom of more complex personality distortions; there is a conflict between the ego and superego, as well as the inability to control impulsive and pleasure-seeking drives, because these influences are rooted in early childhood and later reinforced through reactions to familial and social stresses.[19] As with these theories, other psychoanalytic perspectives focused on family experiences that resulted in unconscious, internal conflicts during early childhood. These conflicts can explain why one engages in delinquent behavior.[20]

HANS EYSENCK: THEORY OF CRIME AND PERSONALITY

For more than 20 years, Hans J. Eysenck developed a theory that linked personality to criminality.[21] Often, discussions of this theory emphasize that human personality can be viewed in three dimensions (i.e., the **PEN model**). He developed the Eysenck Personality Questionnaire to measure individuals on these three dimensions (see Table 6.1). The first dimension is **psychoticism**. Individuals considered to have high psychoticism are associated with being aggressive, cold, egocentric, impersonal, impulsive, antisocial, unempathic, creative, and tough-minded; individuals with low psychoticism are characterized as being empathic, unselfish, altruistic, warm, peaceful, and generally more pleasant.[22]

PEN model: discussions of this theory emphasize that human personality can be viewed in three dimensions: psychoticism, extroversion, and neuroticism

psychoticism: individuals considered to have high psychoticism are associated with being aggressive, cold, egocentric, impersonal, impulsive, antisocial, unempathic, creative, and tough-minded; individuals with low psychoticism are characterized as being empathic, unselfish, altruistic, warm, peaceful, and generally more pleasant

extroversion: in reference to the PEN model, traits associated with extroversion include being sociable, lively, active, assertive, sensation-seeking, carefree, dominant, surgent, and venturesome

neuroticism: in reference to the PEN model, neuroticism is often linked with such traits as being anxious, depressed, tense, irrational, shy, moody, and emotional and having guilty feelings and low self-esteem

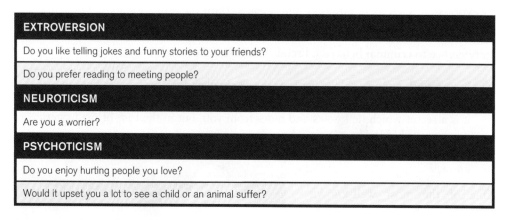

EXTROVERSION

Do you like telling jokes and funny stories to your friends?

Do you prefer reading to meeting people?

NEUROTICISM

Are you a worrier?

PSYCHOTICISM

Do you enjoy hurting people you love?

Would it upset you a lot to see a child or an animal suffer?

Table 6.1 Example Questionnaire Items From the Eysenck Personality Questionnaire–Revised

Source: Miles, J., & Hempell, S. (2004). The Eysenck personality scales: The Eysenck Personality Questionnaire–Revised (EPQ-R) and the Eysenck Personality Profiler (EPP). In M. J. Hilsenroth, D. L. Segal, & M. Hersen (Eds.), *Comprehensive handbook of psychological assessment: Personality assessment* (Vol. 2, pp. 99–100). Hoboken, NJ: John Wiley.

The second dimension is **extroversion**, with the associated traits of being sociable, lively, active, assertive, sensation-seeking, carefree, dominant, surgent, and venturesome. Introverts are usually characterized with the opposite type of traits (e.g., passive, cautious). Most individuals, however, are not exclusively extroverted or introverted; rather, these personality dimensions and associated traits are more on a continuum with a majority of individuals in the middle and not at the extremes. The last dimension is **neuroticism**, or instability, which is linked with such traits as anxiety, depression, guilty feelings, low self-esteem, tension, irrationality, shyness, moodiness, and emotionality.[23]

An Extrovert Thinks:

I was looking forward to that party.

An Introvert Thinks:

Oh, good! The party's cancelled!

These two examples illustrate how an extrovert and an introvert would react to staying home.

Nicole Hahn Rafter provided an insightful description of Eysenck's evolving development of linking criminality and personality.[24] Initially, Eysenck focused on two personality dimensions: neuroticism and extroversion. During this stage of theoretical development, he emphasized the extroversion dimension. Subsequently, he incorporated the psychoticism dimension. Thus, he moved "from his original concept of criminals as extroverts to identifying them with arch-villainous psychopaths."[25] In an effort to explain individual differences in criminality, Eysenck maintained that these can be understood in terms of biology. He offered three arguments: (1) genetics, (2) Pavlovian conditioning, and (3) neurophysiology.

In terms of genetics, or heredity, Eysenck drew on data collected from twins. He stated that "these data . . . demonstrate, beyond any question, that heredity plays an important, and possibly a vital part, in predisposing a given individual to crime."[26] This type of assertion, however, is what made many critics *distrustful* of Eysenck's conclusions.[27] The second argument, Pavlovian conditioning, is an essential part of his biological explanation, which is that

> socialized and altruistic behavior had to be learned and that this learning was mediated by means of Pavlovian conditioning. The newborn and the young child have no social conscience and behave in a purely egocentric manner. They have to acquire a "conscience" through a process of conditioning.[28]

The argument was that it is more difficult to condition extroverts than introverts. Further, he maintained that classical conditioning is associated with moral behavior. Referring to various studies, Eysenck argued that "conscience is . . . a conditioned reflex."[29] The last type of argument was initially based on brain physiology. When he raised this argument, it was relatively undeveloped. Later, he noted that the differences between extroverted and introverted behavior were due to cortical arousal. Eysenck maintained that cortical arousal differs among individuals "with respect to the ease or difficulty with which their level of arousal can be increased (arousability), their usual level of arousal, and the ease with which this arousal level can be maintained."[30]

According to Eysenck, extroverts are characterized by a low level of cortical arousal. To achieve an ideal level of arousal, extroverts need more excitement and stimuli in their environment. Further, they are less susceptible to pain and punishment, and experience less fear and anxiety. For neurotics, the biological link is in the sympathetic part of the autonomic nervous system, which involves the fight and flight reactions. Finally, the cortical arousal level is also associated with psychoticism. Like those scoring high on

JOURNAL ARTICLE

Personality Questionnaire

VIDEO

Pavlovian Conditioning

extroversion, those scoring high on psychoticism have low levels of cortical arousal and are more difficult to condition, as well as more prone to developing antisocial behavior.[31]

Eysenck's model of personality and criminality has received mixed support.[32] For instance, individuals scoring high on psychoticism are often linked to criminal behavior regardless of the methodology (e.g., self-report among the general population or offender samples). Compared with the general population, neuroticism is higher among criminal offender samples. When employing self-report methods, extroversion is usually higher among the general population but not among criminal offender samples.[33]

LAWRENCE KOHLBERG: MORAL DEVELOPMENT

A central feature of Lawrence Kohlberg's theory is that moral development occurs in stages.[34] According to Kohlberg, moral judgment evolves in children in a three-level progression, each level consisting of two stages (see Table 6.2). The **preconventional level of morality** is characteristic of designating what is considered "right" and "wrong." For instance, "telling on your brother is wrong because it is 'tattling,' breaking into the druggist's store is wrong because 'you're not supposed to steal.'"[35] What is deemed "right" and "wrong" is defined by those in authority. Within this level, Stage 1 is characterized as a "punishment and obedience orientation"; rewards and punishments are key components of this stage. An individual follows the rules for his or her benefit as well as to avoid punishment.[36] Stage 2 is when one develops moral relativity. A person recognizes that different people have varying, yet just as valid, justifications for their claims of justice.[37] Thus, an individual views justice as an equal exchange of favors, such as "you scratch my back, I'll scratch yours." Or one may view justice as a "settling of scores," such as "an eye for an eye, a tooth for a tooth."[38]

Stages 3 and 4 on the **conventional level of morality** are what Kohlberg considered the normal adult approaches used to maintain the family and social order. At Stage 3, individuals begin to understand and live by the principle of the golden rule; they appreciate such acts as generosity for those in need and forgiving those who do wrong. At Stage 4, these values of justice are expanded to the social order, such as establishing good citizenship, instilling a strong work ethic, and following the laws of society.[39] Kohlberg identified various types of justice as corrective justice (i.e., impartiality in the application

preconventional level of morality: level of morality characteristic of designating what is considered "right" and "wrong"

conventional level of morality: level of morality considered the normal adult approach used to maintain the family and social order such as the principle of the golden rule and appreciating social order

LEVEL OF MORAL DEVELOPMENT	STAGE OF REASONING
Preconventional	*Stage 1:* Right is obedience to power and avoidance of punishment.
	Stage 2: Right is taking responsibility and leaving others to be responsible for themselves.
Conventional	*Stage 3:* Right is being considerate: "uphold the values of other adolescents and adults' rules of society at large."
	Stage 4: Right is being good, with the values and norms of family and society at large.
Postconventional	*Stage 5:* Right is finding inner "universal rights" balance between self-rights and societal rules—a social contract.
	Stage 6: Right is based on a higher order of applying principles to all humankind; being nonjudgmental and respecting all human life.

Table 6.2 Level of Moral Development

Source: Adapted from Kohlberg, L. (1986). The just community approach to corrections. *Journal of Correctional Education, 37,* 57–58.

of the law and the offender paying his or her debt to society) and commutative justice (i.e., importance of contractual agreements for maintaining social order). Below is an example of commutative justice:

> Question—Is it important to keep a promise to someone you don't know well?
>
> Answer—Yes. Perhaps even more so than keeping a promise to someone you know well. A man is often judged by his actions in such situations, and to be described as being a "man of honour," or a "man of integrity" is very fulfilling indeed.[40]

On the **postconventional level of morality**, at Stage 5 an individual considers such "meta-ethical" issues as "why one should be moral." There is an attempt to balance between an individual's rights and societal rules; this is considered a "social contract" perspective of morality.[41] Kohlberg designated Stage 6 "the moral point of view." A key aspect to this stage is that a person takes equal consideration of each individual's point of view in terms of the moral decision to be made. Various principles are characterized by Stage 6, such as the principle of the maximum quality of life for each, equity or fairness in the distribution of goods and respect, and the principle of utility or benevolence.[42]

An interesting facet to understanding moral development was Carol Gilligan's work, which explored gender differences in terms of moral orientations.[43] Gilligan distinguished between the moral orientations toward "care" and those toward "justice":

> In early childhood, girls often gravitate towards the morality of care, whereas boys often gravitate towards the morality of justice. . . . Males and females alike can develop an awareness of both care and justice; but because of widespread patterns of early experience, girls often orient more towards the former and boys towards the latter.[44]

Gilligan notes that women may construct a problem differently than do men. Thus, women may fail to develop within the constraints of Kohlberg's system of moral development.[45] She noted that Kohlberg's six stages of moral development were based on a study of 84 boys whose development Kohlberg followed for more than 20 years.[46]

JOHN BOWLBY: ATTACHMENT THEORY

Development of **attachment theory** is the combined work of John Bowlby and Mary Ainsworth. Bowlby formulated the basic propositions of the theory; the roots of Bowlby's interest studying separation are in his own early childhood and in his clinical experiences while training as a psychoanalyst prior to World War II.[47] Ainsworth implemented innovated methodology to test some of Bowlby's concepts, as well as to further refine the perspective. While these scholars initially worked independently of each other, both were influenced by the work of Freud and other psychoanalytic theorists.[48] In discussing attachment theory, reference is often made to research examining the effects of separation on mother and infant monkeys. Bowlby cited this research and noted that these types of studies "show plainly not only that the attachment behaviour of young non-human primates is very similar to the attachment behaviour of young children but that their responses to separation are very similar also."[49]

Bowlby maintained that this theoretical perspective has seven essential features:

> *Specificity*—Attachments are selective or "choosy"; these attachments are often focused on one or more individuals, usually with some order of preference.
>
> *Duration*—Attachments are enduring and persistent; these attachments can sometimes last throughout a person's life.

VIDEO

Attachment Theory

postconventional level of morality: when a person attempts to balance between individual rights and societal rules

attachment theory: there are seven essential features of this theoretical perspective focusing on attachment: specificity, duration, engagement of emotion, course of development, learning, organization, and biological function

Engagement of emotion—Some of the most intense and passionate emotions are associated with attachment relationships.

Course of development—In the first 9 months of an infant's life, he or she develops an attachment to a primary figure. This primary figure is the person who provides the most fulfilling and pleasing social interaction.

Learning—While learning does have some influence on a person's attachments, the key component is social interaction.

Organization—Attachment behavior follows cognitive development as well as interpersonal maturation from birth.

Biological function—Attachment behavior has a biological function in terms of survival, which is supported by research on various species.[50]

For example, in terms of *engagement of emotion,* Bowlby discussed the emotion of fear:

In the presence of a trusted companion, fear of situations of every kind diminishes; when, by contrast, one is alone, fear of situations of every kind is magnified. Since in the lives of all of us our most trusted companions are our attachment figures, it follows that the degree to which each of us is susceptible to fear turns in great part on whether our attachment figures are present or absent.[51]

Bowlby's research focused on the effects of early parent–infant interactions and attachments.

Bowlby's interest in early parent–infant interactions evolved from his clinical work with young offenders; his theoretical framework evolved from this work.[52] From 1936 to 1939, Bowlby assessed and treated 88 children between the ages of 5 and 16 at the London Child Guidance Clinic. In his study, "Forty-Four Juvenile Thieves," he stressed the importance of studying the mother–child relationship. As Bowlby noted, inquiries were made into not only the mother's conscious attitude but also her unconscious attitude. He developed a classification procedure to distinguish the various character types. Of the 44 juveniles in his study, 14 were classified affectionless, followed by 13 classified as hyperthymic (i.e., children who tend toward constant overactivity) and 9 designated as depressed.[53] See Box 6.1 for a case history of one of the youths designated as *affectionless.*

MODERN VERSIONS OF PSYCHOLOGICAL PERSPECTIVES OF CRIMINALITY

IQ AND CRIMINAL BEHAVIOR

HISTORICAL OVERVIEW. As noted in an earlier chapter, in the early 1900s, French psychologist Alfred Binet, along with his colleague Theodore Simon, developed what was considered a more quantified measure of intelligence—the **intelligence quotient (IQ)**. Binet noted that this new approach was a "metric scale of intelligence." The Binet-Simon Intelligence Test was initially developed to study intellectual disabilities among French schoolchildren.[54] A Stanford University professor of educational psychology, Lewis M. Terman, revised the Binet-Simon Intelligence Test. Since its publication in 1916, it has been known as the Stanford-Binet Intelligence Test. Two American psychologists often considered Terman's rivals in the area of developing a scaled mental test were Henry H. Goddard and Robert Yerkes.[55]

intelligence quotient (IQ): a quantified measure of intelligence

BOX 6.1: EXAMPLE CASE HISTORY—DEREK B.

History. He was the second of two boys, the elder being a cheerful, normal lad who had never got into trouble. He lived with his mother and father, whose marriage was happy and who appeared to treat the children sensibly and kindly and without discriminating between them. On enquiry into his early history it was found that he was a wanted child and had been breast-fed for three months, after which he throve on the bottle. Indeed he was said to be a happy normal child until the age of 18 months, when he got diphtheria. Because of this he was away in [the] hospital for nine months, during the whole of which he remained unvisited by his parents. In [the] hospital he was said to have been adored by everyone, but when he returned home he was a "little stranger." He refused all food and finally was left to starve for a while. His mother described how "it seemed like looking after someone else's baby. He did not know us, he called me 'nurse' and seemed to have no affection for us at all." She said it was fully 18 months before he settled down, although to an external eye it appeared that in fact he had never done so yet.

Personality. He seemed not to care for anyone except possibly his elder brother, but even with him there were spells of unreasonable temper. Usually he was happiest when playing alone. He was markedly undemonstrative and his schoolteacher commented that emotionally he was "very controlled for a young boy." The mother also remarked on this, saying that he was quite unmoved by either affection or punishment, and she had come to regard him as hard-boiled. On the other hand he was always fighting and was at times destructive of both his own and his brother's toys. The teacher complained particularly of his untruthfulness, "wanton destructiveness" and habits of annoying other children.

Stealing and Truanting. He began school at $4\frac{1}{2}$ and liked it at first. But later he disliked the teacher and wanted his brother's teacher. This led to truanting on and off for about a month. The pilfering was noticed soon after his beginning school. It seems to have been quite undiscriminating, for he was said to pilfer from children's pockets, the teacher's desk, from shops and from his mother. Any money he obtained he spent on sweets which he would share with his brother and other children, but not with his parents. He had been repeatedly beaten both by school authorities and at home for stealing, but the beating had no effect on him beyond making him cry for a few moments.

Examination. On tests he was found to have an [IQ] of 125 and to be slow, careful and deliberate in his work. To the psychiatrist he gave the impression of being an engaging, sociable kid. But in his play there was much violent destructiveness. On many occasions he pilfered toys from the Clinic.

Diagnosis. His superficial geniality was misleading at first. As time went on it was clear that his mother's and school-teacher's accounts of his detachment represented the truth. In view of this, his destructiveness, his hard-boiledness, and his unresponsiveness, he seemed to be a typical case of *Affectionless Character.* This was clearly related to his prolonged hospitalization.

Source: Bowlby, J. (1944). Forty-four juvenile thieves: Their character and home-life. *International Journal of Psychoanalysis,* *25*, 27–28.

Goddard is credited with bringing intelligence testing to the United States.[56] He translated and adapted Binet's model to study immigrants who were coming into the United States. An interesting difference between Goddard's and Binet's assumptions about intelligence or IQ was that Goddard maintained that intelligence or IQ was static or innate; thus, an individual's IQ could not change. He argued that intelligence was passed from generation to generation; intelligence was inherited from parents. As noted earlier in this book, Goddard labeled low IQ as "feeble-mindedness." There were specified levels of feeble-mindedness, such as *moron, imbecile,* and *idiot.*[57] Goddard's *The Kallikak Family: A Study in Hereditary Feeble-Mindedness* has been considered one of the major contributions to the menace, or threat, myth considered to be linked to feeble-mindedness, as well as to the eugenic prescriptions suggested to address such problems of poverty and crime.

Goddard's *The Kallikak Family* was a genealogical study of two branches of one family. One branch had descended from a relationship between Martin Kallikak and a

LEARNING CHECK 6.1

1. According to Freud, this is also designated as a conscience:
   a. Ego
   b. Superego
   c. Libido
   d. Id

2. According to Kohlberg, this level of morality is characteristic of designating what is considered "right" and "wrong":
   a. Preconventional
   b. Conventional
   c. Postconventional
   d. Nonconventional

3. According to Eysenck, which of the following is not associated with one of the three dimensions linked to criminality?
   a. Psychoticism
   b. Extroversion
   c. Anxiety
   d. Neuroticism

Answers located at www.sagepub.com/schram

feeble-minded tavern girl. This union produced generations of indigents, criminals, prostitutes, and alcoholics. The other branch, from Martin's marriage to a Quaker, produced what were considered "good" citizens. When applying the threat, or menace, myth to the Kallikak family and others, eugenicists were not describing what were considered low-functioning *idiots* or *imbeciles* who were considered harmless and often institutionalized. Rather, they claimed that a significant number of Americans, "especially racial and ethnic minorities, did not have the inherited intelligence necessary to control their passions and that these higher-functioning morons were doomed to pauperism and crime."[58]

Between 1888 and 1915, various researchers administered intelligence tests to prisoners and boys in reform schools. For instance, in the early 1900s, the Ohio Board of Administration was convinced that more than 40% of the juveniles incarcerated in the state reformatories were "definitely feeble-minded." Further, the board maintained that it was "folly" to try to reform these juveniles because they were not immoral;

APPLYING THEORY TO CRIME: *RAPE*

Many feminists maintain that when placing rape in a historical context, one needs to realize that women have historically been considered the property of either their fathers or their husbands, and thereby denied equal status within patriarchal societies. Thus, rape has been considered only within the realm of the male's perspective (i.e., a violation of his property) rather than within the realm of a female's perspective (i.e., a violation of her body).[59] In ancient history, according to *lex talionis*—or the "an-eye-for-an-eye" philosophy when dealing with offenders—the father of a raped daughter was allowed to rape the rapist's wife. "Bride capture" involved a man raping a woman to establish a permanent relationship with her.[60]

Some feminists argue that the 19th century approaches to protecting women (e.g., chivalry) were actually efforts among the middle class to control the activities of women working in the public sphere as opposed to the private sphere (i.e., the home). Anne Clark maintains that such efforts perpetuated the myth that as long as "proper" women remained in the home, rather than "roaming the streets," they would not be vulnerable to rape.[61] During this time, it was even more difficult if women attempted to involve the court system to seek justice for the crime of rape.

Some have maintained "that the victim of a sexual assault is actually assaulted twice—once by the offender and once by the criminal justice system."[62] Since the increasing public awareness of rape in the 1970s, various legislative reforms were enacted in an effort to modify rape statutes. Changes in the legal definitions of rape reflect society's changing attitudes regarding this crime. These changes have been especially influenced by the feminist movement. In 1975, the state of Michigan led the country in reforming rape laws. First, it replaced the term *rape* with *criminal sexual conduct*. Second, it identified four degrees of criminal sexual conduct, which were differentiated by the amount of force used, resulting injury, and the age as well as mental state of the victim. This change emphasized the force or coercion used by the perpetrator rather than focusing on the resistance (or lack thereof) of the victim. This shift in perspective incorporated rape with other violent offenses. For instance, a prosecutor does not have to prove beyond a reasonable doubt that a robbery victim did not consent to the offense; thus, why should the prosecutor have to prove beyond a reasonable doubt that a rape victim did not consent to the offense?[63]

A key issue in the definition of rape is whether to include the term *sexual*. One perspective maintains that it is essential to take the "sex out of" rape; rather, rape should be viewed as a crime of violence. Rape is no different than other crimes of violence such as murder and robbery. Another perspective argues that rape is essentially sexual in nature but also violent (i.e., sexual violence). Thus, "to take the sex out of rape is to make it something it is not."[64]

These variations have two important implications regarding measuring rape in the United States. First, because of these differing definitions and procedures, state comparisons are difficult. Second, while some states may have similar legal definitions, the enforcement, prosecution, and conviction procedures may emphasize different legal and possibly extralegal factors.[65]

Given the above definitional issues pertaining to rape, it is essential to note that the Uniform Crime Reports (UCR) define forcible rape as "the carnal knowledge of a female forcibly and against her will. Attempts or assaults to commit rape by force or threat of force are also included."[66] Statutory rape and other sex offenses are not included in the UCR definition of forcible rape. In 2011, 83,425 forcible rape offenses were reported to law enforcement agencies. Of

these, 93.0% were rapes by force, and the remaining were attempts. The rate of forcible rape was about 52.7 rape offenses per 100,000 female inhabitants. When comparing these rates by region, the South has the highest rate per 100,000 female inhabitants at 37.8, followed by the Midwest at 25.3, the West at 24.1, and the Northeast at 12.8 rape offenses per 100,000 female inhabitants.

The Behavioral Science Unit of the FBI has attempted to provide a classification of rapists. Researchers have also attempted to categorize various types of rapists.[67] One such typology was developed by Raymond Knight and Robert Prentky.[68] They classified rapists into four categories: compensatory, displaced-anger, exploitive, and sadistic rapists (see Table 6.3 for a more detailed description of each type).

Four Categories of Rape

Compensatory rapists—Compensatory rapists, also referred to as power-reassurance rapists, reveal the least amount of sexual and general aggression when compared with the other typologies. These individuals also demonstrate little evidence of childhood and adolescent impulsivity, such as running away, involvement in the juvenile justice system, and problems in grammar school. Compared with the other typologies, these offenders most often come from stable families with intact parental marriages; fewer of these individuals experienced neglect and physical abuse.

In reference to adult social characteristics, compensatory rapists average a 10th-grade education level. They often are single and live with either one or both parents; this type of rapist is most likely to be dominated by an aggressive and sometimes seductive mother. They are most likely employed in menial occupations and considered steady and reliable employees. In reference to sexual deviance, the compensatory rapist may be involved in transvestism or such behavior as voyeurism, fetishism, or excessive masturbation.[69]

Displaced-anger rapists—The displaced-anger, or anger-retaliation, rapists had the most chaotic and unstable childhoods. Compared with the other typologies, more of these rapists were either adopted or placed in foster homes. They often come from single-parent homes; as with the exploitive and sadistic groups, a number of these individuals were neglected and abused.[70] In reference to adult social characteristics, the displaced-anger group's primary reason to rape is to hurt women. Rapes by such men are characterized by

(1) the presence of a high degree of nonsexualized aggression or rage, expressed through verbal and physical assaults that clearly exceed what is necessary to force the compliance of the victim; (2) clear evidence, in verbalizations or behavior, of the intent to demean, degrade, or humiliate the victim; (3) *no* evidence that aggression is eroticized or that sexual pleasure is derived from injurious acts; (4) injurious acts are *not* focused on parts of the body that have sexual significance.[71]

This group averages a 9th-grade education. This type of offender perceives himself as athletic and masculine. Thus, he may engage in sports and work in an action-oriented occupation, as well as engage in extramarital affairs. While this offender is often married, he is not violent toward his partner.

(Continued)

APPLYING THEORY TO CRIME: *(CONTINUED)*

Exploitive rapists—Exploitive, or power-assertive, rapists are twice as likely to have some contact with youth services compared with the other groups. Many of these offenders were raised in single-parent families; almost one third lived in foster homes. As with the displaced-anger rapists, a large number of these offenders were physically abused.

In reference to adult characteristics, these rapists have many domestic issues; they also may have experienced a number of unhappy marriages. They are typically well dressed and may frequent singles bars to pick up women. This type of offender may be employed in a traditionally male occupation, such as construction. He attempts to exude an image of masculinity in his physical appearance and demeanor.[72] For this offender, the "sexual behavior is hypothesized to be an impulsive, predatory act. . . . The victim seems to have little or no psychological meaning to the offender, and represents, hypothetically, a masturbatory object."[73]

Sadistic rapists—Of the various typologies, the sadistic rapist is the most dangerous. With this type of offender, as sexual arousal increases, the aggressive nature of the offense emerges; this usually results in the most bizarre and intense forms of sexually aggressive violence.[74] More than half of those designated as sadistic rapists were raised in single-parent homes. Many of these offenders were physically abused; a number of them also experienced some type of sexual deviance during childhood.

In reference to adult characteristics, the sadistic rapist is usually married, and some consider him to be a "good family man." He often lives in a middle-class residential area with low criminal activity; he typically has a better-than-average education and is employed in a white-collar occupation.[75]

Table 6.3 Four Categories of Rapists

Ian could be characterized as an *exploitive rapist* (see Table 6.3). As with many of these types of rapists, Ian was raised in various foster homes from the age of 2. During this time, he was physically abused and neglected. In his adult years, Ian had difficulty establishing and maintaining relationships, especially with women. He had two failed marriages; he had three children by these two women but was not actively involved in their lives. He had a tendency to meet women in situations that did not involve a great deal of emotional intimacy, such as in singles bars.

After his first failed marriage, Ian committed his first rape. He met the woman, Darlene, in a singles bar. They were talking in the bar and drinking quite heavily. Once the bar closed, he suggested that Darlene meet him at his house. She agreed. Soon after they arrived at his house, Ian attacked Darlene. Ian later acknowledged that he never "planned" on raping Darlene. Rather, he stated that it was more of an impulsive act—in the "spur of the moment." He had no ill feelings toward Darlene; in fact, Ian stated that "he had no feelings toward her whatsoever."

One theoretical perspective that could possibly be applied to this offense is Bowlby's *attachment theory*. Due to Ian's unstable childhood, he was unable to form healthy attachments, especially with his mother. Further, these attachments lacked specificity given the various foster homes he was placed in throughout childhood. Related to this, the attachments lacked duration; they were short-lived and sporadic, at best. The problems associated with Ian establishing healthy attachments in childhood were reflected during his adulthood. He had difficulty developing strong relationships, especially with women. This may also have contributed to his ability to rape by perceiving the victim as having "little or no psychological meaning."

rather, they were unmoral.[76] There were critics, however, of such research and the subsequent findings. Edwin Sutherland maintained that the intelligence tests administered were inadequate and there were too many variations of such tests. He also maintained that delinquency is associated more with social and environmental influences than with IQ or intelligence.[77]

RECENT DISCUSSIONS ON IQ AND CRIMINAL BEHAVIOR. For decades, the link between IQ and criminal behavior was neither studied nor discussed often in the literature. This

COMPARATIVE CRIMINOLOGY: *SEXUAL OFFENSES*

Ranking of Countries According to Sexual Offenses or Incidents Against Women

Sexual assault/rape offenses are some of the most difficult crimes for which to obtain accurate numbers. This is especially problematic when comparing such offenses across various countries. Specifically, "perceptions as to what is unacceptable sexual behavior may differ significantly across countries, even in the current era of increasingly globalized norms and values."[78] One question on the International Crime Victimization Survey asked the following:

> People sometimes grab, touch, or assault others for sexual reasons in a really offensive way. This can happen either at home or elsewhere, for instance, in a pub, the street, at school, on public transport, in cinemas, on the beach, or at one's workplace. Over the past five years has anyone done this to you?[79]

In terms of victimization, only those incidents that occurred in the previous year were included. It is essential to stress that this item covers a broad range of behaviors; these range from rape and attempted rape to less serious offenses. Table 6.4 summarizes the rates of sexual offenses or incidents against women among the various countries.

Van Dijk (2008) highlighted a few key findings from these analyses. In the group with the highest rates, the first 10 countries are considered to be "low gender equality." Low gender equality is when the social position of women is rather weak; women are oftentimes considered inferior in various social contexts, such as the family and the workplace. When looking at countries such as Finland, Denmark, the United States, the Netherlands, Canada, Switzerland, the United Kingdom, Germany, and New Zealand, their rates are relatively high considering that these countries are deemed to have higher gender equality. Citing Kangaspunta's work,[80] Van Dijk states that this may be because individuals living in countries with a more liberal view of women are more likely to report such sexual incidents or crimes.

FIFTEEN COUNTRIES WITH THE HIGHEST RATES					
1 Papua, New Guinea	11.8	6 Swaziland	6.2	11 Namibia	4.8
2 Colombia	10.2	7 Lesotho	5.7	12 Peru	4.7
3 Nigeria	8.8	8 Costa Rica	5.5	13 Serbia and Montenegro	4.6
4 India	7.0	9 Zambia	5.4	14 Finland	4.3
5 Albania	6.7	10 Botswana	5.0	15 Denmark	3.8
FIFTEEN COUNTRIES WITH MEDIUM-HIGH RATES					
16 United States	3.5	28 Germany	2.5	45 Austria	1.3
20 Netherlands	3.2	29 New Zealand	2.4	46 Brazil	1.3
21 Canada	3.1	36 Bolivia	1.8	49 Hong Kong, China	1.2
22 Switzerland	3.1	39 Mexico	1.7	51 Greece	1.1
25 United Kingdom	3.0	40 Japan	1.7	52 Italy	0.9
FIFTEEN COUNTRIES WITH THE LOWEST RATES					
58 Turkey	17.9	63 Italy	16.6	68 Japan	10.8
59 France	17.8	64 Spain	13.7	69 Portugal	9.7
60 Austria	17.2	65 Greece	13.5	70 Philippines	9.1
61 Australia	16.9	66 Croatia	12.9	71 Hong Kong, China	7.8
62 Korea, Rep.	16.7	67 Hungary	12.6	72 Azerbaijan	7.7

Table 6.4 Ranking of Countries According to Sexual Offenses or Incidents Against Women

Source: Van Dijk, J. (2008). *The world of crime: Breaking the silence on problems of security, justice, and development across the world.* Thousand Oaks, CA: Sage, p. 85.

Sources: ICVS, 1996–2005.

Alfred Binet, a French psychologist, developed a measure of intelligence known as the IQ test.

changed, however, in the 1977 study by Travis Hirschi and Michael Hindelang.[81] Hirschi and Hindelang analyzed the history of the research on the link between IQ and delinquency. They maintained that recent research on intelligence and delinquency suggests that (a) the relation is at least as strong as the relation of either class or race to official delinquency, and (b) the relation is stronger than the relation of either class or race to self-reported delinquency.

In reference to official delinquency, they analyzed various studies such as Hirschi's research on more than 3,600 boys in California.[82] Using these data, the results revealed that family status and IQ are independently related to official delinquency. Wolfgang and his colleagues' study of 8,700 boys in Philadelphia revealed a strong association between IQ and delinquency independent of class.[83] In reference to self-reported delinquency, West found that 28.4% of the worst quarter of his sample on self-reported delinquency had low IQs compared with 16.6% of the remaining three quarters.[84] Hirschi and Hindelang noted that "however delinquency is measured, IQ is able to compete on at least equal terms with class and race, the major basis of most sociological theories of delinquency."[85]

This study led to a resurgence in research on intelligence testing within the criminological perspective. Recent studies have revealed that certain types of intelligence are more important than others. For instance, several studies have shown that low verbal intelligence has the most significant influence on predicting delinquent and criminal behavior.[86] This resurgence peaked with the 1994 publication of Richard Herrnstein and Charles Murray's *The Bell Curve*. In their preface, Herrnstein and Murray stated the following:

> We are not indifferent to the ways in which this book, wrongly construed, might do harm. We have worried about them from the day we set to work. But there can be no real progress in solving America's social problems when they are as misperceived as they are today. What good can come of understanding the relationship of intelligence to social structure and public policy? Little good can come without it.[87]

While the authors changed the terminology of *moron, imbecile,* and *idiot* to relatively benign terms such as *cognitively disadvantaged,* their argument was consistent with the feeble-mindedness research of the early 20th century. Thus, people with low IQ scores are somewhat destined to be unsuccessful in school, become unemployed, produce illegitimate children, and commit crime. Herrnstein and Murray also maintained that IQ or intelligence is essentially innate, or genetically determined. Thus, there is small chance of one improving one's IQ or intelligence.[88] Stephen Tibbetts noted that *The Bell Curve* resulted in a public outcry. Symposiums at major universities and other venues essentially condemned Herrnstein and Murray's findings. Some professors at public universities were sued in court because they used this book in their classes. Further, the book received critical reviews from other scientists.[89]

JAMES Q. WILSON AND RICHARD J. HERRNSTEIN: *CRIME AND HUMAN NATURE*

In their book *Crime and Human Nature,* Wilson and Herrnstein reviewed a considerable number of criminological studies that examined the influence of genetic and familial factors on criminal behavior.[90] Lawrence Wrightsman noted that such a shift in focus may be due to the changing political climate. During the 1960s, the dominant liberal political climate was one of optimism; there was a perception that any social problem could be solved. Environmental or sociological explanations of crime were more "palatable," while biological explanations "lost favor" among many social scientists. In the 1980s, however, there was a political shift to a more conservative perspective. Wrightsman maintained that this pendulum shift was more tolerant of hereditary factors being considered to explain criminal behavior.[91] In this vein, conservatives are more likely to consider causes of crime within the individual as well as to blame the behavior on the criminal's lack of moral sense; liberals are more likely to consider the causes of crime in society, such as unequal distribution of wealth. Thus, "conservatives are much more likely to see criminals as different from normal citizens, while liberals are more likely to see them as people who have simply reacted differently to different situations they find themselves in."[92]

Wilson (at the time, a Harvard University political scientist) and Herrnstein (a Harvard University psychologist) never explicitly "named" their theory,[93] but Jack Gibbs has suggested that they use the label *operant-utilitarian theory of criminality,* since they often use concepts associated with operant psychology.[94] They maintained that there had been an overemphasis on sociological explanations for criminal behavior:

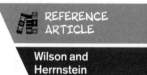

REFERENCE ARTICLE

Wilson and Herrnstein

> The existence of biological predispositions means that circumstances that activate criminal behavior in one person will not do so in another, that social forces cannot deter criminal behavior in 100 percent of a population, and that the distributions of crime within and across societies may, to some extent, reflect underlying distributions of constitutional factors. *Perhaps the simplest thing to say at this point is that crime cannot be understood without taking into account individual predispositions and their biological roots* [italics added].[95]

They attempted to explain street crime by demonstrating how human nature develops and evolves from the interaction of three factors:

1. *Social environment.* While broad societal values have often been neglected as explanations, they maintained that the shift in American culture from valuing restraint and discipline to the recent narcissistic "me-first" orientation has a strong influence on the individual level and has contributed to the increasing crime rate during the previous two decades.

2. *Family relationships.* Parents who are uncaring, inconsistent in the treatment of their children, or unskilled in dispensing rewards and punishments contribute to their children's criminal behavior. Further, a child from a broken home, or a single-parent household, is not necessarily an influential factor; rather, it is the parent's failure to teach the child the consequences of his or her actions.

3. *Biological makeup.* Qualities considered influential include gender, low intelligence, impulsiveness, and body type. These are at least partly hereditary.[96]

The third factor, *biological makeup,* is considered the most controversial aspect of Wilson and Herrnstein's theoretical perspective. They stressed that this theory was not one of predestination. Rather, they argued that the question of whether criminals are "born or made" is poorly phrased. The word *born* implies that some part of criminality may be due, categorically and permanently, to assigned constitutional factors (e.g., genetics); the word *made* implies that some aspect of criminality may be due, categorically and permanently, to social factors. They maintained that such a viewpoint "neglects, obviously, the complex interactions that exist between those causes."[97]

Wilson and Herrnstein contend that at any time, a person can choose between committing a crime and not committing a crime. The consequences of committing a crime consist of rewards and punishments. The greater the ratio of net rewards of crime to net rewards of noncrime, the greater the tendency to commit the crime.[98] Further, constitutional factors, such as intelligence and impulsivity, can influence an individual's ability to judge future and immediate rewards and punishments. Thus, "aggressive and impulsive males with low intelligence are at a greater risk for committing crimes than are young males who have developed 'the bite of conscience,' which reflects higher cognitive and intellectual development."[99] In reference to intelligence, Wilson and Herrnstein argued that social scientists have maintained that individuals identified as offenders have an average IQ of 92, which is about 8 points below the population average. Further, they contend that a low IQ may result in offenders' inability to think past "short-term" situations or difficulty understanding society's rules and the consequences of their actions.[100]

There have been various criticisms of Wilson and Herrnstein's theoretical perspective.[101] One is that they failed to empirically test their terms, such as *ratio of rewards*. Specifically, they did not adequately operationalize these terms; this makes it difficult for researchers to test their theory. Another concern was the focus on street and predatory crimes, such as murder, robbery, and burglary. They did not include other offenses such as white-collar crimes. As Gibbs questioned, "Are some white-collar crimes predatory?"[102] Some argued that while Wilson and Herrnstein objectively selected and presented relevant literature, they may have actually selectively reviewed literature that supported their theory. Thus, "although readers were given the impression that the authors' arguments were based on solid *science* and, therefore, should be *believed,* critics asserted that, in more than one instance, these arguments were based on shaky evidence."[103]

PSYCHOPATHY AND CRIME

David Lykken distinguished between the terms *sociopath* and *psychopath*. **Sociopath** refers specifically to antisocial personalities attributed to social or familial dysfunction. **Psychopath** refers to individuals whose antisocial behavior may be a result of a defect or abnormality within themselves, rather than in their rearing or socialization. In his classic book *Mask of Sanity,* Hervey Cleckley maintained that psychopaths are intelligent, self-centered, glib, superficially charming, verbally shallow, and manipulative. In terms of emotions, these individuals lack essential human characteristics such as empathy and remorse. Behaviorally, psychopaths engage in irresponsible behavior, are prone to seek novelty and excitement, and often engage in moral transgressions or antisocial acts.[104]

While there were various attempts to develop an assessment tool measuring psychopathy, it was not until the mid-1980s that major advances were made. Robert Hare developed the Psychopathy Checklist–Revised (PCL-R) to examine psychopathy in adult samples. His scale adapted some of Cleckley's concepts of psychopathic individuals, as well as including such factors as impulsivity and criminological components (e.g., criminal versatility).[105] The Hare PCL-R includes scales measuring two factors: (1) the callous, selfish, remorseless use of others, and (2) a chronically unstable and antisocial lifestyle.[106]

While a majority of the research on psychopathy has considered it as one construct, other studies in the adult literature have focused on possible subtypes or subgroups of psychopathy.[107] One subgroup is consistent with Cleckley's original concept of the *primary* psychopath:

> [An individual] who displays certain characteristics that are maladaptive and pathological (e.g., lack of conscience, irresponsibility, failure to learn from

sociopath: refers specifically to antisocial personalities that are due to social or familial dysfunction

psychopath: refers to individuals whose antisocial behavior may result from a defect or abnormality within themselves rather than in their rearing or socialization experience)—as well as key traits that appear ostensibly adaptive, or at least nonpathological (e.g., low anxiety, interpersonal charm, absence of irrational thinking).[108]

Another subgroup also has many of the same *maladaptive* traits as the primary psychopath. However, this subtype, or *secondary* psychopath, seems to be more prone to exhibit extensive symptoms of psychological turmoil and emotional reactivity. Also, these individuals tend to be more reactive, antagonistic, and impulsive; they are also more at risk for engaging in self- and other-destructive behavior such as drug use/abuse, suicidal ideation/gestures, and interpersonal aggression.[109]

Various theories have attempted to explain psychopathy. Lykken suggested the *low fear-quotient theory.* He maintained that all individuals have an innate propensity to fear certain stimuli, such as loss of support, snakes, or strangers. Individuals subsequently associate, or condition, fear of stimuli and situations that they have previously experienced with pain or punishment. This is referred to as an innate *fear quotient;* this fear quotient varies from person to person. Primary psychopaths are at the low end of this fear-quotient continuum. Further, most of the normal socialization process relies on punishing antisocial behavior. However, "someone who is relatively fearless will be relatively harder to socialize in this way"[110] (see Box 6.2).

Another explanation of psychopathy is *inhibitory defect* or *underendowment.* Some psychopathic individuals seem to act impulsively without assessing the situation, appreciating the dangers, or considering the consequences. This perspective maintains that lesions in certain areas of the brain can cause a decrease in inhibitory control in animals as well as humans. This view does not argue that *all* psychopaths have lesions or qualitative defects in their frontal cortex areas; rather, frontal lesions can produce a syndrome similar to psychopathy.[111]

The interpersonal and affective factors associated with psychopathy often are related to a socially deviant lifestyle, including irresponsible and impulsive behavior; these behaviors tend to ignore or violate social rules and mores. While not all psychopaths have any type of formal contact with the criminal justice system, the interpersonal, affective, and behavioral features of psychopathy place them at a high risk for aggression and violence.[112] With the

VIDEO

Psychopathy

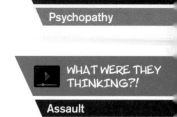

CRIME IN THE NEWS

Psychopathy

WHAT WERE THEY THINKING?!

Assault

BOX 6.2: EXAMPLE OF FEARLESSNESS

Lykken provided the following example of a child who demonstrated fearlessness. The letter was written by the mother of a teenage daughter in response to an article Lykken wrote for a popular magazine:

Your article on fearlessness was very informative. I was able to identify with many of the traits. However, being thirty-six and a single parent of three children, I have managed to backpack on the "edge" without breaking my neck. I have a 14-year-old daughter who seems to be almost fearless to anything in her environment. She jumps out second-story windows.

When she was in first grade, I came home from work one afternoon and found her hanging by her fingers from our upstairs window. I "calmly" asked her what she was doing. She replied that she was "getting refreshed." Later, she stated that she did things like that when she needed a lift—that she was bored and it made her feel better. Nancy is bright, witty, attractive, charismatic, and meets people easily. She tends to choose friends who are offbeat, antisocial, and into dope, alcohol, etc. During her month's visit here with me, she stole money from my purse, my bank card, etc., etc.

Source: Lykken, D. T. (1996). Psychopathy, sociopathy, and crime. *Society, 34,* 32.

LEARNING CHECK 6.2

1. Goddard maintained that intelligence or IQ . . .
   a. was influenced by one's environment
   b. was influenced by one's socialization
   c. was static or innate
   d. did not influence criminality

2. Wilson and Herrnstein argued that street crime is associated with human nature and maintained that human nature develops and evolves from the interaction of three factors. Which of the following is **NOT** one of those three factors?
   a. Social environment
   b. Peer relationships
   c. Family relationships
   d. Biological makeup

3. According to Cleckley, this is an individual who displays certain characteristics that are maladaptive and pathological, as well as key traits that appear ostensibly adaptive or at least nonpathological:
   a. Primary
   b. Secondary
   c. Sociopath
   d. Nonpsychopath

Answers located at www.sagepub.com/schram

widespread adoption of the PCL-R to assess psychopathy, there is empirical evidence on the association between psychopathy and criminal behavior.[113] Research has revealed that while psychopathy occurs in about 1% of the general population, these individuals make up a significant proportion of the prison population.[114]

Hare stressed that while psychopathy is closely associated with antisocial and criminal behavior, it should not be confused with criminality in general.[115] He noted that psychopaths are *qualitatively* different from other individuals involved in criminal behavior. Specifically, he noted that psychopaths have a distinct criminal career in terms of the number and type of antisocial behaviors as well as the ages when they engage in these behaviors. Also, the motivation to engage in these antisocial behaviors differs between psychopaths and nonpsychopaths.

In terms of treatment of psychopaths, most clinicians and researchers are less than optimistic about successful outcomes. A major reason is that unlike most other types of offenders, psychopaths do not experience personal distress and do not appreciate the problems associated with their attitudes and behavior. Further, when they do seek treatment, it is usually in an effort to benefit their situation, such as seeking probation and parole, rather than to improve themselves. Thus, "it is not surprising that they derive little benefit from traditional treatment programs, particularly those aimed at the development of empathy, conscience, and interpersonal skills."[116]

MENTAL HEALTH AND THE CRIMINAL JUSTICE SYSTEM

Research has revealed that the proportion of male and female jail detainees with a mental health disorder is significantly higher than in the general population.[117] Based on a 2006 Bureau of Justice Statistics Report, 56% of state prisoners, 45% of federal prisoners, and 64% of jail inmates had a mental health problem. Almost 25% of both state prisoners and jail inmates who had a mental health problem had served three or more prior incarcerations.[118] Some have referred to the "in and out" of prison and/or jail among offenders with mental health disorders as "the revolving door."[119] Various issues are associated with mental health and the criminal justice system. In this section, we briefly present some of these issues, beginning with treatment approaches.

TREATMENT

Different types of treatment methods have been implemented to address problems linked to criminality, including coping and problem-solving skills, conflict resolution, empathy, and relationships with peers, parents, and other adults.

WHY DO THEY DO IT?

ADAM LANZA

On December 14, 2012, 20-year-old Adam Lanza burst into Sandy Hook Elementary School, in Newtown, Connecticut. He was wearing a bullet-proof vest and carrying various assault weapons. Upon entering the school, he passed through two rooms, shooting school staff and elementary school students as he went. Afterward, Lanza killed himself. Lanza killed 20 children and six school staff members before his rampage was done. A secondary investigation revealed that prior to Lanza's arriving at Sandy Hook Elementary School, he had fatally shot his mother. This was the deadliest school shooting since the 2007 rampage at Virginia Tech. A disturbing distinction between these two shootings, however, is that the victims involved in the Sandy Hook attack included children ranging from kindergarten to fourth grade.[120]

Friends of the family reported that Lanza suffered from Asperger's syndrome, a form of autism. After finishing high school, Lanza spent a great deal of time alone; many commented that he was "reserved" and did not demonstrate any type of violent behavior. However, John Wlasuk, who played Babe Ruth baseball with Lanza as a child, would sometimes accompany his father, a plumber, to the Lanza home. Wlasuk stated that Lanza spent a great deal of time in the basement playing video games, many of them violent.

In the basement, Lanza had posters of military weapons. A former adviser of the Newtown High School tech club, Richard Novia, stated that Lanza was placed in a special program for those children considered at risk of being bullied. Novia, however, did not recall Lanza ever being bullied in school.[121]

During the days following this tragic event, the country went through periods of grief, mourning, shock, and anger. Governor Dannel Malloy stated that "shortly after the initial horror and the immediate grief over what occurred at Sandy Hook Elementary School . . . there was one question on the lips of many of our residents: How do we make sure this never happens again."[122] There has been a great deal of focus among the media, citizens, and policymakers on two central concerns arising from this massacre: mental health issues and access to weapons and ammunition.

One reporter noted that we still know very little about Lanza. Apparently, he spent most of his time in his room; he socialized via computer, especially with gamers. He would order computer parts and buy books without leaving his room. In fact, after the shooting, the police investigation revealed that Lanza had destroyed the hard drive on his computer. This may have provided the only true insight into his thoughts and motives.[123] Many have asked, "Why did he do it?" This is especially troubling given that he had no connection with his victims. Could there be an association between Asperger's syndrome and violent behavior? Some studies have suggested a link between violent crime and Asperger's syndrome.[124] Some also want to consider other factors such as his inclination to play violent video games, limited human contact, and accessibility to weapons.

For instance, in 1997 the **Thinking for a Change** program was developed by Glick, Bush, and Taymans, in cooperation with the National Institute of Corrections. Thinking for a Change is an integrated cognitive behavioral change program that includes cognitive restructuring, social skill development, and development of problem-solving skills. The program was designed to be used with offender populations in prisons, jails, community corrections, and probation and parole settings.[125] Generally, cognitive intervention is

> an approach that focuses on the ways that offenders think. Thinking includes a wide array of skills and processes, such as problem-solving skills, the ability to empathize with others and victims, the ability to formulate and then achieve plans for the future, and the ability to foresee the consequences of one's own behavior.[126]

Thinking for a Change: an integrated cognitive behavioral change program that includes cognitive restructuring, social skill development, and the development of problem-solving skills

JOURNAL ARTICLE

Treatment

A major impetus to developing this program was based on the experience that criminal behavior was more vulnerable to positive social change when offenders were able to apply, and incorporate, both cognitive restructuring and cognitive skills programs.[127]

In reference to studies evaluating the Thinking for a Change program, Golden, Gatchel, and Cahill's study revealed some "mixed" results concerning recidivism.[128] They concluded that the program does improve problem-solving skills among those who have completed the program. These skills may subsequently deter them from engaging in future criminal activity. The researchers also noted that future research might consider exploring whether "booster sessions," such as an aftercare group or relapse prevention measures, could further deter future criminal behavior. While cognitive-behavioral approaches have been applied to various types of programs such as case management, psychologically oriented treatments, and psychoeducational programs, such applications have, according to Wilson, resulted in there being no differences between offenders who participate in a problem-solving skills development program and those who do not.[129]

MENTAL HEALTH COURTS

The concept of **mental health courts** developed from the drug court model in the late 1980s. The first mental health court was created in 1997 in Broward County, Florida. In 2000, President Clinton signed the America's Law Enforcement and Mental Health Project bill. This bill authorized the establishment of up to 100 mental health courts and allocated $10 million a year, for up to 4 years, to maintain these courts.[130] As with drug courts, a major reason for establishing mental health courts was to address the large proportion of individuals with mental illnesses involved in the criminal justice system. Thus, "like drug courts and other 'problem-solving courts,' . . . mental health courts move beyond the criminal court's traditional focus on case processing to address the root causes of behaviors that bring people before the court."[131] The goals of mental health courts include increasing public safety for communities, increasing treatment participation and quality of life for offenders, and enhancing the use of resources in various communities.[132]

AUDIO

Mental Health Courts

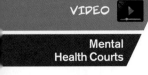

VIDEO

Mental Health Courts

Based on a "working definition," mental health courts share some common features. First, this is a specialized court for offenders with mental health illnesses. Second, as noted above, this court focuses more on problem-solving approaches. Third, participants in this court are identified through a series of mental health screenings and assessments. Fourth, these offenders voluntarily participate in a judicially supervised treatment plan. Finally, there are incentives for adherence to the treatment, as well as sanctions for nonadherence.[133] There are, however, variations among the different mental health courts, such as target population, charge accepted (i.e., misdemeanor or felony), plea arrangement, intensity of supervision, program duration, and type of treatment available.

Most of the mental health court participants suffer from serious mental illnesses. The term *mental illness* covers a broad range of psychological disorders. Within the group of disorders considered serious are those illnesses that are severe and persistent, such as schizophrenia, schizoaffective disorder, bipolar disorder, severe depression, and anxiety disorders. Most states, when determining the criteria for participating in mental health courts, consider offenders' level of functioning as well as "severe and persistent" disorders to prioritize their access to mental health services. Some mental health courts accept individuals with a broad range of mental conditions.

INSANITY DEFENSE

Society has often been challenged with the idea that a mentally ill person should not be held criminally responsible for his or her actions.[134] The idea of excusing offenders for

mental health courts: established to address the large proportion of individuals with mental illnesses involved in the criminal justice system their criminal actions due to a mental disease has been in existence for centuries.[135] **Insanity** is not a medical term; rather, it is a legal term. In this context, questions such as the following are raised:

- Is the person so insane that he or she cannot make a valid will?

- Is the person so insane that he or she should be civilly committed?

- Is the person so insane that he or she cannot be tried for his or her alleged crime?[136]

The general rationale for an insanity defense is that a person should not be punished for engaging in a criminal act if he or she could not refrain from committing the act. The law is established to punish those individuals who make the wrong choices; thus, those people who do not have free choice, due to a mental illness, should not be punished for such acts.[137]

Mental health courts, modeled after drug courts, attempt to address the issues that bring a person to court.

The standards for establishing an insanity defense vary extensively among the different states. Four states—Kansas, Montana, Idaho, and Utah—do not allow for an insanity defense. However, Montana, Idaho, and Utah do have a provision under which an offender can receive a guilty but insane, or mentally ill, verdict.[138] Among the states that do allow an insanity defense, there are essentially four types of tests—again, with modified versions as well. These include the M'Naghten rule, irresistible impulse test, Durham test, and American Law Institute's Model Penal Code (see Table 6.5).

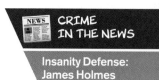

CRIME IN THE NEWS

Insanity Defense: James Holmes

THE M'NAGHTEN RULE. This is the oldest rule for determining insanity.[139] The M'Naghten case introduced the modern concept of insanity into English Common Law, which later

TEST	LEGAL STANDARD BECAUSE OF MENTAL ILLNESS	FINAL BURDEN OF PROOF	WHO BEARS THE BURDEN OF PROOF
M'Naghten	"Didn't know what he was doing or didn't know it was wrong"	Varies between proof by a balance of probabilities on the defense to proof beyond a reasonable doubt on the prosecutor	
Irresistible impulse	"Could not control his conduct"		
Durham	"The criminal act was caused by his mental illness"	Beyond reasonable doubt	Prosecutor
Brawner-A.L.I.	"Lacks substantial capacity to appreciate the wrongfulness of his conduct or to control it"	Beyond reasonable doubt	Prosecutor
Present Federal Law	"Lacks capacity to appreciate the wrongfulness of his conduct"	Clear and convincing evidence	Defense

Table 6.5 Various Insanity Defense Standards

Source: Morris, N. (n.d.). Insanity defense. *Crime File*. Washington, DC: National Institute of Justice, U.S. Department of Justice, p. 3. Retrieved from https://www.ncjrs.gov/pdffiles1/Digitization/100742NCJRS.pdf

insanity: the idea of excusing offenders for their criminal actions due to a mental disease has been in existence for centuries. The term *insanity* is not a medical term; rather it is a legal term influenced law in the United States. In 1843, Daniel M'Naghten shot Edward Drummond, who was the secretary to the British prime minister, Sir Robert Peel. M'Naghten thought that Peel, along with the "Tories," was involved in a conspiracy against him. He believed that the only feasible way to resolve this issue was to kill Peel. Unfortunately, M'Naghten mistook Drummond for Peel. The issue of insanity was formally introduced in M'Naghten's trial. He was subsequently acquitted by a jury on the grounds of insanity.[140] As noted in Table 6.5, the legal standard is that "he didn't know what he was doing or didn't know it was wrong." Specifically, the **M'Naghten rule** is as follows:

1. Every person is presumed sane unless the contrary can be proven.

2. A person suffering a "partial" delusion should be dealt with as if the circumstance of the delusion was real.

3. To establish a defence on the grounds of insanity, it must be clearly proved that

   o at the *time of committing the act,*

   o the accused was laboring under such a *defect of reason,*

   o from a *disease of the mind,*

   o as *not to know the nature and quality of the act he was doing*

   o and if he did know it (the nature and quality of the act he was doing), that *he did not know what he was doing was wrong.*[141]

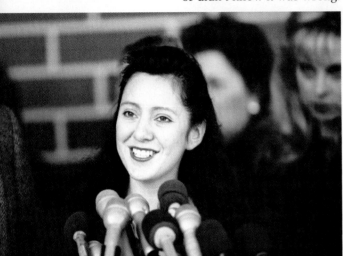

A jury found Lorena Bobbitt not guilty due to insanity under the irresistible impulse test.

M'Naghten rule: the M'Naghten case introduced the modern concept of insanity into English Common Law. The legal standard is that "he didn't know what he was doing or didn't know it was wrong"

irresistible impulse: one standard for the insanity defense. Offenders can claim that, due to a mental disease, they were unable to control their behavior

Durham: offenders are not criminally responsible, even if they are aware of their conduct, if this behavior was the "product of mental disease or defect"

IRRESISTIBLE IMPULSE. In 1897, the federal courts, and subsequently many state courts, included the **irresistible impulse** test with the M'Naghten "right–wrong" test. With this test, offenders can claim that, due to a mental disease, they were unable to control their behavior.[142] The standard for this test is that the individual could not control his or her conduct. One well-known case that used this defense was that of Lorena Bobbitt. In 1993, Lorena Bobbitt severed her husband's penis with a kitchen knife.

During the testimony, Mrs. Bobbitt stated that minutes after her drunken husband raped her, she was drinking a glass of water in the kitchen. It was at this time that she noticed a 12-inch knife. She picked up the knife and cut off her husband's penis while he was sleeping. She further testified that she had not realized what she had done until later. She noticed the knife in one hand and her husband's penis in the other. The defense argued that, given the abuse from her husband and also her various mental illnesses, after her husband raped her, Mrs. Bobbitt experienced an "irresistible impulse" to retaliate against him.[143]

DURHAM. In the 1954 case *Durham v. United States*, the court included a volitional or free choice component to the insanity defense. Thus, according to the **Durham** rule, offenders are not criminally responsible, even if they are aware of their conduct, if this behavior was the "product of mental disease or defect."[144] Judge David Bazelon noted that the M'Naghten rule was too narrow. The court argued that the test should incorporate the situation in which psychopathic disorders are qualifying conditions.[145]

AMERICAN LAW INSTITUTE'S MODEL PENAL CODE.
About one year after the Durham decision, the **American Law Institute's Model Penal Code (ALI/MPC)** developed the substantial capacity test. Due to vague and contradictory rules about insanity, a number of states adopted the ALI test. The test includes the following, in Section 4.01 of the Model Penal Code:

> A person is not responsible for criminal conduct if at the time of such conduct as a result of mental disease or defect he lacks substantial capacity either to appreciate the criminality (wrongfulness) or his conduct or to conform his conduct to the requirements of the law.[146]

A key difference between the M'Naghten and ALI/MPC tests is that the M'Naghten test stipulates that the offender must demonstrate *total* mental impairment; the ALI/MPC test stipulates that the offender must demonstrate a lack of *substantial capacity.*

LEARNING CHECK 6.3

1. Some have referred to the "in and out" of prison and/or jail among offenders with mental health disorders as . . .
    a. the downward spiral
    b. the revolving door
    c. the elevator system of justice
    d. the inverted sieve

2. Mental health courts were modeled after . . .
    a. the American Psychological Association's Model Health Court
    b. civil court procedures
    c. drug courts
    d. family courts

3. For this standard, the court included a volitional or free choice component to the insanity defense:
    a. M'Naghten rule
    b. Irresistible impulse
    c. Durham
    d. ALI/MPC

Answers located at www.sagepub.com/schram

REFERENCE ARTICLE

Mental Health and Crime

AUTHOR PODCAST

Mental Illness

American Law Institute's Model Penal Code (ALI/MPC): One standard for the insanity defense. The ALI/MPC test stipulates that the offender demonstrate a lack of *substantial capacity*

CONCLUSION

This chapter summarized theories that focus on psychological aspects of criminality rather than sociological aspects. According to Mischel, there are various fundamental assumptions of psychological theories of criminality.[147] Some of these assumptions include the following:

1. Personality is the major motivational element within individuals because it is the seat of drives and the source of motives.

2. Crimes result from abnormal, dysfunctional, or inappropriate mental processes within the personality.

3. Criminal behavior, although condemned by the social group, may be purposeful for the individual insofar as it addresses certain felt needs.

4. Normality is generally defined by social consensus.

5. Defective, or abnormal, mental processes may have a variety of causes, including a diseased mind, inappropriate learning or improper conditioning, the copying of inappropriate role models, and adjustment to inner conflicts.[148]

This chapter started with early psychological perspectives such as psychoanalysis, dimensions of an individual's personality (e.g., psychoticism, extroversion, and neuroticism) and criminal behavior, moral development, and attachment to significant others. The following section presented more current psychological perspectives, beginning with the controversial discussion concerning intelligence and criminality. Next, we reviewed the theoretical perspective some have named *operant-utilitarian theory of criminality*, which maintains that various factors influence criminal behavior, including biological factors such as gender, low intelligence, impulsiveness, and body type. We concluded this section with various issues pertaining to mental health in the criminal justice system.

At the beginning of this chapter, we presented the case of Albert Fish. It is interesting to note that while the jurors acknowledged that Fish was insane, they still argued he should be executed. This raises some interesting questions in terms of mental health and the criminal justice system. While this case was heard more than 70 years ago, these issues are central to many horrific crimes we read about in the newspaper or see on the news today. Can a person be insane but still guilty of committing a crime?

SUMMARY OF THEORIES IN CHAPTER 6

THEORY	CONCEPTS	PROPONENTS	KEY PROPOSITIONS
Psychoanalytic perspective	The id, ego, and superego; anxiety, defense mechanisms, and the unconscious	Sigmund Freud, August Aichhorn	Individuals may be unaware of their unconscious experiences; they seek some form of expression until these experiences are brought to their awareness. Attempt to uncover unconscious motives of individuals engaging in criminal behavior.
Theory of crime and personality	Personality can be viewed in three dimensions: psychoticism, extroversion, and neuroticism (the PEN model)	Hans Eysenck	Initially, Eysenck focused on two personality dimensions (neuroticism and extroversion) in terms of how they are linked to criminality; later, he incorporated the psychoticism dimension.
Moral development	Three levels of morality: preconventional, conventional, and postconventional. Within each level are two stages.	Lawrence Kohlberg	Depending on an individual's level of moral development, he or she will perceive issues such as right and wrong, avoiding punishment, responsibility, societal rules, and respecting human life in a different form of reasoning.
Attachment theory	Seven essential features: specificity, duration, engagement of emotion, course of development, learning, organization, and biological function.	John Bowlby, Mary Ainsworth	Individuals may react in certain ways if they experienced some type of separation or if they have weak attachments to significant others.
Operant-utilitarian theory of criminality	Overemphasis on sociological explanations; human nature develops and evolves from the interaction of three factors: social environment, family relationships, and biological makeup.	James Q. Wilson, Richard J. Herrnstein	Crime cannot be understood without considering the individual predispositions and their biological makeup. Constitutional factors, such as intelligence and impulsivity, can influence an individual's ability to judge future and immediate rewards and punishments.
Low fear-quotient theory	Fear quotient; fear quotient continuum; normal socialization process; psychopathy	David Lykken	Individuals have an innate propensity to fear certain stimuli, or an innate *fear quotient*. Psychopaths are at the low end of this fear-quotient continuum.

KEY TERMS

American Law Institute's Model Penal Code (ALI/MPC)

attachment theory

conventional level of morality

Durham

ego

extroversion

id

insanity

intelligence quotient (IQ)

irresistible impulse

mental health courts

M'Naghten rule

neuroticism

PEN model

postconventional level of morality

preconventional level of morality

psychoanalytic perspective

psychopath

psychoticism

sociopath

superego

Thinking for a Change

STUDENT STUDY SITE

Visit the student study site at **www.sagepub.com/schram** to access links to the video, audio, city and state rankings, author podcasts, and SAGE journal and reference articles featured in this chapter, as well as additional study tools, including eFlashcards, web quizzes, web resources, and chapter outlines.

DISCUSSION QUESTIONS

1. What are some of the key principles of Freud's psychoanalytic perspective?

2. How did Aichhorn apply some of these principles to juvenile offenders?

3. What is the PEN model?

4. How would you distinguish the various levels of moral development?

5. What are the key features of attachment theory?

6. What are some of the main issues regarding the link between intelligence and criminality?

7. According to Wilson and Herrnstein, what are the three factors associated with street crime and human nature?

8. How would you distinguish between a psychopath and other criminal offenders?

9. What are the key differences between the M'Naghten, irresistible impulse, Durham, and ALI/MPC tests?

WEB RESOURCES

American Bar Association

http://www.americanbar.org/aba.html

IQ Comparison Site

http://www.iqcomparisonsite.com/iqbasics.aspx

CHAPTER 7

Social Structure Theories of Crime I

Early Development and Strain Models of Crime

INTRODUCTION

This chapter will examine explanations of criminal conduct that emphasize the differences among varying groups in societies, particularly in the United States. Such differences among groups are easy to see in everyday life, and many theoretical models have been developed that place the blame for crime on observed inequalities and/or cultural differences among groups. In contrast to the theories presented in previous chapters, social structure theories disregard any biological or psychological variations across individuals. Rather than emphasize physiological factors, social structure theories assume that crime is caused by the way societies are structurally organized.

These social structure theories vary in many ways, most notably in what they propose as the primary constructs and processes causing criminal activity. For example, some structural models place an emphasis on variations in economic or academic success, whereas others focus on differences in cultural norms and values. Still others concentrate on the actual breakdown of the social structure in certain neighborhoods and the resulting social disorganization that occurs from this process (which we will examine in the next chapter). Regardless of their differences, all the theories examined in this chapter emphasize a common theme: Certain groups of individuals are more likely to break the law due to disadvantages or cultural differences resulting from the way society is structured.

The most important distinction of these social structure theories, as opposed to those discussed in previous chapters, is that they emphasize group differences instead of individual differences. In other words, structural models tend to focus on the macro level of analysis, as opposed to the micro level (note: these units of analysis were discussed in the first chapters of this text). Therefore, it is not surprising that social structure theories are commonly used to explain the propensity of certain racial/ethnic groups to commit crime, as well as the overrepresentation of the lower class in criminal activity.

As you will see, these theoretical frameworks were presented as early as the 1800s and reached their prominence in the early to mid-1900s, when the political, cultural, and economic climate of society at that time was most conducive to such explanations. Although social structural models of crime have diminished in popularity in recent decades,[1] there is much validity to propositions in the theories discussed in this chapter, and there are numerous applications for social structure theories in contemporary society.

EARLY THEORIES OF SOCIAL STRUCTURE: EARLY TO LATE 1800S

EARLY EUROPEAN THEORISTS: COMTE, GUERRY, AND QUETELET

Most criminological and sociological historians trace the origin of social structure theories to the research done in the early to mid-1800s by a number of European researchers, with the most important including Auguste Comte, Andre-Michel Guerry, and Adolphe Quetelet.[2] Although

CASE STUDY

THE BLACK BINDER BANDIT

A recent news story reported on a jobless man who was arrested for committing a dozen bank robberies across the Phoenix valley. The man, Cristian Alfredo Urquijo, 39, told authorities that he did it to survive and that "desperation was a great motivator." He was accused of robbing at least a dozen banks between 2010 and 2011. The criminal complaint noted that he had been laid off from work, was unable to find employment, and robbed the Phoenix-area banks to survive. He went on to say, "It's pretty simple. It's black and white. I don't have a job, I had to work, and I rob to survive." During his crime spree, authorities called him "The Black Binder Bandit" because he typically hid a revolver in a black binder and also would usually place the stolen money in this binder.

> **"IT'S PRETTY SIMPLE. IT'S BLACK AND WHITE. I DON'T HAVE A JOB, I HAD TO WORK, AND I ROB TO SURVIVE."**

Urquijo pleaded guilty to nine counts of bank robbery, three counts of armed bank robbery, and one count of use of a firearm in a crime of violence, which carries an enhanced sentence. He had originally been charged with 16 counts of bank robbery, but as often happens in plea negotiations, the counts were reduced. He did admit that he robbed at least 12 banks and also that he obtained more than $49,000 from these bank robberies.

It is obvious that this man committed these crimes because he wanted to provide for himself in an economic recession. This is just one of many examples of individuals who are strongly motivated to commit crimes—even the major federal crime of bank robbery—to deal with the economic strain or frustration of not being able to "get ahead" or achieve the American Dream of success. This chapter discusses the evolution of theories that address this concept of trying to provide for oneself or succeed while dealing with societal and economic dynamics in American society. Specifically, this chapter reviews the development of anomie/strain theory, starting with its origins among early social structure theorists, such as Durkheim, and moving to its further development by Merton. The chapter also examines the development of various strain models of offending, as well as the most modern versions of strain theory (e.g., general strain theory). We will also examine the empirical research findings on this perspective, which reveal that this framework remains one of the dominant theoretical explanations of criminal behavior in modern times. We will finish this chapter by examining the policy implications suggested by this perspective for explaining criminal behavior, and we will further discuss the case of "The Black Binder Bandit" toward the end of this chapter.

It should be noted that the Federal Bureau of Investigation (FBI) typically assigns nicknames (such as "The Black Binder Bandit") to serial bank robbers. The FBI does so for a very important reason: The public is more likely to take note of serial bank robbers when there is a catchy moniker or nickname attached to them. Apparently, this strategy is useful, because bank robbery actually has a much higher clearance rate than other types of robbery. Other notable nicknames of serial bank robbers in the past few years are "The Mesh-Mask Bandit" (still at large in Texas; wears a mesh mask), "The Geezer Bandit" (still at large in Southern California; authorities believe that the offender may be a young person disguising himself as an elderly person), and "The Michael Jackson Bandit" (still at large in Southern California; wears one glove during robberies). Although all these bank robbery suspects are still "at large," many have been caught as a result of making their nicknames notable to the public.

As surveillance photos show, Urquijo typically carried into the bank a black binder, in which he hid a revolver and the money he acquired from the bank robbery.

we will not discuss the various concepts, propositions, and research findings from their work, it is important to note that all their work was largely inspired by the social dynamics that resulted from the Industrial Revolution (defined by most historians as beginning in the mid-1700s and ending in the mid-1800s), which was in full swing at the turn of the 18th century and continued throughout most of the 1800s. Societies were quickly transitioning from primarily agriculture-based economies to more industrial-based economies, and this transition inevitably led to populations moving from primarily rural farmland to dense urban cities, which seemed to cause an enormous increase in social problems. These social problems ranged from failure to properly dispose of waste and garbage, to constantly losing children and not being able to find them, to much higher rates of crime (which continue to grow in urban areas, compared with suburban and rural areas).

The problems associated with such fast urbanization, as well as the shift in economics, led to a drastic change in basic social structures in Europe, as well as the United States. In addition to the extraordinary implications of the Industrial Revolution on the Western world, other types of revolutions were also affecting social structure. One of the first important theorists in the area of social structure theory was Auguste Comte (1798–1857); in fact, Comte is widely credited with coining the term *sociology*, because he was the first to be recognized for emphasizing and researching concepts based on more macro-level factors, such as social institutions (e.g., economic factors).[3] Although such conceptualization is elementary by today's standards, it had a significant influence on the sociological thinking that followed.

Soon after, the first modern national crime statistics were published in France in the early 1800s, and a French lawyer named Andre-Michel Guerry (1802–1866) published a report that examined these statistics and concluded that property crimes were higher in wealthy areas but violent crime was much higher in poor areas.[4] Some experts have claimed that this report likely represents the first study of scientific criminology,[5] and this was later expanded and published as a book. Ultimately, Guerry concluded that opportunity, in the sense that the wealthy had more to steal, was the primary cause of property crime. Interestingly, this conclusion is supported by recent U.S. Department of Justice statistics that show that property crime is just as common, if not more so, in middle- to upper-class households but that violent crime is not.[6] It is clear, as Guerry stated centuries ago, that there is more to steal in the wealthier areas and that poor individuals will use opportunities to steal goods and currency from wealthy households or establishments.

Cities such as New York tend to grow in predictable ways, but extreme urbanization in the 1800s and early 1900s caused crime rates to soar due to lack of infrastructure and methods to handle fast population growth.

Adolphe Quetelet (1796–1874) was a Belgian researcher who, like Guerry, examined French statistics in the mid-1800s. Besides showing relative stability in the trends of crime rates in France, such as in age distribution and female-to-male ratios of offending, Quetelet also showed that certain types of individuals were more likely to commit crime.[7] Specifically, Quetelet showed that young, male, poor, uneducated, and unemployed individuals were more likely to commit crime than were their counterparts,[8] which has also been supported by modern research. Similar to Guerry, Quetelet concluded that opportunities had a lot to do with where crime tended to be concentrated, in addition to the demographic characteristics.

Adolphe Quetelet's (1796–1874) research was seminal in the study of city crime, especially the introduction of the concept of relative deprivation and the influence this had on crime rates.

However, Quetelet added a special component by identifying the fact that greater inequality or gaps between wealth and poverty in the same place tend to excite temptations and passions. In other words, areas that exhibited large differences in wealth, with many poor and many wealthy in close proximity, had the biggest problems. This is a concept referred to as **relative deprivation** and is a quite distinctive condition from that of just a state of poverty.

For example, a number of deprived areas in the United States do not have high rates of crime, likely because virtually everyone is poor so people are generally content with their lives relative to their neighbors. However, in areas of the country where there are very poor people living in close proximity to very wealthy people, this causes animosity and feelings of deprivation compared with others in the area. Studies have supported this hypothesis,[9] and this is one of the likely explanations for why Washington, D.C., which is perhaps the most powerful city in the world but also has a large portion of severely rundown and poor areas, has such a high crime rate compared with any other jurisdiction in the country.[10] Modern studies have also supported this hypothesis in showing a clear linear association between higher crime rates and localities with more relative deprivation. For example, in more modern times, David Sang-Yoon Lee found that crime rates were far higher in cities that had wider gaps in income; specifically, the larger the gap between the 10th and 90th percentiles, the greater the crime levels.[11]

relative deprivation: the perception that results when relatively poor people live in close proximity to relatively wealthy people

In addition to the concept of relative deprivation, Quetelet also showed that areas with the most rapidly changing economic conditions also showed high crime rates (this will be discussed later in the chapter when we review Durkheim). Quetelet is perhaps best known for this comment: "The crimes . . . committed seem to be a necessary result of our social organization. . . . Society prepares the crime, and the guilty are only the instruments by which it is executed."[12] This statement makes it clear that crime is a result of societal structure and not of individual propensities or personal decision making. Thus, it is not surprising that Quetelet's position was controversial at the time when he wrote (when most theorists were focusing on free will and deterrence) and that he was rigorously attacked by critics for removing all decision-making capabilities from his model of behavior. In response, Quetelet argued that his model could help lower crime rates by leading to social reforms that address the inequalities of the social structure (such as those between the wealthy and the poor).[13]

One of the essential points of Guerry's and Quetelet's work is the positivistic nature of their conclusions. Specifically, they both concluded that the distribution of crime is not random; rather, it is the result of certain types of persons committing certain types of crime in particular places, largely due to the way society is structured and distributes resources. This perspective of criminality strongly supports the tendency of crime to be clustered in certain places, as well as among certain persons in these places. Such findings support a structural, positivistic perspective of criminality through which criminality is seen as being deterministic and, thus, caused by factors outside of an individual's control. So in some ways, the early development of structural theories was in response to the failure of the Classical approach to crime control. We will see that as the 19th century drew to a close, Classical and deterrence-based perspectives of crime fell out of favor, while social structure theories and other positivistic theories of crime, such as the structural models developed by Guerry and Quetelet, attracted far more attention.

DURKHEIM AND THE CONCEPT OF ANOMIE

Although influenced by earlier theorists (e.g., Comte, Guerry, and Quetelet), Emile Durkheim (1858–1916) was perhaps the most influential theorist in modern structural perspectives on criminality.[14] As discussed above, like most other social theorists of the 19th century, he was strongly affected by the political (e.g., American and French) revolutions and the Industrial Revolution. In his doctoral dissertation (1893) at the University of Paris—the first sociological dissertation at that institution—Durkheim developed a general model of societal development largely based on the economic/labor distribution, in which societies are seen as evolving from a simplistic mechanical society toward a multilayered organic society (see Figure 7.1).

As outlined in Durkheim's dissertation, titled *The Division of Labor in Society,* primitive mechanical societies exist as those in which all members essentially perform the same functions, such as hunting (typically males) and gathering (typically females). Although there are a few anomalies (e.g., medicine man), virtually everyone experiences essentially the same daily routine. Such similarities in daily routine and constant interaction with like members of the society lead to a strong uniformity in values, which Durkheim called the **collective conscience**. The collective conscience is the degree to which individuals of a society think alike, or as Durkheim put it, the totality of social likenesses.

Due to very little variation in the distribution of labor in these primitive **mechanical societies,** or those with "mechanical solidarity," the individuals in such societies tend to share similar norms and values, which creates a simple-layered social structure with a strong collective conscience. Because people have more or less the same jobs and mostly interact with similar individuals, they tend to think and act alike, which creates a strong solidarity among members. In mechanical societies, law functions to enforce the conformity of the group. However, as societies progress toward more modern, **organic societies** in the Industrial Age (most historians mark the Industrial Revolution as beginning in the 1750s and ending in the 1860s), the distribution of labor becomes more highly specified. There is still a form of solidarity in organic societies, called "organic

collective conscience: according to Durkheim, the extent to which people in a society share similarities or likeness; the stronger the collective conscience, the less crime in that community

mechanical societies: in Durkheim's theory, these societies were rather primitive with a simple distribution of labor (e.g., hunters and gatherers) and thus a high level of agreement regarding social norms and rules because nearly everyone is engaged in the same roles

This type of urban decay and deterioration is key in theories that emphasize neighborhood environment and how it contributes to high crime rates in certain city areas.

solidarity," because people tend to depend on other groups in the society through the highly specified division of labor, and law's primary function is to regulate interactions and maintain solidarity among the groups.

For example, modern researchers at universities in the United States tend to be trained in extremely narrow topics, some as specific as the antennae of certain species of ants. On the other hand, some individuals are gathering trash from cans on the same streets every single day. The antennae experts probably have little interaction with or in common with the garbage collectors. According to Durkheim, moving from such universally shared roles in mechanical societies to such extremely specific roles in organic societies results in huge cultural differences, which leads to giant contrasts in normative values and attitudes across such groups. Thus, the collective conscience in such societies is weak, largely because there is little agreement on moral beliefs or opinions. Therefore, the preexisting solidarity among the members breaks down and the bonds are weakened, which creates a climate for antisocial behavior.

Durkheim was clear in stating that crime is not only normal but necessary in all societies. Because Durkheim saw even crime as needed in society, his theory is often considered a good representation of functionalism, which assumes that virtually all types of behaviors or groups (such as crime and criminals) serve some important role in a given community. Specifically, he claimed that all social behaviors, especially crime, provide essential functions in a society. To clarify, Durkheim claimed that crime was needed for several reasons. First, crime is important because it defines the moral boundaries of societies. Few people know or realize what is against the societal laws until they see someone punished for a violation. This reinforces their understanding of both what the rules are and what it means to break the rules. Furthermore, the identification of rule breakers creates a bond among

organic societies: in the Durkheimian model, those societies that have a high division of labor and thus a low level of agreement about societal norms, largely because everyone has such different roles in society

MECHANICAL SOCIETIES	ORGANIC SOCIETIES
← INDUSTRIALIZATION →	
XX---XX	
Primitive	Modern
Rural	Urban
Agricultural-based economy	Industrial-based economy
Simple division of labor (few divisions)	Complex division of labor (many specialized divisions)
Law used to enforce conformity	Law used to regulate interactions among divisions
Typically stronger collective conscience	Typically weaker collective conscience

Figure 7.1 Durkheim's Continuum of Development From Mechanical to Organic Societies

the other members of the society, perhaps through a common sense of self-righteousness or superiority.

In later works, Durkheim explained that this need for bonding is what makes crime so necessary in a society. Given the possibility that a community does not have any law violators, the society will change the legal definitions of what constitutes a crime to define some of its members as criminals. Examples of this are prevalent, but perhaps the most convincing is that of the Salem witch trials, in which hundreds of individuals were accused and tried for an almost laughable offense, and more than a dozen executed. Although this case is hard to relate to, Durkheim would say it was inevitable because crime was so low in the Massachusetts Bay Colony (historical records confirm this) that the society had to come up with a fabricated criterion for defining certain members of the population as offenders.

Other examples are common in everyday life, but the most readily apparent are those in which a group of people are thrown together. The fastest way for such a group to bond is to unite over a common enemy, which often means forming into cliques and ganging up on others in the group. As college students can usually relate to, in a group of three or more roommates, two or more of the individuals will quickly join together and complain about the others in the housing unit. This is an inevitable phenomenon of human interaction and group dynamics that has always existed throughout the world across time and place. As Durkheim said, even in

Emile Durkheim's (1858–1916) theories on the progression of societies from mechanical to organic, as well as the "collective conscience" and "anomie," have heavily influenced many modern theories of crime.

> a society of saints . . . crimes . . . will there be unknown; but faults which appear venial to the layman will create there the same scandal that the ordinary offense does in ordinary consciousnesses. . . . This society . . . will define these acts as criminal and will treat them as such.[15]

This is why law enforcement should always be cautious in "cracking down" on gangs, especially during relatively inactive periods, because crackdowns will likely make the gangs stronger by giving members a common enemy. Like all societal groups, when a common enemy rears its head, the persons in the group (even those who do not typically get along) will come together and "circle the wagons" to protect themselves via strength in numbers. This usually produces a powerful bonding effect, and one that many sociologists and especially gang researchers have consistently observed.[16]

While traditional (mostly mechanical) societies could count on relative consensus in regard to moral values and norms, this sometimes led to too much control and stagnation of creative thought. However, Durkheim claimed that progress typically depends on deviating from established moral boundaries in society, especially one in the more mechanical stage. There are many examples of this, including virtually all religious icons. For example, Jesus, Buddha, and Mohammed were all criminally persecuted for deviating from societal norms in the times when they preached. Political heroes have also been prosecuted and incarcerated as criminals, such as Mahatma Gandhi in India, Nelson Mandela in South Africa, and Dr. Martin Luther King Jr. in the United States. Perhaps one of the most compelling cases is that of scientist and astronomer Galileo, who proposed a theory that Earth was not the center of the universe. Even though he was right, he was persecuted for this theory because of the demand for strict adherence to the beliefs of his society. It is obvious that Durkheim was accurate in saying that the normative structure in some societies is so strong that it hinders progress and that crime is the price societies pay for progress.

In contrast to the problems of more primitive mechanical societies, modern societies do not have such extreme restraint against deviations from the established norms. Rather, almost the opposite is true; there are too many differences across groups because the division of labor is highly specialized. Thus, the varying roles in society, such as farmers versus scientific researchers, have become quite different due to the natural transition from primitive societies to more modern, specialized groups found in our contemporary societies. This leads to extreme differences in the cultural values and norms of the various groups. In other words, there is a breakdown in the collective conscience because there is really no longer a "collective" nature in society. Therefore, law no longer is primarily interested in defining the norms of society but, rather, is focused on governing the interactions that take place among the different classes. According to Durkheim, law provides a service in regulating such interactions as societies progress toward more organic (more industrial) forms.

Importantly, Durkheim emphasized that human beings, unlike other animal species that live according to their spontaneous needs, have no internal mechanism to signal when their needs and desires are satiated. Therefore, the selfish desires of humankind are limitless, and the more an individual has, the more he or she wants. In other words, people are greedy by nature, and without something to tell them what they need and deserve, they will never feel content.[17] According to Durkheim, it is society that provides the mechanism for limiting human individuals' insatiable appetite for more and more. Specifically, he claimed that only society has the power necessary to create laws that tell citizens where the limits are drawn on their selfishness and passions.

Durkheim also noted that in times of rapid change, society fails in this role of regulating desires and expectations. This rapid change can be due to numerous factors, such as war or social movements (such as the changes seen in the United States in the 1960s). For Durkheim, the transitions he likely had in mind were those that affected the time in which he wrote—namely, just after the American and French Revolutions, and also immediately following the Industrial Revolution. Durkheim claimed that with rapid change, the ability of society to serve as a regulatory mechanism breaks down and the selfish, greedy tendencies of individuals are uncontrolled, causing a state Durkheim called **anomie**, or "normlessness." Societies in such anomic states would experience increases in many social problems, particularly criminal activity.

Durkheim was clear that it really did not matter whether the rapid change was for good or bad; either way, it would have negative effects on society. For example, whether the U.S. economy was improving (such as in the late 1960s) or quickly tanking (such as in the 1930s, during the Great Depression), according to Durkheim both of these would produce more criminal activity due to the lack of stability in regulating human expectations and desires. Interestingly, both of these periods (the late 1960s and 1930s) showed the greatest crime waves of the 20th century, particularly for murder.[18] Another fact that supports Durkheim's predictions is that middle- and upper-class individuals have higher suicide rates than those from lower classes. This is consistent with the idea that it is better to have stability, even if it means always being poor, than it is to have instability at higher levels of income.

In his most widely known work, *Suicide,* Durkheim applied his theoretical model to an act that was (and often still is) considered an individual decision—namely, the taking of one's own life. This was a major step for several reasons. First, Durkheim took an act—suicide—that would seem to be the ultimate form of free choice or free will, and he showed that this decision to take one's own life is largely determined by external, social factors. To clarify, Durkheim claimed that suicide was a "social fact," meaning that it was a product of meanings and structural aspects that result from interactions among persons.

Specifically, Durkheim showed that the rate of suicide was significantly lower among individuals who were married, young, and adherents of religions that were more interactive and communal (e.g., Judaism). All these characteristics boil down to one aspect: The more social interaction and bonding with the community, the less suicide. So Durkheim concluded that

anomie: a concept originally proposed by Durkheim, which meant *normlessness* or the chaos that takes place when a society (e.g., economic structure) changes very rapidly variations in suicide rates are due to differences in social solidarity or bonding to society. Examples of this are still seen today, as in the recent reports of high rates of suicide among persons who live in extremely rural areas, such as Alaska (which has the highest rate of juvenile suicide), northern portions of Nevada, and Wyoming and Montana. Another way of looking at the implications of Durkheim's conclusions is that social relationships are what make people feel happy and fulfilled. If we are isolated or have weak bonds with society, we will likely be depressed and discontent with our lives.

The second reason Durkheim's examination of suicide was important was that he showed that in times of both rapid economic growth and rapid decline, suicide rates increased. Although researchers later argued that crime rates did not always follow this pattern,[19] he used quantified measures to test his propositions as the positivistic approach recommended. In the least, Durkheim created a prototype of how theory and empirical research could be combined in testing differences across social groups. This theoretical framework would be drawn on heavily for one of the most influential and accepted criminological theories of the 20th century—strain theory.

LEARNING CHECK 7.2

1. Durkheim's model emphasized the evolution of more primitive _____ types of societies to more advanced forms of _____ types of societies.
   a. mechanical/organic
   b. organic/mechanical

2. Durkheim's proposed theory included the concept of "anomie," which can best be defined as _____.
   a. stability
   b. normlessness
   c. status quo
   d. deprived
   e. ritualistic

3. Durkheim wrote an entire book on what type of behavior?
   a. Murder
   b. Robbery
   c. Rape
   d. Burglary
   e. Suicide

Answers located at www.sagepub.com/schram

STRAIN THEORIES

The one thing that all forms of strain theory have in common is their emphasis on a sense of frustration in crime causation, hence the name "strain" theory. Although the theories differ regarding what exactly is causing the frustration, as well as in the way individuals cope (or don't) with such stress and anger, they all identify the strain placed on individuals as the primary causal factor in the development of criminality. Another common feature of strain theories is that they all trace their origin to the seminal theory of Durkheim, as well as to Robert K. Merton's theoretical framework.

MERTON'S STRAIN THEORY

When formulating his theory in the 1930s, Merton drew heavily on Durkheim's idea of anomie in developing his theory of structural strain.[20] As we shall see in this chapter, although Merton altered the way anomie was defined, it is apparent that Durkheim's theoretical framework was a vital influence in the evolution of strain theory. By combining Durkheimian concepts and propositions with an emphasis on American culture, Merton's structural model became one of the most popular perspectives in criminological thought in the early 1900s and remains one of the most cited theories of crime in criminological literature.

CULTURAL CONTEXT AND ASSUMPTIONS OF STRAIN THEORY

Some have claimed that Merton's seminal piece in 1938 was perhaps the most influential theoretical formulation in criminological literature, and one of the most frequently cited papers in sociology.[21] Although partially due to its strong foundation in previous structural theories, the popularity of Merton's strain theory is likely more related to the timing of its publication. As we have discussed previously, virtually every theory addressed in this book became popular when it did because the political and social climate at the time desired that type of theory for its fit with the current perspective on how the world works. Perhaps no theory better represents this phenomenon than strain theory.

Virtually all historians would agree that the most significant social issue in the 1930s was the economy. The Great Depression, largely a result of the stock market crash in 1929, affected virtually every aspect of life in the United States. Not only did unemployment and extreme poverty soar, but suicide rates rose and crime rates skyrocketed, particularly murder rates.[22] So it is not surprising that there was fertile ground in American society for a theory of crime that placed virtually all the blame on the economic structure in the United States.

Not only was society ready for a perspective such as strain theory, but on the other side of the coin, Merton was highly influenced by what he saw happening to the country during the Great Depression. Specifically, he observed how much the economic institution impacted almost all other social factors, particularly crime. He watched how the breakdown of the economic structure drove people to kill themselves or others, not to mention the rise in property crimes, such as theft. After all, many individuals who had once been successful were now poor, and some felt driven to crime for survival. Notably, Durkheim's hypotheses regarding crime and suicide were supported during this time of rapid change, and Merton apparently realized that the framework simply had to be updated and supplemented.

One of the key assumptions distinguishing strain theory from Durkheim's perspective is that Merton altered his version of what "anomie" means, a definition we will explore below. Specifically, Merton discussed the nearly universal socialization of the American Dream in U.S. society. To clarify, this is the idea that as long as someone works hard and pays his or her dues, that person will achieve every goal in the end. According to Merton, the socialized image of the goal is material wealth, whereas the socialized concept of the means of achieving the goal is hard work (e.g., education, labor). So the conventional model of the American Dream was consistent with the Protestant Work Ethic of working hard for a long time and knowing you will be repaid in the distant future.

Furthermore, Merton claimed that nearly everyone is socialized to believe in the American Dream, no matter what economic class they are raised in. There is some empirical support for this belief, which makes sense because virtually all parents, even if they are poor, want to instill in their children a hope for the future, particularly if one is willing to work hard in school and/or at a job. In fact, parents and society usually use celebrities as examples of this process—namely, those individuals who started off poor and rose to wealth. Modern examples include former Secretary of State Colin Powell, Dallas Mavericks owner Mark Cuban, Oscar winner Hilary Swank, and Hollywood director/screenwriter Quentin Tarantino, not to mention Arnold Schwarzenegger, who went from teenage immigrant to Mr. Olympia and governor of California.

These stories epitomize the American Dream, but parents and society do not always teach the reality of the situation. As Merton points out, while a small percentage of persons can rise from the lower class to become materially successful, the vast majority of poor children really don't have much chance of ever obtaining such wealth. So it is this near-universal socialization of the American Dream, without it being obtainable in most cases, that causes most of the strain and frustration in American society. Furthermore, Merton claims that most of the strain and frustration is not necessarily due to the failure to achieve conventional goals (i.e., wealth) but, rather, to the differential emphasis placed on the material goals and the de-emphasis of the importance of the conventional means.

MERTON'S CONCEPT OF ANOMIE AND STRAIN. Merton claimed that an ideal society would feature an equal emphasis on the conventional goals and means in society. However, in many societies, one of these aspects would be emphasized more than the other. Merton claimed that the United States epitomized the type of society that emphasizes goals far above means. This disequilibrium in emphasis between the goals and means of societies is what Merton called **anomie**. So, like Durkheim's, Merton's anomie was a negative state for society; however, the two men had different explanations for how this state of society came about. While Durkheim believed that anomie was primarily caused by a society transitioning too fast to maintain its regulatory control over members, for Merton, anomie represented too much focus on the goals of wealth in the United States, at the expense of the conventional means.

There are numerous examples of how the goals are emphasized more than the means in our society, but perhaps the best way to illustrate this is through hypothetical situations. Which of the following two men would be more respected by youth (or even adults) in our society: (1) John, who has his PhD in physics but lives in a one-bedroom apartment because he can find only a job as a postdoctoral student for a stipend of $25,000 a year, or (2) Joe, who is a relatively successful drug dealer who owns a four-bedroom home, drives a Hummer, dropped out of school in the 10th grade, and makes about $90,000 a year? In years of asking this question in our classes, the answer, with few exceptions, is usually Joe, the drug dealer. After all, he appears to have obtained the American Dream, with little emphasis on how he achieved it.

JOURNAL ARTICLE

Merton's Adaptations

Still another way of supporting Merton's idea that America is too focused on the goal of material success is to ask you, the reader, to think about why you are taking the time to read this chapter and/or to attend college. Specifically, the question is this: If you knew for a fact that you would not get a better employment position by studying this book or, furthermore, by earning a college degree, would you be learning this material just for your own edification? In more than a decade of posing this question to about 10,000 students in university courses, one of the authors of this book has found that only about 5% (usually less) of respondents said "yes." Interestingly, when asked the reason they would put all this work into attending classes, many of them said they would do it for the partying or social life. Ultimately, it appears that most college students would not be engaging in the hard work it takes to educate themselves if it weren't for some payoff at the end of the task. In some ways, this supports Merton's claim that the emphasis is on the goals, with little or no intrinsic value placed on the work itself (i.e., the means). This phenomenon is not meant to be disheartening or a negative statement; after all, it is only meant to exhibit the reality of American culture and to show that it is quite common in our society to place an emphasis on the goal of financial success, as opposed to hard work for hard work's sake.

Merton went on to say that individuals, particularly those in the lower class, eventually realize that the ideal of the American Dream is a lie, or at least a false illusion for the vast majority of people. For example, people can work very hard in school and then get stuck in jobs that will never produce the type of material success promised them via the dream they were socialized to believe in. This revelation of the truth will likely take place when people are in their late teens to mid-20s, the time when crime tends to peak.

According to Merton, this is when the frustration or strain is evident, which is consistent with the peak of offending at the approximate age of 17. Therefore, some individuals begin to innovate ways that they can achieve the goals of society (i.e., material success) without having to use the conventional means of attaining them. Obviously, this is often through criminal activity. However, not all individuals deal with strain in this way; after all, most people who are poor do not resort to crime. To Merton's credit, one of the good things about his theory is that he explained that individuals deal in different ways with the limited economic structure of society. Merton referred to these variations in dealing with the revelation of the economic structure as adaptations to strain.

ADAPTATIONS TO STRAIN. There are five **adaptations to strain,** according to Merton. The first of these is **conformity,** in which persons buy into the conventional goals of society but also buy into the conventional means of working hard in school or labor.[23] This would include the vast majority of the readers of this book, in the sense that, like most of you, conformists want to achieve material success and are willing to do so by conventional means such as educational effort and diligent work. As the label suggests, these individuals are conforming to the goals and means that society suggests. Another adaptation to strain is **ritualism.** Ritualists do not seek to achieve the goals of material success, probably because they know they don't have a realistic chance of obtaining such success. However, they do buy into the conventional means in the sense that they like to do their jobs or are happy just making ends meet. For example, studies have shown that some of the most content and happy people in society are those that don't seek to become rich; rather, they are quite content with their blue-collar jobs and often have a strong sense of pride in the work they do, even if it is sometimes menial. To clarify, such a person considers his or her work a type of ritual and performs it without a goal in mind; rather, the work itself is a form of intrinsic goal. Ultimately, conformists and ritualists tend to be at low risk for offending, in contrast to the other adaptations to strain.

The other three adaptations to strain are far more likely to lead to criminal offending: **innovation, retreatism,** and **rebellion.** Perhaps most likely to become predatory street criminals are the innovators, who Merton claimed greatly desire the conventional goals of material success but are not willing to engage in conventional means of obtaining those goals. Obviously, drug dealers and professional auto thieves, as well as many other variations of chronic property criminals (e.g., bank robbers), fit this adaptation. To clarify, as their name suggests, they are innovating ways to achieve material goals without doing the hard work usually needed to succeed. However, innovators are not always criminals. In fact, many of them are the most respected individuals in our society. For example, some entrepreneurs have used the capitalistic system of our society to produce useful products and services (e.g., the men who designed Google for the Internet) and have made a fortune at young ages without advanced college educations or years of work at a company. Another example is successful athletes who sign multimillion-dollar contracts at age 18. So it should be clear that not all innovators are criminals.

The fourth adaptation to strain is retreatism, in which individuals do not seek to achieve the goals of society or buy into the idea of conventional hard work. There are many varieties of this adaptation, such as persons who become homeless by choice or persons who isolate themselves in desolate places without human contact. A good example of a retreatist is Ted Kaczynski, the Unabomber, who left a good position as a professor at University of California at Berkeley to live in an isolated Montana cabin, which had no running water or electricity, and did not interact with humans for many months at a time. Other types of retreatists, perhaps the most likely to be criminal, are those who actively disengage from social life and try to escape via psychologically altering drugs. All these forms of retreatists seek to drop out of society altogether, thus refusing to buy into the means or goals of society.

The last adaptation to strain, according to Merton, is rebellion—the most complex of the five adaptations. Interestingly, rebels buy into the idea of societal goals and means, but they do not buy into the conventional goals and means currently in place. Most true rebels are criminals by definition, largely because they are trying to overthrow the established societal structure. For example, the founders of the United States were all rebels because they actively fought the governing state (English rule) and clearly committed treason in the process. Had they lost or been captured during the American Revolution,

adaptations to strain: as proposed by Merton, the five ways that individuals deal with feelings of strain; see conformity, innovation, rebellion, retreatism, and ritualism

conformity: in strain theory, an adaptation in which an individual buys into the conventional means of success and also buys into conventional goals

ritualism: in strain theory, an adaptation to strain in which an individual buys into the conventional means of success (e.g., work, school, etc.) but does not buy into the conventional goals

innovation: in strain theory, an adaptation to strain in which an individual buys into the conventional goals of success but does not buy into the conventional means for getting to the goals

retreatism: in strain theory, an adaptation to strain in which an individual does not buy into the conventional goals of success and also does not buy into the conventional means they would have been executed as the criminals they were by law. However, because they won the war, they became heroes and presidents. Another example is Karl Marx, who will be discussed later in this text. He bought into goals and means of society, just not those of the current American culture. Rather, he proposed socialism/communism as a means to the goal of utopia. So there are many contexts in which a rebel can become a criminal, but sometimes rebels end up becoming heroes.

Merton also noted that one individual can represent more than one adaptation to strain. Perhaps the best example is the Unabomber, who started out as a conformist in that he was a respected professor at University of California, Berkeley, well on his way to tenure and promotion. He then seemed to shift to a retreatist state, isolating himself from society (as mentioned above). Later, he became a rebel who bombed innocent people in his quest to implement his own goals and means—as described in his manifesto, which he coerced several national newspapers to publish (and which subsequently resulted in his apprehension, because his brother read it and informed authorities that he thought his brother had written it!).

Finally, some have applied an athletic analogy to these adaptations, which often helps in translating them to actual, everyday behavior.[24] In a basketball game, conformists will play to win, but they will always play by the rules and won't cheat to win. Ritualists will play the game just because they like to play, and they don't care about winning. Innovators will play to win, and they will break any rules they can to triumph in the game. Retreatists don't like to play and obviously don't care about winning. Finally, rebels will not like the rules on the official court, so they will try to steal the ball and play by their own rules on another court. Although this is a somewhat simplistic analogy, it is likely to help readers remember the adaptations and perhaps enable them to apply these ways of dealing with strain to everyday situations, such as resorting to criminal activity.

LEARNING CHECK 7.3

1. According to Merton's theory, which type of individual deals with strain by emphasizing the conventional goals of success, without any consideration for the conventional means of gaining such success?
   a. Ritualists
   b. Conformists
   c. Retreatists
   d. Rebels
   e. Innovators

2. According to Merton's theory, which type of individual deals with strain by emphasizing the conventional means of gaining success, without any consideration for the conventional goals of such success?
   a. Ritualists
   b. Conformists
   c. Retreatists
   d. Rebels
   e. Innovators

3. According to Merton's theory, which type of individual deals with strain by emphasizing the conventional goals of success, as well as strongly considering the conventional means for gaining such success?
   a. Ritualists
   b. Conformists
   c. Retreatists
   d. Rebels
   e. Innovators

Answers located at www.sagepub.com/schram

EVIDENCE AND CRITICISMS OF MERTON'S STRAIN THEORY

Although Merton's framework, which emphasized the importance of the economic structure, appeared to have a high degree of face validity during the Great Depression, many scientific studies showed mixed support for strain theory. While research that examined the effects of poverty on violence and official rates of various crimes has found relatively consistent support (albeit weaker effects than strain theory implies), a series of studies of self-reported delinquent behavior found little or no relationship between social class and

rebellion: in strain theory, an adaptation to strain in which an individual buys into the idea of conventional means and goals of success but does not buy into the current conventional means or goals criminality.[25] Furthermore, the idea that unemployment drives people to commit crime has received little support.[26]

On the other hand, some experts have argued that Merton's strain theory is primarily a structural model of crime that is more a theory of societal groups than of individual motivations.[27] Therefore, some modern studies have used aggregated group rates (i.e., macro-level measures) to test the effects of deprivation, as opposed to using individual (micro-level) rates of inequality and crime. Most of these studies provide some support for the hypothesis that social groups and regions with higher rates of deprivation and inequality have higher rates of criminal activity.[28] In sum, there appears to be some support for Merton's strain theory when the level of analysis is the macro level and official measures are being used to indicate criminality.

CRIME IN THE NEWS

Robbery

WHAT WERE THEY THINKING?!

Robbery

However, many critics have claimed that these studies do not directly measure perceptions or feelings of strain, so they are only indirect examinations of Merton's theory. In light of these criticisms, some researchers have focused on the disparity in what individuals aspire to in various aspects of life (e.g., school, occupation, social life) versus what they realistically expect to achieve.[29] The rationale of these studies is that if an individual has high aspirations (i.e., goals) but also has low expectations of actually achieving the goals due to structural barriers, then that individual is more likely to experience feelings of frustration and strain. Furthermore, it was predicted that the larger the gap between aspirations and expectations, the stronger the sense of strain. Of the studies that examined discrepancies between aspirations and expectations, most did not find evidence linking a large gap between these two levels with criminal activity. In fact, several studies found that for most antisocial respondents there was virtually no gap between aspirations and expectations. Rather, most of the subjects (typically young males) who reported the highest levels of criminal activity tended to report low levels of both aspirations and expectations.

Surprisingly, when aspirations were high, it seemed to inhibit offending, even when expectations to achieve those goals were unlikely. One interpretation of these findings is that individuals who have high goals will not jeopardize their chances for obtaining such aspirations, even when they realize their chances are slim. On the other hand, individuals who don't have high goals are likely to be indifferent to their future and, in a sense, have nothing to lose. So without a stake in conventional society, this predisposes them to crime. While this conclusion supports social control theories (discussed in the following chapters), it does not provide support for strain theory.

Some critics have argued that most studies on the discrepancies between aspirations and expectations have not been done correctly. For example, Farnworth and Leiber claimed that it was a mistake to examine the differences between educational goals and expectations, or differences between occupational goals and expectations, which is what most of these studies did.[30] Rather, they proposed testing the gap between economic aspirations (i.e., goals) and educational expectations (i.e., means of achieving these goals). Not only does this make sense, but Farnworth and Leiber found support for a gap between these two factors being predictive of criminality. However, they also report that persons who reported having low economic aspirations were more likely to be delinquent, which supports the previous studies they criticized. Another criticism of this type of strain theory study is that it is possible that simply reporting a gap between expectations and aspirations does not necessarily mean that the individuals actually feel strained; rather, researchers have simply, and perhaps wrongfully, assumed that a gap between the two measures indicates feelings of frustration.[31]

Other criticisms of Merton's strain theory include some historical evidence and its failure to explain the age–crime curve. Regarding the historical evidence, it is hard to understand why some of the largest increases in crime took place during a period of relative economic prosperity—namely, the late 1960s. Crime increased more than ever before (that we have measures for) between 1965 and 1973, which were generally good economic years in the United States. Therefore, if strain theory is presented as the primary explanation for criminal activity, it would probably have a hard time explaining this historical era. On the other hand, it can be argued that the growth in the economy in the 1960s and early 1970s may have caused even more disparity between rich and poor, thereby producing more relative deprivation.

The other major criticism of strain theory is that it does not explain one of the most established facts in the field: the age–crime curve. Specifically, in virtually every society in the world, across time and place, predatory street crimes (e.g., robbery, rape, murder, burglary, larceny, etc.) tend to peak sharply in the teenage years to early 20s and then drop off quickly, certainly before age 30. However, most studies show that feelings of stress and frustration tend to continue rising after age 30 and do not diminish significantly. For example, suicide rates tend to be just as high or higher as one ages, with persons over 55 showing the highest rates of suicide.

On the other hand, it can be argued that the reason why strain continues or even increases as one ages but the rates of crime go down is that individuals develop coping mechanisms for dealing with their frustrations. This idea seems to make sense, and while Merton never discussed (outside of the adaptations) actual methods of coping with strain, a variation of Merton's theory—general strain theory—did emphasize this concept. Before we cover general strain theory, we will discuss two other variations of Merton's theory that were developed within a 5-year period (1955–1960) to explain gang formation and behavior using a structural strain framework.

VARIATIONS OF MERTON'S STRAIN THEORY: COHEN, AND CLOWARD AND OHLIN

COHEN'S THEORY OF LOWER-CLASS STATUS FRUSTRATION AND GANG FORMATION

In 1955, Albert Cohen presented a theory of gang formation that used Merton's strain theory as a basis for why individuals resort to such group behavior.[32] In Cohen's model, young males from lower classes are at a disadvantage in school because they lack the normal interaction, socialization, and discipline instituted by educated parents of the middle class, which is in line with Merton's original framework of a predisposed disadvantage among underclass youth. According to Cohen, such youths are likely to experience failure in school due to this lack of preparation in conforming with middle-class values, so they fail to live up to what is considered the "middle-class measuring rod," which emphasizes factors such as motivation, accountability, responsibility, deferred gratification, long-term planning, respect for authority and property, and controlling emotions.

Like Merton, Cohen emphasized the youths' internalization of the American Dream and fair chances for success, leading to frustration when they fail to be successful according to this middle-class standard. This strain that they feel due to failure in school performance and respect among their peers, often referred to as "status frustration," leads them to develop a system of values that is contrary to middle-class standards and values. Some have claimed that this represents a Freudian defense mechanism known as **reaction formation**, which involves adopting attitudes or committing behaviors that are the opposite of what is expected—a form of defiance and avoidance of guilt for not living up to the assumed standards. According to Cohen, these lower-class male youths will adopt a normative value system that defies the very values they are expected to live up to. Specifically, instead of abiding by middle-class norms of obedience to authority, school achievement, and respect for authority, these youths change their normative beliefs to

reaction formation: a Freudian defense mechanism applied to Cohen's theory of youth offending, which involves adopting attitudes or committing behaviors that are opposite of what is expected value the opposite characteristics: Namely, they value malicious, negativistic, and non-utilitarian delinquent activity.

For example, these youths will begin to value destruction of property and skipping school, not because these behaviors lead to a payoff or success in the conventional world but simply because they defy the conventional order. In other words, they turn the middle-class values upside down and consider activity that violates the conventional norms and laws, thereby psychologically and physically rejecting the cultural system placed on them without benefit of equal preparation and fair distribution of resources. Furthermore, Cohen claimed that while these behaviors do not appear to have much utility or value, they are quite valuable and important from the perspective of the strained youth. Specifically, they do these acts to gain respect from their peers (those who have gone through the same straining experiences and reactionary formation), which they could not gain through school performance and adherence to middle-class normative culture.

Cohen stated that he believed this tendency to reject middle-class values is the primary cause of gangs, because a number of these lower-class individuals who have experienced the same strains (i.e., status frustration) and experiences form a group—a classic example of "birds of a feather flock together." Cohen claimed that not all lower-class males resort to crime and join a gang in response to this structural disadvantage. Other variations, beyond that of the **delinquent boy**, described above, are the **college boy** and the **corner boy**. The "college boy" responds to his disadvantaged situation by dedicating himself to overcoming the odds and competing in the middle-class schools despite his unlikely chances for success. On the other hand, the "corner boy" responds to the situation by accepting his place in society as a lower-class individual who will somewhat passively make the best of life at the bottom of the social order.

As compared with Merton's original adaptations, Cohen's delinquent boy is probably most similar to rebellion, because the delinquent boy rejects the means and goals (middle-class values and success in school) of conventional society and replaces them with new means and goals (negativistic behaviors and peer respect in a gang). Some would argue that delinquent boys should be seen as innovators, because their goal is ultimately the same: peer respect. But the peers involved completely change, so we argue that through the reaction formation process, the delinquent boy actually creates his own goals and means that go against the conventional, middle-class goals and means. Regarding the college boy, the adaptation that seems to fit best is conformity, because the college boy continues to believe in the conventional goals (i.e., financial success/achievement) and means (i.e., hard work via education/labor) of middle-class society. Finally, the corner boy probably best fits the adaptation of ritualism, because he knows that he likely will never achieve the goals of society, so he essentially resigns himself to not obtaining financial success. At the same time, he does not resort to predatory street crime but, rather, holds a stable blue-collar job or makes ends meet in other typically legal ways. Some corner boys who end up simply collecting welfare and giving up on work altogether may actually become more like the adaptation of retreatism, because they have virtually given up on the conventional means (hard work) of society, as well as the goals.

At the time when he developed his theory, official statistics showed that virtually all gang violence—and most violence, for that matter—was concentrated among lower-class male youths. However, with the development of self-report studies in the 1960s, his theory was shown to be somewhat overstated in the sense that middle-class youths were well represented in committing delinquent acts.[33] Other studies have also been critical of Cohen's theory, particularly the portions that deal with his proposition that crime rates will increase after youths drop out of school and join a gang. Although the findings are mixed, many studies have found that delinquency is often higher before the youths drop out of school and may actually decline once they drop out and become employed.[34] Some critics have pointed out that such findings discredit Cohen's theory, but this is not

CRIME IN THE NEWS

Delinquents

delinquent boy: a type of lower-class male youth, identified by Cohen, who responds to strains and status frustration by joining with similar others in a group to commit crime

college boy: a type of lower-class male youth who has experienced the same strains and status frustration as his peers but responds to his disadvantaged situation by dedicating himself to overcoming the odds and competing in the middle-class schools despite his unlikely chances for success

corner boy: a type of lower-class male youth who has experienced the same strains and status frustration as others but responds to his disadvantaged situation by accepting his place in society as someone who will somewhat passively make the best of life at the bottom of the social order. As the label describes, they often hang out on corners necessarily true. After all, delinquency may be peaking right before the youths drop out because that is the time when they feel most frustrated and strained, whereas delinquency may be decreasing after they drop out because some of the youths are raising their self-esteem by earning a wage and taking pride in holding a job.

Still, studies have clearly shown that lower-class youths are far more likely to have problems in school, and that school achievement is consistently linked with criminality.[35] Furthermore, there is little dispute that much of delinquency represents malicious, negativistic, and non-utilitarian activity. For example, what do individuals have to gain from destroying mailboxes or tagging walls? This is an act that will never gain much in the lines of money or any other form of payoff aside from peer respect. So, ultimately, it appears that there is some face validity to what Cohen proposed, in the sense that some youths engage in behavior that has no other value than earning peer respect, even though that behavior is negativistic and non-utilitarian according to the values of conventional society. Regardless of some criticisms of Cohen's model, he provided an important structural strain theory of the development of gangs and lower-class delinquency.

CLOWARD AND OHLIN'S THEORY OF DIFFERENTIAL OPPORTUNITY

Five years after Cohen published his theory, Richard A. Cloward and Lloyd E. Ohlin presented yet another structural strain theory of gang formation and behavior.[36] Similar to Merton and Cohen, Cloward and Ohlin assumed that all youths, including those in the lower class, are socialized to believe in the American Dream and that when they realize they are blocked from conventional opportunities they become frustrated and strained. What distinguishes Cloward and Ohlin's theory from the previous strain theories is that they emphasized three different types of gangs that form based on the characteristics of the social structure in the neighborhood. To clarify, the nature of gangs varies according to the availability of illegal opportunities in the social structure. So whereas previous strain theories focused only on lack of legal opportunities, Cloward and Ohlin's model emphasized *both legal and illegal* opportunities, and the availability (or lack) of these opportunities largely determined what type of gang would form in that neighborhood—hence the name *differential opportunity theory*. Furthermore, the authors acknowledged Edwin Sutherland's (see Chapter 9) influence on their theory, and this influence is evident in their focus on the neighborhood associations that largely determine what type of gang will form. According to differential opportunity theory, the three types of gangs are criminal gangs, conflict gangs, and retreatist gangs.

Criminal gangs are those that form in lower-class neighborhoods that have an organized structure of adult criminal behavior. Such neighborhoods are so organized and stable that the criminal networks are often known and accepted by the conventional portion of individuals in the area. The adult gangsters in these neighborhoods mentor the youth and take them under their wing. This can pay off for the adult criminals, too, because youth can often be used to do the "dirty work" for the criminal enterprises in the neighborhood without risk of serious punishment if caught. The successful adult offenders supply the youth with the motives and techniques for committing crime. So while members of criminal gangs were blocked from legal opportunities, they are offered ample opportunities in the illegal realm.

Due to the strong organization and stability of such neighborhoods, criminal gangs tend to reflect this high degree of organization and stability. Therefore, criminal gangs primarily commit property or economic crimes, with the goal of making a profit through illegal behavior. These crimes can range from "running numbers" as local bookies to "fencing" stolen goods to running businesses that are a front for vice crimes (e.g., prostitution, drug trading). Regardless of the type, they all involve making a

VIDEO
Youth Violence

JOURNAL ARTICLE
Differential Opportunity

AUDIO
Gangs

criminal gangs: a type of gang identified by Cloward and Ohlin that forms in lower-class neighborhoods with an organized structure of adult criminal behavior. Such gangs tend to be highly organized and stable profit illegally, and there is often a system or structure in which the criminal activity takes place. Furthermore, these criminal gangs are most like the Merton adaptation of innovation (discussed previously in this chapter) because the members still want to achieve the goals of conventional society (financial success). Because of the strong organizational structure of these gangs, individuals who are highly impulsive or uncontrolled are not as conducive to this type of gang as those who have self-control and are good at planning for the future.

Examples of criminal gangs are seen in movies depicting highly organized neighborhoods (often consisting of primarily one ethnicity)—movies such as *The Godfather, A Bronx Tale, State of Grace, Sleepers, New Jack City, Clockers, Goodfellas, Better Luck Tomorrow,* and many others that were partially based on real events. All these depictions involve a highly structured hierarchy in a criminal enterprise, which is largely a manifestation of the organization of the neighborhood. All the Hollywood motion pictures also involve stories about the older criminals in the neighborhood taking younger males from the neighborhood under their wing and training them in the ways of the criminal network. Furthermore, virtually all ethnic groups have examples of this type of gang/neighborhood; for example, in looking at the list of movies above, there are Italian American, Irish American, African American, and Asian American representations. Thus, criminal gangs can be found across the racial and ethnic spectrum, largely because all groups have certain neighborhoods that exhibit strong organization and stability.

Organized crime syndicates are typically found in neighborhoods with more structured criminal organizations, which mentor youth in these neighborhoods and result in a prevalence of criminal gangs.

conflict gangs: a type of gang identified by Cloward and Ohlin that tends to develop in neighborhoods with weak stability and little or no organization; gangs are typically relatively disorganized and lack the skills and knowledge to make a profit through criminal activity

Conflict gangs are another type of gang that Cloward and Ohlin identified. Conflict gangs tend to develop in neighborhoods that have weak stability and little or no organization. In fact, the neighborhood often seems to be in a state of flux because people are constantly moving in and out of the area. Because the youth in the neighborhood do not have a solid crime network or adult criminal mentors, they tend to form together as a relatively disorganized gang. Due to this disorganization, they typically lack the skills and knowledge to make a profit through criminal activity. Therefore, the primary illegal activity of conflict gangs is violence. This violence is used to gain prominence and respect among themselves and the neighborhood, but due to the disorganized nature of the neighborhood, as well as the gang itself, conflict gangs never quite achieve the respect and stability of criminal gangs. The members of conflict gangs tend to be more impulsive and lack self-control compared with members of criminal gangs, largely because there are no adult criminal mentors to control them.

According to Cloward and Ohlin, conflict gangs are blocked not only from legitimate opportunities but also from illegitimate opportunities. If applying Merton's adaptations, conflict gangs would probably fit the category of rebellion best, largely because none of the other categories fits well. But it can be argued that conflict gangs have rejected the goals and means of conventional society and implemented their own values, which emphasize violence. Examples of motion pictures that depict this type of breakdown in community structure and result in a mostly violent gang culture include *Menace to Society, Boyz in the Hood, A Clockwork Orange, Colors, The Outsiders,* and others that emphasize the chaos and violence that results when neighborhood and family organization is weak.

Finally, if an individual is a "double failure" in both the legitimate and illegitimate worlds, meaning he or she can't achieve success in school or status in a local gang, that person may join other such people to form a retreatist gang. **Retreatist gangs** are made up of those individuals who have failed to succeed in the conventional world and also could not achieve status in the criminal or conflict gangs of their neighborhoods. Because members of retreatist gangs are no good at making a profit from crime (like criminal gang members) or at using violence to achieve status (like conflict gang members), their primary form of offending is usually drug usage. Like Merton's retreatist adaptation to strain, members of retreatist gangs often simply want to escape from reality. Therefore, the primary activity of the gang is usually getting high, which is well represented in such movies as *Trainspotting, Drug-Store Cowboy,* and *Panic in Needle Park.* In all these movies, the only true goal of the gangs is to get stoned and escape from the world in which they have failed.

There were a number of empirical studies and critiques of Cloward and Ohlin's theory, with much of the criticism being similar to that of Merton's strain theory—specifically, that there is little evidence that gaps between what lower-class youth aspire to and expect to achieve are predictive of feelings of frustration and strain, or that such gaps are predictive of gang membership or criminality.[37] Another criticism of Cloward and Ohlin's theory is the inability to find empirical evidence that supports their model of the formation of three types of gangs and their specialization in offending. While some research supports the existence of gangs that appear to specialize in certain forms of offending, many studies find that the observed specialization of gangs is not exactly the way Cloward and Ohlin proposed.[38] Additional studies have shown that many gangs tend not to specialize but, rather, engage in a wider variety of offending behaviors.

Despite the criticisms of Cloward and Ohlin's model of gang formation, their theoretical framework inspired policy, largely due to the influence of their work on Attorney General Robert Kennedy. In fact, Kennedy asked Ohlin to assist in developing federal policies regarding delinquency, which resulted in the Juvenile Delinquency Prevention and Control Act of 1961. Cloward and Ohlin's theory was a major influence on the Mobilization for Youth project in New York City, which along with the federal legislation stressed creating education and work opportunities for youth. Although evaluations of this program showed little effect in reducing delinquency,[39] it was impressive that such theorizing about lower-class male youths could have such a large impact on policy interventions.

Ultimately, the variations of strain theory presented by Cohen and Cloward and Ohlin provided additional revisions that seemed at the time to advance the validity of strain theory. However, as discussed above, most of these revisions were based on official statistics that showed lower-class male youths as committing the most crime, which was later shown by self-reports to be exaggerated.[40] Due to the realization that most of the earlier models of strain were not empirically valid for most criminal activity, strain theory became unpopular for several decades. But during the 1980s, another version of strain was devised by Robert Agnew, who rejuvenated the interest in strain theory by devising a theory that made the theory more general and applicable to a larger variety of crimes and forms of deviance.

GENERAL STRAIN THEORY

In the 1980s, Robert Agnew proposed general strain theory, which has a much larger range of behavior due to not concentrating on simply the lower class and provides a more applicable model for the frustrations that all individuals feel in everyday life.[41] Unlike other strain theories, which all assumed the internalization of the American

Many gangs thrive more on violence than on profit-making activities. Such gangs, called conflict gangs, tend to be more territorial and are often found in neighborhoods lacking the structure provided by established crime syndicates.

VIDEO

Motorcycle Gangs

retreatist gangs: a type of gang identified by Cloward and Ohlin that tends to attract individuals who have failed to succeed in both the conventional world and the criminal or conflict gangs of their neighborhoods

Retreatist gangs that focus on recreational substance use form among individuals who have failed in terms of both conventional and illegal opportunities.

Dream and the resulting frustration when it was revealed as a false promise to those of the lower classes, general strain theory does not necessarily rely on this assumption. Rather, this theoretical framework assumes that people of all social classes and economic positions deal with frustrations in routine daily life, which virtually everyone can relate to.

Specifically, previous strain theories, such as the models proposed by Merton, Cohen, and Cloward and Ohlin, focused on individuals' *failure to achieve positively valued goals* that they had been socialized to work toward. Like these previous models, general strain theory also focuses on this source of strain; however, general strain theory emphasizes two additional categories of strain: *presentation of noxious stimuli* and *removal of positively valued stimuli* (see Figure 7.2). In addition to the failure to achieve one's goals, Agnew claimed that the presentation of noxious stimuli (i.e., bad things) in one's life could cause major stress and frustration. Examples of noxious stimuli would include an abusive parent, a teacher who always picks on one student, or a boss who puts undue strain on one employee. These are just some of the many negative factors that can exist in one's life, and the examples of this category of strain are endless.

The other strain category Agnew identified was the removal of positive stimuli (i.e., good things), which is likely the largest cause of frustration. Examples of removal of positively valued stimuli include the loss of a good job, loss of the use of a car for a period of time, or loss of a loved one. Like the other two sources of strain, examples of removal of positive aspects are infinite, and these may have varying degrees of influence depending on the individual. To clarify, one person may not feel much frustration from losing a job or divorcing his or her spouse, whereas another person may experience severe anxiety or depression from such events.

AUTHOR PODCAST

Anger

PERSONAL PERSPECTIVE

Anger

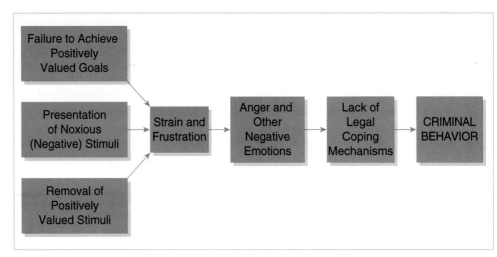

Figure 7.2 Model of General Strain Theory

Source: http://upload.wikimedia.org/wikipedia/commons/thumb/c/ca/
Mertons_social_strain_theory.jpg/728px-Mertons_social_strain_theory.jpg

WHY DO THEY DO IT?

CHRISTOPHER DORNER

Christopher Dorner went on a shooting spree, killing police officers and innocent victims in retaliation for his termination from the LAPD.

In early February 2013, Christopher Dorner went on a killing spree in Southern California that resulted in four people dead, including two police officers, and three officers wounded. His intent was to murder as many law enforcement officers as possible, especially those whom he blamed for losing his job with the Los Angeles Police Department (LAPD), where he had served as an officer from 2005 to 2008. One of the initial victims of his killing spree included the daughter (and her fiancé) of the LAPD captain who unsuccessfully represented him in his appeal of charges of misconduct while on patrol.

Dorner made his intentions quite clear in a "manifesto" he wrote and posted on his Facebook page just before he began his killing spree. In this manifesto, he listed many individuals he planned to stalk and kill, as well as celebrities and others whom he claimed to admire, such as the actor Charlie Sheen. He also made very clear in the manifesto that his goal was to get the LAPD to admit that his termination was in retaliation for reporting excessive force by a fellow officer. After his initial killings, he fled to Big Bear, California, in San Bernardino County, where he burned his truck and holed up in a vacant residence.

Dorner's rampage led to one of the largest manhunts in LAPD history, involving many other agencies in the search. These agencies included the San Bernardino County Sheriff's Office and several federal agencies, such as the U.S. Fish & Wildlife agency, whose agent finally spotted Dorner and exchanged gunfire with him just before the siege that took place at the cabin near the small town of Angelus Oaks, California, in the San Bernardino National Forest.

Despite Dorner's killing of innocent victims, many people came out to support him for taking a stand against the LAPD. Although the authors of this book find it hard to believe, he did gain much support in stalking and killing police officers and their family members. Perhaps Dorner gained this support by articulating his reasons, albeit

sometimes delusionally (e.g., praising drug-addicted, sex-crazed celebrities), in his manifesto.

Dorner shot himself in the head during the mountain siege, after an intense gun battle that killed two more officers. (It is notable that one of the coauthors of this book [Tibbetts] lives in Angelus Oaks. The official population, according to the 2010 Census, is 535.) Law enforcement authorities used incendiary devices to force Dorner out of the cottage, which elicited an outcry from some of Dorner's supporters, who saw this as an attempt to kill the suspect by whatever means available. Regardless of the motives of law enforcement officers, Dorner was neutralized.

So why did Dorner do it? Given the reasons laid out in his manifesto, he likely was feeling frustrated or strained after being fired from the LAPD, as well as being relieved from his service in a U.S. Naval Reserve unit on February 1, 2013. So in addition to an unstable psychological state (which his manifesto reveals, along with documented past domestic issues with several of his former romantic partners), he was likely acting out a deep-seated anger that stemmed from his being fired by the LAPD. Thus, general strain theory, which places a focus on anger, as well as lack of more conventional coping mechanisms, is likely the best theory for explaining why Dorner took out his frustrations by killing both law enforcement officers and innocent family members of persons against whom he wanted to exact revenge.

Sources: Cart, J., & Stevens, M. (2013, February 12). Dorner manhunt: Fish and Wildlife officers make the big break. *Los Angeles Times.* Retrieved from http://latimesblogs.latimes.com/lanow/2013/02/dorner-manhunt-fish-and-wildlife-officers-make-the-big-break.html; Lloyd, J., Ebright, O., Pamer. M., & Tata, S. (2013, February 28). Charred human remains found in rubble of Big Bear-area cabin. *NBC News.* Retrieved from http://www.nbclosangeles.com/news/local/Christopher-Dorner-LAPD-Manhunt-Search-Big-Bear-190902721.html.

Individuals experience stressors every day, and general strain theory emphasizes the importance of stress and anger in increasing the likelihood of engaging in criminal behavior, especially when individuals have not developed healthy coping mechanisms.

VIDEO ▶

Christopher Dorner

Ultimately, general strain theory proposes that these three categories of strain (failure to achieve goals, noxious stimuli, and removal of positive stimuli) will lead to stress and a propensity to feel *anger*. Anger can be seen as a primary mediating factor in the causal model of the gender strain framework. In other words, it is predicted that to the extent that the three sources of strain cause feelings of anger in an individual, that individual will be predisposed to commit crime and deviance. However, Agnew was clear in stating that if an individual can somehow cope with this anger in a positive way, then such feelings do not necessarily have to result in criminal activity. These coping mechanisms vary widely across individuals, with certain strategies working better for some people than for others. For example, some people destress by working out or running, whereas others do so by watching television or a movie. One type of activity that has shown relatively consistent success in relieving stress is laughter, which psychologists are now prescribing as a release of stress. Another is yoga, which largely includes simple breathing techniques such as taking several deep breaths, which is physiologically shown to enhance release of stress (see any studies on stress reduction done in the past few decades).

Although he did not originally provide details on how coping mechanisms work or explore the extant psychological research on these strategies, Agnew specifically pointed to such mechanisms in dealing with anger in prosocial ways. The primary prediction regarding coping mechanisms is that individuals who find ways to deal with their stress and anger in a positive way will no longer be predisposed to commit crime, whereas individuals who do not find a healthy, positive outlet for their anger and frustrations will be far more likely to commit crime. Obviously, the goal is to reduce the use of antisocial and negative coping to strain, such as drug usage, aggression, and so forth, which are either criminal in themselves or increase the likelihood of offending.

Fortunately, recent research and theoretical development has more fully examined various coping mechanisms and their effectiveness in reducing anger and, thus, preventing criminal activity (see below). Obviously, in focusing on individuals' perceptions of stress and anger, as well as their personal abilities to cope with such feelings, general strain theory places more emphasis on the micro level of analysis. Still, due to its origins in structural strain theory, it is included in this chapter and is typically classified as belonging to the category of strain theories that includes the earlier, more macro-level-oriented theories. Additionally, recent studies and revisions of the theory have attempted to examine the validity of general strain theory propositions at the macro, structural level.[42]

Since general strain theory was first proposed in the mid-1980s, there has been a vast amount of research examining various aspects of the theory.[43] For the most part, studies have generally supported the model. Specifically, most studies find a link between the three categories of strain and higher rates of criminality, as well as the link between the sources of strain and feelings of anger or other negative emotions (e.g., anxiety, depression).[44] However, there have been criticisms of the theory, and especially of the way the theory has been tested.

For example, similar to the problems with using objective indicators to measure perceptions of deterrence (as discussed in previous chapters), it is important for strain research to measure subjects' perceptions and feelings of frustration, not simply the occurrence of certain events themselves. Unfortunately, some studies have looked only at the latter, and the validity of such findings is questionable.[45] Fortunately, a number of other studies have directly measured subjective perceptions of frustration, as well as personal feelings of anger.[46]

Such studies have found mixed support for the hypothesis that certain events lead to anger[47] but less support for the prediction that anger leads to criminality, and this link is particularly weak for nonviolent offending.[48] On the other hand, the most recent studies have found support for the links between strain and anger, as well as anger and criminal behavior, particularly when coping variables are considered.[49] Still, many of the studies that do examine the effects of anger incorporate indicators of anger using time-stable "trait" measures, as opposed to incident-specific "state" measures that would be more consistent with the situation-specific emphasis of general strain theory.[50] This is similar to the methodological criticism, discussed in other chapters in this text, that has been leveled against studies of self-conscious emotions, particularly shame and guilt; namely, when it comes to measuring emotions such as anger and shame, criminologists should choose their measures carefully and make sure the instruments are consistent with the theory they are testing. Thus, future research on general strain theory should employ more effective, subjective measures of straining events and situational states of anger.

LEARNING CHECK 7.4

1. According to Agnew, which of the following is NOT one of the key reasons why individuals become strained or frustrated?

    a. Failure to acquire goals/expectations

    b. Dealing with negative stimuli

    c. Loss of positive stimuli

    d. Low self-control

2. Which type of adaptation to strain did Cohen NOT label/identify in his theory?

    a. Corner boy

    b. Drug boy

    c. College boy

    d. Delinquent boy

3. Which of the following types of gang did Cloward and Ohlin NOT label/identify in their theory of gangs?

    a. Ritualistic gangs

    b. Conflict gangs

    c. Criminal gangs

    d. Retreatist gangs

Answers located at www.sagepub.com/schram

Regardless of the criticisms of general strain theory, it is hard to deny its face validity. After all, virtually everyone can relate to the tendency to react differently to similar situations based on what type of day they are having. For example, we all have days when everything seems to be going great—it is Friday, you receive accolades at work, and you are looking forward to a nice weekend with your friends or family. If someone says something derogatory to you or cuts you off in traffic on such a day, you will probably be inclined to let it go. On the other hand, we also all have days when everything seems to be going horribly wrong—it is Monday, you get blamed for mishaps at work, and you have a fight with your spouse or significant other. On a day such as this, if someone yells at you or cuts you off in traffic, you may be more inclined to respond aggressively. Or perhaps more commonly, you will overreact and snap at a loved one or friend when he or she didn't do much to deserve it; this is a form of displacement in which a cumulative buildup of stressors causes us to lash out. In many ways, this supports general strain theory and its prevalence in everyday life.

SUMMARY OF STRAIN THEORIES

The common assumption found across all variations of strain theory is that crime is far more common among individuals who are under a great degree of stress and frustration,

WHY DO THEY DO IT?

GANG LU

Gang Lu was a PhD graduate at University of Iowa in 1991 when he entered a meeting of his former academic department and shot and killed several faculty members (including the chair of his PhD dissertation committee and two other committee members). He also shot and killed a student, his former roommate and winner of the elite Spriestersbach Dissertation Prize—awarded to an outstanding PhD candidate for exemplary research in the field of physics, including a $2,500 reward and nominating the winner as a candidate for a prize on the national level. After Lu shot these people, he proceeded to another building, where he shot and killed the associate vice president for academic affairs and the campus grievance officer, to whom Lu had made numerous complaints about not being nominated/chosen as a candidate for the Spriestersbach prize. In addition to the prize money, Lu believed that winning this award would have helped him get hired as a tenure-track professor.

He also shot a temporary student employee in the grievance office; she was paralyzed but survived the attack. Apparently, the president of the university was also on Lu's "hit list," but he happened to be out of town the day of the shootings. Lu was later found dead in a campus room, where he had shot himself in the head. Lu used a .38-caliber revolver in the attack.

So why did Lu perform this massacre? It is likely that one of the primary reasons can be explained by both traditional and general strain theories examined in this chapter. Specifically, he failed to obtain positively valued goals (the dissertation award) despite high expectations, which is consistent with the original version of strain theory proposed by Merton. However, anger over not winning the award and his complaints going unaddressed was clearly a key factor in his actions, and this anger is best explained by Agnew's general strain theory, which was also discussed in this chapter as a more recent and robust framework regarding how strain and frustration can increase propensities to commit crimes. Lu obviously did not deal or cope with this frustration and anger in a healthy way, which is also key in general strain theory; those with healthy coping mechanisms to strain and stress are typically fine, but those who can't deal with it in a positive way are likely to be predisposed to violence or other illegal activity.

A movie—titled *Dark Matter*—starring Meryl Streep and Aiden Quinn and largely based on this event was released in 2007 and won the Sloan Prize at the Sundance Film Festival that year. It is not a factual depiction of what occurred in this case, but it hits close to the mark in portraying why Lu might have committed this act.

Sources: Beard, J. A. (1997, June 24). The fourth state of matter. *New Yorker*. Retrieved from http://www.newyorker.com/arch ive/1996/06/24/1996_06_24_080_TNY_CARDS_000376447; Eckhardt, M. L. (2001, November 1). 10 years later: U. Iowa remembers fatal day. *Daily Iowan*; Marriott, M. (1991, November 3). Gunman in Iowa wrote of plans in five letters. *New York Times*. Retrieved from http://www.nytimes.com/1991/11/03/us/gunman-in-iowa-wrote-of-plans-in-five-letters.html.

especially those who can't cope with or handle such stress in a positive way. The origin of most variations of strain theory can be traced to Durkheim's and Merton's concept of anomie, which essentially means a state of chaos or normlessness in society due to a breakdown in the ability of societal institutions to regulate human desires, thereby resulting in feelings of strain.

Although different types of strain theories were proposed and gained popularity at various points throughout the 20th century, they all became accepted during eras that were politically and culturally conducive to such perspectives, especially regarding the differences across the strain models. For example, Merton's formulation of strain, which emphasized the importance of the economic institution, was developed and became popular during the Great Depression. Then, in the late 1950s, two strain theories that focused on gang formation were developed by Cohen and by Cloward and Ohlin; they became popular among politicians and society due to the focus on official statistics suggesting that most crime at that time was being committed by lower-class, inner-city male youths, many of whom were gang members. Finally, Agnew developed his general strain model in the mid- to late 1980s, during a period when a number of general theories of crime were being developed (e.g., Gottfredson and Hirschi's low self-control theory and Sampson and Laub's developmental theory); so such models were popular at that time, particularly those that emphasized personality traits (such as anger) and experiences of individuals. So all the variations of strain, like all the theories discussed in this book, were manifestations of the periods in which they were developed and became widely accepted by academics, politicians, and society.

POLICY IMPLICATIONS OF STRAIN THEORY

Although this chapter deals with a wide range of theories regarding social structure, the most applicable policy implications are those suggested by the most recent theoretical models of this genre. Thus, we will focus on policies that are most relevant in contemporary times and are key factors in the most modern versions of this perspective. Specifically, the factors that are most vital for policy implications regarding social structure theories are those regarding educational and vocational opportunities and programs that develop healthy coping mechanisms to deal with stress.

Empirical studies have shown that intervention programs that focus on educational and/or vocational training and opportunities are needed for high-risk youths, because those that do not have much motivation for such endeavors can have a significant impact on reducing their offending rates.[51] Specifically, providing an individual with a job, or the preparation for such, is key to building a more stable life, even if the position is not a high-paying job. Thus, the individual is less likely to feel stressed or "strained." In modern times, people are lucky to have a stable job, and this must be communicated to our youth. And ideally they will find some intrinsic value in the work they perform.

VIDEO

Robbery

STATE CRIME RANKINGS

Robberies

APPLYING THEORY TO CRIME: *BANK ROBBERY*

Bank robbery is a special type of robbery that, unlike the everyday "street" robberies we discussed in a previous chapter, is within the jurisdiction of the FBI, as opposed to local police authorities. Robbery is defined by the FBI in its Uniform Crime Reports (UCR) as "the taking or attempting to take anything of value from the care, custody, or control of a person or persons by force or threat of force or violence and/or putting the victim in fear." So bank robbery is a special form of robbery but robbery nonetheless. A working definition of bank robbery is the act of entering a bank when it is open (or when some person is on the premises) to take money or other goods, and then taking them

by force or threat of force. It should be noted that if a break-in occurs at a bank and no one is there, it is typically defined as a burglary (see Chapter 4).

Each year, the FBI puts together a comprehensive review of the many thousands of bank robberies in the United States, which we will review below. But first, it is important to mention that there is no established, systematically collected database of bank robberies for other countries throughout the world. In fact, virtually all other countries simply include bank robberies with other types of robbery that occur in a given year. With that said, the United States likely is well represented in the

world in terms of bank robbery. We say that with confidence given the data from the FBI.

In 2009, the FBI reported that at least 5,943 bank robberies were committed in the United States. Notably, this did not include more than 100 bank burglaries (those occurring when the bank was closed); as you may recall from a previous chapter, robberies are inherently violent, so someone must be present for a robbery to occur. From these 5,943 bank robberies in 2009, the FBI reported that the "loot" taken (including cash, securities, checks, and other property)

(Continued)

APPLYING THEORY TO CRIME: *(CONTINUED)*

totaled more than $45 million. The amount of the loot recovered was about $8 million, which means that most of the stolen cash and property were likely never recovered.

Some interesting statistics about these bank robberies in 2009 (largely because such distributions do not tend to differ much from year to year) include gender and race of offender, day of the week, time of day, type of bank, areas of bank involved, and modus operandi. Regarding gender, the vast majority of bank robbers were male (6,822; note: this number exceeds the number of incidents because sometimes there are multiple offenders in these bank robberies) versus female (431). This statistic backs up data previously reviewed in the text showing that males commit the overwhelming majority of violent crimes; in this case, females make up less than 6% of all bank robbers. In terms of race, black robbers (3,344) outnumbered white offenders (2,973), despite making up only about 15% of the general population; thus, blacks in the United States are at least 7 times (or 700%) more likely to engage in bank robbery than are whites. This is likely due to their high rates of poverty in our nation, which makes sense especially in terms of the theories reviewed in this chapter.

Another notable factor in the etiology of bank robbery in the United States is that of day of the week, as well as time of day. Regarding day, the modal category for day in 2009 is Friday (1,236), which makes sense because offenders may be thinking about getting money for weekend activities. Friday is followed by Monday (1,116) and Tuesday (1,102), perhaps because offenders didn't have the foresight

to anticipate the weekend but feel that they need to make up for what they spent on the weekend (just an educated guess), or perhaps they believe the banks have the most money on hand those days. Consistent with this theory, Saturday is the least likely day for bank robberies.

One of the more consistent predictors of bank robbery is the time of day when most robbers hit banks. In the 2009 report, as well as for the past few decades, bank robbers were most likely to offend between 9:00 a.m. and 1:00 p.m., with the highest peak coming in the hour between 10:00 a.m. and 11:00 a.m. A theory for why offenders seem to choose this time most often is that they want some of the money that flows in during the first hour (with most banks opening at 9:00 a.m.) but want to avoid the "lunch-hour" banking rush, when there are many witnesses.

Another factor highlighted by the FBI's 2009 report is that of the type of bank location robbed. In 2009, the main office was rarely robbed, whereas the primary robberies were among branch offices (5,683 robberies), with other locations such as in-store branches and other remote facilities robbed infrequently. Also, in 2009 metropolitan banks were robbed far more often (2,886 robberies) than were banks in suburban, small cities or rural locations. Additionally, in 2009 nearly all the bank robberies were carried out at the bank counter (5,735 robberies), as opposed to the vault/safe, safe deposit boxes, office area, drive-in/walk-up, armored vehicles, or other areas.

Finally, and this may come as a surprise given the current Hollywood

depictions of "takeover robberies," such as in the movies *Heat* and *The Town,* the vast majority of bank robberies in 2009 (as well as for every year in the past few decades) were committed using demand notes, usually presented to the teller at the counter. In 2009, the FBI report showed that the demand note approach was used in 3,269 of the bank robberies for that year, which is consistent with previous years. In fact, weapons were used (or threatened) only in a minority of the bank robberies in 2009, consistent with previous years.

It is likely that bank robbery is largely driven by unemployment and/or poverty, especially during hard economic times. In one notable recent incident, a jobless man was arrested for committing a dozen bank robberies across the Phoenix valley. The man, Cristian Alfredo Urquijo, discussed in the case study at the beginning of this chapter, told authorities that he did it to survive and that "desperation was a great motivator."

Urquijo's case is reflective of some of the various theories discussed in this chapter, especially those regarding strain theory. After all, we are talking about a man who, up to that time, appeared to have a clean record. However, when he was suddenly unemployed, he innovated a new way to obtain the money he needed to survive. In addition, according to general strain theory, when positive stimuli are removed (such as a stable job), individuals are more likely to engage in criminal offending, especially when such illegal acts are attempts to replace the lost positive stimuli (in this case, income from work).

Sources: FBI. (2010). *Bank crime statistics 2009: Federal insured financial institutions, January 1, 2009–December 31, 2009.* Washington, DC: Author; Reuters (2011, August 23). Jobless Arizona bank robber says he "stole to survive." Retrieved from http://www.reuters.com/article/2011/08/24/us-arizona-bankrobber-idUSTRE77N0AS20110824.

COMPARATIVE CRIMINOLOGY: BANK ROBBERY

Ranking U.S. States on Bank Robbery and Notable Findings From Other Nations

This box continues the book's theme of comparing the United States with foreign nations in terms of various aspects of criminology and criminal justice (see Comparative Criminology 1.1 in Chapter 1, which provides an introduction to this feature). In the case of bank robbery, there is no systematic database for occurrences of this crime across various nations. So we are largely going to compare various states and regions of the United States and then discuss some findings from other foreign nations.

First, it must be said that bank robbery in the United States has declined significantly over the past two decades, which is consistent with other violent crimes (e.g., homicide) during this most recent time period. For the most recent year for which preliminary data are available (2010), bank robberies once again declined. In 2010, there were just over 5,600 bank robberies (a significant decrease [by about 400] from 2009), in which the offenders got away with about $42 million (of that, authorities recovered about $8 million). As in previous years, the vast majority of these offenses were committed at the bank counter via a demand note. Of course, there are many other types of bank robberies, such as "takeover" robberies (which usually include more than one armed offender forcing everyone in the bank to "get down"), as well as other types. But regardless of type or modus operandi of the robberies, they are all counted the same in most FBI data because they were all attempted or true bank robberies.

In 2010, California, as usual, recorded by far the most bank robberies, at 805 for the year; Texas was a distant second at 464. It should be said that California does have more people than any other state, but even when accounting for the population, California remains overrepresented in bank robberies compared with virtually all states. The other primary states that had high bank robbery numbers were Ohio (263) and Florida (243). Just for comparison among U.S. states, it is notable that North Dakota had only two bank robberies in 2010. Once again, it is important to note that North Dakota has a far lower population than the other states discussed above, but even when standardizing the rates per capita, North Dakota is far lower in bank robberies than those other jurisdictions.

Virtually no foreign nations keep, or at least release publically, records on bank robbery (at least on the

government level) as the FBI does in the United States. Rather, most countries tend to lump incidents of bank robbery in with other types of robbery. Therefore, in this comparative section, we will simply examine some of the statistics and findings that have been provided regarding bank robberies in various countries.

As in the United States, bank robberies in Canada in recent years took place in more urban areas. In fact, banks in only seven cities in Canada were responsible for about 66% of all bank robberies, despite having only about 30% of bank branches. The same can be said for the United Kingdom, where London has only about 10% of bank branches but reported about 39% of the bank robberies in the whole United Kingdom. The concentration of bank robberies in urban areas is largely attributed to their location, especially regarding the nearby highways or freeways that allow for more opportunity to escape via fast-moving traffic. Furthermore, a recent study showed that one third of the banks robbed in the United Kingdom were robbed again soon after, specifically in the following 3 months. However, the same can be said for banks in the United States; if a particular bank is robbed, it greatly increases its chances of being robbed again, especially if the first robbery was successful (i.e., the offenders were not caught).

A study by the Australian Institute of Criminology examined more than 800 bank robberies that occurred in Australia between 1998 and 2002. It was found that the majority (55%) of the incidents were committed by a lone offender, similar to incidents in the United States. This study also found that pairs or multiple offenders inflicted the most injuries on victims at the scene and used disguises most often.

Overall, the trends regarding bank robberies in other similar, industrialized countries seem highly consistent with the trends in the United States. It is important to note that recent developments in crime prevention (e.g., bulletproof teller windows) and biometric technology (e.g., video, fingerprint scanners) make it much harder to access the vaults of various banks in the countries we have discussed. Perhaps this is why bank robberies have fallen dramatically in most of these countries, especially in the United States—even in Southern California, where bank robberies occur less than half as often as they did a decade ago.

(Continued)

COMPARATIVE CRIMINOLOGY: *(CONTINUED)*

Ultimately, although the rates of bank robberies vary across nations, many of the countries that are most like the United States (e.g., Canada, the United Kingdom, Australia) appear to have the same trends in the way bank robberies are committed. So perhaps the most intriguing conclusion is that offenders tend to think the same way across various countries. Still, given that most of the countries in the world do not report specific data on bank robberies, we are going only on what official data has been reported by the countries discussed above. Hopefully, in the future, there will be more readiness among nations to report rates and characteristics of bank robbery.

Sources: Australian Institute of Criminology. (2003, July). *Bank robbery in Australia*. Canberra: Author. Retrieved from http://www.aic.gov.au/publications/current%20series/cfi/41-60/cfi053.html; Federal Bureau of Investigation. (2010). *Bank crime statistics 2009: Federal insured financial institutions, January 1, 2009–December 31, 2009*. Washington, DC: Author; Home Office. (n.d.). *Policy: Reducing and preventing crime*. Retrieved from http://www.crimereduction.homeoffice.gov.uk/repeatvictimisation02.htm; Richey, W. (2011, April 5). Which state has the most bank robberies? FBI releases its annual report. *Christian Science Monitor*. Retrieved from http://www.csmonitor.com/USA/Justice/2011/0405/Which-state-has-the-most-bank-robberies-FBI-releases-its-annual-report.

Another key area of recommendations from this perspective involves developing healthy coping mechanisms to strain. After all, every individual deals with stress virtually every day. The key is not to avoid stress or strain, because that is impossible. Rather, the key is to develop healthy, legal ways to cope with such strain. Many programs have been created to train individuals on how to develop coping mechanisms for handling such stress without resorting to antisocial behavior. There has been some success in such "anger-management" programs, particularly the ones that take a cognitive-behavioral approach, which teaches individuals to think before they act and often involves role playing.[52]

CONCLUSION

This chapter examined the theories that emphasize inequitable social structure as the primary cause of crime. We examined early perspectives that established that societies vary in the extent to which they are stratified, as well as the consequences that result from inequalities and complexities of such structures. Early European researchers showed that certain types of crimes were clustered in different areas based on their socioeconomic levels. These early models set the stage for later theoretical development in social structure models of crime, especially strain theories.

Our examination of strain theories explored theoretical models stating that individuals and groups who are not offered equal opportunities for achieving success can experience feelings of stress and frustration and, in turn, develop dispositions toward committing crime. There have been many versions of strain theories proposed by scholars over the past century, with some focusing on economics and others emphasizing school performance, neighborhood dynamics, or many other factors beyond economic ones that can also produce frustration among individuals.

We also examined the policy recommendations suggested by the various strain theoretical models, which included the need to help provide individuals with educational and job opportunities, as well as paying more attention to developing healthy coping mechanisms to deal with the daily stressors we all face. Some of these programs have shown success in reducing the level of criminality from stress and frustrations, especially recent programs that have helped high-risk individuals develop better coping mechanisms to deal with such stressors. These programs hold much promise for future interventions.

Finally, we followed up on our initial case study of a jobless man—Cristian Alfredo Urquijo, or "The Black Binder Bandit"—arrested for committing a dozen bank robberies across the Phoenix valley. He confessed to authorities that he engaged in these bank robberies to survive and that "desperation was a great motivator," as he had been laid off and could not find a stable job. This "Black Binder Bandit," so nicknamed because he often hid a revolver in a black binder, is a good representation of some of the theories discussed in this chapter, especially those regarding strain theory.

SUMMARY OF THEORIES IN CHAPTER 7

THEORY	CONCEPTS	PROPONENTS	KEY PROPOSITIONS
Early European social structure theories	Relative deprivation	Adolphe Quetelet	Areas that have the greatest differences in wealth in close proximity (i.e., very poor living near very rich) tend to have the highest crime rates.
Early European social structure theories		Andre-Michel Guerry	Violent crime rates tend to be highest in poor areas, whereas property crimes tend to cluster in more wealthy areas.
Early strain theory	Mechanical vs. organic societies Anomie Collective conscience	Emile Durkheim	Societies evolve from mechanical to organic, with the former having a limited division of labor/roles, which strengthens the "collective conscience" of members. As the division of labor increases in the move to more organic society, the collective conscience breaks down and results in "normlessness" or anomie.
Merton's strain theory	Anomie (different meaning from Durkheim's) Adaptations to strain	Robert K. Merton	U.S. economic structure causes a differential emphasis on the goals ("wealth") compared with the conventional means of obtaining the goals, which results in anomie. Individuals with limited access to success and wealth adapt to such strain in different ways, with many innovating ways to achieve the goals via illegal methods instead of through legitimate means.
Lower-class frustration theory	Reaction formation Corner boy College boy Delinquent boy	Albert Cohen	Lower-class youth are not prepared for school and are at a disadvantage because schools are based on middle-class norms. Due to failure at school, they socialize with other failures and defy the middle-class norms/rules ("reaction formation"), which leads to gang formation. Different adaptations to this frustration exist, with delinquent boys being the most likely to commit crimes.
Differential opportunities theory	Criminal gangs Conflict gangs Retreatist gangs	Richard A. Cloward and Lloyd E. Ohlin	Gangs in lower-class city areas are a manifestation of the type of neighborhood structure that exists there, as well as the ability of youths to be accepted by adult criminal enterprises. Some youths are given opportunities to engage in illegal structures (e.g., the mafia), and others are blocked from these illegitimate opportunities as well as legitimate ones.
General strain theory	Failure to obtain goals Loss of positive stimuli Presentation of noxious stimuli Coping mechanisms (or lack thereof)	Robert Agnew	This greatly expanded the sources of strain to include everything that had been presented by previous models (economics, school frustration, etc.) and also added much more in the sense of having constant stressors (noxious stimuli) and the loss of positive aspects in one's life. It also added the component of coping mechanisms and individuals' ability to deal with stress in a healthy way.

KEY TERMS

adaptations to strain	conformity	mechanical societies	retreatism
anomie	corner boy	organic societies	retreatist gangs
collective conscience	criminal gangs	reaction formation	ritualism
college boy	delinquent boy	rebellion	
conflict gangs	innovation	relative deprivation	

STUDENT STUDY SITE

Visit the student study site at **www.sagepub.com/schram** to access links to the video, audio, city and state rankings, author podcasts, and SAGE journal and reference articles featured in this chapter, as well as additional study tools, including eFlashcards, web quizzes, web resources, and chapter outlines.

DISCUSSION QUESTIONS

1. How does sociological positivism differ from biological or psychological positivism?

2. Which of the early sociological positivism theorists do you think contributed the most to the evolution of social structure theories of crime? Why? Do you think their ideas still hold up today?

3. Can you think of modern examples of Durkheim's image of mechanical societies? Do you think such societies have more or less crime than modern organic societies?

4. What type of adaptation to strain do you think fits you most? Least? What adaptation do you think best fits your professor? Your postal delivery worker? Your garbage collector?

5. Do you know people you went to school with who fit Cohen's model of status frustration? What did they do in response to the feelings of strain?

6. How would you describe the neighborhood where you or others you know grew up, in terms of Cloward and Ohlin's model of organization/disorganization? Can you relate to the types of gangs they discussed?

WEB RESOURCES

Emile Durkheim

http://www.emile-durkheim.com

http://durkheim.uchicago.edu/Biography.html

Strain theory

http://www.criminology.fsu.edu/crimtheory/week8.htm

http://socialscience.stow.ac.uk/criminology/criminology_notes/strain_theory.htm

http://www.criminology.fsu.edu/crimtheory/agnew.htm

CHAPTER 8

Social Structure Theories of Crime II

Social Disorganization and Subcultures

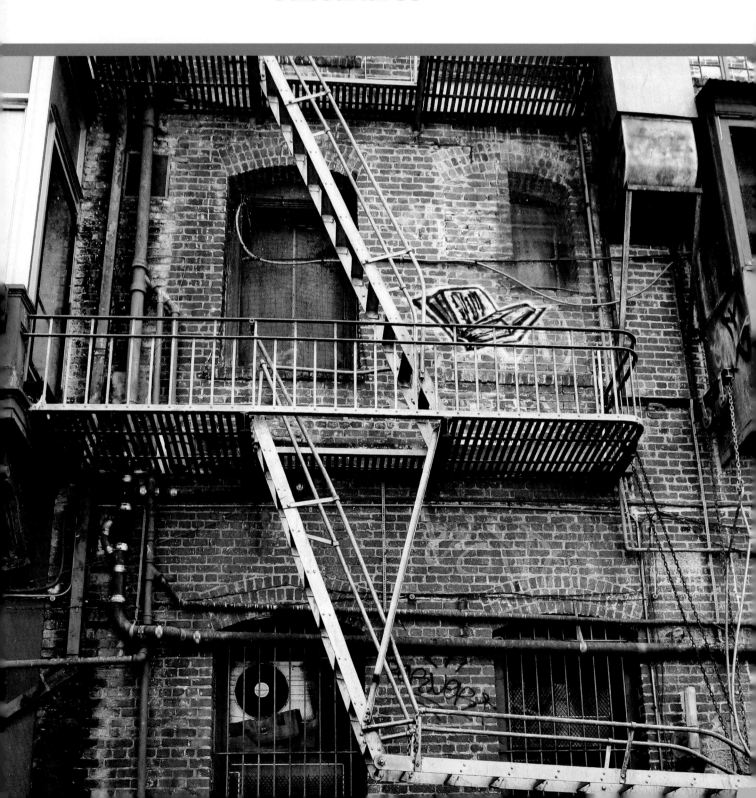

INTRODUCTION

This chapter will continue our survey of key social structure theories that have been proposed by criminologists to explain criminal behavior. The previous chapter discussed early social structure theories that evolved in Europe in the 19th century, as well as more modern versions of strain theory. In this chapter, we will focus on a different type of social structure framework, which emphasizes the risk factors and social dynamics in certain neighborhoods. Specifically, we will examine the Chicago School of criminology, which is otherwise known as the Ecological School or theory of social disorganization, for reasons that will become clear by the end of this chapter. The Chicago School perspective places a high emphasis on the impact of the neighborhood where a youth lives in determining his or her criminal behavior.

The Chicago School evolved in that location because the city at that time (late 19th century to early 20th century) desperately needed answers to dealing with its exponentially growing problem of delinquency and crime. Thus, this became a primary focus in the city. A significant portion of the Chicago perspective involved the transmission of cultural values to other peers, and even intergenerational transmission, as the older youths relayed their antisocial values and techniques to the younger children. Thus, the cultural/subcultural perspective is also a key area of this theoretical model. This cultural aspect of the Chicago model will also be examined in this chapter, as well as other subculture frameworks of offending behaviors.

THE ECOLOGICAL SCHOOL AND THE CHICAGO SCHOOL OF CRIMINOLOGY

Despite its name specifying one city, the **Chicago School of criminology** represents one of the most valid and generalizable theories we will discuss in this book, in the sense that many of its propositions can be readily applied to the growth and evolution of virtually all cities around the world. The Chicago School, which is often referred to as the Ecological School or the theory of social disorganization, also represents one of the earliest examples of balancing theorizing with scientific analysis, along with guiding important programs and policy implementations that still exist and thrive in contemporary times. Perhaps most important, the development of the Chicago School of criminology was the epitome of using theoretical development and scientific testing to help improve conditions in society when it was most needed, which can be appreciated only by understanding the degree of chaos and crime that existed in Chicago in the late 1800s and early 1900s.

CULTURAL CONTEXT: CHICAGO IN THE 1800S AND EARLY 1900S

Experts have identified 19th century Chicago as the fastest growing city in the history of the United States.[1] Census data show the town growing from about 5,000 people in the early 1800s to more than 2 million people by 1900; put another way, the population more than doubled every decade during the 19th century.[2] This massive rate of growth, which was much

CASE STUDY

LOS ANGELES GANGS

Although most case studies we review in this book are about individuals, in this case we concentrate on groups, which is fitting for this chapter because virtually all the theories we will cover in this section are macro- or group-level theories. A recent scientific study by researchers at University of California, Los Angeles, showed that when Los Angeles gangs and incidents of gang activities are mapped, the places with the highest frequency of violence are on the borders between two or more rival gangs.[3]

WHEN LOS ANGELES GANGS AND INCIDENTS OF GANG ACTIVITIES ARE MAPPED, THE PLACES WITH THE HIGHEST FREQUENCY OF VIOLENCE ARE ON THE BORDERS BETWEEN TWO OR MORE RIVAL GANGS.

This 2012 report showed that, contrary to popular belief, the most dangerous places to be in Los Angeles are not the regions deeply within the territory of a dominant gang but, rather, on the boundaries of gang territories, perhaps due to turf disputes or increased likelihood of encountering rival factions. We shall see that this recently observed phenomenon among established gang territories was to some extent predicted and explained by Chicago School theories of crime and city growth proposed more than half a century ago. We will follow up on this case study toward the end of this chapter.

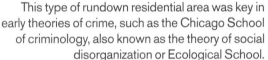

This type of rundown residential area was key in early theories of crime, such as the Chicago School of criminology, also known as the theory of social disorganization or Ecological School.

Modern criminological research was born in Chicago in response to the chaos created by an influx of immigrants and children who had little supervision, which led to delinquency.

faster than that seen in other large U.S. cities such as Boston, Baltimore, New York, Philadelphia, and San Francisco, was due to Chicago's centrally located geographic position; in other words, it was in many ways "landlocked," because although it sits on Lake Michigan, there was no water route to the city from the Atlantic Ocean until the Erie Canal opened in 1825, which opened the Great Lakes region to shipping (including migration of people). Three years later, the Baltimore and Ohio Railroad—the first U.S. passenger train with a route from a mid-Atlantic city to central areas—started operating. These two transportation advancements created a continuous stream of (im)migration to the Chicago area, which only increased with the completion of the transcontinental railroad in 1869, linking both coasts with the midwestern portions of the country.[4]

It is important to keep in mind that in the early to mid-1800s, many large U.S. cities had virtually no formal social agencies such as we have today to handle problems of urbanization. For example, there were no social workers, building inspectors, garbage collectors, or even police officers. Once police agencies did start in some of these cities, their duties often included tasks we associate with other agencies, such as finding lost children and collecting garbage, primarily because there weren't other agencies to perform these tasks. Therefore, communities were largely responsible for solving their own problems, including crime and delinquency. However, by the late 1800s Chicago was largely made up of citizens who did not speak a common language and did not share one another's cultural values. This phenomenon is consistent with Census Bureau data from that era that show 70% of Chicago residents were foreign-born and another 20% were first-generation American. Thus, it was almost impossible for these citizens to organize themselves to solve community problems, because in most cases they could not even understand one another. This resulted in the type of chaos and normlessness that Durkheim predicted would occur when urbanization and industrialization occurred too rapidly; in fact, Chicago represented the archetypal example of a society in an anomic state, with almost

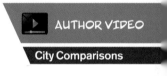

AUTHOR VIDEO

City Comparisons

Chicago School of criminology: theoretical framework of criminal behavior that emphasizes the environmental impact of living in a high-crime neighborhood, applies ecological principles to explain how cities grow, and highlights levels of neighborhood organization to explain crime rates a complete breakdown in control. There were many manifestations of this breakdown in social control, but one of the most notable was that children were running wild on the streets in gangs, with little intervention from the adults in the neighborhoods. So delinquency was soaring, and it appeared that the gangs were controlling the streets as much as any other group.

So the leaders and people of Chicago needed theoretical guidance to develop solutions to their problems, particularly regarding the high rates of delinquency. This was a key factor in why the Department of Sociology at the University of Chicago became so important and dominant in the early 1900s. Essentially, modern sociology developed in Chicago because the city needed it to solve its social problems. Thus, Chicago became a type of laboratory for the sociological researchers, and they developed a number of theoretical models of crime and other social ills that are still empirically valid today.

ECOLOGICAL PRINCIPLES IN CITY GROWTH AND CONCENTRIC CIRCLES

In the 1920s and 1930s, several new perspectives of human behavior and city growth were offered by sociologists at the University of Chicago. The first relevant model was proposed by Robert E. Park, who claimed that much of human behavior, especially the way cities grow, follows the basic principles of ecology that had been documented and applied to wildlife for many years at that point.[5] Ecology is essentially the study of the dynamics and processes through which plants and animals interact with the environment. In an application of Darwinian theory, Park proposed that the growth of cities follows a natural pattern and evolution.

Specifically, Park claimed that cities represent a type of complex organism that has a sense of unity formed from the interrelations among citizens and groups in the city. Park applied the ecological principle of symbiosis to explain the dependency of the various citizens and units on one another: Everyone is better off working together as a whole. Furthermore, Park claimed that all cities contain identifiable clusters, which he called **natural areas**, where the group has taken on a life or organic unity by itself. To clarify, many cities have neighborhoods that are primarily made up of one ethnic group or are distinguished by certain features. For example, Hell's Kitchen, Times Square, and Harlem represent areas of New York City that have each taken on a unique identity; however, each of them contributes to the whole—namely, the makeup and identity of the city. The same can be seen in other cities, such as Baltimore, which in a 2-mile area has the Inner Harbor, Little Italy, and Fells Point, with each area complementing the others. From Miami to San Francisco to New Orleans, all cities across America—and throughout the world, for that matter—contain these identifiable natural areas.

Applying several other ecological principles, Park also noted that some areas (or species) may invade and dominate adjacent areas (species), causing the recession of previously dominant areas (species). The dominated area or species can either recede and migrate to another location or die off. In wildlife, this can be seen in the incredible proliferation of a weed called kudzu. Kudzu grows at an amazing pace and has large leaves. It grows on top of other plants, trees, fields, and even houses, covering everything in its path and stealing all the sunlight. Introduced in the 1800s at a world exposition, this weed was originally used to stop erosion but got out of control, especially in the Southeastern region of the United States. Now this weed costs the government more than $350 million each year in destruction of crops and other fauna. This is a good example of a species that invades, dominates, and causes the recession of other species in the area. As is often the case, kudzu was not a completely natural phenomenon; it was synthetically introduced to this country at a world expo.

AUDIO
Urban Violence

VIDEO
High Crime Areas

natural areas: Chicago School's idea that all cities contain identifiable clusters, such as a Chinatown or Little Italy, and neighborhoods that have low or high crime rates

A similar example is the introduction of buffalo on Santa Catalina Island, off the coast of Southern California, in the 1930s. About three dozen buffalo were originally imported to the island for a movie shoot, and the producers decided not to spend the money to remove them afterward; so they have remained and multiplied. Had this occurred in many other parts of the United States, it would not have caused a problem; however, the largest mammal native to the island before the buffalo "invaded" was a 4-pound fox. So the massive buffalo, which have multiplied into the many hundreds (to the point where officials recently deported several hundred to their native Western habitat), have destroyed much of the environment, driving to extinction some plants and animals unique to Catalina Island. Similar to the invasion of kudzu, the buffalo came to dominate the environment, and other species died off.

Park claimed that a similar process occurs in cities, where some areas invade other zones or areas and the previously dominant area must succeed or die off. This is easy to see in modern times with what is known as *urban sprawl*. Geographers and urban planners have long acknowledged the detriment caused to traditionally stable residential areas when businesses move in. Some of the most recent examples involve the battles of longtime home owners against introduction of malls, businesses, and other industrial centers in a previously zoned residential district. Media have documented such fights, especially with the proliferation of such establishments as Wal-Mart or Super Kmarts in areas where residents perceive (and perhaps rightfully so) their presence as an invasion. Such an invasion can create chaos in a previously stable residential community, due to increased traffic, a transient population, and, perhaps most important, crime.

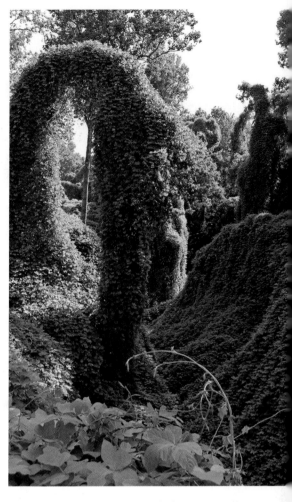

Kudzu covers other plants and hogs their sunlight. The Ecological/ Chicago School of criminology applied this type of natural process to show how a criminal element invades and comes to dominate certain areas.

Furthermore, some cities are granting power to such development through eminent domain, in which the local government can take land from the home owners to rezone and import businesses.

At the time when Park developed his theory of ecology, he observed the trend of businesses and factories invading the traditionally residential areas of Chicago, which caused chaos and breakdown in stability in those areas. Readers, especially those who were raised in suburban or rural areas, can likely relate to this, in that when they go back to where they grew up or even currently live, they can often see fast growth. Such development can devastate the informal controls (i.e., neighborhood networks, family ties, etc.) in these areas due to the "invasion" of a highly transient group of consumers and residents who do not have strong ties to the area.

This leads to a psychological indifference toward the neighborhood, in which no one cares about protecting the community any longer. Those who can afford to leave the area do, and those who can't afford to leave will simply remain until they can save enough money to move. After all, especially in the time when Park presented his theory of ecology in the 1920s, when factories moved into the area it often meant a lot of smoke billowing out of chimneys. No one wanted to live in such a state, particularly at a time when there was no real understanding of pollution and virtually no filters on such smokestacks. In fact, certain parts of Chicago, as well as all other cities in America, were perpetually covered by smog from these factories. In highly industrial areas, it appeared to be always snowing or overcast due to the constant and vast coverage of smoke and pollutants

CRIME IN THE NEWS

High Crime Areas

The American Buffalo was introduced to Catalina Island and destroyed much of the native plant life. This is an example of a foreign element creating chaos and destruction, as crime does in residential areas.

The Chicago/Ecological model proposed that as factories invaded and dominated residential areas, the residents who could afford to leave did and those left were the poor and deprived, which increased risk of crime.

across the sky. So it is easy to see how such "invasions" by factories and businesses can completely disrupt the previously dominant and stable residential areas of a community.

Park's ideas became even more valid and influential with the complementary perspective offered by Ernest W. Burgess.[6] Burgess proposed a theory of city growth in which cities were seen as growing not simply on the edges but from the inside outward. To clarify, while it is easy to see cities growing on the edges, as in the example of urban sprawl described above, Burgess claimed that the source of the growth is in the center of the city. Specifically, the growth of the inner city puts pressure on the adjacent zones of the city, which in turn begin to grow into the next adjacent zones (following the ecological principle of "succession" identified by Park). This type of development is referred to as "radial growth," meaning it begins on the inside and ripples outward.[7]

An example of radial growth can be seen by watching a drop of water fall into the center of a bucket filled with water. The waves from the impact will form circles that ripple outward. This is exactly how Burgess claimed that cities grow. Although the growth of cities is most visible on the edges, largely due to development of businesses and homes where only trees or barren land existed before, the growth on the edges originates from pressure forming in the very heart of the inner-city area. Another good analogy is the "domino effect," because pressure from the center leads to pressure to grow in the next zone, which leads to growth in the adjacent zones, and so forth.

To his credit, Burgess also specified the primary zones all cities appear to have, which included five pseudo-distinctive natural areas (in a constant state of flux due to growth). Burgess exhibited these zones as a set of concentric circles (see Figure 8.1). The first, center circle was called Zone I, the central business district (on the chart, it is labeled "The Loop" because that is what downtown Chicago is called, even today). This area of a city contains the large business buildings (modern skyscrapers), which include banking establishments, chambers of commerce, the courthouse, and other essential business and political centers such as police headquarters, the post office, and so forth. The adjacent area, just outside the business district, was the "factory zone" (unnumbered), which is perhaps the most significant in terms of causing crime, because it invaded the previously stable residential zones in Zone II—identified as the transition zone or **zone in transition**. Zone II is appropriately named, because it was truly in a state of transition from residential to industrial, primarily because this was the area of the city where businesses and factories were invading residential areas. Zone II was the area most significantly subjected to the ecological principles suggested by Park—namely, invasion, domination, recession, and succession. This is the zone subsequent theorists focused on in criminological theorizing, and it is based on the encroachment of factories and/or businesses in areas that were previously stable residential communities.

According to Burgess's theory of concentric circles, Zone III was the "workingmen's homes," largely made up of relatively modest homes and apartments; Zone IV consisted of higher-priced family dwellings and more expensive apartments; and Zone V was considered the suburban or commuter zone. These outer three zones identified by Burgess were of less importance in terms of distinction, primarily because as a general rule, the farther a family could move out of the city, the better in terms of social organization and the lower the rate of social ills (e.g., poverty, delinquency). The important point of this theory of concentric circles is that the growth of each inner zone puts pressure on the next zone to grow and push on the next zone.

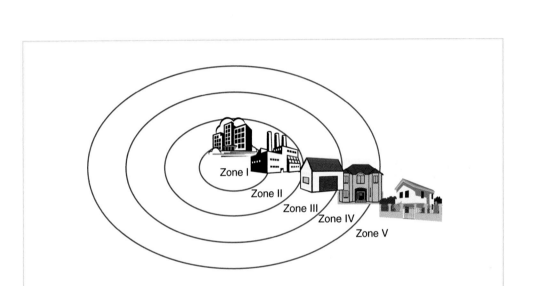

Figure 8.1 Major Zones of the City of Chicago

Source: R. Park, E. W. Burgess, & R. D. McKenzie (Eds.), *The city.* Chicago: University of Chicago Press.

It is easy for readers to see examples of this model of **concentric circles**. Whether you live on the East Coast or the, West Coast, or in the middle regions of the United States, all you have to do is drive on a highway that enters a major city to see real-life evidence of the validity of this perspective. For example, whether you drive on Interstate 95 through Baltimore or Interstate 5 through Los Angeles, you will see the same pattern of city structures as you travel through the city. As you approach each of the cities, if you look closely you will see suburban wealth in the homes and buildings (often hidden by trees off the highway). As you get closer to the cities, you will see the homes and buildings deteriorate in terms of value. From the raised highway system near Baltimore and Los Angeles, it is readily apparent when you enter Zone II, due to the prevalence of factories and the highly deteriorated nature of these areas. Many of the factories developed through the 20th century have been abandoned or are limited in use, so many of these factory zones feature rusted-out or demolished buildings. This is also often the location of subsidized or public housing. In other words, this is where the people who can't afford to live anywhere else live. Finally, as you enter the inner-city area of skyscrapers, the conditions improve drastically, because this is where the major businesses have invested their money; it appears to be a relative utopia compared with Zone II.

AUDIO

Murder

zone in transition: in the Chicago School, this zone (Zone II) was once residential but is becoming more industrial because of invading factories; tends to have the highest crime rates

concentric circles: model proposed by Chicago School theorists that assumes that all cities grow in a natural way with the same five zones

REFERENCE ARTICLE

Concentric Zone Model

VIDEO ▶

Urban Planning

This theory does not apply just to U.S. cities, and we challenge readers to find any major city throughout the world that did not develop this way. In modern times, some communities have tried to plan their development, and other communities have experienced the convergence of several patterns of concentric circles due to central business districts (i.e., Zone Is) starting in what were previously suburban areas (i.e., Zone Vs). However, for the most part, the theoretical framework of concentric circles still has a great deal of support. In fact, even cities found in Eastern cultures have evolved this way. Therefore, Park's application appears to be correct: Cities grow in a natural way across time and place, and abide by the natural principles of ecology.

SHAW AND MCKAY'S THEORY OF SOCIAL DISORGANIZATION

Clifford Shaw and Henry McKay drew heavily on their colleagues at the University of Chicago in devising their theory of social disorganization, which became known as the Chicago School theory of criminology.[8] Shaw had been producing excellent case studies on the individual (i.e., micro) level for years before he took on theorizing on the macro (i.e., structural) level of crime rates.[9] However, once he began working with McKay, he devised perhaps the most enduring and valid model for why certain neighborhoods have more social problems, such as delinquency, than others.

In this model, Shaw and McKay proposed a framework that began with the assumption that certain neighborhoods in all cities have more crime than other parts of the city—most of them located in Burgess's Zone II, which is the zone in the transition from residential to industrial, due to the invasion of factories. According to Shaw and McKay, the neighborhoods that have the highest rates of crime typically have at least three common problems (see Figure 8.2): physical dilapidation, poverty, and heterogeneity (which is a fancy way of saying a high cultural mix). Shaw and McKay noted other common characteristics, such

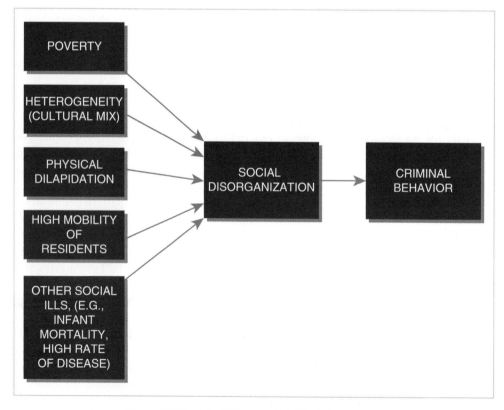

Figure 8.2 Model of Shaw and McKay's Theory of Social Disorganization

as a highly transient population, meaning that people constantly move in and out of the area, as well as unemployment among the residents of the neighborhood.

As noted in Figure 8.2, other social ills are included as antecedent factors in the theoretical model. The antecedent social ills tend to lead to a breakdown in social organization, which is why this model is referred to as the theory of social disorganization. Specifically, it is predicted that the antecedent factors of poverty, heterogeneity, and physical dilapidation will lead to a state of social disorganization, which in turn will lead to crime and delinquency. This means that the residents of a neighborhood that fits the profile of having a high rate of poor, culturally mixed residents in a dilapidated area cannot come together to solve problems, such as delinquency among the neighborhood's youth.

One of the most significant contributions of Shaw and McKay's model was that they demonstrated that the prevalence and frequency of various social ills—be it poverty, disease, low birth weight, or other problems—tend to overlap with higher delinquency rates. Regardless of what social problem is measured, higher rates of social problems are almost always clustered in the zone in transition. It was in this area that Shaw and McKay believed there was a breakdown in informal social controls and that children began to learn offending norms from their interactions with peers on the street, through what they called "play activities."[10] Thus, the breakdown in the conditions of the neighborhood leads to social disorganization, which in turn leads to delinquents learning criminal activities from older youth in the neighborhood. Ultimately, the failure of the neighborhood residents to organize themselves allows the older youth to govern the behavior of the younger children. Basically, the older youth in the area provide a system of organization where the neighborhood cannot; so younger children follow them instead.

Shaw and McKay supplied data to support these theoretical propositions. Specifically, they demonstrated through data from the U.S. Census and city records that neighborhoods with high rates of poverty, physical dilapidation, and a high cultural mix also had the highest rates of delinquency and crime. Furthermore, the high rates of delinquency and other social problems were consistent with Burgess's framework of concentric circles, in that the highest rates were observed for the areas in Zone II, the zone in transition. However, there was an exception to the model; the Gold Coast area along the northern coast of Lake Michigan was notably absent from the high rates of social problems, particularly delinquency, that existed throughout the otherwise consistent model of concentric circles and neighborhood zones.

So Shaw and McKay's findings were as predicted, in the sense that high delinquency rates were apparent in the area of the city where factories were invading the residential district. Furthermore, Shaw and McKay's longitudinal data showed that it did not matter which ethnic groups lived in Zone II (zone in transition), because all groups (with the exception of Asians) who lived in that zone had high delinquency rates while they lived there. On the other hand, once most of each ethnic group moved out of Zone II, their delinquency rates decreased significantly.

This finding rejects the notion of social Darwinism, because it is obvious that the culture is not what influences crime and delinquency but, rather, the criminogenic nature of the environment. After all, if ethnicity or race made a difference, the delinquency rates in Zone II would fluctuate based on who lived in that area, but these rates did not differ. Rather, the zone determined the rates of delinquency, regardless of what ethnic or racial groups were living there at the time.

REACTION AND RESEARCH FOR SOCIAL DISORGANIZATION THEORY

Over the past few decades, the Chicago School theoretical framework has experienced an enormous amount of attention from researchers.[11] Virtually all the research

LEARNING CHECK 8.1

1. In Shaw and McKay's theoretical model, which zone was predicted to be the highest in crime and delinquency rates, largely due to other social problems there?

   a. Central business district

   b. Zone in transition

   c. Zone VI

   d. Zone V

2. Which unit of analysis does Shaw and McKay's theory focus on?

   a. Macro level

   b. Micro level

   c. Situational level

Answers located at www.sagepub.com/schram

has supported Shaw and McKay's version of social disorganization and the resulting high crime rates in neighborhoods that exhibit such deprived conditions. Modern research has supported the theoretical model proposed by Shaw and McKay, specifically in terms of the high crime rates in disorganized neighborhoods. Also, it is quite true that virtually every city that one can drive through on an elevated highway (e.g., Richmond, Virginia; Baltimore, Maryland; Los Angeles, California) visually supports Shaw and McKay's model of crime in concentric circles. Specifically, one can see while driving into almost all cities that the pattern of dilapidated structures surrounds the inner-city area, which is the zone of transition. Preceding (and following) this layer of dilapidated structures, one encounters a layer of houses and residential areas that seem to increase in quality as the driver gets closer to (or farther away from) the inner-city area.

However, critics have raised some valid concerns regarding the original model. Specifically, it has been argued that Shaw and McKay's original research did not actually measure their primary construct: social disorganization. Although this criticism was accurate in calling out Shaw and McKay on not measuring their primary intervening variable, recent research has shown that the model is valid even when measures of social disorganization are included in the model.[12] Such measures of social disorganization include simply asking members of the neighborhood how many neighbors they know by name or how often they observe unsupervised peer groups in the area.

Additional criticisms of Shaw and McKay's formulation of social disorganization also focus on the emphasis the theory places on the macro, or aggregate, level of analysis. After all, while their theory does a good job predicting which neighborhoods will have higher crime rates than others, the model does not even attempt to explain why most youths in the worst areas do not become offenders. Furthermore, their model does not attempt to explain why some, albeit a very small amount of, youths in the best neighborhoods (in Zone V) choose to commit crime. However, the previous case studies completed and published by Clifford Shaw attempted to address the individual (micro) level of offending.

Also, there was one notable exception to Shaw and McKay's proposition that all ethnic/racial groups would have high rates of delinquency and crime while they lived in Zone II. Evidence showed that when Japanese residents made up a large portion of residents in this zone in transition, they had very low rates of delinquency. Thus, as in most theoretical models in social science, there was an exception to the rule.

Perhaps the biggest criticism of Shaw and McKay's theory, which has yet to be adequately addressed, deals with their blatant neglect in targeting the most problematic source of criminality in the Zone II, transitional zone, neighborhoods. Their findings seem to point undoubtedly to the invasion of factories and businesses into residential areas as a problem, yet the researchers did not focus on slowing such invasions as a recommendation. This is

AUDIO

Social Networking Crime

REFERENCE ARTICLE

Social Disorganization

APPLYING THEORY TO CRIME: *STALKING*

January is National Stalking Awareness Month, as designated by the U.S. Department of Justice. Although this suggests an unprecedented interest in stalking—including the first-ever national survey sponsored by the National Institute of Justice, a branch of the U.S. Department of Justice (Tjaden & Thoennes, 1998)—the number of studies on stalking is still limited. Despite a recent surge in laws to combat stalking passed in virtually every state and the District of Columbia, very little is known about the most common stalkers, how much stalking occurs, and so forth.

To define it, *stalking* generally refers to threatening or harassing behavior an individual repeatedly engages in (e.g., making harassing phone calls, following a person, leaving numerous messages, continuously appearing at a person's home or place of work). Unfortunately, legal definitions vary from state to state. However, regardless of the definition, there is a strong link between stalking and other forms of violence in intimate relationships (Tjaden & Thoennes, 1998), with 81% of women who were stalked by a current or former partner also being physically abused by that person.

Women are significantly more likely to be stalked, with recent estimates showing that females are twice as likely as males to be victimized in this way (Tjaden & Thoennes, 1998). A recent study by the Bureau of Justice Statistics (Baum, Catalano, & Rand, 2009) concluded that a pattern of decreasing risk for such stalking victimization is evident for persons in higher-income households. This study also showed that a large portion of stalking victims experienced some form of cyberstalking, such as e-mail or text messages, and almost half (46%) of all victims felt fear of not knowing what would happen next. Importantly, more than half of stalking victims lost more than a week of work due to this victimization.

These findings relate to the theories covered in this chapter in the sense that with the advancement of technology and media, there seems to be a certain cultural element that encourages stalking. After all, Twitter, Facebook, and other social networking sites enable the "following" of individuals, and some individuals, given their unstable state, tend to have problems drawing appropriate lines regarding intrusion into others' lives. Much more study must be done to determine how to discourage and decrease the recent surge in stalking, because the current increase in such cyber-related networking will likely only increase stalking in the near future. For example, a recent story from 2009 showed how a Bronx man was sentenced to 40 years in prison for international stalking, harassment, and so forth (see the FBI report for this case here: http://www.fbi.gov/newyork/press-releases/2009/nyfo091609.htm).

Sources: Baum, K., Catalano, S., & Rand, M. (2009). *Stalking victimization in the United States*. Washington, DC: Bureau of Justice Statistics; Tjaden, P., & Thoennes, N. (1998). *Stalking in America: Findings from the National Violence Against Women Survey*. Washington, DC: National Institute of Justice, U.S. Department of Justice.

likely due to political and financial concerns, being that the owners of the factories and businesses were financing their research and later funded their primary policy implementation. Furthermore, this neglect is represented in their failure to explain the exception of the Gold Coast in their results and conclusions.

Despite the criticisms and weaknesses of the Chicago School perspective on criminology, this theory resulted in one of the largest programs to date attempting to reduce delinquency rates. Clifford Shaw was put in charge of establishing the Chicago Area Project, which established centers in the most crime-ridden neighborhoods of Chicago. These neighborhood centers sought to create activities for youth, as well as to establish ties between parents and officials in the neighborhood. Although this program was never scientifically evaluated, it still exists, and many cities have implemented programs based on this model. For example, Boston implemented a similar program that was evaluated by Walter Miller.[13] This evaluation showed that while this project was effective in establishing relationships and interactions between local gangs and community groups, as well as providing more educational and vocational opportunities, the program appeared to fail in reducing delinquent or criminal behavior. Thus, the overall conclusion reached by

VIDEO

Stalking

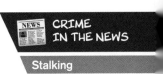
CRIME IN THE NEWS

Stalking

experts was that the Boston project and other similar programs, such as the Chicago Area Project, typically fail to prevent criminal behavior.[14]

CULTURAL AND SUBCULTURAL THEORIES OF CRIME

Cultural/subcultural theories of crime assume that there are unique groups in society that socialize their children to believe that certain activities that violate conventional law are good and positive ways to behave. Although it is rather difficult to find large groups of people or classes that fit this definition, it is somewhat likely that there are subcultures or isolated groups of individuals who buy in to a different set of norms than the conventional, middle-class set of values.

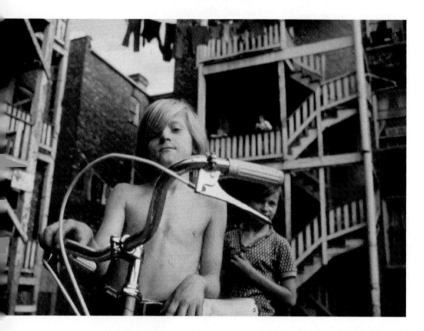

EARLY THEORETICAL DEVELOPMENTS AND RESEARCH IN CULTURAL/ SUBCULTURAL THEORY

One of the key developments of cultural theory has been largely attributed to the 1967 work of Franco Ferracuti and Marvin E. Wolfgang, who examined the violent themes of a group of inner-city youths from Philadelphia.[15] Ferracuti and Wolfgang's primary conclusion was that violence is a culturally learned adaptation to deal with negative life circumstances and that learning such norms occurs in an environment that emphasizes violence over other options.[16] These researchers based their conclusion on an analysis of data that showed great differences in rates of homicide across racial groups. However, Ferracuti and Wolfgang were clear that their theory was based on subcultural norms. Specifically, they proposed that no subculture can be totally different from or totally in conflict with the society of which it is a part.[17] This **cultural/subcultural theory** brings the distinction of culture and subculture to the forefront.

The distinction between a culture and a subculture is that a culture represents a distinct, separate set of norms and values among an identifiable group of people that are summarily different from that of the dominant culture. For example, communism is distinctly different from capitalism because it emphasizes equality over competition, and it values utopia (i.e., everyone gets to share all profits) over the idea that the best performer gets the most reward. So it can be said that communists have a different culture than capitalists. However, there is a substantial difference between a culture and a subculture, which is typically only a pocket of individuals who may have a set of norms that deviate from conventional values. Therefore, what Ferracuti and Wolfgang concluded is not so much a cultural theory as a subcultural theory.

This is also seen in the most prominent (sub)culture theory, which was presented by Walter Miller.[18] Miller presented a theoretical model that proposed that the entire lower class had its own cultural value system. In this model, virtually everyone in the lower

Cultural/subcultural theorists claim that residents in such environments have a different normative code or moral values than do those in mainstream society, which often are counter to the law and conventional culture.

cultural/subcultural theory: perspective on criminal offending that assumes that many offenders believe in a normative system distinctly different from and often at odds with the norms accepted by conventional society class believed in and socialized the values of six **focal concerns**: fate, autonomy, trouble, toughness, excitement, and smartness. Fate was the concern of luck, or whatever life dealt you; it disregarded responsibility and accountability for one's actions. Autonomy was the value of independence from authority. Trouble was the concern of staying out of legal problems, as well as getting into and out of personal difficulties (e.g., pregnancy). Toughness was maintaining your reputation on the street in many ways. Excitement was the engagement in activities (some illegal) that helped liven up an otherwise mundane existence of being lower class. Smartness was an emphasis on "street smarts" or the ability to con others. Miller claimed that these six focal concerns were emphasized and taught by members of the lower class as a culture or environment (or "milieu," as stated in the title of his work).

A more recent subculture model proposed by Elijah Anderson has received a lot of attention in the past few years.[19] This theory focuses on African Americans and claims that due to deprived conditions in the inner cities, black Americans feel a sense of hopelessness, isolation, and despair. Anderson clearly notes that while many African Americans believe in middle-class values, these values have no value on the street, particularly among young males. According to Anderson, "the code of the streets"—also the title of his book—is to maintain one's reputation and demand respect. For example, to be disrespected ("dissed") is considered grounds for a physical attack. Masculinity and control of one's immediate environment are treasured characteristics; this is perceived as the only thing these young men can control, given the harsh conditions they live in (e.g., unemployment, poverty, etc.).

CRITICISMS OF CULTURAL THEORIES OF CRIME

The studies on cultural theories of crime, at least in the United States, show that no large groups blatantly deny the middle-class norms of society. Specifically, Miller's model of lower-class focal concerns simply does not exist across the entire lower class. Studies consistently show that most adults in the lower class attempt to socialize their children to believe in conventional values, such as respect for authority, hard work as positive, delayed gratification, and so forth, and not the focal concerns that Miller specified in his model. Even Ferracuti and Wolfgang admitted that their research findings led them to conclude that their model was more of a subcultural perspective and not one of a distinctly different culture. So there are likely small groups or gangs that have subcultural normative values, but that does not constitute a completely separate culture in society. Perhaps the best subculture theories are those presented by Cohen and Cloward and Ohlin (see the previous chapter), in their variations of strain theory that emphasize the formations of gangs among lower-class male youths, which we discussed earlier in this chapter. Therefore, it can be concluded that if there are subcultural groups in our society, they seem to make up a small percentage of the population, which somewhat negates the cultural/subcultural perspective of criminality.

> **LEARNING CHECK 8.2**
>
> 1. Which theorist proposed the theory of lower-class focal concerns?
>   a. Burgess
>   b. Shaw
>   c. Anderson
>   d. Miller
>
> 2. Which theorist wrote a significant book on inner-city, African American subculture titled *The Code of the Streets*?
>   a. Burgess
>   b. Park
>   c. Anderson
>   d. Miller
>
> Answers located at www.sagepub.com/schram

focal concerns: primary concept of Miller's theory, which asserts that all members of the lower class focus on concepts they deem important: fate, autonomy, trouble, toughness, excitement, and smartness

COMPARATIVE CRIMINOLOGY: *VIOLENCE AGAINST FEMALES*

Cross-Regional Rates of Intimate Violence Committed Against Females

In this section, we compare various regions based on their rates of intimate violence against females. This box is relevant to the chapter because countries with higher rates of violence against females tend to have cultural norms that are more permissive of such violence within families.

As shown in Figure 8.3, the region of the world with by far the highest annual percentage of females 15 and over being victimized by violence from intimate partners was the Middle East. The second highest region was Africa, but it was a distant second. The leading theory for why these two regions, and especially the Middle East, are so high is the extreme patriarchy—or dominance of males—prominent in most countries in those regions.

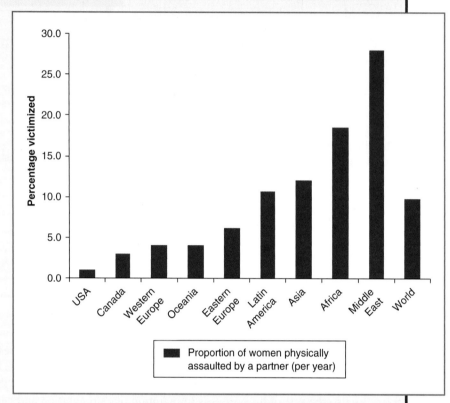

Figure 8.3 Percentages of Women, 15 Years and Older, Victimized by Violence From Intimate Partners Over the Past 12 Months

Sources: Independently run, dedicated surveys of violence against women in 72 countries. United Nations. (2006). *In-depth study on all forms of violence against women.* Report to the Secretary-General, New York, United Nations. (A/61/122/Add.1.)

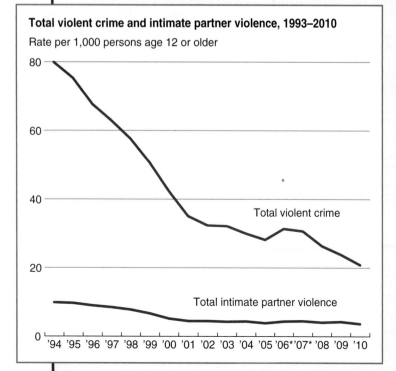

Total violent crime and intimate partner violence, 1993–2010

Rate per 1,000 persons age 12 or older

Figure 8.4 Total Violent Crime and Intimate Partner Violence, 1993–2010 (Rate per 1,000 Persons Age 12 or Older)

Note: Estimates based on two-year rolling averages beginning in 1993. Includes rape or sexual assault, robbery, aggravated assault, and simple assault committed by current or former spouses, boyfriends, or girlfriends.

*Due to methodological changes, use caution when comparing 2006 NCVS criminal victimization estimates to other years. See *Criminal Victimization, 2007,* NCJ 224390, BJS website, December 2008, for more information. Source: Bureau of Justice Statistics, National Crime Victimization Survey, 1993–2010.

COMPARATIVE CRIMINOLOGY: (CONTINUED)

Consistent with this conclusion, Van Dijk (2008) points out that perhaps the most comprehensive studies of domestic abuse in modern times were done in Germany and surveyed more than 11,000 teenagers about their experiences with domestic violence in their homes. One consistent finding was that rates or percentages of violence against mothers reported by children of immigrants were significantly higher, with extremely high rates among those from Turkey (32%), Yugoslavia (25%), and Russia (20%). Another interesting pattern was that the immigrant families who had resided in Germany for longer periods had higher rates of violence,

which Van Dijk claimed suggested "growing tensions between spouses after a longer exposure of women to German norms and values concerning gender equality" (p. 88).

It is also notable that the World Health Organization (2004) estimated annual economic costs in the United States due to intimate partner violence at about $13 billion. One bit of good news is that intimate partner violence has dropped significantly in the United States in recent years (see Figure 8.4), showing a 64% drop between 1994 and 2010.

Sources: Bureau of Justice Statistics. (2012). *Intimate partner violence, 1993–2010.* Washington, DC: U.S. Department of Justice; Van Dijk, J. (2008). *The world of crime.* Thousand Oaks, CA: Sage; World Health Organization. (2004). *The economic dimensions of interpersonal violence.* Geneva, Switzerland: Author.

POLICY IMPLICATIONS

Many of the policy implications suggested by the theoretical models proposed in this chapter are rather ironic. Regarding social disorganization, a paradox exists, in the sense that the very neighborhoods most desperately in need of becoming organized to fight crime are the same inner-city ghetto areas that are, by far, the most difficult places to cultivate such organization (e.g., neighborhood watch or "Block Watch" groups). Rather, the neighborhoods that do have high levels of organization tend to be those that already have low levels of crime, because the residents naturally "police" their neighbors' well-being and property since they have a stake in keeping the area crime free. Although there are some anecdotal examples of success in neighborhood watch programs, the majority of the empirical evidence is "almost uniformly unsupportive" of this approach's ability to reduce crime in such neighborhoods. Furthermore, many studies of these neighborhood watch programs find that in a notable number of communities these groups actually increase the fear of crime, perhaps due to the heightened awareness of crime issues in such areas.

Also, as explained above, perhaps the most prominent program that resulted from the Chicago School/social disorganization model—the Chicago Area Project—and similar programs have been deemed failures in reducing crime rates among the participants. Still, there have been some advances in trying to get residents of high-crime areas organized to fight crime. To clarify, the more specific the goals of neighborhoods regarding crime reduction, such as more careful monitoring of high-level offenders (e.g., more intensive supervised probation) and better lighting in dark places, the more effective the implementation will be.

Regarding cultural/subcultural programs, some promising intervention and outreach programs have been suggested by such models of offending. There are now many programs that attempt to build prosocial attitudes (along with other health and opportunity aspects) among high-risk youth, often young children. For example, a recent program called Peace Builders, which focuses on children in early grades, was shown by a recent evaluation to be effective in producing gains in conflict resolution, development of

WHY DO THEY DO IT?

WHITEY BULGER

Whitey Bulger (James Joseph "Whitey" Bulger, Jr.) is perhaps the most notorious gangster from the South Boston area, which is saying a lot given the history and tradition of organized crime in "Southie," as they call it. Bulger was a key figure of a criminal organization from the early 1970s to the mid-1990s and head of this organization for much of that time. Under heat from authorities, he fled in 1994, and for 12 years he was on the FBI's "Ten Most Wanted" list. Bulger was apprehended with his long-term girlfriend, Catherine Greig, in Santa Monica, California, in 2011, and is currently awaiting trial for 19 murders and various other charges.

Bulger is believed to have been largely in charge of narcotics distribution and extortion rackets in the Southie area during most of the 1980s and early 1990s, along with the violence inherent to such a position. Interestingly, most sources show that he was also an FBI informant during at least some of this time period.

Perhaps most related to this chapter, Bulger was seen locally as a type of Robin Hood figure, considered by most people on the streets as a sort of guardian protecting the interests of the neighborhood or local area. After all, Bulger had been a key element of organized crime in that area for many years, and this led to a subcultural/cultural climate placing him as an authority for all that happened in that locale. Furthermore, much of his business dealt with narcotics distribution and extortion, so his motives fit the other theories in this chapter of being largely based on finding criminal opportunities despite the relatively poor and deprived conditions of the South Boston region.

So why did he do it? As alluded to before, Bulger likely saw the draw of organized crime as being his only way to accomplish the higher financial and/or social status that could be obtained in the South Boston area. After all, there were not many legitimate opportunities open to him given his early criminal record, not to mention the deprivation and lack of stable employment in that region. Furthermore, he probably also desired to become an important figure in the subculture/culture of that area, and the only likely way to do that was to become a prominent figure in the organized crime syndicates.

Whitey Bulger (1929–) was the head of one of the most notorious organized crime syndicates in Boston until he was apprehended in Southern California in 2011. He is being processed in criminal court.

Sources: MacKenzie, E., & Karas, P. (2004). *Street soldier: My life as an enforcer for "Whitey" Bulger and the Boston Irish Mob.* Hanover, NH: Steerforth; Weeks, K., & Karas, P. (2009). *Brutal: My life inside Whitey Bulger's Irish Mob.* New York: HarperCollins.

VIDEO ▶

Whitey Bulger

prosocial values, and reductions in aggression, and a follow-up showed that these attributes were maintained for a long period of time. Another recent antiaggression training program for foster-home boys showed much success in increasing levels of empathy, self-efficacy, and attribution style among boys who had exhibited early-onset aggression. Ultimately, there are effective programs out there that promote prosocial norms and culture. More efforts should be devoted to promoting such programs that will help negate the antisocial cultural norms of individuals, especially among high-risk youths.

CONCLUSION

In this chapter, we examined theoretical perspectives proposing that the social organizations in neighborhoods that are broken-down and dilapidated are unable to control delinquency and crime in those areas. Furthermore, we discussed how this model of crime was linked to processes derived from ecological principles. This type of approach has been tested numerous times, and virtually all studies show that the distribution of delinquents and crime activity is consistent with this model.

We then discussed the ability of cultural and subcultural theories to explain criminal activity. Empirical evidence shows that cultural values do make a contribution to criminal behavior but that the existence of an actual alternative culture in our society has not been found. However, some pockets of certain subcultures, particularly regarding inner-city youth gangs, certainly exist and provide some validity for the subculture perspective of crime. Furthermore, the Chicago perspective plays a role because it is typically in the inner-city areas (i.e., zones of transition) where these subcultural groups form.

We also examined some policy implications suggested by these theoretical models. Regarding social disorganization, we noted the paradox that exists: The very neighborhoods most desperately in need of becoming organized to fight crime are the same inner-city ghetto areas that are, by far, the most difficult places to cultivate such organization (e.g., neighborhood watch groups). On the other hand, the neighborhoods that do have high levels of organization tend to be those that already have low levels of crime, because the residents naturally "police" their neighbors' well-being and property since they have a stake in keeping the area crime free. Still, there have been some advances in organizing residents of high-crime areas to fight crime. Regarding the cultural and subcultural perspectives, we examined some of the intervention and outreach programs suggested by such models of offending.

Finally, it is important to follow up on the case study we discussed at the beginning of this chapter, which involved a 2012 UCLA-led study finding that the most dangerous areas of Los Angeles were not deep within established gang territories but, rather, near the boundaries or border areas among rival gangs. This makes sense and can be explained by several of the frameworks presented in this chapter. Specifically, the natural areas discussed by Park and the zones identified by Shaw and McKay seem to be relatively safe and sound when there is some stability; it is when they are disrupted—such as in the zone in transition, where residential areas are being invaded by factories or big-box stores—that chaos tends to ensue. It appears that this is exactly the same case in terms of gangs and gang territories. So although much of the Ecological/Chicago School framework was proposed more than 50 years ago, it can still be applied to contemporary city dynamics and crime rates in metro areas worldwide.

SUMMARY OF THEORIES IN CHAPTER 8

THEORY	CONCEPTS	PROPONENTS	KEY PROPOSITIONS
Ecological/Chicago School perspectives on city growth	Natural areas Concentric circles	Robert E. Park and Ernest W. Burgess	Virtually all cities grow in a natural way, whereby they form distinct areas that tend to grow in a radial fashion from the center outward, forming rings of concentric circles.
Social disorganization theory	Various zones in the city Zone in transition Factory zone	Clifford Shaw and Henry McKay	Nearly all cities experience large growth of factories around the city center, which invades residential areas and essentially creates a state of transition and instability, which leads to chaos and higher crime and delinquency rates.
Subcultural theories		Marvin E. Wolfgang and Franco Ferracuti; Elijah Anderson	Some groups of people have normative structures that deviate significantly from the mainstream culture, which inevitably leads to illegal behavior.
Lower-class focal concerns	Six focal concerns (that go against middle-class norms)	Walter Miller	The lower class has an entirely separate culture and normative value system (i.e., focal concerns), which in many ways values the opposite of many middle-class standards.

KEY TERMS

Chicago School of criminology

concentric circles

cultural/subcultural theory

focal concerns

natural areas

zone in transition

STUDENT STUDY SITE

Visit the student study site at **www.sagepub.com/schram** to access links to the video, audio, city and state rankings, author podcasts, and SAGE journal and reference articles featured in this chapter, as well as additional study tools, including eFlashcards, web quizzes, web resources, and chapter outlines.

DISCUSSION QUESTIONS

1. Can you identify and discuss another example of the ecological principles of invasion, domination, and succession among animals or plants that was not discussed in this chapter?

2. Can you see examples of the various zones that Shaw and McKay described in the town or city where you live (or nearest you)? Try obtaining a map or sketching a plot of the town or city closest to your home and then draw the various concentric circles where you think the zones are located.

3. What forms of organization and disorganization have you observed in your own neighborhood? Try to supply examples of both, if possible.

4. Can you provide modern-day examples of different cultures and subcultures in the United States? What regions, or parts of the country, would you say have cultures that are more conducive to crime?

5. Do you know people who believe most or all of Miller's focal concerns? What social class do they belong to? What are their other demographic features (age, gender, urban/rural, etc.)?

6. Do you know individuals who seem to fit either Ferracuti and Wolfgang's cultural theory or Anderson's model of inner-city youth street code? Why do you believe they fit such a model?

WEB RESOURCES

Chicago School of criminology

http://www.helium.com/items/865770-an-overview-of-the-chicago-school-theories-of-criminology

http://suite101.com/article/the-chicago-school-of-criminology-a301917

Subcultural theories

http://socialscience.stow.ac.uk/criminology/criminology_notes/subcultures_deviance.htm

http://www.criminology.fsu.edu/crimtheory/wolfgang.htm

CHAPTER 9

Social Process and Control Theories of Crime

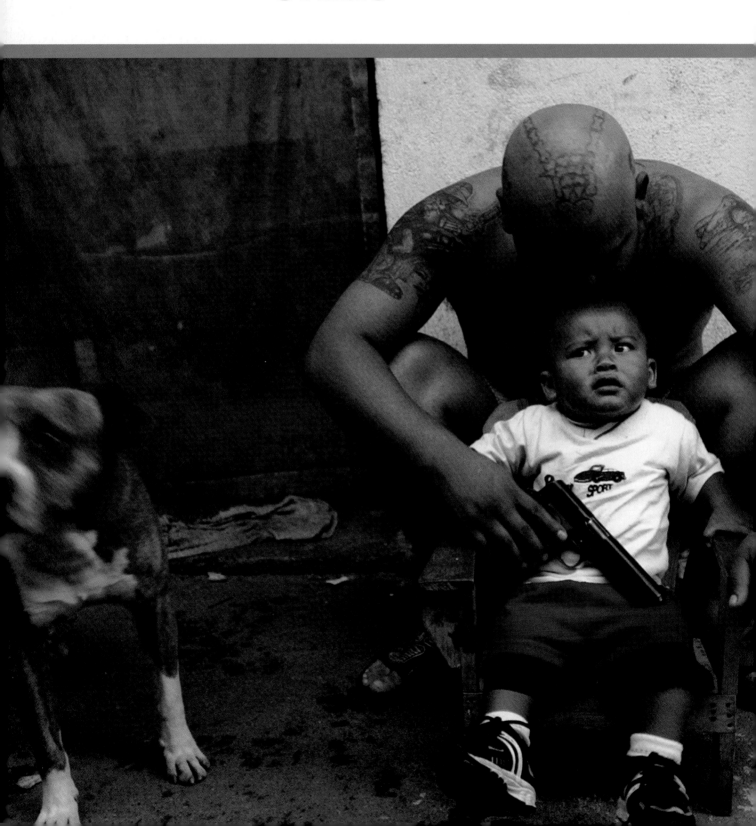

INTRODUCTION

People learn rules, morals, and values through a process of socialization. Early socialization usually occurs with the family. During this stage, children start learning how to behave. Ideally, they learn what behavior is appropriate when at home and in public. Socialization also takes place later in life and outside of the family context. As individuals grow older, other influential agents of socialization become school and peers. The workplace, community and religious organizations, and countless other entities also contribute to the socialization process.

Most people who have no understanding of criminological theory understand that socialization is important and, possibly, connected to how one behaves later in life. It is well-known, for instance, that broken homes,[1] poor parental control,[2] and child abuse and neglect[3] often lead to certain problems. For example, a child who suffers repeated abuse may be inclined to abuse his or her children in adulthood. Even if one is fortunate enough to grow up in a fully functional family, other outside factors—such as being bullied in school or ridiculed in the workplace—can contribute to inappropriate behavior.[4]

In short, people are influenced by numerous sources, which is why it is useful to examine the role of socialization in criminal behavior. Theories that claim socialization is linked to criminal activity are known as *social process theories*. Social process theories examine how individuals interact with other individuals and groups. These theories focus carefully on how behavior is learned, internalized, and transmitted between individuals.

This chapter begins with social process theories known as **learning theories**. Learning theories attempt to explain how and why individuals learn criminal, rather than conforming, behavior. Learning theorists believe that individuals are "socialized" in criminal behavior. For example, learning theorists argue that delinquent peers may contribute to a person's decision to violate the law. Next, we discuss **control theories**. Control theories focus on social or personal factors that *prevent* individuals from engaging in selfish, antisocial behaviors.

A useful way to distinguish between learning and control theories is as follows: Learning theories are concerned with why individuals are socialized into criminal activity (e.g., by witnessing domestic violence over a period of years and then acting abusively in adulthood). By contrast, control theories are concerned with why individuals are *not* socialized into conforming behavior. That is, what is it about one's surroundings and upbringing that leads one to follow the rules of society despite a natural disposition to offend?

LEARNING THEORIES

In this section, we review theories that explain the social processes of *how* and *why* people engage in criminal behavior through learning. Unlike other theories that assume we are born with offending tendencies (e.g., control theories), virtually all learning theories assume that our attitudes and

THE SON OF JEFF HALL

On May 1, 2011, around 4:00 a.m., police found Jeff Hall dead on his living room couch. His 10-year-old son had shot him with a handgun. Just hours before shooting his father, the boy was showing off the gift his father had given him—a leather belt with a silver insignia of the Nazi SS. Jeff Hall led a chapter of the National Socialist Movement (NSM) in Riverside, California. The NSM is considered the nation's largest neo-Nazi party.

Interestingly, while many involved in the NSM are alienated from their families or have difficulty explaining their beliefs, Mr. Hall was open with his five children about his activities. In fact, his home was the NSM's Southern California headquarters. The movement focused a great deal of energy on illegal immigration. He invested his own personal funds on night-vision goggles and ham radio licenses to conduct "border patrols." Mr. Hall also bragged to others that he was teaching his son to use night-vision equipment as well as to shoot a gun.[5]

In January of 2013, the boy, then 12 years old, was found criminally responsible for killing his father. The judge noted that while the boy had endured years of abuse and neglect, he did realize that killing was wrong. The judge also stated that "Hall's attempts to indoctrinate his son

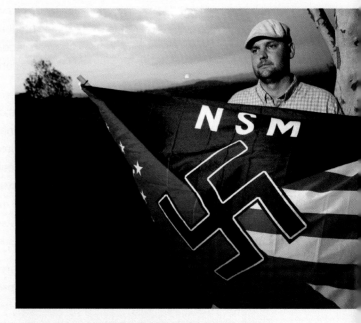

Jeff Hall, pictured here holding the NSM flag, was shot to death by his 10-year-old son.

into the hate group corrupted the thought process of a disturbed boy who already had displayed violent tendencies."[6] The 12-year-old boy was found guilty of second-degree murder and for using a gun in the commission of a felony. He could be held in juvenile detention until he is 23 years old. When reading about Jeff Hall and his son, there are many issues one should think about. For instance, where did the boy learn how to shoot a gun? Was this boy "born" violent, or was violence something he learned from firsthand experience?

IN JANUARY OF 2013, THE BOY, THEN 12 YEARS OLD, WAS FOUND CRIMINALLY RESPONSIBLE FOR KILLING HIS FATHER.

behavioral decisions are acquired via communication after we are born; so individuals enter the world with a blank slate (often referred to as the tabula rasa). Thus, learning theories seek to explain how criminal and noncriminal behavior is learned through cultural values people internalize and acquaintances they make. A key feature of learning theories is recognizing the influence of peers and significant others on an individual's behavior. Three learning theories are discussed in this section, starting with differential association theory.

DIFFERENTIAL ASSOCIATION THEORY

Edwin H. Sutherland is considered one of the most influential criminologists of the 20th century. In the third edition of *Principles of Criminology*, Sutherland fully introduced his **differential association theory**.[7] He was especially interested in explaining how criminal values and attitudes could be culturally transmitted from one generation to the next. Sutherland was greatly influenced by Shaw and McKay's concept of social disorganization[8] (see Chapter 8). He was also influenced by Gabriel Tarde's imitation theory,[9] which, as its name suggests, claims that people imitate one another. Tarde formulated three laws of imitation: (1) People imitate one another in proportion as they are in close contact, (2) often the superior is imitated by the inferior, and (3) when two mutually exclusive methods or approaches come together, one method can be substituted for another.[10]

ELEMENTS OF DIFFERENTIAL ASSOCIATION THEORY. Sutherland presented his theory of differential association with nine specific statements.[11] The statements are listed below in italics, and each statement is followed by a brief interpretation and clarification.

1. *Criminal behavior is learned.* Criminal behavior is not inherited; rather, a person needs to be trained, or educated, in crime.

2. *Criminal behavior is learned in interaction with other persons in a process of communication.* In most instances, this communication is verbal. However, communication can also be nonverbal in nature.

3. *The principal part of the learning of criminal behavior occurs within intimate personal groups.* Sutherland distinguished personal and impersonal groups. Personal communications between family and friends, he theorized, will have more of an influence than impersonal communications, such as those occurring with simple acquaintances, as well as through the movies and other entertainment media.

4. *When criminal behavior is learned, the learning includes (a) techniques of committing the crime, which are sometimes very complicated, sometimes very simple; and (b) the specific direction of motives, drives, rationalizations, and attitudes.* Criminals learn from others the techniques, methods, and motives necessary to sustain their behavior.

5. *The specific direction of motives and drives is learned from definitions of the legal codes as favorable or unfavorable.* Individuals may associate with others who define the legal codes as rules that should be observed; these individuals, however, may also associate with others whose definitions favor violating these legal codes.

6. *A person becomes delinquent because of an excess of definitions favorable to violation of law over definitions unfavorable to violation of law.* Sutherland noted that this is the essence of differential association. Individuals can have associations that favor both criminal and noncriminal behavior patterns. A person will engage in criminal behavior when there is an *excess* of definitions that favor violating the law.

7. *Differential associations may vary in frequency, duration, priority, and intensity.* Frequency and duration refer to how often and how long associations occur. Priority

JOURNAL ARTICLE

Differential Association

learning theories: theoretical models that assume that criminal behavior of individuals is due to a process of learning from others the motivations and techniques for engaging in such behavior

control theories: theories of criminal behavior that emphasize the assumption that humans are born selfish and that their tendencies toward aggression and offending must be controlled

differential association theory: a theory of criminal behavior that emphasizes association with significant others (peers, parents, etc.) in learning criminal behavior refers to whether an individual has developed a strong sense of lawful behavior during early childhood. Intensity is not precisely defined.

8. *The process of learning criminal behavior by association with criminal and anticriminal patterns involves all of the mechanisms that are involved in any other learning.* This statement asserts that the process of learning criminal behavior is similar to the process of learning other types of behavior.

9. *While criminal behavior is an expression of general needs and values, it is not explained by those general needs and values, since noncriminal behavior is an expression of the same needs and values.* Sutherland argued that motives, needs, and values as explanations for criminal behavior are inadequate because they are also explanations for noncriminal behavior. For instance, needing money is a motivation for a thief to steal as well as for a student to get a part-time job. This final proposition was largely an argument against the other dominant social theories of crime at the time when Sutherland wrote—namely, strain theory, which emphasized economic goals and means in predicting criminal activity.[12]

To further elaborate on these principles, it is important to understand the cultural context when Sutherland developed his theory in the early to mid-20th century. At that time, most academics, and society for that matter, believed that there was something abnormal or different about criminals. For example, Sheldon's body type theory was popular in the same time period, as was the use of IQ (intelligence quotient) to pick out persons who were of lower intelligence and predisposed to crime (both of these theories are covered in Chapter 4). So the common assumption at the time when Sutherland created the principles of differential association theory was that there was something essentially wrong with individuals who committed crime.

AUDIO
Deviant Behavior

In light of this common assumption, it was extremely profound for Sutherland to propose that criminality is learned just as any conventional activity is learned. He asserted that any normal individual, when exposed to definitions and attitudes favorable toward crime, will learn both the motivations and techniques for engaging in illegal behaviors. Furthermore, he proposed the idea that the various learning mechanisms and processes—namely, social interaction—involved in developing criminality are identical to the learning processes of virtually all conventional activities, such as reading, playing football, or riding a bike.

Almost everyone learns to swim or ride a bike from friends, parents, or teachers. In contrast, almost no one learns how to do these activities from reading a book. Instead, we typically learn the techniques (e.g., how to float in a pool or balance and turn on a bike) as well as motivations (e.g., it is pleasurable and fun to do with friends) for engaging in such activities from our significant others. According to Sutherland, crime is learned the same way—through interactions with individuals with whom we are close—and from them we learn both the techniques (e.g., how to hot-wire a car) and the motivations (e.g., taking a "joyride" in a stolen car can be a thrill). Although in modern times most people and researchers take it for granted that criminal behavior is learned, the idea was quite radical when Sutherland presented his theory of differential association.

Still, differential association theory is just as deterministic as were the earlier theories that emphasized biological factors (e.g., stigmata, body types, etc.) or psychological factors (e.g., low IQ). In other words, Sutherland strongly felt that if a person was receiving from significant others and internalizing a higher ratio of definitions that breaking the law is beneficial, then that person certainly would engage in illegal behavior (see Principle 6 above). So there is virtually no room for any possible free choice or decision making in this model of criminal activity. In contrast, individuals' propensities to commit crimes are determined through social interactions with significant others. Thus, individuals do not actually make decisions to commit (or not commit) criminal acts; rather, we are predetermined to do so, which makes differential association theory as highly positivistic (i.e., deterministic) as any of the preexisting positivistic theories we reviewed in Chapter 4 (e.g., Lombroso's theory of born criminals).

However, the primary distinction of differential association theory from the earlier positivistic theories is that instead of biological or psychological traits being emphasized as primary factors in causing criminality, it is social interaction and learning. In fact, Sutherland was quite clear in asserting that individual differences in terms of physiological functioning have nothing to do with the development of criminality. It should be noted at this point that this hard stance against biological and psychological factors being relevant as risk factors in criminal activity has been negated by the extant empirical research, which clearly shows that such variations in physiological functioning do in fact significantly influence criminal behavior. In defense of Sutherland, this body of research does suggest that such physiological factors may affect individuals' criminality largely due to the effects of such detriments on the learning processes of people in everyday life.

CLASSICAL CONDITIONING. At the time when he developed his theory of differential association, Sutherland used the dominant psychological theory of learning of the early 20th century. This learning model was called **classical conditioning** and was primarily developed by Pavlov.[13] Classical conditioning assumes that animals, as well as people, learn through associations between stimuli and responses. The organism, animal, or person is a somewhat passive actor in this process, meaning that the individual simply receives various forms of stimuli and responds in natural ways. Furthermore, the organism (or individual) will learn to associate certain stimuli with certain responses over time.

REFERENCE ARTICLE

Classical Conditioning

In developing the theory, Pavlov performed seminal research that showed that dogs, which are naturally afraid of loud noises, could be quickly conditioned not only to be less afraid of loud bells but actually to desire and salivate at their ringing. A dog naturally salivates when presented with meat; so when this unconditioned stimulus (meat) is presented, a dog will always salivate (unconditioned response) in anticipation of eating the meat. Pavlov demonstrated through a series of experiments that if a bell (conditioned stimulus) is always rung at the same time as the dog is presented with meat, then the dog will learn to associate what was previously a negative stimulus (loud bell) with a positive stimulus (food). Thus, the dog will quickly begin salivating at the ringing of a bell, even when meat is not presented. When this occurs, it is called an unconditioned response, because it is not natural; however, it is a powerful and effective means of learning, and it can sometimes take only a few occurrences of coupling the ringing bell with meat before the unconditioned response takes place.

VIDEO

Conditioning

A common, real-life example that virtually everyone can relate to is associations related to songs or smells. Specifically, probably every reader has heard a song on the radio that reminded her or him of a good (or bad) event that occurred years before while that same song was playing. It can seem as though we are reexperiencing that event in our minds when we hear the song. Similarly, people diagnosed with post-traumatic stress disorder can reexperience traumatic events from exposure to certain stimuli. For example, the sound of a car backfiring can remind a war veteran of being under fire in combat. A similar phenomenon occurs with odors, in the sense that a certain scent, such as a particular perfume or cologne, can remind us of someone we once dated. Another version of this experience is when a spouse has to leave for a long time and the pillow retains his or her natural scent; this can hold a powerful association with memories and often elicits strong emotions (responses) in the partner or spouse left behind. On a more simple level, the smell of a turkey cooking in the oven may automatically remind us of Thanksgiving (or other holidays).

classical conditioning: a learning model that assumes that animals, as well as people, learn through associations between stimuli and responses

These are just a couple of the many types of associations typically experienced by people in everyday life, and there are many other forms of this type of learning that virtually all persons experience but may not realize they are experiencing. Still, all involve the primary components of classical conditioning, in that they all include a stimulus (e.g., a song), an association with the stimulus, and the resulting response (e.g., good/bad feelings). This is still a highly supported learning model.

Another modern use of this learning model in humans is the prescribed administration of drugs that make people ill when they drink alcohol.[14] Alcoholics are often prescribed drugs that will make them feel sick, often to the point of throwing up, if they ingest any alcohol. The idea behind these drugs is primarily that users will learn to associate feelings of sickness with drinking and that this will thus curb the desire to consume alcohol. One important barrier to this strategy is that many alcoholics do not consistently take the drugs, so they often slip back into addiction. However, in defense of this strategy, if alcoholics were to maintain their prescribed drug regimen, it would likely work, because people do tend to learn effectively through association, which in this case is feelings of nausea (the response) associated with ingesting alcohol (the stimulus).

A similar form of the classical conditioning learning model was prominently used in the critically acclaimed 1964 novel (and subsequent motion picture) *A Clockwork Orange*. In this novel, the author, Anthony Burgess, tells the story of a juvenile murderer who is "rehabilitated" by doctors who force him to watch hour after hour of violent images while simultaneously giving him drugs that make him sick. In the novel, the protagonist is "cured" after only 2 weeks of this treatment, having learned to consistently associate violence with sickness. However, once he is released he lacks the ability to choose violence and other antisocial behavior, which is seen as losing his humanity. Therefore, the ethicists order a reversal treatment and make him back into his former self, a violent predator. Although a fictional piece, *A Clockwork Orange* is probably one of the best illustrations of the use of classical conditioning in relation to criminal offending and rehabilitation.

REACTION TO DIFFERENTIAL ASSOCIATION THEORY. Since Sutherland's nine statements were published, they have been subjected to significant scrutiny and interpretation. Researchers have been critical of his statements and have also pointed to several "misinterpretations" of his work.[15] For example, some people assume that Sutherland's theory is concerned only with associations between criminals. If this were the only relevant type of association, then the theory would be invalid, because some people have an extensive association with criminal behavior patterns but are not considered criminals. These people include police officers, corrections officers, and judges.

As indicated, Sutherland theorized that crime occurs when associations favorable to violation of the law "outweigh" associations favorable to conforming to the law. But measuring this ratio and understanding when the balance tips in favor of a criminal lifestyle is all but impossible.[16] Still, some empirical studies have found support for differential association variables, particularly in the area of white-collar crime. For example, one recent study involving a sample of 133 graduate business students found that participants would go against their friends' and professors' opinions and commit corporate crime if they felt that their coworkers and superiors at work agreed with the illegal behavior.[17] This study found that the influence of associating with people who have a different set of values—in this case, strong corporate attitudes—on a daily basis can have a powerful effect on criminal decision making, even to the point where individuals will do things they know their family and friends feel are immoral. The context of this and other corporate crime studies is interesting because Sutherland actually coined the term *white-collar crime* and did much of the seminal work on that topic (for more discussion, see Chapter 13). So perhaps it is not so surprising that much of the support for differential association theory is found in the context of corporate crime.

On a related note, Sutherland theorized that criminal associations lead to crime but that the reverse is plausible. That is, one may commit crime and then seek out individuals with attitudes similar to one's own.[18] This is similar to the "Which came first, the chicken or the egg?" debate. Do youths learn to commit crime once they start hanging out with delinquent peers, or do the youths that commit crime start hanging out with similar people (i.e., birds of a feather flock together)? After a rather lengthy literary debate, most recent research points to the occurrence of both causal processes: Criminal associations cause more crime, *and* committing crime causes more criminal associations.[19]

Another interesting criticism that has been leveled at differential association theory is the argument that if criminal behavior is learned and people are born with a blank slate (i.e., tabula rasa), then who first committed crime if no one taught that person the techniques and motives for it? After all, if someone was the first to do it, then who could expose that person to the definitions favorable to violation of law? Furthermore, what factor(s) caused that individual to do it first if it was not learned? If the answers to these questions involve any other factor(s) than learning—which they must, because the theory's assumption is that there was no one to teach this behavior—then the action cannot be explained by learning theories. This is a criticism that cannot be addressed, so it is somewhat ignored in the scientific literature.

At the same time, however, some research is supportive of Sutherland's theory. For example, researchers have found that young criminals are "tutored" by older ones,[20] that criminals sometimes maintain associations with other criminals prior to their delinquent acts,[21] and that the deviant attitudes, friends, and acts are closely connected.[22] Unfortunately, many of Sutherland's principles are somewhat vague and cryptic, which does not lend the theory to easy testing.[23] Related to this issue, perhaps one of the biggest problems with Sutherland's formulation of differential association is that he used primarily one type of learning model—classical conditioning—to formulate most of his principles, which neglects the other important ways we learn attitudes and behavior from significant others. This may be an important reason why his principles are so hard to test, especially in light of more current models of his framework that have incorporated other learning models that are easier to test and provide more empirical validity.

Do you think children are influenced by video games, movies, and other forms of media?

Finally, Sutherland was adamant that such learning about how and why to commit crime occurred *only* through social interaction with significant others and *not* via any media role models, such as those in movies or on the radio. Although not surprising in our modern times, it was not long before another theorist, Daniel Glaser, proposed an alternate theory that included the important influence that such media can play in behavior. We will now review Glaser's theory.

GLASER'S CONCEPT OF DIFFERENTIAL IDENTIFICATION. As stated above, Sutherland claimed that learning of criminal definitions could take place only through social interactions with significant others, as opposed to reading a book or watching movies. However, in 1956 Daniel Glaser proposed the idea of **differential identification**, which allows for learning to take place not only through people close to us but also through other reference groups, even distant ones such as sports heroes or movie stars whom the

differential identification: a theory of criminal behavior similar to differential association theory, the major difference being that this theory takes into account associations with persons and images presented in the media

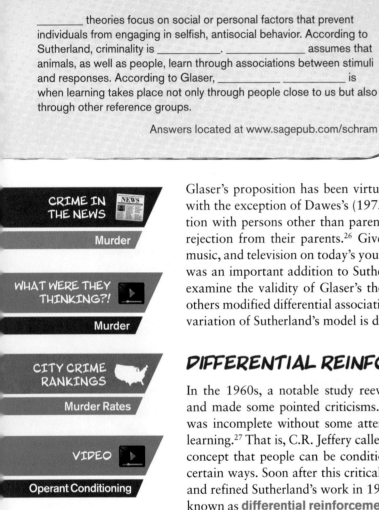

individual has never actually met or corresponded with.[24] Glaser claimed that it did not matter much whether the individual had a personal relationship with the reference group(s); in fact, he claimed that they could even be imaginary, such as fictitious characters in a movie or book. Thus, "a person pursues criminal behavior to the extent that he identifies himself with real or imaginary persons from whose perspective his criminal behavior seems acceptable."[25] The important thing, according to Glaser, was that the individual identify with the person or character and thus behave in ways that fit the norm set of this reference group or person.

Glaser's proposition has been virtually ignored by subsequent criminological research, with the exception of Dawes's (1973) study of delinquency, which found that identification with persons other than parents was strong when youths reported a high level of rejection from their parents.[26] Given the profound influence of video games, movies, music, and television on today's youth culture, it is obvious that differential identification was an important addition to Sutherland's framework. Thus, far more research should examine the validity of Glaser's theory in contemporary society. Although Glaser and others modified differential association, the most notable, respected, and empirically valid variation of Sutherland's model is differential reinforcement theory.

DIFFERENTIAL REINFORCEMENT THEORY

In the 1960s, a notable study reevaluated Sutherland's differential association theory and made some pointed criticisms. One of the primary criticisms was that the theory was incomplete without some attention to the more modern psychological models of learning.[27] That is, C.R. Jeffery called out the failure of Sutherland's model to include the concept that people can be conditioned, via rewards or punishments, into behaving in certain ways. Soon after this critical review, Robert Burgess and Ronald Akers criticized and refined Sutherland's work in 1966.[28] The product of this follow-up was what is now known as **differential reinforcement theory**. Burgess and Akers argued that by integrating Sutherland's work with contributions from the field of social psychology—namely, the learning models of **operant conditioning** and **modeling/imitation**—decisions to commit criminal behavior could be more clearly understood.

ELEMENTS OF DIFFERENTIAL REINFORCEMENT THEORY

In their 1966 article, Burgess and Akers presented seven propositions to summarize differential reinforcement theory (see Table 9.2 on page 224)—often referred to as social learning theory in the criminological literature—which largely represent efficient modifications of Sutherland's original nine principles of differential association. The influence of the relatively new (in 1966) learning models proposed by social psychologists is illustrated in their first statement, as well as throughout the seven principles. Although differential reinforcement incorporates the elements of classical conditioning learning models in its framework, the first proposition clearly states that the essential learning mechanism in social behavior is operant conditioning; so it is vital to understand what operant conditioning is and how it is valid at all times in an individual's life. The inclusion of both modern (e.g., operant conditioning and modeling) and classic models of learning (e.g., classical conditioning) explains why differential reinforcement theory is also commonly referred to as the social learning theory of crime.

differential reinforcement theory: a theory of criminal behavior that emphasizes various types of social learning, specifically classical conditioning, operant conditioning, and imitation or modeling

operant conditioning: a learning model based on the association between an action and feedback following the action

APPLYING THEORY TO CRIME: *MURDER*

In this section, we provide an example of a person (named Trent) who committed murder, largely due to influences from social interactions with his peers, who were fellow gang members. This illustrates an example of Sutherland's differential association theory, which will be discussed further below. But before we get to the actual example, it is important to understand murder or criminal homicide, as well as some current statistics on this criminal act.

According to common law, as well as traditionally in the United States, the crime of murder is defined as the "unlawful killing of a human being by another human being with malice aforethought."[29] However, proving malice aforethought is sometimes difficult, because, under the modern interpretation, it is not necessary to prove either malice as it is commonly defined, nor forethought. Therefore, it is preferable not to rely upon this misleading expression for an understanding of murder.[30]

According to the Federal Bureau of Investigation (FBI) Uniform Crime Reports (UCR), murder and nonnegligent manslaughter is defined as the "willful (nonnegligent) killing of one human being by another."[31] The UCR Program does not include such incidents as deaths caused by negligence, suicide, or accident; justifiable homicides; or attempts to murder or assaults to murder, which are counted as aggravated assaults.[32] Based on the 2011 report, the FBI summarized the following key findings concerning murder:

- About 14,612 people were murdered nationwide in 2011. This is a 0.7% decrease from 2010 and a 10.0% decrease from 2002.

- Almost 44% of murders were reported in the South, the most populated region, followed by 21.0% reported in the West, 20.6% reported in the Midwest, and 14.8% reported in the Northeast.

Table 9.1 provides a summary of the types of weapons used in these murders. Note that more than two thirds of the murders involved a firearm (67.8%), followed by knives or cutting instruments (13.4%).

There are instances when individuals, accused of murder, provide some type of defense to justify their criminal actions. For instance, *self-defense* is most often used as a defense in homicide cases. The defendant must show some evidence of the following to make such a claim:

- Unlawful force was threatened against him or her.

- Danger of harm was imminent.

TYPE	NUMBER OF OFFENSES (2011)	PERCENTAGE DISTRIBUTION
Firearms	8,583	67.8%
Knives or cutting instruments	1,694	13.4%
Blunt objects (clubs, hammers, etc.)	496	3.9%
Personal weapons (hands, fists, feet, etc.)	728	5.7%
Poison	5	*
Explosives	12	0.1%
Fire	75	0.6%
Narcotics	29	0.2%
Drowning	15	0.1%
Strangulation	85	0.7%
Asphyxiation	89	0.7%
Other weapon or weapon not stated	853	6.7%

Table 9.1 Murder by Weapon

*Less than 1/10 of 1%.
Source: FBI. (2011). *Crime in the United States, 2011.* Washington, DC: U.S. Department of Justice, n.p.

(Continued)

- He or she was not the aggressor.
- He or she fully believed that danger existed.
- Force was necessary to avert the danger.
- The type and amount of force used was necessary.

The jury is then required to determine whether the defendant's perception of the need of self-defense, or the degree of force used, was reasonable.[33]

Another defense is the *insanity defense.* Throughout American history, the insanity defense has varied. We discuss this in more detail in Chapter 6. A well-known case using a diminished-capacity defense occurred in 1978, when Dan White shot and killed San Francisco Mayor George Moscone and San Francisco Supervisor Harvey Milk. His diminished-capacity defense was termed the "Twinkie Defense" by the media. It was based on psychological testimony revealing that Dan White's junk-food diet

exacerbated a chemical imbalance in his brain. Thus, he was not deemed legally responsible for these deaths.[34]

To clarify key aspects of differential association, we apply this perspective to the crime of murder. Trent had a troubled family life and difficulties in school. He did not easily establish and maintain close relationships with his family or friends. When Trent was 12 years old, he was befriended by a couple of boys in his neighborhood. He would spend a great deal of time with these boys, and these boys were part of a local gang. In this gang, Trent learned how to shoplift, burglarize homes and businesses, and sell drugs. He also learned how to use a gun. Soon he began to incorporate beliefs such as, one has to "take what one wants" rather than "work hard and wait for the rewards." This attitude illustrates an excess of definitions favorable to violating the law over definitions unfavorable to violating the law.

When Trent was 16 years old, he and some of his fellow gang

members spotted a man driving a very expensive car. They decided to carjack the automobile at any cost. They waited until the man was at a red light and pulled their car alongside his. Given his previous internalization of the techniques and motivations provided by fellow gang members, as well as their encouragement just prior to the incident, Trent got out of the passenger-side door and told the man to get out of his car. The man refused, so Trent shot him once in the head. Trent then dragged the man out of the car and slid into the driver's seat and drove away. A number of eyewitnesses immediately called 911. Two days later, Trent was arrested and charged with murder.

Incorporating Sutherland's differential association, we can argue that Trent learned to engage in criminal activity through his friends. This learning process also involved Trent being exposed to definitions and attitudes favorable toward crime, which ultimately resulted in Trent committing murder because he wanted an automobile "at any cost."

Source: FBI.

---

modeling/imitation: a major factor in differential reinforcement theory that proposes that much social learning takes place via imitation or modeling of behavior

DIFFERENTIAL REINFORCEMENT THEORY PROPOSITIONS
1. Criminal behavior is learned according to the principles of operant conditioning.
2. Criminal behavior is learned both in nonsocial situations that are reinforcing or discriminative and through that social interaction in which the behavior of other persons is reinforcing or discriminative for criminal behavior.
3. The principal part of the learning of criminal behavior occurs in those groups which comprise the individual's major source of reinforcements.
4. The learning of criminal behavior, including specific techniques, attitudes, and avoidance procedures, is a function of the effective and available reinforcers, and the existing reinforcement contingencies.
5. The specific class of behaviors which are learned and their frequency of occurrence are a function of the reinforcers which are effective and available, and the rules or norms by which these reinforcers are applied.
6. Criminal behavior is a function of norms which are discriminative for criminal behavior, the learning of which takes place when such behavior is more highly reinforced than noncriminal behavior.
7. The strength of criminal behavior is a direct function of the amount, frequency, and probability of its reinforcement.

Table 9.2 Differential Reinforcement Theory Propositions

Source: Burgess, R., & Akers, R. (1966). A differential association-reinforcement theory of criminal behavior. *Social Problems, 14,* 146.

COMPARATIVE CRIMINOLOGY: *HOMICIDE*

Homicide Rates per World Subregion

In this section, we examine findings from data provided by the sixth to eighth United Nations Crime Surveys and data from the World Health Organization[35] regarding homicide rates in various world subregions.[36]

The data in Figure 9.1 reveal that of the world subregions included in this study, Southern Africa has, by far, the highest rate of homicide at 31.5 (per 100,000/year). The second highest region—Central America—is a distant second at 15.8, and the third-ranking subregion—South America—is close to the second at 15.5. It is also notable that the world average is 8.2, which would likely be significantly lower except for having such a high outlier at the top (Southern Africa). In fact, if we removed the world ranking from this report, and chose to use the median (instead of the mean or average) as our measure of central tendency of the 16 subregions presented in the report, then the world average would be about 5.8 (per 100,000/year).

Also notable is North America (which of course includes the United States) at a rate of 6.8, which is below the world average (8.2). Perhaps most interesting is the rate reported for North Africa (0.8), which is the lowest reported, despite being on the same continent as the highest recorded rate (Southern Africa). This just goes to show how certain locations, often in close proximity, can be entirely different in terms of crime. This can also be seen on a more local level, such as in cities in Southern California (e.g., Mission Viejo, Thousand Oaks) that are some of the safest communities in the United States virtually every year, while some close cities in that region (e.g., Compton, San Bernardino) typically have some of the highest rates of crime. It is quite amazing that some of the cities in our nation or regions in the world can have such drastic differences regarding crime rates. This just goes to show how variant places can be, even if they are relatively close in proximity or in the same geographic area.[37]

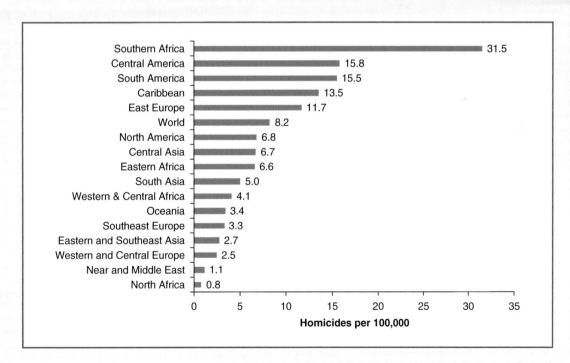

Figure 9.1 Homicides per 100,000 Population, per World Subregion (2002)

Sources: 6th to 8th UN Crime Surveys; WHO, 2002.

(Continued)

COMPARATIVE CRIMINOLOGY: *(CONTINUED)*

RANK AND CITY	RATE	RANK AND CITY	RATE	RANK AND CITY	RATE
1 New Orleans, LA	20.8	17 Philadelphia, PA M.D.	9.1	37 Oakland-Fremont, CA M.D.	7.7
2 Detroit-Livonia-Dearborn, MI M.D.*	18.2	17 Sherman-Denison, TX	9.1	38 Pensacola, FL	7.6
3 Flint, MI	13.8	21 Bakersfield, CA	9.0	39 Lafayette, LA	7.5
4 Macon, GA	12.0	21 Hot Springs, AR	9.0	39 Peoria, IL	7.5
5 Danville, VA	11.3	21 Pine Bluff, AR	9.0	41 Mobile, AL	7.4
6 Salinas, CA	10.7	21 Salisbury, MD	9.0	42 Houston, TX	7.3
7 Merced, CA	10.5	25 Miami-Dade County, FL M.D.	8.9	43 Jacksonville, FL	7.2
8 Florence, SC	10.4	26 Albany, GA	8.7	43 Panama City-Lynn Haven, FL	7.2
8 Jackson, MS	10.4	27 Memphis, TN-MS-AR	8.6	43 Richmond, VA	7.2
10 Baltimore-Towson, MD	10.3	28 Shreveport-Bossier City, LA	8.4	46 Durham-Chapel Hill, NC	7.1
11 Augusta, GA-SC	10.2	29 Kansas City, MO-KS	8.2	47 Columbus, GA-AL	7.0
11 Rocky Mount, NC	10.2	29 Lake Charles, LA	8.2	47 Goldsboro, NC	7.0
13 Yakima, WA	10.0	31 Vallejo-Fairfield, CA	8.1	47 Montgomery, AL	7.0
14 Hinesville, GA	9.7	32 Atlantic City, NJ	8.0	50 Jackson, MI	6.9
15 Longview, TX	9.6	32 Tucson, AZ	8.0	50 Newark-Union, NJ-PA M.D.	6.9
16 Stockton, CA	9.2	32 Visalia-Porterville, CA	8.0	50 Victoria, TX	6.9
17 Detroit (greater), MI	9.1	35 Philadelphia (greater) PA-NJ-MD-DE	7.8		
17 Monroe, LA	9.1	35 St. Louis, MO-IL	7.8		

Table 9.3 Murder Rate in 2010

National Rate = 4.8 Murders per 100,000 Population

*metropolitan division

DIFFERENTIAL REINFORCEMENT THEORY PROPOSITIONS

Differential reinforcement theory may appear, in many ways, to be no different than rational choice theory (see Chapter 3). This is true to some extent, because both models focus on punishments and reinforcements that occur after an individual offends. Differential reinforcement theory, however, can be distinguished from the rational choice perspective in that it assumes humans are born with an innate capacity for rational decision making, whereas the differential reinforcement perspective assumes individuals are born with a blank slate (i.e., tabula rasa) and thus must be socialized and taught how to behave through various forms of conditioning (e.g., classical and operant conditioning) and modeling. Also, differential reinforcement theory is far more deterministic than rational choice theory, in the sense that the former assumes that individuals have virtually no free will or free choice (behavior is based on the definitions, beliefs, rewards, punishments, etc., that individuals are subject to after their previous behaviors), whereas the latter is based almost entirely on the assumption that individuals do indeed have the ability to make their own choices and tend to make calculated decisions based on the contextual circumstances of a given situation. Thus, it is clear that differential reinforcement theory has different assumptions, as well as distinctive concepts, that clearly distinguish it from rational choice models of behavior. We will now review some of the key concepts that differential reinforcement theory proposed that were important additions to the differential association model and that made it a far more robust and valid theory for explaining criminal behavior.

JOURNAL ARTICLE

Differential Reinforcement

OPERANT CONDITIONING

Operant conditioning was primarily developed by B. F. Skinner,[38] who coincidentally was just across campus from Edwin Sutherland when he was developing differential association theory at Indiana University; just as it is now, academia tended to be too intradisciplinary and intradepartmental. If Sutherland had been aware of Skinner's studies and theoretical development, he likely would have included it in his original framework of differential association theory. However, operant conditioning was not well-known or researched at the time Sutherland developed his theory of differential association; rather, he simply incorporated the dominant learning model of his time—classical conditioning. So it was up to others, such as Burgess and Akers, to later incorporate operant conditioning (as well as Bandura's social learning principles, discussed below) into Sutherland's theoretical model.

To explain it simply, operant conditioning is concerned with how behavior is influenced by reinforcements and punishments. Operant conditioning assumes that the animal or human is a proactive player in seeking out rewards, not just a passive entity that simply receives stimuli, which is what classical conditioning assumes. Specifically, certain behaviors are encouraged through reward (**positive reinforcement**) or through avoidance of punishment (**negative reinforcement**). For example, if a child is given a toy or video game for doing well on his or her report card, that is a positive reinforcement. On the other hand, if a child who has been confined to his or her room after school for a week for not doing homework is then allowed to start playing with friends again after school because she or he did a good job on homework the following week, this is a negative reinforcement because the child is now being rewarded via the avoidance of something negative. Like different types of reinforcement, punishment also comes in two forms. Thus, behavior is discouraged, or weakened, via adverse stimuli (positive punishment) or lack of reward (negative punishment). A good example of positive punishment would be putting a child in a "timeout," where he or she is forced to sit alone for many minutes—a punishment that tends to be quite effective with young children. Another form of positive punishment—perhaps the best example—is "spanking," but this has been frowned on in recent times because it is certainly a positive form of a negative stimulus. So anything that directly presents negative sensations or feelings is a positive punishment. On the other hand, if parents take away their child's opportunity to go on an outing with friends (say to a movie or theme park) because he or she skipped school, this is an example of negative punishment because the parents are removing a positive aspect or reward.

One notable example of operant conditioning is teaching a mouse to successfully run a maze. When the mouse takes the right paths and finishes the maze quickly, it is either positively reinforced (e.g., rewarded with a piece of cheese) or negatively reinforced (e.g., not shocked with an electric prod, as it was when it chose the wrong path). On the other hand, when the mouse takes wrong turns or does not complete the maze in adequate time, it is either positively punished (e.g., shocked with electricity) or negatively punished (e.g., not given the cheese). Mice, like humans, tend to learn the correct behavior extremely fast using such consistent implementation of punishments and reinforcements.

Especially in humans, such principles of operant conditioning can be found even at very early ages. In fact, many of us have implemented such techniques (or been subjected to them) without really knowing they were called operant conditioning. For example, during "toilet training," we teach our children to use the toilet, rather than urinating and defecating in their pants. To reinforce the act of going to the bathroom on a toilet, we

positive reinforcement: a concept in social learning in which people are rewarded by receiving something they want

negative reinforcement: a concept in social learning in which people are rewarded through removal of something they dislike

Referring to Bandura's theory of imitation/modeling, do you think the boy pictured learned this hand sign by observing others?

encourage the correct behavior by presenting positive rewards, which can be as simple as showing extreme pleasure and hugging the child or giving the child a "treat." While modern parents rarely use spanking in toilet training, there is an inherent positive punishment for children who use the bathroom in their pants; specifically, they have to stay in their dirty diaper for a while and face the embarrassment most children feel when this happens. Also, negative punishments are present in such situations because they do not get the positive recognition or treats, so the rewards are absent as well.

A large amount of research has shown that humans learn attitudes and behavior best through a mix of punishments and reinforcements throughout life. For example, studies have clearly shown that rehabilitative programs that appear to work most effectively in reducing recidivism in offenders are those that have many opportunities for rewards, as well as threats for punishments. To clarify, empirical research that has combined the findings from hundreds of studies of rehabilitation programs has demonstrated that the programs that are most successful in changing the attitudes and behavior of previous offenders are those that offer at least four reward opportunities for every one punishment aspect of the program.[39] So whether it is training children to use the toilet or altering criminals' thinking and behavior, operant conditioning is a well-established form of learning that makes differential reinforcement theory a more valid and specified model of offending than differential association.

Thus, whether deviant or conforming behavior occurs and continues "depends on the past and present rewards or punishment for the behavior, and the rewards and punishment attached to alternative behavior."[40] This is in stark contrast to Sutherland's differential association model, which looked only at what happens before an act (i.e., classical conditioning), not what happens after (i.e., operant conditioning). Burgess and Akers's model looks at both what occurs before the act and what occurs afterward. Thus, illegal behavior is likely to occur, as Burgess and Akers theorized, when its perceived rewards outweigh the potential punishments for committing such acts.

BANDURA'S THEORY OF IMITATION/MODELING

Burgess and Akers emphasized another learning model in their formulation of differential reinforcement theory, which was *imitation and modeling*. Given that Sutherland's original formulation of differential association theory was somewhat inspired by Tarde's concept of imitation,[41] it is surprising that his nine principles did not adequately emphasize the importance of modeling in the process of learning behavior. Similar to the neglect of acknowledging Skinnerian models of operant conditioning, Sutherland's failure to focus on imitation and modeling was likely due to the fact that the primary work by Albert Bandura in this area had not become well-known at the time when differential association theory was being formulated.[42]

Bandura demonstrated, through a series of theoretical and experimental studies, that a significant amount of learning takes place absent virtually any form of conditioning, or responses to a given behavior. To clarify, he claimed that individuals can learn even if they are not punished or rewarded for a given behavior (i.e., operant conditioning) or exposed to associations between stimuli and responses (i.e., classical conditioning). Instead, Bandura proposed that people learn much of their attitudes and behavior from simply observing the behavior of others—namely, through mimicking others. This type of phenomenon is often referred to as "monkey see, monkey do"—but not just monkeys do this. Social psychological research has clearly established that humans, as well as most animal species, are physiologically "hardwired" (meaning it is instinctive) to observe and learn the behavior of others, especially those older in years, to see what behavior is essential for success and survival.

The most important finding of Bandura's experiments was that simply observing the behavior of others, especially adults, can have profound learning effects on the behavior of children. To clarify, in Bandura's experiments, a randomized experimental group of children watched a video of adults acting aggressively toward a Bo-Bo doll (a blow-up plastic doll), and a control group of children did not watch such illustrations of adults beating up the dolls. These different groups of children were then sent into a room containing Bo-Bo dolls. The experimental group who had seen the adult behavior mimicked this behavior by acting far more aggressively toward the dolls than did the children in the control group, who had not seen the adults beating up the dolls. So although the experimental group was not provided with previous associations or rewards for being more aggressive toward the dolls, the children who had seen adults act more aggressively became far more aggressive themselves (compared with the control group) simply because they were imitating or modeling what they had seen the older people do.

In light of these findings, Bandura's theory of modeling and imitation has implications not only for the criminal behavior of individuals but also for the influence of television, movies, video games, and so on. The influences demonstrated by Bandura simply supported a phenomenon we can see in everyday life—namely, the source of fashion trends, such as wearing low-slung pants or baseball hats a certain way. These types of styles tend to ebb and flow based on respected persons (often celebrities) wearing clothing a certain way, which leads to many people, typically youth, mimicking that behavior. This can be seen very early in life, with parents having to be careful what they say and do because their children, as young as 2 years old, will imitate them. For example, this is why parents often must change their language when in the presence of toddlers. This continues throughout life, especially in teenage years, as young people imitate the "cool" trends and styles, as well as behavior. Of course, sometimes this behavior is illegal, but individuals are often simply mimicking the way their friends or others are behaving, with little regard for potential rewards or punishments. Thus, Bandura's theory of modeling and imitation adds a great deal of explanation to a model of learning, and differential reinforcement theory included such influences; Sutherland's model of differential association did not, largely because the psychological perspective had not yet been developed.

In watching an adult smoke a cigarette, this child could later mimic this behavior and try to smoke a cigarette as well.

REACTION TO DIFFERENTIAL REINFORCEMENT THEORY

Just as Sutherland's work has been interpreted and criticized, so too has that of Burgess and Akers. For instance, Reed Adams criticized the theory for incorrectly and incompletely applying the principles of operant conditioning. Further, Adams noted that the theory does not adequately address the importance of "nonsocial reinforcement."[43] Nonsocial reinforcement can be considered self-reinforcement. For example, if someone gets enjoyment out of abusing others, then the person can be considered "reinforced" through nonsocial means.

Perhaps the most important criticism of differential reinforcement theory is that it appears tautological, which means that the variables and measures used to test its validity are true by definition. To clarify, studies testing this theory have been divided into four groups of variables or factors: associations, reinforcements, definitions, and modeling.

Some critics have noted that if individuals who report that they associate with those who offend are rewarded for offending, believe offending is good, and have seen many of their significant others offend, they will be more likely to offend. In other words, if your friends and/or family are doing it, there is little doubt that you will also do it.[44] For example, critics would argue that a person who primarily hangs out with car thieves, knows he will be rewarded for stealing cars, believes stealing cars is good and not immoral, and has observed many respected others stealing cars will inevitably commit auto theft himself. However, it has been well argued that such criticisms of tautology are not valid because none of these factors necessarily make offending by the respondent true by definition.[45]

Differential reinforcement theory has been criticized in the same way as Sutherland's theory has, in the sense that delinquent associations may take place after criminal activity, rather than before. However, Burgess and Akers's model clearly addresses this area of criticism, because differential reinforcement covers what comes after the activity. Specifically, it addresses the rewards or punishments that follow criminal activity, whether those rewards come from friends, parents, or other members or institutions of society.

It is arguable that differential reinforcement theory may have the most empirical validity of any contemporary (nonintegrated) model of criminal offending, especially considering that studies have examined a variety of behaviors, ranging from drug use to property crimes to violence. The theoretical model has also been tested in samples across the United States, as well as in other cultures such as South Korea, with the evidence being quite supportive of the framework. Furthermore, a variety of age-groups have been examined, ranging from teenagers to middle-aged adults to the elderly, with all studies providing support for the model.[46] Specifically, researchers have empirically tested differential association–reinforcement theory and found that the major variables of the theory have a significant effect in explaining marijuana and alcohol use among adolescents.[47] The researchers concluded that the "study demonstrates that central learning concepts are amenable to meaningful questionnaire measurement and that social learning theory can be adequately tested with survey data."[48] Other studies have also supported the theory when attempting to understand delinquency, cigarette smoking, and drug use.[49]

One recent empirical study—a meta-analysis of virtually all the scientific studies that have tested differential reinforcement/social learning theory—concluded that there was considerable variation in the magnitude and stability of key variables in the theory.[50] Specifically, in this comprehensive study, the effects of all variables—differential association, definitions, modeling/imitation, and differential reinforcement—were typically significant predictors. However, the study showed that although the former two concepts (differential association and definitions) showed stronger magnitude in terms of explaining criminal behavior, the latter two (differential reinforcement and modeling/imitation) had only modest effects on such behavior. Overall, the model appeared to be relatively supported by the extant empirical evidence. Therefore, the inclusion of three psychological learning models—namely, classical conditioning, operant conditioning, and modeling/imitation—appears to have made differential reinforcement one of the most valid theories of human behavior, especially in regard to criminal behavior. Thus, it appears that differential reinforcement/social learning theory is one of the more valid theories in terms of explaining criminal behavior, perhaps due to the theory's incorporation of so many distinct concepts and learning theories in its primary assumptions and propositions.

NEUTRALIZATION THEORY

Neutralization theory is associated with Gresham Sykes and David Matza's *Techniques of Neutralization*[51] and Matza's *Drift Theory*.[52] Like Sutherland, both Sykes and Matza claimed that social learning influences delinquent behavior, but they also claimed that most criminals hold conventional beliefs and values. More specifically, Sykes and Matza argued that most criminals are still partially committed to the dominant social order. According to Sykes and Matza, youths are not immersed in a subculture committed to extremes of either complete conformity or complete nonconformity. Rather, these individuals vacillate, or *drift,* between these two extremes:

> The delinquent *transiently* exists in a limbo between convention and crime, responding in turn to the demands of each, flirting now with one, now the other, but postponing commitment, evading decision. Thus, he [or she] drifts between criminal and conventional action.[53]

While still partially committed to conventional social order, youths can *drift* into criminal activity and avoid feelings of guilt for these actions by justifying or rationalizing their behavior. Why is it called neutralization theory? People justify and rationalize behavior through "neutralizing" it, or making it seem less serious. In other words, individuals make up situational excuses for behavior they know is wrong, and they do this to alleviate the guilt they feel for committing such immoral acts. In many ways, this technique for alleviating guilt resembles Freud's defense mechanisms (see Chapter 6), which allow our mind to forgive ourselves for the bad things we do, even though we know they are wrong. So the specific techniques of neutralization outlined by Sykes and Matza in 1957, which we consider next, are much like excuses for inappropriate behavior.

TECHNIQUES OF NEUTRALIZATION

Sykes and Matza developed methods, or **techniques of neutralization,**[54] that people use to justify their criminal behavior. These techniques allow people to neutralize their criminal and delinquent acts by making them look as though they are conforming to the rules of society. Individuals are then freed to engage in criminal activities without serious damage to their self-image. These five techniques of neutralization include the following:

1. *Denial of responsibility.* Denial of responsibility is more than just claiming that deviant acts are an accident. Rather, individuals may claim that due to outside forces (e.g., uncaring parents, bad friends, poverty), they are not responsible or accountable for their behavior. Statements such as, "It wasn't my fault," are extremely common among both youth and adult offenders.

2. *Denial of injury.* Criminals may evaluate their wrongful behavior in terms of whether anyone was hurt by it. For instance, vandalism may be considered "mischief"; stealing a car may be viewed as "borrowing." Sometimes society agrees with people who evaluate their wrongfulness in this manner, designating these activities as "pranks."

3. *Denial of the victim.* While criminals may accept responsibility for their actions and admit these actions caused an injury, they neutralize them as being a rightful retaliation or punishment. Criminals may perceive themselves as avengers and the victim as the wrongdoer. For instance, vandalism is revenge on an unfair teacher, and shoplifting is retaliation against a "crooked" store owner. Another variation is when shoplifters claim that no one is getting hurt because the stores have theft insurance, failing to acknowledge that stores raise their prices to alleviate such losses and higher insurance premiums.

4. *Condemnation of the condemners.* Criminals may also shift the focus of attention from their deviant acts to the motives and behavior of those who disapprove of these actions. They may claim the condemners are hypocrites, deviants in disguise, or compelled by personal spite. For instance, one may claim that police are corrupt, teachers show favoritism, or parents "take it out" on their children. Thus, criminals neutralize their behavior through "a rejection of the rejectors."[55]

JOURNAL ARTICLE

White-Collar Crime

techniques of neutralization: a theory that suggests that individuals, especially in their teenage years and early adulthood, make excuses to alleviate guilt related to committing certain criminal acts

5. *Appeal to higher loyalties.* Criminals may sacrifice the rules of the larger society for the rules of the smaller social groups to which they belong, such as a gang or peer group. They do not necessarily deviate, because they reject the norms of the larger society. Rather, their higher loyalty is with these smaller groups; thus, they subscribe to the norms of these groups over general social norms. They may claim that one must "always help a buddy" or "never squeal on a friend." Another example of this neutralization technique is antiabortion radicals who shoot doctors who perform abortions; they claim they are appealing to a higher loyalty (a supreme being), which relieves them from responsibility and guilt.

Sykes and Matza emphasized that the techniques of neutralization may not be strong enough to protect individuals from their own internalized values and the reactions of conforming others. Instead, neutralization techniques lessen "the effectiveness of social controls" and "lie behind a large share of delinquent behavior."[56]

One area where techniques of neutralization have been applied is white-collar crime. Several studies have examined the tendency to use such excuses to alleviate guilt for engaging in behavior that professionals know is wrong. For example, a recent study that examined the decision making of 133 students in a graduate business program found that not only did neutralizing attitudes have significant effects on the respondents' decisions to commit corporate crime (involving distributing a dangerous drug) but the older students—namely, those with more seniority and experience in the business world—were more likely to employ techniques of neutralization.[57]

Furthermore, studies of corporate crime have identified two more common types of excuses that white-collar criminals use in their illegal activities.[58] Specifically, the two techniques of neutralization that experts have observed primarily among corporate criminals are "defense of necessity" and "metaphor of the ledger." *Defense of necessity* implies that an individual should not feel shame or guilt about doing something immoral as long as the behavior is perceived as necessary. Often in the corporate world, the climate puts pressure on the bottom line, and all that matters is making a larger profit, no matter what behavior is used; in other words, criminal activity is often seen as a necessity.

The other neutralizing technique found primarily in corporate settings is *metaphor of the ledger,* which essentially is the belief that an individual or group has done so much good (e.g., provided a useful product or service for public consumption) that he or she is entitled to mess up by doing something illegal (e.g., "cooking the books" or knowingly distributing a faulty, dangerous product). Many of us likely use this latter technique often, especially when it comes to studying or writing a paper right before the test or deadline. At times when we know we should be working, we may often say something along the lines of, "I worked hard yesterday, so even though I am not close to being finished, I deserve to go out with my friends to the beach today." This is a good example of using the fact that you did a good thing to justify doing something you know you probably shouldn't if you want to do well on the test or paper. So it is not just in corporate climates that these neutralizing techniques—seven altogether—are used to alleviate guilt. Regular people, especially college students and professors, use them all the time.

REACTION TO NEUTRALIZATION THEORY

Studies that have attempted to empirically test neutralization theory are, at best, inconclusive. Robert Agnew argued that there are essentially two general criticisms of studies that support neutralization theory.[59] The first challenge is that several researchers have improperly measured the acceptance of neutralization techniques. Based on his research on neutralization among incarcerated adults, one researcher noted that the relationships between vocabularies of motive and criminal behavior are more subtle, complex, and situation-specific than previously recognized. The major tasks for subsequent neutralization research are to empirically distinguish between neutralization and unconventional commitment.[60]

Second, researchers have expressed concern that criminals may use techniques of neutralization *prior* to committing a criminal offense. This ordering, they claim, is just as plausible as when neutralization *follows* a criminal act.[61] This uncertain time-order problem is due to research conducted at a single point in time. Additional research conducted over time could prove supportive of neutralization theory. However, some would argue that the temporal ordering problem is not a major criticism of the theory, because some individuals may be predisposed to make up such rationalizations for their behavior regardless of whether they do it before or after the offending act. Such a propensity may be related to low self-control theory, which we examine later in this chapter.

CONTROL THEORIES

The learning theories discussed in the previous section assume that individuals are born with a conforming disposition, or at least a blank slate (i.e., tabula rasa). By contrast, control theories assume that all people would naturally commit crimes if not for restraints on the selfish tendencies that exist in every individual. Social control perspectives of criminal behavior thus assume that there is some type of basic human nature and that all human beings exhibit antisocial tendencies toward being violently aggressive and taking from others what they want. Therefore, such control theories are more concerned with explaining why individuals *don't* commit crime or deviant behaviors. Specifically, control theorists rhetorically ask, "What is it about society, human interaction, and other factors that causes people *not* to act on their natural impulses?"

The assumption that people have innate antisocial tendencies is a controversial one because it is nearly impossible to test. Nevertheless, some recent evidence supports the idea that human beings are inherently selfish and antisocial by nature. Specifically, researchers have found that most individuals are oriented toward selfish and aggressive behaviors at a very early age, with such behaviors peaking at the end of the second year (see Figure 9.2).[62] Such studies are observational and examine children interacting with their peers. But it is clear from such studies that young individuals are predisposed toward selfish, physically aggressive behavior.

An example of antisocial dispositions appearing early in life was reported by Tremblay and LeMarquand, who found that for most young children (particularly boys), aggressive behaviors peaked at 27 months. These behaviors included hitting, biting, and kicking.[63] Their research is not isolated; virtually all developmental experts acknowledge that toddlers exhibit a tendency to show aggressive behaviors toward others. We are sure virtually all readers can relate to this, even if they don't have children of their own. All one needs to do is observe a typical preschool playground, and one will see numerous "felonies" occur in a short period of time. The bottom line is that the "terrible twos" is a

LEARNING CHECK 9.2

Burgess and Akers, in their *differential reinforcement theory*, integrated Sutherland's work with the learning models of _____ conditioning and modeling/imitation. The differential reinforcement perspective assumes that individuals are born with a _____ _____. According to Sykes and Matza, youths engaging in criminal behavior are still partially committed to the dominant _____ _____. People use certain methods, or _____ _____, to justify their criminal behavior.

Answers located at www.sagepub.com/schram

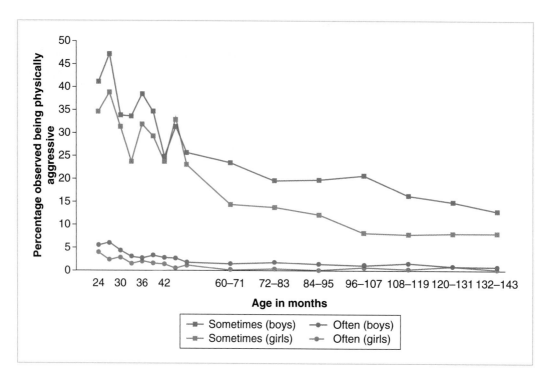

Figure 9.2 Frequencies of Hitting, Biting, and Kicking at Ages 2 to 12 Years

true phenomenon; most individuals exhibit a high tendency toward violence, as well as stealing from others, at this time in life. This line of research would seem to support the notion that people are predisposed toward antisocial, even criminal, behavior.

Control theorists do not necessarily assume that people are predisposed toward crime in a way that remains constant throughout life. On the contrary, research shows that most individuals begin to desist from such behaviors after age 2. This trend continues until about age 5, with only the most aggressive individuals (i.e., chronic offenders) continuing into higher ages. Furthermore, this extreme desistance from engaging in such antisocial behavior supports the control perspective in explaining criminal behavior, especially in the long term, because it is clear from these scientific studies that something must be controlling virtually all individuals (who previously showed tendencies toward aggressive, antisocial behavior) to inhibit themselves from carrying out their natural propensities to fight and take at will.

When considering potential factors that inhibit individuals from following their instincts, it is important to note that at the same time selfish and aggressive behaviors decline, self-consciousness is formed. Specifically, it is around age 2 when individuals begin to see themselves as entities or beings; prior to age 2, children have no understanding that they are people. Subsequently, during this second year, various social emotions—such as shame, guilt, empathy, and pride—begin to appear, largely because they become possible in knowing that they are part of a society.[64] This observation is critical because it is what separates control theories from the classical school of criminology and the predispositional theories that we already discussed. According to control theories, without appropriate socialization or personal inhibitions, people will act on their "preprogrammed" tendency toward crime and deviance.

In short, control theories claim that all individuals have natural tendencies to commit selfish, antisocial, and even criminal behavior. So what curbs this natural propensity?

Many experts believe the best explanation is that individuals are socialized and controlled by social attachments and investments in conventional society. Others claim that there are internal mechanisms (such as self-control or self-conscious emotions, such as shame, guilt, etc.), but even those are likely a product of the type of environment in which one is raised. This assumption regarding the vital importance of early socialization is probably the primary reason why control theories are currently among the most popular and accepted theories for criminologists.[65] We will now discuss several early examples of these control theories.

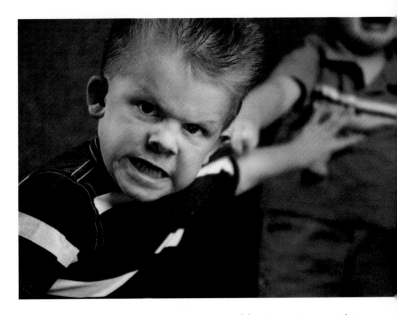

Most experts agree that toddlers, particularly boys, exhibit a tendency toward aggression.

EARLY CONTROL THEORIES OF HUMAN BEHAVIOR

THOMAS HOBBES

Although control theories are found in a variety of disciplines, perhaps the earliest notable form of social control in explaining deviant behavior is found in a perspective offered by the 17th century Enlightenment philosopher Thomas Hobbes (see Chapter 2). Hobbes claimed that the natural state of humanity was one of greediness and self-centeredness, which led to a chaotic state of constant warfare among individuals. In this state, Hobbes claimed that individuals were essentially looking out for their own well-being, and without any law or order there was no way to protect themselves.[66] But Hobbes also theorized that this constant state of chaos created such fear among many individuals that it resulted in them coming together to rationally develop a pact that would prevent such chaos. This became the concept of a society. Hobbes claimed that by creating a society and forming binding contracts (or laws), this would alleviate the chaos by deterring individuals from violating others' rights. However, despite such laws, Hobbes doubted that the innately greedy nature of humans would be completely eliminated. Rather, the existence of such innate selfishness and aggressiveness was exactly why the use of punishments was necessary, their purpose being to induce fear in the societal members who choose to violate the societal law. In a way, Hobbes was perhaps the first deterrence theorist, in the sense that he was the first notable theorist to emphasize the use of punishment to deter individuals from violating the rights of others.

REFERENCE ARTICLE

Hobbes

EMILE DURKHEIM'S IDEA OF COLLECTIVE CONSCIENCE

Consistent with Hobbes's view of individuals being naturally selfish, Emile Durkheim proposed a theory of social control in the late 1800s that suggested humans have no internal mechanism to let them know when they are fulfilled.[67] To this end, Durkheim coined the terms *automatic spontaneity* and *awakened reflection*. Automatic spontaneity can be understood in reference to animals' eating habits. Specifically, animals stop eating when they are full and are content until they are hungry again; they don't start hunting again right after they have filled their stomachs. In contrast, awakened reflection concerns the fact that humans do not have such an internal, regulatory mechanism. People often acquire resources beyond what is immediately required. Durkheim went so far as to say that "our capacity for feeling is in itself an insatiable and bottomless abyss."[68] This is one of the reasons Durkheim believed crime and deviance are quite normal, even essential, in any society.

Durkheim's "awakened reflection" has become commonly known as greed. People tend to favor better conditions and additional fulfillment because we apparently have no biological or psychological mechanism to limit such tendencies. As Durkheim noted, the selfish desires of mankind "are unlimited so far as they depend on the individual alone. . . . The more one has, the more one wants."[69] Thus, society must step in and provide the "regulative force" that keeps humans from acting too selfishly.

One of the primary elements of this regulative force is the **collective conscience**, which is the extent of similarities or likenesses that people share. For example, almost everyone can agree that homicide is a serious and harmful act that should be avoided in any civilized society. The notion of collective conscience can be seen as an early form of the idea of social bonding, which has become one of the dominant theories in criminology, discussed later in this chapter.[70]

According to Durkheim, the collective conscience serves many functions in society. One such function is the ability to establish rules that inhibit individuals from following their natural tendencies toward selfish behavior. Durkheim also believed that crime allows people to unite together in opposition against deviants. In other words, crime and deviance allow conforming individuals to be "bonded" together in opposition against a common enemy, as can be seen in everyday life. This enemy consists of the deviants who have not internalized the code of the collective conscience.

Many of Durkheim's ideas hold true today. Just recall a traumatic incident you may have experienced with other strangers (e.g., being stuck in an elevator during a power outage, weathering a serious storm, being involved in a traffic accident). Incidents such as this bring people together and permit a degree of bonding that would not take place in everyday life. Crime, Durkheim argued, serves a similar function.

How is all this relevant today? Most control theorists claim that individuals commit crime and deviant acts not because they are lacking in any way but because certain controls have been weakened in their development. This assumption is consistent not only with Durkheim's theory but with a Freudian model of human behavior we discussed in Chapter 6.

FREUD'S CONCEPT OF ID AND SUPEREGO

Although psychoanalytic theory would seem to have few similarities with a sociological positivistic theory, in this case it is extremely complementary. One of Freud's most essential propositions is that all individuals are born with a tendency toward inherent drives and selfishness due to the id domain of the psyche.[71] According to Freud, not only are all people born with id drives; they all have an equal amount of such motivations toward selfishness. Another one of Freud's assumptions is that this inherent, selfish tendency must be countered by controls produced from the development of the superego. According to Freud, the superego, which is the domain of the psyche that contains our conscience (see Figure 9.3), is formed through the interactions that occur between a young infant/child and significant others. As you can see, the control perspective has a long history that can be found in many philosophical and scientific disciplines.

VIDEO ▶

Freud's Concepts

collective conscience: according to Durkheim, the extent to which people in a society share similarities or likenesses; the stronger the collective conscience, the less crime in that community

EARLY CONTROL THEORIES OF CRIME

Throughout the 1950s and 1960s, criminologists borrowed and built on some of the ideas just discussed. Until that time, most research in the criminological literature was dominated by the learning theories discussed earlier in this chapter or by social structure theories, such as the Chicago School or Merton's strain theory (see Chapters 7 and 8). While early control theories may not be particularly popular in this day and age, they were vitally important because they laid the groundwork for future theoretical development.

REISS'S CONTROL THEORY

One of the first control theories of crime was proposed by Albert Reiss in 1951. Reiss claimed that delinquency was a consequence of weak controls that resulted in weak ego or superego controls among juvenile probationers.[72] Reiss assumed that there was no explicit motivation for delinquent activity; rather, he claimed that it would occur in the absence of controls or restraints against such behavior.

Like Freud, Reiss believed that the family was the primary entity through which deviant predispositions were discouraged. Furthermore, Reiss claimed that a sound family environment would provide for an individual's needs and the essential emotional bonds that are so important in socializing individuals. Another important factor in Reiss's model was close supervision, not only by the family but also by the community. He claimed that individuals must be closely monitored for delinquent behavior and adequately disciplined when they break the rules.

Personal factors, such as the ability to restrain one's impulses and delay gratification, were also important in Reiss's framework. These concepts are similar to later, more modern concepts of control theory that have been consistently supported by empirical research.[73] For this reason, Reiss was ahead of his time when he first proposed his control theory. Although the direct tests of Reiss's theory have provided only partial support for it, Reiss's influence is apparent in many contemporary criminological theories.[74]

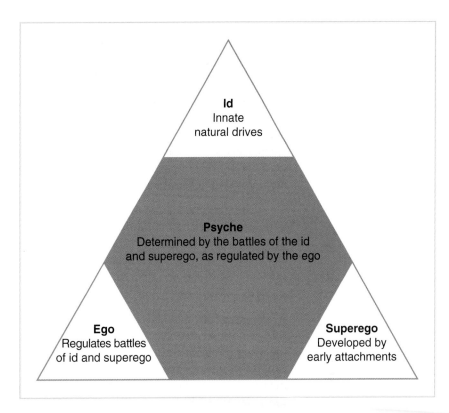

Figure 9.3 Freud's Model of the Three Domains of the Psyche

According to Reiss's model, close supervision by the family discourages deviant predispositions.

TOBY'S CONCEPT OF STAKE IN CONFORMITY

Soon after Reiss's theory was presented, a similar theory was developed. In 1957, Jackson Toby proposed a theory of delinquency and gangs.[75] He claimed that individuals were more inclined to act on their natural tendencies when the controls on them were weak. Like most other control theorists, Toby claimed that such inclinations toward deviance were distributed equally across all individuals. Further, he emphasized the concept of a *stake in conformity* that supposedly prevents most people from committing crime. The stake in conformity Toby was referring to is the extent to which individuals are *invested* in conventional society. In other words, how much is a person willing to risk by violating the law?

Studies have shown that stake in conformity is one of the most influential factors in individuals' decisions to offend. For example, individuals who have nothing to lose are much more likely to take risks and violate others' rights than are those who have relatively more invested in social institutions.[76]

One distinguishing feature of Toby's theory is his emphasis on peer influences in terms of both motivating and inhibiting antisocial behavior, depending on whether most of one's peers have low or high stakes in conformity. Toby's stake in conformity has been used effectively in subsequent control theories of crime.

NYE'S CONTROL THEORY

A year after Toby introduced the stake in conformity, F. Ivan Nye (1958) proposed a relatively comprehensive control theory that placed a strong focus on the family.[77] Following the assumptions of early control theorists, Nye claimed that no significant positive force causes delinquency, because such antisocial tendencies are universal and would be found in virtually everyone if not for certain controls usually found in the home.

Nye's theory consists of three primary components of control. The first component is *internal control,* which is formed through social interaction. This socialization, he claimed, assists in the development of a conscience. Nye further claimed that if individuals are not given adequate resources and care, they will follow their natural tendencies toward doing what is necessary to protect their interests.

Nye's second component of control is *direct control,* which consists of a wide range of constraints on individual propensities to commit deviant acts. Direct control includes numerous types of sanctions, such as jail and ridicule, and the restriction of one's chances to commit criminal activity.

Nye's third component of control is *indirect control,* which occurs when individuals are strongly attached to their early caregivers. For most children, it is through an intense and strong relationship with their parents or guardians that they establish an attachment to conventional society. However, Nye suggested that when the needs of an individual are not met by caregivers, inappropriate behavior can result.

As shown in Figure 9.4, Nye predicted a U-shaped curve of parental controls in predicting delinquency. Specifically, he argued that either no controls (i.e., complete freedom) or too much control (i.e., no freedom at all) would predict the most chronic delinquency. Instead, he believed that a healthy balance of freedom and parental control was the best strategy for inhibiting criminal activity. Some recent research supports Nye's prediction.[78] We will see later in this chapter that contemporary control theories, such as Tittle's control–balance theory, draw heavily on Nye's idea of having a healthy balance of controls and freedom.[79]

RECKLESS'S CONTAINMENT THEORY

Another control theory, known as containment theory, has been proposed by Walter Reckless.[80] This theory emphasizes both *inner containment* and *outer containment,* which can be viewed as internal and external controls. Reckless broke from traditional assumptions of social control theories by identifying predictive factors that *push* and/or *pull* individuals toward antisocial behavior. However, the focus of his theory remained

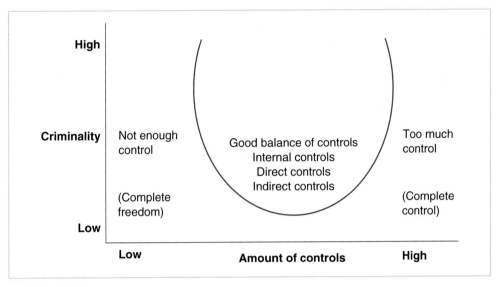

Figure 9.4 Nye's Control Theory

Source: Tibbetts, S., & Hemmens, C. (2010). *Criminological Theory: Text/Reader.* Thousand Oaks, CA: SAGE Publications., p. 456.

on the controlling elements, which can be seen in the emphasis placed on "containment" in the theory's name.

Reckless claimed that individuals can be *pushed* into delinquency by their social environment, such as by a lack of opportunities for education or employment. Furthermore, he pointed out that some individual factors, such as brain disorders or risk-taking personalities, could push some people to commit criminal behavior. Reckless also noted that some individuals could be *pulled* into criminal activity by hanging out with delinquent peers, watching too much violence on television, and so on. All told, Reckless went beyond the typical control theory assumption of inborn tendencies. In addition to these natural dispositions toward deviant behavior, containment theory proposes that extra pushes and pulls can motivate people to commit crime.

Reckless further claimed that the pushes and pulls toward criminal behavior could be enough to force individuals into criminal activity unless they are sufficiently *contained* or controlled. Reckless claimed that such containment should be both internal and external. By *inner containment,* he meant building a person's sense of self. This would help the person resist the temptations of criminal activity. According to Reckless, other forms of inner containment include the ability of individuals to internalize societal norms. With respect to *outer containment,* Reckless claimed that social organizations, such as school, church, and other institutions, are essential in building bonds that inhibit individuals from being pushed or pulled into criminal activity.

Reckless described a visual image of containment theory, which we present in Figure 9.5. The outer circle (Circle 1) in the figure represents the social realm of pressures and pulls, whereas the innermost circle (Circle 4) symbolizes a person's individual-level pushes to commit crime. In between these two circles are the two layers of controls—namely, external containment (Circle 2) and internal containment (Circle 3). The structure of Figure 9.5 and the examples included in each circle are those specifically noted by Reckless.[81]

While some studies have shown more general support for containment theory, other studies have shown that some of the components of the theory, such as internalization of rules, seem to have much more support in accounting for variation in delinquency than do other factors, such as self-perception.[82] In other words, external factors may be more important than internal ones. Furthermore, some studies have noted weaker support for

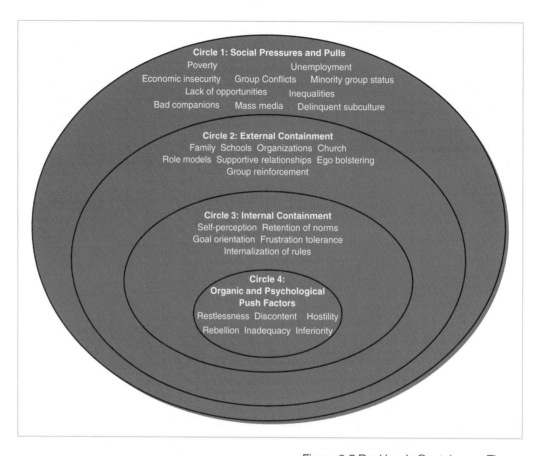

Figure 9.5 Reckless's Containment Theory

Source: Tibbetts, S., & Hemmens, C. (2010). *Criminological Theory: Text/Reader.* Thousand Oaks, CA: SAGE Publications., p. 458.

Reckless's theory among minorities and females. Thus, the model appears to be most valid for white males.[83]

One of the problems with containment theory is that it does not go far enough toward specifying the factors that are important in predicting criminality. For example, an infinite amount of concepts exist that could potentially be categorized as either a "push" or "pull" toward criminality, or as an "inner" or "outer" containment of criminality. Thus, the theory could be considered too broad and not specific enough to be of practical value. To Reckless's credit, though, containment theory has increased the exposure of control theories of criminal behavior. And although support for containment theory has been mixed, there is no doubt that it has influenced other, more recent control theories.[84]

MODERN SOCIAL CONTROL THEORIES

As the previous sections attest, control theory has been around, in various forms, for some time. Modern social control theories, to which we now turn our attention, build on these earlier versions of social control but also add a level of depth and sophistication. Two modern social control theories that we consider here are Matza's drift theory and Hirschi's social bonding theory.

MATZA'S DRIFT THEORY

The theory of *drift*, presented by David Matza in 1964, claims that individuals offend at certain times in their lives when social controls, such as parental supervision, employment, and family ties, are weakened.[85] In developing his theory, Matza criticized earlier theories and their tendency to predict too much crime. For example, theories such as those of the Chicago School would wrongfully predict that all individuals in bad neighborhoods will commit crime. Likewise, strain theory predicts that all poor individuals will commit crime. Obviously, this is not true. Thus, Matza claimed that there is a degree of determinism (i.e., Positive School) in human behavior but also a significant amount of free will (i.e., Classical School). He called this perspective **soft determinism**, which is the gray area between free will and determinism. This is illustrated in Figure 9.6.

ASSUMPTION OF COMPLETE FREE WILL	SOFT DETERMINISM	ASSUMPTION OF TOTAL ("HARD") DETERMINISM
Belief held by classical theorists	A sort of middle-ground position	Belief held by positive theorists
Assumes all behavior is the result of decisions freely chosen by a person		Assumes all behavior is the result of factors (e.g., economy, upbringing, peers) determining behavior

Figure 9.6 Matza's Concept of Soft Determinism as the Middle-Ground Stance Between Two Extreme Assumptions of Criminal Behavior

Returning to the basics of Matza's theory, he claimed that individuals offend at times in life when social controls are weakened. As is well-known, the time when social controls are most weakened for the majority of individuals is during their teenage years. It is at this time that parents and other caretakers stop having a constant supervisory role. At the same time, teenagers generally do not have too many responsibilities—such as careers or children—that would inhibit them from experimenting with deviance. This is consistent with the well-known age–crime relationship; most individuals arrested are in their teenage years (see Figure 9.7).[86] Once sufficient ties are developed, people tend to mature out of criminal lifestyles.

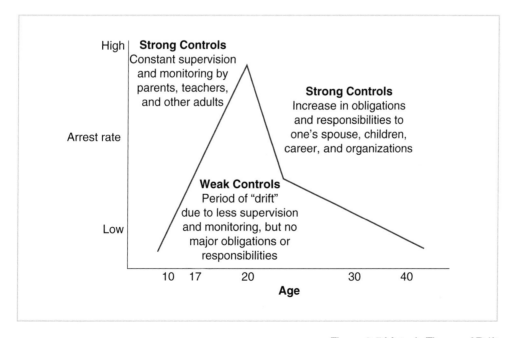

Figure 9.7 Matza's Theory of Drift

Source: Tibbetts, S., & Hemmens, C. (2010). *Criminological Theory: Text/Reader.* Thousand Oaks, CA: SAGE Publications., p. 460.

soft determinism: the assumption that both determinism and free will play a role in offenders' decisions to engage in criminal behavior

San Francisco 49er fans and Oakland Raider fans clash in the stands during a preseason NFL game.

Matza further claimed that when supervision is absent and ties are minimal, the majority of individuals are the most "free" to do what they want. Where, then, does the term *drift* come from? As shown in Figure 9.7, it is during the times when people have few ties and obligations that they will "drift" in and out of delinquency. Matza pointed out that previous theories are unsuccessful in explaining this age–crime relationship. For example, he claimed that "most theories of delinquency take no account of maturational reform; those that do often do so at the expense of violating their own assumptions regarding the constrained delinquent."[87]

Matza insisted that "drifting" is not the same as a commitment to a life of crime. Instead, it is "experimenting" with questionable behavior and then rationalizing it. The way youth rationalize behavior that they know to be wrong is through the learning of techniques of neutralization, discussed earlier in this chapter.

Drift theory goes on to say that individuals do not reject the conventional normative structure. On the contrary, much offending is based on neutralizing or adhering to *subterranean values* that they have been socialized to use as a means of circumventing conventional values. This is basically the same as asserting one's independence, which tends to occur with a vengeance during the teenage years.

As discussed in Chapter 7, subterranean values are quite prevalent and underlie many aspects of our culture. For example, while it is conventional to believe that violence is wrong, boxing and other injury-prone sports are some of the most popular spectator activities. Such phenomena create an atmosphere that readily allows neutralization or rationalization of criminal activity.

We will see other forms of subterranean values when we discuss risk-taking and low self-control later in this chapter. In many contexts (such as business), risk-taking and aggressiveness are seen as desirable characteristics; so many individuals are influenced by such subterranean values. This, according to Matza, adds to individuals' likelihood of "drifting" into crime and delinquency.

Matza's theory of drift seems sensible on its face, but empirical research examining the theory has been mixed.[88] One of the primary criticisms of Matza's theory, which even he acknowledged, is that it does not explain the most chronic offenders, the people responsible for the vast majority of serious, violent crimes. Chronic offenders often offend long before and well past their teenage years, which clearly limits the predictive value of Matza's theory.

Despite its shortcomings, Matza's drift theory does appear to explain why many people offend exclusively during their teenage and young adult years but then grow out of it. Also, the theory is highly consistent with several of the ideas presented by control theorists, including the assumption that (1) selfish tendencies are universal, (2) these tendencies are inhibited by socialization and social controls, and (3) the selfish tendencies appear at times when controls are weakest. The theory goes beyond the previous control theories by adding the concepts of soft determinism, neutralization, and subterranean values, as well as the idea that in many contexts selfish and aggressive behaviors are not wrong but are actually desirable behaviors.

HIRSCHI'S SOCIAL BONDING THEORY

Perhaps the most influential social control theory was presented by Travis Hirschi in 1969.[89] Hirschi's theory of **social bonding** takes an assumption from Durkheim that "we are all animals, and thus naturally capable of committing criminal acts."[90] However, as Hirschi acknowledged, most humans can be adequately socialized to become tightly bonded to conventional entities, such as families, schools, communities, and the like. Hirschi claimed also that the stronger a person is bonded to conventional society, the less prone to engaging in crime he or she will be. More specifically, the stronger the social bond, the less likely that an individual will commit criminal offenses.

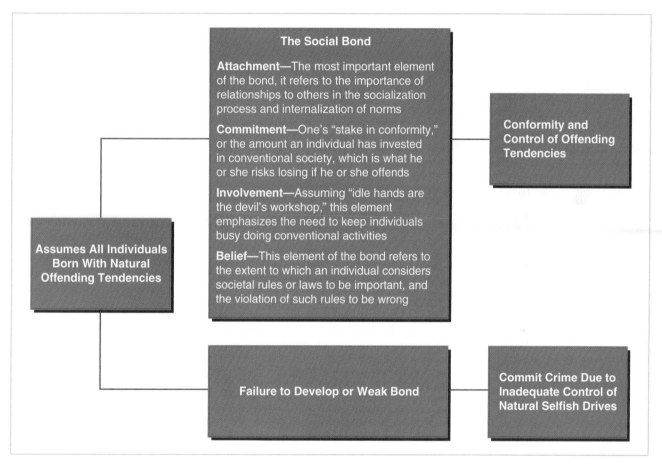

Figure 9.8 Hirschi's Social Bonding Theory

Source: Tibbetts, S., & Hemmens, C. (2010). *Criminological Theory: Text/Reader.* Thousand Oaks, CA: SAGE Publications., p. 462.

As shown in Figure 9.8, Hirschi's social bond is made up of four elements: (1) attachment, (2) commitment, (3) involvement, and (4) belief. The "stronger" or more developed a person is in each of the four elements, the less likely he or she will be to commit crime. Let us now consider each element in detail.

The most important factor in the social bond is *attachments,* which consist of affectionate bonds between an individual and his or her significant others. Attachment is vitally important for the internalization of conventional values. Hirschi claimed that "the essence of internalization of norms, conscience, or superego thus lies in the attachment of the individual to others."[91] Hirschi made it clear, as did Freud, that strong early attachments are the most important factor in developing a social bond. Commitment, involvement, and belief, he argued, are contingent on adequate attachment to others. That is, without healthy attachments, especially early in life, the probability of acting inappropriately increases.

social bonding: a control theory that assumes that individuals are predisposed to commit crime and that conventional bonds prevent or reduce offending. This bond is made up of four constructs: attachments, commitment, involvement, and moral beliefs regarding committing crime.

According to Hirschi, participating in conventional activities can inhibit delinquent and criminal activity.

Commitment, the second element of Hirschi's social bond, is the investment a person has in conventional society. This has been explained as one's "stake in conformity," or what is at risk of being lost if one gets caught committing crime. If a person feels that much will be lost by committing crime, then he or she will probably not do so. In contrast, if someone has nothing to lose, what is to prevent that person from doing something he or she may be punished for? The answer is, of course, not much. And this, some theorists claim, is why it is difficult to control so-called "chronic offenders" who have nothing to lose. Trying to instill a "commitment" to conventional society in such individuals is extremely difficult.

Another element of the social bond is *involvement,* which is the time spent in conventional activities. The assumption is that time spent in constructive activities will reduce time devoted to illegal behaviors. This element of the bond goes back to the old adage that "idle hands are the devil's workshop."[92] Hirschi claimed that taking an active role in all forms of conventional activities can inhibit delinquent and criminal activity.

The last element of the social bond is *beliefs,* which have generally been interpreted as moral beliefs concerning the laws and rules of society. This is one of the most examined, and consistently supported, aspects of the social bond. Basically, individuals who feel that a course of action is against their moral beliefs are much less likely to pursue it than are individuals who don't see a breach of morality in such behavior. For example, we all probably know some people who see drunk driving as a serious offense because of the injury and death it can cause. However, we also probably know individuals who don't see a problem with such behavior. The same can be said about speeding in a car, shoplifting from a store, or using marijuana; people differ in their beliefs about most forms of criminal activity.

Hirschi's theory has been tested by numerous researchers and has, for the most part, been supported.[93] However, one criticism is that the components of the social bond may predict criminality only if they are defined in a certain way. For example, with respect to the "involvement" element of the bond, studies have shown that not all conventional activities are equal when it comes to preventing delinquency. Only academic or religious activities seem to have consistent effects on inhibiting delinquency. In contrast, many studies show that teenagers who date or play sports actually have an increased risk of committing crime.[94]

Another major criticism of Hirschi's theory is that the effects of "attachments" on crime depend on whom one is attached to. As explained earlier in this chapter, studies have clearly and consistently shown that attachment to delinquent peers is a strong predictor of criminal activity.

Finally, some evidence indicates that social bonding theory may better explain reasons why individuals start offending but not reasons why people continue or escalate in their offending. One reason for this is that Hirschi's theory does not elaborate on what occurs after an individual commits criminal activity. This is likely the primary reason why some of the more complex integrated theories of crime (some of which are discussed below) often attribute the initiation of delinquency to a breakdown in the social bond. However, they typically see other theories (such as differential reinforcement) as being better predictors of what happens after the initial stages of the criminal career.[95]

Despite the criticism it has received, Hirschi's social bonding theory is still one of the most accepted theories of criminal behavior.[96] It is a relatively convincing explanation for criminality because of the consistent support it has found among samples of people taken from all over the world.[97]

INTEGRATED SOCIAL CONTROL THEORIES

It is worthwhile to briefly discuss the two integrated models that most incorporate the control perspective into their frameworks. These two integrated models are control–balance theory and power–control theory. Both have received considerable attention in the criminological literature.

TITTLE'S CONTROL–BALANCE THEORY

Presented by Charles Tittle in 1995, control–balance theory proposes that (1) the amount of control to which one is *subjected* and (2) the amount of control one can *exercise* determine the probability of deviance occurring. The "balance" between these two types of control, he argued, can even predict the *type* of behavior likely to be committed.[98]

Tittle argued that a person is least likely to offend when he or she has a balance of controlling and being controlled. Further, the likelihood of offending will increase when these factors become imbalanced. If individuals are more controlled (Tittle calls this control deficit), then the theory predicts that they will commit predatory or defiant acts. In contrast, if an individual possesses an excessive level of control (Tittle calls this control surplus), then he or she will be more likely to commit acts of exploitation or decadence. Note that excessive control is not the same as excessive self-control. Tittle argues that people who are controlling—that is, who have excessive control over others—will be predisposed toward inappropriate activities.

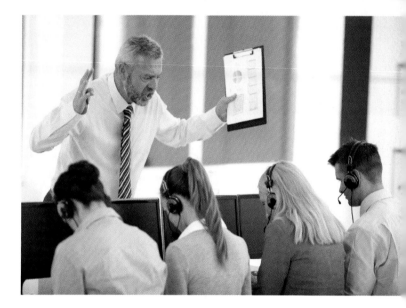

These employees may feel "out of balance" because they are being controlled rather than exercising control.

Initial empirical tests of control–balance theory have reported mixed results, with both surpluses and deficits predicting the same types of deviance.[99] Additionally, researchers have uncovered differing effects of the control–balance ratio on two types of deviance that are contingent on gender. This finding is consistent with the gender-specific support found for Reckless's containment theory, described earlier in this chapter.[100]

HAGAN'S POWER–CONTROL THEORY

Power–control theory is another integrated theory proposed by John Hagan and his colleagues.[101] The primary focus of this theory is on the level of patriarchal attitudes and structure in the household, which are influenced by parental positions in the workforce. Power–control theory assumes that in households where the mother and father have relatively similar levels of power at work (i.e., balanced households), mothers will be less likely to exert control over their daughters. These balanced households will be less likely to experience gender differences in the criminal offending of the children. However, households in which mothers and fathers have dissimilar levels of power in the

Power–control theory focuses on the patriarchal attitudes and structure in the household.

workplace (i.e., unbalanced households) are more likely to suppress criminal activity in daughters. Additionally, assertiveness and risky activity among the males in the house will be encouraged. This assertiveness and risky activity may be a precursor to crime.

Most empirical tests of power–control have provided moderate support for the theory, while more recent studies have further specified the validity of the theory in different contexts.[102] For example, one recent study reported that the influence of mothers, not fathers, on sons had the greatest impact on reducing the delinquency of young males.[103] Another researcher has found that differences in perceived threats of embarrassment and formal sanctions varied between more patriarchal and less patriarchal households.[104] Finally, studies have also started measuring the effect of patriarchal attitudes on crime and delinquency.[105] Power–control theory is a good example of a social control theory in that it is consistent with the idea that individuals must be socialized and that the gender differences in such socialization affect how people will act throughout life.

A GENERAL THEORY OF CRIME: LOW SELF-CONTROL

In 1990, Hirschi, along with his colleague Michael Gottfredson, proposed a general theory of **low self-control**, which is often referred to as the general theory of crime.[106] This theory has led to a significant amount of debate and research in the field since its appearance, more so than any other contemporary theory of crime. Like the previous control theories of crime, this theory assumes that individuals are born predisposed toward selfish, self-centered activities and that only effective child rearing and socialization can create self-control among persons. As shown in Figure 9.9, without such adequate socialization (i.e., social controls) and reduction of criminal opportunities, individuals will follow their natural tendencies to become selfish predators. Furthermore, the general theory of crime assumes that self-control must be established by age 10. If it has not formed by that time, according to the theory, individuals will forever exhibit low self-control.

Although Gottfredson and Hirschi still attribute the formation of controls to the socialization process, the distinguishing characteristic of this theory is its emphasis on the individual's ability to control himself or herself. That is, the general theory of crime assumes that people can take a degree of control over their own decisions and, within certain limitations, "control" themselves.

The general theory of crime is accepted as one of the most valid theories of crime.[107] This is probably because it identifies only one primary factor that causes criminality—low self-control. But low self-control may actually consist of a series of personality traits, including risk taking, impulsiveness, self-centeredness, short-term orientation, and quick

CRIME IN THE NEWS

Parenting and Crime

low self-control: a theory that proposes that individuals either develop self-control by age 10 or do not. Those who do not will manifest criminal or deviant behaviors throughout life

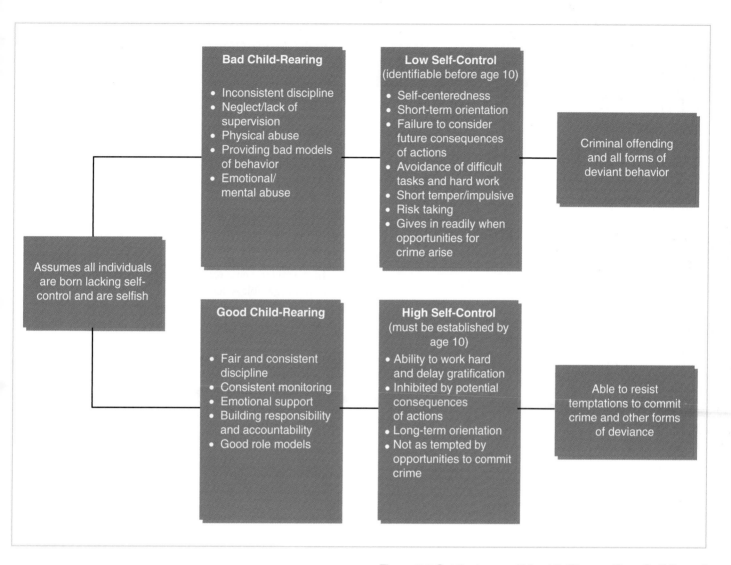

Figure 9.9 Gottfredson and Hirschi's Theory of Low Self-Control

temper. For example, recent research has supported the idea that inadequate child-rearing practices tend to result in lower levels of self-control among children and that these low levels produce various risky behaviors, including criminal activity.[108]

PSYCHOLOGICAL ASPECTS OF LOW SELF-CONTROL

Criminologists have recently claimed that low self-control may be due to the emotional disposition of individuals. For example, one study showed that the effects of low self-control on intentions to commit drunk driving and shoplifting were tied to individuals' perceptions of pleasure and shame. More specifically, the findings of this study showed that individuals who had low self-control had significantly lower levels of anticipated shame but significantly higher levels of perceived pleasure in committing both drunk driving and shoplifting.[109] These results suggest that individuals who lack self-control will be oriented toward gaining pleasure and taking advantage of resources but also toward avoiding negative emotional feelings (e.g., shame) that are primarily induced through socialization.

LEARNING CHECK 9.3

1. Which theorist(s) developed the theory of drift?
   a. Gottfredson and Hirschi
   b. Tittle
   c. Hagan
   d. Matza

2. Which theorist(s) developed the integrated theory of power–control?
   a. Gottfredson and Hirschi
   b. Tittle
   c. Hagan
   d. Matza

3. Which theory emphasizes the concepts of control deficit and control surplus?
   a. Theory of drift
   b. Social bonding theory
   c. Differential reinforcement theory
   d. Control–balance theory

Answers located at www.sagepub.com/schram

PHYSIOLOGICAL ASPECTS OF LOW SELF-CONTROL

Low self-control can also be tied to physiological factors. Interestingly, research has shown that chronic offenders show greater arousal toward danger and risk taking than toward the possibility of punishment.[110] This arousal has been measured by monitoring brain activity in response to certain stimuli. The research suggests that individuals are *encouraged* to commit risky behavior due to physiological mechanisms that reward their risk-taking activities by releasing "pleasure" chemicals in the brain.[111]

In a similar vein, recent studies show that chronic gamblers tend to get a physiological "high" (a sudden, intense release of brain chemicals similar to that following a small dose of cocaine) from the activity of betting, particularly when they are gambling with their own money and risking a personal loss.[112] Undoubtedly, there exists a minority group of individuals who thrive off of risk-taking behaviors significantly more than others do. This suggests that there are not just psychological differences among people but also physiological differences that may explain why certain individuals favor risky behaviors.

Researchers have also found that criminal offenders generally perceive a significantly lower level of internal sanctions (e.g., shame, guilt, embarrassment) than do nonoffenders.[113] So, in summary, a select group of individuals appear to derive physiological and psychological pleasure from engaging in risky behaviors while simultaneously being less likely to be inhibited by internal emotional sanctions. Such a combination, Gottfredson and Hirschi claimed, is dangerous and helps explain why some impulsive individuals often end up in prison.

Finally, the psychological and physiological aspects of low self-control may help explain the gender differences observed between males and females. Specifically, studies show that females are significantly more likely than males to experience internal emotional sanctioning for offenses they have committed.[114] In other words, there appears to be something innately different about males and females that helps explain the differing levels of self-control each possesses.

CRIME IN THE NEWS

Aileen Wuornos

AUTHOR VIDEO

Distinguishing Theories

SUMMARY OF CONTROL THEORIES

Control perspectives are among the oldest and most respected explanations of criminal activity. The fundamental assumption that humans have an inborn, selfish disposition that must be controlled through socialization distinguishes control theories from other theories of crime. The ability of the control perspective to remain among the most popular criminological theories demonstrates its legitimacy as an explanation of behavior. This is likely due to the dedication and efforts of criminologists who are constantly developing new and improved versions of control theory, many of which we have discussed here.

WHY DO THEY DO IT?

AILEEN WUORNOS

A mug shot of Aileen Wuornos

Aileen Wuornos, a serial killer, was one of the few females executed recently (October 2002). Wuornos killed at least seven men in Florida in the late 1990s, largely off interstate or state highways. These men were likely looking for prostitutes, but instead of servicing them, Wuornos shot them numerous times, typically with a small-caliber handgun, and hid their bodies, most of which were later recovered.

Wuornos was born in Michigan in 1956 with the name Aileen Carol Pittman, but she later took her mother's maiden name. She never met her father, probably because he was in prison for the rape and attempted murder of a young girl when she was born. Wuornos's father, diagnosed as schizophrenic, hanged himself in prison. When Wuornos was young, her mother abandoned her, leaving her with her maternal grandparents, both of whom were alcoholics. Wuornos subsequently developed into a prototypical offender, participating in various delinquent activities, such as using drugs, as early as age 11. She would often exchange sexual favors for cigarettes, drugs, and even food. She claimed that during her early years, her grandfather sexually molested her and beat her when he was drunk.

According to Wuornos, she dropped out of school early (at age 14), after an associate of her grandfather raped her and she became pregnant. She gave up the child for adoption. When her grandmother died from liver failure, she came under court authority as a ward of the state. At age 15, she left and began her life as a prostitute.

To make a long story short, Wuornos was charged with numerous crimes (assault, driving under the influence, disorderly conduct, firing a gun from a moving vehicle) before she ever got to Florida. But it was there that she married 69-year-old Lewis Fell (Wuornos was 20 at the time). He took out a restraining order on her and annulled the marriage after she beat him with a cane. She was later sentenced to prison for a variety of offenses, including forgery, theft, grand theft auto, resisting arrest, and operating under a false identity. She was released in the late 1980s, but after this time in prison, Wuornos flourished as a killer, actively preying on men.

So why did she do it? As described by the theories presented in this chapter, specifically various social control theories (such as Hirschi's theory of social bonding) and socialization theories (e.g., differential association theory, differential reinforcement theory), Wuornos never had much of a chance to form strong social bonds with conventional society, nor was she adequately socialized. Smith (2003) stated this well: "Everything was against Aileen Wuornos, right from the beginning" (p. 147). To clarify, because her father was absent before she was born and her mother abandoned her, Wuornos never had a chance to form bonds with her parents. Her only associations with significant caretakers in early life were with her grandparents, who were both negative role models as highly abusive alcoholics. With this lack of early social bonds, as well as the negative associations she observed from her caretakers, it is not surprising that she resorted to early delinquent and later predatory crimes. Wuornos engaged in such behaviors out of selfishness and personal satisfaction, and without any empathy for her victims, because that was what her experience in the world taught her to do. It is likely that her perspective was to look out for herself and do whatever she wanted, regardless of how it affected others.

As mentioned above, she was sentenced to death for committing multiple murders and executed in Florida in 2002. Her story was later portrayed in the movie *Monster*, for which Charlize Theron, playing Wuornos, received an Academy Award.

Sources: Kennedy, D., & Nolin, R. (1994). *On a killing day: The bizarre story of convicted murderer Aileen Lee Wuornos*. New York: S. P. I. Books; Smith, J. D. (2003). *100 most infamous criminals*. New York: Metro Books.

CONCLUSION

In the first section, we discussed learning theories. These theories focus on the process of *how* and *why* individuals learn criminal behavior, including the techniques, justifications, and underlying values. These theories also give substantial attention to significant people involved in the socialization process—specifically, family, friends, and important others. Learning theories continue to be helpful in our understanding of criminal behavior, as shown by virtually all empirical studies that have evaluated the validity of these theoretical models. If we theorize that individuals learn various techniques, justifications, and values that influence their potential to engage in criminal activity, then these individuals can also learn how to engage in law-abiding behavior.

In the latter half of this chapter, we examined a large number of control theories, which assume that individuals are essentially born naturally greedy and selfish and that we have to be controlled to resist acting on these inherent drives. Although the many different control theories have some unique distinctions, they all share one key underlying assumption: They all assume that people must be socialized in such a way that their learning of right and wrong will control the antisocial tendencies they are born with.

In this chapter, we discussed a wide range of theories that may appear to be quite different. However, it is important to remember that all the criminological theories covered in this chapter share an emphasis on social processes as the primary reason why individuals commit crime. This is true for the learning theories, which propose that people are taught to commit crime, as well as for the control theories, which claim that people offend naturally and must be taught *not* to commit crime. Despite their seemingly opposite assumptions of human behavior, the fact is that learning and control theories both identify socialization, or the lack thereof, as the key cause of criminal behavior.

SUMMARY OF THEORIES IN CHAPTER 9

THEORY	CONCEPTS	PROPONENTS	KEY PROPOSITIONS
Differential association	Criminal behavior is learned in interaction with other persons; learning occurs within intimate personal groups; learned definitions are favorable or unfavorable to the legal code; associations vary in frequency, duration, priority, and intensity.	Edwin Sutherland	Criminality is learned just like any conventional activity; any normal individual, when exposed to definitions and attitudes favorable toward crime, will learn both the motivations and techniques for engaging in illegal behaviors.
Differential reinforcement theory	Criminal behavior is learned according to the principles of operant conditioning and modeling/imitation; criminal behavior is learned in both nonsocial and social interactions; learning occurs in groups that make up the individual's major source of reinforcements.	Robert Burgess and Ronald Akers	Assumes individuals are born with a blank slate and socialized and taught how to behave through classical and operant conditioning, as well as modeling; behavior occurs and continues depending on past and present rewards and punishments.
Techniques of neutralization	Criminals are still partially committed to the dominant social order; there are five techniques of neutralization to justify criminal behavior.	Gresham Sykes and David Matza	Individuals can engage in criminal behavior and avoid feelings of guilt for these actions by justifying or rationalizing their behavior; since they are partially committed to the social order, such justifications help them engage in criminal behavior without serious damage to their self-image.
Early control theories	Individuals are naturally born selfish and greedy, and they must be socialized by others to control their inherent desires and drives.	Sigmund Freud, Jackson Toby, Albert Reiss, F. Ivan Nye, Walter Reckless, and others	Most of the early theorists emphasized the need for external societal controls to counter people's inner drives; Reckless called such a process "containment," in the sense that if such drives are not contained, there is little to stop a person from doing what is natural, which is to offend.
Theory of drift	Soft determinism, meaning that offending behavior is the result of both free will/decision making *and* deterministic factors outside of our control.	David Matza	Offending typically peaks in the teenage years because that is the time when social controls are weakest; that is, we are no longer being monitored constantly by caretakers, and the adulthood control factors of marriage, employment, etc., have not yet kicked in.
Social bonding theory	The social bond is made up of four elements: attachments, commitment, involvement, and moral beliefs.	Travis Hirschi	A simple theory in the sense that as each of the four elements of the social bond grows stronger, the likelihood of offending lessens due to being more bonded to conventional society.

THEORY	CONCEPTS	PROPONENTS	KEY PROPOSITIONS
Control-balance theory	Control deficit and control surplus	Charles Tittle	Individuals who either are too controlled by others or have too much control over others are more likely to commit crimes, compared with people who have a healthy balance between the two.
Power–control theory	Balanced and unbalanced households	John Hagan	Households in which the parents have similar types of jobs are more balanced and tend to control their sons and daughters more equally than in unbalanced households, where the parents have different jobs, which leads to more controls placed on daughters than on sons.
Low self-control theory	Bad child rearing	Michael Gottfredson and Travis Hirschi	Bad parenting (abusive, inconsistent, lack of monitoring, neglectful) results in lack of development of self-control, which then leads to criminality and risky behaviors.

KEY TERMS

classical conditioning

collective conscience

control theories

differential association theory

differential identification

differential reinforcement theory

learning theories

low self-control

modeling/imitation

negative reinforcement

operant conditioning

positive reinforcement

social bonding

soft determinism

techniques of neutralization

STUDENT STUDY SITE

Visit the student study site at **www.sagepub.com/schram** to access links to the video, audio, city and state rankings, author podcasts, and SAGE journal and reference articles featured in this chapter, as well as additional study tools, including eFlashcards, web quizzes, web resources, and chapter outlines.

DISCUSSION QUESTIONS

1. What distinguishes learning theories from other criminological theories?

2. What distinguishes differential association from differential reinforcement theory?

3. What did differential identification add to learning theories?

4. Which technique of neutralization do you use/relate to the most? Why?

5. Which technique of neutralization do you find least valid? Why?

6. Which element of Hirschi's social bond do you find you have the highest levels of?

7. Which element of Hirschi's social bond do you find you have the lowest levels of?

8. Can you identify someone you know who fits the profile of a person with low self-control?

9. Which aspects of the low self-control personality do you think you fit?

10. Regarding Matza's theory of drift, do you think this relates to when you or your friends have committed crimes in your lives? Why or why not?

WEB RESOURCES

Social learning theories

http://sociology.about.com/od/Sociological-Theory/a/Social-Learning-Theory.htm

http://psychology.about.com/od/developmentalpsychology/a/sociallearning.htm

Control theories

http://www.oxfordbibliographies.com/view/document/obo-9780195396607/obo-9780195396607-0091.xml

http://www.youtube.com/watch?v=pvwd8R5_OGs

http://www.everydaysociologyblog.com/2008/11/gottfredson-and.html

CHAPTER 10

Labeling Theory and Conflict/ Marxist/Radical Theories of Crime

INTRODUCTION

During the 1960s and 1970s, one of the most prominent paradigms to rival traditional theoretical explanations of crime was radical and/or critical criminology.[1] Traditional criminology theories (e.g., classical and positive) were considered a part of mainstream criminology; they had a tendency to support the status quo and the dominant ideologies of that time. Critical criminology, however, was initially based on a critique of both the state and the political economy of crime and crime control.[2] While this earlier radical criminological perspective continued for a relatively brief time, this framework is typically used as a gauge for assessing whether theories in the 1980s and 1990s were evolving or devolving.[3]

By the late 1980s and early 1990s, this radical perspective was transforming. First, the paradigm was designated as *critical* rather than *radical*. Second, while the earlier radical paradigm primarily focused on Marxist and neo-Marxist frameworks of class, state, and social control, the critical paradigm began to broaden its focus and diversify. A common feature of the earlier radical and subsequent critical perspectives, however, is their "anti-establishment stances or criticisms, their pursuits of transformation of one kind or another, and their relative appreciations for the political economy of crime and crime control."[4]

This chapter presents several critical criminology theories. We start with a discussion on labeling theory. Next, we focus on selected contributions to the conflict perspective, including the conservative (pluralist) and the Marxist/radical. Additional critical perspectives are reviewed, including peacemaking criminology, restorative justice, and left realism. This chapter concludes by presenting examples of policies and programs related to the labeling and conflict theories of crime.

LABELING THEORY

As with fashions, ideas can be influenced by changing fads, even ideas that attempt to explain crime.[5] **Labeling theory** came to the forefront during a time when various assumptions concerning societal authority were being questioned and reexamined. Near the end of the 1950s, the unfair and inequitable treatment of underprivileged individuals in society was becoming a widespread concern for many Americans. As a result, protests and demonstrations were held to fight for civil rights and women's rights. Others were also questioning the legitimacy of political authority regarding U.S. foreign policy in Vietnam. Thus, many protested the United States' involvement in the Vietnam War; a number of these protests were held on college campuses.

Within this broader societal context, scholars were also beginning to question existing explanations of crime. These scholars maintained that too much emphasis was placed on explaining individual characteristics contributing to criminal behavior. These scholars were concerned with the structure of social class and power; thus, the labeling perspective is not overly concerned with questions of why an individual engages in deviant behavior. Rather, this perspective focuses on such questions as, Who applies

As students read this chapter, they should consider the following questions:

- What are the basic assumptions of labeling theory?

- What are the key differences between primary deviance and secondary deviance?

- What are the different types of deviant behavior, as categorized by Becker?

- What are the main processes involved in stereotyping, retrospective interpretation, and negotiation, as presented by Schur?

- What are the major limitations of labeling theory?

- What are some of the key features of the consensus view of the law?

- What are the distinguishing features of conservative (pluralist) and critical–radical perspectives?

- What are some of the key features of Marxist theory as they relate to criminological theories?

- What are the major limitations of conflict theories?

- Who are the key contributors of alternative perspectives such as peacemaking criminology, the restorative justice perspective, and left realism?

CASE STUDY

E-WASTE DUMPING AND DEVELOPING NATIONS

Various environmental groups have raised concerns about rich, developed countries exporting "hand-me-down" electronics equipment to developing nations, sometimes referred to as "electronic waste" or "e-waste." According to the U.S. Environmental Protection Agency, more than 4.6 million tons of e-waste ended up in U.S. landfills in 2000. E-waste contains toxic chemicals that can release toxins into the atmosphere, negatively impacting communities near such landfills and the environment. Incineration of e-waste can release heavy metals such as lead and mercury into the air. Thus, some developed counties have exported this e-waste to developing counties.[6]

The Basel Action Network (BAN), a nonprofit group comprising a worldwide network of environmental activists, issued a report that stresses the need to curtail unregulated free trade of e-waste to developing nations. Major U.S. personal computer vendors have recycling programs for e-waste. In many instances, however, this e-waste is sold to brokers for disposal and ends up in countries such as Nigeria and Asia. According to the BAN report, this growing trade is not driven by altruism but by the profits that can be made from "dumping" this waste, without any concern for the consequences.[7]

Research conducted on behalf of the INTERPOL Pollution Crime Working Group has demonstrated

One example of an e-waste dumping site. Consider the harmful effects of this material.

a major potential for informal criminal networks to profit from the illegal export of e-waste to developing countries. This potential criminal gain is when "unscrupulous operators are able to profit from disposing of waste cheaply and illegally abroad instead of taking the environmentally responsible but more expensive option of full recycling to remove and neutralise toxic materials."[8] This type of criminal activity is not what some would consider "traditional" crime (e.g., robbery, larceny). How would a "traditional" theoretical explanation of crime help us understand this form of criminal activity? At the end of this chapter, we will address this question.

> ACCORDING TO THE U.S. ENVIRONMENTAL PROTECTION AGENCY, MORE THAN 4.6 MILLION TONS OF E-WASTE ENDED UP IN U.S. LANDFILLS IN 2000.

the deviant label to whom? Who establishes and enforces the rules?[9] Specifically, these scholars argued that it is important to understand how criminal, or deviant, behavior is defined or labeled. Furthermore, these scholars were interested in how society reacts to this labeled behavior.

FOUNDATION OF LABELING THEORY

Labeling theory was influenced by **symbolic interactionism**, especially from the works of Charles Horton Cooley, William I. Thomas, George Herbert Mead, and Erving Goffman. Symbolic interactionism focuses on how an individual's personality and thought processes evolve through social interactions such as symbolic language and gestures. Cooley argued that an individual gains a sense of his or her social self through primary groups or significant others.[10] Thus, if a child learns how to spell a word correctly and a teacher tells her that she did an excellent job, that child will feel a sense of pride and pleasure. If, however, the child misbehaves in the classroom and the teacher reprimands her, she may feel a sense of shame and embarrassment. Cooley identified this process of obtaining one's self-image through the "eyes of others" as the *looking-glass self*. This also illustrates the influence of *primary groups*. Cooley noted that primary groups are those characterized by intimate and personal interactions.[11] Some of the most important primary groups are the neighborhood and play groups, and especially the family.[12]

While Cooley essentially focused on the process of self-formation during childhood, Thomas was concerned with the later years, specifically when the adult self is redefined.[13] Further, Thomas maintained that to understand human behavior, one needs to understand the "total situation," which consists of objective factors as well as an individual's subjective definitions of those factors.[14] One needs to understand the "definition of the situation."[15]

Mead identified two types of social interaction—nonsymbolic interaction and symbolic interaction. Nonsymbolic interaction occurs when individuals respond to gestures or actions. For instance, two dogs may go through a series of gestures (e.g., snarling, growling, baring teeth). The dogs are responding to each other's gestures. These responses are dictated by preexisting tendencies to respond in certain ways. These dogs are *not* responding to the intention of the gestures; therefore, these animal interactions are devoid of any conscious or deliberate meaning.[16] Symbolic interaction occurs when individuals interpret each other's gestures and act based on the meaning of those gestures. Mead was primarily interested in symbolic interaction. Specifically, Mead was concerned with the "*interpretation,* or ascertaining the meaning of the actions or remarks of the other person, and *definition,* or conveying indications to another person as to how he is to act [italics in original]."[17] Symbolic interactionism emphasizes how human behavior and social relationships are developed through social interactions. This perspective focuses on how an individual's behavior is intertwined with another's.

An essential component of symbolic interactionism is that individuals who are stigmatized as being deviant are predisposed to take on a deviant self-identity.[18] Goffman defined stigma as an "attribute that is deeply discrediting" and that diminishes the individual "from a whole and usual person to a tainted, discounted one."[19] He maintained that stigmatized individuals differ from "normals" in terms of how society reacts to them. Subsequently, society attributes a wide range of deficiencies based on the original perceived flaw. In the next section, we further explore how symbolic interactionism influenced labeling theory.

FRANK TANNENBAUM

Many scholars identify the origins of the labeling perspective in Frank Tannenbaum's 1938 publication, *Crime and the Community*. Drawing on the school of symbolic interactionism, Tannenbaum focused on the process that occurs after an individual has

AUDIO

E-waste

VIDEO

E-waste

AUDIO

Symbolic Interaction

labeling theory: theoretical perspective that assumes that criminal behavior increases because certain individuals are caught and labeled as offenders; their offending increases because they have been stigmatized

symbolic interactionism: proposes that many social interactions involve symbolism, which occurs when individuals interpret each other's words or gestures and act based on the meaning of those gestures

Do some people stigmatize people who are homeless? How do some people react to these individuals?

been caught and designated as violating the law. He maintained that there is a gradual shift from the definition of the specific act as evil to the definition of the individual as evil.[20]

The "community's point of view," or the social reaction to illegal behavior, is designated the **dramatization of evil**. According to Tannenbaum, the process of making the criminal involves tagging, defining, and identifying the individual as such, resulting with that person becoming the very thing he or she is described as being.[21] Tannenbaum contends that the first dramatization of evil has a greater influence on "making the criminal" than any other experience.

Along with the dramatization of evil, Tannenbaum argued that acts are not inherently good or bad; rather, there are differing degrees of good and bad. The social reactions also influence how those behaviors will be labeled. Furthermore, these behaviors are placed within a context that includes such factors as a person's social status and the social setting. For instance, society might react differently to an attorney drinking a glass of wine at dinner than to a homeless person drinking a bottle of wine on a street corner.

EDWIN M. LEMERT

In his 1951 book, *Social Pathology*, Edwin Lemert made a significant contribution to the labeling perspective by distinguishing between primary deviance and secondary deviance. **Primary deviance** is behavior that is situational or occasional. A person uses excuses or rationalizations to justify his or her deviant behavior. These behaviors continue to be considered "primary deviations or symptomatic and situational as long as they are rationalized or otherwise dealt with as functions of a socially acceptable role."[22] Lemert argued that this process occurs either through *normalization* (i.e., a problem of everyday life) or through minimal controls that do not seriously hinder individuals' getting along with each other.[23] Thus, a person engaging in primary deviant behavior perceives the behavior as bad; this individual, however, does not perceive himself or herself as a bad person.

> **Secondary deviance** is deviant behavior, or social roles based upon it, which becomes a means of defense, attack, or adaptation to the overt and covert problems created by the societal reaction to primary deviation. In effect, the original "causes" of the deviation recede and give way to the central importance of the disapproving, degradational, and isolating reactions of society.[24]

A person engaging in secondary deviant behavior uses this behavior as a way to defend against, or adjust to, the various problems related to the social reactions to his or her primary deviance.

The sequence of interaction that results in secondary deviation essentially consists of the following: (1) primary deviation; (2) social penalties; (3) further primary deviation; (4) stronger penalties and rejections; (5) further deviation, possibly with hostilities and resentment toward those imposing the penalties; (6) crisis reaching the tolerance quotient, expressed in formal action by the community stigmatizing the deviant; (7) strengthening of the deviant conduct as a reaction to the stigmatizing and penalties; and (8) ultimate

dramatization of evil: a concept proposed by Tannenbaum in relation to labeling theory; states that when relatively minor laws are broken, the community tends to dramatize it

primary deviance: in labeling theory, the type of minor, infrequent offending people commit before they are caught and labeled as offenders

secondary deviance: in labeling theory, the more serious, frequent offending people commit after they have been caught and labeled as offenders

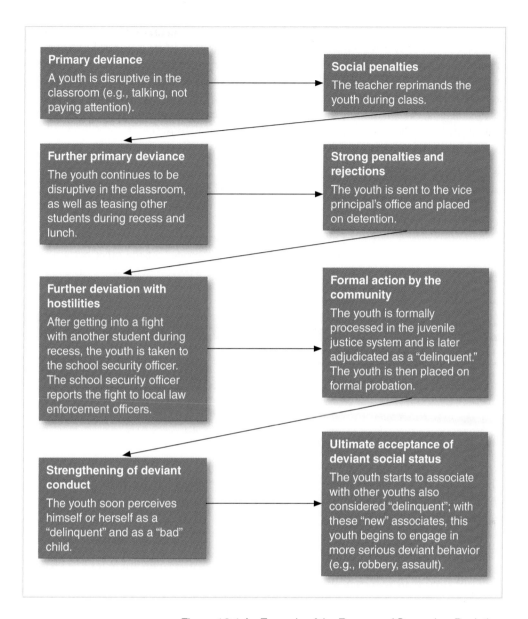

Figure 10.1 An Example of the Process of Secondary Deviation

Source: Adapted: from Lemert, E. M. (1951). *Social pathology: A systematic approach to the theory of sociopathic behavior*. New York: McGraw-Hill, p. 77.

acceptance of the deviant social status and efforts at adjusting to the associated role.[25] (See Figure 10.1 for an example of the process of secondary deviation.) A key aspect of secondary deviance is not only society's reaction to the individual's behavior but also the individual's response to that reaction. According to this perspective, when the societal reaction and label are integrated into an individual's self-image, they will likely lead to the amplification of deviance.

HOWARD S. BECKER

In 1963, another major contribution to the labeling perspective was Howard S. Becker's *Outsiders: Studies in the Sociology of Deviance*. Becker argued that the term *outsiders* refers to those individuals considered by others to be deviant; these labeled individuals are deemed to be "outside" the circle of the "normal" members of the group.[26] Furthermore, deviance is created by society. Social groups create deviance by making the rules, whose infraction is considered deviance, and by applying those rules to particular people and labeling them as outsiders.[27] A key aspect to labeling deviance is realizing that certain groups have the power to impose rules, and subsequently labels, on other groups. This power differential results in groups with this "authority" to designate other individuals as deviants and outsiders.

Becker argued that deviance has two dimensions. One dimension is that only those behaviors considered deviant by others are truly deviant. The second dimension is whether a behavior or an act conforms to a certain rule. With this conceptual framework, Becker developed a typology of deviant behavior (see Figure 10.2). Two of the four types of behavior are both correctly perceived by society. A person engaging in conforming behavior obeys the rules, and society perceives that person as obeying the rules. At the other extreme, the **pure deviant** is an individual who disobeys the rules and is perceived by society as doing so.

	OBEDIENT BEHAVIOR	RULE-BREAKING BEHAVIOR
Perceived as deviant	Falsely accused	Pure deviant
Not perceived as deviant	Conforming	Secret deviant

Figure 10.2 Typology of Deviant Behavior

Source: Becker, H. S. (1963). *Outsiders: Studies in the sociology of deviance.* New York: Free Press, p. 20.

The remaining two types of behavior are more problematic. First, the **falsely accused** is an individual who has been identified as disobeying the rules when he or she did not violate the rules. For instance, a juvenile occasionally associates with a group of delinquents and is arrested with these youths one night on suspicion of burglary. This juvenile will show up in the official statistics as a delinquent, along with other juveniles who actually engaged in delinquent behavior. Researchers, using official data, will attempt to develop an understanding of delinquency, including this youth who was falsely accused. Second, the **secret deviant** is an individual who violates the rules of society, without society reacting to this behavior. These individuals are able to avoid detection; thus, they are not labeled as deviant. Self-report studies reveal that a large number of individuals fall into this group.[28]

EDWIN M. SCHUR

In the late 1960s, Edwin M. Schur's work also made a significant contribution to the labeling perspective.[29] He addressed some of the criticisms and misunderstandings of the labeling perspective. First, he noted that some scholars maintained that this perspective failed to distinguish adequately between deviance and nondeviance. The labeling perspective, however, attempts to explain the *varieties of the deviant experience* rather than just the "mere counting and classifying of deviating acts and individuals."[30] Second, Schur mentioned that various criticisms argued that the labeling perspective was too narrow—for instance, that the focus was on the ascribed aspects of the deviant status rather than on the deviant motivation. Third, Schur cited critics who maintained that this perspective failed to explain some forms of deviance.

One reason for this confusion and controversy was the failure of labeling theorists to provide a concise definition of deviance that can be used when conducting research. He provided the following working definition:

pure deviant: based on Becker's typology, an individual who disobeys the rules and is perceived as doing so

falsely accused: based on Becker's typology, when an individual has been identified as disobeying the rules but did not violate the rules

secret deviant: based on Becker's typology, an individual who violates the rules of society but elicits no reaction from society

VIDEO

Hate Crimes

Human behavior is deviant *to the extent that* it comes to be viewed as involving a *personally discreditable* departure from a group's normative expectations, *and it elicits* interpersonal or collective reactions that serve to "isolate," "treat," "correct," or "punish" *individuals* engaged in such behavior [italics in original].[31]

Schur argued that the terms *deviant* and *delinquent* are what sociologists designate as an ascribed status and not an achieved status. Specifically, an ascribed status is a social position an individual occupies not only due to the consequence of that individual's actions but also as a result of the actions of others.[32]

Schur identified key factors in the labeling process, including stereotyping, retrospective interpretation, and negotiation. **Stereotyping** is usually associated with racial prejudice and discrimination. Citing the work of Piliavin and Briar,[33] Schur argued that stereotyping can also occur in police encounters with juveniles. During the various decision-making stages of these encounters (e.g., bringing the juvenile into the station, type of disposition to invoke), police react to various cues from the juvenile. These cues include the youth's group affiliations, age, race, grooming, dress, and demeanor.[34]

The second key factor, **retrospective interpretation**, was defined as the process by which an individual is identified as a deviant and thereafter viewed in a "new light."[35] Through this process, an individual is given a new personal identity. The most dramatic way of initiating this process is through a public **status-degradation ceremony**, such as a criminal trial.[36] Schur contended that the individual's character, both past and present, is reexamined. In terms of youths adjudicated as delinquent, retrospective interpretation is applied through such terms as *delinquency proneness* and *predelinquent*. Studies focus on these adjudicated delinquents to identify certain "indicators" of such behavior after these youths have been labeled delinquent.

The last key factor, **negotiation**, is more noticeable in cases involving adults rather than juveniles, usually in instances that use plea bargaining in criminal trials. This negotiation process, however, is still present when working with juveniles. For instance, alleged delinquents may try to influence their disposition by exploiting the relationship between the image they present and the probable outcome of their case. Citing Aaron Cicourel's work on juveniles,[37] Schur noted that a juvenile who is "appealing and attractive," wants to be liked, and relates in a friendly manner to those around him or her is a prime candidate for clinical interpretations rather than criminal imputations.[38]

BASIC ASSUMPTIONS OF LABELING THEORY

Referring to works such as those by Tannenbaum, Lemert, and Becker, Clarence Schrag identified the following basic assumptions of labeling theory:

1. *No act is intrinsically criminal.* The law designates an act as a crime; thus, crimes are defined by politically influential and organized groups.

2. *Criminal definitions are enforced in the interest of the powerful.* While the law incorporates detailed guidelines, as well as definitions and procedures, the implementation of the law can vary by decisions of local officials and other social leaders.

If you saw this woman walking in a store, would you perceive her as a potential shoplifter? Why or why not?

VIDEO

Stereotyping

stereotyping: in labeling theory, usually associated with racial prejudice and discrimination

retrospective interpretation: in labeling theory, the process by which an individual is identified as a deviant and thereafter viewed in a "new light"

3. *A person does not become a criminal by violating the law.* Rather, a person becomes a criminal by authorities designating him or her as such.

4. *The practice of dichotomizing individuals into criminal and noncriminal groups is contrary to common sense and research.* Self-report and other unofficial sources reveal that most acts committed by criminals conform with the law, while some actions of "conformists" violate the law. Thus, the criminal label designates an individual's legal status and not his or her behavior.

5. *Only a few persons are caught in violating the law even though many individuals may be equally guilty.* The act of "getting caught" begins the labeling process. When an individual is labeled as a criminal, he or she may become one of a few that many can blame for the ills of society (i.e., a scapegoat).

6. *While the sanctions used in law enforcement are directed against the individual and not just the criminal act, the penalties for such an act vary according to the characteristics of the offender.* Therefore, the decisions of many authorities appear to reflect the perspective, "Once a criminal, always a criminal, but some are more criminal than others."

7. *Criminal sanctions also vary according to other characteristics of the offender.* Further, these sanctions tend to be more severe among males, the young, the unemployed or underemployed, the poorly educated, members of the lower classes, members of minority groups, transients, and residents of deteriorated urban areas.

8. *Criminal justice is founded on a stereotyped conception of the criminal as a pariah—a willful wrongdoer who is morally bad and deserving of the community's condemnation.* The criminal justice system is based on a free-will perspective that allows for the condemnation and rejection of the identified offender.

9. *Confronted by public condemnation and the label of an evil man, it may be difficult for an offender to maintain a favorable image of himself.* Thus, labeling is a process that produces, eventually, identification with a deviant image and subculture and, subsequently, the "rejection of the rejectors."[39]

Although some might add to, or modify, these assumptions, the above represent a comprehensive analysis of labeling theory as it is generally discussed and used in criminological theory, research, and policy.[40]

RESEARCH ON LABELING THEORY

Researchers from various disciplines have conducted empirical studies of labeling theory using different types of research methods. In the field of criminal justice, a central focus of research for a number of studies was the process of deviance amplification due to labeling an individual as a criminal or a delinquent. Examples of this line of research include examining the relationship between the severity of a juvenile court disposition and future

AUTHOR VIDEO

Labeling Theory

PERSONAL PERSPECTIVE

Prison Culture

status-degradation ceremony: the most dramatic way to initiate the process of giving an individual a new identity, such as a criminal trial

negotiation: one of the key factors identified by Schur (i.e., labeling process); more noticeable in cases involving adults rather than juveniles (e.g., plea bargaining)

WHY DO THEY DO IT?

MICHAEL JACKSON

In January 1994, Michael Jackson and the family of a 13-year-old youth reached an out-of-court settlement reported to be between $15 million and $20 million. This settlement followed allegations of Jackson sexually molesting the youth. In December 2003, the Santa Barbara County District Attorney's Office filed formal charges against Jackson. In April 2004, a grand jury indicted Jackson on charges of molesting another young boy. Jackson pled not guilty; the testimony and the closing arguments lasted for almost 14 weeks. Subsequently, the jury deliberated for about 32 hours stretched over 7 days. They returned a verdict of "not guilty."[41]

In this example, the question, "Why do they do it?" refers to those people who may have labeled Jackson. For instance, even though he was acquitted, has Jackson been labeled? Further, did the act of "getting caught" begin the labeling process for Jackson? Was getting caught and the decision making of the criminal justice system a function of offender, rather than of offense characteristics? Did age, socioeconomic class, and race play a part in establishing patterns of differential criminal justice decision making?

offending,[42] parental labeling and delinquency,[43] perceived teacher disapproval and subsequent delinquency,[44] racial differences between negative labeling and criminal behavior,[45] labeling youth as delinquent or mentally ill based on their dress or taste in music (e.g., punk, heavy metal) and future criminal behavior,[46] and the effects of processing status offenders and subsequent delinquent behavior.[47]

As mentioned previously, research from various disciplines has used labeling theory to study different types of phenomena. Using a field experimental method, Richard Schwartz and Jerome Skolnick examined the effect of an employee's criminal court record on the reactions of potential employers.[48] The researchers constructed four employment folders that differed only with respect to the applicant's reported record of criminal court involvement. The results revealed that only one employer demonstrated an interest in the convicted folder, three in the tried-but-acquitted folder, six in the tried-but-acquitted folder (including a letter from the judge), and nine in the no-criminal-record folder. The researchers concluded that "the individual accused but acquitted has almost as much trouble finding even an unskilled job as the one who was not only accused of the same offense, but also convicted."[49]

Rosenhan examined how the label of "insanity" can influence the behavior and perceptions of hospital staff.[50] Eight individuals from various backgrounds, but deemed "sane," applied for admission to different mental hospitals. Upon their arrival at the hospitals, each individual pretended to hear voices, a symptom of schizophrenia. When questioned about their backgrounds and significant life events, they all gave truthful and accurate responses. All but one individual was labeled schizophrenic. After their admission, these individuals were responsible for demonstrating their sanity. The various hospital staff treated them as schizophrenic patients. Subsequently, these individuals were discharged from the hospital, with a diagnosis of schizophrenia "in remission."

CRITIQUES OF LABELING THEORY

There have been various critiques of labeling theory, including the following:

1. The various propositions to be tested are not adequately specified. This lack of specificity does not allow researchers to empirically examine the relationship between significant variables. Charles Tittle notes that advocates of labeling theory argue "that the particular strength of labeling theory lies in its resistance to formalization and in its vagueness and ambiguity, since such features alert us to important aspects of social life which are themselves relativistic and elusive."[51]

2. Due to the lack of satisfactory data and empirical research, evaluating the adequacy of labeling theory has been difficult. Furthermore, since the theory is vague with respect to its propositions, it is difficult to obtain additional information from research conducted for other purposes.[52] Additional refinement is needed, especially with respect to deviance amplification.[53]

3. Labeling theory focuses on the *reaction* to criminal and/or deviant behavior. It avoids the question of causation; specifically, why do some individuals commit a certain act while others do not?[54]

4. Labeling theory focuses on the "reactors" rather than the "actors." Thus, it views the "actor" or "labellee" as overly passive.[55] John Hagan emphasized that labeling theory would likely benefit empirically from the recognition of a *reciprocal* relationship in terms of the actor and reactor, stimulus and response, and preexisting differences and "reaction effects."[56]

5. Labeling should be viewed as a perspective rather than a theory. Specifically, it is neither a theory in the strictest sense nor does it focus exclusively on the act of the labeling itself. Rather, it is one approach to studying a general area of human activity.[57] Erich Goode argues that labeling theory is not a theory; in fact, he also maintains that it may not even be a perspective. Instead of examining deviance in general, the theory examines specific features of deviance.[58]

In 1975, Charles Wellford argued that labeling theory had weaknesses as an explanatory model of criminal behavior.[59] Eighteen years later, along with his former student Ruth Triplett, Wellford commented on the future of labeling theory in understanding deviant and criminal behavior. They maintained that the future of labeling theory could be promising, especially in terms of social thought or symbolic interactionism.[60]

Some scholars have been examining more complex versions of labeling theory.[61] For instance, some are interested in *shaming*.[62] David R. Karp maintains that the previous terms associated with labeling theory (e.g., *primary* and *secondary deviance*) have been replaced with other terms, such as *shame*.[63] Specifically, the central issue now is the potential of shaming as a tool of formal social control. Shaming involves self-labeling or self-stigmatizing. The concept of shaming is not new, especially when we look at how society has dealt with individuals considered to be deviant and/or criminal (e.g., the stocks, the "scarlet letter").[64]

CRIME IN THE NEWS

Theft

CONFLICT PERSPECTIVES

Most of the theories presented in the previous chapters are based on what are generally referred to as the **consensus perspective** of law. In the 18th and 19th centuries, consensus perspectives of law were identified as "social contract theories." These theories stressed that law serves a necessary social function (i.e., functionalism). A major proponent of this perspective, Thomas Hobbes, argued that without either law or the state, individuals would pursue their self-interests without considering how these pursuits

consensus perspective: theories that assume that virtually everyone is in agreement on the laws and therefore assumes no conflict in attitudes regarding the laws and rules of society

APPLYING THEORY TO CRIME: *LARCENY-THEFT*

Hammurabi, the King of Babylon in 1780 B.C., was the earliest known ruler to publicly provide the people with a body of laws. His "Code of Laws" includes various references to the crime of theft:

- If anyone steals the property of a temple or of the court, he shall be put to death, and also the one who receives the stolen thing from him shall be put to death.

- If anyone steals cattle or sheep, or an ass, or a pig or a goat, if it belonged to a god or to the court, the thief shall pay thirtyfold therefor; if they belonged to a freed man of the king he shall pay tenfold; if the thief has nothing with which to pay he shall be put to death.

- If anyone takes a male or female slave of the court, or a male or female slave of a freed man, outside the city gates, he shall be put to death.[65]

According to the Federal Bureau of Investigation (FBI) Uniform Crime Reports (UCR), larceny-theft is the "unlawful taking, carrying, leading, or riding away of property from the possession or constructive possession of another." Examples of larceny-theft include "bicycles, motor vehicle parts and accessories, shoplifting, pocket-picking, or the stealing of any property or article that is not taken by force and violence or by fraud." Thus, such crimes as embezzlement, confidence games, forgery, and check fraud are not counted as theft.[66] Based on the 2011 report, the FBI summarized the following key findings concerning larceny-theft:

- There were an estimated 6,159,795 larceny-thefts nationwide.

- When comparing the 2010 and 2011 larceny-theft rates, there was a drop of 0.7%.

- Larceny-thefts accounted for an estimated 68.0% of property crimes.

- The average value of property taken during larceny-thefts was $987 per offense. When the average value was applied to the estimated number of larceny-thefts, the loss to victims was more than $6 billion.

- The largest portion of reported larcenies (24.8%) was thefts from motor vehicles (except accessories).[67]

Table 10.1 provides a summary of larceny-theft by type from *Crime in the United States, 2011.*

The National Crime Victimization Survey (NCVS) collects data to provide additional insight into what is referred to as the *dark figure* of crime (e.g., crimes unreported to law enforcement). In reference to property crimes, such as larceny-theft, the NCVS does not include those affecting businesses or other commercial establishments; rather, the NCVS collects data on households. Some key summary findings, based on 2011 data, include the following:

- In 2011, members of U.S. households experienced about 17.1 million property victimizations (this includes larceny-theft, as well as other types of property crimes).

- In 2011, 51.2% of property crimes were reported to police.

- About 12.8 million property thefts occurred in 2011.

- About 104.2 per 1,000 households experienced property thefts during this time period.[68]

In an effort to further illustrate key aspects of labeling theory, we apply this perspective to the crime of larceny-theft. Jeff was a 15-year-old boy who was getting into some "minor" trouble at home (e.g., not cleaning his room, talking back to his mother). At one point, Jeff's mother decided to punish him by taking away his allowance. Jeff was quite upset about this, because he was planning to buy a DVD with his allowance. He decided to get this DVD by shoplifting from a nearby discount store; however, Jeff got caught stealing. The police were called, and Jeff was formally processed in the juvenile justice system and adjudicated as a delinquent. Afterward, many of Jeff's teachers, other kids at school, and neighbors knew he was caught stealing and processed through the juvenile justice system.

Initially, Jeff thought that he had made a "stupid" decision to steal the DVD. He never considered himself a thief; he stole the DVD in large part because he was angry that his mother took his allowance. However, after Jeff realized that many people around him, such as teachers, schoolmates, and neighbors, considered him a thief, he started to identify himself as a thief as well. So Jeff decided that if people were going to consider him a thief, he might as well start stealing more property. One evening, a neighbor left her garage door open. Jeff snuck in the garage and stole a bicycle. Identify some key features of labeling theory (e.g., self-fulfilling prophecy, secondary deviance, offense escalation) in this scenario.

(Continued)

APPLYING THEORY TO CRIME: *(CONTINUED)*

TYPE	NUMBER OF OFFENSES (2011)	PERCENTAGE DISTRIBUTION	AVERAGE VALUE
Pocket-picking	23,150	0.4%	$539
Purse-snatching	23,642	0.4%	$412
Shoplifting	940,903	17.5%	$199
From motor vehicles (except accessories)	1,330,396	28.4%	$818
Motor vehicle accessories	434,832	8.1%	$540
Bicycles	189,428	3.5%	$367
From buildings	635,582	11.8%	$1,443
From coin-operated machines	17,055	0.3%	$368
All others	1,774,967	33.1%	$1,564

Table 10.1 Larceny-Theft by Type

STATE CRIME RANKINGS

Larceny-Thefts

CITY CRIME RANKINGS

Larceny-Theft Rates

could affect others. To avoid such a lawless condition, individuals enter into an agreement, or consensus, to sacrifice their self-interests in an effort to form a society for the common good of all people.[69] Criminologists from this consensus perspective maintain that (1) law reflects the need for social order, (2) law is a product of value consensus, (3) law is an impartial system that protects public rather than private interests, and (4) where differences between groups exist, law is the neutral mechanism that helps individuals resolve their conflicts.[70]

Around the 1950s, conflict theory began to challenge the assumptions associated with the consensus and functional models of criminology.[71] There are various conflict theoretical perspectives. They all share a critical position concerning the existing social order; they differ, however, as to their conceptualization of the nature of social order.[72] Generally, there are two forms of conflict theory: conservative (pluralist) and critical-radical. The primary focus of conservative (pluralist) conflict theories is power and the use of that power; this theoretical framework views society as consisting of diverse interest groups competing for power.[73] George Vold, Austin Turk, and Richard Quinney have made major contributions to the conservative (pluralist) conflict theoretical perspective. The other form of conflict theory, critical-radical, can be traced back to the writings of Karl Marx; this theoretical framework views contemporary society as being dominated by a unified, capitalist ruling class.[74] William Chambliss and Robert Seidman, as well as Mark Colvin and John Pauly, have incorporated Marxist themes to understand crime and criminals.

THE CONSERVATIVE (PLURALIST) CONFLICT PERSPECTIVES

GEORGE VOLD

In his 1958 book *Theoretical Criminology,*[75] George Vold introduced **group conflict theory**. Prior to introducing this theory, Vold provided an interesting evaluation of

COMPARATIVE CRIMINOLOGY: *LARCENY-THEFT*

Ranking Countries by Rate of Larceny-Theft

The FBI considers larceny a major Index crime in the United States. However, according to Van Dijk,[76] there is likely no suitable, or comparable, equivalent to larceny in the various world statistics. The closest equivalent presented is for pickpocketing, which is somewhat similar in that there is no threat of violence, which would then make the crime robbery.

The best and most recent data are drawn from the International Crime Survey (years 1996–2005), which is basically broken into different continental regions. As Figure 10.3 shows, Africa leads the world in pickpocketing rates, with Asia and Latin America and the Caribbean tying for a close second. Eastern Europe had the fourth highest rate. All these regions were shown to be quite high in terms of pickpocketing. This should not come as much of a surprise, given that these same regions (or countries within these regions) tend to have the highest scores regarding robbery and/or burglary.

It makes sense that countries or regions that have high rates on one type of property crime (such as burglary) will also have high rates for other forms of property crime, such as pickpocketing and larceny.

Sign warning tourists of pickpockets

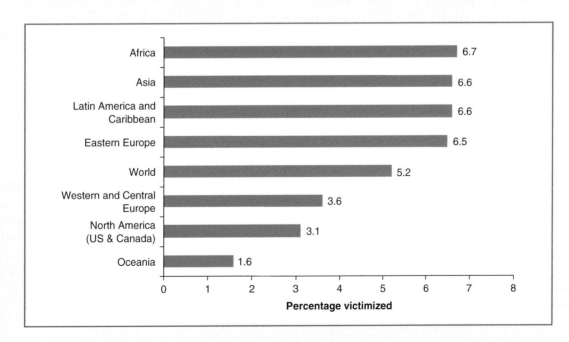

Figure 10.3 Percentages of the Public in Urban Areas Victimized by Pickpocketing During the Past 12 Months, by World Region

Source: FBI. (2012). *Crime in the United States, 2011.* Retrieved from http://www.fbi.gov/about-us/cjis/ucr/crime-in-the-u.s/2011/crime-in-the-u.s.-2011/tables/larceny-theft-table various theoretical perspectives.[77] He noted that, historically, there have been two basic types of criminological theories: *spiritualism* and *naturalism*. *Spiritual* explanations are influenced by "otherworld" powers. However, these explanations "cannot be considered scientific, even if some thoughtful and intelligent people believe that they represent the best explanation of crime." *Natural* explanations are more systematic and scientific. Vold identified three types of naturalistic theories: (1) those that focus on the individual, (2) those that emphasize group and intergroup relations, and (3) those that are "eclectical," including various factors that might explain criminal behavior.[78] In the preface of his book, Vold stated,

> No special plea is made for any particular theoretical position examined, though it should be clear that there is some preference for approaches that recognize and make more explicit the concept of crime as a by-product of the struggle for power in the group structure of society.[79]

Thus, he focused on the issue of conflicting group interests. Vold argued that part of human nature is that people's lives are a part of, and a product of, their group associations. Individuals are fundamentally group-involved beings. These groups usually evolve out of situations in which individuals have common interests and common needs that can be further promoted through some type of collective action. Subsequently, "groups come into conflict with one another as the interests and purposes they serve tend to overlap, encroach on one another, and become competitive."[80]

A key aspect to group conflict theory is recognizing the *social process* view of society as a collection of various groups that are held together in a dynamic equilibrium of opposing group interests and efforts. This social process involves a continuous struggle to maintain, or enhance, the position of one's own group within the context of these other competing groups. Conflict is an essential component to this social process. Thus, "these social interaction processes grind their way through varying kinds of uneasy adjustment to a more or less stable equilibrium of balanced forces, called social order or social organization."[81] Vold stressed that the conflict between these groups to maintain, or enhance, their own interests is especially apparent through the legislative political process.

In reference to crime, Vold maintained that the process of lawmaking, lawbreaking, and law enforcement reflects essential and fundamental conflicts between group interests, as well as the struggles among groups for control of state police power. Subsequently, criminal behavior is the course taken by less powerful groups who could not promote and defend their interests and purposes in the legislative process.[82]

Group conflict theory focuses only on those situations in which criminal behavior is a result of conflicting group interests. Generally, these types of crimes include (1) crimes arising from political protest, (2) crimes resulting from labor disputes, (3) crimes arising from disputes between and within competing unions, and (4) crimes arising from racial and ethnic clashes.[83] Group conflict theory, however, does not explain more individual types of behavior such as rape and robbery.

The importance of Vold's contribution is that it offered another explanation of understanding crime—*critical criminology*. Like many new approaches to explaining crime, Vold's is not as well defined or soundly based as those that followed.[84] These are discussed below.

AUSTIN TURK

In his 1969 book, *Criminality and Legal Order*, Austin Turk stated that "nothing and no one is intrinsically criminal; criminality is a definition applied by individuals with the

group conflict theory: Vold argued that part of human nature is that people's lives are a part, and a product, of their group associations; groups come into conflict with one another due to conflicting and competitive interests power to do so, according to illegal and extra-legal, as well as legal criteria."[85] While this appears to reflect the assumptions of labeling theory, Turk argued that one also needs to recognize the milieu that establishes the social categories.[86]

According to Turk, society is characterized by conflict arising among various groups seeking to establish or maintain control over one another. Thus, criminology should focus on differences between the status and role of legal *authorities* and *subjects*.[87] Individuals in society become accustomed to living with the social roles of authorities and subjects in such a manner that these roles are not questioned. While consensus theorists would contend that social order occurs through the internalization of the norms reflected in the law, Turk maintained that social order is based in a consensus–coercion balance preserved by the authorities.

Turk's "theory of criminalization" (i.e., the process of being labeled a criminal) occurs through the interaction between those who enforce the law and those who violate the law. This interaction is influenced by various social factors. One such social factor is the congruence of cultural and social norms.[88] Cultural norms are associated with verbal formulations of values (e.g., the law as written); social norms are associated with actual behavior patterns (e.g., the law as enforced). Conflict will occur between authorities and subjects regarding the congruence of the cultural and social norms.

Two additional social factors are the level of organization and the level of sophistication of both the authorities and the subjects. It is assumed that authorities are organized, since organization is essential for establishing and maintaining power. Conflict is more likely when subjects are also organized. Turk defined sophistication as the understanding of patterns in the behavior of others, which is then used in an effort to manipulate them. When either the subjects or authorities are less sophisticated, conflict is more likely to occur. For instance, when authorities are less sophisticated, they may have to use more overt forms of coercion to achieve their goals, as opposed to more subtle approaches.[89]

Another social factor is the power differential between enforcers and violators. Criminalization will most likely occur when the enforcers (e.g., the police, prosecutors, and judges) have a great deal of power compared with the resisters. Finally, realism of moves is another essential social factor. Conflict will most likely occur when either the enforcers or resisters engage in inappropriate or unsuitable behavior. For instance, an unrealistic move would be a motorist, while driving her car alongside a highway patrol officer, lighting up a marijuana cigarette. A realistic move would be when she smokes a marijuana cigarette in the privacy of her home.

In a subsequent article, Turk attempted to develop a model of social deviance and proposed various "working premises."[90] Turk also stressed that his proposed **nonpartisan conflict perspective** differs from a **partisan conflict perspective**. For instance, Richard Quinney (discussed below) argued for the partisan conflict perspective:

> In understanding criminal justice—its theory and practice under capitalism—we provide a theory and a practice that has as its objective changing the world. The importance of criminal justice is that it moves us dialectically to reject the capitalist order and to struggle for a new society. We are engaged in socialist revolution.[91]

Turk stressed the importance of nonpartisan conflict theory. Specifically, he maintained that the ideological position or the political utilities of theories are irrelevant when assessing the validity of knowledge claims.[92] Thus, *truth* should be independent of an individual's political ideology or personal values.

WHAT WERE THEY THINKING?!

Murder

nonpartisan conflict perspective: according to Turk, the ideological position or political utilities of theories are irrelevant when assessing the validity of knowledge claims; *truth* should be independent of political ideology or personal values

partisan conflict perspective: according to Quinney, provides a theory and practice with the purpose of changing the world; associated political objective

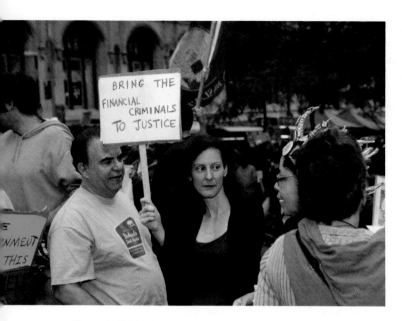

These individuals are protesting those whom they perceive as "financial" criminals.

RICHARD QUINNEY

Drawing from Vold's comments as well as from social interaction and labeling theory, Quinney provided a different explanation of criminal behavior. He set forth six propositions that described his social reality of crime. These propositions are as follows:

Proposition 1 (definition of crime): Crime is a definition of human conduct that is created by authorized agents in a politically organized society.

This proposition reflects assumptions of labeling theory. Quinney maintained that crime is created. Further, he argued that this proposition avoids the more commonly used "clinical perspective," which focuses on the quality of the act and assumes some type of individual pathology. Crime is considered a process that culminates in defining persons and behaviors as criminal.[93]

Proposition 2 (formulation of criminal definitions): Criminal definitions describe behaviors that conflict with the interests of the segments of society that have the power to shape political policy.

Quinney stressed that those groups who have the power to represent their interests in public policy are able to regulate the formulation of these criminal definitions. These interests are essentially based on desires, values, and norms. The formulation of criminal definitions is one of the most obvious indications of conflict in society. Specifically, formulating criminal law, such as legislative statutes, administrative rulings, and judicial decisions, allows these powerful segments of society to protect and perpetuate their own interests.[94]

Proposition 3 (application of criminal definitions): Criminal definitions are applied by the segments of society that have the power to shape the enforcement and administration of criminal law.

These interests of the powerful groups cannot be effectively protected by just formulating criminal law; rather, it is also essential that these groups protect their interests by *applying* these criminal definitions. Furthermore, the likelihood that criminal definitions will be applied differs according to the extent to which the behaviors of the powerless groups conflict with the interests of powerful groups. These powerful groups usually do not directly apply the criminal law. Instead, they delegate the enforcement and administration of law to authorized legal agents.[95]

Proposition 4 (development of behavior patterns in relation to criminal definitions): Behavior patterns are structured in segmentally organized society in relation to criminal definitions, and within this context persons engage in actions that have relative probabilities of being defined as criminal.

Individuals in segments of society that are not represented in formulating and applying the criminal definitions are more likely to act in a manner that will be defined as criminal.

Individuals in segments of society that are represented in formulating and applying the criminal definitions are less likely to act in a manner that will be defined as criminal. As this process of formulating and applying criminal definitions continues, those individuals identified as criminal begin to perceive themselves as criminal and subsequently learn to play the role. This process results in these individuals engaging in behavior that increases their chances of being defined as criminal.[96]

Proposition 5 (construction of criminal conceptions): Conceptions of crime are constructed and diffused in the segments of society by various means of communication.

Quinney noted that the "real world" is a social construction. Social reality is constructed through various processes that include the type of "knowledge" they develop, the ideas they are exposed to, the manner in which they select information that fits the "world" they are developing, and how they interpret these conceptions. As a result, individuals behave in reference to the social meanings they attach to their experiences. Within this broader context of constructing social reality, the concept of crime is also constructed. These conceptions are constructed by communication. Furthermore, the most fundamental conceptions are those of the powerful segments of society; these conceptions are usually incorporated into the social reality of crime.[97]

Proposition 6 (the social reality of crime): The social reality of crime is constructed by the formulation and application of criminal definitions, the development of behavior patterns related to criminal definitions, and the construction of criminal conceptions.

Quinney maintained that the previous five propositions can be accumulated into a composite. The theoretical framework for the social reality of crime describes, as well as explains, factors that increase the probability of crime in society, which subsequently results in the social reality of crime (see Figure 10.4).[98]

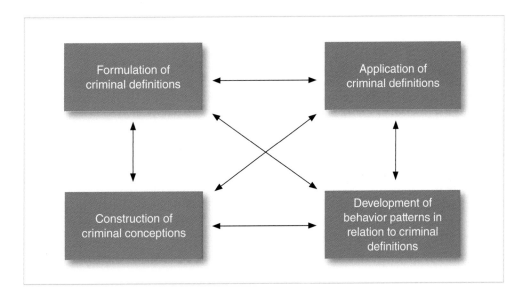

Figure 10.4 Model of the Social Reality of Crime

Source: Quinney, R. (1970). *The social reality of crime.* Boston: Little, Brown, p. 24.

THE RADICAL CONFLICT PERSPECTIVES

While it is difficult to summarize the various conservative (pluralist) conflict perspectives, this is even more challenging with the radical conflict perspectives. Criminologists within this perspective have covered a broad range of interests, including Marxism (discussed below) and left realism (discussed at the end of this chapter). Regardless of these various positions, the recent radical conflict perspectives can be traced to the writings of Karl Marx.[99]

MARXIST CRIMINOLOGY

Marx wrote very little about crime and criminal behavior. Radical criminologists, however, applied his ideas concerning social class to understanding crime. His philosophy was greatly influenced by the poor economic conditions following the Industrial Revolution. He argued that societies are characterized by class struggles. These class struggles are essentially based on the economic organization of a society.[100]

VIDEO

Marxism

Marx focused on the means of production. Society is divided into two classes based on the means of production. The superordinate class, or **bourgeoisie**, owns the means of production (e.g., factories); the subordinate class, or **proletariat**, works for those who own the means of production. This division of labor results in class struggles:

> The division of labor offers us the first example . . . that . . . as long as a cleavage exists between the particular and the common interests, . . . man's own deed becomes an alien power opposed to him, which enslaves him instead of being controlled by him. For as soon as labor is distributed, each man has a particular, exclusive sphere of activity, which is forced upon him and from which he cannot escape.[101]

bourgeoisie: a class or status Marx assigned to the dominant, oppressing owners of the means of production; believed to create and implement laws that helped retain their dominance over the working class

proletariat: in Marx's conflict theory, the oppressed group of workers exploited by the bourgeoisie; they never profit from their own efforts because the upper class owns and controls the means of production

Awareness of common interests among members in a class was designated as *class consciousness*. Alternatively, not being aware of these common interests was identified as *false consciousness*. This false consciousness causes the proletariat to believe that maintaining the capitalist system is in their best interest, rather than in the interest of the bourgeoisie.

Generally, criminologists have incorporated Marxist ideology in three ways. First, they have maintained that the law is a tool of the ruling class. The law represents the interests of the ruling class, essentially perpetuating concepts of capitalism. Second, they argue that all crime, in capitalist countries, is a product of a class struggle. When the accumulation of wealth and property is emphasized, this produces individualism and competition, which can result in conflict between, as well as within, classes. Third, scholars need to address the relationships between the mode of production and understanding crime.[102]

WILLIAM CHAMBLISS AND ROBERT SEIDMAN

In their book *Law, Order, and Power*, William Chambliss and Robert Seidman used a Marxist perspective to provide a critical understanding of the American justice system. Compared with the consensus perspective, the conflict perspective provides a very different framework when attempting to explain the criminal justice system. They argued that the myth (i.e., consensus perspective) regarding the operation of the law includes such concepts as, that it represents the values of society as a majority, it operates through a value-neutral government controlled by the people, and it serves the best interests of society.[103]

From a conflict perspective, Chambliss and Seidman stressed that society is made up of various groups that are in conflict. The law is a tool for those in power (i.e., the ruling class), functioning to provide coercive power in conflict.[104] They maintained that the myth of the operation of the law is revealed daily:

> We all know today that blacks and the poor are not treated fairly or equitably by the police. We know that judges have discretion and in fact make policy (as the Supreme Court did in the school desegregation cases). We know that electoral laws have been loaded in the past in favor of the rich, and the average presidential candidate is not a poor man, that one-fifth of the senators of the United States are millionaires.
>
> It is our contention that, far from being primarily a value-neutral framework within which conflict can be peacefully resolved, the power of the state is itself the principal prize in the perpetual conflict that is society.[105]

JOURNAL ARTICLE

Marxist Criminology

They maintained that the relationship between power and the use of the law extends to various institutions such as the legislatures, law enforcement, and especially the appellate courts.

In reference to the appellate courts, judges make rulings that have a lasting effect on future cases. Through their socialization process and privileged social position, these judges "are necessarily biased in favor of ensuring that courts are more available to the wealthy than to the poor, and tend to produce solutions in the interests of the wealthy."[106] Chambliss and Seidman also examined how law enforcement agencies are connected to the powerful and wealthy political structure. The specific points of this assertion are listed in Table 10.2.

FUNCTIONING OF LAW ENFORCEMENT AGENCIES
1. The agencies of law-enforcement are bureaucratic organizations.
2. An organization and its members tend to substitute for the official goals and norms of the organization's ongoing policies and activities, which will maximize rewards and minimize the strains on the organization.

3. This goal-substitution is made possible by:
   a. the absence of motivation on the part of the role-occupants to resist pressures toward goal-substitution.
   b. the pervasiveness of discretionary choice permitted by the substantive criminal law, and the norms defining the roles of the members of the enforcement agencies.
   c. the absence of effective sanctions for the norms defining the roles in those agencies.

4. Law enforcement agencies depend for resource allocation on political organizations.
5. It will maximize rewards and minimize strains for the organization to process those who are politically weak and powerless and to refrain from processing those who are politically powerful.
6. Therefore it may be expected that law-enforcement agencies will process a disproportionately high number of the politically weak and powerless, while ignoring the violations of those with power.

Table 10.2 Functioning of Law Enforcement Agencies

Source: Chambliss, W., & Seidman, R. (1971). *Law, order, and power.* Reading, MA: Addison-Wesley, p. 269.

COLVIN AND PAULY'S INTEGRATED STRUCTURAL-MARXIST THEORY

In their integrated structural-Marxist theory of delinquency, Mark Colvin and John Pauly maintain that structures of control have various "patterns associated with work, families, school, and peer groups and that those patterns form the mechanisms for the reproduction of the class structure."[107] Parents' socialization and discipline practices with their children are influenced by their workplace experiences. Working-class parents in an unstable workplace setting experience more coercive controls. As a result, these parents tend to enforce an uneven and erratic family control structure that fluctuates between being lax and highly punitive. Working-class parents with steadier, long-term employment tend to enforce a more utilitarian compliance structure in the family. Their children can usually expect predictable consequences for their behavior. Parents who are characterized as "white-collar workers" tend to enforce a more normative family compliance structure, which results in more positive bonds with their children. Such socialization and discipline practices influence delinquent behavior; specifically, there are significant positive associations between more physical and punitive parental discipline practices and delinquent behavior.[108]

Another essential aspect of the reproduction of labor and capitalist production relations is the school experience. Colvin and Pauly contend that

> parents' bonds engendered by workplace control structures are reproduced in the child through family controls; the child's initial ideological orientation toward authority is most likely to be reinforced in school control structures by mechanisms which render the child suitable for eventual placement in a workplace control structure similar to that of the parent. Thus, inequality and the class structure are subtly reproduced.[109]

Some studies have maintained that school control structures correlate with delinquent behavior. For instance, positive bonds with school have been associated with lower levels of delinquency.

In reference to peer associations, Colvin and Pauly suggest that such associations act as a mediator between delinquent behavior and the other control structures of family and school. Youths with similar bonds to family and school will be drawn to one another and subsequently share comparable values and experiences. For instance, juveniles in advanced educational tracks, which reinforce positive bonds, form peer associations that consist of more normative and compliant structures that discourage delinquent behavior. Alternatively, youths in lower educational tracks, characterized by more alienated bonds with family and school, form peer associations that reinforce more negative, delinquent behavior.[110]

The integrated structural-Marxist theory reveals how various theoretical perspectives have been incorporated in an attempt to provide a more comprehensive understanding of criminal behavior. This perspective begins with a "structural-Marxist" perspective, which opens with the premise that social relations are grounded in the process of capitalist material production. This perspective also incorporates aspects of learning theory, strain theory, control theories, and labeling theory.

ADDITIONAL EXPLANATIONS OF CRIME USING A MARXIST FRAMEWORK

In their book *Adolescent Subcultures and Delinquency,* Herman Schwendinger and Julia Siegel Schwendinger incorporated a Marxist framework to explain adolescent subcultures and delinquency.[111] They based this theoretical explanation on extensive observations and interviews conducted from the 1950s through the 1980s. They argued that previous theoretical explanations of delinquency are inadequate and maintained that it is essential to incorporate structural conditions, especially economic conditions, under which certain peer groups develop and that promote delinquent behavior.

A capitalistic economic system is conducive to developing and maintaining various social class relationships that are primarily reproduced in individuals' places in the labor force. The Schwendingers contend that certain *stratified networks* of adolescent groups negotiate those relationships between the broader social context (e.g., socioeconomic conditions) and patterns of delinquent behavior among peer groups. These adolescent groups may be designated by such labels as "rich kids" and "poor kids." These groups may violate the law more often than other youths; however, both groups represent subcultures that have historically evolved with the rise of capitalism. Their lifestyles may reveal conspicuous consumption or other status accompaniments.[112]

For instance, these *stratified networks* can be enhanced in the public school system. Most adolescents in the United States attend public schools that help youths develop the skills needed to eventually participate in the labor force. Resources, however, are not equally distributed among youths. Some adolescents benefit more than others due to economic and cultural privileges awarded to certain ethnic, racial, or occupational groups.

Steven Spitzer applied a Marxian perspective to understanding deviance. He argued that one of the most essential functions of the superstructure in capitalist societies is the regulation and management of problem populations. These groups are problems when they question or disturb the following:

1. Capitalist modes of appropriating the product of human labor (e.g., when the poor "steal" from the rich)

2. The social conditions under which capitalist production takes place (e.g., those who refuse or are unable to perform wage labor)

3. Patterns of distribution and consumption in capitalist society (e.g., those who use drugs for escape and transcendence rather than sociability and adjustment)

4. The process of socialization for productive and non-productive roles (e.g., youth who refuse to be schooled or those who deny the validity of "family life")

5. The ideology which supports the functioning of capitalist society (e.g., proponents of alternative forms of social organization.[113]

Problem populations have similar characteristics, but a key factor is that their behavior, personal qualities, and/or position threatens the social relations of production.

Official control of these individuals is determined by how much of a problem they pose for the continuation of a capitalist society. Those individuals who are passive and do not attempt to disrupt society are viewed by the dominant class as *social junk*. Social junk rarely comes to the attention of officials except when attempts are made to regulate or contain these individuals. Examples of what Spitzer called social junk are the aged, handicapped, and mentally ill. Those individuals who question established relationships, especially relations to production and domination, are designated as *social dynamite*. Officials usually deal with social dynamite through the legal system. Examples of individuals considered to be social dynamite are political activists and criminals.[114]

RESEARCH ON CONFLICT THEORIES

Research using a conflict perspective can be categorized into one of two broad approaches: (1) studies examining laws that are formulated in the interests of those in power and (2) studies examining the differential processing of certain individuals in the criminal justice system.[115] Research from the first approach includes examining vagrancy laws[116]

LEARNING CHECK 10.3

According to Marx, the _____ owned the means of production; the _____ worked for those who owned the means of production.

_____ and _____ maintained that law enforcement agencies are connected to the powerful and wealthy political structure.

Colvin and Pauly contend that working-class parents in an unstable workplace environment experience more _____ controls.

Answers located at www.sagepub.com/schram

and the Marijuana Tax Act.[117] One example of a more current study using the first approach is Amanda Robinson's research on public reaction to a domestic violence pro-arrest policy.[118] Robinson hypothesized that there would be differences in support for the criminalization of domestic violence between powerful groups (i.e., middle- and upper-class white men) and less powerful groups (i.e., women, minorities, and the economically and educationally disadvantaged). The analyses revealed that there were differences by age, education, income, and gender; these differences supported the conflict perspective.

Various studies have used the second approach to examine differential processing of individuals in the criminal justice system. A number of studies have explored whether race and ethnicity are significant factors during various stages of criminal justice processing: intake diversion,[119] arrests,[120] juvenile justice dispositions,[121] and felony dispositions.[122]

Other aspects of the criminal justice system were examined using this approach. Malcolm Holmes hypothesized that the number of threatening acts and people was directly related to the number of police brutality civil rights criminal complaints filed with the U.S. Department of Justice.[123] The results revealed that the presence of threatening people (percentage black, percentage Hispanic, and majority/minority income inequality) was positively related to the mean number of civil rights criminal complaints. Mitchell Chamlin tested two hypotheses: (1) Increases in the size of threatening groups (e.g., blacks, Hispanics, and the poor) will increase the level of hostility between crime control agents (e.g., law enforcement officers) and civilians, and (2) these increased levels of hostility will enhance the volatility of police–citizen encounters, resulting in increased rates of police killings.[124] The results revealed that economic inequality did not have an effect on police killings. Support for the increase in population size of racial minorities, however, was related to "mutually suspicious interactions between civilians and police."

CRITIQUES OF CONFLICT PERSPECTIVES

George Vold and his colleagues presented some of the limitations associated with the conflict perspective.[125] First, while there have been advancements in research methodologies, especially with the use of more sophisticated techniques using multivariate analyses, there is still a fundamental problem when testing conflict theory; specifically, a similar finding may be interpreted in more than one way:

> If a direct effect of race on the decision to arrest or the length of a sentence is found, controlling for hosts of other factors, what does this mean? It could be evidence of widespread racial prejudice in society, manifested in unequal treatment of minorities by criminal justice system actors. On the other hand, it could represent systematic and institutionalized protection of those in power (whites) from the threatening group (blacks).[126]

Thus, some studies that reveal unequal treatment of individuals of different races haphazardly and erroneously assume support for conflict theory.

Second, some research studies testing conflict theory are unable to distinguish between alternative explanations. For instance, some studies (such as those discussed in the previous

WHY DO THEY DO IT?

TED KACZYNSKI

Mug shot of Theodore "Ted" Kaczynski

In 1978, the explosion of what was considered a primitive homemade bomb sent to a Chicago university started Theodore Kaczynski's "reign of terror." Over the next 17 years, these bombs were either hand-delivered or mailed, resulting in three deaths and 24 injuries. In 1979, an FBI task force, including the Bureau of Alcohol, Tobacco, Firearms, and Explosives and the U.S. Postal Inspection Service, was formed to investigate what was designated as the UNABOM (<u>un</u>iversity and <u>a</u>irline <u>bom</u>bing targets) case. This task force, which grew to more than 150 full-time investigators, analysts, and others, attempted to recover bomb components and examined the lives of the victims in an effort to identify the bomber.[127]

In 1995, the unidentified "Unabomber" sent the FBI a 35,000-word essay that explained, from his perspective, the reasons for these bombs, as well as his views on the ills of modern society. The following is just one item among the 232 listed in the manifesto:

> 4. We therefore advocate a revolution against the industrial system. This revolution may or may not make use of violence; it may be sudden or it may be a relatively gradual process spanning a few decades. We can't predict any of that. But we do outline in a very general way the measures that those who hate the industrial system should take in order to prepare the way for a revolution against that form of society. This is not to be a POLITICAL revolution. Its object will be to overthrow not governments but the economic and technological basis of the present society.[128]

FBI director Louis Freeh and Attorney General Janet Reno agreed with the task force's recommendation to publish the essay, with the hope that a reader could identify the author. This manifesto was printed in the *Washington Post* and the *New York Times*.

While thousands of people offered various suspects, one stood out. In January of 1996, in his family home in Illinois, David Kaczynski found papers, written by his brother Theodore (Ted), that contained Unabomer-like rhetoric. David Kaczynski notified the FBI. Linguistic analysis revealed that the author of these documents was most likely the author of the manifesto as well. On April 3, 1996, Ted Kaczynski was arrested in his remote mountain cabin in Stemple Pass, Montana. During the search of his cabin, investigators found a large number of bomb components, 40,000 handwritten journal pages, descriptions of Unabomber crimes, and one live bomb ready for mailing. Following his guilty plea in January of 1998, Ted Kaczynski was incarcerated in an isolated cell in a Colorado supermax prison.[129]

Are any features of this type of offense reflected in the various theories that have been discussed? For instance, in reference to Steven Spitzer's work, would Ted Kaczynski be considered social dynamite? Why or why not?

section) attempt to reveal that in areas where threatening groups (e.g., minorities and the poor) pose an increasing threat to those in power, there is an increase in law enforcement activity. These researchers, when finding such a positive relationship, argue that this supports conflict theory. There may, however, be alternative explanations. For example, nonwhites may *want* or *need* more law enforcement protection than do whites. Or non-whites may encounter different types of social problems that require more social services.

Finally, few attempts have been made to develop and test well-constructed conflict theories. As demonstrated in the previous section, there are variations of the conflict perspective. As a result, many empirical studies do not adequately specify which conflict propositions on conflict theory are being tested. Vold and his colleagues cited a study conducted by Lanza-Kaduce and Greenleaf, however, that addresses this problem by specifically identifying how Turk's theory of norm resistance can be operationalized and tested when examining encounters between police and citizens.[130] "Their effort is encouraging, in that it shows that a particular conflict theory can be tested empirically, if the researcher is careful to be true to the original theory."[131]

CRIME IN THE NEWS

Ted Kaczynski Manifesto

ADDITIONAL CRITICAL THEORIES

We finish up the chapter with a brief discussion of three other critical criminological theories: (1) peacemaking criminology, (2) the restorative justice perspective, and (3) left realism.

CRIME IN THE NEWS

Manifestos

PEACEMAKING CRIMINOLOGY

Peacemaking criminology has incorporated three intellectual traditions: religious, feminist, and critical.[132] Generally, peacemaking criminology contends that rather than using punishment and retribution as a means of social control, society should attempt reconciliation through mediation and dispute settlement.[133] Individually and collaboratively, Harold Pepinsky and Richard Quinney have been involved in developing peacemaking criminology.[134] Figure 10.5 is a theoretical model of peacemaking criminology. This model consists of five basic elements—social structure, crimes, social harms, the criminal justice system, and peacemaking alternatives:

> Peacemaking criminology research, in its strictest sense, will opt to examine how people in our present times become affected by and, in turn, affect these five basic elements within the peacemaking criminology theoretical model. Leaving out an element would lead, in a peacemaking criminology view, to an incomplete understanding of crime and how to address crime in a humane way.[135]

A key aspect to this model is recognizing that the world needs to be understood in terms of its interconnections rather than focusing on individual elements.

John Wozniak identified three predominate themes of peacemaking criminology. The first theme is types of crime and social harms. A common approach among peacemaking criminologists is to focus on different crimes (i.e., violation of a law) in the same context as other social harms (i.e., physical, mental, or social damages or injuries that are not violations of law in the strictest sense).[136] A key tenet of peacemaking criminology is to realize how different types of crime are inextricably related to different types of social harm.

The second theme is the types of peacemaking frameworks or perspectives. A general review of the literature reveals that many peacemaking criminology scholars tend to deviate from mainstream criminology theories in their research. Rather, they tend to focus on the type of theories that begin with questioning existing political, economic, and underlying ideologies of the status quo. They also maintain that answers to violence and social harm, as well as the injustices associated with such harm, are essentially outside the criminal justice system.[137] Not only is peacemaking criminology diverse; it is also optimistic. For instance, this approach encourages individuals working in the field of criminal justice to believe that society could be reorganized in a way that would result in human reactions conducted in a more humane manner.

The third theme is the types of peacemaking alternatives.[138] Peacemaking alternatives are quite diverse with respect to confronting crimes and social harms. Wozniak selected

peacemaking criminology: incorporates three intellectual traditions: religious, feminist, and critical; contends that society should attempt reconciliation through mediation and dispute settlement

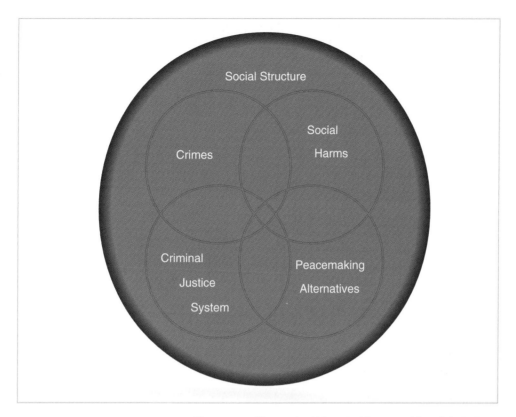

Figure 10.5 Theoretical Model of Peacemaking Criminology

Source: Wozniak, J. F. (2001). Toward a theoretical model of peacemaking criminology: An essay in honor of Richard Quinney. *Crime and Delinquency, 48,* 221.

various examples to illustrate this point. Within the feminist tradition of peacemaking, he cited how researchers examining sexual assault led to the promise of community "Take Back the Night" marches, sexual assault centers, rape crisis programs, Men and Women Committed to Stopping Violence Against Women, and watchdog programs committed to monitoring the treatment of victims.[139] Another scholar's research endeavors directed attention toward the Alternatives to Violence Project for prisons, as well as transformation of the correctional center to a healing center that advocates for the teaching of nonviolent techniques.[140]

RESTORATIVE JUSTICE PERSPECTIVE

Retributive justice refers to the repair of justice through a one-sided approach of imposing punishment; **restorative justice** refers to the repair of justice by reaffirming a shared consensus of values, involving a joint or multisided approach.[141] Restorative justice emphasizes the victim, the community, and the offender. The restorative justice framework is based on the balanced approach (see Figure 10.6).

> The Balanced Approach mission addresses the public need for 1) sanctioning based on accountability measures which attempt to restore victims and clearly denounce and provide meaningful consequences for offensive behavior; 2) offender rehabilitation and reintegration; and 3) enhanced community safety and security. It does this by articulating three system goals directed toward the three primarily "client/customers" of the system—the victim, the offender, and the community. These system goals, which also govern the response to each offense, are: accountability; competency development; community protection.[142]

retributive justice: refers to the repair of justice through a one-sided approach of imposing punishment

restorative justice: refers to the repair of justice by reaffirming a shared consensus of values involving a joint or multisided approach; emphasizes victim, community, and offender

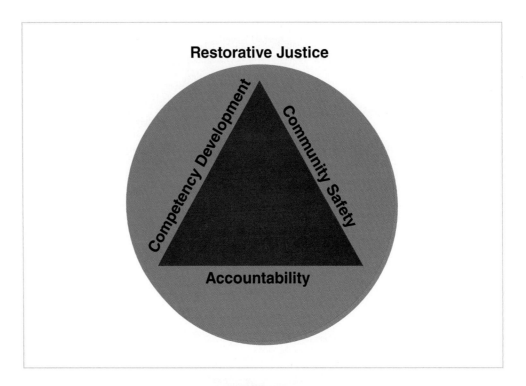

CLIENT/CUSTOMERS	GOALS	VALUES
Victims	Accountability	When an offense occurs, an obligation to victims and community incurs.
Youth	Competency Development	Offenders who enter the juvenile justice system should exit more capable than when they entered.
Community	Community Protection	Juvenile justice has a responsibility to protect the public from juveniles in the system.

Source: Adapted from Maloney, D., Romig, D., & Armstrong, T.(1988). *Juvenile probation: The balanced approach.* Reno,. NV: National Council of Juvenile and Family Court Judges.

Figure 10.6 The Balanced Approach

Source: Bazemore, G., & Umbreit, M. (1997). *Balanced and restorative justice for juveniles: Framework for juvenile justice in the 21st century.* Washington, DC: Office of Juvenile Justice and Delinquency Prevention, p. 14.

To further illustrate how the restorative justice perspective differs from a more traditional and retributive perspective, Gordon Bazemore and Mark Umbreit compared these two perspectives (see Table 10.3) and found key differences. For instance, retributive justice focuses on public vengeance as well as punishment exacted through an adversarial process. Restorative justice is more inclusive in that it considers not only the offender but the victim and the community.

Wheeldon argued that although there have been definitional challenges, existing restorative justice programs share key principles. The first is focusing on harms. Such harms include those suffered by communities. The second is to root procedures in the communities where such harms occurred. Such procedures or processes include understanding the community's part in crime commission as well as prevention. When the community is involved in this process, there is an acceptance that even those individuals not personally harmed by a specific crime continue to have an interest in the resolution of this offense. The third is the moral potential for restorative justice. This is related to the spiritual or religious traditions as well as a sense of humanism.[143]

RETRIBUTIVE JUSTICE	RESTORATIVE JUSTICE
Crime is an act against the state, a violation of a law, an abstract idea	Crime is an act against another person or the community
The criminal justice system controls crime	Crime control lies primarily in the community
Offender accountability defined as taking punishment	Accountability defined as assuming responsibility and taking action to repair harm
Crime is an individual act with individual responsibility	Crime has both individual and social dimensions of responsibility
Punishment is effect (a) threat of punishment deters crime (b) punishment changes behavior	Punishment alone is not effective in changing behavior and is disruptive to community harmony and good relationships
Victims are peripheral to the process	Victims are central to the process of resolving a crime
The offender is defined by deficits	The offender is defined by capacity to make reparation
Focus on establishing blame or guilt, on the past (did he/she do it?)	Focus on problem solving, on liabilities/obligations, on the future (what should be done?)
Emphasis on adversarial relationship	Emphasis on dialogue and negotiation
Imposition of pain to punish and deter/prevent	Restitution as a means of restoring both parties; goal of reconciliation/restoration
Community on sideline, represented abstractly by state	Community as facilitator in restorative process
Response focused on offender's past behavior	Response focused on harmful consequences of offender's behavior; emphasis on the future
Dependence upon proxy professionals	Direct involvement by participants

Table 10.3 Retributive and Restorative Justice Assumptions

Source: Bazemore, G., & Umbreit, M. (1997). *Balanced and restorative justice for juveniles: Framework for juvenile justice in the 21st century.* Washington, DC: Office of Juvenile Justice and Delinquency Prevention, p. 15.

LEFT REALISM

Jock Young identified four major processes that have transformed criminological thinking: (1) the etiological crisis due to rising crime rates; (2) the crisis in penalty in terms of the failure of prisoners, as well as a reappraisal of the role of police; (3) the increased awareness of victimization and of crimes that had previously gone "unnoticed"; and (4) a growing public demand and criticism of public service efficiency and accountability.[144] In the 1980s, some theorists were questioning the narrow focus of Marxism and other radical theories.[145]

The major criticism was that these theoretical perspectives placed too much emphasis on the notion that crime is a result of the capitalist system and the abuses of those in the "elite" class. As a result, this focus fails to recognize that crime also exists in socialist countries; it ignores how crime challenges those in the lower classes who are often victims of violence; and this narrow emphasis results in weak crime-control approaches that do not adequately address the problem of crime. This critical perspective was identified as **left realism**. Realism contends that previous criminological theories are incomplete in that they emphasize only one part of the square of crime: the state (as in labeling theory, neoclassicism), the public (as in control theory), the offender (as in positivism), or the victim (as in victimology). One of the major goals of left realism is to provide an analysis of crime on all levels, as well as to develop a range of policy recommendations.[146]

left realism: contends that previous criminological theories have been incomplete in that they emphasize only one part of the square of crime; attempts to provide an analysis of crime on all levels and develop a range of policy recommendations

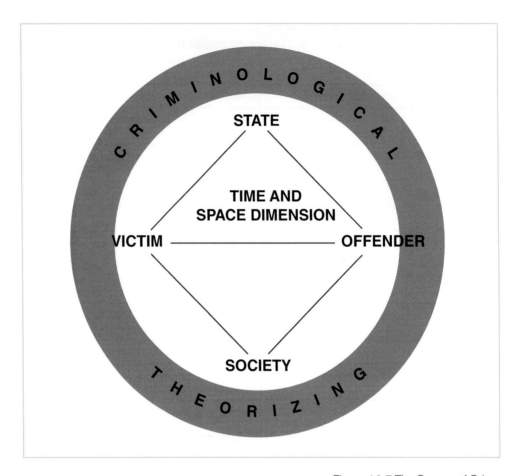

Figure 10.7 The Square of Crime

Source: Matthews, R., & Young, J. (1992). Reflections on realism. In J. Young & R. Matthews (Eds.), *Rethinking criminology: The realist debate* (pp. 1–23). London: Sage, p. 20.

Criminological realism refers to the notion of the *square of crime*. This term is "shorthand" and serves as a reminder that crime occurs at the intersection of a number of lines of force. One should not view crime solely in terms of victims and offenders without also including the role of the state and public opinion.[147] This square of crime is illustrated in Figure 10.7.

Left realists stress the necessity of a crime-control strategy in a capitalist society. It is essential that this crime-control strategy protect those individuals from the lower and working classes who are more vulnerable to becoming victims of crime and also experience a more intense fear of crime. In fact, this increased fear of crime has provided for the right wing to adhere to a "law-and-order" campaign that is repressive to many of these individuals.[148]

POLICIES RELATED TO LABELING AND CONFLICT THEORIES OF CRIME

A major policy implication of labeling research is that if deviance amplification occurs, the criminal justice agency, especially the juvenile justice system, should strive to divert certain individuals from formal processing to avoid the negative effects of such labeling.[149] In reference to policies related to the labeling perspective, a general approach has been to incorporate diversion programs, particularly for juveniles. Diversion occurs when a juvenile is not formally processed in the juvenile justice system (e.g., adjudication or incarceration); rather, these youths may be referred to some type of program such as treatment or work. Some would maintain that when a youth is diverted out of the juvenile justice system, he or she avoids the *label* of "juvenile delinquent." Thus, "by keeping juveniles out of the system, the labeling impact of courts and judges will be reduced. Juveniles will also develop less of the secondary deviance patterns that result from being labeled by the system as 'delinquent.'"[150]

One example of a diversion program is youth courts (also known as peer courts or teen courts). Youth courts are typically for juveniles between the ages of 10 and 15 years old who have no prior arrests and are charged with less serious law violations (e.g., shoplifting, vandalism). In most cases, these youths are provided with an option to participate in this program rather than continue through the formal juvenile justice system. These courts differ from other programs in that the juveniles determine the disposition; however, adults do oversee the program.[151]

An example of policies that reflect the conflict theoretical perspective relates to crack and cocaine legislation.[152] In the mid-1980s, crack cocaine was becoming more prevalent and receiving a great deal of media attention. Crack was characterized as inducing violence, highly addictive, and a major problem in urban areas. This public perception led to the quick passage of two federal sentencing laws: the Anti-Drug Abuse Act of 1986 and the Omnibus Anti-Drug Abuse Act of 1988.

These sentencing laws used a 100-to-1 ratio between the amount of crack and powder cocaine needed to instigate mandatory sentences for trafficking, as well as minimum penalties for simple possession of crack cocaine. For instance, possession with the intent to distribute 500 grams or more of powder cocaine carried a 5-year sentence; possession with the intent to distribute 5 grams of crack cocaine carried a 5-year sentence. These laws resulted in crack users and dealers receiving harsher penalties than users and dealers of powder cocaine.

These sentencing laws have been challenged. First, some argue that these differences resulted in racial disparity. About two thirds of crack users are white or Hispanic; most individuals convicted of possession in federal courts were African American. According to the U.S. Sentencing Commission, in 1994, defendants convicted of crack possession were 84.5% black, 10.3% white, and 5.2% Hispanic. Second, some maintained that the sentences were unconstitutional on the grounds that (1) they denied equal protection or due process, (2) the penalties constituted cruel and unusual punishment, and (3) the statutes were unconstitutionally vague.

On August 3, 2010, President Barack Obama signed the Fair Sentencing Act. This law lessens the disparity between mandatory minimum sentences for crack and powder cocaine offenses. Specifically, it reduces the sentencing disparity to 18 to 1. Thus, a person convicted of selling 28 grams of crack will face a 5-year mandatory minimum, just as will a person who is convicted of selling 500 grams of powder cocaine.

CONCLUSION

An overriding theme of this chapter was to illustrate various theoretical perspectives that challenge the traditional criminological theories and dominant ideologies. These critical perspectives question various assumptions that were considered as "given" in the traditional perspectives. We started this chapter with labeling theory. A major aspect of the labeling perspective is critically examining how deviant behavior is defined and who has the power to define this behavior as such.

The next section presented various conflict perspectives. These different perspectives, however, share a common assumption—conflict is natural to society. While it is difficult to generally categorize these conflict perspectives, we grouped them in two categories. The first was conservative (pluralist) theories. Conservative (pluralist) conflict theories emphasize power and the use of power. The second was critical–radical theories. These perspectives have incorporated Marxist themes to understand crime and criminals. We concluded this chapter by presenting three additional critical perspectives—peacemaking criminology, the restorative justice perspective, and left realism.

It is essential that readers appreciate how these diverse criminological theories have evolved. A major contribution of these critical theoretical perspectives is that they provide an additional lens not previously considered in traditional, mainstream criminological theories. These critical perspectives also emphasize that attempts to understand individual criminal behavior need to incorporate the broader societal context.

After studying these theoretical perspectives, students should reconsider the case study on e-waste dumping at the beginning of this chapter. Think about issues such as whether wealth and privilege are key factors in how this type of activity is defined (e.g., as a crime) as well as how such definitions are enforced.

SUMMARY OF THEORIES IN CHAPTER 10

THEORY	CONCEPTS	PROPONENTS	KEY PROPOSITIONS
Labeling theory	Not overly concerned with questions of why an individual engages in deviant behavior; rather, it is important to understand how criminal, or deviant, behavior is defined or labeled, as well as how society reacts to this behavior.	Frank Tannenbaum, Edwin Lemert, Howard Becker, Edwin Schur	No act is intrinsically criminal; criminal definitions are enforced in the interest of the powerful; an individual does not become a criminal by violating the law; penalties for a criminal act vary according to the characteristics of the offender; criminal justice is based on a stereotyped conception of the criminal; public condemnation may make it difficult for an offender to sustain a positive self-image.
Conservative (pluralist) conflict perspectives	Conflict is an essential component; groups have competing interests; society is made up of groups with different levels of power; group interests are reflected in various aspects of society, especially in the legislative political process.	George Vold, Austin Turk, Richard Quinney	Conflict arises between various groups seeking to establish or maintain control over one another; the law is an essential tool used to reflect the interests of those powerful groups; differences in power are reflected in who defines behavior as criminal.
Radical conflict perspectives	Modes of production influence various aspects of the social structure, including the criminal justice system, family, and school.	Various	Similar propositions to those of conservative (pluralist) conflict perspectives, with an emphasis on wealth and social class.

KEY TERMS

bourgeoisie

consensus perspective

dramatization of evil

falsely accused

group conflict theory

labeling theory

left realism

negotiation

nonpartisan conflict perspective

partisan conflict perspective

peacemaking criminology

primary deviance

proletariat

pure deviant

restorative justice

retributive justice

retrospective interpretation

secondary deviance

secret deviant

status-degradation ceremony

stereotyping

symbolic interactionism

STUDENT STUDY SITE

Visit the student study site at **www.sagepub.com/schram** to access links to the video, audio, city and state rankings, author podcasts, and SAGE journal and reference articles featured in this chapter, as well as additional study tools, including eFlashcards, web quizzes, web resources, and chapter outlines.

DISCUSSION QUESTIONS

1. What are the major assumptions of labeling theory?

2. According to Lemert, how does an individual get labeled as a "deviant"?

3. According to Becker, what two behaviors are incorrectly perceived by society?

4. Is labeling a theory, a perspective, or neither?

5. What key features distinguish the consensus model of law from the conflict model of law?

6. How has Marxist theory been incorporated to explain crime?

7. What are some of the limitations of conflict theories?

8. What are the key features of peacemaking criminology?

9. How has the restorative justice perspective incorporated the offender, victim, and community?

10. What are some examples of policies that reflect the labeling and conflict perspectives?

WEB RESOURCES

Critical criminology

http://wcr.sonoma.edu/v3n2/hil.html

Restorative Justice Online

http://www.restorativejustice.org/

CHAPTER 11

Feminist Theories of Crime

INTRODUCTION

Feminist criminology evolved when various assumptions and stereotypes about women in criminal justice were being questioned. Such questions included women as professionals as well as women as offenders and victims. This chapter begins with a brief history of feminism in the United States. To provide a better understanding of feminist theories of crime, it is essential to stress that there is no *one* feminist perspective. Rather, there are various feminist perspectives. Some of these feminist perspectives are discussed in the subsequent section. Next, this chapter discusses traditional theories of female crime, followed by feminist critiques of previous research focusing on women. We then present issues pertaining to understanding crime and criminal behavior that have been raised in feminist research. Finally, we discuss various policy and program recommendations based on theories and research grounded in a feminist perspective.

A BRIEF HISTORY OF FEMINISM IN THE UNITED STATES

Feminism is a belief that women and men are inherently of equal worth. Because most societies privilege men as a group, social movements are necessary to achieve equality between women and men, with the understanding that gender always intersects with other social hierarchies.[1]

Most scholars contend that feminism has evolved in three major waves. The **first wave of feminism** started in the mid-1800s when women demanded the right to vote.[3] A major event associated with this first wave occurred in 1848. About 300 women and men met in Seneca Falls, New York. At the Seneca Falls Convention, these participants established a "Declaration of Sentiments" as well as 12 resolutions. This declaration was modeled after the Declaration of Independence. The Declaration of Sentiments stressed the need for reforms in marriage, divorce, property, and child custody laws. A major criticism of this convention was that the focus was primarily on white, upper-class women. Thus, working-class and black women were essentially invisible.

These "invisible" women, however, did contribute to the 19th century women's rights movement. For instance, Sojourner Truth delivered her well-known speech at an 1851 women's rights convention in Akron, Ohio.[4] She delivered an impromptu speech that included her well-known question, "Ain't I a woman?" In this speech, she attempted to persuade the audience to support women's rights. The feminist views were "taking a beating all evening." Eventually, a man claimed that women needed to be protected with chivalrous acts. It was at this time that Sojourner Truth rose and replied with her speech.[5]

The peak of the first wave was between 1870 and 1928. This time period is characterized by intense activity toward winning women the right to vote as well as achieving educational and social reforms. While many women from various backgrounds were involved in these reforms, those women who were particularly involved in the antislavery and temperance movements worked together to secure women the right to vote.[6] In 1920, the Nineteenth Amendment to the Constitution was passed, giving the vote

LEARNING OBJECTIVES

As students are reading this chapter, they should consider the following topics:

- Compare and contrast the first, second, and third waves of feminism.

- Identify the key features of the various feminist perspectives.

- Describe how traditional theories of crime perceived female offenders.

- Identify some of the problems associated with traditional research methods.

- Describe feminist pathways research.

- Discuss how multicultural feminism differs from previous feminist perspectives.

- Describe some key critiques of feminist criminological theories.

- Discuss what is meant by "the personal is the political."

- Describe praxis.

- Identify some of the significant rape reforms.

- List and describe some of the fundamental factors of gender-specific programming.

ELIZABETH ESCALONA

On July 12, 2012, 23-year-old Elizabeth Escalona pled guilty to injury to a child in a Dallas, Texas, court. During her sentencing, Escalona admitted that she had abused her 2-year-old daughter, Jocelyn Cedillo. She further stated, "I hit her, I kicked her constantly and she didn't deserve that. . . . I want everybody to know that I'm not a monster. I love my kids." Apparently, Escalona was getting frustrated over potty training Jocelyn. On September 7, 2011, she superglued her daughter's hands to the wall and repeatedly beat her. Evidence photos revealed that Jocelyn suffered from numerous bruises, cuts, and bite marks prior to being taken to Children's Medical Center Dallas; she remained in a coma for 2 days. The prosecutor sought a 45-year sentence; the judge sentenced Escalona to 99 years. She will be eligible for parole in 30 years.

Escalona is the mother of five children. Four of her children were placed in foster care and then with their maternal grandmother. The fifth child was born to Escalona while in jail and was subsequently placed with the grandmother as well. Escalona testified that she had been molested and abused by her boyfriends. She was a recovering marijuana and cocaine addict; she was raising her children on child support payments in a bug-infested one-bedroom apartment.

The prosecutor noted that Escalona was once considered a dangerous juvenile delinquent, a gang member who started smoking marijuana at the age of 11. During the sentencing hearing, the prosecutor played recordings of a teenage Escalona threatening to kill her mother.[2]

> ESCALONA IS THE MOTHER OF FIVE CHILDREN. FOUR OF HER CHILDREN WERE PLACED IN FOSTER CARE AND THEN WITH THEIR MATERNAL GRANDMOTHER. THE FIFTH CHILD WAS BORN TO ESCALONA WHILE IN JAIL AND WAS SUBSEQUENTLY PLACED WITH THE GRANDMOTHER AS WELL.

After reading this case, one may ask, "How could a mother do that to her child?" Do we as a society perceive such offenses committed by a mother *differently* than similar offenses committed by a father? If so, we need to explore how gender influences our attitudes about criminal behavior as well as criminal offenders. At the end of this chapter, we will address this question.

to women. With the passage of the Nineteenth Amendment, many of the suffragists believed that women had indeed become men's equals.[7]

The **second wave of feminism** developed in the 1960s when other marginalized groups were also challenging the status quo (e.g., civil rights movement, prisoners' rights movement).[8] Feminists of this wave argued that to be fully liberated, women needed to have equal access to economic opportunities and sexual freedoms as well as civil liberties. Some women advocated a reformist, liberal agenda, whereas others pushed for a more revolutionary, radical program of change and action.[9] The liberal political perspective was influenced by the Civil Rights Act of 1964, which banned racial discrimination as well as sex discrimination. The radical political perspective was influenced by both the civil rights and student movements of the 1960s.[10]

This 1970 postage stamp commemorated the 50th anniversary of women securing the right to vote.

Many liberal feminists were joining emerging women's *rights* groups such as the National Organization for Women (NOW), the National Women's Political Caucus, and the Women's Equity Action League. Most radical feminists were involved with women's *liberation* groups, which were much smaller and more personally focused. Among these groups were the Women's International Terrorist Conspiracy from Hell (WITCH), the Redstockings, the Feminists, and the New York Radical Feminists.[11] It was in this social context, within these emerging political perspectives, that feminist criminology began to question assumptions and stereotypes concerning women in criminal justice. This included women as professionals as well as women as offenders and victims.

The **third wave of feminism** evolved around the late 1980s into the 1990s. This wave of feminism is an extension as well as a response to the shortcomings of the second wave.[12] Some have maintained that this third wave coincides with the birth of Generation X; in fact, the literature associated with the third wave often describes younger women's experiences of frustration with the second wave of feminism.[13] The one major theme of third wave feminism is willingness to accommodate difference, diversity, and change:

> They seem to be feminist sponges, willing and able to absorb some aspects of all the modes of feminist thought that preceded the third wave's emergence on the scene. Third-wave feminists are particularly eager to understand how gender oppression and other kinds of human oppression co-create and co-maintain each other . . . [D]ifference is the way things are. Moreover, contradiction, including self-contradiction, is expected and even willingly welcomed.[14]

More than any other group of feminists, the third-wave feminist perspective has provided a voice for many women who otherwise did not identify with previous feminist perspectives, especially women of color.

KEY TERMS OF FEMINIST PERSPECTIVES

Before discussing the various feminist perspectives, it is essential for readers to appreciate key terms associated with these perspectives. A few of these key terms are *sex, gender, chivalry, paternalism,* and *patriarchy.*

AUDIO

Feminism

REFERENCE ARTICLE

Feminism

first wave of feminism: started in the mid-1800s when women demanded the right to vote

second wave of feminism: developed in the 1960s when other marginalized groups were also challenging the status quo (e.g., civil rights movement, prisoners' rights movement). Feminists of this wave argued that to be fully liberated, women needed to have equal access to economic opportunities and sexual freedoms as well as civil liberties

VIDEO ▶

Women's Rights

VIDEO ▶

Feminism

third wave of feminism: evolved around the late 1980s and into the 1990s; an extension of as well as a response to the shortcomings of the second wave

sex: sex differences typically refer to biological variations such as reproductive organs and hormones

gender: gender usually refers to social definitions of what it means to be a *woman* or a *man*

chivalry: pertains to behaviors and attitudes toward certain individuals that treat them as though they are on a pedestal

paternalism: denotes that women need to be protected for their own good. In a broader social context, paternalism implies independence for men and dependence for women

patriarchy: a social, legal, and political climate based on male dominance and hierarchy. A key aspect to this ideology is that women's nature is biologically, not culturally, determined

Differences between women and men have usually been identified as either sex or gender differences. **Sex** differences typically refer to biological characteristics, such as reproductive organs and hormones. **Gender** differences usually refer to social definitions of what it means to be a "woman" or a "man." These social definitions may include characteristics such as appearance and occupation. It is confusing when the terms *sex* and *gender* are used interchangeably; sometimes individuals will use these terms imprecisely and assume that everyone understands the difference between sex and gender.[15]

West and Zimmerman illustrate the complexity of the concepts of sex and gender by distinguishing between *sex, sex category,* and *gender.*[16] As mentioned above, *sex* is determined through the use of socially agreed on biological criteria. An individual is located in a *sex category* by applying socially determined criteria of sex. By applying these criteria, society has defined sex as a binary category through sex categorization. *Gender* is not a set of characteristics or a variable or a role. Rather, gender is a product of social "doings." *Gender* is activity considered appropriate for a person's sex category. These activities are determined through social constructions of sex and sex category. "Doing gender" is a continuous activity embedded in everyday interactions. By understanding the independence of these constructs, people can question whether differences between women and men are due to sex or to social constructions of gender.

Chivalry pertains to behaviors and attitudes toward certain individuals that treat them as though they are on a pedestal.[17] Chivalrous behavior is more complex than just preferential treatment. Engaging in a chivalrous relationship usually entails a bartering system in which men hold a more powerful status than do women. Social class and race/ethnicity are also intertwined with such treatment. Women of certain social classes and racial/ethnic backgrounds are considered more worthy of chivalrous treatment than other women. This is best illustrated by Sojourner Truth's speech "Ain't I a Woman?" The idea of **paternalism** denotes that women need to be protected for their own good. In a broader social context, paternalism implies independence for men and dependence for women. Both chivalry and paternalism suggest that certain individuals or groups need protection because they are weak and helpless. This protection can also lead to various types of control.

The Latin word *pater* refers to the social role of a father as opposed to the biological role of a father. Patriarchal societies exclude women from the exercise of political responsibilities; **patriarchy** refers to the subordinate role of women and male dominance.[18] Thus, patriarchy is a social, legal, and political climate based on male dominance and hierarchy. A key aspect to this ideology is that women's nature is biologically, not culturally, determined.[19]

FEMINIST PERSPECTIVES ON GENDER

As noted previously, it is essential to provide readers with a general understanding that there is no *one* feminist perspective. Rather, there are various feminist perspectives. This section gives readers a summary of these different perspectives of gender. These summaries "are crude and oversimplified, but they offer a starting point for different ways of conceptualizing gender in social and political theory."[20]

TRADITIONAL OR CONSERVATIVE PERSPECTIVE

Kathleen Daly and Meda Chesney-Lind highlighted key features of the **traditional or conservative perspective**. First, they maintained that from this perspective, the causes of gender inequality are due to biological sex differences, including hormonal differences (e.g., greater testosterone production in males) or reproductive capacities (e.g., female child bearing and lactation). Second, they identified the process of how gender is formed. The conservative perspective stresses that social behavior is based on these biological sex differences. These biological sex differences can be amplified to explain social behavior, such as greater strength and innate aggression among males as well as innate nurturing and caregiving among females. Unlike the other feminist perspectives, the conservative perspective does not offer any strategies for social change, since men's and women's behaviors reflect evolutionary adaptations of sex differences.[21]

LIBERAL FEMINISM

Liberal feminism, also termed *mainstream feminism,* is founded on political liberalism, which holds a positive view of human nature as well as the ideals of liberty, equality, justice, dignity, and individual rights. A major feature of liberal feminism is that women should receive the same rights and treatment as men.[22] This perspective purports that gender inequality is due to women's blocked opportunities to participate in various aspects of the public sphere, such as education, employment, and political activity.[23] (See Table 11.1 for an example of a liberal feminist agenda.) Strategies for social change are devised to free women from oppressive gender roles—for instance, performing only those jobs associated with the traditional feminine personality (e.g., nursing, teaching, and child care).[24]

There are generally two types of liberal feminists: classical and welfare. Both approaches rely a great deal on legal remedies to address gender inequality. Classical liberal feminists support limited government and a free market as well as political and legal rights. Central facets of this approach are freedom of expression, religion, and conscience. Welfare liberal feminists favor government involvement in providing citizens, particularly underprivileged individuals, with housing, education, health care, and social security. They also maintain that the market should be limited through significant taxes and restricting profits.[25]

A major criticism of the liberal feminist perspective is that it primarily focuses "on the interests of white, middle-class, heterosexual women."[26] Specifically, within the area of feminist criminology, some argue that the liberal perspective poses "men as the criminal yardstick." This results in equating justice with equality and not considering other influential standpoints such as race/ethnicity and social class.[27] Joanne Belknap maintains that

> prison reform for women would not be nearly as effective in achieving equality with men's prisons if the only goal was to allow the same access to health care, vocational, educational, legal, and treatment programs. While these would be significant advances, it is also necessary to request reforms that address women prisoners' experiences, needs, and histories that differ from male prisoners.[28]

Another area where the "equal treatment" doctrine is problematic is in sentencing. Specifically, sentencing reforms aimed at reducing race- and class-based disparities in sentencing for male offenders "may yield equality with a vengeance" for female offenders.[29] Thus, "equality defined as equal treatment of men and women . . . forestalls more fundamental change and in some instances may worsen women's circumstances."[30]

RADICAL FEMINISM

Radical feminism evolved from the women's liberation movement of the 1960s. This perspective emphasizes the importance of personal feelings, experiences, and relationships. Gender is a system of male dominance, and women's biology is the main cause of patriarchy.[31]

JOURNAL ARTICLE

Liberal Feminism

traditional or conservative perspective: causes of gender inequality are due to biological sex differences, and social behavior is based on the biological sex differences; does not offer any strategies for social change since men's and women's behaviors reflect evolutionary adaptations of sex differences

liberal feminism: one of the areas of feminist theories of crime that emphasize the assumption that differences between males and females in offending were due to the lack of female opportunities in education, employment, etc., compared with males

	BILL OF RIGHTS FOR WOMEN
I.	That the U.S. Congress immediately pass the Equal Rights Amendment to the Constitution to provide that "Equality of rights under the law shall not be denied or abridged by the United States or by any State on account of sex," and that such then be immediately ratified by the several States.
II.	That equal employment opportunity be guaranteed to all women, as well as men, by insisting that the Equal Employment Opportunity Commission enforces the prohibitions against racial discrimination.
III.	That women be protected by law to ensure their rights to return to their jobs within a reasonable time after childbirth without the loss of seniority or other accrued benefits, and be paid maternity leave as a form of social security and/or employee benefit.
IV.	Immediate revision of tax laws to permit the deduction of home and child-care expenses for working parents.
V.	That child-care facilities be established by law on the same basis as parks, libraries, and public schools, adequate to the needs of children from the pre-school years through adolescence, as a community resource to be used by all citizens from all income levels.
VI.	That the right of women to be educated to their full potential equally with men be secured by Federal and State legislation, eliminating all discrimination and segregation by sex, written and unwritten, at all levels of education, including colleges, graduate and professional schools, loans and fellowships, and Federal and State training programs such as the Job Corps.
VII.	The right of women in poverty to secure job training, housing, and family allowances on equal terms with men, but without prejudice to a parent's right to remain at home to care for his or her children; revision of welfare legislation and poverty programs which deny women dignity, privacy, and self-respect.
VIII.	The right of women to control their own reproductive lives by removing from the penal code laws limiting access to contraceptive information and devices, and by repealing penal laws governing abortion.

Table 11.1 NOW's 1967 Bill of Rights for Women

Source: NOW Bill of Rights (Adopted at NOW's first national conference, Washington, D.C., 1967). In R. Morgan (Ed.), *Sisterhood is powerful.* New York: Random House, pp. 513–514. Reprinted with permission of the National Organization for Women.

The cause of gender inequality, according to this perspective, is based on men's need or desire to control women's sexuality and reproductive potential. Further, the process of gender formation is founded on the power relations between men and women, in which boys and men view themselves as superior to and having a right to control girls and women. These relations are further intensified through heterosexual sexuality, as defined by men.[32]

Radical feminists maintain, in principle, that sexism is the first, most widespread form of human oppression. They do not, however, agree on the nature or function of this sexism or on what strategies are needed for social change. Rosemarie Tong identified two types of radical feminism: libertarian and cultural.[33] Radical-libertarian feminists assert that an exclusively feminine gender identity will most often limit a woman's development as a full human person. They encourage women to become androgynous individuals who embody both (good) masculine and (good) feminine characteristics. Radical-cultural feminists argue that women should be strictly female/feminine. They should not try to be like men. Women should emphasize such values and virtues as interdependence, community, connection, sharing, emotion, body, trust, absence of hierarchy, nature, immanence, process, joy, peace, and life. Alternatively, women should not emphasize such values as independence, autonomy, intellect, will, wariness, hierarchy, domination, culture, transcendence, product, asceticism, war, and death.

Tong noted that this distinction, while not perfect,

> helps explain not only why some radical feminists embrace the concept of androgyny and others eschew it, but also why some radical feminists view both sex and reproduction as oppressive, even dangerous for women and why others view these aspects as liberating, even empowering for women. . . . *[R]adical feminists are not afraid to take exception to each other's views* [italics added].[34]

PERSONAL PERSPECTIVE ▶

Machismo

....

radical feminism: emphasizes the importance of personal feelings, experiences, and relationships; gender is a system of male dominance, and women's biology is the main cause of patriarchy

Suggested strategies for social change among some radical feminists include overthrowing patriarchal relations, developing methods of biological reproduction to permit women's sexual autonomy, and establishing women-centered social institutions and women-only organizations. Other radical feminists celebrate gender differences, particularly women's special capacities or talents; however, these feminists do not pose gender differences in the framework of power relations.[35]

One of the criticisms of radical-libertarian and radical-cultural feminism is that they need to reconcile the split between themselves in an effort to avoid polarization, particularly in the area of sexuality. Even though radical-libertarian feminists are hesitant about consensual heterosexuality, they maintain that these relationships can be pleasurable for women. Radical-cultural feminists warn against the dangers of heterosexuality and have implied that there is no such thing as consensual heterosexuality. Thus, according to this view, "only lesbians are capable of consensual sex in a patriarchal society."[36] Citing Ann Ferguson, a socialist feminist, Tong notes that there is no one universal "function" for human sexuality.[37]

MARXIST AND SOCIALIST FEMINISM

Some scholars maintain that while it is possible to distinguish between **Marxist feminism** and **socialist feminism**, it is difficult, particularly because these two perspectives' differences are more an issue of emphasis than of substance.[38] Marxist feminism places gender in the context of production methods. The burdens of physical and social reproduction in the home are operated and reinforced in a male-dominated economic and political order.[39] The causes of gender inequality are due to hierarchical relations of control with the increase of private property and ownership among men. Class relations are primary, and gender relations are secondary.[40] An insightful example of such gender and class relations is housework. Traditionally, housework has been delegated to women; however, housework does not produce surplus value or profit. Thus, some do not consider this labor (see Table 11.2). Marxist feminism focuses essentially on work-related inequalities, as well as enhancing our understanding of the trivialization of women's work in the home (e.g., raising children, doing housework) and the tedious, poorly paid jobs predominately occupied by women.[41] In fact, a study conducted by the University of Michigan revealed that having a husband creates an extra 7 hours of housework each week for women. Overall, however, the amount of housework performed by U.S. women has dropped considerably since 1976 (see Figure 11.1).[42]

Socialist feminism attempts to synthesize radical and Marxist feminism. This perspective attempts to integrate concepts such as male domination and political–economic relations. Social feminists focus on gender, class, and racial relations of domination. They differ from Marxist feminists in that both class and gender relations are deemed primary.[43] Within the socialist feminism perspective, there are two general themes: (1) two-system explanations of women's oppression and (2) interactive-system explanations of women's oppression. Under the two-system explanations, these emphases are less committed to the Marxist-founded framework. Rather, they maintain that patriarchy, not capitalism, may be women's ultimate worst enemy.[44] The interactive-system explanations attempt to illustrate that both capitalism and patriarchy are equal contributors to women's oppression; they are interdependent. These feminists use terms such as *capitalist patriarchy* or *patriarchal capitalism*.[45]

POSTMODERN FEMINISM

Postmodern feminism is a more contemporary intellectual movement that has been modified and adapted by feminist theory. This perspective rejects the traditional assumptions about truth and reality; the emphasis is more on the plurality, diversity, and multiplicity of women as distinct from men.[46] Tong argues that the relationship between

▶ VIDEO

Marxist Feminism

Marxist feminism: a perspective of crime that emphasizes men's ownership and control of the means of economic production; similar to critical or radical feminism but distinguished by its reliance on the concept of economic structure

socialist feminism: feminist theories that moved away from economic structure (e.g., Marxism) and placed a focus on control of reproductive systems; believes that women should take control of their own bodies and reproductive functions via contraceptives

postmodern feminism: a perspective that says women as a group cannot be understood, even by other women, because every person's experience is unique; therefore, there is no need to measure or research such experiences

	MINS/ DAY	HRS/ YEAR	HOUSE- HOLD WORK	$ PER HOUR	$ PER PERSON/ YR	TOTAL 97 $ (MILLIONS)	GDP VALUE
Cooking/Washing Up	57	347	29%	$ 9.20	$ 3,190	**$ 2,444**	15%
Cleaning/Laundry	40	243	20%	$ 9.20	$ 2,239	**$ 1,715**	10%
Shopping	38	231	19%	$ 9.20	$2,127	**$ 1,629**	10%
Maintenance/Repair	14	85	7%	$ 9.20	$ 784	**$ 600**	4%
Other Housework	29	176	15%	$ 9.20	$ 1,623	**$ 1,243**	8%
Primary Child Care	25	152	10%	$7.58	$ 1,153	**$ 883**	5%
Total Household	202	1229	100%	$9.02	$ 11,084	**$ 8,490**	51%
Voluntary Work	29	176		$13.02	$ 2,292	**$ 1,755**	9%
Total Unpaid Work	231	1405			$ 13,376	**$ 10,245**	60%

Table 11.2 Economic Value of Labor Inputs Into Unpaid Work by Activity, Nova Scotia, 1997

Source: Colman, R. (1998). *The economic value of unpaid housework and child-care in Nova Scotia,* p. 103. Retrieved from http://www .gpiatlantic.org/publications/summaries/houseworksumm.pdf.

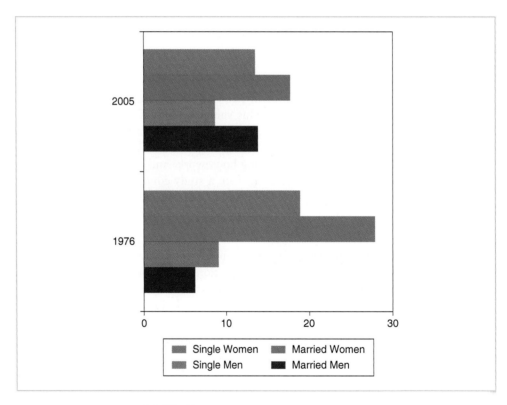

Figure 11.1 Weekly Hours of Basic Housework by Gender and Marital Status

Source: Kotz, D. (2008, April 7). Wives do more housework, study shows. *U.S. News & World Report.* http:// health.usnews.com/health-news/blogs/on-women/2008/04/07/wives-do-more-housework-study-shows

postmodernists and feminists is "uneasy."[47] For instance, similar to all postmodernists, postmodern feminists reject ideas centered on an absolute world that is "male" in style (e.g., phallogocentric). They also reject any attempts to provide a single explanation or steps women must take to achieve liberation (i.e., a feminist "to-do list"). Those who identify themselves as postmodern feminists "invite each woman who reflects on their writings to become the kind of feminist she wants to be. There is, in their estimation, no single formula for being a 'good feminist.'"[48]

However, this emphasis on diversity, and "no single formula for being a 'good feminist,'" poses dilemmas for feminists:

> The emphasis on diversity in postmodernism, however, ignores the need for political entities . . . that can pursue collective political action on women's issues. If one calls for unity among women, one assumes that women are an entity that has "essentially" the same interests. . . . Thus, the marriage between postmodernism and feminism poses a threat to the political agenda of feminists.[49]

One suggested approach to addressing this dilemma is to adopt a stance of "positionality" or "both/and." An individual does not need to choose between the postmodern focus on multiplicity and feminist politics. Rather, when a person is engaged in politics, he or she can act as though women (or African Americans or poor people) are a group united around a similar cause or purpose. In other situations, however, that person realizes and appreciates women's (or other groups') diversity.[50]

ADDITIONAL FEMINIST PERSPECTIVES

Additional feminist perspectives include ecofeminism as well as global and postcolonial feminism. Ecofeminism was developed around the 1980s to examine relations between environmental issues and women's issues. It sprang from the growing global environmental crisis. Ecofeminists perceive domination—of women, minority groups, animals, and the Earth—as the essential problem, rather than patriarchy.[51] This perspective, however, contains many varieties, such as nature ecofeminism, radical-cultural ecofeminism, and spiritual ecofeminism.[52]

Global and postcolonial feminism emerged in the mid-1970s. This is an international women's movement founded in the commonalities of women's lives, such as low economic status. This perspective critically explores the impact of development, patriarchal religions, international trafficking in women, and the Westernization of the Third World.[53] While feminists from First World nations (i.e., those nations that are heavily industrialized, located primarily in the Northern Hemisphere) are essentially interested in issues revolving around sexuality and reproduction, a number of Third World feminists (i.e., those in economically developing nations, located primarily in the Southern Hemisphere) are concerned not only with gender issues but with political and economic issues as well.[54]

In the next section, we provide a brief overview of the traditional theories of female criminality. This context will provide readers with a better understanding of the development of feminist criminology.

TRADITIONAL THEORIES OF FEMALE CRIME

From antiquity to the present, cultures have categorized women into "either/or" roles.[55] One such pervasive conceptualization is the Madonna/whore duality. This cultural ideology has been reflected and perpetuated by the criminal justice system. It is grounded in

COMPARATIVE CRIMINOLOGY: *TRAFFICKING IN PERSONS*

Ranking Regions/Countries as Most Likely for Trafficking in Persons

In this section, we examine the findings and conclusions of studies regarding trafficking in persons, largely collected by the U.N. Office on Drugs and Crime (UNODC). The findings of these recent studies regarding the prevalence of trafficking in persons in certain countries, including the main origin countries as well as the main transit and main destination countries, are enlightening in several ways. The majority of trafficking in persons cases are for the purpose of sexual exploitation (77%), followed by those for the purpose of labor exploitation (23%). More than 50% of the victims are women, and more than 40% are minors (mostly girls).

Van Dijk synthesized some of the data from the UNODC published in 2006,[56] as well as a study by Kriistina Kangaspunta regarding the prevalence of trafficking in persons in the year 2002.[57] As shown in Table 11.3, the top five countries with the highest frequencies of trafficking in persons for country of origin (starting with the highest) were Russia, Ukraine, Thailand, Nigeria, and the Republic of Moldova (notably, the United States did not make the top 10 countries of origin). The top five main transit countries (those through which trafficked

persons were sent) were (starting with the highest) Albania, Bulgaria, Hungary, Poland, and Italy. Finally, the top five destination countries were (starting with the highest) Belgium, Germany, Greece, Italy, and the Netherlands. Notably, the United States ranked 10th in destination countries.

As with data collected through official sources, this information may be more a reflection of the investigative activities of the police, or lack thereof, than of the extent of such crimes. This may be due to various reasons. First, not all countries are committed, or able, to conduct investigations or prosecutions of such cases. Second, trafficking in persons is not criminalized in some countries, so prosecutions of these crimes may be designated as something other than trafficking. Van Dijk maintains that if governments are not forthcoming about such crimes, the international media can be a helpful resource. Further, since trafficking in persons is a transnational crime, "reports on cases of human trafficking coming from destination countries often provide information about where the victims were recruited and through which countries they were transported."[58] Thus, while some countries, such as countries of origin or transit, may not acknowledge such criminal activities, information obtained from destination countries can be useful.

	MAIN COUNTRIES OF ORIGIN	MAIN TRANSIT COUNTRIES	MAIN DESTINATION COUNTRIES
1	Russian Federation	Albania	Belgium
2	Ukraine	Bulgaria	Germany
3	Thailand	Hungary	Greece
4	Nigeria	Poland	Italy
5	Republic of Moldova	Italy	The Netherlands
6	Romania	Thailand	Israel
7	Albania	—	Turkey
8	China	—	Japan
9	Belarus	—	Thailand
10	Bulgaria	—	United States
11	Lithuania	—	—

Table 11.3 Most Frequently Cited Countries of Origin, Transit, and Destination of Trafficking in Persons (2002)

Sources: Kangaspunta, K. (2003). Mapping the inhuman trade: Preliminary findings of the database on trafficking in human beings. *Forum on Crime and Society, 3*, 81–105; United Nations Office on Drugs and Crime (UNODC). (2006). *Trafficking in persons: Global patterns*. Vienna.

two contrasting perceptions of the female "nature" or sexuality. The Madonna image personifies women as faithful and submissive wives, as well as nurturing mothers. The whore image portrays women as temptresses who prey on a man's sexuality and self-control. Inherent in this dichotomization are class and racial/ethnic assumptions. The Madonna image was primarily restricted to women from white, middle- to upper-class backgrounds.[59]

Young further argued that black women have not experienced this "good/bad" dichotomy.[60] Rather, stereotypes of black women have essentially been "bad." Young attempted to identify the gender role characterizations that have been attributed to black females. For instance, the characterization of the black female as a matriarch has revealed two negative images—the *Amazon* (domineering, strong, assertive, independent, and masculine) and the *sinister Sapphire* (dangerous, castrating, and treacherous toward black men). Another instance of contradictory images is founded on myths concerning a black woman's sexuality—*mammy* (long-suffering, patient, nurturing, and asexual) and *seductress* (loose, immoral, and sexually depraved).[61] Young argues that black women in American society have been victimized by their double status as blacks and as women. Specifically, discussions of blacks have focused on the black man and discussions of females have focused on the white woman. Rather than being considered as a primary focus, black women have been on the periphery of understanding in terms of their position relative either to black males or to white females. Thus, "these images have influenced the way in which black female victims and offenders have been treated by the criminal justice system."[62]

Another pervasive cultural perception is "femininity." The concept of femininity is made up of various traits such as gentleness, sensitivity, nurturance, and passivity. Comparatively, traits associated with masculinity include intelligence, aggressiveness, independence, and competitiveness.[63] These conceptualizations become problematic when such traits are assumed to be inherent to an individual's sex or are considered as "biological fact."[64] Gender roles guided by concepts of femininity and masculinity are considered to be sex-linked behaviors as well as traits.[65] Related to the conceptualization of femininity was the cult of true womanhood. The attributes of true womanhood comprised four virtues: piety, purity, submissiveness, and domesticity.[66]

This photo of a Victorian woman illustrates what is referred to as the cult of true womanhood.

Theories of female criminality emerged within this cultural context and the prevailing assumptions regarding women (e.g., the Madonna/whore duality, femininity, and the cult of true womanhood). When contextualized, the development of such theoretical constructs illustrates that "those women who do commit offenses are judged to be either criminal by nature or pathological because they deviate from the 'true' biologically determined nature of women which is to be law abiding."[67] Nicole Rafter Hahn argued that a woman was usually deemed "bad" if she had one of the following characteristics: (1) She was indecisive and lacked "moral fortitude," (2) she was promiscuous, or (3) she was irresponsible, because she was loosening not only her morals and values but also those of her mate and descendants.[68]

The following sections briefly review some of the early theories of female crime that reflect and incorporate these negative perceptions. Specifically, we will discuss such theorists as Cesare Lombroso, W. I. Thomas, Sigmund Freud, and Otto Pollak.

CESARE LOMBROSO

One of the earliest theorists focusing on the female offender was **Cesare Lombroso**.[69] In his book *The Female Offender*, Lombroso emphasized the physiological and psychological determinants of female criminality rather than socializing factors or social–structural constraints.[70] For instance, Lombroso summarized some of the anomalies associated with prostitutes and other female offenders. He noted that prostitutes essentially do not have any wrinkles but are more likely to have moles, hairiness, large jaws and cheekbones, and anomalous teeth (see Table 11.4). According to Lombroso, women who committed homicides often had cranial depressions as well as prominent cheekbones.

	14 TO 24 YEARS		25 TO 49 YEARS.		50 YEARS & OVER.	
	Normal 54. Percent	Criminal 20. Percent	Normal 72. Percent	Criminal 41. Percent	Normal 32. Percent	Criminal 9. Percent
Deep frontal, horizontal wrinkles	9.2	25	41.7	53.6	90.6	88.8
Deep fronto-vertical wrinkles	1.8	—	6.9	7.3	40.6	71
Crow's-feet	5	12.5	20	33	78	88.8
Wrinkles under the eye-lids	1.8	—	15	14.6	46.6	44.4
Naso-labial wrinkles	25.9	25	69.5	63.3	96.7	100
Zygomatic wrinkles	—	—	5.5	12.2	28.1	22.2
Goniomental wrinkles	—	25	36.1	31.7	53.1	44
Labial wrinkles	—	—	6.9	12.2	28.1	44

Table 11.4 An Example of Lombroso's Summary Data Collected on Female Offenders–Wrinkles

Source: Lombroso, C. (1898). *The female offender.* New York: D Appleton, p. 72.

Cesare Lombroso:

one of the earliest theorists focusing on the female offender; his book emphasized the physiological and psychological determinants of female criminality rather than socializing factors or social–structural constraints

Lombroso implemented a typology for female offenders similar to the one he did for male offenders. He begins the chapter "The Born Criminal" by citing sexist comments such as the following Italian proverb: "Rarely is a woman wicked, but when she is she surpasses the man."[71] Other traits of this born criminal include a lack of the maternal instinct (which was regarded as a biological trait), as well as an excessive desire for revenge, cruelty, greed and avarice, love of dress and ornaments, a lack of religious feeling, and untruthfulness. When summarizing traits of the occasional criminal, Lombroso notes that occasional offenders can be divided into two classes—one that includes the milder types of born criminals and another that differs only slightly from the normal, or "consisting of normal women in whom circumstances have developed the fund of immorality which is latent in every female."[72] Although this theory has been refuted, this "biological determinism" perspective is entrenched in some theories of female criminality. For instance, while more sophisticated and technical, this biological determinism is evident with premenstrual syndrome explanations of female crime.[73]

W. I. THOMAS

W. I. Thomas argued that there are basic biological differences between males and females. For instance, maleness is "katabolic," which denotes the animal force that uses the destructive release of energy, resulting in the potential for creative work. Femaleness is "anabolic," which denotes motionless, lethargic, and conservative energy.[74] Thus, females were seen as passive and motionless, while males were seen as active and dynamic.[75] In his subsequent work, Thomas focused on female delinquency. This work was noted for a transition from physiological explanations to more sophisticated theoretical explanations that incorporate physiological as well as psychological and social–structural explanations.[76]

Thomas maintained that humans essentially have four desires: (1) the desire for new experience, (2) the desire for security, (3) the desire for response, and (4) the desire for recognition.[77] The desire for new experience and the desire for response were the two wishes that influenced criminal behavior. Therefore, Thomas argued that a woman who went into prostitution did so to satisfy a desire for excitement and response; for a woman, prostitution was the most likely option to satisfy those needs.[78] Environmental factors were also incorporated in Thomas's work. For instance, he maintained that "when crime and prostitution appear as professions they are the last and most radical expressions of loss of family and community organization."[79]

SIGMUND FREUD

Many early theories of female deviance embraced the psychoanalytic writings of **Sigmund Freud**. Many of these theories evolved from two key concepts: (1) the structure of the personality and (2) the psychosexual stages of development of the child.[80] Freud perceived women as anatomically inferior—biologically destined to be wives and mothers. The basis for this inferiority is that women's sex organs are inferior to men's sex organs. This is further argued by noting that the girl assumes that she has lost her penis as a punishment; as a result of this assumption, she is traumatized and matures with a sense of envy and vengeance. The boy also realizes that the girl has lost her penis; he fears a similar punishment and is wary of the girl's envy and vengeance. Thus, "women are exhibitionistic, narcissistic, and attempt to compensate for their lack of a penis by being well dressed and physically beautiful."[81] The Freudian orientation is not just restricted to this form of penis envy for understanding female deviant behavior. Freud also maintained that women are inferior because they are more concerned with personal matters and have very little interest in social issues.[82]

Within this perspective, a deviant woman attempts to be a man. Such a woman is forcefully rebellious. This drive to accomplishment is due to her longing for a penis. Since this drive will never be fulfilled, the result is that the woman will become "neurotic." According to the Freudian orientation, the best way to treat such a woman is to help her adjust to her sex role. Thus, this reflects "the notion of individual accommodation that repudiates the possibility of social change."[83]

OTTO POLLAK

In his 1950 book *The Criminality of Women*, **Otto Pollak's** concluding statement was that "the criminality of women reflects their biological nature in a given cultural setting."[84] Pollak argued that women are more criminal in nature than many have generally

REFERENCE ARTICLE
The Female Offender

CRIME IN THE NEWS
Prostitution

WHAT WERE THEY THINKING?!
Prostitution

W. I. Thomas: argued that there are basic biological differences between males and females

Sigmund Freud: originated psychoanalysis, founded on the perception of resistance used by individuals when therapists attempt to make them conscious of their unconscious; perceived women as anatomically inferior

Otto Pollak: argued that women are more criminal in nature than has been generally perceived; suggested that criminologists should address the unknown criminality of women perceived. He suggested that criminologists should address the following three questions: (1) Are those crimes in which women seem to participate exclusively, or to a considerable extent, offenses that are known to be greatly underreported? (2) Are women offenders generally less often detected than are men offenders? (3) Do women, if apprehended, meet with more leniency than do men?[85] This unknown criminality is essentially due to women's deceitful nature and the "masked" quality of female criminality. He maintained that "the criminality of women is largely masked criminality."[86]

Pollak supported his theory of "hidden" criminality by noting such factors as the relative weakness of a woman, which make deceit necessary as a defense; that all oppressed classes use subversion as a common tactic; that a woman's socialization teaches her to conceal many things, such as menstruation, aggression, and marital frustration; and that the biology of the female enables her to deceive (i.e., she can fake an orgasm, while a man cannot).[87]

> Man must achieve an erection in order to perform the sex act and will not be able to hide his failure. His lack of positive emotion in the sexual sphere must become overt to the partner, and pretense of sexual response is impossible for him, if it is lacking. Woman's body, however, permits such pretense to a certain degree and lack of orgasm does not prevent her ability to participate in the sex act.[88]

It is interesting to stress that while Pollak did consider biological factors, he incorporated sociological factors as well. Like the other theorists we have discussed above, these sociological factors were based on assumptions and prejudices.[89]

In her classic essay on female crime, Dorie Klein revealed that theorists such as Lombroso, Thomas, Freud, and Pollak focused primarily on women's biology (i.e., their sexuality) or some type of psychological problem. Klein argued that these theorists focused on women's sexuality or other stereotypical traits, such as women being manipulative, to explain criminal behavior. They did not, however, examine economic, political, or social factors that provide a more comprehensive understanding of female criminality.[90]

FEMINIST CRITIQUES OF PREVIOUS RESEARCH STUDYING WOMEN AND CRIME

Feminist scholars have argued that science reflects the social values and concerns of dominant societal groups.[91] Subsequently, research in the social sciences has often ignored women and issues of concern to women, or has created differences between women and men, girls and boys that are not "natural, essential, or biological."[92] Studies of women and crime have also been either marginalized or "invisible."[93] In 1977, Carole Smart noted that women have not been *entirely* ignored in the study of crime and deviance. The quality of work, however, is questionable at best. She stressed the importance of contextualizing female criminality within a broader framework: moral, political, economic, and sexual spheres.[94]

From a critical, feminist perspective, Ngaire Naffine conducted an extensive review of the literature pertaining to female criminality. Her review examined such theoretical perspectives as strain theory, differential association, masculinity theory, the Control School, labeling theory, and the women's liberation thesis (discussed below).[95] With the exception of the women's liberation thesis, female criminality was rarely a major focus of these various theoretical perspectives. In fact, these theories were primarily based on adult and juvenile male offenders. If female criminality was mentioned, in most instances these explanations were founded on sexist assumptions and biases.

It is essential to understand that the inclusion of women does not necessarily imply that the study is using a feminist framework. To illustrate this point, feminists note that research using either an "add-and-stir" approach or a sex roles approach do not incorporate key feminist concepts:

1. **Add women and stir.** One approach to eliminating the "male centeredness" (i.e., androcentrism) of traditional analyses is the "add-and-stir" approach. That is, one uses an existing theoretical perspective based on males and "adds" women. Feminists argue, however, that if one merely "adds women and stirs" in a perspective or schema established by an androcentric analysis, the experiences of women will be marginalized or ignored. Women's experiences would then be located "as compared to men's" perspective. Many scholars contend that a great deal of criminological research incorporates this approach. Thus, although women are not necessarily invisible, their experiences and representation are infrequent and distorted.[96]

2. **Sex roles.** Another approach to conducting research on women has been to focus on the social construction of *sex roles,* currently referred to as *gender roles.*[97] Research using this approach has been criticized primarily because there is a tendency to perceive these roles as being almost sex linked, without incorporating a larger context as to how these roles have been defined or "determined." This approach can lead to a form of biological determinism due to the limited explanation or theoretical understanding of the conceptualization of roles.[98] (The "Why Do They Do It?" case on page 300 further illustrates this idea of "the conceptualization of roles" as related to a sex offender.) Candace West and Don Zimmerman proposed that it is essential to move beyond this approach of sex role, or gender role, studies. Instead, the focus of research should be "what is involved in doing gender as an ongoing activity embedded in everyday interaction."[99]

The first of the modern gender-based perspectives on crime tried to understand female criminality rather than provide a more gender-sensitive approach to criminal behavior. The liberation thesis is one example of such a theoretical perspective. Another example of a gender-based perspective is John Hagan's power–control theory. While this is not a feminist theory, it is an integrated theory informed by feminism.[100]

LIBERATION THESIS

The **liberation thesis**, also referred to as the emancipation hypothesis, attempts to link the women's liberation movement with female crime rates. While there were various explanations for the changing female crime rates, two predominant explanations were (a) the increased opportunities for women to participate in the labor force and, thus, increased opportunities to commit certain types of crime, and (b) the changing self-concept and identity of women and girls due to the consciousness-raising aspects of the movement.[101] Two often-cited scholars of this perspective are Freda Adler and Rita Simon. It is essential to stress that these perspectives were offered during the second wave of feminism. Thus, they were influenced by what was occurring in the broader social context of that time.

VIDEO

Mary K. Letourneau

add women and stir: when one uses an existing theoretical perspective based on males and "adds" women

sex roles: research using the sex role approach has been criticized primarily because of the tendency to perceive these roles as being almost sex-linked, without incorporating a larger context for how these roles have been defined, leading to a form of biological determinism

liberation thesis: also referred to as the emancipation hypothesis; attempts to link the women's liberation movement with female crime rates

WHY DO THEY DO IT?

MARY K. LETOURNEAU

When Mary K. Letourneau was 34 years old, she was married to Steve Letourneau, a cargo specialist for Alaska Airlines, and mother to their four children. Letourneau was a well-respected elementary school teacher in Burien, Washington. On March 4, she was arrested on charges of second-degree child rape. She was pregnant by her 12-year-old student, Vili Fualaau. On August 7, 1997, Letourneau pled guilty to two counts of child rape. However, she maintained that her relationship with Fualaau was loving and consensual rather than predatory. In November, she was sentenced to 7 years and 5 months in prison. Judge Linda Lau initially suspended the sentence under the condition that she not have any contact with

Fualaau. In February, the judge found out that Letourneau did have further contact with the student, and she was subsequently sent to prison. Letourneau was pregnant with their second child.

Letourneau was released from prison on August 4, 2004. Hours after her release, Fualaau, now 21 years of age, filed a motion to vacate the sentencing order that barred any further contact between him and Letourneau.

This story captured the attention of many across the world. More than 100 reporters and photographers from national and international news organizations covered the sentencing hearing. One television producer noted that if this were a 35-year-old man who impregnated a 13-year-old girl, he would be in prison and there would most likely be little coverage of the story. However, this case involved a 35-year-old woman and a 13-year-old boy. Some would argue that she did not fit the stereotype of a sex offender. Do you think she is a sex offender? Do some people view male sex offenders differently than they view female sex offenders?

In her 1975 book *Sisters in Crime,* Adler argued that as women continue to strive for equality with men, they will also have more opportunities to commit crimes that were previously unavailable to them due to occupational discrimination:

> Women are closing many of the gaps, social and criminal, that have separated them from men. The closer they get, the more alike they look and act. . . . The simplest and most accurate way to grasp the essence of women's changing patterns is to discard dated notions of femininity. That is a role that fewer and fewer women are willing to play. In the final analysis, women criminals are human beings who have basic needs and abilities and opportunities. Over the years these needs have not changed, nor will they. But women's abilities and opportunities have multiplied, resulting in a kaleidoscope of changing patterns whose final configuration will be fateful for all of us.[102]

CRIME IN THE NEWS

Mary K. Letourneau

As the position of women becomes similar to that of men, this will result in women obtaining not only legitimate opportunities in the labor force but illegitimate opportunities as well.[103]

In her 1975 book *Women and Crime,* Simon proposed a similar argument.[104] She did differ from Adler, however, with respect to the types of crime that would be influenced by the women's movement. Adler maintained that due to women's liberation, the violent crime rate among women would increase. Simon suggested that only the property crime rates among women would increase and that the violent crime rates among women would, in fact, decrease because women's frustrations would lessen as they were provided more opportunities in employment and education.[105]

Naffine outlined the assumptions of the women's liberation theory: (1) The liberation movement can be linked to an increase in female crime, (2) the increase in female crime is a function of women becoming more masculine, and (3) these increases in female crime are due to women becoming actively competitive with men.[106] There are various problems with these assumptions, including the assumption about the relation between enhanced structural opportunities and the increase in women's offending rates. Statistics have revealed that women have not achieved equality in those high-paying and managerial professions.[107] There have been additional criticisms of the liberation thesis, including the manipulation of statistics and attempts to support the assumption that gender equality "produces" increases in crime rates among women.[108]

POWER-CONTROL THEORY

John Hagan and his colleagues developed the **power–control theory**, incorporating a conflict-oriented theory with social control theory.[109] The power–control theory attempted to explain gender differences in delinquency rates by including family dynamics. Specifically, Hagan argued that youths from families characterized as patriarchal (i.e., mother has lower status than father) revealed greater gender differences in delinquency rates compared with youths from more egalitarian homes (i.e., parents have same status or mother is the only parent in the home) (see Figure 11.2).

The argument was that female youths from more egalitarian families were encouraged to engage in risk-taking behaviors—just as their brothers were. Risk-taking behavior is considered to be related to delinquent behavior. Alternatively, female youths from patriarchal families were encouraged to avoid risk-taking behavior—unlike their brothers. Thus, these female youths were less likely to engage in delinquent behavior.

An integral aspect to the relationship between family dynamics, gender, and delinquency rates was social class. Hagan and his colleagues stressed the importance of class structure

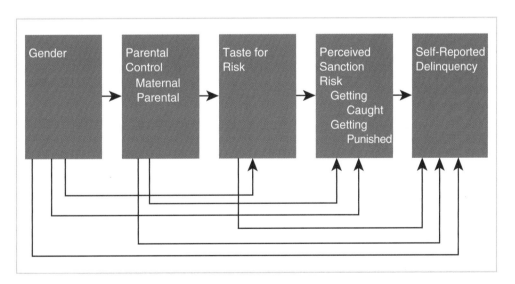

Figure 11.2 Causal Model of Gender and Delinquency

Source: Hagan, J., Gillis, A. R., & Simpson, J. (1985). The class structure of gender and delinquency: Toward a power-control theory of common delinquent behavior. *American Journal of Sociology, 90,* 1157.

power–control theory: integrated theory of crime that assumes that, in households where the mother and father have relatively similar levels of power at work, mothers will be less likely to exert control over daughters, and in households where mothers and fathers have dissimilar levels of power in the workplace, mothers will be more likely to suppress criminal activity in daughters but not in sons

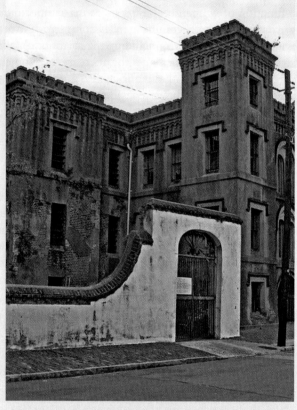

Built in 1802, the Old City Jail in Charleston, South Carolina, housed Lavinia Fisher and her husband, John.

On February 18, 1820, Lavinia Fisher and her husband, John Fisher, were hanged on the gallows in Charleston, South Carolina, for multiple robberies and murders. During the early 1800s, the Fishers operated a hotel called the Six Mile Wayfarer House, which was located 6 miles from Charleston, South Carolina. Men visiting Charleston started going missing—all after staying at the Six Mile Wayfarer House. After numerous reports of these missing men, authorities initiated an investigation. But given the couple's popularity and the lack of evidence, the authorities halted the investigation.

The local townspeople, however, were not satisfied and assembled a group of vigilantes who attempted to stop the activities occurring at the hotel. Apparently, they were satisfied with their endeavors and returned to Charleston. At around the same time, John Peeples was traveling from Georgia to Charleston. He stopped at the Six Mile Wayfarer House to see if they had an available room. Lavinia greeted Mr. Peeples and informed him they did not have a room but invited him to tea and dinner. Mr. Peeples was attracted to Lavinia's beauty and charm. She asked him numerous questions. After some time, she informed Mr. Peeples that a room was available. During this time, Lavinia kept pouring tea for him; he did not like tea, but rather than appearing rude by refusing the tea, he poured it out when she was not looking.

Soon, Mr. Peeples grew uncomfortable. He noticed that Lavinia's husband, John, was shooting him odd glances while he talked to Lavinia; also, Mr. Peeples was worried that he provided Lavinia with too much information and thought he may be a target for robbery. So he decided to rest in the chair by the door rather than in the bed. Later in the evening he was awakened by a loud noise. He realized that the bed he should have been sleeping in had disappeared into a deep hole in the floor. Mr. Peeples jumped out of the window and quickly informed the authorities. The police arrested John and Lavinia Fisher, along with two men working with them. The police thoroughly searched

the Six Mile Wayfarer House, uncovering hidden passages throughout the hotel, items that could be linked to various travelers who had been reported missing, tea laced with an herb that puts a person to sleep, a mechanism that opened the floorboards underneath the bed, and almost 100 sets of human remains in the basement.

Some have considered Lavinia Fisher to be the first known female serial killer in the United States. Why do you think Lavinia Fisher was involved with robbing and murdering numerous men visiting the Six Mile Wayfarer House? Do you think there is a biological explanation? Do you think there may be a psychological explanation? Or do you think there are other factors that one should consider in explaining her criminal activity?

Source: South Carolina legends: Lavinia Fisher—First female American serial killer. Retrieved from http://www.legendsofamerica.com/sc-laviniafisher.html. See also Orr, B. (2010). *Six miles to Charleston: The true story of John and Lavinia Fisher.* Charleston, SC: History Press.

in the gender–delinquency relationship. While in all classes males are freer to engage in delinquent behavior than females, males in more powerful classes are the freest to engage in such behavior compared with males in less powerful classes.[110] As a result, individuals—especially those from various social classes—experience power relationships in the larger society differently. Specifically, the social reproduction of gender relations refers to those activities, institutions, and relationships that are involved in maintaining and reinforcing gender roles. These activities include those individuals responsible for caring for, protecting, and socializing children for their adult roles. According to this theoretical perspective, family class structure shapes the social reproduction of gender relations, which then influences rates of delinquency.[111] These power relationships in the larger society are reflected in the family relationships. Evaluations of the power–control theory reveal inconsistent findings;[112] others have maintained that the power–control theory is just a variation of the liberation thesis (i.e., the mother's liberation causes the daughter's criminal behavior).[113]

FEMINIST PERSPECTIVES ON UNDERSTANDING CRIME AND CRIMINAL BEHAVIOR

In 1987, Sandra Harding asked the question, "What's new in feminist analyses?" She provided three characteristics or features that distinguish feminist research.[114] The first feature is that the empirical and theoretical bases emanate from women's experiences. These bases, or resources, question as well as challenge traditional understandings of what has been considered human activity, as defined by white, European, middle-class men. By examining *women's experiences,* various issues are raised that contradict traditional research. The second feature of feminist analyses was the new purpose *for* women, whereas traditional analyses have primarily been for men. Research questions and answers are not "to pacify, control, exploit, or manipulate women." Furthermore, this research is implemented to meet the needs of women and to understand as well as voice their experiences. The final characteristic of feminist research was locating the researcher in the same critical plane as the subject matter. Harding initiated this discussion by stressing that the sources of social power need to be examined. Specifically, she provided an example of how numerous studies have focused on the "peculiar mental and behavior characteristics" of women. Only recently, however, have there been studies on the "bizarre mental and behavioral characteristics of psychiatrists."[115]

Feminist scholars have raised various concerns with traditional research methods. Below, we briefly discuss two of these issues: (1) objectivity and subjectivity, and (2) qualitative "versus" quantitative analyses.

OBJECTIVITY AND SUBJECTIVITY

Objectivity refers to being "neutral," "value free," or "unbiased." Feminist scholars challenge research claims of objectivity. In fact, they maintain that such claims are tautological; "value-free" (i.e., objective) research is a value. Furthermore, feminist scholars argue that the standards to assess objectivity are founded on biases established by, and for, individuals of privilege. Science and its practice are influenced by the values and experiences of its practitioners.[116] These practitioners are primarily from privileged backgrounds (i.e., white, middle-class males);[117] thus, androcentric and sexist biases are implicit in the standards implemented for conducting scientific research.[118] In the context of feminist jurisprudence, Catharine MacKinnon noted that "objectivity—the nonsituated, universal standpoint, whether claimed or aspired to—is a denial of the existence or potency of sex inequality that tacitly participates in constructing reality from the dominant point of view."[119]

Carolyn Wood Sherif provided additional challenges concerning "objective" research.[120] Her criticisms were primarily directed toward psychological research, but the issues that

AUTHOR PODCAST

Feminist Perspective

objectivity: refers to being "neutral," "value free," or "unbiased." Feminist scholars challenge research claims of objectivity she raised can be directed to various types of social science research. She maintained that biases can occur at different points in the research process, including what to study, how to study the participants, and which behaviors or attitudes of the participants will be observed or ignored:

> The opportunity starts when a researcher decides what to study and it continues to widen during decisions about how to study the subject. . . . The researcher decides, of course, often in highly arbitrary ways dictated by custom in previous research, not by what the person does or is doing in daily life. . . . The researcher makes all of these decisions, often forgetting at times that he or she is a human being who is part of the research situation too.[121]

Feminist researchers acknowledge their biases and argue that other researchers need to do so as well. "In doing so, the false idealization of objectivity and the criticisms of subjectivity become meaningless and irrelevant."[122]

QUALITATIVE "VERSUS" QUANTITATIVE ANALYSES

On the surface, the major distinction between these two types of analyses appears to be how the data are represented: **qualitative** is nonnumerical, and **quantitative** is numerical. But feminist researchers have raised questions regarding qualitative and quantitative methods. Toby Epstein Jayaratne and Abigail J. Stewart noted that quantitative methods translate individuals' experiences into predefined categories designated by the researchers. This method distorts women's experiences and results in "silencing women's own voices."[123] Those scholars advocating qualitative methods maintain that women's understandings, emotions, and actions must be explored in those women's own terms.

Researchers advocating quantitative methods maintain that although these methods can be, and have been, used to distort women's experiences, they need not be. As this discourse continues, emphasizing *only* qualitative methods for feminist research has also been critiqued. For instance, Jacquelyn White and Richard Farmer conducted a study on sexual violence and implemented a multiple-strategic approach. They argued that it is essential to recognize that *both* the qualitative and quantitative methods have strengths and weaknesses:

> Empirical analytic methods cannot help us know the phenomenological experiences of a beautiful sunset, nor can we know the phenomenological experience of a rape survivor using traditional research paradigms. Conversely, subjective reports shed little light on the incidence and prevalence of sexual assault. There is, however, much that can be learned from both subjective methods and traditional scientific approaches when applied to the study of sexual aggression and victimization.[124]

It is essential to note that issues relevant to these types of research methods have been "politicized"—specifically, one method (i.e., quantitative) being deemed more "scientific" than the other (i.e., qualitative). However, one method is not "inherently" superior to the other; rather, these methods are only different approaches to understanding reality.

FEMINIST CRIMINOLOGY

Feminist criminology evolved, primarily from liberal feminists, with the realization and objection that gender was essentially ignored and excluded from criminological theory.[125] This exclusion was difficult to understand given that gender was such a strong predictor of criminal behavior.[126] Further, feminists recognized the limitations of critical and radical criminological perspectives given the primary focus on economic disparities without

AUTHOR VIDEO ▶

Feminist Perspective

qualitative: nonnumerical research methods; often compared with quantitative research methods

quantitative: numerical research methods; often compared with qualitative research methods examining the issues of race and gender. Thus, "early feminist criminologists demanded that analyses of crime include consideration of gender in ways that had not occurred before."[127]

Twenty years after her essay on female crime, Dorie Klein included an afterword; she maintained that feminist criminologists need to address three major challenges: (1) continue to search for the scientific basis of theories of men's and women's criminal behavior, (2) reexamine gender and racial/ethnic biases in the social sciences, and (3) develop a new definition of crime.[128] Joanne Belknap gave an overview of the potential of various traditional criminological theories to provide insight in examining gender differences and similarities in understanding criminal behavior. Some of the traditional criminological theories that do have some promise in this area of understanding include differential association theory and strain and general strain theory.[129]

Kathleen Daly and Meda Chesney-Lind identified the following five elements that distinguish feminist thought from other forms of social and political thought:

REFERENCE ARTICLE

Female Offenders

1. Gender is not a natural fact but a complex social, historical, and cultural product; it is related to, but not simply derived from, biological sex differences and reproductive capacities.

2. Gender and gender relations order social life and social institutions in fundamental ways.

3. Gender relations are constructs of masculinity and femininity and are not symmetrical but are based on an organizing principle of men's superiority and social and political–economic dominance over women.

4. Systems of knowledge reflect men's views of the natural and social world; the production of knowledge is gendered.

5. Women should be at the center of intellectual inquiry, not peripheral, invisible, or appendages to men.[130]

AUDIO

Female Inmates

When addressing whether there can be a feminist criminology, Daly and Chesney-Lind maintained that feminist theories and research should be incorporated in any criminologist's study of crime. Incorporating such perspectives entails more than just a focus on women or sexism. Rather, these approaches provide an opportunity to study unexplored aspects of men's crime and forms of justice, as well as forms of theory construction and verification. Thus, they argued that the promise of feminist thought has barely been realized.[131]

Almost 20 years after Daly and Chesney-Lind's article on feminist criminology, Amanda Burgess-Proctor argued that for contemporary third-wave feminist criminologists, it is essential to build on the foundation laid by previous feminist criminologists.[132] Specifically, she maintained that feminist criminology needs to embrace all sources of oppression without prioritizing gender. Thus, feminist criminology should incorporate an intersectional framework, informed by **multiracial feminism**, which includes such defining social characteristics as race, class, gender, sexuality, nationality, and age.[133]

One feminist framework that has been used to explore the experiences of women in the criminal justice system is **pathways research**:

> A feminist approach to understanding the etiology of females' (and sometimes males') offending is termed by some as "pathways to crime." . . . [T]his approach attempts to determine life experiences, particularly childhood ones, that place one at risk of offending. The pathways research indicates that traumas such as physical and sexual abuse and child neglect are not only defining features in the lives of many female offenders, but also these traumas are often related to one's likelihood of committing crimes.[134]

multiracial feminism: an intersectional framework that includes such defining social characteristics as race, class, gender, sexuality, nationality, and age

pathways research: typically collects data, usually through interviews, at one point in time that provide retrospective inquiry as to an individual's life and life experiences

Before and after pictures of a woman who uses methamphetamine. One may question how this woman got to this point in her life—in other words, her pathway.

Whereas life course research collects longitudinal data over the course of an individual's life, pathways research typically collects data, usually through interviews, at one point in time that provides retrospective inquiry as to an individual's life and his or her life experiences.[135] Some feminists have argued that the pathways perspective has provided researchers with a greater understanding of how a woman's offending is influenced by the social conditions of her life as well as by her being a women in a patriarchal society.[136]

Recently, a growing area of research has been using the pathways framework. Barbara Owen conducted what she termed a "quasi-ethnography" of women incarcerated in the Central California Women's Facility.[137] This methodology included in-depth interviews with these women as well as detailed observations of everyday life. When inquiring about these women's lives prior to prison, Owen identified three key issues that were central pathways to their incarceration—multiplicity of abuse in their pre-prison lives; family and personal relationships, especially those involving male partners and children; and their spiraling marginality and subsequent criminality.[138] A majority of these incarcerated women experienced various forms of physical, sexual, and emotional abuse in their lives. In addition, the abuse of drugs and alcohol was a key factor for many of these women prior to their incarceration. Many also experienced poverty as well as early parenthood. The spiraling marginality shared by many of these women included limited educational and vocational preparation, which resulted in a lack of employment opportunities. Owen concluded her book by noting that "this description of the lives of women in prison then is offered as a starting point for constructive dialogue and public policy concerning the lives and experiences of women on their own terms."[139]

Other examples of research focuses incorporating a pathways perspective include women incarcerated in an Iranian prison;[140] transferring female juveniles to adult court;[141] drug abuse among women;[142] sexual assault victimization and suicidal behavior;[143] and the development of antisocial behavior.[144]

CRITIQUES OF FEMINIST THEORIES

A number of criticisms concerning feminist theories have been raised by feminist scholars. In the 1960s, women of color challenged feminism by arguing that these perspectives essentially focused on the experiences of white middle-class women.[145] After reviewing feminist theory in sociology, Janet Saltzman Chafetz argued that the current topic among feminist scholars is the intersection of race, class, and gender.[146] A number of feminist scholars maintain that examining difference, rather than equality, is a major emphasis of current feminist studies.

While some feminist scholars maintain that this shift in focus has revitalized feminist theory,[147] others assert that it has introduced new conflicts in feminist studies.[148] Maxine Baca Zinn and Bonnie Thornton Dill stress, however, that while there may be problems when focusing on difference,

> our perspectives take their bearings from social relations. Race and class difference are crucial, we argue, not as individual characteristics . . . but insofar as they are primary organizing principles of a society which locates and positions groups within that society's opportunity structures.[149]

Some feminist scholars emphasize the importance of examining the interlocking, or intersection, of race, class, and gender.[150] The development of an intersectional perspective on gender and race is rooted in the work of scholars focusing on women of color.[151]

Amanda Burgess-Proctor identified key conceptual factors that distinguish multiracial feminism from other feminist perspectives.[152] First, multiracial feminism claims that gender relations do not exist in a vacuum; rather, men and women are also characterized by their race, class, sexuality, age, physical ability, and other social locations of inequality. Second, multiracial feminism stresses the importance of recognizing the ways intersecting systems of power and privilege interact on all social–structural levels. Third, multiracial feminism is founded on the concept of *relationality*; this "assumes that groups of people are socially situated in relation to other groups of people based on their differences."[153] Other key conceptual facets to multiracial feminism include appreciating the interaction of social structure and women's agency, implementing various methodological approaches, and an emphasis on understandings founded on the lived experiences of women. This evolving perspective uses various terms such as *multiracial feminism, multicultural feminism*, and *U.S. Third World feminism*.[154]

Another issue that has been raised by feminist scholars is that, when conducting research on women, it is essential that one avoid placing these women as *either* offenders *or* victims. This has been referred to as the "blurred boundaries" theory of victimization and criminalization. As Mary Gilfus notes, "criminalization is connected to women's subordinate position in society where victimization by violence coupled with economic marginality related to race, class, and gender all too often blur the boundaries between victims and offenders."[155] This false categorization of women as *either* offenders *or* victims does not provide an enhanced understanding about women who commit crime.

LEARNING CHECK 11.4

When one uses an existing theoretical perspective based on males and adds women, this is referred to as "_____." The _____ is also referred to as the emancipation hypothesis. The _____-_____ theory attempts to explain gender differences in delinquency rates by including family dynamics. Some scholars maintain that approaches to assess _____ are based on biases established by, and for, individuals of privilege. The _____ research approach attempts to determine life experiences, particularly childhood ones, that place one at risk of offending.

Answers located at www.sagepub.com/schram

APPLYING THEORY TO CRIME: ROBBERY

Again, referring to the King of Babylon, Hammurabi, and the "Code of Laws," there are a few references to the crime of robbery:

- If a man has committed highway robbery and has been caught, that man shall be put to death.

- If the highwayman has not been caught, the man that has been robbed shall state on oath what he has lost and the city or district governor in whose territory or district the robbery took place shall restore to him what he lost.[156]

According to the FBI's Uniform Crime Reports, robbery is defined as "the taking or attempting to take anything of value from the care, custody, or control of a person or persons by force or threat of force or violence and/or by putting the victim in fear."[157] Below are some key findings on robbery; these are based on the report *Crime in the United States, 2011:*

- An estimated 354,396 robberies occurred nationwide in 2011.

- When comparing the 2010 and 2011 robbery rates, the rate decreased by 4%.

- An estimated $409 million in losses were attributed to robberies in 2011.

- The average dollar value amount of property stolen per reported robbery was $1,153. Banks were listed as the highest average dollar loss at $4,704 per offense.

- Strong-arm tactics were used in 42.3% of the robberies, firearms were used in 41.3%, knives and cutting instruments were used in 7.8%, and other dangerous weapons were used in 8.7% of robberies in 2011.

Table 11.5 is a summary of robbery by type from *Crime in the United States, 2011.*

As noted previously, the National Crime Victimization Survey collects data to provide additional information concerning crime and victims in the United States. In reference to robberies, some key findings, based on 2011 data, are listed below:

- The number of robbery victims decreased by 2% from 2010 (568,510) to 2011 (556,760).

- Among male robbery victims, 53% of offenders were strangers and 34% nonstrangers; among female robbery victims, 40% of offenders were strangers and 48% nonstrangers.

- In 2011, 42% reported there was no weapon involved in the robbery, compared with 43% who reported there was a weapon; slightly less than 15% did not know.[158]

To illustrate key aspects of feminist pathways, we apply this perspective to the crime of robbery-theft. Lindsay was a 24-year-old woman incarcerated in a midwestern correctional facility for women. She was sentenced to 15 years for armed robbery. One may ask how Lindsay got to this point in her life. What pathways did she take during her life that resulted in her incarceration? To answer these questions, one could conduct an in-person interview with Lindsay

and attempt to gain a more in-depth understanding of her life prior to being incarcerated.

After listening to Lindsay's past experiences, one obtains a greater understanding of how key aspects of her life led her down the pathway to incarceration. Lindsay was one of four children. Her father left her mother when she was 2 years old. She had a very unstable family life. When Lindsay was 5 years old, her mother married a man named John. Both her mother and John abused drugs and alcohol. John was physically abusive to Lindsay, her siblings, and her mother. John started sexually abusing Lindsay when she was 12 years old. During this time, Lindsay had a difficult time in school, both academically and socially.

At 15 years of age, Lindsay ran away. She was living on the streets and started abusing drugs, especially crack cocaine. When she was 17 years old, Lindsay met Matt, a 25-year-old involved in various criminal activities, including theft and drug sales. Although the relationship was quite tumultuous, Lindsay and Matt had a child. Eventually, Matt left Lindsay and the child. A year later, Lindsay lost custody of her child due to abuse and neglect. Lindsay continued to abuse drugs. To support her drug habit, Lindsay engaged in various criminal activities, including prostitution, shoplifting, burglary, and robbery.

LOCATION	NUMBER OF OFFENSES (2011)	PERCENT DISTRIBUTION	AVERAGE VALUE
Street/highway	127,403	43.8%	$785
Commercial house	37,885	13.0%	$1,783
Gas or service station	7,009	2.4%	$890
Convenience store	14,863	5.1%	$667
Residence	49,361	17.0%	$1,489
Bank	5,777	2.0%	$4,704
Miscellaneous	48,878	16.8%	$1,050

Table 11.5 Robbery by Location

Source: Federal Bureau of Investigation. (2012). *Crime in the United States, 2011.* Washington, DC: U.S. Department of Justice, n.p.

COMPARATIVE CRIMINOLOGY: *ROBBERY*

Rates of Robbery Across Different Continents and Regions of the World

Continuing with our comparisons between the United States and foreign nations in terms of various aspects in criminology and criminal justice, in this section, we examine findings from relatively recent data provided from the International Crime Victimization Survey.

As shown in Table 11.6, Latin America and the Caribbean was the world region that reported the highest percentage of citizens who had been victims of robbery, which was 3 times higher than the global average. The second highest was Africa, but this percentage was significantly lower than

that of the leading region. Van Dijk noted that a high number of robberies in Latin America were committed with a firearm. Furthermore, he pointed out Brazil, Mexico, and Argentina as having high rates of armed robberies. He also noted the most common form of robbery in modern times in these Latin American countries, which involves "express robberies," named after American Express credit cards. These robberies involve a victim being held at gunpoint or knifepoint until he or she withdraws money from the bank, typically from an automatic teller machine (ATM). Such chronic forms of these various types of robbery are likely the reason why Latin America and the Caribbean lead the world in terms of robbery.[159]

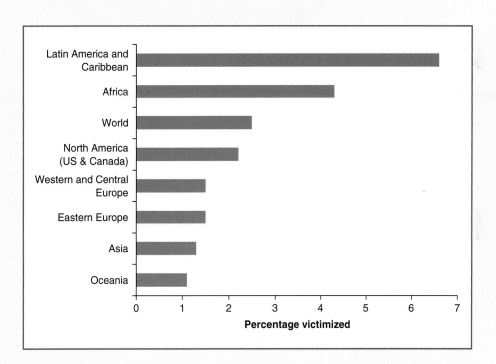

Table 11.6 Percentages of the Public Victimized by Robbery in the Course of 1 Year, by World Region

Source: ICVS, 1996–2005.

Lisa Maher critiqued both traditional and feminist research with respect to the importance of not overemphasizing or ignoring **women's agency**.[160] The more traditional approach often overlooks the social locations of women's marginalization and places too much emphasis on female offenders as "active subjects" who pursue criminal opportunities. This places women with "overendowed" agency. On the other end of the spectrum, more associated with some feminist research, women are denied agency. Thus, "women are portrayed as the passive victims of oppressive social structures, relations, and substances, or some combination thereof."[161] These women are then situated as submissive objects that are mere instruments for the reproduction of determining social structures.

POLICIES BASED ON FEMINIST THEORIES OF CRIME

A key aspect to understanding policies based on feminist theories of crime is that some policies are not always directly related to crime. Rather, feminist perspectives also incorporate broader social issues that are connected to criminal behavior.[162] Thus, aspects of policies related to feminist theories of crime are reflected in broader concepts of feminism. For instance, feminist researchers emphasize the importance of *reflexivity*.[163] This is when research empowers women; this form of research takes women's experiences seriously and centers on the idea that **"the personal is the political"**:

> Feminist work has demonstrated that even the most apparently private interactions have political consequences and motivations. The inextricable connections between the personal and the political means that what happens to "the individual" is not merely the result of individual processes. As a consequence, it is unsatisfactory to treat individuals as if they were isolated from society—at the very least because this cannot give an accurate picture of people and their lives.[164]

This phrase "The personal is the political" refers to the notion that the "private sphere" (e.g., sexuality and domestic life) is as structured by power relations involving gender, sexuality, race, class, and age as the "public sphere" (e.g., waged work outside the home, party politics, and state institutions).[165]

Another aspect related to feminism is **praxis**. According to Donovan, praxis does not refer just to consciousness raising. Rather, praxis also refers to "the development of alternative arrangements that will themselves provide models for change and will in the process change consciousness.[166] Praxis also implies building alternative institutions, such as the establishment of rape crisis centers and shelters, as well as changes in personal relationships. Generally, praxis is when theory translates into action. One of the most essential opportunities for praxis centers on the pursuit of social justice.[167]

Influenced by the women's movement (i.e., the second wave of feminism), our understanding and the legal response to rape have undergone substantial changes.[168] For instance, the Schwendingers theorized how rape myths have pervaded the legal sphere of society, as exemplified by the belief that if a rape victim did not "fight back" or resist, as well as demonstrate physical evidence of such a confrontation, then she must have initially given her consent and afterward "changed her mind."[169] In the past, this myth has been significant in laws that required a demonstration of resistance. However, the Schwendingers provided the following analogy to elucidate the misconceptions associated with this myth:

> Businessmen may forcibly resist theft of their property. But no law *demands* this kind of personal resistance as a condition for the lawful protection of his property rights. Women's rights, on the other hand, seem to be another matter [italics in original].[170]

Legislative reforms were enacted in an effort to modify state rape statutes. Searles and Berger asserted that the major goals of the legislative reforms included (1) increasing the reporting of rape and enhancing the prosecution and conviction in rape cases, (2) improving the treatment of rape victims involved in the criminal justice process, (3) achieving comparability between the legal treatment of rape and other violent offenses, (4) prohibiting a broader range of coercive sexual conduct, and (5) expanding the range of persons protected by the law.[171] Four major types of legislative reforms were identified: (1) redefinition of the offense, (2) evidentiary reforms, (3) statutory offenses, and (4) penal structure.[172]

....

women's agency: the more traditional approach overlooks social locations of women's marginalization and places too much emphasis on female offenders as "active subjects" who pursue criminal opportunities. On the other end, women are denied agency and situated as mere instruments for the reproduction of determining social structures

"The personal is the political": refers to the notion that the "private sphere" is as structured by power relations involving gender, sexuality, race, class, and age as the "public sphere"

praxis: refers not just to consciousness raising but also to the establishment of alternative arrangements that will provide models for change, which then change consciousness

THE VALENTINE FOUNDATION OUTLINED 14 FACTORS THAT SHOULD BE INCORPORATED IN A GENDER-SPECIFIC PROGRAM FOR GIRLS:
1. Ask girls who they are, what their lives are like, and what they need.
2. Allow girls to speak up and actively participate in the services they receive.
3. Assist girls with their family relationships and help them deal with family issues.
4. Assist girls in becoming grounded in some form of spirituality.
5. Allow staff more time and opportunity for building trusting relationships with girls.
6. Allow girls the safety and comfort of same-gender environments.
7. Provide girls with mentors who reflect girls' lives and who model survival, growth, and change.
8. Assist girls with child care, transportation, and safe housing issues.
9. Maintain a diverse staff who reflect the girls served.
10. Weave a multicultural perspective through programming.
11. Teach girls strategies to overcome domestic violence, physical and sexual abuse, and substance abuse.
12. Understand that relationships are central to girls' lives; help girls maintain important connections without sacrificing themselves to their relationships.
13. Connect girls with at least one capable and nonexploitive adult for an ongoing supportive relationship.
14. Promote academic achievement and economic self-sufficiency for girls.

Table 11.7 Factors Associated With Gender-Specific Programs for Girls

Source: Valentine Foundation and Women's Way. (1990). *A conversation about girls.* Bryn Mawr, PA: Valentine Foundation.

Another example of how feminist criminologists have informed policies is in the area of **gender-specific programming**. The Office of Juvenile Justice and Delinquency Prevention established a funding opportunity to enhance programs specifically targeted to juvenile girls.[173] Such programming gives females an increased sense of community. This sense of community has been associated with juveniles developing and integrating a healthy identity.[174] Table 11.7 outlines factors associated with gender-specific programs for girls.

There have been efforts to incorporate these key factors of gender-specific services for female juvenile offenders. For instance, Bond-Maupin and her colleagues argued that intake officials recognized an appreciation of how gender, class, and race influence the lives of female juveniles.[175] Other studies have also recommended that agencies providing services to female juveniles incorporate gender-specific or gender-responsive programs.[176] Such programming has also been recommended for adult female offenders with substance abuse problems,[177] as well as for adult female prisoners.[178]

JOURNAL ARTICLE LINK

Programs for Girls

gender-specific programming: programs targeted to juvenile girls; gives females an increased sense of community that has been associated with developing and integrating a health identity

CONCLUSION

In an effort to provide a context for feminist theories of crime, this chapter started with a brief history of feminism in the United States. Many describe this history in terms of waves (i.e., first, second, and third waves). As noted at the beginning of this chapter, it is essential for readers to understand that there is no *one* feminist perspective. Thus, this section presented various feminist perspectives, such as liberal feminism, radical feminism, Marxist and socialist feminism, and postmodern feminism.

The next portion of this chapter presented traditional theories of female crime. This brief overview gave readers an enhanced appreciation of the development of feminist criminology. These traditional theories were developed by such scholars as Cesare Lombroso, W. I. Thomas, Sigmund Freud, and Otto Pollak. The next section provided feminist critiques of previous research that focused on women and crime. Such critiques include using an "add-women-and-stir" approach and implementing a sex roles perspective.

Subsequently, we discussed various aspects pertaining to feminist perspectives on understanding crime and criminal behavior. This discussion included problems feminist scholars have raised pertaining to traditional research methods such as objectivity and subjectivity, as well as qualitative "versus" quantitative analyses. This section also presents a brief overview of multiracial feminism and how it differs from previous feminist perspectives. We also illustrate one example of research within a feminist perspective—feminist pathways. Key critiques of feminist theories were also raised in this section. These criticisms include earlier feminist theories focusing on the experiences of white, middle-class women; placing women as *either* offenders *or* victims; and ignoring women's agency.

We concluded this chapter with a discussion of policies based on feminist theories of crime. Two related concepts pertaining to any feminist research presented in this section were "the personal is the political" and praxis. We reviewed such policies as early rape reform efforts, as well as the current trend of providing gender-specific programs for female offenders.

At the beginning of this chapter, we presented the case study of Elizabeth Escalona, who pled guilty to injury to a child. We asked if some individuals would perceive such offenses committed by a mother *differently* than they would similar offenses committed by a father. Some may answer "yes" to this question; others may contend that this is due to stereotypes such as the perception that women have a biologically determined sense of maternal and nurturing capabilities. Also note that the case study discussion included references to Escalona's prior life experiences leading up to her abusing her daughter—in other words, pathways to crime.

SUMMARY OF THEORIES IN CHAPTER 11

THEORY	CONCEPTS	PROPONENTS	KEY PROPOSITIONS
Traditional theories of female crime	Dichotomize women into "either/or" roles in terms of sexuality; femininity; the cult of true womanhood; emphasize biological and psychological factors	Various (e.g., Cesare Lombroso, W. I. Thomas, Sigmund Freud, Otto Pollak)	Emphasized physiological and psychological explanations to understand female criminality, rather than social factors; particular emphasis on stereotypical assumptions of women and sexuality.
Liberation thesis	Increased opportunities for women to participate in the labor force; changing self-concept and identity of women; liberation movement	Freda Adler Rita Simon	As opportunities for women in the legal sphere are enhanced, so are opportunities for women in the illegal sphere; increases in female crime are due to women becoming actively competitive with men.
Power–control theory	Family dynamics; patriarchal families; egalitarian families; social class	John Hagan et al.	Youths from patriarchal families have greater gender differences in delinquency rates compared with youths from egalitarian families; individuals experience power relationships in the broader social context, especially those from different social classes.
Feminist criminology	Gender is not a natural fact but a complex social, historical, and cultural product; gender relations order social life; gender relations are constructs of masculinity and femininity based on organizing principle of men's superiority; systems of knowledge reflect men's view of the natural and social world; women should be at the center of intellectual inquiry	Various	Continue to search for the scientific basis of theories of men's and women's criminal behavior; reexamine gender and racial/ethnic biases in the social sciences; develop a new definition of crime; recognize the ways interesting systems of power and privilege interact on all social–structural levels.

KEY TERMS

add women and stir	Marxist feminism	power–control theory	Sigmund Freud
Cesare Lombroso	multiracial feminism	praxis	socialist feminism
chivalry	objectivity	qualitative	"The personal is the political"
first wave of feminism	Otto Pollak	quantitative	
gender	paternalism	radical feminism	third wave of feminism
gender-specific programming	pathways research	second wave of feminism	traditional or conservative perspective
liberal feminism	patriarchy	sex	W. I. Thomas
liberation thesis	postmodern feminism	sex roles	women's agency

STUDENT STUDY SITE

Visit the student study site at **www.sagepub.com/schram** to access links to the video, audio, city and state rankings, author podcasts, and SAGE journal and reference articles featured in this chapter, as well as additional study tools, including eFlashcards, web quizzes, web resources, and chapter outlines.

DISCUSSION QUESTIONS

1. How would you distinguish the first, second, and third waves of feminism?

2. What are the key features of the various feminist perspectives?

3. How did traditional theories of crime perceive female offenders?

4. What are some of the problems associated with traditional research methods when studying gender?

5. What are some of the key concepts associated with feminist thought?

6. What is feminist pathways research?

7. How does multicultural feminism differ from previous feminist perspectives?

8. What are some critiques of feminist criminological theories?

9. What is meant by "the personal is the political"?

10. What is praxis?

11. What are some of the major rape reforms?

12. What are the key factors of gender-specific programming?

WEB RESOURCES

National Organization for Women (NOW)

http://now.org/

American Society of Criminology Division on Women and Crime

http://ascdwc.com/

CHAPTER 12

Developmental/Life-Course Perspectives of Criminality

INTRODUCTION

This chapter discusses the development of the life-course perspective in the late 1970s and its influence on modern research on criminal trajectories. During this period, criminological theorists and researchers began to realize that tracking the offending patterns of certain individuals over their lifetimes would add much to the understanding of why such individuals commit more offenses at certain points in their lives. The same type of examination also shows why individuals reduce, or even stop, offending after certain significant life events (e.g., getting a good job, getting married, having children).

Thus, this chapter focuses on explaining the various concepts in the life-course perspective, such as early onset, desistence, frequency of offending, and factors involved in criminal careers. Perhaps the best indicator for predicting future chronic, habitual offenders is when they were first arrested, labeled "early onset." To clarify, when an individual is arrested prior to age 14, this is likely the best indicator that the person is at high risk of becoming a habitual offender. Another important factor is when the person committed his or her most serious offenses. The other aspects of developmental theory are also insightful in our understanding of why individuals commit crime, especially in terms of when they commit most of their offenses (i.e., frequency), and perhaps more so regarding why they desist or stop offending. We will also discuss the criticisms and arguments against this developmental/life-course perspective. Finally, we will review the current state of research regarding the perspective of life-course or developmental theory.

To clarify, this chapter presents one of the most current and progressive approaches toward explaining why individuals engage in criminal activity—namely, **developmental theories** of criminal behavior. Developmental theories are explanatory models of criminal behavior that follow individuals throughout their life course of offending, thus explaining the development of offending over time. Such developmental theories represent a break with past traditions of theoretical frameworks, which typically focused on the contemporaneous effects of constructs and variables on behavior at a given point in time. Prior to the 1970s, virtually no traditional theories attempted to explain the various stages (e.g., onset, desistence) of individuals' criminal careers, and certainly no models differentiated the varying factors that are important at each stage. Developmental theories have been prominent in modern times, and we believe that readers will agree that developmental theories, also known as the life-course perspective, have added a great deal to our understanding and thinking about why people engage in criminal behavior.

BASIC CONCEPTS AND EARLY DEVELOPMENTAL THEORY

Developmental theories are distinguished by their emphasis on the evolution of individuals' criminality over time. Developmental theories tend to look at the individual as the unit of analysis, and such models focus on the various aspects of the onset, frequency, intensity, persistence/duration, desistence, and other aspects of the individual's criminal career. The onset of offending is when the offender first begins offending, and desistence is when an

LEARNING OBJECTIVES

As students are reading this chapter, they should consider the following questions:

- How do developmental or life-course theories differ from other theoretical perspectives presented in this book?

- How do various concepts or factors that are important in life-course/developmental perspectives, such as onset, frequency of offenses, duration of offending, seriousness of the offenses, desistence of offending, etc., play key roles in when individuals offend and why they do so at certain times in their lives?

- What are some of the primary criticisms or weaknesses of the life-course/developmental perspective? Which theories are clearly "antidevelopmental"?

- Which specific theories in the developmental/life-course genre seem best to account for specific transitions or trajectories either toward or away from crime?

- Which theories account for different types of offenders, such as chronic or habitual offenders versus individuals who offend only during certain times in their lives?

CASE STUDY

THE TEEN BURGLAR

A news story from the spring of 2012 reported that a 14-year-old boy had been arrested in Tennessee in connection with nearly 100 burglaries in the north Nashville area of Tennessee.[1] Officers said the teen was linked to these burglaries over the previous 2 years (making him 12 when he started offending). According to police, he had a specific and consistent modus operandi, or method of operation. Specifically, he would kick in back doors, enter, and steal whatever he could grab quickly, such as flat-screen TVs or video games. Officers noted his creativity and innovation, which included using a go-kart as his getaway vehicle, driving from house to house through back alleys. The police also mentioned that he had lost both parents and likely didn't have much guidance or anyone looking out for him. They had evidence tying him to the burglaries, such as fingerprints and items found inside his home, which likely is the reason he admitted to many of the break-ins. It is unfortunate that this boy had such a poor family life and so little parental supervision, but one must wonder what inspired him to commit more than 100 residential burglaries, starting when he was 12 years old! We will revisit this case in our conclusion, with additional insight into why he may have committed these crimes.

> ONE MUST WONDER WHAT INSPIRED HIM TO COMMIT MORE THAN 100 RESIDENTIAL BURGLARIES, STARTING WHEN HE WAS 12 YEARS OLD!

individual stops committing crime. Frequency refers to how often the individual offends at certain times, whereas intensity is the degree of seriousness of the offenses he or she commits at certain times in the offending career. Persistence or duration involves the length of an individual's criminal career in terms of time from onset to final offense. Finally, desistence refers to when the criminal career of an individual ends and he or she opts out of offending (or at least doesn't get caught again).

Experts have long debated and examined these various aspects of the development of criminal behavior. Perhaps the earliest notable focus on such development was presented in 1950 and after by Sheldon and Eleanor Glueck of Harvard University, who for more than 40 years performed research that examined the development of criminal careers among 1,000 boys (500 were persistent delinquents, and 500 were not).[2] The Gluecks examined a plethora of variables, ranging from their subjects' IQ scores to their body types to their personalities, as well as multiple sociological factors. The data from this research have been utilized by researchers in modern times, primarily Robert Sampson, John Laub, and their colleagues, in exploring the various reasons why individuals offend early in life, as well as why some desist and others continue to offend, sometimes throughout their lives.[3] Many other studies have followed this model of examining a multitude of factors that may influence the development of individuals, especially in terms of criminality.

Virtually all studies on the life-course/developmental perspective show that most individuals who get arrested are never arrested again.[4] However, for those who offend many times, a certain pattern emerges. This pattern involves an escalation from minor-status offending (e.g., truancy, underage drinking, smoking tobacco), usually committed early in their preteen or early teenage years. This then leads to some higher level petty crimes (e.g., shoplifting, smoking marijuana) and then to far more serious criminal activity, such as robbery and aggravated assault, and eventually murder and rape. This development of criminality is shown across every study that has ever been performed and demonstrates that, with very few exceptions, people begin with relatively minor offending and progress toward more serious, violent offenses.[5]

Although this trend is undisputed, other issues remain unresolved. For example, studies have not yet determined when police contact or an arrest becomes *early onset*. Most empirical studies draw the line at age 14, so any arrest or contact prior to this time is considered early onset.[6] However, other experts disagree and say this line should be drawn earlier (say at 12 years old) or even later (such as at 16 years old). Still, however it is defined, early onset is one of the most important predictors of any of the measures we have for determining who is most at risk for developing serious, violent offending behavior. Given extensive research, the current "cut-off" age is still considered age 13.[7]

Another key area is persistence or duration of offending. This has become one of the most researched components of the developmental perspective.[8] A great example of persistence in offending is represented by the story of a 41-year-old man named Kevin Holder in Lincoln, Nebraska, who has been arrested 226 times.[9] Some may instantly think that Mr. Holder has just committed simple misdemeanors, but that is not the case. Rather, his past offenses include assault, resisting arrest, assault on a police officer, and

Chronic offending often starts with minor offenses, such as truancy, smoking, and underage drinking, but then escalates to more serious offenses, such as burglary, robbery, and assault.

developmental theories: perspectives of criminal behavior that emphasize the evolution of individuals' criminality over time, with the individual as the unit of analysis

Kevin Holder has been arrested at least 226 times for a variety of offenses.

violation of a restraining order. What is even more shocking is that he was nowhere near the top rank in terms of number of arrests in that one county in Lincoln, Nebraska; he ranked No. 40! So there were 39 offenders in that county who had been arrested more frequently. In fact, the authorities there reported that a few had more than 500 arrests. This is an example, albeit extreme, of what is meant by persistence or duration of a criminal career.

Perhaps the most discussed and researched aspect of developmental theory is *offender frequency*, referred to as *lambda*. Estimates of lambda, or average frequency of offending by criminals over a year period, vary greatly.[10] Some estimates of lambda are in the high single digits, and some are in the triple digits. Given this large range, it does not do much good in estimating the frequency of most offenders. Rather, the frequency depends on many, many variables, such as what types of offenses the individual commits. Perhaps if we were studying only drug users or rapists, it would make sense to determine lambda, but given the general nature of most examinations of crime, such estimates are not typically useful. Thus, the frequency of offending, even within crime type, varies so widely across individuals that we question its use in understanding criminal careers.[11] Still, it can sometimes be useful to have an estimate of lambda or frequency, such as if a researcher is investigating a specific type of offense or particular group of offenders.

It is notable that the developmental/life-course perspective has recently become one of the most dominant theories in explaining criminality. A study conducted in 2008 surveyed 387 criminologists to discover which theories each of them considered the most viable explanations for serious/persistent criminal behavior.[12] This study found that life-course/developmental theory was ranked No. 2 for most accepted theoretical explanation of serious crime (after social learning theory, which was ranked No. 1). This perspective made a giant leap in ranking from similar surveys done in past years.[13]

Before we discuss the dominant models of developmental theory, it is important to discuss the opposing viewpoint, which is that of complete stability in offending. Such counterpoint views assume that the developmental approach is a waste of time because the same individuals who show antisocial behavior at early ages (before age 10) are those who will exhibit the most criminality in their teenage years, 20s, 30s, 40s, and so on. This framework is most notably represented by the theoretical perspective proposed by Gottfredson and Hirschi in their model of low self-control.

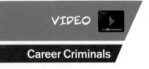

ANTIDEVELOPMENTAL THEORY: LOW SELF-CONTROL THEORY

In 1990, Travis Hirschi, along with his colleague Michael Gottfredson, proposed a general theory of low self-control as the primary cause of all crime and deviance (see prior discussion in Chapter 9); this is often referred to as the *general theory of crime*.[14] This theory has led to a significant amount of debate and research in the field since its appearance, more than any other contemporary theory of crime. Like other control theories of crime that we previously discussed (see Chapter 9), this theory assumes that individuals are born predisposed toward selfish, self-centered activities and that only effective child rearing and socialization can create self-control. Without such adequate socialization (i.e., social controls) and reduction of criminal opportunities, individuals will follow their natural tendencies to become selfish predators.

The general theory of crime assumes that self-control must be established by age 10. If it has not formed by that time, according to the theory, individuals will forever exhibit low self-control. This assumption of the formation of low self-control by age 10 is the oppositional feature of this theory compared with the developmental perspective. Once low self-control is set at age 10, there is no way to develop it afterward, the authors assert. In contrast, developmental theory assumes that people can, indeed, change over time.

Like others, Gottfredson and Hirschi attribute the formation of controls to socialization processes in the first years of life; the distinguishing characteristic of this theory is its emphasis on the individual's ability to control him- or herself. That is, the general theory of crime assumes that people can exercise a degree of control over their own decisions and, within certain limitations, control themselves. The general theory of crime is accepted as one of the most valid theories of crime.[15] This is probably due to the parsimony, or simplicity, of the theory, because it identifies only one primary factor that causes criminality—low self-control.

But low self-control may actually consist of a series of personality traits, including risk taking, impulsiveness, self-centeredness, short-term orientation, and quick temper. Recent research has supported the idea that inadequate child-rearing practices tend to result in lower levels of self-control among children and that these low levels of self-control produce various risky behaviors, including criminal activity.[16] It is important to note that even this theory has a developmental component in the sense that it proposes that self-control develops from parenting practices during the early years; thus, even this most notable antidevelopment theory actually includes a strong developmental aspect (see Figure 12.1).

In contrast to Gottfredson and Hirschi's model, one of the most dominant and researched frameworks of the past 20 years, another sound theoretical model shows that individuals can change their life trajectories in terms of crime. Research shows that certain events or realizations can lead people to alter their frequency or incidence of offending, sometimes to zero. To account for such extreme transitions, we must turn to the dominant life-course model of offending, which is Sampson and Laub's developmental model of offending.

LEARNING CHECK 12.1

1. According to the text, how do developmental/life-course theories of crime differ from traditional explanatory models?
   a. Developmental models focus more on group rates of crime.
   b. Developmental theories tend to put more emphasis on the state of the economy.
   c. Developmental models emphasize following individuals through various stages in their lives.
   d. Developmental theories focus more on the political changes that occur.

2. According to the text, which of the many concepts/factors in developmental theory seems to offer the best chance for predicting future criminality?
   a. Desistence
   b. Early onset
   c. Duration
   d. Frequency (lambda)

3. According to a study discussed in the text, a recent survey of 387 criminologists found that they ranked developmental/life-course theory where among all existing theoretical perspectives in ability to explain serious criminal behavior?
   a. No. 1
   b. No. 2
   c. No. 4
   d. No. 7

Answers located at www.sagepub.com/schram

VIDEO

Cycle of Violence

AUDIO

Self-Control

COMPARATIVE CRIMINOLOGY: *CHILD ABUSE*

Some Exploratory Studies on Child Abuse in Other Countries

Unfortunately, there is no systematic global data collection regarding child abuse; however, the World Health Organization (WHO, 2002) estimated that there were about 57,000 homicides of children under 15 in just the year 2000. This study also found that perpetrators of child abuse had witnessed violence against their mothers when they were young. This is consistent with studies that repeatedly find links between childhood exposure to domestic violence and violent offending at older ages (see discussion in Van Dijk, 2008, p. 88). This phenomenon is commonly referred to as the "cycle of violence."

Van Dijk (2008) points out that perhaps the most comprehensive studies of child abuse in modern times were done in Germany, surveying more than 11,000 teenagers about their experiences with domestic violence. One consistent finding was that children of immigrants reported significantly higher rates/percentages of violence against mothers, with extremely high rates among those from Turkey (32%), Yugoslavia (25%), and Russia (20%). Another interesting pattern was that the immigrant families that had resided in Germany for longer periods had higher rates of domestic violence, which Van Dijk claimed suggested "growing tensions between spouses after a longer exposure of women to German norms and values concerning gender equality" (p. 88).

Also notable, WHO (2004) estimated that annual economic costs in the United States due to child abuse totaled about $94 billion. And although traditionally rare, there is a growing trend to punish much more severely parents and caretakers who abuse children, which also adds to the costs in terms of processing and incarcerating offenders. For example, in October 2012, a 23-year-old Texas woman was sentenced to 99 years in prison for such abuses as gluing her daughter's hands to the wall and beating her as punishment for potty-training setbacks. (Read more about this story here: http://abcnews.go.com/US/texas-mom-glued-daughters-hands-wall-99-years/story?id=17436643.)

Sources: Van Dijk, J. (2008). *The world of crime*. Thousand Oaks, CA: Sage; World Health Organization. (2002). *World report on violence and health*. Geneva: Author; World Health Organization. (2004). *The economic dimensions of interpersonal violence*. Geneva: Author.

MODERN DEVELOPMENTAL/ LIFE-COURSE PERSPECTIVES

REFERENCE ARTICLE

Life-Course Perspective

PERSONAL PERSPECTIVE

Transitions

SAMPSON AND LAUB'S DEVELOPMENTAL MODEL

One of the best-known and best-researched developmental theoretical models to date is that of Robert Sampson and John Laub.[17] Sampson and Laub have proposed a developmental framework largely based on a reanalysis of original data collected by Sheldon and Eleanor Glueck in the 1940s. As a prototype developmental model, individual stability and change are the primary foci of their theoretical perspective.

Most significantly, Sampson and Laub emphasized the importance of certain events and life changes that can alter an individual's decisions to commit (or not commit) criminal actions. Although based on a social control framework, this model contains elements of other theoretical perspectives. First, Sampson and Laub's model assumes, like other developmental perspectives, that early antisocial tendencies among individuals, regardless of social variables, are often linked to later adult criminal offending. Furthermore, some social-structure factors (e.g., family structure, poverty, etc.) also tend to lead to problems in social and educational development, which then lead to crime. Another key factor in this development of criminality is the influence of delinquent peers or siblings, which further increases an individual's likelihood for delinquency.

However, Sampson and Laub also strongly emphasize the importance of **transitions**, or specific events (e.g., marriage, stable employment) that are important in altering

transitions: events important in altering trajectories toward or away from crime, such as marriage or employment

trajectories: paths people take in life, often due to life transitions

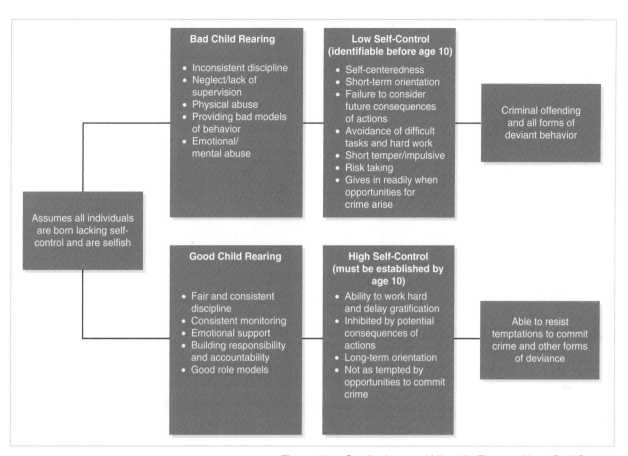

Figure 12.1 Gottfredson and Hirschi's Theory of Low Self-Control

Source: Tibbetts, S. G. (2012). *Criminological theory: The essentials* (p. 602). Thousand Oaks, CA: Sage.

long-term trends in behavior, which are referred to as trajectories. **Trajectories** are more nonspecific, longitudinal patterns of behavior either toward or away from committing crime and are typically the cumulative result of certain or many specific transitions, such as marriage, employment, having children, or enlisting in military service, which drastically change a person's criminal career. Sampson and Laub show sound evidence that many individuals who were once on a path toward a consistent form of behavior—in this case, serious, violent crime—suddenly (or gradually) halted due to such a transition or series of transitions. In some ways, this model is a more specified form of David Matza's theory of drift, which we discussed in Chapter 9, in which individuals tend to grow out of crime and deviance due to the social controls imposed by marriage, employment, and so on.

Still, Sampson and Laub's framework contributed much to the knowledge of criminal offending by providing a more specified and grounded framework that identified the ability of individuals to change their criminal trajectories via life-altering transitions, such as the possible effect of marriage on a man or woman, which is quite profound. In fact, recent research has consistently shown that marriage and full-time employment significantly reduced the recidivism of California parolees, and other recent

Robert Sampson and John Laub are key theorists in the developmental/life-course perspective

Studies have shown that getting married and obtaining steady employment significantly reduce the offending rates of even chronic offenders.

Moffitt's developmental theory or taxonomy: a theoretical perspective proposing that criminal acts are committed by (1) adolescence-limited offenders or (2) life-course persistent offenders

studies have shown similar results from employment in later years.[18] Other types of transitions, such as getting a great job that one would never want to lose or having children, are also examples of transitions that can radically alter an individual's trajectory away from criminal offending.

MOFFITT'S DEVELOPMENTAL TAXONOMY

Another primary developmental model that has had a profound effect on the current state of criminological thought and theorizing is Terrie **Moffitt's developmental theory or taxonomy,** proposed in 1993.[19] Moffitt's framework distinguishes two types of offenders: **adolescence-limited offenders** and **life-course persistent offenders.** Adolescence-limited offenders make up most of the general public and include all persons who committed offenses when they were teenagers or young adults. Their offending was largely caused by association with peers and a desire to engage in activities exhibited by the adults they were trying to emulate. Such activities are a type of rite of passage and quite normal among all people who have normal social interactions with their peers in teenage or young adult years. It should be noted that a small percentage (about 1–3%) of the population are nonoffenders who, quite frankly, do not have normal relations with their peers and therefore do not offend at all, even in adolescence.

On the other hand, there exists another, smaller group of offenders, referred to in this model as *life-course persistent offenders*. This small group, estimated to account for 4% to 8% of all offenders—albeit the most violent and chronic—commit the vast majority

WHY DO THEY DO IT?

HENRY EARL

Henry Earl is, according to all available sources, the most arrested individual on record, at least in recent times. Hailing from the area of Lexington, Kentucky (Fayette County), Earl was born in 1949 and has since done quite an impressive job of getting himself arrested, especially after he turned 21. Specifically, Earl is on record for being arrested well over 1,300 times since 1970. Although the actual number is disputed, and likely growing every month, recent official reports from the local jurisdictions show that Earl has been arrested for more than 1,352 offenses and has spent more than 15 years in jail. Despite being jailed for much of his life, Earl appears to make up for lost time when he is not incarcerated, as the data show.

Although many of his arrests were for public intoxication, he also had a number of more serious charges, including third-degree trespassing, and various charges of disorderly conduct. Readers are probably wondering how this man could still be on the streets, but the most likely explanation is that virtually all his arrests were for nonviolent, nontheft, and nondrug (except alcohol) violations, which tend not to get much jail time. However, one would think that after the first hundred arrests, not to mention the first thousand, the judges would try to put this public nuisance away for a long time. Apparently, that is not the case. Earl's last reported arrest was in October 2012, so he is seemingly still active and perhaps trying to achieve a record of arrests that may be hard for anyone to beat.

This goes to show a couple of things that relate to this chapter. First, if someone is highly motivated to commit crime, he or she can easily find ways to do so. After all, anyone can simply leave the house and commit numerous felonies against neighbors, people driving by on the street,

and so forth—not to mention what that person is capable of outside of his or her neighborhood. Second, there is virtually no way to deter or stop a person from committing a crime he or she is highly motivated to commit, especially if that person has nothing to lose. Obviously, Earl has nothing at stake in terms of conventional society.

This case is notable in the context of developmental/life-course criminology. Although a highly extreme case study, it reveals that normal development, such as key transitions in life, as noted by Sampson and Laub's theory, clearly don't apply in this case. Some individuals have an extremely high predisposition to offend, an even higher disposition than Gottfredson and Hirschi's theory of low self-control may have imagined possible. Regardless, this amazingly strong disposition toward such antisocial behavior is likely due to major failures in all areas of development throughout Earl's life course, beginning with his genetics, early development, and adolescence.

Henry Earl, arrested more than 1,300 times, is widely considered the most arrested individual in U.S. history.

Sources: Henry Earl: Setting the record straight. (2008, September 25). *The Smoking Gun.* Retrieved from http://www.thesmokinggun.com/documents/crime/henry-earl-setting-record-straight; Lexington-Fayette Urban County Government, Division of Community Corrections. (n.d.). *JailWebsite.com.* Retrieved from http://jail.lfucg.com/Secure/Account/Login.aspx?ReturnUrl=%2fQueryProfile.aspx%3foid%3d137&oid=137.

Terrie Moffitt developed the most renowned and studied developmental framework, which not only identified different types of offenders but also provided a causal etiology for why chronic, persistent offenders differ from relatively normal individuals who commit crime only during their adolescent years.

AUTHOR PODCAST

Terrie Moffitt

JOURNAL ARTICLE

Moffitt's Theory

adolescence-limited offenders: a type of offender who commits crimes only during adolescence and desists in his or her 20s or adulthood

life-course persistent offenders: a type of offender who starts offending early and persists through adulthood

of the serious, violent offenses in any society, such as murder, rape, and armed robbery. In contrast to the adolescence-limited offenders, the disposition of life-course persistent offenders toward offending is caused by an entirely different model: an interaction between neurological problems and the disadvantaged or criminological environments in which they were raised.

For example, if an individual has only neurological problems or only came from a poor, disadvantaged environment, then that individual will be unlikely to develop a life-course persistent trajectory toward crime. However, if a person has both neurological problems and came from a disadvantaged environment, then that individual will have a very high likelihood of becoming a chronic, serious, violent offender. This proposition, which has been supported by empirical studies,[20] suggests that it is important to pay attention to what happens early in life.

Because illegal behaviors are normal among teenagers or young adults, more insight can be gained by looking at the years prior to age 12 to determine who is most likely to become a chronic, violent offender. Life-course persistent offenders begin offending very early in life and continue to commit crime far into adulthood, even middle age, whereas adolescence-limited offenders tend to engage in criminal activity only during their teenage and young-adult years. Moffitt's model suggests that more than one type of development explains criminality. Furthermore, this framework shows that certain types of offenders commit crime due to entirely different causes and factors.

THORNBERRY'S INTERACTIONAL MODEL OF OFFENDING

A final major developmental theory was presented by Terrence Thornberry in 1987.[21] This model incorporated empirical evidence that addressed an extremely important aspect never before addressed in criminological theory. Specifically, Thornberry's interactional theory was the first to emphasize reciprocal, or feedback, effects in the causal modeling of the theoretical framework. To clarify, this was the first widely acknowledged model that presented certain factors, such as peer associations, both as a predictor variable and as a factor that is subsequently influenced by other factors that follow it temporally, such as offending. In other words, negative peer influences predict future offending, but such offending can then cause even more negative peer influence, thus leading to even more criminality.

As a basis for his model, Thornberry combined social control and social learning models. According to Thornberry, both of these theories try to explain criminality in a straightforward, causal process and are largely targeted toward a certain age population.[22] Thornberry uniquely claims that the processes of both social control and social learning theory affect each other in a type of feedback process.

Thornberry's interactional model incorporates five primary theoretical constructs, which are synthesized in a comprehensive framework to explain criminal behavior. These five concepts are commitment to school, attachment to parents, belief in conventional values (these first three are taken from social control and bonding theory), adoption of delinquent values, and association with delinquent peers (these last two are drawn from social learning and differential association–reinforcement theory). These five constructs, which most criminologists would agree are important in the development of criminality, are obviously important in a rational model of crime; so at first, it does not appear that Thornberry has added much to the understanding of criminal behavior. Furthermore, Thornberry's model clearly points out that different variables will have greater effects

APPLYING THEORY TO CRIME: *ARSON*

Arson is a serious crime in terms of Federal Bureau of Investigation (FBI)/Uniform Crime Reports (UCR) standards; it is categorized as a Part I/Index crime. According to Winslow and Zhang (2008), the FBI did not seriously consider arson an Index crime until around 1978, when it was realized that incidents of arson had increased more than 3,100% between the years 1951 and 1977. Thus, the authorities at the U.S. Department of Justice in charge of the FBI and UCR decided that arson should be added to the other seven Index crimes. The FBI definition of arson is "any willful or malicious burning or attempting to burn, with or without intent to defraud, a dwelling house, public building, motor vehicle, or aircraft, personal property of another, etc." As you can see, this is a wide definition, which is why there are so many different types of arson. After all, some youths start fires for excitement, some business owners start fires to cash in on insurance claims, and pyromaniacs light fires to fulfill a psychological compulsion to burn things, whereas others burn crime scenes to destroy evidence or to get revenge on others. There are even more reasons to start illegal fires, but they all fall under this category of arson.

The reason why we are discussing arson in this chapter is because it is the only Part I/Index offense primarily committed by young people (under 14). The vast majority of arsonists are male. Furthermore, early onset of offending (a key factor of the developmental perspective) is often seen in an act of arson—"boys playing with fire." And although such youths often do not realize the implications of their actions, it still often causes much property damage and sometimes costs lives. Given the prevalence and clustering of arson in young ages, we are discussing it in this chapter; however, the act of arson spans a variety of ages and motives.

According to recent reports by the FBI, there were about 58,871 official reports/incidents of arson in the United States in 2009. The average damage/loss due to arson in that year was $17,411. Arsons involving structures (e.g., residential, public, storage, etc.) accounted for about 45% of the total, whereas mobile property (e.g., vehicles) and other types of property (e.g., crops, fences, etc.) accounted for about 28% and 27%, respectively. Incidents of arson contributed to a total loss of more than a billion dollars in 2009 alone. This shows the need for further prevention of this Index offense and reveals why it is a top priority for the FBI and other agencies in the federal government.

Perhaps this is why many programs have been formed to prevent arson, especially among youths. Various types of intervention programs have been started to try to curb high-risk "fire-setters." And, as mentioned before, this is one of the early predictors or "red flags" that developmental/ life-course researchers examine in determining the likelihood someone will become a chronic offender. As many readers have likely heard, serial killers often have a history of cruelty toward domesticated animals (such as dogs and cats), or a history of bed-wetting. Early engagement in arson is another of these early key predictors of a chronic criminal career, such as in the case of David "Son of Sam" Berkowitz, who killed at least six victims and wounded seven others with a .44 caliber handgun over the course of about a year (1976–1977) in New York City. Berkowitz had a long record of committing arsons earlier in his life.

On the other hand, some youths simply are bored or are being experimental and don't ever intend harm to anyone or anything. However, early incidents of arson are certainly a "red flag" in developmental theory and should be taken seriously.

Sources: U.S. Department of Justice. (2009). *Uniform crime report.* Washington, DC: Author; Winslow, R., & Zhang, S. (2008). *Criminology: A global perspective.* Upper Saddle River, NJ: Pearson, p. 42.

at certain times; for example, he claims that association with delinquent peers will have more effect in the mid-teenage years than at other ages.

What Thornberry adds beyond other theories is the idea of reciprocity or feedback loops, which no previous theory had mentioned, much less emphasized. In fact, much of the previous criminological literature spent much time debating whether individuals become delinquent and then start hanging out with similar peers or whether individuals start hanging out with delinquent peers and then begin engaging in criminal activity. This has been the traditional "chicken-or-egg" question in criminology for most of the 20th century—namely, "Which came first, delinquency or bad friends?" It has often

▶ VIDEO

Arson

▶ WHAT WERE THEY THINKING?!

Arson

COMPARATIVE CRIMINOLOGY: *ARSON*

Comparing Arson Rates in the United States With Those in Other Countries

Here, we examine the findings and conclusions of a particular study conducted in November 2007 by John R. Hall, Jr., of the Fire Analysis and Research Division, National Fire Protection Association.

Hall's (2007) findings regarding arson in the United States revealed that civilian fire deaths due to arson dropped significantly between 1990 (850 deaths) and 2005 (490 deaths) (p. 8). This was compared with the same measure for three other industrialized countries—the United Kingdom, Japan, and Canada. The United Kingdom, for civilian fire deaths in those same years, reported about 90 in 1990 and about 100 in 2005, which reveals that the United Kingdom's incidence of arson actual rose, while the incidence in the United States dropped significantly. The same was true for data from Japan, which also showed an increase in deaths from 1990 to the most recent year available, 2003. Canada had about the same number of civilian deaths during this period, and the number of incidents was relatively stable. Therefore, Hall concluded:

In the United Kingdom and Japan, the trends in intentional fires have been upward, in contrast to the trend in the U.S. In Canada, there has been no consistent trend up or down in set fires, in total or as a share of all fires, or in associated losses. (p. 6)

Although these figures are based on numbers and not rates of arson, it appears that the United States has gone down significantly in frequency of arson in recent years, whereas some of the most similar industrialized countries have either seen a rise or remained stable.

Regarding the rankings for arson rates among states in 2009 (see Table 12.1), there is not much of a consistent pattern. Although two Mid-Atlantic states are ranked in the top three, with Maryland ranked as a high outlier at No. 1 (with a rate of 8.6 per 100,000 population) and Delaware ranked at No. 3 (with a rate of 6.7), no other nearby states appear in the top 10. Furthermore, although Oklahoma was ranked as No. 2 (7.1 per 100,000 population), many other Western states had the lowest rates of arson for that year. Specifically, South Dakota, Wyoming, North Dakota, and Texas were among the six states with lowest rates of arson. Thus, we can conclude that there was no consistent pattern in terms of region in the United States.

ALPHA ORDER					
RANK AND STATE	**RATE**	**RANK AND STATE**	**RATE**	**RANK AND STATE**	**RATE**
33 Alabama	3.4	9 Louisiana	6.0	30 Ohio	3.5
7 Alaska	6.2	8 Maine	6.1	2 Oklahoma	7.1
30 Arizona	3.5	1 Maryland	8.6	6 Oregon	6.3
38 Arkansas	3.1	48 Massachusetts	1.6	14 Pennsylvania	5.3
30 California	3.5	38 Michigan	3.1	11 Rhode Island	5.8
17 Colorado	5.0	27 Minnesota	3.6	37 South Carolina	3.2
43 Connecticut	2.8	5 Mississippi	6.5	49 South Dakota	1.5
3 Delaware	6.7	13 Missouri	5.5	20 Tennessee	4.2
47 Florida	2.1	33 Montana	3.4	44 Texas	2.7
27 Georgia	3.6	11 Nebraska	5.8	21 Utah	4.1
42 Hawaii	2.9	10 Nevada	5.9	38 Vermont	3.1
14 Idaho	5.3	19 New Hampshire	4.7	25 Virginia	3.7
Illinois**	NA	25 New Jersey	3.7	17 Washington	5.0
23 Indiana	3.9	4 New Mexico	6.6	41 West Virginia	3.0
33 Iowa	3.4	24 New York	3.8	33 Wisconsin	3.4
27 Kansas	3.6	21 North Carolina	4.1	46 Wyoming	2.2
16 Kentucky	5.1	45 North Dakota	2.5		

RANK ORDER					
RANK AND STATE	**RATE**	**RANK AND STATE**	**RATE**	**RANK AND STATE**	**RATE**
1 Maryland	8.6	17 Washington	5.0	33 Montana	3.4
2 Oklahoma	7.1	19 New Hampshire	4.7	33 Wisconsin	3.4
3 Delaware	6.7	20 Tennessee	4.2	37 South Carolina	3.2
4 New Mexico	6.6	21 North Carolina	4.1	38 Arkansas	3.1
5 Mississippi	6.5	21 Utah	4.1	38 Michigan	3.1
6 Oregon	6.3	23 Indiana	3.9	38 Vermont	3.1
7 Alaska	6.2	24 New York	3.8	41 West Virginia	3.0
8 Maine	6.1	25 New Jersey	3.7	42 Hawaii	2.9
9 Louisiana	6.0	25 Virginia	3.7	43 Connecticut	2.8
10 Nevada	5.9	27 Georgia	3.6	44 Texas	2.7
11 Nebraska	5.8	27 Kansas	3.6	45 North Dakota	2.5
11 Rhode Island	5.8	27 Minnesota	3.6	46 Wyoming	2.2
13 Missouri	5.5	30 Arizona	3.5	47 Florida	2.1
14 Idaho	5.3	30 California	3.5	48 Massachusetts	1.6
14 Pennsylvania	5.3	30 Ohio	3.5	49 South Dakota	1.5
16 Kentucky	5.1	33 Alabama	3.4	Illinois**	NA
17 Colorado	5.0	33 Iowa	3.4	District of Columbia**	NA

Table 12.1 Reported Arrest Rate for Arson in 2009
National Rate = 3.8 Reported Arrests per 100,000 Population*

Source: CQ Press using reported data from the Federal Bureau of Investigation
"Crime in the United States 2009" (Uniform Crime Reports, September 13, 2010, http://www.fbi.gov/ucr/ucr.htm)

*By law enforcement agencies submitting complete reports to the FBI for 12 months in 2009. These rates based on population estimates for areas under the jurisdiction of those agencies reporting. Arrest rate based on the FBI estimate of reported and unreported arrests for arson is 4.0 arrests per 100,000 population.

**Not available.

Hall, J. R., Jr. (2007, November). *Intentional fires and arson*. Quincy, MA: Fire Analysis and Research Division, National Fire Protection Association. Retrieved from http://www.nfpa.org/assets/files/MbrSecurePDF/OS.arson.pdf.

been referred to as the *self-selection* versus *social learning* debate; in other words, do certain individuals decide to hang out with delinquents based on their previous behavior, or do they learn criminality from delinquents with whom they associate? One of the major contributions of **Thornberry's interactional model** is that he directly answered this question.

Specifically, Thornberry noted that most, if not all, contributors to delinquency (and criminal behavior itself) are related reciprocally. Thus, Thornberry postulated that engaging in crime leads to hanging out with other delinquents and that hanging out with delinquents leads to committing crimes. It is quite common for individuals to commit crime and then

Thornberry's interactional model: the first major perspective to emphasize reciprocal, or feedback, effects in the causal modeling of the theoretical framework start hanging out with peers who are doing the same, and it is also quite common for people to start hanging out with delinquent peers and then start committing crimes. Furthermore, it is perhaps the most likely scenario for a person to be offending and also dealing with both the influences of past experiences and peer effects (see Figure 12.2).

As mentioned previously, Thornberry considers the social control and bonding constructs, such as attachments to parents and commitment to school, which are some of the most essential predictors of delinquency. Like other theoretical models of social bonding and control, Thornberry's model puts the level of attachment and commitment to conventional society ahead of the degree of moral beliefs that individuals hold regarding criminal offending. However, lack of such moral beliefs leads to delinquent behavior, which in turn negatively affects the level of commitment or attachment an individual may have built in his or her development. As Thornberry claimed,

> While the weakening of the bond to conventional society may be an initial cause of delinquency, delinquency eventually becomes its own indirect cause precisely because of its ability to weaken further the person's bonds to family, school, and conventional beliefs.[23]

Thus, the implications of this model are that variables relating to social control or bonding and other sources cause delinquency, which then becomes, in itself, a predictor and cause for the breakdown of other important causes of delinquency and crime.

Terrence Thornberry proposed one of the most complex, albeit accurate, models for how various factors interact with one another in the development of individuals in terms of predicting delinquency and criminality.

A CASE STUDY AND EMPIRICAL EVIDENCE FOR THORNBERRY'S INTERACTIONAL MODEL. As an example case study, consider a person we shall call Johnny, who has an absent father and a mother who uses inconsistent discipline and sometimes inflicts harsh physical abuse on her son. He sees his mother's state of constant neglect and abuse as proof that belief in conventional values is wrong, and he becomes indifferent toward governmental laws; his main goal is to survive and be successful. Because of his mother's psychological and physical neglect, Johnny pays no attention to school and turns to his older peers for guidance and support. These peers guide him toward behavior that gives him both financial rewards (by selling what they steal) and status in their group (respect for performing well in illegal acts). At some point, Johnny gets caught, and this makes the peers who taught him how to engage in crime proud while also alienating him from the previous bonds he had with his

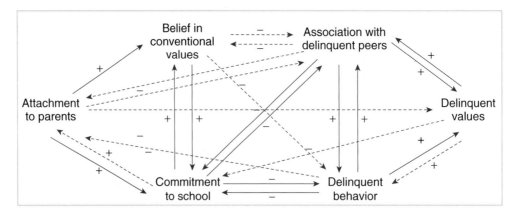

Figure 12.2 A Reciprocal Model of Delinquent Involvement at Middle Adolescence

Source: Tibbetts, S. G., & Hemmens, C. (2010). *Criminological theory: A text/reader* (p. 718). Thousand Oaks, CA: Sage.

school, where he may be suspended or expelled, and with his mother, who further distances herself from him. This creates a reciprocal effect, or feedback loop, to the previous factors— lack of attachment to his mother and lack of commitment to school. The lowered level of social bonding and control of conventional institutions and factors (mother, school) and increased influence of delinquent peers then leads Johnny to commit more frequent and more serious crimes.

Such a model, although complex and hard to measure, is logically consistent, and the postulates are sound. However, the value of any theory has to be determined by the empirical evidence supporting its validity. Much of the scientific evidence regarding Thornberry's empirical model has been contributed by Thornberry and his colleagues.

Although the full model has yet to be tested, the researchers "have found general support for the reciprocal relationships between both control concepts and learning concepts with delinquent behavior."[24] One test of Thornberry's model used the longitudinal Rochester Youth Development Study to test its postulates.[25] This study found that the estimates of previous unidirectional models (nonreciprocal models) did not adequately explain the variation in the data. Rather, the results supported the interactional model, with delinquent associations leading to increases in delinquency, delinquency leading to reinforcing peer networks, and both directional processes working through the social environment. In fact, this longitudinal study demonstrated that, once the participants had acquired delinquent beliefs from their peers, the effects of these beliefs had further effects on their future behavior and associations, which is exactly what Thornberry's theory predicts.[26]

Another empirical test of Thornberry's interactional model examined the age-varying effects of the theory.[27] This study incorporated hierarchical linear modeling in investigating a sample of the National Youth Survey. The results showed that, while the effects of delinquent peers were relatively close to predictions, peaking in the mid-teenage years, the predictions regarding the effects of family on delinquency were not found to be significant in the periods expected, although family was important during adolescence.

Finally, it should be said that in many ways Thornberry's interactional model is far more developmental than others discussed here because it gives equal weight to the traditionally

LEARNING CHECK 12.2

1. According to the text, which developmental theory focuses on transitions and trajectories in our life course as reasons for causing individuals to reduce their criminal offending— transitions such as getting married or obtaining a job one doesn't want to lose?
   a. Moffitt's developmental taxonomy
   b. Thornberry's interactional model
   c. Sampson and Laub's developmental theory
   d. Gottfredson and Hirschi's theory of low self-control

2. According to the text, which developmental theory focuses on two different types of offenders—namely, life-course persistent offenders and adolescence-limited offenders?
   a. Moffitt's developmental taxonomy
   b. Thornberry's interactional model
   c. Sampson and Laub's developmental theory
   d. Gottfredson and Hirschi's theory of low self-control

3. According to the text, which developmental theory focuses on certain factors having different influences at certain times in a person's life, as well as the reciprocal or feedback effects of subsequent variables or behaviors on the earlier antecedent factors, creating a feedback loop?
   a. Moffitt's developmental taxonomy
   b. Thornberry's interactional model
   c. Sampson and Laub's developmental theory
   d. Gottfredson and Hirschi's theory of low self-control

4. According to the text, which theoretical model is considered "antidevelopmental" in the sense that it proposes that once an individual has an early propensity toward criminality, it is virtually impossible to change that propensity and such a person will likely continue offending?
   a. Moffitt's developmental taxonomy
   b. Thornberry's interactional model
   c. Sampson and Laub's developmental theory
   d. Gottfredson and Hirschi's theory of low self-control

Answers located at www.sagepub.com/schram

separate theoretical frameworks combined into his model, in the sense that both are considered antecedent and reciprocal in their effects on criminal behavior. Thornberry's model is likely the most convoluted framework we examine in this book, but it also sheds much light on what is happening in real life among individuals. After all, not only do certain factors, such as family influences, play a part in our peer influences, but peer influences come back and influence familial factors. So although readers may find such a model highly complicated, that is how human behavior works. We live in and experience a complicated world, with numerous interactions among a plethora of constantly occurring factors.

POLICY IMPLICATIONS

Many—perhaps an infinite number of—policy implications can be derived from developmental theories of criminality. Thus, we will focus on the most important, which are those policies emphasizing the prenatal and perinatal stages of life; the most significant and effective interventions can occur during this time. If policymakers hope to reduce early risk factors for criminality, they must insist on universal health care for pregnant women, as well as for their newborn infants through the first few years of life. The United States is one of the few developed nations that does not guarantee this type of maternal and infant medical care and supervision. Doing so would go a long way toward avoiding the costly damages (costly in many ways) of criminal behavior among youths at risk.[28] In fact, in one of the most recent publications regarding this issue, J. C. Barnes stated that "hundreds of studies have shown support for the notion that life-course-persistent offending is often preceded by deficiencies in pre-, peri-, and postnatal care that result in structural and/or functional brain abnormalities."[29]

Furthermore, there should be legally mandated interventions for pregnant women who are addicted to drugs or alcohol. Although this is a highly controversial topic, it appears to be a no-brainer that women who suffer from such addictions may become highly toxic to the child they carry and should receive closer supervision and more health care. Perhaps no other policy implementation would have as much influence in reducing future criminality in children as making sure their mothers do not take toxic substances while pregnant.[30]

An additional concern is inadvertent exposure to toxins, such as lead, which has shown an alarming causal connection to persistent criminality. In a very recent review of the evidence regarding such toxins, particularly lead, John Wright stated that "a series of studies shows a consistent link between pre- and postnatal lead ingestion and delinquency in adolescence and criminal behavior in adulthood."[31] Although lead is just one of the many toxins likely to affect the development of an individual's brain, it is currently the most prominent of the various toxins that can predispose a young person toward criminality. Thus, the exposure to lead or any other toxins should be monitored, especially in certain areas where such toxins are known to exist.

Other policy implications include assigning special caseworkers for high-risk pregnancies, such as those involving low birth weight or low Apgar scores. Another advised intervention would be to organize a centralized medical system that provides a flag for high-risk infants who have numerous birth or delivery complications so that the doctors seeing them for the first time are aware of their vulnerabilities.[32] Finally, universal preschool should be funded and provided for all young children; studies have shown that this leads to better performance, both academically and socially, once they enter school.[33]

Ultimately, as the many developmental theories have shown, many concepts and stages of life can have a profound effect on the criminological trajectories lives can take. However, virtually all these models propose that the earlier stages of life are likely the most important in determining whether an individual will engage or not engage in criminal activity throughout life. Therefore, policymakers should focus their efforts on providing care and interventions within this time period.

COMPARATIVE CRIMINOLOGY: *CRIME RATES*

Comparing Crime Rates of U.S. Cities

Given that this is the developmental theory chapter and we have explored all the major Part I or Index crimes in the UCR, as well as examining international comparisons for each of them, we thought it would be beneficial to concentrate on comparing various cities in the United States. So in this unique Comparative Criminology box, we are going to compare the crime rates of cities in the United States based on their total score on the UCR Crime Index for the year 2010. This measure includes rates for seven of the Index crimes for each city; these seven are murder, forcible rape, aggravated assault, robbery, burglary, motor vehicle theft, and larceny-theft. Remember, these are comparisons based on rates per capita (not numbers), so they are somewhat fair comparisons regardless of the number of citizens in a given city. Notably, this study and ranking include only cities with populations of 75,000 or more.

Table 12.2 shows rankings on the total crime Index score for 2010. The "worst," or highest, ranking on this score was Miami Beach, Florida, followed by Springfield, Missouri; St. Louis, Missouri; Little Rock, Arkansas; and Macon, Georgia. It is notable that

Missouri had two cities in the top three on this ranking—perhaps a result of Missouri being "Ground Zero" for methamphetamine production in recent years.

On the other end of the list, the safest cities in the United States, according to this score, are Fishers, Indiana; Ramapo, New York; Mission Viejo, California; Irvine, California; and Lake Forest, California. It is notable that California had three cities in the top five "safest cities" (and the next safest on the list was Murrieta, also in California).

Breaking down the study to focus on only the most serious offense—murder—the rankings change quite a bit (see Table 12.3). Specifically, in terms of murder rates in 2010, the city with by far the highest rank is New Orleans, Louisiana, followed by Flint, Michigan; Camden, New Jersey; St. Louis, Missouri; Baltimore, Maryland; Detroit, Michigan; and Newark, New Jersey. Notably, Michigan had two cities in the top six cities for murder, and New Jersey had two cities in the top seven.

It is likely that the gross deprivation and poverty in virtually all these cities are key in their high murder rates. These same cities seem to have been in the top 10 for murder over the past decade or so.

Source: Morgan, K. O., Morgan, S., & Santos, R. B. (2012). *City crime: Rankings 2011–2012.* Los Angeles: CQ Press.

RANK AND CITY	RATE	RANK AND CITY	RATE	RANK AND CITY	RATE
1 Miami Beach, FL	10,918.3	15 Orlando, FL	7,550.9	29 North Charleston, SC	6,848.9
2 Springfield, MO	10,530.2	16 New Haven, CT	7,383.7	30 Dayton, OH	6,827.8
3 St. Louis, MO	9,440.8	17 Cincinnati, OH	7,257.4	31 Atlanta, GA	6,812.8
4 Little Rock, AR	9,192.3	18 Chattanooga, TN	7,203.4	32 St. Petersburg, FL	6,801.5
5 Macon, GA	8,959.3	19 Detroit, MI	7,200.3	33 Cleveland, OH	6,797.7
6 Jackson, MS	8,594.7	20 Tacoma, WA	7,199.6	34 Camden, NJ	6,753.8
7 Salt Lake City, UT	8,504.9	21 Columbus, OH	7,195.5	35 Oklahoma City, OK	6,744.1
8 Everett, WA	8,257.6	22 Columbia, SC	7,053.0	36 Kansas City, MO	6,710.6
9 Spokane, WA	8,024.7	23 Yakima, WA	7,045.3	37 Lawton, OK	6,612.3
10 Flint, MI	7,917.1	24 San Antonio, TX	6,952.1	38 Fayetteville, NC	6,562.4
11 Columbus, GA	7,827.1	25 Buffalo, NY	6,921.9	39 Topeka, KS	6,546.4
12 Memphis, TN	7,796.6	26 Stockton, CA	6,920.1	40 Tulsa, OK	6,522.2
13 Springfield, IL	7,683.4	27 Rochester, NY	6,893.5	41 Rockford, IL	6,452.2
14 Knoxville, TN	7,586.5	28 Lafayette, LA	6872.2	42 Edinburg, TX	6,433.5

...CONTINUED

RANK AND CITY	RATE	RANK AND CITY	RATE	RANK AND CITY	RATE
43 Amarillo, TX	6,433.0	46 Fort Smith, AR	6,367.3	49 Berkeley, CA	6,305.7
44 South Bend, IN	6,407.1	47 Independence, MO	6,362.0	50 Milwaukee, WI	6,279.5
45 Winston-Salem, NC	6,382.2	48 Lubbock, TX	6,316.0		

Table 12.2 Crime Rate in 2010
National Rate = 3,345.5 Crimes per 100,000 Population*

Source: CQ Press using reported data from the FBI "Crime in the United States 2010"

*Includes murder, rape, robbery, aggravated assault, burglary, larceny-theft, and motor vehicle theft.

RANK AND CITY	RATE	RANK AND CITY	RATE	RANK AND CITY	RATE
1 New Orleans, LA	49.1	18 Richmond, CA	20.3	35 Milwaukee, WI	15.5
2 Flint, MI	48.5	19 Rochester, NY	20.1	36 Miami, FL	15.4
3 Camden, NJ	46.8	20 Miami Gardens, FL	20.0	37 Chicago, IL	15.2
4 St. Louis, MO	40.5	21 Richmond, VA	19.9	38 Vallejo, CA	14.9
5 Baltimore, MD	34.8	22 Philadelphia, PA	19.6	39 Norfolk, VA	14.5
6 Detroit, MI	34.5	23 Peoria, IL	19.2	40 Portsmouth, VA	14.1
7 Newark, NJ	32.1	24 Cleveland, OH	19.0	41 Yakima, WA	14.0
8 Compton, CA	26.6	25 West Palm Beach, FL	18.8	42 Tulsa, OK	13.7
9 Macon, GA	24.7	26 New Haven, CT	18.4	43 Rockford, IL	13.4
10 Jackson, MS	23.5	27 Trenton, NJ	18.0	44 Memphis, TN	13.2
11 Dayton, OH	22.3	28 Inglewood, CA	17.8	44 Salinas, CA	13.2
12 Oakland, CA	22.0	29 Pittsburgh, PA	17.6	46 Hammond, IN	13.1
13 Washington, DC	21.9	30 Kansas City, KS	17.4	47 Little Rock, AR	13.0
14 Kansas City, MO	21.1	31 Atlanta, GA	17.3	47 Shreveport, LA	13.0
15 Buffalo, NY	20.7	32 Stockton, CA	16.8	49 Longview, TX	12.8
15 Hartford, CT	20.7	33 Bridgeport, CT	15.8	50 Antioch, CA	12.7
17 Cincinnati, OH	20.5	34 San Bernardino, CA	15.6	50 Lakeland, FL	12.7

Table 12.3 Murder Rate in 2010
National Rate = 4.8 Murders per 100,000 Population

Source: Morgan, K. O., Morgan, S., & Santos, R. B. (2012). *City crime: Rankings 2011–2012* (p. 202). Los Angeles: CQ Press.

CONCLUSION

This chapter presented a discussion of the importance of developmental or life-course theories of criminal behavior. This perspective is relatively new compared with other traditional theories explored in this text—becoming popular in the late 1970s—but did not become a mainstream or popular perspective until the 1990s to now. Ultimately, this is one of the most cutting-edge areas of theoretical development, and life-course theories are likely to be the most important frameworks in the future of the field of criminological theory.

- Developmental or life-course theory focuses on the individual and following such individuals throughout life to examine their offending careers. This perspective puts a lot of emphasis on life events, often referred to as transitions (such as getting married or becoming employed in a stable job), which significantly affect an individual's trajectory in criminal behavior. In-depth consideration of changes during the life course are of highest concern, especially regarding general conclusions that can be made about the factors that tend to increase or decrease someone's likelihood to continue offending.

- Life-course perspectives emphasize such concepts as onset, frequency of offending, duration of offending, seriousness of offending, desistence of offending, and other factors that play key roles in when individuals offend and why they do so—or don't do so—at certain times in their lives. There are many critics of the developmental or life-course perspective, particularly those who buy into the low self-control model. This model is antidevelopmental in the sense that it assumes that propensities for crime do not change over time but, rather, remain unchanged throughout life.

- One of the developmental models that has received the most attention is that of Sampson and Laub, which emphasizes transitions in life (e.g., marriage, military service, employment, etc.) that alter trajectories either toward or away from crime. Moffitt's developmental theory of chronic offenders (whom she labeled life-course persistent offenders) versus more normal offenders (whom she labeled adolescence-limited offenders) is the developmental model that has received the most attention over the past decade, and much of this research is supportive of the interactive effects of biology and environment combining to create chronic, habitual offenders. Another key developmental theory is Thornberry's interactional model, which emphasizes different types of influences of certain factors at different times in our development, as well as the reciprocal or "feedback" effects of certain outcome variables on previous antecedent factors. This type of "feedback loop" can often result in a person becoming caught in a vicious cycle of criminality, which can become hard to escape.

- To follow up on the case study we discussed at the opening of this chapter, the Thornberry model is likely the best explanation for the case of the 14-year-old Tennessee boy arrested in connection with nearly 100 burglaries in the north Nashville area. Given that his parents had been absent for quite some time, as well as the rewards (or property) he was obtaining in stealing from these homes, the youth experienced success and then kept repeating the same illegal acts that allowed him to survive and be successful. Therefore, this created a cycle in which he lacked support from society, which forced him to do what it took to stay alive. When this paid off the first time, he naturally kept doing the same thing, time after time. Although this example may seem rather extreme, it is likely that many more individuals also face extremely deprived conditions that essentially force them to engage in high levels of criminal activity.

- In this chapter, we also examined the policy implications of this developmental approach, which emphasize the need to provide universal care for pregnant mothers as well as their newborn infants. Other policy implications include legally mandated interventions for mothers who are addicted to toxic substances (e.g., alcohol, drugs) and assignment of caseworkers for high-risk infants and children, such as those with birth or delivery complications. Such interventions would go a long way toward sparing society from the many problems (e.g., financial, victimization, etc.) that will persist without such interventions. Ultimately, a focus on the earliest stages of intervention will provide the "biggest bang for our buck."

- Ultimately, the chapter discussed life-course/developmental theory as one of the most important perspectives in criminology today, in terms of empirical validity of the theoretical framework and the growing attention being given to the model in the research and discussion in criminological literature.

SUMMARY OF THEORIES IN CHAPTER 12

THEORY	CONCEPTS	PROPONENTS	KEY PROPOSITIONS
Developmental/ life-course theory	Early onset, duration, persistence, frequency, desistence from crime	Various	Focus is on following individuals through life.
Developmental/ life-course theory	Transitions and trajectories	Sampson and Laub	Individuals can change and stop offending despite early propensities, especially when positive transitions occur (e.g., marriage, employment).
Developmental/ life-course theory	Life-course persistent offenders and adolescence-limited offenders	Moffitt	There are two primary types of offenders. The life-course type are more chronic offenders who start early and continue throughout life; the adolescence-limited type offend only during teenage years to early 20s and then grow out of it.
Developmental/ life-course theory	Interactions among predictive factors and reciprocal effects	Thornberry	Key predictive factors have differential effects at certain times in life. These variables tend to influence or interact with each other and cause "feedback loops," or reciprocal effects, in which an outcome variable influences a prior antecedent variable, such as when being caught offending causes further tension in parental relationships.
Antidevelop-mental theory	Low self-control	Hirschi and Gottfredson	Assumption that once low self-control disposition is formed by age 10, there is no way to change or develop away from criminality.

KEY TERMS

adolescence-limited offenders

developmental theories

life-course persistent offenders

Moffitt's developmental theory or taxonomy

Thornberry's interactional model

trajectories

transitions

STUDENT STUDY SITE

Visit the student study site at **www.sagepub.com/schram** to access links to the video, audio, city and state rankings, author podcasts, and SAGE journal and reference articles featured in this chapter, as well as additional study tools, including eFlashcards, web quizzes, web resources, and chapter outlines.

DISCUSSION QUESTIONS

1. What characteristic distinguishes developmental theories from traditional theoretical frameworks?

2. What aspects of a criminal career do experts consider important in such a model? Describe all the aspects they look at in a person's criminal career.

3. Discuss the primary criticisms regarding the developmental perspective, particularly that presented by Gottfredson and Hirschi. Which theoretical paradigm do you consider the most valid? Why?

4. What transitions or trajectories have you seen in your life or your friends' lives that support Sampson and Laub's developmental model? What events encouraged offending or inhibited it?

5. Given Moffitt's dichotomy of life-course persistent and adolescence-limited offenders, which of these should be given more attention in research? Why do you feel this way?

WEB RESOURCES

Developmental theories of crime

cooley.libarts.wsu.edu/garina/Soc3612/Documents/Lecture_20.ppt

Terrie Moffitt's theory

http://en.wikipedia.org/wiki/Terrie_Moffitt%27s_developmental_theory_of_crime

www.wpic.pitt.edu/research/famhist/PDF_Articles/APA/BF16.pdf

Sampson and Laub's model

http://harvardmagazine.com/2004/03/twigs-bent-trees-go-stra.html

Thornberry's interactional model

http://www.jstor.org/stable/1143788?seq=12

CHAPTER 13

White-Collar Crime, Organized Crime, and Cybercrime

INTRODUCTION

This chapter examines a large group of offenses that do not generally fit in the traditional concept of predatory street crimes, such as murder, rape, assault, burglary, and motor vehicle theft. Rather, the types of offending examined in this chapter include various types of white-collar, organized, and computer (or cyber) crimes. Although these crimes do not get near the amount of attention traditional street crimes (e.g., murder) get on the evening news or in newspapers, readers may be surprised to learn that these forms of offending cause far more damage to society, in terms of both property/financial losses and violence, than do all the street crimes combined. The first section covers those crimes generally referred to as *white-collar, corporate,* or *occupational.* This section provides students with a general overview of such topics as defining, measuring, and curbing white-collar crime, as well as discussing different types of crimes.

The next section presents various issues pertaining to organized crime, including types of organized crime groups and different criminal justice responses to these types of offenses. While in years past, clear distinctions were made between organized and white-collar crime, recently some researchers have maintained that these two types of offenses may be similar, rather than fundamentally distinct.[1] The last portion of this chapter illustrates how difficult it is for the criminal justice system to "keep up" with technological advances, specifically in the area of cybercrime (also referred to as hi-tech crime, computer crime, e-crime, or electronic crime).

WHITE-COLLAR CRIME

Despite years of being relatively ignored by researchers, **white-collar crime** is currently receiving much attention, probably due to high-profile chief executive officers (CEOs) and celebrities, such as Martha Stewart, being convicted of illegal business practices. Such types of corruption have existed since the earliest businesses formed many centuries ago, with historical records showing a high prevalence of unethical practices by businesses and governments throughout human civilization. However, white-collar crime is perhaps more emphasized today due to the global, multibillion-dollar nature of corporations in the modern world. Despite its presence throughout history, it is amazing that white-collar crime did not gain much attention from criminological researchers until the 1940s and remained a relatively low priority until the past few decades. This section examines the way the concept is defined and how it has evolved to the present day, with particular emphasis on its huge impact on modern societies, especially in the United States.

DEFINITIONS AND HISTORY OF WHITE-COLLAR CRIME

Experts in the area of white-collar crime consider it one of the most difficult concepts to define, with little consistency from researcher to researcher.[2] The first prominent acknowledgment of "white-collar crime" as an important concept for criminologists to study was presented at an American

LEARNING OBJECTIVES

While reading this chapter, students should consider the following topics:

- Understand and articulate the criteria experts use to distinguish white-collar crime from traditional forms of offending, as well as criticisms of these criteria.

- Understand and articulate the ways corporate crimes harm society in terms of physical and property damage, as well as in weakening the moral fabric of society.

- Understand the impact of corporate violations against the environment.

- Explain the function of the Occupational Safety and Health Administration in enforcing labor regulations.

- Appreciate the complexity in defining organized crime.

- Identify key historical events that have influenced and shaped organized crime.

- Discuss the different types of criminal organizations identified by the criminal justice system.

- Identify the various criminal justice responses to organized crime.

- Discuss how different theoretical explanations can be applied to enhance our understanding of organized crime.

- Appreciate the similarities and differences between traditional forms of crime and cybercrime.

- Identify various types of cybercrimes, such as hacking, identity theft, child pornography, Internet fraud, and cyberstalking.

- Appreciate some of the challenges associated with the investigation of cybercrime.

- Discuss some of the legislation that has been enacted to address cybercrime.

- Apply some "traditional" theoretical perspectives to explaining cybercrime.

MARTHA STEWART

In March of 2007, Martha Stewart was convicted of conspiracy, obstruction of an agency proceeding, and making false statements to federal investigators. Stewart is well known for her cooking talents and decorating suggestions, but she is also an extremely successful businesswoman; she founded the Martha Stewart Living Omnimedia Corporation. In 2001, biotech company ImClone Systems, Inc., was waiting for approval from the U.S. Food and Drug Administration (FDA) on a cancer drug. A day before the FDA denied approval for the cancer drug, Stewart sold her ImClone stock. She did so on a tip from her broker, Peter Bacanovic, who said that the ImClone chief executive was dumping his stock.

Stewart maintained that she was not acting on insider information; rather, she had arranged to sell her stock when it was at a certain price. As noted above, Stewart was not convicted of insider trading. She was convicted, essentially, of lying to investigators.[3] Stewart received a 5-month prison sentence in Danbury Federal Correctional Institution; in addition, she received another 5 months of house arrest and 2 years under supervision of a probation officer, as well as a fine of $30,000. Interestingly, on the next Friday after her sentencing, stock in her Martha Stewart Living Omnimedia Corporation rose from $2.63 to $11.27.[4] Does this fit your perception of crime? Does she fit the description of a criminal? Do you think she was treated differently than other offenders who had lied to investigators?

A DAY BEFORE THE FDA DENIED APPROVAL FOR THE CANCER DRUG, STEWART SOLD HER IMCLONE STOCK.

Sociological Society (ASS) conference in 1939 by **Edwin Sutherland**,[5] who coined the term *white-collar crime* and is generally considered the most prominent criminologist of the 20th century (for this and other work, such as the formation of differential association theory; see Chapter 9). In this presentation, which was the ASS Presidential Address, Sutherland did not provide a clear definition of white-collar crime but, rather, simply presented a variety of cases that seemed to apply.[6] For example, Sutherland discussed the racketeering cases against Chicago's Al Capone, as well as the Federal Trade Commission investigations of automobile companies that falsely advertised low-interest-rate loans and the false claims of some of Hearst's publications, such as *Good Housekeeping*. His discussion also included cases in which judges and various officials accepted bribes or engaged in other unethical practices in which they abused the power of their positions. Perhaps the reason why Sutherland did not provide a clear definition of crime in his address was because he first needed to convince other academics that white-collar crime is an actual, serious form of criminal activity, which at the time took some convincing. After all, perhaps the most profound statement he made in his address was: "White-collar crime is real crime."[7]

Before we discuss the contents and importance of Sutherland's Presidential Address, it is important to note that there was a notable history of research in the study of corporate and occupational crimes—even back to the ancient Greeks, who had issued decrees against those who forced up prices of imported grain, the penalty for which was death for that person and his entire family.[8] Although most textbooks claim that Sutherland introduced the concept of corporate, occupational, or industrial crimes, that is not true. Specifically, prior to Sutherland's address, there were numerous scientific studies on "white-collar bandits," "robber-barons," "corporate crime," "muckrakers," and "industrial crime," all of which refer to forms of corporate, industrial, occupational, or political corruption.[9] In fact, some of these studies are considered seminal, classic studies on the topic, such as Matthew Josephson's classic *The Robber Barons: The Great American Capitalists*[10] and George Anderson's *The Consolidation of Gas Companies in Boston*,[11] published in 1934 and 1905, respectively—well before Sutherland's address. So although Sutherland is often considered the scholar who created the concept of white-collar crime, this is far from true. There were many notable studies on corporate, occupational, and industrial offending prior to his 1939 address. Although similar terms, such as *white-collar bandits*, had been used many times before, Sutherland does deserve credit for coining the term *white-collar crime* and, more important, for bringing far more attention to the topic by making it the primary focus of his ASS Presidential Address, which was prominently reported by the mainstream press and significantly increased public attention for this type of offending.

At the end of Sutherland's Presidential Address at the ASS conference in 1939, he provided a summary list of his four primary propositions, the first (implying its importance) being that "white-collar criminality is real criminality, being in all cases in violation of the criminal law," which is a vague and weak definition.[12] In addition to this Presidential Address, Sutherland also published a study in 1945 on the prevalence of white-collar crime (discussed below); again, a clear definition of the concept was not provided.[13] However, in 1949 Sutherland published two works that supplied definitions, albeit still somewhat vague, for white-collar crime. One of these was *White-Collar Crime*,[14] in

Al Capone's mug shot, taken by the Chicago police after his 1931 arrest

AUTHOR PODCAST

White-Collar Criminals

VIDEO

Al Capone

white-collar crime:
criteria include (1) upper-class offender, (2) work-related violations, (3) work-related violations of blue-collar workers excluded, and (4) regular crimes committed by upper-class persons excluded

Edwin Sutherland:
coined the term *white-collar crime;* generally considered the most prominent criminologist of the 20th century

which he provided the definition in a footnote. In this footnote, Sutherland stated that white-collar crime

> may be defined approximately as a crime committed by a person of respectability and high social status in the course of his occupation . . . [which] excludes many crimes of the upper class, such as . . . murder . . . since these are not customarily a part of their occupational procedures . . . and refer[s] principally to business managers and executives.[15]

There are a number of things to note about this definition, which was perhaps the first somewhat specific explanation ever provided, although still relatively vague compared with those of more modern researchers. First, as you can see from the wording, particularly use of the word *approximately*, even Sutherland (the man who coined the term) appears to lack confidence in what "white-collar crime" means.[16] However, the definition contains some key distinctions that separate it from descriptions of typical street crimes.

The first necessary condition is that the offenders are at the top of the socioeconomic structure, which is somewhat inherent due to the requirement of having a "white-collar" job, as opposed to a "blue-collar" job or no job at all. According to this portion of Sutherland's definition, if a clerk at a fast-food restaurant steals money from the register, it is not considered white-collar crime because, although the person committed the crime while engaging in work-related duties, he or she clearly does not hold a white-collar position. Later, we will discuss modern criticisms of this requirement in defining white-collar crime.[17] Another key element of this definition is that offenses by upper-class individuals are considered white-collar crime only if employment related. A business executive may be a serial killer or a drug dealer, but if these violations do not pertain to his actual job, then they do not count as white-collar crime. Finally, the definition notes that this term refers "principally" to business executives, but such a word is vague (once again suggesting Sutherland's lack of confidence in specifying the exact meaning of the term) and therefore allows some deviation from including only violations committed by executives. Still, it is clear that the person must have a white-collar position to qualify, even if not a manager or high-ranking officer in the corporation.

The second relevant publication by Sutherland in 1949 was a brief, five-page entry titled "The White Collar Criminal" in Branham and Kutash's *Encyclopedia of Criminology*.[18] Despite its relative obscurity, this entry seemed to provide the most straightforward definition of this form of offending. Specifically, he wrote that the

> white-collar criminal is defined as a person with high socioeconomic status who violates the laws designed to regulate his occupational activities. . . . The white collar criminal should be differentiated . . . from the person of lower socio-economic status who violates the regular penal code or the special trade regulations which apply to him, and . . . from the person of high socio-economic status who violates the regular penal code in ways not connected with his occupation.[19]

For the most part, this definition is highly consistent with Sutherland's first definition, taken from *White-Collar Crime*. Specifically, in both definitions, Sutherland stipulates four criteria constituting white-collar crime: (1) the offender is upper-class, (2) the committed violations are work related, (3) the work-related violations of blue-collar workers are excluded, and (4) regular crimes (i.e., those occurring outside of employment) committed by upper-class persons are excluded. Also in the encyclopedia entry, Sutherland stated that the laws violated by white-collar offenders are sometimes in the regular penal code but often found only in regulatory or trade codes (many of which are now created and enforced by agencies such as the Securities and Exchange Commission, or SEC).

Perhaps the most important consequence of Sutherland's creation of the term *white-collar crime*, and his definition and promotion of the concept, was the almost immediate attention, particularly empirical studies, focused on the topic.[20] Although many of these studies failed to apply his definitional criteria to the offenses they examined, and some clearly deviated from the parameters set by his criteria, there is no doubt that Sutherland's writings and presentations between 1939 and 1949—not to mention his subsequent work in the area—got the ball rolling in terms of research and theoretical development regarding white-collar crime. Still, despite the criteria established by Sutherland, the term *white-collar crime* was both criticized and loosely applied to a variety of behaviors, particularly by the researchers of the 1940s through the 1960s, while others questioned the limits that had been set or the use of the term *criminal* in such situations.

Teamsters striking outside factory

For instance, some argued that many, if not most, of the persons Sutherland referred to had not been convicted in criminal court and therefore could not be considered "criminals" who had committed "crimes."[21] Sutherland responded to this argument by noting the need to emphasize the actual harm done by such acts and to acknowledge that what these individuals did was in violation of the mandate of legal codes, and that these factors should be emphasized more than the criminal justice system and/or society was doing in response to such offenders.[22] Unfortunately, even today white-collar criminals are far less likely than traditional street criminals to be investigated, caught, charged, and convicted, let alone sentenced to significant prison time. Perhaps the epitome of this type of minor "wrist-slapping" is seen in the case of Michael Milken (see Why Do They Do It? on the next page), who admitted to stealing about a billion dollars via illegal business practices and was ordered to pay back only about 60% of that, also spending only a few years in prison. (He later received a standing ovation in Congress after donating some money—likely stolen via insider trading—to prostate cancer research—likely because he had just been diagnosed with this disease.)

Some of these criminologists acknowledged considering the criteria established by Sutherland when determining whether the offenses they were examining deserved the label "white-collar crime." For example, one researcher explicitly questioned whether embezzlers were white-collar offenders, considering that many of them were not persons of high status, although most had committed their crimes during the course of their occupational duties.[23] A similar consideration was expressed by a researcher who examined individuals who had violated war time regulations regarding meat rationing, involving unauthorized distribution and/or consumption (i.e., the black market).[24] Other experts outright claimed that Sutherland's definitional criteria were far too restrictive and should allow for inclusion of any offenders working for a business.[25] These are just a couple of the many examples of offending that fall in the "gray area" between white-collar crimes and regular types of crime, as well as what is considered a true crime or criminal.

Another major cause of confusion when it comes to defining white-collar crime is that a variety of other terms have evolved that are typically used synonymously, although some would argue that these terms do have distinctions. These terms include, but are not limited to, *corporate crime, organizational crime, occupational crime, upperworld crime,*

▶ VIDEO

White-Collar Crime

NEWS CRIME IN THE NEWS

Corporate Crime

WHY DO THEY DO IT?

MICHAEL MILKEN

Soon, federal investigations of the junk-bond division of Drexel Burnham Lambert, Inc., resulted in Milken pleading guilty to six securities violations. He was sentenced to 10 years in prison but served only 22 months. He was also fined more than $1 billion and banned, for life, from the securities business, as well as from associating with any broker, dealer, or other investment professional.[28]

During the 1980s, Michael Milken was operating a $200-billion junk-bond business. Junk bonds are often unsecured or partially secured but, due to the high risk, are sometimes referred to as high-yield bonds.[26] Milken's personal compensation for these investments was $550 million in 1987; he earned more than $1 billion in a 4-year period. To put this in perspective, "every minute of every day and night, Mr. Milken earned about $1,046. . . . As he headed home from work he was close to breaking the $1 million mark."[27]

It has been more than 15 years since Milken was released from prison. During this time, he has lived through prostate cancer and raised millions of dollars for medical research. He has also sought a presidential pardon. Prior to President Bush leaving office in 2009, Milken was refused such a pardon. President Clinton also refused Milken's petition 8 years earlier. Interestingly, a number of influential individuals support his pardon; others, however, including some from the Justice Department and Wall Street, oppose it.[29]

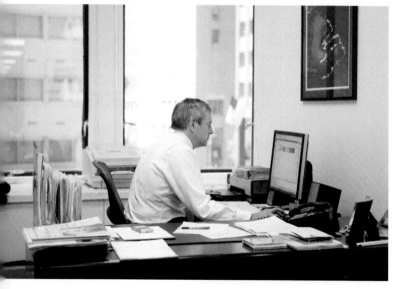

Corporate workers have plenty of opportunities to commit white-collar crimes and are often under pressure from the corporation to engage in such activities, especially when the company is not performing well.

business crime, and *suite crime* (as opposed to traditional *street crime*).[30] Some have even claimed that there is virtually no distinction between white-collar crime and organized crime (this issue will be discussed further in a later section in this chapter).[31] The many different terms used to identify white-collar crime add to the difficulty in developing a clear, explicit definition of this behavior. For example, a strong argument has been made regarding the difference between occupational crime and corporate crime: The former includes offenders at all levels of the business/social structure, whereas the latter is generally crime committed by managers or executives (often under the direction of the CEO or board of directors).[32]

One summary of the early scientific works on white-collar crime, particularly regarding definitional issues, concluded that the primary criterion is that the acts occur in relation to the offender's occupational role, which the author claimed was more important than the types of offending or the person's socioeconomic standing.[33] Unfortunately, there is also debate over what behaviors are considered a part of one's occupational role and, thus, what activities constitute white-collar crime. Even in more recent times, experts have offered refined definitions, such as suggesting that the primary criterion is abuse of a position of authority or trust.[34] Still other theorists go as far as to claim that there is no reason at all to distinguish white-collar crimes from traditional crimes.[35] Interestingly, some recent recommendations have been to go back to using Sutherland's original criteria,[36] an idea that appears to be gaining support.[37]

Despite such pointed criticisms and ongoing disagreements among criminologists about a clear definition of white-collar crime, a short list of the general categories of various white-collar offenses includes (1) fraud, (2) labor violations, (3) manufacturing violations, (4) unfair business practices, (5) abuse of authority, and (6) regulatory or administrative violations.[38] Each of these categories contains many specific forms of crime; in this chapter, some examples will be provided for each general type and variations discussed.

Examples of fraud include tax evasion and false advertising. Labor violations, discussed in detail later, include different forms of harassment and dangerous working conditions that can cause injuries and death. Manufacturing violations include the production and distribution of unsafe consumer

products, as well as environmental violations (e.g., toxic-waste dumping). The category of unethical business practices has likely gotten the most attention in the media recently, due to the prosecution and/or conviction of many high-ranking business executives in the United States. Examples of unfair business practices include insider trading, bid rigging, antitrust violations, and illegal mergers. Perhaps one of the better known categories for criminal justice practitioners is abuse of authority, which can take many forms, including bribery, extortion, brutality, kickbacks, and so forth. Finally, a host of rules and codes established by federal, state, and local agencies govern the functioning of businesses and other organizations; offenses against these codes are considered regulatory/administrative violations and include copyright, trademark, and patent infringements. There are literally thousands of other examples for these categories, but we have tried to provide some of the more common forms for each general grouping of white-collar offenses.

INCIDENCE AND IMPACT ON SOCIETY

After his Presidential Address to the ASS, Sutherland published a key study regarding corporate crime and violations by most of the largest companies in the United States at that time (the 1940s).[39] In this seminal study, Sutherland examined the decisions of courts and regulatory commissions against the 70 largest mercantile and industrial corporations in the nation. Considering that the study was done in the 1940s, the findings are quite startling. Sutherland found that a total of 547 adverse decisions had been made against these 70 companies, with an average of almost eight decisions per corporation. Even more surprising was the prevalence of the substantiated rule violations; specifically, every single one of the corporations that Sutherland included in his sample had a decision against it, which implies that all highly successful businesses in the United States had engaged in unethical practices (and been caught).

Perhaps most shocking, virtually every corporation committed more than one offense, with 97.1% recidivating. It appears that being caught and charged once did not do much to deter the businesses from engaging in unethical behaviors again. Readers should keep in mind that corporate crime is usually not discovered when it occurs, so the fact that almost every business in this study was caught more than once implies that the most successful companies actively and repeatedly engage in unethical activity for a profit. Interestingly, although Sutherland made a strong argument that all these activities were criminal, only 9% (49 out of the 547) of the decisions were made by criminal courts. The others were made mostly by federal or state oversight agencies, which often lack the power that criminal courts can wield in terms of punishment and/or stigma.

It is amazing that every highly successful company in the United States was found by an authoritative body to have committed a rule violation, and most had committed more than a handful of such violations. When comparing these rates of violations, some may argue that there were a higher percentage of companies committing such violations in the 1940s due to less regulation of the rules. However, that doesn't seem like a strong argument, because there was enough regulation to catch every single company (of the top 70) engaging in unethical practices and, furthermore, enough to catch most of them numerous times.

Has the increased amount of laws, regulatory codes, and investigation lowered this rate of violations among modern corporations? The scientific answer is that we do not know for sure if the rate is higher or lower, because there was no stable, consistent measure of such violations from the 1940s to now. But given the recent revelations regarding the extensive amount of grossly unethical practices at some of the nations most respected and "successful" corporations—especially those with strong political ties, such as Enron (see Why Do They Do It? on the next page), and others (e.g., WorldCom and Adelphia)—there has not likely been a significant reduction in the incidence of corporate criminality in the past 60 years.

After all, other investigations of the largest businesses in the nation have all found that corporate misbehavior is not the exception but the norm; in fact, it appears that the more successful the company, the more it has been charged with violations. For example, one analysis of the 582 largest manufacturing and retail/service corporations in the United States from 1975 to 1976 found that 60% of the corporations had at least one violation, and this was in just the 2-year period of the study! Close to half the companies had more than one violation, and some had more than 30 violations in this short period of time, which of course represents a chronic state of corporate offending.[40]

Furthermore, a review of corporate crime among the Fortune 500 companies found that well over half (62%) were involved in at least one violation between 1975 and 1984, while a more recent analysis found that every one (100%) of the 25 largest Fortune 500 corporations had been convicted of a violation between 1977 and 1990.[41] A recent review of the evidence of the rate (and causes) of modern white-collar crime concluded:

> The reality of corporate crime in U.S. society changes little from year to year. Corporate crime is rampant; corporations are criminal recidivists . . . and corporate crime is treated with kid gloves by government agencies and the criminal justice system.[42]

ECONOMIC COSTS

There is now little doubt that white-collar crime causes far more financial damage to society than all other crimes combined. As one recent review concluded:

> The general public loses more money *by far* . . . from price fixing and monopolistic practices and from consumer deception and embezzlement than from all the property crimes in the Federal Bureau of Investigation's Index combined. Yet these far more costly acts are either not criminal, or, if technically criminal, not

WHY DO THEY DO IT?

ENRON

Enron Corporation was founded in 1985 by Kenneth Lay. It was an energy company based in Houston, Texas. When Enron was established, natural gas and energy were produced, transmitted, and sold by state-regulated monopolies. These procedures were largely ineffectual. Enron creatively transformed energy supplies into financial instruments, which subsequently could be traded online like stocks and bonds.[43] In 15 years, Enron grew to become the United States' seventh largest company, with about 21,000 staff in more than 40 countries.[44] Apparently, the problems developed when Enron moved from trading energy to other trading ventures. So, "for a time, Enron swept its failures into creative hiding places, but ultimately the truth came out, confidence in the company collapsed."[45]

Enron attempted to hide its losses in an effort to protect company profits. The following is just one example of such an attempt:

> Enron invested a bunch of money in a joint venture with Blockbuster to rent out movies online. The deal flopped eight months later. But in the meantime Enron had secretly set up a partnership with a Canadian bank. The bank essentially lent Enron $115 million in exchange for Enron's profits from the movie venture over its first 10 years. The Blockbuster deal never made a penny, but Enron counted the Canadian loan as a nice, fat profit.[46]

The fallout of one of the largest bankruptcies in U.S. history included several high-level executives being sentenced to prison and thousands of people losing their jobs and retirement savings.[47]

prosecuted, or if prosecuted, not punished, or if punished, only mildly. In any event, although the individuals responsible for these acts take more money out of the ordinary citizen's pocket than our Typical Criminal, they rarely show up in arrest statistics and almost never in prison populations.[48]

Some modern estimates by the FBI's Uniform Crime Reports have put the cost of all street crimes at close to $17 billion for the year 2002.[49] In a shocking comparison, just one act of corporate crime (Enron) in the early years of the millennium resulted in estimated losses of $60 billion, and the Savings and Loan Industry bailout from 1989 is estimated to cost taxpayers $473 billion by the year 2020 (showing the long-term consequences of such events).[50]

So the "suite" crimes committed by Enron caused more than 3 times the financial damage of all "street" crimes combined, not to mention the impact of the Savings and Loan bailout. And these are just *two* cases discovered and brought to public attention. Furthermore, a "very conservative" estimate of the total economic costs from white-collar crimes each year is about $500 billion, about 30 times (i.e., 3,000%) greater than the total for combined street crimes.[51] Some readers will be surprised to know that this works out to an average loss of about $1,800 per person annually from corporate crimes, compared with the estimated loss of about $60 per person from combined street crimes. And yes, we are all paying for such corporate crimes, because such losses, bailouts, recovery funds, and so forth typically come out of federal or state funds, which means taxpayers are picking up the bill.

PHYSICAL COSTS

The financial cost of white-collar crime is not the most disturbing type of damage that results from corporate misbehavior. Most experts now agree that the scientific evidence clearly shows "corporate crime kills, maims, and injures enormously larger numbers of innocent people than all street crimes combined."[52] Empirical studies are consistent regarding the high numbers of deaths and physical injuries that directly result from the wrongdoings of business executives.

For example, one study showed that a conservative estimate of how many individuals die annually due to corporate crime is at least 105,000 persons, which includes about 55,000 employees who were harmed while working (including occupational illnesses), another 30,000 consumer deaths from unsafe products, and at least 20,000 citizen deaths from a variety of types of environmental pollution.[53] Of course, these estimates do not include how many persons are dying from falsely prescribed or marketed pharmaceutical drugs, which likely totals many thousands each year and, due to the aging population in the United States, is probably increasing every year—as is the number of people who die from criminally negligent nursing home or medical care.

Finally, these estimates do not include the estimated 4.7 million Americans harmed (but not killed) at work, which includes 4.4 million persons who suffered physical injuries and 300,000 who contracted occupational illnesses (getting sick due to work conditions),[54] with a high percentage of these directly due to corporate crime. These workplace injuries are far more common than injuries due to traditional street crimes and, on average, are more serious than the common wounds suffered from assaults on the street. This was measured by comparing the number of workdays missed due to work-related injuries/illnesses versus workdays missed due to violent assaults; the average number of days missed from work was higher for those injured on the job.

JOURNAL ARTICLE

Corporate Fraud

It is important to keep in mind that there are only about 15,000 homicides due to street crimes in the United States each year (it was far higher in the early 1980s).[55] So compared with the previous estimates of annual deaths, it appears that corporate crime causes at least 7 times (and likely 10 times) more deaths than do traditional street crimes (i.e., 1,000% more deaths from corporate crimes than street crimes). Furthermore, it also appears that while the rate of homicides and assaults due to street crimes has been cut in half over the past 25 years (with most of this decrease coming in the past 15 years), there is no indication that deaths or injuries due to corporate crimes have decreased; on the contrary, there is evidence that such injuries are on the rise.[56] A recent review of the empirical evidence comparing the damages between traditional and white-collar crime concluded: "The total of all violent crime and all property crime combined is less of a threat to society than the crime committed by corporations."[57]

BREAKDOWN IN SOCIAL FABRIC

Beyond the relatively high levels of economic and violent damage caused by white-collar crimes, a number of theorists have made the argument that these "suite" crimes are also far worse than "street" crimes in terms of the damage done to the moral and social fabric of society.[58] To clarify, they argue that corporate crime creates a higher level of immorality in American society because of the nature of hypocrisy typically inherent in the offenders and/or offending. After all, these offenders are often individuals who are looked up to by other members of society, and they are often persons, such as community leaders, politicians, or judges, who have condemned and even prosecuted others for street crimes that didn't inflict near the damage of their own "suite" crimes. As Clinard and Yeager (1980) claim in their classic work:

It is hypocritical to regard theft and fraud among the lower classes with distaste and to punish such acts while countenancing upper-class deception and calling it "shrewd business practice." A review of corporate violations and how they are prosecuted and punished shows who controls what in law enforcement in American society and the extent to which this control is effective; . . . corporate crime is generally surrounded by an aura of politeness and respectability rarely if ever present in cases of ordinary crime.[59]

Furthermore, most high-profile businesses guilty of corporate wrongdoing had strong political ties to certain groups—namely, the Republican Party. Specifically, an analysis showed that virtually every corporate violator made more contributions to the Republican Party (with a generally more pro-business or laissez-faire [hands-off] attitude) than to the Democratic Party.[60] However, the history of corporate and white-collar violations clearly is on both sides of the aisle, in terms of political ideology.

When we poll our students about how serious they perceive white-collar crime to be compared with street crimes, they often claim that they don't care much about white-collar crime because it doesn't directly affect them. But indeed it does! After all, who will be paying for the Enron fallout, the Savings and Loan scandal of the late 1980s, fraudulent insurance claims, and the other thousands of corporate violations each year? American taxpayers and consumers. Furthermore, we are far less likely to be injured or killed by traditional street offenders than by corporate offenders, whether from unsafe pharmaceuticals, hazardous consumer products, or dangerous working conditions.

Ultimately, we hope readers will consider the argument that the damage caused by white-collar crimes outweighs the damage inflicted by all traditional street crimes combined, in terms of property, violence, and destruction of the fabric of society. We will now examine several notable forms of white-collar crime. Although there are hundreds of varieties of corporate offending, due to space limitations, we concentrate here on what we consider to be the most influential and/or fastest growing types of white-collar crime: violations against the environment, labor violations, and organized crime (i.e., racketeering).

Pollution and chemical runoff have plagued many cities with various toxins over the years. Only in the past few decades have officials tried to curb this threat to individuals.

CRIMES AGAINST THE ENVIRONMENT

Although forms of pollution have existed throughout human civilization, the real turn for the worst for the environment was the Industrial Revolution (mid-1700s to mid-1800s), which is generally considered by historians to be one of the most important periods in the world's history (and our nation's in particular) in terms of progress. After all, that period resulted in a dramatic shift from rural-based economies to industrial-based economies.

In the preindustrial period, the farmers were dependent on the land; so for the most part, they treated it well. Once the Industrial Revolution hit, there were countless numbers of factories and plants that had no concern for the environment, and this resulted in unprecedented dumping of deadly chemicals and waste products into bodies of water, toxins being released from endless streams of smoke coming out of factory chimneys, and massive destruction of majestic forests and natural resources. However, there was virtually no understanding of the damage being done, and pollution was not acknowledged as a concept, let alone a problem.

LEARNING CHECK 13.2

1. According to the text, studies show what percentage of the largest 25 corporations in the Fortune 500 were convicted of a violation between 1977 and 1990?

   a. 20%

   b. 40%

   c. 60%

   d. 80%

   e. 100%

2. According to the text, white-collar/corporate crimes cost U.S. society far more each year in terms of injuries/deaths than all street crimes combined. True or false?

   Answers located at www.sagepub.com/schram

AUDIO

Environmental Crime

CRIME IN THE NEWS

Labor Violations

In the 20th century, it became obvious that much damage had been done; so efforts have since been made to repair and restrict harm against the environment. Many laws and regulations were passed, and entire federal, state, and local agencies were created, such as the most prominent federal agency, the **Environmental Protection Agency** (EPA; see http://www.epa.gov/). The EPA is not a Cabinet agency, but the administrator (appointed by the president) is normally given Cabinet rank; so he or she certainly has almost daily contact with the president of the United States.

The EPA, started in 1970, is charged with protecting human health and safeguarding the natural environment, which is quite a burden.[61] For instance, the United States contains 30,000 waste sites, along with more than 10 billion pounds of toxic chemicals that pose a significant threat of pollution.[62] Furthermore, the EPA estimates that there are about 60,000 deaths—mostly among the elderly and young children—each year in the United States as a direct result of toxic particles emitted from manufacturing plants. Also, in one recent year, the EPA identified 149 manufacturing plants throughout the nation where air in nearby communities was tested as being toxic and dangerous.[63]

The EPA often works with the U.S. Department of the Interior and U.S. Department of Agriculture in developing and enforcing regulations to protect the environment from corporate crimes. These include laws against air pollution, against water pollution, for preserving forests and other natural areas, for appropriate hazardous waste disposal, and for protecting endangered species. This has been one of the most common areas of corporate violation over the past few decades, and the EPA has been busy. Although the vast majority of the near-20,000 people working for the EPA are doing their best to protect us and the environment, imagine their shock, as well as the public's, when it was discovered that EPA executives in the early 1980s were committing corporate crime. Specifically, Rita Lavelle was appointed by President Reagan and put in charge of a large fund to clean up the most extreme cases of corporate pollution resulting from improper disposal of hazardous waste.[64] She participated in questionable decisions with some of the most chronic corporate polluters and used the dispersal of monies for political purposes; she was later convicted on four felony counts in 1983. So again, here is an example of the hypocrisy of white-collar crime and how it destroys the moral fabric of society. After all, why should any business respect the environmental codes when the very people who create and enforce the codes have been known to engage in high levels of corruption?

Environmental Protection Agency: started in 1970, charged with protecting human health and safeguarding the natural environment

LABOR VIOLATIONS

One of the more common corporate violations involves crimes against the people who work for the business. Like environmental crimes, these types of offenses became far more common during and after the Industrial Revolution. Labor violations range from hiring illegal workers (e.g., children) to exploiting workers to keeping unsafe work conditions, and many more variations.

The primary legislation developed to investigate labor violations is the **Occupational Safety and Health Act** (OSHA), passed in 1970. Among other things, this act made it a misdemeanor to cause the death of a worker by willfully violating safety laws; this remains a misdemeanor to this day.[65] Unfortunately, the maximum jail time for this offense was 6 months, which some theorists have noted is half the maximum term for a person caught riding a wild burro on federal lands.[66] OSHA inspectors are charged with establishing and enforcing standards for the safety of American workers; however, that means overseeing 115 million workers, which is near impossible, especially with only about 2,500 inspectors. So they remain busy and often find violators.

For example, OSHA conducted about 40,000 inspections in 2003 alone, finding about 83,600 violations.[67] Violators are sometimes fined, but even then these fines are usually relatively low in relation to the profits being made by the companies. Also, OSHA almost never pursues criminal charges; between 1970 and 2002, OSHA referred only 151 cases to the Department of Justice for criminal prosecution, despite finding tens of thousands of violations each year. Of these 151 cases, only 11 resulted in prison sentences, with the maximum being 6 months. A comprehensive analysis of 170,000 workers killed during the 20-year period from 1982 to 2002 revealed that OSHA investigated only about 24% of these cases, and even in the cases where willful safety violations occurred, the fines were typically $70,000 or less and jail time was extremely rare.[68]

This photograph illustrates the dangerous conditions associated with child labor. In 1836, Massachusetts was the first state to pass a minimum-age law for workers.

Thus, it is obvious that little enforcement or deterrence is involved in labor violations, even by OSHA. So corporations simply have little or nothing to lose by even willfully violating the labor regulations and codes. Interestingly, labor issues, especially regarding worker unions, are often related to the next category of white-collar crime we will discuss—organized crime and racketeering.

TRANSNATIONAL COMPARISONS OF WHITE-COLLAR/CORPORATE CRIME

Although most of this chapter emphasizes white-collar and corporate crimes in the United States, it is now clear that similar crimes happen just as often, if not more, throughout various regions of the world. Unfortunately, the occurrence of such illegal activities is not measured well in virtually any of these regions, including the United States. Still, there are some indicators of such corporate offending across many countries, provided by the International Crime Victimization Survey (ICVS), the Corruption Perception Index, and Transparency International—with most of the focus on bribes among business experts (see Comparative Criminology: Bribery).

REFERENCE ARTICLE

Corporate Crime

In terms of more street-level corruption (such as bribing police officers or other local authorities), which is the best measure we have for the less-developed countries, one recent study by Van Dijk collected data from 92 countries and examined both the data from ICVS and Transparency International surveys from the early 2000s. These surveys focused on the percentage of the general public involved in paying bribes to local officials in a given year.[69] This study reported that such corruption was highest in two regions of the world: West/Central Africa and East Africa (South Asia ranked a distant third). These were by far the regions with the highest percentage of households reporting paying bribes

Occupational Safety and Health Act: among other things, made it a misdemeanor to cause the death of a worker by willfully violating safety laws

COMPARATIVE CRIMINOLOGY: *BRIBERY*

Ranking Countries as Likeliest for Companies to Pay or Offer Bribes to Win or Retain Business

In this section, we examine findings and conclusions from the Transparency International Annual Report of 2003, which since 1999 has administered among business experts in 15 emerging market countries global surveys regarding the propensity of international companies to offer or pay bribes to win or retain business in their nations.[70]

This comparison is applicable to the chapter in the sense that it provides a relatively recent analysis of the extent to which countries are perceived to be corrupt in terms of soliciting bribes to encourage business opportunities in their countries. The portion of the Transparency International report that we are concerned with here is the ranking of countries based on responses of business experts to the question of how likely the companies from certain countries are to pay or offer bribes to win or retain business in that country. It should be noted that rankings are based on a scale of 10 (zero perceived propensity to pay bribes) to 1 (highest perceived propensity to pay bribes), with higher scores indicating lower likelihood for paying bribes. So the higher the score, the better the country's businesses are rated in terms of ethics, at least as related to offering bribes.

According to the findings in the Transparency International report (see Table 13.1), the country that scored the highest on this rating—meaning it had the lowest level of perceived propensity to receive bribes—is Australia; Sweden and Switzerland closely followed.[71] This is not too surprising given the international respect for business ethics in these countries, especially in Sweden and Switzerland. However, our focus is on the countries that scored lowest on this measure, which were

Russia and China, as well as the category of Domestic Companies. It is likely that the final Domestic Companies category scored lowest on this rating because virtually all respondents being offered bribes experienced this in their own countries. But this is basically a "wash," or constant, because it can be assumed that most of the experts surveyed largely deal with companies in their own country; so we will not explore that category.

Regarding Russia and China, this low ranking is very much in line with other rankings of corporate corruption, such as bribe taking and ICVS rankings of countries.[72] Furthermore, neither of these countries are members of the Organisation for Economic Co-operation and Development (OECD), which was adopted in 1997 after an urgent request by the U.S. government and other nations.[73] Ratified by the majority of industrialized countries, an obligation from the OECD requires countries to criminalize payment of bribes in their government legislation. Russia and China are not part of that coalition, and, as shown by the results, their reluctance to join is connected to their failure to crack down on bribery tactics.

Notably, the United States ranked below the middle of the group, coming in at number 13 out of 21 countries. Obviously, this is not good, because our nation is perceived by many leading experts to be below average in terms of ethical business practices. This is alarming, because so many economically competing nations, such as Canada, the United Kingdom, Germany, and France, scored better on this ranking. On the other hand, we were perceived as the same as or less corrupt than other rival nations (in terms of economic viability), such as Japan, Italy, and South Korea. Still, this relatively recent ranking shows that the United States is largely perceived as being relatively corrupt in terms of paying or offering bribes to win or retain contracts for business in our country.

RANKING BY COUNTRY		
RANK	COUNTRY	SCORE
1	Australia	8.5
2	Sweden	8.4
3	Switzerland	8.4
4	Austria	8.2
5	Canada	8.1
6	Netherlands	7.8
7	Belgium	7.8

8	United Kingdom	6.9
9	Singapore	6.3
10	Germany	6.3
11	Spain	5.8
12	France	5.5
13	United States	5.3
14	Japan	5.3
15	Malaysia	4.3
16	Hong Kong	4.3
17	Italy	4.1
18	South Korea	3.9
19	Taiwan	3.8
20	People's Republic of China	3.5
21	Russia	3.2
22	Domestic companies	1.9

Table 13.1 Ranking of countries, based on responses to the question: "In the business sectors with which you are most familiar, how likely are companies from the following countries to pay or offer bribes to win or retain business in this country?"

Source: Transparency International, Annual Report, 2003.

to local authorities. Given the extreme deprivation in such areas, these results reveal that persons in even the lowest forms of power (e.g., police officers) likely take advantage of their relatively high status by victimizing those they can. Although this type of street-level corruption is often not seen as white-collar crime in the United States, we must understand that in many regions of the world, the local police authorities are the equivalent of our white-collar workers and CEOs.

At this time, it is virtually impossible to estimate the level of various white-collar crimes and corporate crimes committed in the numerous countries of the world. It is hoped that in the near future, far more information will be available regarding how often various countries are victimized by a larger range of white-collar and corporate crimes.

THEORETICAL EXPLANATIONS OF WHITE-COLLAR CRIME

Although historically the empirical research on theories explaining white-collar crime was limited, in the past few decades there has been a significant increase in attention to this area. A recent review of the extant scientific research testing the empirical validity of various theories discussed previously in this book found that some theories performed better than others in explaining white-collar crime.[74] Specifically, various studies were examined regarding the theories of differential association/social learning, techniques of neutralization, deterrence/rational choice, cultural/subcultural, routine activities/opportunity, strain, and low self-control theory and the political/economic ideologies of capitalism versus communism/socialism.

Regarding the conclusions that can be reached from this recent review of the empirical research, the theory of differential association, techniques of neutralization, and other social learning principles are extremely valid in understanding the influence of the corporate world. In white-collar crime, however, it is not a person's significant others (e.g., friends, family, etc.) who form the important definitions of doing "good" but, rather, their supervisors and fellow professional colleagues, who are most likely to affect decisions to act unethically in business practices. Furthermore, this is consistent with the use of excuses or neutralization techniques to allow an individual to do what he or she knows is inherently wrong for the good of a higher authority (e.g., company, supervisors, loyalty to colleagues, etc.). In fact, one recent study showed that executive MBA candidates, who had much experience in the corporate world, were significantly more likely to use neutralization techniques in explaining why they agreed to marketing and selling an admittedly dangerous drug than were normal MBA students, who had far less experience in the corporate world.[75]

This may help explain why there is virtually no evidence for deterrence at the corporate level; after all, studies have shown that the more often a company is caught for violations, the more likely it is to engage in such acts in the future. This is easily understood by the simple fact that the companies that have been caught have gotten away with such violations for many years without being caught, and they know that the potential benefits far outweigh any sanctions they may face if they are caught for a few of their total violations. Relatedly, portions of rational choice theory are strongly supported by empirical research, in the sense that violating ethical business rules often gains much in terms of financial profit and/or employer recognition. This also relates to the cultural/subcultural findings regarding motivations to commit white-collar crime, which clearly show the significant cultural emphasis in most companies that focus solely on making a profit; thus, any other normative value system pales in comparison with helping contribute to the profit margin. And once a person starts working in a company, that individual tends to take on the mentality or normative culture of the company, with few exceptions. After all, that company is paying individuals and providing their livelihood; so it is only natural that a person would start internalizing the subcultural beliefs and goals promoted by the group directly responsible for his or her success or survival.

Such subcultural influences of peers and supervisors in a corporate environment likely take over as the dominating force, especially regarding the teaching of ethics for business majors at most universities. Such moral beliefs are key in social bonding theory, as well as a key conditional variable in many rational choice theories of offending. However, as said before, studies show that the cultural norms of one's environment seem to overwhelm university-led ethical training.[76] Not surprisingly, an individual will typically follow the orders of superiors and/or subcultural pressures among colleagues to make a profit for the company, despite any ethical principles learned in school or from personal beliefs.

Regarding opportunity theories, such as routine activities theory, the ready-made opportunity to commit various white-collar crimes is quite attractive, especially given the low likelihood of being caught and the ease of achieving economic gain via one's everyday job. After all, there doesn't seem to be much of a downside to engaging in illegal and unethical behavior in most white-collar positions, especially when one sees on the news that even when someone is caught and convicted, that person usually doesn't spend any time in prison. And even when such persons do serve time, it is often at a minimum-security facility—quite a difference from serving "hard time." So there doesn't seem to be much certainty or severity of punishment, but there is likely to be a huge payoff or promotion if one does engage in unethical practices. Given the current enforcement of laws against illegal behaviors among white-collar professionals, it only makes sense to engage in criminal activity. Until more certain enforcement and far more severe penalties are mandated, it is highly unlikely that the perceptions and motivations of white-collar workers will change, especially given the constant opportunities to engage in such activity.

Regarding strain theory, especially institutional anomie theory, there is believed to be an American cultural value of monetary success, which often takes priority over other important social factors (i.e., family, friends, education, etc.). This strain for success, or even greed, has its source in both individuals and corporations. Furthermore, the source of strain for monetary gain emanates from both internal and external sources to the company, ranging from the internal performance of specific employees to more macro-level economic trends in the market.

In terms of conflict theory, especially regarding the overall political or economic ideology of various corporations (such as across various countries), studies show that whether a company is based in more communistic countries versus more capitalistic countries, the goal is profit. Specifically, studies have shown that white-collar crime existed at a high rate in more socialist and communist countries.[77] This is likely due to these countries not having much enforcement against such practices, since they are believed not to exist in such idealistic societies. But greed is a universal pattern, so you will find it everywhere, in any society and at any time.

After reviewing all the relevant empirical studies for each of the theories above, the authors concluded:

> The majority of empirical research in white-collar crime thus far has been built off traditional theories that were originally developed to explain conventional crimes. However, white-collar and conventional offenders . . . are distinctly different. . . . Our next step should be to move beyond conventional explanations.[78]

We agree with this assessment, and more topic-specific theories must be created to understand fully the reasons and motivations for committing white-collar crime. This is also true of another form of corporate-related offending, which we will discuss next—organized crime and racketeering.

ORGANIZED CRIME

For decades, the American public has had a curious fascination with organized crime. For instance, when John Dillinger was gunned down by the Federal Bureau of Investigation in 1934, there were photographs of his body in the morgue. In fact, the Cook County (Chicago) morgue allowed the public to view his body. The public enjoys watching movies or television programs that depict the so-called mob lifestyle, such as *The Godfather*, *Goodfellas*, and *The Sopranos*. However, many of these movies and television programs contain some myths or "entertainment" license. In this chapter, we provide students with a general overview of issues pertaining to organized crime, beginning with a definition and followed by the historical context of organized crime in the United States. Next we will review different types of criminal organizations, as well as criminal justice responses to organized crime. We will conclude this section with a brief outline of various theoretical explanations for this type of criminal activity.

JOURNAL ARTICLE

Organized Crime

DEFINITION OF ORGANIZED CRIME

In the 1986 *Report to the President and the Attorney General*, the President's Commission on Organized Crime noted that when defining organized crime, the problem is not in the

APPLYING THEORY TO CRIME: *WHITE-COLLAR CRIME*

In this section, we discuss several theories that seem to explain some of the reasons why individuals engage in various forms of white-collar crime. First, it should be apparent that although most crimes don't pay well, white-collar crime often does come with a large payoff. Second, the individuals in white-collar positions tend to have a low likelihood of getting caught; even if they are caught, they are typically not punished severely. So given the obvious failure of traditional, formal deterrence theory in trying to explain this phenomenon, we must turn to other theoretical frameworks.

Despite its similarity to traditional deterrence, one theoretical model that has shown much promise in understanding criminal decision making in the corporate world is rational choice theory. In a recent review of the extant research, Paternoster and Tibbetts (forthcoming) concluded that one of the key reasons for the empirical support of rational choice theory over formal deterrence theory is that the informal pressures and controls that exist within a corporation often override any possible deterrent effect from authorities outside the organization. Rational choice theory places an emphasis on accounting for such informal factors and, thus, is an improvement over models focused on formal sanctions, or lack thereof.

Additional theoretical models found to be helpful in explaining white-collar crime include the social process/learning models of differential association/reinforcement theory, which place an emphasis on the influence of significant others in individuals' decisions of whether or not

to engage in illegal behavior (Akers, 1985; Sutherland, 1939). A study by Piquero, Tibbetts, and Blankenship (2005) showed that several components of the differential association theoretical framework did, in fact, predict intentions to make unethical business decisions in a scenario presented to participants (MBA students). The scenario involved a drug that was known to cause detrimental (even fatal) side effects. However, it wasn't the perceived attitudes of peers or family or business professors that led to higher intentions to commit the unethical act of further marketing and selling the dangerous drug; it was the attitude of coworkers and the perceived beliefs of their employers/bosses that actually had a greater impact on participants' decision to commit this illegal act.

Thus, it appears that social learning theory is supported for white-collar crime but not in the same way as for most street crimes, which typically are more influenced by family or good friends. Rather, the influence of such social learning factors in predicting white-collar/corporate crime is actually more due to the differential associations and reinforcements present in the workplace environment. These findings are consistent with additional research that has examined the validity of cultural/subcultural theory in understanding white-collar crime, with the vast majority of findings supporting the use of this framework in corporate offending (Shover & Hochstetler, 2002; for a recent review of these studies, see Schoepfer & Tibbetts, 2012). What virtually all the studies reveal is that the climate in the corporation plays a much stronger role in individuals' decisions to commit white-collar

crime than do other associations or learning from significant others, such as parents, peers, and/or professors from their college years.

Another theory tested in the Piquero et al. (2005) study was that of techniques of neutralization, which are strategies used by offenders to alleviate their guilt for committing an act they know is wrong. In this study, there were numerous such neutralization techniques examined, and it was found that several of them (e.g., denial of responsibility, appeal to higher loyalties) were highly important in decisions to engage in illegal corporate activity. The participants noted the importance of making a profit for their company as trumping any type of hesitation in making their decision, despite what friends or family would think.

Ultimately, the rational choice perspective has been supported as an important framework for understanding individuals' perceptions and intentions to engage in illegal business practices. Also, the social learning theories of differential association/reinforcement, as well as the concepts of techniques of neutralization, appear to be highly influential among individuals in their decisions to engage in unethical behavior when it comes to white-collar crime. These theories are consistent with the empirical validity found for cultural and subcultural models of unethical corporate decision making.

Other theories can help explain why individuals engage in white-collar crime, but the three theories discussed in this section are the most supported models for understanding crime in the corporate realm.

Sources: Akers, R. L. (1985). *Deviant behavior: A social learning approach* (3rd ed.). Belmont, CA: Wadsworth; Paternoster, R., & Tibbetts, S. G. (forthcoming). White-collar crime and perceptual deterrence. In N. Shover (Ed.), *The Oxford handbook on white-collar crime.* Oxford, UK: Oxford University Press; Piquero, N. L., Tibbetts, S. G., & Blankenship, M. B. (2005). Examining the role of differential association and techniques of neutralization in explaining corporate crime. *Deviant Behavior, 26,* 159–188; Schoepfer, A., & Tibbetts, S. G. (2012). From early white-collar bandits and robber barons to modern-day white-collar criminals: A review of the conceptual and theoretical research. In D. Shichor, L. Gaines, & A. Schoepfer (Eds.), *Reflecting on white-collar and corporate crime: Discerning readings* (pp. 63–83). Long Grove, IL: Waveland; Shover, N., & Hochstetler, A. (2002). Cultural explanation and organizational crime. *Crime, Law and Social Change, 37,* 1–18; Sutherland, E. H. (1939). *Principles of criminology* (3rd ed.). Philadelphia: Lippincott.

word *crime*; rather, the difficulty is with the term *organized*.[79] One approach to defining organized crime is to incorporate a typology. This typology includes such factors as the means of obtaining the goals (e.g., violence, theft, corruption) and the reasons for engaging in such activities—an economic objective (e.g., through common crime, illegal business, or legal business) or a political objective (e.g., through the existing order, against the existing order).[80]

While there is no agreed-on definition of organized crime, Howard Abadinsky listed various factors associated with this type of criminal activity, as identified by law enforcement agencies and researchers.[81]

1. Organized crime is nonideological.

2. Organized crime is hierarchical.

3. Organized crime has limited or exclusive membership.

4. Organized crime perpetuates itself.

5. Organized crime is willing to use illegal violence and bribery.

6. Organized crime consists of specialization or division of labor.

7. Organized crime is monopolistic.

8. Organized crime is governed by rules and regulations.

HISTORICAL CONTEXT OF ORGANIZED CRIME IN THE UNITED STATES

No sooner had crime become profitable in America than it became organized. And no sooner did it become organized than it became a regular part of the American way of life, thanks to the cooperation and collusion of government officials. Organized crime did not begin with twentieth century Prohibition. It began with the colonial pirates.[82]

Some argue that pirates during the American colonial era were a form of organized crime group. These pirates developed a well-structured, hierarchical organization; engaged in nonideological goals; and had a restricted membership.[83]

Crime at the end of the piracy era was essentially disorganized. By the turn of the 19th century, New York City was the "entrepreneurial center" of the country. Many immigrants entered the country to seek freedoms, opportunities, and fortunes. These factors also made New York the center for conspiracies, crooks, and criminals.[84] In the 1850s, gangs began to dominate the criminal arena. These gangs included the Forty Thieves, the Hudson Dusters, the Short Tails, and the Dead Rabbits; they evolved when groups of immigrants banded together for protection as well as for the exploitation of other immigrants. These gangs eventually formed partnerships with the political machines of the time in an effort to control their vice enterprises.[85] One notorious political machine was **Tammany Hall**. Tammany Hall got its name from the Indian Chief Tammaned. It was founded in 1789 to oppose the ruling conservative Federalist party. A primary strength of Tammany Hall was its skill to elect candidates to the state legislature in Albany and to the board of aldermen in New York City.[86]

In 1919, the Eighteenth Amendment to the Constitution was passed, outlawing the manufacture, sale, distribution, and transportation of alcoholic beverages.[87] Prohibition created an opportunity for criminals. Even with the passage of the Eighteenth Amendment, they recognized the need for a major infrastructure to meet the public demand for alcohol, including production, transportation, and importation. Prohibition and the

organized crime: sometimes defined through a typology, such as the means of obtaining the goals and the reasons for engaging in such activity: an economic objective or a political objective

Tammany Hall: a notorious Democratic political machine in New York City from the 1790s through the 1960s, with major influence in city and state politics

THE TAMMANY TIGER LOOSE.—"What are you going to do about it?"
(The first use of the famous Tiger symbol)

This cartoon appeared in *Harper's Weekly* in November 1871, the day before the election.

VIDEO ▶

Prohibition

Chicago political machine created one of the most notorious criminal organizations in this country's history. One of the most infamous of these criminals, epitomizing Chicago during Prohibition, was Al Capone.[88] Prohibition provided an opportunity to transform Italian, Jewish, and Irish gangsters into more powerful groups. The profits earned from illegally supplying alcohol were great; however, even with a more powerful position, many of these gangs continued to operate as they did in their "wild early days."[89] This would oftentimes result in violence among various gangs to obtain control over this illegal market.

In response to the need for tax revenue during the Great Depression, the state of Nevada legalized gambling in 1931. Bugsy Siegel was the first prominent criminal to realize the potential of legalized gambling.[90] In 1947, the Flamingo Hotel in Las Vegas, Nevada, was opened. This opening designated the onset of organized crime control of the legal gambling industry.[91] Given their experience as "bootleggers," organized crime groups had the business acumen to control gambling. Many of the lavish hotels, such as the Flamingo, were controlled, albeit through hidden interests, by organized crime. Usually, monies were "skimmed" before being counted for tax purposes; this money was distributed to the organized crime bosses in proportion to their "hidden" ownership. In fact, from 1973 to 1983, at least $14 million was skimmed from just one hotel, the Stardust. Today, Las Vegas is not controlled by organized crime; rather, casinos are now major corporate entities.[92]

In 1986, the President's Commission on Organized Crime noted that of the various developments in organized crime during the preceding 20 years, three developments are significant. One is the increasing awareness that other organized crime groups exist. While many are ethnic based, others originated in U.S. prisons and outlaw motorcycle gangs. Another development is the success of law enforcement against the leadership, membership, and associates of *La Cosa Nostra*, which is considered by some to be the best-known organized crime group in the past 30 years. The third significant development is organized crime's involvement in drug trafficking:[93] "It is essential that we broaden our view to include all significant facets of organized crime. There will be little lasting benefit in disabling *La Cosa Nostra* if other groups successfully claim its abandoned criminal franchise."[94]

Today there is growing concern over organized crime groups using advances in technology to engage in various criminal activities. While we specifically discuss cybercrime in the following section, Zambo claimed that cybergangs are organized in a similar fashion to the Mafia; the major difference is that cybergangs operate completely online.[95] Examples of such crimes include credit card cloning, phone card piracy, computer viruses, child pornography, electronic banking fraud, music piracy, counterfeit medicine, and software piracy.[96]

TYPES OF CRIMINAL ORGANIZATIONS

As stated above, it is essential that law enforcement recognize that organized crime is not synonymous with the Mafia. In this section, we begin with a brief discussion of the

Mafia followed by discussion of other types of criminal organizations, including outlaw motorcycle gangs, prison gangs, and urban street gangs.

THE MAFIA

The origins of the Mafia are unclear. One opinion is that the Mafia evolved as a 9th century response to Arabic domination of Sicily. Another view is that the Mafia evolved in Palermo, Italy, in 1282 as a political organization to free Sicily from French domination. The group's rallying cry was "*Morte alla Francia Italia anela*" ("Death to the French is Italy's cry"). The acronym of this pledge is MAFIA.[97] The true origins of the term *Mafia* are convoluted by assorted use and personal preference.[98] Some of the most common references are listed in Table 13.2. Originally, the Mafia was similar to an extended social family. While not necessarily related by blood, members were related by home village and Sicilian nationality. The members took an oath, swearing under punishment of death to a code of silence. Initially, the Mafia was a self-protection group; by the 1860s, however, they had expanded to criminal activities such as smuggling, cattle rustling, and extortion.[99] While the term *Mafia* referred to beauty, perfection, grace, and excellence, the term Mafioso referred to characteristics of a man, such as pride, self-confidence, and an "arrogant" attitude.[100]

In 1878, the Italian government began concentrated efforts to eliminate the Sicilian Mafia. Thus, many Sicilian Mafiosi immigrated to the United States, settling in major urban cities such as Boston, Chicago, Kansas City, New Orleans, New York, and St. Louis.[101] The Mafiosi in the United States were similar to other immigrants. When these criminals entered the United States, they assimilated with others but continued their criminal activities. From 1890 to the 1920s, the Mafiosi preyed on other immigrants by forcing their participation in the protection scam. This was known as *La Mano Nero*, or "The Black Hand." Soon their activities expanded to other crimes, especially during Prohibition.[102]

Michael Lyman and Gary Potter pose an interesting question: "Does the Mafia really exist?" They provide arguments from both positions. From the "yes" position, they note that there have been high-profile trials on such "mob bosses" as Al Capone, Sam Giancana, "Lucky" Luciano, Vito Genovese, and John Gotti. While the convictions of these "bosses" did not result in total disbanding of the organization, they did provide law enforcement the opportunity to survey, monitor, arrest, interview, and collaborate with members of the Mafia and other organized crime groups. Some also maintain that

JOURNAL ARTICLE

The Mafia

Term	Definition
Maffia	Tuscan word for *misery*
Mauvia	French word for *bad*
Ma-afir	Arabic tribe that settled in Sicily
MAFIA	*Mazzini autorizza furti incendi auvelenamenti*, or Massini authorizes thefts, arson, and poisons
Mu'afy	Arabic word meaning "protects from death in the night"
Mafia	The name of a stone quarry in Sicily
I Mafiusi di la Vicaria	The title of a play written in 1860 by Guiseppe Rizzotto, *The Heroes of the Penitentiary*.

Table 13.2 Common References to the Term *Mafia*

Source: Albini, J. (1971). *Mafia: Genesis of a legend.* New York: Appleton-Century-Crofts, p. 83.

Mafia: similar to an extended social family; members took an oath swearing, under punishment of death, to a code of silence. It started as a self-protection group, but by the 1860s expanded to criminal activities such as smuggling, cattle rustling, and extortion.

Mafioso: referred to characteristics of a man, such as pride, self-confidence, and a sense of "arrogant" behavior in 1963, Joe Valachi revealed information about the structure of the Mafia, claiming that there were about 25 Italian gangs throughout the United States, referred to as "families."

From the "no" position, some argue that there is no single organization known as the Mafia; rather, there are loosely structured criminal gangs, some of which are of Italian descent. These Italian gangs, or families, do exist but are not as organized or structured as thought by law enforcement and the media. These individuals maintain, however, that by claiming the existence of a well-organized Mafia, law enforcement agencies can justify their existence.[103]

OUTLAW MOTORCYCLE GANGS

During the late 1940s, **outlaw motorcycle gangs** (OMGs) evolved as disorganized and unruly groups made up of disgruntled World War II veterans. Through the decades, the tough-guy image was perpetuated and membership increased, along with the organization and sophistication of these groups.[104] Soon, some of these groups' behavior was more rebellious than openly criminal.[105] In fact, OMG members refer to themselves as "one-percenters":

> Some years ago . . . the American Motorcycle Association . . . [estimated] that outlaw motorcyclists comprised less than one per cent of the motorcycling population. Outlaw gangs immediately seized on the figure as a reflection of their belief that they are rebels, operating outside society's laws and norms.[106]

While the 1% figure is meaningless today, members refer to themselves as "one-percenters" to flaunt their status as lawless outsiders.

OMGs today are secretive and close-knit groups with selective membership. Membership in OMGs is symbolized by "colors," which are often displayed on denim or leather jackets with embroidered patches sewn on the back. These patches display a gang logo and may also include "rockers" that identify the name of the gang and home city of the chapter. The colors are the member's most prized possession and represent his primary commitment—to the gang and its criminal lifestyle. The outrageous treatment of women who associate with the members is also part of the OMG lifestyle. Women are considered less important than the gang itself or the member's motorcycle. In some gangs, women are used to generate money through prostitution as well as for the transportation of drugs and weapons.[107]

Some of the most notorious OMGs include the Hells Angels, the Outlaws, the Bandidos, and the Pagans (see Table 13.3). Among these, the Hells Angels are regarded as the wealthiest and most powerful of the OMGs. They have not only an extensive membership in the United States but also chapters in Brazil, Canada, Colombia, Australia, New Zealand, Japan, and seven Western European countries. The Hells Angels also have a sophisticated and wide-ranging counterintelligence structure as protection from arrest and prosecution.[108] There are sophisticated but smaller OMGs, including the Vagos (in the West and Southwest), the Warlocks (in the region of Pennsylvania, New Jersey, and Delaware), the Dirty Dozen (in Arizona), the Gypsy Jokers (in the Pacific Northwest), and the Sons of Silence (in Colorado).[109]

PRISON GANGS

Some have attributed the growth of prison gangs to the 1964 U.S. Supreme Court decision **Cooper v. Pate**. As a result of this decision, prisoners were allowed to sue state officials in federal court, which resulted in a great deal of litigation and changed prison conditions in the 1970s. Gangs grew in the more liberal prison environment. Prior to *Cooper v. Pate*, only Washington and California reported the existence of prison gangs; by 1984, this number had risen to more than 60% of state and federal prisons reporting gang activity. By the 1990s, some of these prison gangs had evolved into well-organized

VIDEO ▶

OMGs

outlaw motorcycle gangs: the tough-guy image of these groups was perpetuated and membership increased, along with organization and sophistication. Soon, behavior of some groups was less rebellious and more openly criminal; some members refer to themselves as "one-percenters."

Cooper v. Pate: as a result of this decision, prisoners were allowed to sue state officials in federal court, which resulted in much litigation and changed the prison conditions in the 1970s.

PAGAN'S MOTORCYCLE CLUB CONSTITUTION

CLUB ORGANIZATION

The Pagan motorcycle club is run by the Mother Club. The Mother Club has last and final say so on all club matters. Any violation of the constitution will be dealt with by the Mother Club.

CHAPTER ORGANIZATION

Six (6) members needed to start a chapter. No new chapter may be started without approval of the Mother Club.

PRESIDENT

Runs chapter under the direction of the Mother Club. Keeps chapter organized, makes sure chapter business is carried out, inspects all bikes before runs and makes President meetings.

SERGENT-AT-ARMS

Makes sure President's orders are carried out.

VICE-PRESIDENT

Takes over all President's duties when the President is not there.

SECRETARY-TREASURER

In charge of minutes of meetings and treasury. No members may change chapters without the Mother Club Members permission in his area. All present chapter debts are paid and is approved by the president of the new chapter he wishes to change to. If a member has a snival, he must use chain of command, in other words, (1) His Chapter President, (2) Mother Club member in area, (3) President of Club.

MEETINGS

1. Chapters must have one organized meeting per week.

2. Chapter meetings are attended by members only.

3. Members must be of sound mind (straight) when attending meetings.

4. If a Mother Club member attends a meeting and a member is fouled-up, he will be fined by the Mother Club member.

5. Miss three (3) meetings in a row, and you're out of the club.

6. Members must attend meeting to leave club and turn in his colors and everything that has the name PAGANS on it. (T-shirts, Wrist Bands, Mugs, Etc.)

7. If a member is thrown out of the club or quits without attending meeting, he loses his colors, motorcycle, and anything that says PAGANS on it, and probably an ass kicking.

8. When a member is traveling, he must attend meeting of the area he is traveling in.

9. If a vote is taken at a meeting and member is not there, his vote is void.

10. Member must have colors with him when attending meeting.

BIKES

1. All members must have a Harley Davidson 750-1200 CC.

2. If a member is not of sound mind or too fouled-up to ride his motorcycle in the opinion of another member, his riding privilege may be pulled by said member until he has head together.

3. All bikes must be on the road April 30th, or otherwise directed by the Mother Club.

4. All members must have a motorcycle license.

MANDATORIES

Two (2) mandatories, July 4, and Labor Day, Mother Club may call additional mandatories if need be.

FUNERALS

1. If a member dies in a chapter, it is necessary for all members in his chapter to attend funeral.

2. Chapter is in charge of taking care of all funeral arrangements, parties, police, procession, etc.

...CONTINUED

PARTIES
Pagan parties are Pagan parties only. Each chapter must throw (1) party or run a year.

RESPECT
1. Respect is to be shown to all Mother Club members, officer members, member's personal property, Bike, Old Lady, House, Job, etc. In other words, if it's not yours, "Don't Mess With It."
2. No fighting among each other is allowed, any punches to be thrown will be done by the Sgt.-at-Arms or a Mother Club Member.
3. No stealing from members.
4. Respect your Colors.

COLORS
1. President gets colors from Mother Club member in area when new members is voted in.
2. When a member leaves club, the president of his chapter turns over his colors to the Mother Club member in his area.
3. Respect your Colors, don't let anyone take them from you except the president of your chapter or a Mother Club member.
4. No colors are worn in a cage, except during funerals and loading or unloading a bike from a truck.
5. Nothing will be worn on the back of your jacket except your colors, Diamond, 13 Patch.
6. No Hippie shit on the front.
7. Colors are to be put on cut off denim jackets only.
8. The only member who may keep his colors if he leaves the club is a Mother Club Member.

OLD LADIES
1. Members are responsible for their Old Ladies.
2. Members may have more than one (1) Old Lady.
3. Members may not discuss club business with their Old Lady.
4. No Old Ladies Allowed at meetings.
5. No property patch is worn on an Old Lady. So if you see a chick you better ask before you leap.

PROSPECTS
1. Prospect must be at least 18 years old.
2. Prospect must be sponsored by one member who has known him at least one year.
3. Sponsor is responsible for respect.
4. Prospect must have motorcycle.
5. Prospect must ride his bike to meeting at time of being voted into club.
6. Prospect can not do any drugs.
7. Prospects can not carry weapons at meetings and Pagan functions, unless otherwise directed by the President.
8. No stealing from Prospects.
9. Prospects must attend all meetings and club functions.
10. Prospect must do anything another member tells him to, that a member has done or would be willing to do himself.
11. Prospect must be voted in by all members of the chapter and Three (3) Mother Club Members.
12. Prospect must pay for his colors before received them.
13. Prospects period is determined by Mother Club Member.
14. Pagan's M.C. is a motorcycle club and a non-profit organization.

Table 13.3 Pagan's Motorcycle Club Constitution

Source: From Abadinsky, H. *Organized crime*, 6e (pp. 234–235). © 2000 Wadsworth, a part of Cengage Learning, Inc. Reproduced by permission.

crime groups. These gangs were different from previous gangs primarily in their demand for absolute obedience to the "parent" group. For instance, the "death oath," or "blood in and blood out," requires the member to remain a member forever.[110] Specifically, this oath requires that to become a member, an inmate must kill or assault another prisoner or staff member; if a member wants to leave the gang, then his blood "will be spilled."[111]

Organized in the late 1950s, one of the oldest prison gangs is the Mexican Mafia, whose members are primarily Mexican Americans from Southern California.[112] In some prisons, the Mexican Mafia controls homosexual prostitution, gambling, and narcotics. Both inside and outside prison, the Mexican Mafia is involved in burglary, assault, robbery, extortion, drug trafficking, and contract killing. Another major prison gang is La Nuestra Familia, considered an enemy of the Mexican Mafia. This prison gang was established in Soledad Prison (California) in 1967. La Nuestra Familia's outside prison operations include a protection racket, similar to more traditional organized crime groups. The Texas Syndicate originated in Folsom Prison (California) in 1974. The members are predominately Mexican Americans from the El Paso and San Antonio region. The gang has a reputation for being one of the most violent. The Black Guerilla Family was established at San Quentin Prison by black activist prisoner George Jackson in 1966. This gang is closely associated with the Crips street gang. The Black Guerilla Family is controlled by a central committee consisting of generals, captains, lieutenants, and soldiers. The Aryan Brotherhood is a motorcycle-oriented, white-supremacist gang founded in San Quentin Prison in the 1960s. The Aryan Brotherhood's criminal activities include extortion, protection rackets, drug trafficking, and contract killing.[113]

URBAN STREET GANGS

Using Maltz's[114] characteristics associated with organized crime groups, Dennis Kenney and James Finckenauer evaluated whether urban street gangs could be deemed organized crime groups. The first characteristic of organized crime groups is *corruption*. At this time, there is no evidence to support the notion that urban street gangs systematically engage in paying off public officials in an effort to avoid arrest and prosecution. The second characteristic, *violence* or the threat of violence, is a major feature of urban street gangs. The third characteristic, *continuity*, is a feature for certain street gangs. Some gangs, such as social or party gangs, are more spontaneous; they exist as a gang for a short period of time and quickly split up. The fourth characteristic is *multiple enterprises*. The drug "business" is essentially the only enterprise for urban street gangs. While some may be involved in other types of crime, such as property crime, they do not run illegal business enterprises such as gambling, prostitution, and loans.

Structure and involvement in legitimate businesses is the fifth characteristic. While some street gangs appear to have some type of organizational structure, there does not seem to be a great deal of expansion from illegal business into legitimate business. The last characteristic is *sophistication, discipline, and bonding*. While some gangs engage in sophisticated activities, such as speaking in code over the telephone, most gangs do not. In reference to discipline, many urban gangs, especially those involved in the drug business, do stress the need for discipline. Finally, many street gangs emphasize bonding, such as rituals and initiation rites.[115]

CRIMINAL JUSTICE RESPONSES TO ORGANIZED CRIME

CHICAGO CRIME COMMISSION

In 1919, a group of Chicago businessmen, concerned about Chicago's "gangland" reputation, formed the Chicago Crime Commission. While some would argue that the Commission

Ranking Regions/Countries as Most Likely for Organized Crime

In this section, we examine the findings and conclusions of various studies regarding organized crime, which typically includes certain elements, such as use of extreme violence, corruption of public officials (such as police and judicial officers), penetration of the legitimate economy (often through money laundering), and interference in the political process.[116] The findings of these recent studies on prevalence of organized crime across various regions/countries are surprising in many ways.

One of the key measures of organized crime in the world is the Organized Crime Perception (OCP) Index, which is a combined measure using data from various sources, such as the World Economic Forum (a survey of CEOs of large companies), the World Bank and European Bank of Reconstruction and Development, and The Merchant International

Group Ltd (an internationally active security consultancy group). Although many factors go into the OCP Index, it is generally considered the most accurate measure to determine how much organized crime is perceived and how much is actually present in most regions/countries around the world.[117]

According to the OCP Index, the traditional notion of Mafia-type activities being concentrated in Italy and other nearby locations can be largely dispelled. As seen in Figure 13.1, the countries with the highest scores on the OCP Index as compared with unsolved homicides has Italy ranked about in the middle in terms of Mafia-type activities, as well as with a relatively low ranking in terms of rates of unsolved homicides. Rather, the countries of Colombia, Venezuela, Zimbabwe, and the Russian Federation have the highest scores on both Mafia-type activities and rates of unsolved homicides. (Note: The United States was absent from this comparison.)

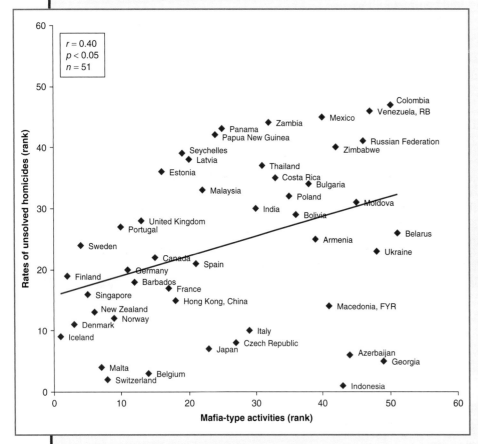

Figure 13.1 Prevalence of Mafia-Type Activities as Perceived by Business Leaders and/or Security Experts and Rates of Unsolved Homicides (Ranked Variables)

Sources: World Economic Forum, Global Competitiveness Reports, 1997–1998 to 2003–2004; Merchant International Group, 2004; BEEPS, 2002; 8th UN Crime Survey.

In addition, Van Dijk correlated the OCP Index with another index that measured high-level corruption in many countries.[118] The findings of this analysis, as shown in Figure 13.3, reveal that the highest scoring countries on both organized crime and political corruption included Iraq (the highest on both scores), Ukraine, Nigeria, Haiti, Pakistan, Venezuela, and the Russian Federation. It is interesting to note that the United States scored relatively low on both these measures. Given the noticeably high prevalence of organized crime and political corruption in the United States (as suggested by constant media reports of political corruption and recent arrests for organized crime), it is shocking that we are doing better than most countries on these two types of criminal

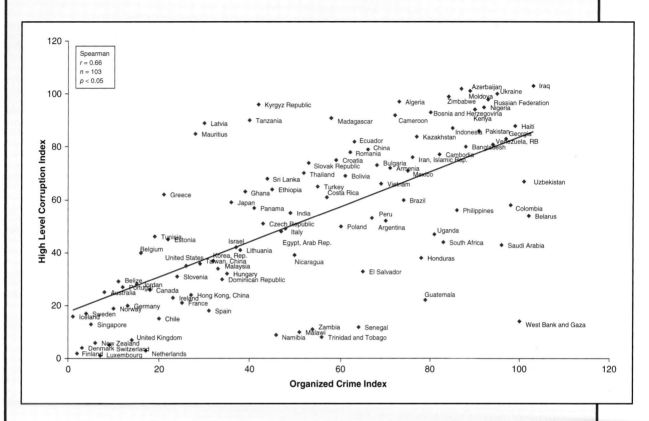

Figure 13.2 Prevalence of Perceived Organized Crime and Regional Scores on Composite Index Measuring High-Level Corruption/State Capture

Sources: World Economic Forum, Global Competitiveness Reports, 1997–1998 to 2003–2004; Merchant International Group, 2004; BEEPS, 2002; Buscaglia & Van Dijk, 2003.

activity—at least according to these various measures. It is also notable that the countries that scored relatively higher on both organized crime and political corruption in this analysis were from scattered regions of the world, including the Middle East, Asia, Africa, North America/the Caribbean, and South America. Probably the only area that scored low on this analysis was the Australian continental region.

Thus, it can be concluded that organized crime is prevalent in virtually all parts of the world, as is political corruption. So the myth of Mafia-type organizations being largely present in Italy and the United States can be absolutely dismissed. Organized crime is alive and well throughout virtually all societies, and as shown in the results in Figure 13.2, is likely to be correlated with political corruption as well.

was "a self-serving exercise in hypocrisy,"[119] it was able to demonstrate the city's crime problem through a successful public relations campaign. For instance, the public relations committee introduced the "Public Enemy" list prior to J. Edgar Hoover's version.

THE WICKERSHAM COMMISSION

To assess the effect of Prohibition on criminal activity, the **Wickersham Commission** was formed in 1929. The findings from the commission revealed that organized criminal activity flourished around bootlegging activities. The commission recommended a

Wickersham Commission: formed in 1929, the commission found that organized criminal activity flourished around bootlegging operations.

more in-depth study of organized crime and its criminal activities. This study did not occur, however, until years later. This delay was attributed to various factors, including the well-publicized arrests and prosecutions of organized crime "bosses" such as Al Capone and "Lucky" Luciano, giving the public a sense that law enforcement and the criminal justice system were successfully deterring such activities. Further, the public's attention was focused on such social concerns as the Great Depression and World War II. Given these "diversions," organized crime prospered, and it was not until the formation of the Kefauver Committee that there was an extensive investigation into organized crime.[120]

THE KEFAUVER COMMITTEE

In May of 1950, Senator Estes Kefauver became chair of the Special Committee to Investigate Organized Crime in Interstate Commerce. The **Kefauver Committee** was charged with three responsibilities:

1. Conducting an extensive study and investigation to assess whether organized crime uses the services, or avenues, of interstate commerce to promote any transactions that violate federal or state law

2. If such transactions do occur, investigating the identification of the persons, firms, or corporations involved

3. Determining whether such interstate criminal operations were responsible for developing corrupting influences in violation of federal or state laws[121]

During Kefauver's term as chair, the committee heard from more than 600 witnesses in Miami, Tampa, New Orleans, Kansas City, Cleveland, St. Louis, Detroit, Los Angeles, San Francisco, Las Vegas, Philadelphia, Washington, Chicago, and New York.[122]

The Kefauver Committee provided invaluable information on organized crime; however, the committee did not provide support for the existence of an international Mafia conspiracy:[123]

> Neither the Senate Crime Committee in its testimony nor Kefauver in his book presented any real evidence that the Mafia exists as a functioning organization. . . . The only other "evidence" presented . . . is that certain crimes bear "the earmarks of the Mafia."[124]

THE MCCLELLAN COMMITTEE

In the early 1960s, the Senate Permanent Subcommittee on Investigation, chaired by Senator John McClellan, was formed to investigate labor racketeering in the country's trade unions. In 1963, the committee held televised hearings, including the testimony of Joseph Valachi, the first "made member" of the Genovese crime family to testify on Italian American organized crime:[125]

> Valachi was a barely literate, low-echelon soldier whose firsthand knowledge of organized crime was limited to street-level experiences. Much of the information attributed to him is obviously well beyond his personal experience. . . . Nevertheless, this did not prevent his disclosures from becoming the core of a chapter on organized crime in the final report of the President's Commission on Law Enforcement and Administration of Justice.[126]

Valachi's testimony did not result in any convictions; further, the McClellan Committee failed to recommend a specific definition of organized crime. These hearings, however, did contribute to the government's understanding of this type of criminal activity.[127]

Kefauver Committee: in 1950, charged with three responsibilities that focused on whether organized crime used services of interstate commerce to engage in illegal activities and identifying the persons, firms, or corporations involved in such activities

THE PRESIDENT'S COMMISSION ON LAW ENFORCEMENT AND THE ADMINISTRATION OF JUSTICE

In 1965, President Lyndon Johnson established the President's Commission on Law Enforcement and the Administration of Justice; there were nine different task forces, one of which was the Task Force on Organized Crime. In its 1967 report to the commission, the task force noted:

> Today the core of organized crime in the United States consists of twenty-four groups operating as criminal cartels in large cities across the Nation. . . . To date, only the Federal Bureau of Investigation has been able to document fully the national scope of these groups, and the FBI intelligence indicates that the organization as a whole has changed its name from the Mafia to *Cosa Nostra*.[128]

The commission maintained that gambling was the largest source of revenue for organized crime, followed by loan sharking and narcotics trafficking.[129] The task force continued efforts initiated by the Kefauver Committee. Further, the task force made various recommendations, including a witness protection program, special federal grand juries, and legislation allowing electronic surveillance.[130]

ORGANIZED CRIME CONTROL ACT OF 1970

As a result of the President's Commission on Law Enforcement and the Administration of Justice, Congress passed the Organized Crime Control Act in 1970. A key component of this legislation was Title 9—specifically, the **Racketeer Influenced and Corrupt Organizations (RICO) Act.** It would take nearly a decade, however, for authorities to adequately apply RICO. There are three criminal penalties for RICO violations, which can be applied simultaneously: (1) a fine of no more than $25,000, (2) a prison term of no more than 20 years (for each racketeering count), and (3) the forfeiture of any interest obtained or maintained in the course of state violations.[131]

THE PRESIDENT'S COMMISSION ON ORGANIZED CRIME

Under Executive Order Number 12435, President Reagan created the President's Commission on Organized Crime in 1983. During its 3 years of existence, the commission produced five reports. Some of the key issues highlighted by the commission included the problem of money laundering, labor union racketeering, and "mob lawyers." The commission avoided the primary focus on Italian American organized crime, focusing also on Colombian cocaine cartels and other criminal groups, such as outlaw motorcycle clubs.[132]

The commission also provided a more meaningful definition of organized crime. Further, in an effort to enhance its understanding of organized crime groups, the commission developed a contingency model that highlighted levels of involvement of members and nonmembers; these levels included the criminal group (i.e., the core of the organized crime unit), the protectors (e.g., corrupt public officials, businesspersons, judges, attorneys, financial advisers), specialized support (i.e., those who provide services that facilitate organized crime, such as pilots, chemists, arsonists, and hijackers), user support (i.e., consumers of organized crime's illegal goods and services, such as drug users, and people knowingly buying stolen goods), and social support (i.e., those who provide the perception of legitimacy of these criminal groups, such as politicians who seek the support of organized crime members and community leaders who invite these crime members to social gatherings).[133]

THEORETICAL EXPLANATIONS OF ORGANIZED CRIME

Dennis Kenney and James Finckenauer noted that while there had been some positive developments in understanding organized crime, there were criticisms that this type of

Racketeer Influenced and Corrupt Organizations (RICO) Act: provides for enhanced criminal and civil penalties for individuals engaging in activities with criminal organizations

LEARNING CHECK 13.3

The President's Commission on Organized Crime noted that when defining organized crime, the problem is with the word _____. Outlaw motorcycle gangs refer to themselves as "_____-percenters." Some have attributed the growth of prison gangs to the 1964 U.S. Supreme Court decision _____. A key component of the _____ was the Racketeer Influenced and Corrupt Organizations (RICO) Act.

Answers located at www.sagepub.com/schram

criminal activity lacked a sound theoretical framework.[134] Kenney and Finckenauer reviewed various theoretical perspectives that attempt to provide an understanding of organized criminal behavior, such as cultural transmission, culture conflict, and strain theories, as well as low self-control theory. Another theoretical perspective they discussed was ethnicity and ethnic succession:

> Organized crime has been described as being "caused" by the efforts of successive immigrant groups to make it in America. Cut off from legitimate opportunities for achieving socioeconomic and political success, immigrants have been forced by circumstances to climb . . . the "queer ladder" of upward social mobility, namely, crime, and especially organized crime.[135]

Another theoretical perspective presented was enterprise theory. This perspective maintains that the legitimate marketplaces do not provide an opportunity for customers to obtain goods and services; thus, illicit entrepreneurs fill this void by providing such goods and services themselves.[136]

They concluded this chapter with an outline of a theory proposed by Peter Reuter.[137] Reuter was attempting to understand under what circumstances some gangs are deemed organized crime groups. He contends that adult gangs are primarily in existence for economic purposes—specifically, to make money. Another key characteristic is the supply and demand conditions that help organized crime flourish. Thus, according to Reuter, three factors affect the extent of organized crime in a particular city:

1. Illegal market opportunities (e.g., gambling, drugs, and loan sharking) that are contingent on coordinated groups of people in frequent interaction

2. The extent of recent migration of significant ethnic groups into the community, allowing for recruitment as well as potential clients for goods and services

3. The strength and corruptness of local political authority[138]

Kenney and Finckenauer stress that Reuter's "mini-theory" provides an exploratory foundation for conceptual and empirical research in an effort to enhance our understanding of organized criminal behavior. Further, a sound theoretical framework is essential to providing effective intervention to prevent and control organized crime.

AUDIO

Cybercrime

CYBERCRIME

In September 2011, Tony Perez, a 21-year-old Indiana man, was sentenced in U.S. District Court in Virginia after admitting to operating an online business that sold counterfeit credit cards encoded with stolen account information. He received a 14-year federal prison sentence and was ordered to pay $2.8 million in forfeiture and a $250,000 fine. Perez used various online personas in criminal "carding forums," Internet discussion groups established to assist in buying and selling stolen financial account information, as well as through other avenues and services to promote credit card fraud. The U.S. Secret Service, upon executing a search warrant at Perez's apartment, found thousands of fraudulent transactions totaling more than $3 million.[139]

Cybercrime is a relatively new area of criminal activity. As there have been tremendous advances in technology in recent years, there have also been tremendous advances for criminal opportunities using this technology. In this chapter, we provide a brief definition of *cybercrime,* followed by a general overview of various types of cybercrime, such as hacking, identity theft, and cyberstalking. Next, we present some of the criminal justice responses to cybercrime. We conclude this section by reviewing some theoretical explanations of cybercrime.

DEFINITION OF CYBERCRIME

Scholars have recognized some of the issues surrounding terms and definitions for crimes committed by electronic means, terms such as *computer crime, computer-related crime,* and *cybercrime.* There is a question of whether this process of definitional clarification is "hyper-defining":

> The result of such hyper-definition is to negate some emerging legislation. This is not to suggest that legislators should cease efforts to specifically criminalize computer-specific criminal activity. Indeed, further legislation should be pursued to enhance prosecutorial toolboxes, not to replace or supplant traditional mechanisms.[140]

Another term was introduced for such crimes—*high-technology crime.* This refers to any criminal act involving the use of high-technology devices. Examples of high-technology devices include computers, telephones, check-reading machines, and credit card machines. High-technology crimes can comprise traditional crimes committed prior to technological developments and more recent crimes that use high-technology devices.[141] Thus, this term incorporates crimes that may involve *limited use* of computers and networks as well as those that *completely rely* on the use of computers and networks.[142]

Soumyo Moitra acknowledged that there were initially heated debates as to the various definitions for these crimes; however, he maintained that the term *cybercrime* has gained in both usage and popularity. Interestingly, *cybercrime* was derived from the term *cyber-space,* originated by the author William Gibson.[143] Cybercrime was defined as follows: "any unauthorized, or deviant, or illegal activity over the Internet that involves a computer (or computers) as the tool to commit the activity and a computer (or computers) as the target of that activity." **Cybercrime** consists of at least three features: The act was committed using (1) a computer, (2) a "victim" computer, and (3) an intermediary network.[144]

TYPES OF OFFENSES

HACKING

The term *hacker* most likely emerged from the electrical engineering labs at the Massachusetts Institute of Technology (MIT). Like other universities, some MIT students engaged in attention-seeking pranks; these students were called "hacks." From this, the term soon took on the meaning of creative invention, especially as computing was developing as a discipline.[145] However, today individuals who claim to be **hackers** contend that true hackers are concerned with enhancing computer security. Later, the term *cracker* was suggested to replace *hacker* in the media. Although some use this term, it usually refers to an individual who violates copyright protection. In the computer science community, the distinction between these two terms is recognized; outside this community, the two terms often refer to the same activity.[146]

Robert Moore described six general types of hackers: black hat hackers, white hat hackers, gray hat hackers, script kiddies, hactivists, and cyber terrorists:[147]

cybercrime: cybercrime consists of at least three features: The act was committed using (1) a computer, (2) a "victim" computer, and (3) an intermediary network.

hackers: individuals who violate computer security

• *Black hat hackers.* These individuals violate computer security essentially out of malice or for personal gain. They write programs to damage computer systems and networks. Because of these hackers, organizations have had to spend millions of dollars to develop protected computer networks and operating systems.

• *White hat hackers.* These hackers are involved in writing programs to protect systems and networks from being illegally and maliciously accessed. They attempt to hack into targeted computers. If successful, they subsequently notify the computer system's owner of its vulnerabilities.

• *Gray hat hackers.* A blend of black hat and white hat hackers, these individuals may be considered "opportunistic." They may successfully target and access a computer system and then notify the system's owner. Rather than informing the administrator of how the system was exposed, these hackers offer to correct the defect for a fee.

• *Script kiddies.* These hackers are deemed the lowest on the hacker ladder due to their limited technical ability. Essentially, they surf the Internet for hacker utility programs and then launch the programs at a target computer system. Due to their limited technical knowledge, they are considered risky because they are not aware of how programs will affect the attacked computer system. Some well-known hacking attacks, such as the shutting down of the eBay and Amazon websites, were done by script kiddies.

• *Hactivists.* In reference to their methods, these individuals are similar to those hackers described above. They differ, however, in their motives. Hactivists attempt to hack computer systems or networks that will provide them an avenue to spread their political message. They may access the server that stores a webpage and then modify the page to reveal their message.

• *Cyber terrorist.* These individuals access computer systems linked to critical infrastructures, such as water purification, electricity, and nuclear power plants. Such "attacks" can cause damage or even death due to a loss of service. These hackers are relatively new but are gaining attention and inspire a great deal of public fear.[148]

IDENTITY THEFT

Identity theft is defined as "the procuring of this false identity regardless of its use . . . [often] to commit identity fraud, but in some cases, it is used by criminals and terrorists to establish false identities and escape detection."[149] There are generally three different types of identity theft. The first type is when the identity thief assumes the life of the victim. One possible motivation for this form of identity theft is that of someone engaging in organized criminal activities. The trail left behind would lead to someone else, with no affiliation to the criminal organization, rather than to the thief. This type of identity theft is rare, possibly because taking over an individual's life is extremely difficult.

The second form of identity theft is beginning to evolve but has received little attention, perhaps due to the lack of financial or physical harm to its victims. This type of identity theft is "virtual" identity theft. Today, most Internet users create a screen name. Recently, individuals have stolen others' screen names for the purpose of, for example, harassing people or spamming other users.

identity theft: occurs when an individual obtains a false identity to commit identity fraud; can be used by criminals and terrorists to establish false identities and escape detection

The third type of identity theft is the most common. It occurs when a victim's credit identity is stolen, such as his or her Social Security number or other identifying information. Subsequently, the offender will use this stolen information to apply for credit in the victim's name.[150] There are various approaches to obtaining an individual's identity, including the following:

1. *Carding.* This refers to stealing a victim's credit card information and subsequently using the information to purchase items, especially electronics. A key feature of carding is delivery of purchased items. One method has been to have the items delivered to a shipping facility (e.g., Mail Boxes Etc. or The UPS Store) where the offender can open a fake account to store these items.

2. *Dumpster diving.* This method involves offenders obtaining materials, such as credit card carbons or preapproval credit card forms, that include identity information. One new development in this area is dumpster diving in university unions, particularly those that provide postal service for students. Students often receive preapproval notices and usually throw them in the trash immediately.

3. *Credit card skimming.* A majority of companies no longer use slider machines that create credit card carbons. Rather, they use electronic card readers. When a credit card is slipped into this reader, the information is scanned from the magnetic strip on the back of the credit card. Subsequently, this information is sent to a credit card verification service through a call made by the machine. If the card is accepted, then the machine will save the authorization numbers in a separate digital file. Thus, offenders can implement various methods to steal this information during the scanning procedure.

4. *Shoulder surfing.* In this method, when a victim removes his or her credit card to pay for merchandise, the offender peers over the victim's shoulder and memorizes the card number. Interestingly, offenders need not memorize all 16 numbers. Experienced thieves may have a listing that includes information on the first eight numbers associated with the card. For instance, the gold VISA cards begin with a different eight-number sequence than do regular VISA cards. Thus, the offender needs to memorize only half the numbers and the expiration date.[151]

CHILD PORNOGRAPHY

Child pornography portrays children engaged in sexual acts or in a sexual way. These depictions are the same as those in adult pornography except the media (e.g., photographs, video) include images of children, children and adults, or children and animals or objects.[152] As with adult pornography, child pornography exists to meet the demand for such material.[153] During a 1-week period in December 1995, there were 5,651 messages about child pornography posted on four electronic bulletin boards.[154] Further, there are national and international organizations that support pedophiles and child sexual exploitation. One such organization is the North American Men/Boy Love Association (NAMBLA). A review of the literature identified four common categories of users of Internet child pornography:

1. Individuals who encourage prevailing or developing sexual interests in children

2. Individuals who communicate with other sexual offenders who use child pornography as a broader pattern of offending

3. Individuals who are impulsive and curious

4. Individuals who are involved in child pornography for nonsexual reasons, such as financial gain[155]

During the 1980s, federal law enforcement agencies aggressively focused on pursuing those involved in the manufacturing and distribution of child pornography. Such efforts resulted in the belief that the issue of child pornography was a "controllable problem." That all changed, however, with the advent of the Internet.[156] Deputy Assistant Attorney General Kevin V. Di Gregory testified before Congress that

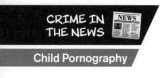

> the trafficking in child pornography by computer users has, in some ways, challenged the progress of nearly eighty years of aggressive child pornography investigation and prosecution. Whereas by the early 1990s, the government has largely eradicated the cottage trade within the United States for this material and distribution was typically limited to trading or sharing between individual pedophiles who actually knew each other, today computer technology has reinvigorated both the commercial and non-commercial distribution of obscene child pornography.[157]

With the ever-growing World Wide Web, there will be a continuous expansion of child pornography. Further, law enforcement efforts are difficult and characterized by legal definitional issues, overlapping jurisdictions, and entrapment problems.[158]

INTERNET FRAUD

Businesses have the option of placing their operations, either entirely or as an added component, on the Internet. While this has allowed legitimate businesses to expand their customer base, it has also given illegitimate businesses or operations an opportunity to engage in fraud via the Internet. Two of the most common types of **Internet fraud** schemes are online auctions and sale of wives and prostitutes.[159]

Yahoo Auctions and eBay are two of the most popular Internet auction sites. Some interesting items have been put up for auction, illustrating that practically anything can be sold:

- *A man's family*. The man promised that the highest bidder would receive a happy family ready for holidays and family events.

- *An island*. The island, apparently located off the coast of the United States, was advertised as ideal for a remote casino resort.

- *Escort services*. The winner was promised an "unforgettable afternoon."[160]

A major problem with online auction fraud is when an individual purchases merchandise but never receives it. Further, since these transactions can occur between a seller and purchaser living in different states or even different countries, there are issues pertaining to investigating and prosecuting these offenses. However, many states have statutes that criminalize fraudulent selling practices, and these statutes would apply to auction fraud cases just as they would to more traditional transactions between a buyer and seller.[161]

Mail-order bride services and solicitation of prostitutes are not new offenses, but engaging in these crimes through the Internet is a relatively new phenomenon. For instance, there are more than 30,000 websites for mail-order brides. There are various types of mail-order bride fraud. One scam is when a woman contacts numerous men and states that she likes their letters. A man may then respond by asking her to visit, usually in the United States. He sends the woman money for the visit, but the woman stops communicating with him after receiving the money. In another type of scam, the woman is actually a man posing as a potential wife.[162]

Internet fraud: when individuals use the Internet to engage in fraud, often identity theft

Online prostitution refers to soliciting sexual acts through the Internet. The Internet can be used for prostitution in two ways. One involves using the Internet to facilitate communication between those seeking the services of prostitutes. The second uses the Internet for electronic communications and websites to facilitate meetings. It is this second form that involves fraudulent activities. One type of fraud occurs when a "date" is scheduled, with a required deposit prior to the arranged meeting. The website obtains the "customer's" credit card information, but the services are never provided.[163]

CYBERSTALKING

The term *stalking* has been in use since the early 1990s to describe a victim being harassed or physically threatened. Prior to this time, a victim of such harassment was informed that nothing could be done to the perpetrator until he or she made a physical attempt that threatened the victim's safety or well-being.[164] After five women were murdered by stalkers, California became the first state in the United States to criminalize this behavior.[165] These statutes, however, did not foresee how stalking behavior would emerge within cyberspace.

Florida statute explicitly defines **cyberstalking** as a

> means to engage in a course of conduct to communicate, or to cause to be communicated, words, images, or language by or through the use of electronic mail or electronic communication, directed at a specific person, causing substantial emotional distress to that person and serving no legitimate purpose.[166]

Cyberstalking includes some of the following actions:

- Monitoring e-mail communication directly or by using some form of spyware or keystroke-logging hardware

- Sending e-mails that threaten, insult, or harass

- Disrupting e-mail communications by inundating a victim's inbox with unwanted mail

- Disrupting e-mail communications by sending a virus

- Using the victim's e-mail identity to send false messages to others or to purchase goods and services (i.e., committing virtual identity theft)

- Using the Internet to seek and collect a victim's personal information and whereabouts[167]

VIDEO

Cyberstalking

Various motivations have been offered as to why someone would stalk another individual. For instance, some may select their victims opportunistically and subsequently get a sense of satisfaction from intimidating them; this is a type of power-assertive motivation.[168] For instance, an abusive ex-husband was involved in a 2-year crusade against his ex-wife through e-mail communications. Although the wife obtained a restraining order against her ex-husband, he continued to send her more than 1,500 pages of threatening e-mails from numerous e-mail accounts. One such e-mail outlined his plans to shoot her children with a rifle and then beat, rape, and mutilate her with sulfuric acid before slashing her spinal cord so she could never walk again.[169] Others may be obsessed with a need to retaliate against their victims for perceived wrongs; this is a type of anger-retaliatory motivation. Gary Dellapenta was a cyberstalker who went to extreme efforts to terrify Randi Barber. He stated that he had an "inner rage" toward her and he was unable to control this rage. He would send messages that were degrading and intended to bring harm to Barber; he arranged to have other people harm her but was unwilling to do so himself.[170]

cyberstalking: when an individual engages in stalking behavior through such means as electronic mail or electronic communication

CRIMINAL JUSTICE RESPONSES TO CYBERCRIME

INVESTIGATION OF CYBERCRIME

Law enforcement has lagged behind the remarkable technological advances and the easy availability of this technology to millions of individuals. A number of large law enforcement agencies have devoted resources to electronic crime investigation; medium-sized agencies may be attempting to develop an electronic crime investigation unit or cross-train detectives from traditional fields. Small agencies, however, do experience computer crime in their area but are often not able to devote the resources for a specialized unit.[171]

Further, law enforcement needs to determine whether they will be *reactive* or *proactive* when investigating the various types of cybercrimes:

> The question facing law enforcement has been whether to handle these crimes in a reactive or proactive manner. Cyberstalking and identity theft are almost always viewed in a reactive manner because a victim's complaint is necessary in order to begin an investigation. However, digital child pornography has become such a widespread problem that many agencies have begun employing proactive investigations in attempts to control the problems that develop from this activity.[172]

For instance, the Federal Bureau of Investigation, through Operation Innocent Images, has been proactively investigating pedophiles for years, and now local and state law enforcement agencies are also implementing these types of investigations. One method has been for the officer to enter various chat rooms, pretending to be a child, usually between the ages of 6 and 14. The officer will spend a great deal of time chatting and interacting with others in an attempt to lure potential *groomers* (i.e., pedophiles). Another method is when the officer arranges a meeting between the groomer and the undercover officer, whom the groomer believes to be a child.[173]

Another important facet to investigating cybercrime involves search warrants. It is essential that operating systems, storage devices, and hard specifications be clearly articulated in the development of a comprehensive search warrant.[174] For instance, investigators may seize additional evidence under the "plain view" exception to search warrant requirements. In reference to computers, however, the concept of "plain view" may not be as clear. The case of *United States v. Carey* (1998) illustrated this point. Patrick Carey was under investigation for possible sale and possession of cocaine. During the arrest, officers observed in plain view a "bong." Subsequently, the officer asked Carey to consent to a search of his apartment. Carey consented to the search and signed a formal written consent. The officers recovered cocaine, marijuana, and hallucinogenic mushrooms. They also confiscated two computers, thinking they could be subject to forfeiture of evidence of drug dealing. The investigators then obtained a warrant to search the files on the computers for evidence related to drugs. Their investigation revealed that Carey had files containing child pornography; he was charged with one count of child pornography. On appeal, Carey challenged the admissibility of the child pornography because it was discovered as a result of a warrantless search. The court ruled that the investigators exceeded the scope of the warrant and reversed Carey's conviction. They noted that "the plain view doctrine may not be used to extend a general exploratory search from one object to another until something incriminating at last emerges."[175]

RELEVANT LEGISLATION

Compared with state legislatures, the U.S. Congress has acted more swiftly to enact legislation establishing computer-specific statutes—specifically, legislation that addresses such crimes as electronic fraud and hacking.[176] Below, we present a brief overview of some legislation focusing on cybercrimes.

COMPUTER FRAUD AND ABUSE ACT. The **Computer Fraud and Abuse Act** (CFAA) was initially enacted in 1984; it was amended in 1986 and has been amended further since that time. It was originally designed to protect national security, financial, and commercial information; medical treatment; and interstate communication systems from malicious acts, including unauthorized access. In addition, the CFAA allows those who have been victims of such crimes to bring a civil suit against violators. The CFAA does not exclude application of other laws such as additional computer crime statutes that broaden the scope of CFAA.[177]

DIGITAL MILLENNIUM COPYRIGHT ACT. During the past several years, the music and video industries have modified their businesses in response to major technological advances. These industries have used the Internet as a vehicle for individuals to purchase (i.e., download) movies and music. A major problem with such availability, however, is Internet piracy.[178] Internet piracy is the "unauthorized copying of copyright material for commercial purposes and the unauthorized commercial dealing in copied materials."[179] The various entities claimed that they were losing millions of dollars due to copyright violations.[180] Under pressure from the motion picture industry, record labels, software publishers, and other entities whose profits are linked to copyrighted material, Congress passed the **Digital Millennium Copyright Act** in 1998. This act incorporates part of the Copyright Act; it criminalizes making, distributing, or using tools, such as software, to evade technological protection measures implemented by copyright owners to prevent access to copyrighted material.[181]

CHILD ONLINE PROTECTION ACT. In 1998, Congress passed the **Child Online Protection Act,** which prohibits individuals from knowingly engaging in communication for commercial purposes that includes material "harmful to minors" and available to minors.[182] Such prohibited material includes pictures, writings, recordings, and videos that are obscene—or what the average person would consider, in the context of minors, to appeal to prurient interests. A violation is a misdemeanor, punishable by up to 6 months' imprisonment and a $50,000 fine for each violation.[183] It is essential to note that this is just one example of legislation that has been enacted to address Internet child pornography. For instance, the Child Pornography Protection Act attempted to prohibit the use of electronically altered photographs depicting child pornography, such as artificial images of children (i.e., virtual images). This act has been challenged on the grounds of vague language and possible violation of the First Amendment right to free speech.[184]

ELECTRONIC COMMUNICATIONS PRIVACY ACT. In 1986 Congress passed the **Electronic Communications Privacy Act,** which regulates the interception of electronic communications by individuals as well as by the government. In reference to investigators, this act regulates the amount of information law enforcement can obtain based on the levels of service. Law enforcement is required to obtain a subpoena for basic subscriber information (e.g., name, address, local and long-distance telephone billing records, length of service, type of service). A court order is needed to acquire transactional information (e.g., records or logs pertaining to the subscriber, such as destinations of outgoing mail). Law enforcement needs to obtain a search warrant for obtaining the actual content of e-mail messages.[185]

THEORETICAL EXPLANATIONS OF CYBERCRIME

Robert Taylor and his colleagues reviewed several theories to explain computer crime.[186] In this section, we highlight a few of these theoretical perspectives to illustrate how theories that have been applied to "traditional" types of criminal behavior can also explain more technologically advanced activities. Routine activities theory contends that

Computer Fraud and Abuse Act: originally designed to protect national security, financial, and commercial information; medical treatment; and interstate communication systems from malicious acts, including unauthorized access; allows victims of such crimes to bring civil suits against violators

Digital Millennium Copyright Act: criminalizes making, distributing, or using tools, such as software, to evade technological protection measures implemented by copyright owners to prevent access to copyrighted material

Child Online Protection Act: prohibits individuals from knowingly engaging in communication for commercial purposes that includes material "harmful to minors" and available to minors

Electronic Communications Privacy Act: regulates the interception of electronic communications by individuals as well as the government

LEARNING CHECK 13.4

_____ hackers are individuals who violate computer security essentially out of malice or for personal gain. The _____ method of Internet fraud occurs when a victim removes his or her credit card to pay for merchandise and the offender peers over the victim's shoulder and memorizes the card numbers. Activities associated with _____ include monitoring e-mail communication; sending e-mails that threaten, insult, or harass; and using the victim's e-mail identity to send false messages to others or to purchase goods and services. The _____ Act was established to address various problems associated with the Internet, including piracy.

Answers located at www.sagepub.com/schram

when a motivated offender, a suitable target, and the absence of a capable guardian converge, a crime will occur. With the rapid increase in use of computers as well as the Internet, the number of suitable targets has also increased. The insufficient software protection for these types of crimes reveals the absence of a capable guardian. Thus, "when motivated offenders are present, they make rational choices by selecting suitable targets that lack capable guardianship."[187] This also lessens the chances of an offender being apprehended.

Social process theories, such as learning theory and differential reinforcement theory, can help explain crimes committed by individuals who develop and spread computer viruses. A person needs to have a certain level of technical competency to write a virus. This often involves a process that includes learning how to write the code necessary to develop a virus. In most instances, this learning does not take place face to face; rather, many learn these skills through chat rooms, bulletin boards, or distance learning. There are also positive reinforcements involved with this type of activity, including the excitement of propagating the virus and infecting systems, "admiration" from one's peer group, and possible financial gains. Negative reinforcements can include experiencing hostility from other virus writers and being wanted by law enforcement.[188]

Social structure theories, specifically strain theory, can be applied when attempting to understand Internet fraud schemes and corporate espionage. From this theoretical perspective, criminal behavior may be linked to blocked legitimate opportunities. Thus, individuals who engage in this type of criminal behavior could be considered "innovators"; they use illegitimate means to attain the conventional goal of success, usually measured by financial gain. Interestingly, Merton initially applied this theoretical perspective to explain blocked legitimate opportunities of those predominantly from the lower class. Contemporary strain theorists, however, have attempted to apply this perspective to those from the middle and upper-middle classes. Specifically, individuals from higher socioeconomic classes may also enjoy a certain amount of success by _perceiving_ that legitimate means to accumulating more wealth are blocked.[189]

CONCLUSION

This chapter presented three general categories of crime that some may not consider as fitting in with traditional street crimes, such as murder, larceny, and assault. This does not mean that these types of crime are not *associated* with more traditional types of offenses. For instance, criminal organizations do engage in murder, and cybercrimes can involve theft. Rather, some would argue that there are unique aspects to these types of offenses that should be recognized. In the first section of this chapter, we attempted to illustrate how scholars have distinguished white-collar crime from traditional forms of offending. This section also explored the various ways corporate crimes have harmed society, as well as responses to these types of offenses.

The next section focused on organized crime. Again, we presented the various complex factors involved in defining organized crime. We then briefly discussed the historical events that have influenced organized criminal behavior, including the criminal justice responses to organized crime. We concluded this chapter with a discussion on cybercrime. This is a relatively new type of criminal activity; thus, there are growing challenges associated with investigating cybercrime, as well as legislation that has been enacted to address it.

At the beginning of this chapter, we presented the case of Martha Stewart. We asked you various questions about your perceptions and descriptions of crime and criminals, as well as whether you thought Stewart received preferential treatment. As noted earlier, in this chapter we attempted to illustrate that criminal behavior is not restricted to what some deem traditional types of offenses; rather, criminal behavior can involve high-level executives and powerful corporations, groups organized around the purpose of engaging in criminal activity, and criminal behavior in which there is no physical contact between the victim and the offender.

KEY TERMS

Child Online Protection Act

Computer Fraud and Abuse Act

Cooper v. Pate

cybercrime

cyberstalking

Digital Millennium Copyright Act

Edwin Sutherland

Electronic Communications Privacy Act

Environmental Protection Agency

hackers

identity theft

Internet fraud

Kefauver Committee

Mafia

Mafioso

Occupational Safety and Health Act

organized crime

outlaw motorcycle gangs

Racketeer Influenced and Corrupt Organizations (RICO) Act

Tammany Hall

white-collar crime

Wickersham Commission

STUDENT STUDY SITE

Visit the student study site at **www.sagepub.com/schram** to access links to the video, audio, city and state rankings, author podcasts, and SAGE journal and reference articles featured in this chapter, as well as additional study tools, including eFlashcards, web quizzes, web resources, and chapter outlines.

DISCUSSION QUESTIONS

1. How does white-collar crime differ from traditional street crimes?

2. How does white-collar crime compare with traditional street crimes in terms of property damage and damage to society? In terms of physical damage, such as injuries and death?

3. Can you provide some recent examples of crimes against the environment in the United States?

4. What impact did OSHA seem to have on corporate labor violations?

5. What are some of the key features that distinguish organized crime from "just" crime?

6. How did Prohibition influence organized crime groups?

7. What are some of the different types of criminal organizations?

8. What are some of the major contributions from the Kefauver Committee?

9. What is RICO?

10. What is Reuter's "mini-theory" to explain and understand organized crime?

11. What are some of the similarities and differences between traditional forms of crime and cybercrime?

12. What are some of the different types of cybercrime?

13. What are some of the difficulties related to search warrants for cybercrimes?

14. What are some of the key statutes enacted by Congress to address problems associated with advanced technology?

15. How have some of the traditional theories of crime been applied to cybercrime?

WEB RESOURCES

CNN news story about WorldCom

http://money.cnn.com/2002/06/28/news/companies/worldcom/index.htm

CNN new story about Bernie Madoff scandal

http://www.cnn.com/2008/POLITICS/12/16/coffee.madoff/index.html?iref=allsearch

Outlaw motorcycle gangs

http://www.youtube.com/watch?v=7BQWQUBwdag

Cyberstalking

http://www.youtube.com/watch?v=BZ6LByl0pgw

CHAPTER 14

Hate Crimes, Terrorism, and Homeland Security

INTRODUCTION

In recent years, increased attention has been given to certain types of criminal activities that were not often discussed in the newspaper, on television, or, for that matter, in criminology textbooks. Specifically, these activities include hate crimes and terrorism. These types of offenses illustrate the multicultural and multinational aspects of crime. It is essential for students to appreciate how crime, and the concept of crime, expands beyond national boundaries. There has been some debate, however, as to whether hate crime offending and terrorism should be considered as similar behavior. While scholars have recognized that there are legal distinctions, some have maintained that there are also similarities, such as motivations, objectives, and perpetrator characteristics.[1] These types of offenses focus on terrorizing a larger social group.[2] Others argue that hate crimes and terrorism are distinct types of behavior, conceptually and empirically. For instance, terrorism is often considered an *upward crime*; these offenses are committed by individuals from a lower social standing. Hate crimes are often deemed *downward crimes*; these offenses are often perpetrated by individuals from a majority or powerful group in society against minority-group victims.[3]

In this chapter, we present a discussion of both hate crimes and terrorism but do so in separate sections. The chapter begins with a discussion on hate crimes; this section presents issues pertaining to hate crimes, such as the definition and legislative responses to these offenses. The next section focuses on terrorism, including the definition and the types and extent of terrorism. The chapter concludes with a section on homeland security that covers such issues as agencies involved in homeland security and potential conflicts regarding civil liberties.

HATE CRIMES

In November of 2002, the Human Rights Watch reported that anti-Muslim **hate crimes** in the United States increased by about 1,700% during 2001. Their report, *We Are Not the Enemy*, was based on research with police, prosecutors, community activists, and victims of hate crimes in Seattle, Dearborn (Michigan), Chicago, Los Angeles, Phoenix, and New York. The Human Rights Watch noted that while most public figures condemned these types of hate crimes against Muslims, a few public figures expressed open discrimination against Muslims:

> Just a week after September 11, a member of Congress, John Cooksey, told a Louisiana radio station, "If I see someone [who] comes in that's got a diaper on his head and a fan belt wrapped around the diaper on his head, that guy needs to be pulled over." . . . Similarly, while speaking to law enforcement officers in Georgia, Representative C. Saxby Chambliss stated: "just turn [the sheriff] loose and have him arrest every Muslim that crosses the state line.". . . Representatives Cooksey and Chambliss both eventually apologized for their remarks.[4]

LEARNING OBJECTIVES

As students read this chapter, they should consider the following questions:

- What are some of the bias motivations associated with hate crimes?

- What is some key anti-hate-crime legislation?

- How would you distinguish terrorist activities from more conventional forms of criminal activities?

- What are the various motivations for engaging in terrorist activities?

- What are some of the different organizational structures associated with terrorist groups?

- What are some of the ways terrorist groups finance their activities?

- What is homeland security?

- What are some of the agencies that make up the Department of Homeland Security?

- What are some of the bureaucratic problems associated with the Department of Homeland Security?

- What is the USA PATRIOT Act?

- What are some of the controversial issues related to civil liberties and the efforts to counter terrorism?

JOHN ROBERT MCGRAHAM

In the 1980s, John Robert McGraham lost his job as a bellhop at the old Ambassador Hotel. He became seriously depressed, and his sisters, Sharon and Susanne, arranged for him to see a therapist. This initially seemed to help John. When the therapist took a month-long vacation, however, he was soon "lost." His sisters tried to have him committed, but John left and began spending a great deal of time on the streets. At one point, he moved in with his mother, but they had problems and his mother asked him to leave. John's sisters would visit him on mid-Wilshire Boulevard in Los Angeles. They would bring him food, money, and clothing. They also brought their children to visit with "Uncle Johnny." The sisters discovered that people in the neighborhood were looking out for John.[5]

ON OCTOBER 9, 2008, JOHN, 55 YEARS OLD, WAS FOUND DEAD. SOMEONE HAD BRUTALLY MURDERED HIM BY DOUSING HIM WITH GASOLINE AND SETTING HIM AFIRE.

was left on the sidewalk in front of a boarded-up dental office on the corner of West Third and Berendo. Local residents tried to help him, but it was too late. A service was held at Immanuel Presbyterian Church; the church was filled to capacity with people who came to honor John. Susanne stated that the perpetrator(s)

targeted him in my mind, and that's the worst kind of person. . . . I hope they give him the full scope of the law because that person went to a gas station, filled up the gas can, drove to the site, poured gasoline on him and then set him on fire. That person had so many opportunities to change [his] mind and . . . didn't.[6]

On October 9, 2008, John, 55 years old, was found dead. Someone had brutally murdered him by dousing him with gasoline and setting him afire. His body

Was this a hate crime? Was John a target because he was homeless? We will address these questions at the end of this chapter.

How does a hate crime differ from a traditional crime? Are there various types of hate crimes? What is the extent of hate crimes in the United States? How has the criminal justice system responded to these crimes? Why do some people engage in these types of offenses? In this section, we attempt to answer these questions.

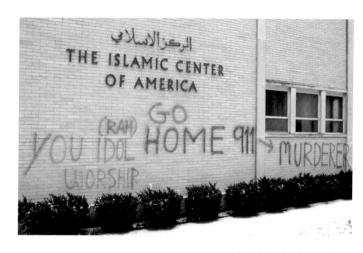

Anti-Muslim hate crime of vandalism

WHAT IS A HATE CRIME?

An incident designated as a hate crime is a traditional offense, such as murder or vandalism, with an additional factor of bias. Congress defined hate crime as follows: "A criminal offense against a person or property motivated in whole or in part by an offender's bias against a race, religion, disability, ethnic origin or sexual orientation."[7] The Federal Bureau of Investigation (FBI) has provided guidelines as to how one can identify a crime as being motivated by bias. The FBI stresses that an individual who commits an offense and has a bias against the victim's race, religion, disability, sexual orientation, and/or ethnicity/national origin is not sufficient grounds to designate the offense a hate crime. Rather, this offense must be *motivated* by bias.[8]

The FBI recognizes the subjective nature of such an assessment; however, it provides various factors to consider when determining if such an offense is a crime motivated by bias:

- The offender and the victim were of different race, religion, disability, sexual orientation, and/or ethnicity/national origin.

- Bias-related oral comments, written statements, or gestures were made by the offender, which indicate his or her bias.

- Bias-related drawings, markings, symbols, or graffiti were left at the crime scene.

- A substantial portion of the community where the crime occurred perceived that the incident was motivated by bias.

- The offender was previously involved in a similar hate crime or is a hate-group member.

- The incident coincided with a holiday or a date of particular significance relating to race, religion, disability, sexual orientation, or ethnicity/national origin.[9]

While a hate crime is not exclusively a federal offense, the federal government can, and does, investigate and prosecute hate crimes as civil rights violations.

WHAT WERE THEY THINKING?!

Hate Crimes

AUDIO

Hate Crimes

TYPES OF HATE CRIMES

The types of hate crimes are identified by bias motivations. Common biases include those against race and religion. There are, however, also biases against rich people, poor people, men with long hair, smokers, drinkers, and people with diseases such as AIDS. The biases reported to the FBI's Uniform Crime Reports (UCR) program are restricted to those mandated by the sanctioning act and subsequent amendments. The bias motivations relevant to hate crimes are as follows: racial (e.g., anti-black, anti-American Indian/Alaskan Native), religious (e.g., anti-Jewish, anti-Islamic), disability (anti-physical disability, anti-mental disability), sexual orientation (e.g., anti-male homosexual, anti-bisexual), and ethnicity/national origin (e.g., anti-Hispanic).[10] Table 14.1 provides examples of various incidents and whether they should be designated as hate crimes.

hate crimes: traditional offenses, such as murder and vandalism, with an additional factor of bias

IS THIS A HATE CRIME?
1. A white juvenile male snatched a Jewish woman's purse and while doing so knocked her down and called her by a well-known and recognized epithet used against Jews. The offender's identity is not known. Although the offender used an epithet against Jews, it is not known whether he belongs to another religious group or whether his motive was anything more than robbery. Because the facts are ambiguous, agencies should not report this incident as bias motivated.
2. While driving through a predominately Mexican American neighborhood, a black male stopped his car to repair a flat tire. A group of Mexican Americans leaving a bar across the street accosted the driver and then attacked him with bottles and clubs. During the attack, the offenders called the victim a well-known and recognized epithet used against blacks and told him that blacks were not welcome in the neighborhood. This incident should be reported as anti-black, because the victim and offenders are of different races, the offenders used a racial epithet, and the facts reveal no reason for the attack other than the stated one (i.e., to keep blacks out of the neighborhood).
3. A small neighborhood bar frequented by gays burned down after being closed for the night. Investigation revealed that the fire was deliberately set, but there were no witnesses or suspects. Although the fire was deliberately set, the fact that the bar was frequented by gays may have been coincidental. Therefore, the incident should not be reported as bias motivated. Two weeks later, three white adult males were arrested on a tip from an informant. They admitted to burning down the bar, saying they did it to keep gays out of the neighborhood. As a result, this incident should now be reported as a bias crime.
4. A group home for persons with psychiatric disabilities who were in transition back into the community was the site of a reported arson. Apparently, neighbors had expressed many concerns about the group home and were angry that the house was located in their community. Shortly before the fire was reported, a witness heard a white male state, "I'll get rid of those 'crazies.' I'll burn them out." An anti-mental disability incident should be reported, because the suspect apparently committed the crime because of his bias against persons with psychiatric disabilities.
5. Overnight, unknown persons broke into a synagogue and destroyed several religious objects. The perpetrators drew a large swastika on the door and wrote "Death to Jews" on a wall. Although valuable items were present, none were stolen. This incident should be reported as anti-Jewish, because the offenders destroyed religious objects, left anti-Semitic words and graffiti behind, and did not appear to be motivated by theft.

Table 14.1 Is This a Hate Crime?

Source: FBI. (1999). *Hate crime data collection guidelines.* Washington, DC: U.S. Department of Justice, pp. 7–8.

JOURNAL ARTICLE

Hate Crimes

AUTHOR VIDEO

Hate Crimes

EXTENT OF HATE CRIMES

In 2011, 1,944 law enforcement agencies reported 6,222 hate crime incidents. These consisted of 7,254 offenses committed by 5,724 offenders and involving 7,697 victims. When examining the bias motivation of these incidents, 46.9% were motivated by a racial bias, followed by sexual-orientation bias (20.8%), religious bias (19.8%), ethnicity/national origin bias (11.6%), and disability bias (0.9%).

Within each of these bias motivation categories, some groups were the predominant target of such crimes. For instance, within the racial group, 72.0% of these offenses were motivated by anti-black bias. The majority of religious bias crimes were anti-Jewish (62.2%). More than half of the sexual-orientation bias crimes were motivated by anti-male bias (57.8%). Of the 891 offenses based on the perceived ethnicity or national origin of the victim, 56.8% were motivated by anti-Hispanic bias. There were 58 offenses motivated by disability bias, of which 35 were driven by anti–mental disability bias.

When reviewing these incidents by offense type (see Table 14.2), 63.7% were crimes against persons and 36.0% were crimes against property. The remaining offenses were against society. Within the crimes against persons, 45.6% were for intimidation, 34.5% simple assault, 19.4% aggravated assault, and 0.2% for murder (four offenses) and forcible rape (seven offenses). Among crimes against property, 81.4% were acts of destruction, damage, and/or vandalism. The remaining 18.6% comprised offenses such as robbery, burglary, larceny-theft, motor vehicle theft, and arson.[11]

OFFENSE TYPE	TOTAL OFFENSES	VICTIM TYPE					
		INDIVIDUAL	BUSINESS/ FINANCIAL INSTITUTION	GOVERNMENT	RELIGIOUS ORGANIZATION	SOCIETY/ PUBLIC[1]	OTHER/ UNKNOWN/ MULTIPLE
Total	7,254	6,016	305	206	208	20	499
Crimes against persons[2]	**4,623**	**4,623**	**NA**	**NA**	**NA**	**NA**	**NA**
Crimes against property:	**2,611**	**1,393**	**305**	**206**	**208**	**0**	**499**
Robbery	131	119	3	0	0	0	9
Burglary	124	87	10	5	10	0	12
Larceny-theft	152	102	38	1	1	0	10
Motor vehicle theft	6	6	0	0	0	0	0
Arson	42	28	4	1	5	0	4
Destruction/ damage/ vandalism	2,125	1,030	243	198	192	0	462
Other[2]	31	21	7	1	0	0	2
Crimes against society[2]	**20**	**NA**	**NA**	**NA**	**NA**	**20**	**NA**

Table 14.2 Hate Crime Offenses by Victim and Offense Type, 2011

Source: FBI. (2012). *Hate crime statistics, 2011*. Retrieved from http://www.fbi.gov/about-us/cjis/ucr/hate-crime/2011/tables/table-6.

[1]The victim type society/public is collected only in the National Incident-Based Reporting System (NIBRS). See Methodology.
[2]Includes additional offenses collected in NIBRS. See Methodology.

ANTI-HATE-CRIME LEGISLATION

Since 1990, Congress has passed various pieces of legislation that have greatly influenced hate crime initiatives and prevention measures. Below, we briefly review some of this legislation.

HATE CRIME STATISTICS ACT OF 1990

On April 23, 1990, the president signed into law the **Hate Crime Statistics Act of 1990**. This was in response to increasing concern about these types of offenses.[12] As part of the UCR program, the attorney general was required to develop guidelines and collect data about crimes that manifest evidence of prejudice based on race, religion, sexual orientation, or ethnicity, including, where appropriate, the crimes of murder, nonnegligent manslaughter, forcible rape, aggravated assault, simple assault, intimidation, arson, and destruction, damage, or vandalism of property.[13]

To develop procedures for collecting national hate crime data, many emphasized avoiding any new data reporting responsibilities for those law enforcement agencies participating in the UCR program. Thus, the collection of hate crime data provides additional information

Hate Crime Statistics Act of 1990: as part of the Uniform Crime Report program, the attorney general was required to develop guidelines and collect data about crimes that manifest evidence of prejudice based on race, religion, sexual orientation, or ethnicity on traditional UCR collection procedures. As mentioned previously, if a traditional offense has been motivated by the offender's bias, the reporting agency is to complete the Hate Crime Incident Report. This form collects information on the location, victim type (e.g., individual, business), number of offenders, race of offender(s), and bias motivation.

VIOLENT CRIME CONTROL AND LAW ENFORCEMENT ACT OF 1994

The **Violent Crime Control and Law Enforcement Act of 1994** amended the Hate Crime Statistics Act to enhance penalties for offenses that involved a motivation bias.[14] Further, to complement the state hate crime penalty-enhancement statutes in the 1994 Crime Bill, Congress passed the Hate Crime Sentencing Enhancement Act. Specifically, this act directed the U.S. Sentencing Commission to enhance hate crime sentences to no fewer than three offense levels. The amendment took effect on November 1, 1995.[15]

CHURCH ARSON PREVENTION ACT OF 1996

From January 1, 1995, to January 7, 1997, the Department of Justice opened 328 investigations of suspicious fires, bombings, and attempted bombings. Of these, 138 attacks were on houses of worship, which were predominantly African American institutions.[16]

In 1996, Congress unanimously enacted the **Church Arson Prevention Act**. This act prohibits

1. the intentional defacement, damage, or destruction of any religious real property, because of the religious, racial, or ethnic characteristics of that property, or

2. the intentional obstruction by force or threat of force, or attempts to obstruct any person in the enjoyment of that person's free exercise of religious beliefs.[17]

The punishment can vary from 1 year imprisonment and a fine to death. The punishment depends on such factors as whether any individuals were injured or killed as a result of the conduct prohibited by this act.

CAMPUS HATE CRIMES RIGHT TO KNOW ACT OF 1997

The **Campus Hate Crimes Right to Know Act of 1997** amends a section of the Higher Education Act of 1965 that provides "for the disclosure of all criminal incidents that manifest evidence of prejudice based on race, gender, religion, sexual orientation, ethnicity, or disability."[18] Findings from the Congressional hearing include the following: The incidence of violence based on bias on college campuses poses a serious national problem; this violence disrupts the tranquility and safety of campuses and results in divisiveness; the existing reporting requirements are inadequate to deal with the problem of hate crimes, since the majority of hate crimes on college campuses do not result in murder, rape, or aggravated assault; and omitting certain hate crimes from official campus crime reports deprives students and their parents of important information needed to protect students and to make informed decisions in choosing a college or university.

MATTHEW SHEPARD AND JAMES BYRD, JR., HATE CRIMES PREVENTION ACT OF 2009

The **Matthew Shepard and James Byrd, Jr., Hate Crimes Prevention Act of 2009** is named after two victims of hate crimes. Matthew Shepard attended the University of Wyoming. In 1998, he was assaulted because he was perceived to be a homosexual; he died from his injuries. Also in 1998, James Byrd, Jr., an African American man, was tied to a truck by white supremacists and then dragged and decapitated. The act states that it is unlawful to willfully cause bodily injury, or attempt to do so, with a dangerous weapon

Matthew Shepard was assaulted because he was perceived to be homosexual.

James Byrd, Jr., was viciously attacked by white supremacists.

when the offense is committed because of the actual or perceived race, color, religion, national origin, gender, sexual orientation, gender identity, or disability of any person.[19] This act gives the FBI authority to investigate violent hate crimes, including those aimed at the gay, lesbian, bisexual, and transgender community.[20]

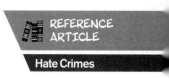

MODEL STATE LEGISLATION: HATE CRIMES/ VIOLENCE AGAINST PEOPLE EXPERIENCING HOMELESSNESS

The National Law Center on Homelessness and Poverty and the National Coalition for the Homeless advocated for state legislation that includes homelessness in hate crime statutes. They proposed a **model state legislation for hate crimes/violence against people experiencing homelessness**. The National Coalition for the Homeless reported that more communities across the country are actively addressing this problem. For instance, in 2008, Alaska added homeless status to a law that establishes more protection for vulnerable populations; in 2004, California passed a law requiring police officer training on hate crimes against persons who are homeless; and Florida passed a law in 2010 that added "homeless status" to hate crime legislation.[21]

The model state legislation designates the following acts as hate crimes motivated by a person's status as homeless:

- Assault, aggravated assault, battery, or aggravated battery on the person

- Acts that deface, damage, or destroy, or attempt to deface, damage, or destroy the personal property of the person

- Acts that result in the death of the person

- Any other crime against the person[22]

> **model state legislation for hate crimes/ violence against people experiencing homelessness:** the National Law Center on Homelessness and Poverty and the National Coalition for the Homeless advocated for state legislation that includes homelessness in hate crimes statutes

WHY DO THEY DO IT?

MATTHEW SHEPARD

On October 9, 1998, a bicyclist was passing through a rural area in Laramie, Wyoming. When he glanced over, he thought he saw a scarecrow tied to a ranch fence. He stopped and realized that the form was not a scarecrow but the burned, battered, and nearly dead body of Matthew Shepard.

Shepard was a 22-year-old student at the University of Wyoming. Prior to his vicious assault that evening, he attended a meeting of the Lesbian, Gay, Bisexual, Transgendered Association. Later, he went to a bar. While he was drinking a beer, two men approached Shepard. The two men stated that they were gay; Shepard also indicated that he was gay. Just after midnight, the two men, Russell Henderson and Aaron McKinney, lured Shepard to Henderson's pickup truck. They beat Shepard inside the truck and then pulled into an isolated part of a rural subdivision. They tied Shepard to a fence and pistol-whipped him with a .357 magnum handgun "while he begged for his life." They stole his wallet and shoes and left him there, where he was discovered by the bicyclist about 18 hours later.[23]

Five days after he was found tied to the fence, Shepard died from his injuries.[24] Henderson pled guilty and received two consecutive life sentences. McKinney was found guilty of felony murder and received two consecutive life terms without the possibility of parole. Shepard's death resulted in outrage across the country; many called for the need to develop federal hate crime legislation. As one writer noted in a *New York Times* opinion piece,

> In a nation sickened by the gratuitous thuggery of his murder, he may do much to dispel the stubborn belief in some quarters that homosexuals are not discriminated against. They are. Hatred can kill. . . . [H]is death makes clear the need for hate-crime laws to protect those who survive and punish those who attack others, whether fatally or not, just because of who they are.[25]

THEORETICAL EXPLANATIONS OF HATE CRIMES

Byers and Crider examined hate crimes against the Amish using routine activities theory.[26] Specifically, they were studying offenders who engaged in acts called "Claping." *Clape* is a derogatory term used by some non-Amish to insult and degrade Old Order Amish. Claping is any act of persecution committed against the Amish. Examples of claping include verbal harassment, blowing up mailboxes, forcing Amish buggies off the road with motorized vehicles, killing Amish-owned animals, and spraying the Amish with fire extinguishers.

The qualitative data supported routine activities theory in that the participants (i.e., offenders) were motivated, the Amish were considered suitable targets, and there was a perception that guardians to discourage these types of crimes were absent. Based on interviews, the offenders revealed various motivations for engaging in these crimes, such as the perception that the Amish are "different," a desire for excitement, and the belief that the Amish deserve such treatment. The Amish were considered suitable targets for various reasons, such as the perceived absence of consequences, the belief that the Amish were inferior, and the belief that they were vulnerable or an "easy target." The participants cited various themes indicating the lack of capable guardians, such as the low probability of getting caught and a belief that society accepted Claping and devalued the Amish.

Waldner and Berg applied a revision of routine activities theory to understanding anti-gay violence.[27] They employed Finkelhor and Asdigian's revised routine activities theory, which includes the concept of *target congruence*.[28] Target congruence is when various personal characteristics of individuals could possibly enhance their vulnerability to victimization since these characteristics have some congruence with the needs and motives of the offenders. Thus, certain offenders are attracted, or respond, to particular types of victims or particular characteristics in victims, making these victims more vulnerable.[29]

Another facet of studying hate crimes is examining individuals' *perceptions* of hate crimes, or how people view such offenses.[30] Plumm and her colleagues implemented a jury simulation model to explore different forms of victim blame involving an assault motivated by bias against sexual orientation.[31] They concluded that jurors may consider various factors in these types of cases. Jurors may not agree that a violent crime motivated by bias should necessarily be deemed a hate crime. Rather, other factors may be considered in the context of attributions of victim blaming. Thus, "prosecution of hate crimes may, therefore, be unsuccessful to the extent that extra-legal factors contribute to victim blaming."[32]

LEARNING CHECK 14.1

The _____ Act is named after two victims of hate crimes. The _____ Act is part of the UCR program. A hate crime is an offense that must be _____ by an individual with a bias against the victim's race, religion, disability, sexual orientation, and/or ethnicity/national origin. _____ theory was applied to understanding hate crimes against the Amish.

Answers located at www.sagepub.com/schram

TERRORISM

In May 2011, Osama bin Laden was killed by Navy SEALs in the U.S. Naval Special Warfare Development Group. He was not found in a remote area near the Pakistani–Afghan border, where he was presumed to be hiding; rather, he was located in a large compound in the city of Abbottabad, about an hour's drive from the Pakistani capital of Islamabad. As noted in *the New York Times*, "Bin Laden's demise is a defining moment in the American-led fight against terrorism, a symbolic stroke affirming the relentlessness of the pursuit of those who attacked New York and Washington on Sept. 11, 2001."[33] President Barack Obama addressed the nation to announce Osama bin Laden's death. Part of his address included the following:

> After nearly 10 years of service, struggle, and sacrifice, we know well the costs of war. These efforts weigh on me every time I, as Commander-in-Chief, have to sign a letter to a family that has lost a loved one, or look into the eyes of a service member who's been gravely wounded. So Americans understand the costs of war. Yet as a country, we will never tolerate our security being threatened, nor stand idly by when our people have been killed. We will be relentless in defense of our citizens and our friends and allies. We will be true to the values that make us who we are. And on nights like this one, we can say to those families who have lost loved ones to al Qaeda's terror: Justice has been done.[34]

Terrorism has existed for hundreds of years. However, after the September 11 attacks, terrorism has become more intertwined with Americans and their lives than in previous years. For instance, we read about it more in the newspapers and have experienced changes in how we travel.

In this section, we attempt to provide students with an overview of terrorism, starting with the question, "What is terrorism?" Next, we provide a brief historical overview of terrorism, as well as a discussion on the context of modern terrorism, such as organizational networks and financial support. We conclude this section with a brief review of some theoretical explanations of terrorism.

VIDEO
Bin Laden

Mumbai attacks
over Taj Majol

WHAT IS TERRORISM?

As noted above, in the past few years, through newspapers, television, the Internet, and personal conversations, we have heard a great deal about terrorism. Given that exposure, how would you define terrorism? What are some key features of terrorism? Who engages in terrorist activities? In this section, we will try to answer the question "What is terrorism?" First, we will discuss issues pertaining to the definition of terrorism. Then we will briefly review various types of terrorism, as well as the extent of terrorism.

DEFINITION OF TERRORISM

In one respect, terrorism is a social construct, meaning it is defined through social and cultural practice. People have varying definitions for the term *terrorism*:

> It is a pejorative term in that it has extremely negative associations and always connotes death and destruction. Society is constantly exposed to the term by the news media, politicians, and popular entertainment venues, and it is applied to a wide variety of actors, conditions, activities, and situations. As a social construct, the term is used to demonize people, societies, and actions.[35]

Today, *terrorism* is a significant word in our vocabulary, evoking highly emotional responses and reactions. Billions of dollars are spent worldwide to control terrorism, and people die every day from acts of terrorism. However, "some people do not seem to bother to define terrorism nor do they consider it worthwhile defining the concept."[36] Thus, there is no clear and concise definition of the word.

During a presentation at the War Crime Research Symposium, Alex Schmid argued that the United Nations has found it difficult to agree on a common definition of terrorism. In fact, various agencies in the U.S. government with interests in counterterrorism missions have different definitions of terrorism (see Table 14.3). In an attempt to distinguish terrorism from other types of criminal activity and irregular warfare, Bruce Hoffman identified terrorism as follows:

- Inevitably political in aims and motives

- Violent or threatens violence

- Designed to have far-reaching psychological consequences beyond the immediate victim or target

- Conducted *either* by an organization with an identifiable chain of command or conspiratorial cell structure *or* by individuals or a small collection of individuals directly influenced, motivated, or inspired by the ideological aims or example of some existent terrorist movement and/or its leaders

- Perpetrated by a subnational group or nonstate entity[37]

TYPOLOGIES OF TERRORISM

Identifying typologies of terrorism helps one focus on the varying forms of violence as well as the social meanings of terrorism while avoiding the controversial debates about

DEFINITIONS OF TERRORISM

1. U.S. House of Representatives Permanent Select Committee on Intelligence (2002): "Terrorism is the illegitimate, premeditated violence or threat of violence by subnational groups against persons or property with the intent to coerce a government by instilling fear amongst the populace."

2. State Department (1984): "Terrorism means premeditated, politically motivated violence perpetrated against noncombatant targets by subnational groups or clandestine agents, usually intended to influence an audience."

3. FBI (1999): "Terrorism is defined as the unlawful use, or threatened use, of force or violence by a group or individual . . . committed against persons or property to intimidate or coerce a government, the civilian population, or any segment thereof, in furtherance of political or social objectives."

4. Department of Defense (2000): "Terrorism is the calculated use of violence or threat of violence to inculcate fear; intended to coerce or to intimidate governments or societies in the pursuit of goals that are generally political, religious or ideological."

Table 14.3 Definitions of Terrorism by Four U.S. Government Agencies

the lack of a concise definition. It is essential to emphasize that while these typologies may enhance our understanding of terrorism, each incident should be appreciated within its particular social, historical, and political context.[38] There are a number of terrorist organizations and terrorist activities around the world.[39] In 2008, the secretary of state identified 44 foreign terrorist organizations, including al Qaeda, the National Liberation Army, the Continuity Irish Republican Army, and the Communist Party of the Philippines/New People's Army.[40] Upon examining worldwide terrorism, Gus Martin developed a typology of terrorism founded on motivation: (1) state sponsored, (2) dissident, (3) religious, and (4) criminal.[41]

State-sponsored terrorism includes terrorist acts that transpire due to the guidance of the state or government against perceived enemies. Targets of this type of terrorism may include politicians and political parties or groups within the host country or in other countries.[42] The U.S. Department of State has identified four countries that are state sponsors of terrorism: Iran, Syria, Sudan, and Cuba.[43] **Dissident terrorism** involves terrorist activities committed by rebellious groups against the government. In some instances, these terrorist acts are committed for power, wealth, and control; some are used to obtain independence. **Religious terrorism** involves terrorist acts legitimized by religious dogma. Terrorism motivated by religious philosophy has been the predominant form for the past several decades.[44] It is essential to stress that religious terrorism should not be associated with just the Muslim religion. For instance, American Christian white supremacists have engaged in various terrorist acts based on their faith and hatred for groups such as African Americans and Jews. **Criminal terrorism** involves engaging in criminal activity for profits, as in the drug cartels in Mexico, for example. Traditional organized crime enterprises, such as the Italian Mafia, profit from criminal activity for personal gain; criminal–political enterprises, such as Sri Lanka's Tamil Tigers, profit from criminal activity to sustain the movement.[45]

EXTENT OF TERRORISM

The **National Counterterrorism Center** (NCTC) provides the Department of State with statistical information on terrorism. This includes information on the number of individuals, including U.S. citizens and dual nationals, killed, injured, or kidnapped by each terrorist group during the preceding year.[46] In its *2011 Report on Terrorism*, the NCTC reported more than 10,000 terrorist attacks occurring in 70 countries. These attacks involved more than 45,000 victims, of which more than 12,500 were fatalities. Compared with the previous year, this was about a 12% decrease in attacks, and a 29% decrease from 2007.

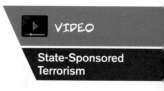
VIDEO

State-Sponsored Terrorism

state-sponsored terrorism: includes terrorist acts that transpire due to the guidance of the state or government against perceived enemies

dissident terrorism: involves terrorist activities against the government that are committed by rebellious groups

religious terrorism: motivated by engaging in terrorist acts that are legitimized by religious dogma

criminal terrorism: terrorism motivated by engaging in criminal activity for profit, such as in the drug cartels in Mexico

National Counterterrorism Center: provides the Department of State with statistical information on terrorism

The NCTC also provided specific information from various regions around the world:

- Africa experienced 978 attacks, an 11.5% increase from 2010. This is largely due to the more aggressive approach of the Nigeria-based terrorist group Boko Haram.

- Attacks in Europe and Eurasia decreased 20%. The greatest decline occurred in Russia, whereas Turkey experienced an increase in terrorist attacks.

- Terrorist attacks in the Western Hemisphere increased almost 40%. This is mostly due to attacks perpetrated by the Revolutionary Armed Forces of Colombia.

- East Asia and the Pacific revealed a decrease in terrorist attacks for a fifth consecutive year.

- The Near East and South Asia endured 7,721 attacks, resulting in 9,236 deaths. A majority of these attacks occurred in three countries: Afghanistan, Iraq, and Pakistan. These three countries accounted for 85% of the attacks in the region and almost 64% of terrorist attacks worldwide.[47]

Most of the attacks that occurred in 2011 were perpetrated by terrorists implementing standard fighting methods such as armed attacks, bombings, and kidnappings (almost 80%). Suicide attacks accounted for 2.7% of terrorist attacks but 21% of all terrorism-related deaths. Improvised explosive devices were the terrorist weapon most often used. One key finding was an increase in suicide attacks from 2010 (264 attacks) to 2011 (279 attacks); Sunni extremists were involved in about 93% of these attacks.[48]

In 2011, more than half of the people killed in terrorist attacks were civilians; of these victims, 755 were children. While terrorism deaths have decreased, there was an increase in such deaths among government representatives and security forces. Figure 14.1 shows the number of deaths, by victim categories, for 2011. Other findings include the following:

- When religious affiliation of terrorism victims could be determined, Muslims have suffered between 82% and 97% of terrorism-related deaths over the past 5 years.

- Muslim majority countries endured the largest number of attacks involving 10 or more deaths, with Afghanistan sustaining the highest number (47), followed by Iraq (44), Pakistan (37), Somalia (28), and Nigeria (12).

- Afghans also endured the highest number of deaths (3,245), followed by the Iraqis (2,958), Pakistanis (2,038), Somalis (1,013), and Nigerians (590).[49]

HISTORICAL CONTEXT OF MODERN TERRORISM

Even though it is difficult to offer a clear and concise definition of terrorism, it is essential that we provide a brief historical overview. Presenting some historical context provides a better understanding of terrorism's origins and helps develop an appreciation of its implications.[50] Terrorism is a type of political warfare; thus, like war, while it retains its consistent nature, the causes, objectives, and motivations of terrorism evolve. The first known terrorist group was the Sicarii, an extremist group of the religious sect of Zealots who tried to banish the Romans and their Jewish collaborators from the Judean region from A.D. 66 to 73. The term *Sicarii* refers to the short sword or *sica*, their weapon of choice.[51] During the 11th century, a Shiite Muslim sect killed politicians and clerics who did not adhere to their form of Islam. These individuals became known as "assassins." Literally, the term *assassin* meant "hashish-eater." This may be a reference to the rumor, possibly false, that these individuals engaged in ritualistic drug use prior to their missions.

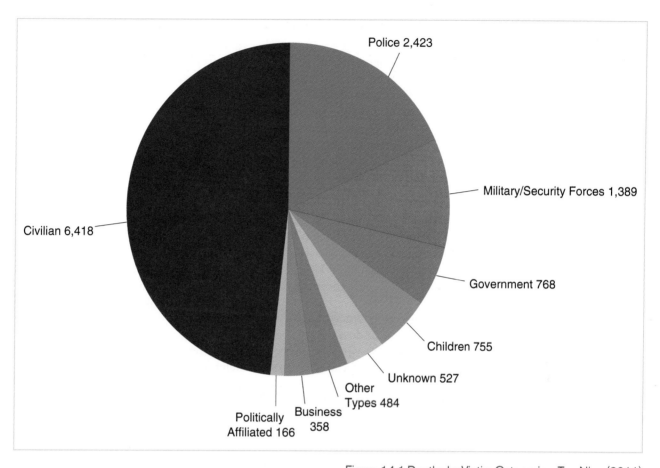

Figure 14.1 Deaths by Victim Categories, Top Nine (2011)

Source: National Counterterrorism Center. (2012). *2011 report on terrorism.* Washington, DC: National Counterterrorism Center, p. 14. Retrieved from http://www.fas.org/irp/threat/nctc2011.pdf.

Like other religiously inspired terrorists, when engaging in terrorist missions, the assassins perceived their deaths as sacrificial and believed that such a death would guarantee entrance into paradise.[52]

THE FRENCH REVOLUTION

The term *terrorism* originated from the *regime de la terreur* (reign of terror) that prevailed during the French Revolution. The regime was intended to consolidate the power of the new revolutionary government and protect it from what were considered "subversive" factors. Terrorism was initially considered a positive action.[53] In 1794, Maximilien Robespierre, the French revolutionary leader, stated that

> terror is nothing other than justice, prompt, severe, inflexible; it is therefore an emanation of virtue; it is not so much a special principle as it is a consequence of the general principle of democracy applied to our country's most urgent needs.[54]

Under this reign of terror, about 40,000 people were executed by guillotine. In fact, Robespierre and his top lieutenants were also put to death when he announced that he would be issuing a new list of subversives; some of the individuals in the revolutionary government feared their names were on this list. Soon, the French Revolution involved individuals turning on each other; the term *terrorism* eventually had a negative connotation, similar to today's value-laden meaning.[55]

LATE 19TH AND EARLY 20TH CENTURY TERRORISM

From the 1800s into the early 1900s, anarchists and socialists were responsible for a great deal of terrorism.[56] Anarchism and radical socialism were leftist ideologies that advocated for the rights of the working class and abhorred central government control, as well as private property.[57] Thus, most of the acts involving the anarchists and socialists were directed toward those perceived as supporters of the oppressive government.[58] For example, many officials in the Serbian government and military were engaged in supporting, training, and arming Balkan terrorist groups, one of which was responsible for the assassination of Archduke Franz Ferdinand on June 28, 1914. This act has been attributed to initiating World War I. Terrorist acts during this time have been labeled *state-sponsored terrorism*.[59]

After World War II, there was shift in terrorist activity; this focus moved from Europe to its various colonies. There was an increase in national movements, as well as resistance to European attempts to continue colonization across the Middle East, Asia, and Africa. These nationalist and anticolonial groups were often involved in activity involving guerrilla warfare. Conflicts occurring in Kenya, Malaysia, Cyprus, and Palestine involved groups who learned how to exploit the increasing globalization of the international media:[60]

> They also began to target innocent civilians from other countries who often had little if anything to do with the terrorists' cause or grievance, simply in order to endow their acts with the power to attract attention and publicity that the attacks against their declared or avowed enemies often lacked. Their intent was to shock and, by shocking, to stimulate worldwide fear and alarm.[61]

These groups realized that terrorism, and the fear of terrorism, could be used to serve their needs.[62]

During the 1960s and 1970s, groups engaging in terrorist activities increased; these groups expanded to include not only nationalists but those who were motivated by ethnic as well as ideological issues. Nationalist groups include the Palestinian Liberation Organization and the Provisional Irish Republican Army; groups motivated by ethnic and ideological issues include the Red Army Faction and the Italian Red Brigades.[63]

CONTEMPORARY TERRORISM

Since the September 11 attacks, terrorism has had a tremendous influence not only in the United States but on the international stage as well. A great deal of emphasis has focused on the threat posed by al Qaeda. Interestingly, "the U.S. view of terrorism nonetheless remains, to a degree, largely ego-centric—despite the current administration's rhetoric concerning a so-called 'Global War Against Terrorism.'"[64] Gus Martin contends that the modern world is challenged by the "New Terrorism," which is characterized by the following:

- Loose, cell-based networks with minimal lines of command and control

- Desired acquisition of high-intensity weapons and weapons of mass destruction

- Politically vague, religious, or mystical motivations

Martin then compared the New Terrorism with traditional terrorism, characterized by the following:

- Clearly identifiable organizations or movements

- Use of conventional weapons, usually small arms and explosives

- Explicit grievances championing specific classes or ethno-national groups

- Relatively surgical selection of targets[65]

APPLYING THEORY TO CRIME: *TERRORISM*

This section applies different theories of crime to one of the primary offenses discussed in this chapter—terrorism. Empirical studies show that the most likely theory to best explain this category of criminal behavior is strain theory, both traditional and more recent versions of this framework (Agnew, 2010; Merton, 1938). Further, social learning perspectives (differential association/reinforcement theory) are another theoretical framework that applies directly to such terrorist activities. Although other theories can also be applied to explaining terrorist behavior, versions of strain theory and social process/learning are currently among the leading theories for understanding why individuals engage in such activities.

Many notable recent acts of terrorism are based on the loss of some key positive element, whether it be land/territory (such as in the Israeli/Palestine conflict) or other types of principles/goals, such as what motivated Timothy McVeigh in his bombing of the Alfred P. Murrah Federal Building in Oklahoma City in 1995. These incidents of terrorism fit well in the framework of strain theory, including both Merton's traditional strain theory and the more modern versions of general strain theory, such as Agnew's. After all, most elements of terrorism are rooted in a feeling of strain or frustration, whether it be frustration with the current government structure or some other source (often anger with another government/state).

Specifically, in the case of the current dispute over land in Israel, the reason people revolt is because many feel that the Palestinian citizens' lands were taken from them (via the ruling by worldwide bodies that concluded that they belong to the state of Israel), which is clearly a case of losing a positive aspect of their livelihood. The Palestinian revolt over the past five decades or so has revealed this frustration and anger at having their land taken from

them. This creates a great amount of strain and frustration, which has resulted in lashing out against the existing Israeli state that they believe took this important positive aspect. This type of anger and strain clearly fits into the general strain theory model of criminal offending, which emphasizes the loss of a positive stimulus (e.g., land/territory), without compensation for this loss.

A recent study by Agnew (2010) has shown that terrorism fits well in the framework of general strain theory, due to the feelings of anger and strain that create strong motivations for engaging in terrorist attacks against those who are primarily to blame for the loss of positive stimuli (in this case, land/territory, the Palestinian state, etc.). And it certainly fits regarding the anger and frustration of the Palestinians in trying to reacquire their land in the face of an overwhelming force—the state of Israel (with the backing of the United States and other governments).

Another example is that of McVeigh, who was responsible for one of the worst cases of domestic terrorism. As a sympathizer of militia movements, McVeigh's goal in his bombings was to try to get revenge against the U.S. federal government regarding its handling of the 1993 siege (which killed 76 people) in Waco, Texas, as well as the killing of militia citizens at Ruby Ridge in 1992. Ultimately, his goals fit well in traditional strain theory (Merton, 1938), especially regarding the adaptation of rebel or rebellion, in which a person desires certain means and goals for society but strongly disagrees with the current conventionally established means and goals and therefore seeks to change them. This is exactly what McVeigh sought to do by bombing the federal building. Unfortunately, many of the victims of his attack were children in the building's day care center. So his act was seen not as an attack on authority or the current political state but, rather,

as a massacre of innocent victims who had nothing to do with the ideological and political climate he was fighting against.

Other theories can also help explain the terrorism we have discussed in this section. For example, the social process/learning theories of differential association/reinforcement (Akers, 1985; Sutherland, 1939) offer a good explanation for why certain individuals engage in terrorist activity. To clarify, these theories emphasize the influence of significant others (e.g., peers, family) in promoting such behavior. Regarding the two notable incidents of terrorism described in this section, it is obvious that both cases involve a social learning element. Specifically, in both the Israeli/Palestinian conflict and the McVeigh bombing of the federal building, certain ideals are being internalized by the offenders via their peers and other significant others. In fact, a rather extensive doctoral dissertation study by Silverman (2002) supported the fact that social learning played an important role in various forms of terrorism. It is quite certain that such social learning factors play a key role in the ongoing conflict within the state of Israel, which appears to be socialized from generation to generation via families and peers, as well as in McVeigh's motivation for bombing the federal building, which was documented by his association with coconspirator Terry Nichols, who taught him how to make explosives.

Ultimately, these two examples of terrorism fit well in the framework of strain theory (both traditional and modern versions), as well as various social learning components. There are other theories that also help explain modern terrorism (e.g., culture theory), but this section has showed that strain theory and social learning theory are two of the most likely explanatory models for understanding modern forms of terrorism.

Sources: Agnew, R. (2010). A general strain theory of terrorism. *Theoretical Criminology, 14*, 131–153; Akers, R. L. (1985). *Deviant behavior: A social learning approach* (3rd ed.). Belmont, CA: Wadsworth; Merton, R. K. (1938). Social structure and anomie. *American Sociological Review, 3*, 672–682; Silverman, A. L. (2002). *Exploratory analysis of interdisciplinary theory of terrorism*. Ann Arbor, MI: UMI; Sutherland, E. H. (1939). *Principles of criminology* (3rd ed.). Philadelphia: Lippincott.

COMPARATIVE CRIMINOLOGY: *TERRORISM*

Quality of Rule of Law and Perceived Cost of Terrorism

Gupta[66] and Schmid[67] examined whether there was a link between the rule of law in a country and the prevalence of terrorist incidents. Their research revealed a negative association between these two factors. For instance, Gupta's research demonstrated that a lack of civil and political rights (i.e., the rule of law is weak) was related to terrorist incidents. Schmid's research also demonstrated a link between his index of terrorism and whether countries observed human rights or engaged in some form of state repression. Citing these works, Van Dijk replicated these studies by using the index of *costs of terrorism for business* as an indicator of terrorism; he used the World Bank index as an indicator of the rule of law.[68]

Figure 14.2 illustrates the results of these analyses. A low score on the rule of law indicates

high quality; a high score on the cost of terrorism indicates high prevalence of terrorist incidents. This figure reveals that terrorism incidents are more common, or thought to be more common, in those countries where the rule of law is weak. Interestingly, there were some countries that were considered "outliers"—specifically, the United States and Israel. Van Dijk concluded that this was due to these countries being susceptible to international terrorism.

Further analyses noted a weak association between police performance and terrorism. Specifically, in those countries that ranked high on the Police Performance Index (i.e., better performing policing), terrorist incidents are considered less of a threat. Van Dijk noted that terrorist "threats seem to be facilitated by institutional failures to maintain the rule of law, including through democratic and effective policing."[69]

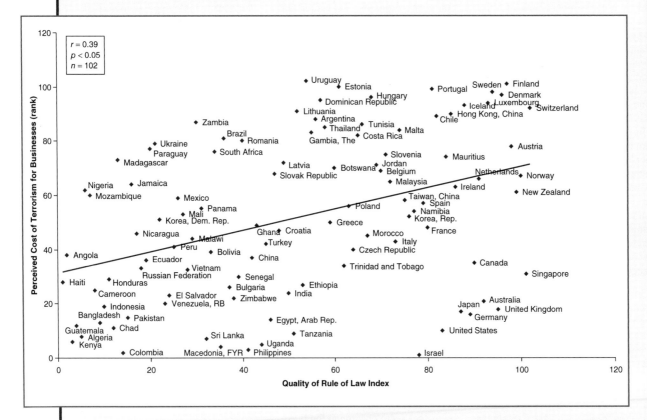

Figure 14.2 Quality of Perceived Cost of Terrorism per Country

Sources: World Economic Forum. (2003). *The Global Competitiveness Report 2002–2003*. New York: Oxford University Press; Kaufmann, D., Kraay, A., & Mastruzzi, M. (2004). *Governance matters III: Governance indicators for 1996–2002*. Policy Research Working Paper 3106. Washington, D.C. World Bank. see www.worldbank.org/wbi/governance/govdata; and the rule of law index (WBI).

CURRENT CONTEXT OF TERRORISM

It is essential that terrorists constantly move, develop more effective tactics, and create new structures to avoid detection. Terrorist groups need to continually change for their prolonged existence. In addition to an organizational structure, a terrorist group also needs to have financial resources. These two factors interact with change. The organizational structure and financial resources are influenced by the strategic philosophy of a given movement.[70]

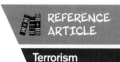

REFERENCE ARTICLE

Terrorism

ORGANIZATIONAL NETWORKS

Jonathan White provided an overview of how terrorist organizational structures have changed over time (see Figure 14.3).[71] The traditional terrorist organization comprised cells; groups of cells formed columns. Members in the cells rarely knew one another. Soon the organization structure was modified to a pyramid, either large or small. The pyramids represent the hierarchical nature of the groups, with the passive and active supporters at the base and the active cadre and command at the top.

During the early 1980s, a new organizational structure developed from the pyramid. The first structural change was the umbrella organization. In this organizational structure, numerous small pyramids are assembled under a sheltering group. This sheltering group manages supplies, acquires resources, develops support structures, and obtains intelligence. The umbrella organization is disconnected from the terrorist activities. In the 1990s, the RAND Corporation identified other types of new organizational structures.[72] One is virtual organizations. This organizational structure evolves through communication, financial, and ideological links. A virtual organization has no central leadership. Another structure is chain organizations. Chain organizations are temporary associations with various groups. These groups gather for a specific operation; upon completion of

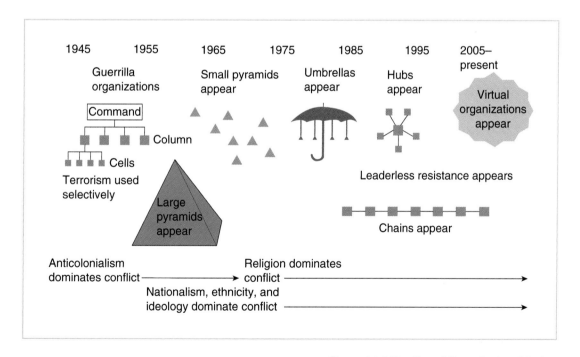

Figure 14.3 Timeline of Organizational Styles

Source: White, J. R. (2012). *Terrorism and homeland security* (7th ed.). Belmont, CA: Wadsworth, p. 77.

that operation, they disperse. Hub organizations are established to manage or support cells; they function similarly to umbrella groups.

FINANCIAL SUPPORT

An essential method to combat terrorism is restricting the financing of such organizations.[73] Limiting their financial resources can result in the following: (1) It can directly or indirectly influence an organization's leadership, morale, and legitimacy (e.g., diminish support from members and other terrorist organizations), and (2) it can have strategic implications (e.g., a group may not have the necessary resources to accomplish a planned attack).[74] For example, in 2003, a terrorist group was planning to simultaneously bomb the Egyptian, American, and other Western embassies in Pakistan. Due to a lack of financial resources, the group focused solely on attacking the Egyptian embassy:

> A short time before the bombing of the [Egyptian] embassy the assigned group . . . told us that they could strike both the Egyptian and American embassies if we gave them enough money. We had already provided them with all that we had and we couldn't collect more money.[75]

Authorities have focused on two general activities to limit terrorist financing: (1) **money laundering** and (2) **fundraising**. While these are two different types of activities, sometimes they are interconnected. Money laundering is a process whereby funds, obtained through illegal activities, are "cleansed."[76] Specifically, this involves a three-step process: (1) The illegally obtained monies are placed into the financial system; (2) these monies are layered, or processed, through the system, usually internationally, and subsequently intermingled with legal monies; and (3) the monies are turned and reintegrated into the legitimate economy.[77]

These ill-gotten monies are obtained through various criminal activities. One such activity is drug trafficking: "If we cannot kill them with guns, . . . we will kill them with drugs."[78] There are documented connections between terrorist groups and drug trafficking, particularly in reference to smuggling pseudoephedrine (used to manufacture methamphetamine). Another criminal activity linked to terrorist financing is fraud, involving credit cards, welfare, Social Security, insurance, food stamps, and coupons.[79]

Terrorist organizations also use fundraising to finance their activities. One such method has been to use charities. The Irish Republican Army has used this method for decades to fund its attacks in Northern Ireland and England.[80] Osama bin Laden used charity fundraising to finance al Qaeda.[81] In November 2008, five former leaders of a U.S.-based Muslim charity, Holy Land Foundation, were convicted of channeling more than $12 million to the Palestinian terrorist group Hamas. Patrick Rowan, assistant attorney general for National Security, stated that "for many years, the Holy Land Foundation used the guise of charity to raise and funnel millions of dollars to the infrastructure of the Hamas terror organization."[82]

INFLUENCE OF THE MEDIA

Much of what the general public knows about terrorism is from the media. Simon Cottle identified the various communication frames used to report on terrorism.[83] These frames include *reporting frames* that are short and blended with facts; *dominant frames* from one authority's viewpoint; *conflict frames* consisting of two perspectives; *contention frames* comprising various positions; *investigative frames* that expose corrupt or illegal behavior; *campaigning frames,* which are the broadcaster's opinion; *reportage frames* comprising comprehensive coverage; *community service frames,* which provide information to the

VIDEO ▶

Money Laundering

....

money laundering: a process whereby funds, obtained through illegal activities, are "cleansed"

fundraising: used by terrorist organizations to finance their activities public; *collective interest frames* that reinforce common values and viewpoints; *cultural recognition frames* that reflect a group's values and norms; and *mythic tales frames* consisting of hero stories.

As noted in the beginning of this section, terrorism is a social construct. One area that can shape the social construction of terrorism is the media; the meanings associated with terrorism can be shaped by the media. Terrorists are also attentive to the power of the media and will increase the use of various forms of media, such as the Internet, to convey their message and purpose.[84] White outlined some of the issues associated with the media and reporting terrorism.[85] One of these issues centers on whether the media present information on terrorism in an unbiased and objective manner. Governments and terrorists attempt to manipulate the news; thus, it is essential that the media take an objective position and "just tell the truth." However, some maintain that this assumption is naive.[86] Another issue is the contention effect. This refers to whether media coverage of a terrorist incident inspires more terrorism. The issue of censorship is also raised when individuals assume that terrorist acts are influenced by irresponsible media coverage and that this coverage can provide terrorists with information. As White noted,

> These new media organizations not only cover the drama but add differing interpretations and flavors to their stories. An Algerian terrorist once said he would rather kill one victim in front of a news camera than one hundred in the desert where the world would not see them. His point should be noted: Modern terrorism is a media phenomenon.[87]

DOMESTIC TERRORISM

While this section has focused on what some designate as *international terrorism*, another form of terrorism has been identified as **domestic terrorism.** The FBI defines domestic terrorism as

> the unlawful use, or threatened use, of force or violence by a group or individual based and operating entirely within the United States or Puerto Rico without foreign direction committed against persons or property to intimidate or coerce a government, the civilian population, or any segment thereof in furtherance of political or social objectives.[88]

Essentially, this is when Americans attack other Americans, often based on extremist ideologies. The FBI contends that domestic terror threats include white supremacists, destructive eco-terrorists, violence-prone antigovernment extremists, and radical separatist groups, among others.[89] See Box 14.1 for some of the FBI's most wanted offenders for domestic terrorism.

Martin maintained that most of the political violence in the United States can be categorized as either *left* or *right*.[90] The *left* applies to those political trends and movements that stress group rights. Examples include labor activism, people's rights, single issues (e.g., environmentalists, peace movements), and questioning traditions.[91] Examples of single-issue groups from the left are the Animal Liberation Front (ALF) and the Earth Liberation Front (ELF). ALF's credo includes the following:

> The Animal Liberation Front (ALF) carries out direct action against animal abuse in the form of rescuing animals and causing financial loss to animal exploiters, usually through the damage and destruction of property. . . . Because ALF actions may be against the law, activists work anonymously, either in small groups or individually, and do not have any centralized organization or coordination.[92]

domestic terrorism: unlawful use, or threatened use, of force or violence by a group or individual based in the United States to intimidate or coerce others to further political or social objectives

BOX 14.1: FBI'S MOST WANTED FOR DOMESTIC TERRORISM

DONNA JOAN BORUP

Unlawful Flight to Avoid Prosecution—Riot, Assault on a Police Officer

Donna Joan Borup is wanted for her alleged participation in the violent disruption of an anti-apartheid demonstration at JFK International Airport in Queens, New York, on September 26, 1981. During the riot, Borup allegedly tossed an acidic substance into the eyes of a Port Authority Police Officer, leaving him partially blind. At the time, Borup was a member of the May 19th Communist Organization, a Marxist-Leninist organization that advocated for armed revolution and the violent overthrow of the United States Government. Borup, along with some accomplices, was arrested and released on bail pending trial in May of 1982.

On May 20, 1982, an arrest warrant was issued for Borup after she failed to appear for her trial on a Queens County indictment that charged her with riot in the first degree and assault in the first degree. On September 14, 1982, a federal arrest warrant was issued for Borup in the Eastern District of New York and she was charged with unlawful flight to avoid prosecution.

Borup has ties to Philadelphia and Horsham, Pennsylvania. She may wear eyeglasses and baggy clothes. Borup is thought to have a photographic memory and is highly intelligent.

JOSEPHINE SUNSHINE OVERAKER

Conspiracy to Commit Arson of United States Government Property and of Property Used in Interstate Commerce; Conspiracy to Commit Arson and Destruction of an Energy Facility; Attempted Arson of a Building; Arson of a Vehicle; Arson of a Building; Destruction of an Energy Facility

REWARD: The FBI is offering a reward of up to $50,000 for information leading to the arrest of Josephine Sunshine Overaker.

On January 19, 2006, a federal grand jury in Eugene, Oregon, indicted Josephine Sunshine Overaker on multiple charges related to her alleged role in a domestic terrorism cell. Overaker was charged with two conspiracy violations related to seventeen incidents, five counts of arson, one count of attempted arson, and one count of destruction of an energy facility. These crimes occurred in Oregon, Washington, California, Colorado, and Wyoming, and date back to 1996. Many of the crimes she is accused of participating in were claimed to be committed by the Earth Liberation Front (ELF) or the Animal Liberation Front (ALF).

Overaker is fluent in Spanish. She is known to use illegal narcotics. Overaker may have a light facial moustache. She was a vegan and may still be. Overaker is an American citizen.

ELIZABETH ANNA DUKE

Unlawful Possession of United States Identification; Conspiracy; Unlawful Storage of Explosives; Unlawful Possession of Firearms and Destructive Devices; Storage and Concealment of Stolen Explosives; Unlawful Possession of Five or More False Identification Documents; Possession of Counterfeit Social Security Cards; Aiding and Abetting; Unlawful Possession of Document-Making Implement

REWARD: The FBI is offering a reward of up to $50,000 for information leading directly to the arrest and conviction of Elizabeth Anna Duke.

Elizabeth Anna Duke is wanted for her alleged involvement in a series of criminal activities during the late 1970s and early 1980s. She was allegedly a member of the radical group known as the May

19th Communist Organization, which advocated communism and the violent overthrow of the United States Government. Duke was arrested in Bucks County, Pennsylvania, in May of 1985 for her alleged participation in this group, but was released on bail. She later fled the jurisdiction and has been a fugitive since October of 1985. A federal arrest warrant was issued for Duke in the Eastern District of Pennsylvania on November 13, 1986, charging her with the aforementioned federal charges.

Duke is known to speak fluent Spanish. She has ties to Texas and is known to travel in the northern United States near the Canadian border.

LEO FREDERICK BURT

Sabotage; Destruction of Government Property; Conspiracy

REWARD: The FBI is offering $150,000 for information leading to the arrest of Leo Frederick Burt.

Leo Frederick Burt is wanted for allegedly participating in the bombing of Sterling Hall, on the campus of the University of Wisconsin, on August 24, 1970.

The blast from the explosion, combined with the fire, resulted in the death of a 33-year-old researcher. Additionally, there were several injuries reported and an estimated $6 million damage to the building and its contents. Reportedly, explosives had been placed in a stolen panel truck, located three blocks from the building, just several days before the blast. Also, a light-colored, late-model vehicle (Corvair) was seen leaving the vicinity of the bombing, and Burt was identified as being in the car.

On September 2, 1970, Leo Burt was indicted federally in Madison, Wisconsin. He was charged with sabotage, destruction of government property, and conspiracy.

ELF was founded in England by a former activist of the group Earthfirst! These individuals separated from Earthfirst! because of that organization's decision to stop engaging in criminal activities. Some consider this group more radical than ALF.[93]

The *right* consists of political trends and movements that stress conventional and traditional principles such as family values, educational content, and social-order politics.[94] Right-wing terrorism is often motivated by racial supremacism and antigovernment viewpoints. Compared with left-wing groups, right-wing terrorist activities are rare, with an attack such as that in Oklahoma City being uncommon.[95] Moralist terrorism is one example of right-wing political violence. Most moral terrorist activities are motivated by a religious doctrine that is considered a "fringe interpretation" of Christianity. Abortion clinics and gay bars have often been the targets of moralist violence.[96] One such group is the Army of God, which opposes abortion and homosexuality. Apparently, the Army of God's ideology is an extreme interpretation of fundamentalist Protestantism. There are some racial supremacist predispositions as well.[97] For instance, on its website, when referring to individuals who have killed doctors who perform abortions, the Army of God used such phrases as these:

- "This is why the shooting of babykilling abortionist George Tiller was Justifiable Homicide."

- "Thank you Scott Roeder for stopping Babykilling abortionist George Tiller from murdering any more innocent children."

- "Now George Tiller will never murder another child."[98]

THEORETICAL EXPLANATIONS OF TERRORISM

Brian Forst noted that "the challenges presented by terrorism are in many ways more formidable than those presented by conventional crime."[99] He identified three general barriers to understanding terrorism. First, while terrorism cases are similar with respect to having a political motive, there are numerous differences as well. For instance, terrorism cases vary by type of extremism (e.g., Islamic, Christian fundamentalist, environmental), connection to a larger network, extent of planning, type of attack (e.g., assassination, hostage taking), ideological justification, nature of target, weapon of choice, and extent of fatalities.

Second, in most instances, terrorists, unlike other criminals, engage in unpredictable activities. These terrorists attempt to create fear and mayhem by purposely operating outside of conventional patterns. For instance, after the September 11 attacks, when terrorist screening procedures overlooked women as suicide bombers, terrorists enlisted women for this type of bombing. These unpredictable patterns are difficult to examine in the data.

Finally, compared with other types of crime, terrorism is difficult to analyze because there is a relatively small amount of reliable data on cases of each major form of terrorism to provide a foundation for statistical inference. As Forst notes, while a few terrorist cases in the United States have provided some empirical analysis, this lack of data "is a curse for empirically oriented analysts interested in understanding terrorism."[100]

Despite these barriers, however, there have been attempts to enhance our understanding of terrorism. As mentioned previously, the National Counterterrorism Center is collecting data on terrorist incidents. This type of information is helpful in developing theoretical models to understand causal factors associated with terrorism. One such model is routine activities theory. In Chapter 3, we discussed key components of routine activities theory. For a crime to occur, there must be willing offenders, suitable targets, and an absence of adequate guardianship.[101] If any one of these factors is unmet or absent, there is no opportunity for a terrorist act to occur. One notable conclusion of this theory in explaining and preventing terrorism is to avoid situations where there is a lack of guardianship. Another factor to consider is diminishing willing offenders, such as by enhancing surveillance of extremists and targeting individuals and groups with terrorist affiliations.

Another theoretical model that could enhance our understating of terrorism is **game theory**. The military uses game theory for teaching, training, and operational studies. Another formal use of this theory is with business and economic games. However, game theory has also been used increasingly to study social and other problems such as political and social processes.[102] This analytic approach assesses various scenarios by applying simulation gaming models.[103] Generally, the analysis of games has two goals. The first goal is to understand why the parties (i.e., players) in competitive situations behave as they do. The second goal is to advise the players of the best way to play the game.[104] Thus, game theory "could prove equally useful for assessing alternative approaches to protecting any prospective target against threats posed by terrorism."[105]

HOMELAND SECURITY

On September 11, 2001, the most horrible attacks of modern international terrorism occurred in the United States. Nineteen al Qaeda terrorists were responsible for these attacks. They were on a suicidal "martyrdom mission" to fight in the name of a holy cause against what they perceived to be an evil enemy from the West. Their purpose was

---

AUTHOR PODCAST 🔊

Terrorism

---

game theory: assesses various scenarios by applying simulation gaming models, usually to understand why parties in competitive situations behave as they do and to advise players of the best way to play the game to attack symbols of American, and Western, interests that they deemed responsible for the continuing domination and exploitation of Muslim countries.[106] These attacks were targeted at the World Trade Center in New York City and the Pentagon in northern Virginia. The attacks resulted in 3,030 deaths and 2,337 injuries. There were 343 firefighters and 75 police officers killed responding to these attacks.[107]

After these attacks, the United States realized the need to develop a national security strategy. In this section, we will first attempt to answer the question "What is homeland security?" including a summary of the origins and definition. Next, we will provide an overview of the organizational structure of **homeland security**, including those agencies responsible for this task and some bureaucratic problems and solutions. Finally, we will cover some of the civil liberty issues that are challenged by national security concerns.

> ## LEARNING CHECK 14.2
>
> _____ includes terrorist acts that transpire due to the direct, or indirect, guidance of the state or government. The term *terrorism* originated from the reign of terror that prevailed during the _____. The traditional terrorist organization comprised _____. Another theoretical model that could enhance our understating of terrorism, used in the military for teaching, training, and operational studies, is _____.
>
> Answers located at www.sagepub.com/schram

WHAT IS HOMELAND SECURITY?

ORIGINS OF HOMELAND SECURITY

When these attacks occurred, it was painfully clear not only that the United States was vulnerable to such attacks but that the country was ill equipped to prevent them. While there was a history of terrorist attacks throughout the world, and there had been a few in the United States, preparing for such attacks was a low priority.[108] The September 11 attacks, as well as the fear of subsequent attacks, "significantly changed the national philosophy and ushered in a new strategy and American defense system. Nonetheless, the country had little foundation from which to build a national prevention strategy."[109]

On October 8, 2001, President George W. Bush issued Executive Order 13228. The order established the Office of Homeland Security as well as the Homeland Security Council. Specifically, it laid the foundation for implementation of a new concept of homeland security as it relates to counterterrorist policies.[110] The initial responsibility of the Office of Homeland Security was to produce the first National Strategy for Homeland Security in 2002. This strategy was to address four questions:

- What is "homeland security," and what missions does it entail?

- What do we seek to accomplish, and what are the most important goals of homeland security?

- What is the federal executive branch doing now to accomplish these goals, and what should it do in the future?

- What should nonfederal governments, the private sector, and citizens do to help secure the homeland?[111]

In 2003, the Department of Homeland Security was created from the Office of Homeland Security.[112] This was considered the most noteworthy transformation of the U.S. government in more than 50 years, primarily because it transformed and realigned "the current

homeland security: a unified national effort to prevent terrorist attacks within the United States, lessen America's vulnerability to terrorism, and minimize the damage resulting from such attacks confusing patchwork of government activities into a single department whose primary mission is to protect our homeland."[113]

DEFINITION OF HOMELAND SECURITY

The 2002 National Strategy for Homeland Security defined homeland security as follows:

> Homeland security is a concerted national effort to prevent terrorist attacks within the United States, reduce America's vulnerability to terrorism, and minimize the damage and recover from attacks that do occur.[114]

This strategy outlined a framework for achieving homeland security, which comprised four general goals: (1) Prevent and disrupt terrorist attacks; (2) protect the American people, critical infrastructure, and key resources; (3) respond to and recover from incidents that do occur; and (4) continue to strengthen the foundation to ensure long-term success.[115]

Upon examining the literature on homeland security, Christopher Bellavita recognized the various definitions of homeland security implemented since the September 11 attacks.[116] These definitions have been developed to address the events that have been the focus of homeland security programming; they include terrorism, all hazards, terrorism and catastrophes, jurisdictional hazards, meta hazards, national security, and security *uber alles* (see Table 14.4 for a detailed list of these definitions). For instance, under the definition of *jurisdictional hazards,* homeland security is founded more on a local jurisdiction and its experiences with various hazards (e.g., hurricanes, wildfires, floods, tornados), rather than on a federal decree. Bellavita asks, "What are the likely incidents that threaten the safety and security of local jurisdictions?" He then proceeds to answer that question by illustrating the various major incidents that occurred in the United States from September 11, 2001, to December 31, 2007 (see Figure 14.4). This information is based on the

HOMELAND SECURITY DEFINITIONS
1. *Terrorism.* Homeland security is a concerted national effort by federal, state, and local governments, by the private sector, and by individuals to prevent terrorist attacks within the United States, reduce America's vulnerability to terrorism, and minimize the damage and recover from attacks that do occur.
2. *All Hazards.* Homeland security is a concerted national effort to prevent and disrupt terrorist attacks, protect against man-made and natural hazards, and respond to and recover from incidents that do occur.
3. *Terrorism and Catastrophes.* Homeland security is what the Department of Homeland Security—supported by other federal agencies—does to prevent, respond to, and recover from terrorist and catastrophic events that affect the security of the United States.
4. *Jurisdictional Hazards.* Homeland security means something different in each jurisdiction. It is a locally-directed effort to prevent and prepare for incidents most likely to threaten the safety and security of its citizens.
5. *Meta Hazards.* Homeland security is a national effort to prevent or mitigate any social trend or threat that can disrupt the long-term stability of the American way of life.
6. *National Security.* Homeland security is an element of national security that works with the other instruments of national power to protect the sovereignty, territory, domestic population, and critical infrastructure of the United States against threats and aggression.
7. *Security Uber Alles.* Homeland security is a symbol used to justify government efforts to curtail civil liberties.

Table 14.4 Definitions of Homeland Security

Source: Bellavita, C. (2008). Changing homeland security: What is homeland security? *Homeland Security Affairs, 4,* 1–2.

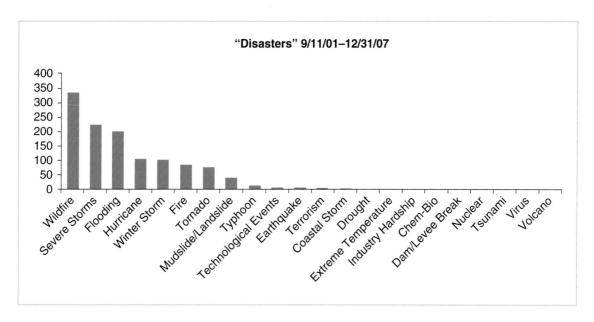

Figure 14.4 Types of Disasters Recorded by FEMA From September 11, 2001, Through December 31, 2007

Source: Bellavita, C. (2008). Changing homeland security: What is homeland security? *Homeland Security Affairs, 4*, 8.

Federal Emergency Management Agency (FEMA) database. Thus, "if homeland security is a part of a doctrine that plans for the most probable incidents, most of the country can safely ignore terrorism as a threat."[117]

ORGANIZATIONAL NETWORK

Since the creation of the **Department of Homeland Security** (DHS), there have been various modifications given the evolving nature of recognizing, and addressing, the range of threats faced by the United States. Eleven days after the September 11 attacks, Pennsylvania governor Tom Ridge was appointed the first director of the Office of Homeland Security. In November 2002, Congress passed the Homeland Security Act, making the DHS into a stand-alone, Cabinet-level department. In February 2005, Secretary Michael Chertoff took office and instigated a review of the DHS's operations, policies, and structures. Subsequently, additional modifications were adopted, including the Post-Katrina Emergency Management Reform Act of 2006 and the Security Accountability for Every Port (SAFE Port) Act of 2006. In 2010, Janet Napolitano was named the third secretary of the DHS. Secretary Napolitano initiated additional reviews of the DHS to further enhance national security.[118] Figure 14.5 shows the department's organizational chart.

AGENCIES RESPONSIBLE FOR HOMELAND SECURITY

In this section, we provide a brief summary of some key agencies within the DHS, including the Transportation Security Administration, U.S. Customs and Border Protection, U.S. Citizenship and Immigration Services, U.S. Secret Service, FEMA, and U.S. Coast Guard (see Figure 14.6).

TRANSPORTATION SECURITY ADMINISTRATION. With the passage of the Aviation and Transportation Security Act, the **Transportation Security Administration (TSA)** was

Department of Homeland Security: a Cabinet department of the U.S. federal government, established in 2003 in response to the September 11 attacks; main responsibilities include protecting the United States from terrorist attacks and responding to terrorist attacks, man-made accidents, and natural disasters

Transportation Security Administration (TSA): provides security for all types of transportation; recruits, assesses, hires, trains, and deploys security officers for commercial airports; and provides screening of all checked luggage

U.S. DEPARTMENT OF HOMELAND SECURITY

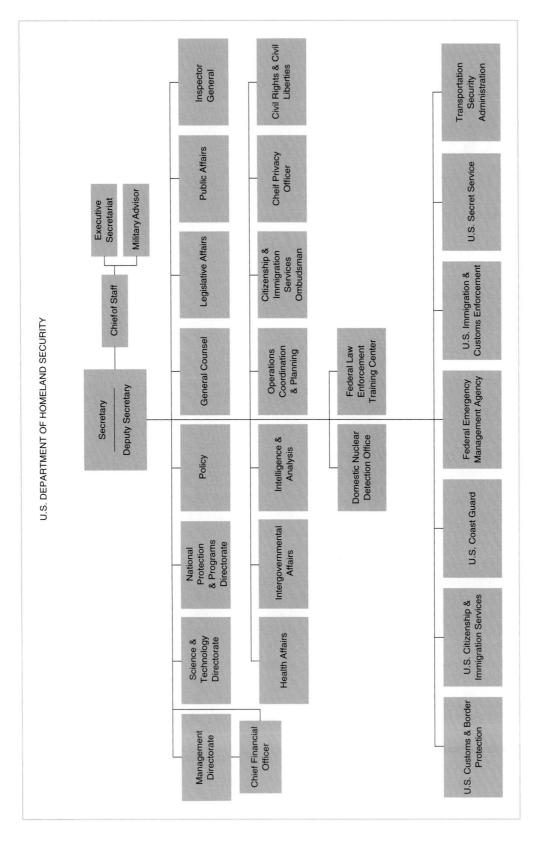

Figure 14.5 Organizational Chart for the Department of Homeland Security

Source: Retrieved from http://www.dhs.gov/xabout/structure/editorial_0644.shtm.

WHO JOINED DHS

Learn more about how the Department of Homeland Security (DHS) was created through the integration of all or part of 22 different federal departments and agencies into a unified, integrated Department and how DHS has become a more effective Department.

CHRONOLOGY OF EVENTS

LEAD UP TO 9/11	TODAY
The U.S. Customs Service (Treasury)	U.S. Customs and Border Protection—inspection, border and ports of entry responsibilities U.S. Immigration and Customs Enforcement—customs law enforcement responsibilities
The Immigration and Naturalization Service (Justice)	U.S. Customs and Border Protection—inspection functions and the U.S. Border Patrol U.S. Immigration and Customs Enforcement—immigration law enforcement: detention and removal, intelligence, and investigations U.S. Citizenship and Immigration Services—adjudications and benefits programs
The Federal Protective Service	U.S. Immigration and Customs Enforcement until 2009; currently resides within the National Protection and Programs Directorate
The Transportation Security Administration (Transportation)	Transportation Security Administration
Federal Law Enforcement Training Center (Treasury)	Federal Law Enforcement Training Center
Animal and Plant Health Inspection Service (part) (Agriculture)	U.S. Customs and Border Protection—agricultural imports and entry inspections
Office for Domestic Preparedness (Justice)	Responsibilities distributed within FEMA
The Federal Emergency Management Agency (FEMA)	Federal Emergency Management Agency
Strategic National Stockpile and the National Disaster Medical System (HHS)	Returned to Health and Human Services, July 2004
Nuclear Incident Response Team (Energy)	Responsibilities distributed within FEMA
Domestic Emergency Support Teams (Justice)	Responsibilities distributed within FEMA
National Domestic Preparedness Office (FBI)	Responsibilities distributed within FEMA
CBRN Countermeasures Programs (Energy)	Science & Technology Directorate
Environmental Measurements Laboratory (Energy)	Science & Technology Directorate
National BW Defense Analysis Center (Defense)	Science & Technology Directorate
Plum Island Animal Disease Center (Agriculture)	Science & Technology Directorate
Federal Computer Incident Response Center (GSA)	US-CERT, Office of Cybersecurity and Communications in the National Protection and Programs Directorate
National Communications System (Defense)	Office of Cybersecurity and Communications in the National Protection and Programs Directorate
National Infrastructure Protection Center (FBI)	Dispersed throughout the Department, including Office of Operations Coordination and Office of Infrastructure Protection
Energy Security and Assurance Program (Energy)	Integrated into the Office of Infrastructure Protection
U.S. Coast Guard	U.S. Coast Guard
U.S. Secret Service	U.S. Secret Service

Figure 14.6 Agencies Transferred to the Department of Homeland Security

Source: Retrieved from http://www.dhs.gov/who-joined-dhs.

established after the September 11 attacks to strengthen the security of the country's transportation system. The TSA issued three mandates: (1) take responsibility for security for all types of transportation; (2) recruit, assess, hire, train, and deploy security officers for 450 commercial airports; and (3) provide screening of all checked luggage for explosives. In March 2003, the TSA was moved from the Department of Transportation to the DHS.[119] Most people assume that the TSA is primarily concerned with airport security; as noted above, however, the TSA is responsible for all types of transportation, including aviation, waterways, rail, highways, public transportation, and pipelines.[120]

U.S. CUSTOMS AND BORDER PROTECTION. To collect tariffs on goods imported into the United States, Congress created the U.S. Customs Service in 1789. This agency was responsible for collecting tariffs, which supported the country's early infrastructure, for more than 125 years.[121] In March 2003, **U.S. Customs and Border Protection (CBP)** was established as part of the DHS. Agencies transferred to the DHS, along with the U.S. Customs Service, include the Department of Agriculture, Animal, and Plant Health Inspection Service; the U.S. Border Patrol; and the U.S. Immigration and Naturalization Service. The CBP is "responsible for securing the borders of the United States while simultaneously facilitating the flow of legitimate trade and travel."[122] CBP's primary law enforcement responsibilities include apprehending criminals and other individuals who attempt to illegally enter the United States, seizing illegal drugs and contraband, and protecting agriculture from harmful pests and diseases.[123]

U.S. CITIZENSHIP AND IMMIGRATION SERVICES. In 2003, the services and functions of the U.S. Immigration and Naturalization Service (INS) were moved to the DHS, and the department was subsequently renamed the **U.S. Citizenship and Immigration Services (USCIS)**. As noted above, the enforcement and inspection functions of INS were moved to CBP.[124] USCIS is responsible for administration of immigration and naturalization adjudication functions. Some of these functions include granting U.S. citizenship, processing immigrant visa and naturalization petitions, adjudicating asylum and refugee applications, and issuing documents for employment authorization.[125]

U.S. IMMIGRATION AND CUSTOMS ENFORCEMENT. **U.S. Immigration and Customs Enforcement (ICE)** was created as the primary investigative arm of the DHS.[126] ICE was created by merging the law enforcement branch of the INS, the intelligence and investigative sections of the former U.S. Customs Service, and the U.S. Federal Protective Services.[127] While CBP focuses on securing U.S. borders, ICE's responsibilities go beyond the borders. Thus, "ICE attempts to identify criminal activities and vulnerabilities that pose a threat to the nation, as well as enforcing economic, transportation, and infrastructure security."[128] The ICE Strategic Plan includes preventing terrorism and improving security; protecting the boarders against illicit trade, travel, and finance; and protecting the borders through enhanced interior immigration enforcement.[129]

U.S. SECRET SERVICE. The **U.S. Secret Service** was created in 1865 to suppress counterfeit currency. After the assassination of President William McKinley in 1901, the Secret Service became responsible for the protection of the president. In 1984, Congress passed legislation making the fraudulent use of credit and debit cards a federal violation; the Secret Service was authorized to investigate these violations. Under the PATRIOT Act of 2001 (discussed below), the Secret Service was authorized to investigate fraud and similar activities related to computers. The U.S. Secret Service was transferred from the Department of the Treasury to the DHS in 2003.[130] As noted in its mission statement,

> the United States Secret Service is to safeguard the nation's financial infrastructure and payment systems to preserve the integrity of the economy, and to protect national leaders, visiting heads of state and government, designated sites and National Special Security Events.[131]

U.S. Customs and Border Protection (CBP): responsible for securing U.S. borders while also monitoring the flow of legitimate trade and travel

U.S. Citizenship and Immigration Services (USCIS): responsible for administration of immigration and naturalization adjudication functions

U.S. Immigration and Customs Enforcement (ICE): focuses on identifying criminal activities and vulnerabilities that may be a threat to the country

U.S. Secret Service: responsible for safeguarding the country's financial infrastructure and payment systems, as well as protecting national leaders and visiting heads of state and government

FEDERAL EMERGENCY MANAGEMENT AGENCY. The **Federal Emergency Management Agency (FEMA)** was created under the Robert T. Stafford Disaster Relief and Emergency Assistance Act of 1988. This act established the statutory authority for most federal response activities to prepare for, protect against, respond to, recover from, and alleviate all types of hazards. In 2003, FEMA became part of the DHS, along with many other agencies.[132] FEMA focuses on four initiatives: (1) Foster a whole community approach to emergency management nationwide, (2) build the country's ability to stabilize and recover from a catastrophic event, (3) build unity of effort and common strategic understanding among the emergency management team, and (4) enhance FEMA's ability to learn and innovate as an organization.[133] When the president declares an area a disaster, FEMA is then initiated to respond. FEMA activities include both short- and long-term responses; these activities also include coordinating with state and local personnel.[134]

U.S. COAST GUARD. Established in 1790, the **U.S. Coast Guard's** primary responsibility was to enforce the country's maritime laws, interests, and environment. The U.S. Coast Guard is one of the five armed forces of the United States; it is now the only military organization within the DHS.[135] The Coast Guard's homeland security role includes the following:

- Protecting ports, the flow of commerce, and the marine transportation system from terrorism

- Maintaining maritime borderer security against illegal drugs, illegal aliens, firearms, and weapons of mass destruction

- Ensuring that the United States can rapidly deploy and resupply military assets by maintaining the Coast Guard at a high state of readiness, as well as by keeping marine transportation open for other military services

- Protecting against illegal fishing and indiscriminate destruction of living marine resources

- Preventing and responding to oil and hazardous material spills

- Coordinating efforts and intelligence with federal, state, and local agencies[136]

BUREAUCRATIC PROBLEMS AND SOLUTIONS

Following the September 11 attacks, the United States took swift action to implement various measures to defend the country from further terrorist attacks. Numerous measures were established, including a major governmental reorganization for such a defense, the DHS. In view of the Boston Marathon bombing on April 15, 2013, there is a question as to whether the government's defense efforts have been effective. Further, "policy discussions of homeland security issues are driven not by rigorous analysis but by fear, perceptions of past mistakes, pork-barrel politics, and insistence on an invulnerability that cannot possibly be achieved."[137]

Since its establishment, there have been problems with the DHS, which is not unusual for a newly developed agency or organization. Larry Gaines and Victor Kappeler noted that one such problem is when conflicting political interests overshadow the organizational imperative. "Politicians were all too often more interested in managing appearances as opposed to solving real problems."[138] The White House and Congress have significant oversight responsibility, as well as authority over the DHS. For instance, about 80 committees and subcommittees in the House and Senate have some form of oversight responsibilities regarding homeland security. Many have realized that this is a problem and have suggested that the secretary of the DHS be given more autonomy to manage the department. However, some politicians are not willing to give up this oversight, especially when such "authority over some aspect of homeland security always plays well with their electorates."[139]

Federal Emergency Management Agency (FEMA): focuses on emergency management and recovery from a catastrophic event on a local and national level

U.S. Coast Guard: the only military organization within the Department of Homeland Security; its role includes protecting ports, maintaining border security, and coordinating intelligence with various government entities

WHY DO THEY DO IT?

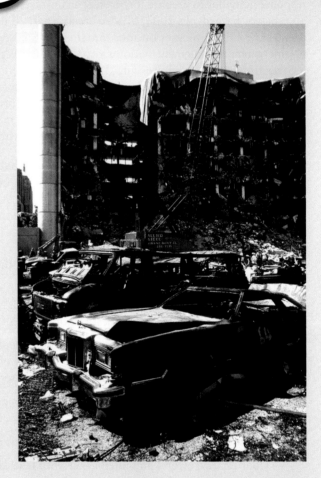

The devastating aftermath from the bombing of the Alfred P. Murrah Federal Building in downtown Oklahoma City

On April 19, 1995, a man parked a rented Ryder truck in front of the Alfred P. Murrah Federal Building in downtown Oklahoma City. Inside the truck was a bomb made out of agricultural fertilizer, diesel fuel, and other chemicals. The man stepped out of the truck and walked to his getaway car. He ignited one timed fuse, then another fuse. At 9:02 a.m., the bomb exploded, causing 168 deaths—including 19 children—along with several hundred injuries. This is still considered the worst act of domestic terrorism in U.S. history, and the following investigation was one of the most exhaustive in FBI history, including more than 28,000 interviews, 43,000 investigative leads, $3\frac{1}{2}$ tons of evidence, and almost a billion items of information. The investigation led to the arrest of Timothy McVeigh.[140]

McVeigh was born on April 23, 1968, in Pendleton, New York. He grew up in a rural community near Buffalo, Niagara, and Canada. His parents separated when he was 10 years old. After graduating from high school, he entered Niagara County Community College. He was there for a short time and went on to take various jobs. In 1987, he got a pistol permit and a job in Buffalo as a guard on an armored car. His coworkers recalled that McVeigh had a *survivalist* mentality—hoarding weapons and food for what he considered to be an imminent breakdown in the social order. In 1988, McVeigh enlisted in the Army. He received an early discharge in the fall of 1991, and by January he was living with his father and working as a security guard. The following year, he began to travel; he met up with two Army friends, Michael Fortier in Kingman, Arizona, and Terry Nichols in Decker, Michigan.[141]

Kingman and Decker were characterized as cities populated by individuals interested in paramilitary, antigovernment, antitax, survivalist, and racist propaganda. McVeigh continued his interest in weapons, as well as adhering to the survivalist movement. After the August 1992 conflict between federal agents and the survivalist Randy Weaver at his cabin in Idaho and the April 1993 conflict in Waco, Texas, with David Koresh and the Branch Davidians, McVeigh was becoming even more antigovernment in his views.[142]

On June 11, 2001, McVeigh, 33, was executed by lethal injection in Terra Haute Federal Prison. In a letter to the *Buffalo News*, McVeigh wrote, "I am sorry these people had to lose their lives. . . . But that's the nature of the beast. It's understood going in what the human toll will be."[143] His accomplices were also convicted. Nichols received a life sentence without the possibility of parole for his part in helping McVeigh build the bomb. Fortier received a 12-year sentence because he failed to warn authorities of McVeigh's plan to bomb the federal building.

As noted previously, the establishment of the DHS—a major governmental reorganization—occurred in a rapid fashion. This resulted in a great deal of confusion among the newly formed departments and other agencies. Many would assume that the DHS has exclusive responsibility for homeland security; however, other agencies such as the Department of Defense, the FBI, and the Treasury Department also have major interests in homeland security. A related problem in this rapid reorganization is **mission distortion**. Those agencies involved in this reorganization not only acquired new responsibilities but also were expected to continue with their agency's missions prior to the merge. Thus, "homeland security duties, for the most part, were simply added to the agencies' original or traditional responsibilities."[144]

ISSUES RELATED TO CIVIL LIBERTIES

In recent years, efforts to counter terrorism have posed some serious challenges for civil liberties. For instance, some countries have engaged in torture to counter terrorism; other countries have disregarded monitoring of detention centers to prevent torture. Further, other countries have returned persons suspected of being involved with terrorist activities to countries where they may be tortured for these activities; this is a violation of international law, or *non-refoulement*. In this section, we briefly review some of the serious challenges to civil liberties as they relate to counterterrorism efforts.[145]

THE TORTURE DEBATE

Gus Martin highlighted the issues concerning whether counterterrorist methods of torture should be used on terrorist suspects. This came to the forefront when there were reports of abuse at the U.S.-controlled Abu Ghraib prison, outside of Baghdad.[146] Once the Abu Ghraib prison was under U.S. control, there were several thousand civilian prisoners, including women and teenagers. They were picked up during random military sweeps and at highway checkpoints. These prisoners fell into three broadly designated categories: common criminals, security detainees suspected of "crimes against the coalition," and a few suspected "high-value" leaders of the insurgency against the coalition forces.

General Janis Karpinski, an Army reserve brigadier general, was named commander of the 800th Military Police Brigade and put in charge of the military prisons in Iraq. Later, General Karpinski was suspended and an investigation into the Army's prison system launched. Major General Antonio Taguba submitted his report, not meant for public release, on the conditions of the prison.[147] His report including the following:

> Breaking chemical lights and pouring the phosphoric liquid on detainees; pouring cold water on naked detainees; beating detainees with a broom handle and a chair; threatening male detainees with rape; allowing a military police guard to stitch the wound of a detainee who was injured after being slammed against the wall in his cell; sodomizing a detainee with a chemical light and perhaps a broom stick, and using military working dogs to frighten and intimidate detainees with threats of attack, and in one instance actually biting a detainee.[148]

Subsequently, incriminating photographs were released, several of which were broadcast on CBS's *60 Minutes 2*. As a result, various criminal courts martial were convened and numerous guards convicted and imprisoned.

According to Martin, the torture debate continues. On one side is the issue that the practice of torture has historically been disdained by the United States, both morally and as a questionable interrogation technique. On the other side, however, is that during a war on

mission distortion: occurred when those agencies involved in the reorganization of the Department of Homeland Security acquired new responsibilities and also were to continue with their agency's missions prior to the merge terrorism, one needs to consider the definition of torture. Further, one needs to determine whether certain forms of coercion, whether physical or psychological, are justifiable in this context. Martin then asks whether the following techniques should be considered torture:

- Waterboarding, during which prisoners feel as though they are drowning
- Sexual degradation, whereby prisoners are forced to pose in painful positions for performance of sex acts
- Stress positions, whereby prisoners are forced to pose in painful positions for extended periods
- Creating a chronic state of fear
- Environmental stress, accomplished by adjusting a detention cell's temperature
- Sleep deprivation
- Disorientation about one's whereabouts or the time of day
- Sensory deprivation, such as depriving suspects of sound or light[149]

He concludes this discussion by noting that policymakers are still involved in this debate and disagree as to whether certain situations necessitate the use of such techniques on terrorist suspects.

HUMAN RIGHTS

The United Nations has defined **human rights** as universal values and legal guarantees that protect individuals against actions or omissions, primarily by government agents, that infringe on their fundamental freedoms, entitlements, and human dignity. Further, these human rights include "respect for, and protection and fulfillment of, civil, cultural, economic, political and social rights as well as the right to development."[150] These rights are universal, meaning they are owed to all human beings.

Generally, there are two controversial areas involving the intersection of human rights with terrorism and homeland security.[151] The first is that terrorist attacks on innocent people violate the right of people to be free from such violence. Terrorists, however, justify their use of physical violence by maintaining that people are not innocent, because they live within the governmental system.[152] The second is that governments must recognize the human rights of their adversaries. Governments often justify inhumane actions against terrorists by arguing that such terrorists have forfeited their right to humane treatment due to their use of violence.[153]

The United Nations stressed that the issue of human rights within the context of terrorism and counterterrorism measures has often focused on the protection of civil and political rights. There has been little attention to how terrorism and counterterrorism measures affect economic, social, and cultural rights. Thus, "greater efforts must . . . be made to understand and address the linkages between terrorism and the enjoyment of economic, social, and cultural rights."[154]

human rights: universal values and legal guarantees that protect individuals against actions or omissions, primarily by government agents, that infringe on their fundamental freedoms, entitlements, and human dignity

THE CONSTITUTION

The U.S. Constitution is the supreme law in the United States. It establishes the organizational framework of the government, including the relationship between federal and state governments, as well as U.S. citizens. The Bill of Rights, the first 10 amendments to the Constitution, also regulates the authority of government. Cole and Dempsey argue that some of the United States' fundamental rights are being challenged by new government policies focused on addressing terrorism. These fundamental rights include the presumption of innocence, the right to counsel, the right to confront witnesses, the right of access to the courts, and privacy rights.[155] One of the most controversial of these new government policies is the USA PATRIOT Act (discussed below).

An interesting facet involves the Equal Protection Clause for noncitizens:

> It might be argued that because noncitizens do not have a vested interest in American society the way that citizens do, they are more apt to commit acts of terrorism, even if they are no more practically capable of doing so. And, therefore, the distinction between citizens and aliens in counterterrorism law is appropriate. But this is plainly a false premise.[156]

Cohen concluded that the compromise to the Equal Protection Law after the September 11 attacks is not only problematic from a practical perspective when combating terrorism; it also undermines the most basic foundational principle of American government. Thus, the court needs to renew its commitment to the concept of equality under the law.

REFERENCE ARTICLE

USA PATRIOT Act

USA PATRIOT ACT OF 2001

Following the attacks on September 11, 2001, Congress responded quickly by passing the Uniting and Strengthening America by Providing Appropriate Tools Required to Intercept and Obstruct Terrorism Act (i.e., the **USA PATRIOT Act**) on October 26, 2001. The USA PATRIOT Act consists of 10 sections, or titles, that provide new powers for government operations.[157] The act focuses on four significant areas of concern for homeland security: (1) the collection of communications information and data, (2) conducting foreign intelligence investigations, (3) controlling money laundering, and (4) funding and enhancing national border security.[158] Examples of these provisions include the following:

- Revisions of the standards for government surveillance, including federal law enforcement access to private records

- Enhancement of electronic surveillance authority, such as tapping into e-mail, electronic address books, and computers

- The use of "roving wiretaps" by investigators, which permit surveillance of an individual's telephone conversations on any phone anywhere in the country

- Requiring banks to identify sources of money deposited in some private accounts and requiring foreign banks to report on suspicious transactions

- The use of nationwide search warrants

- Deportation of immigrants who raise money for terrorist organizations

- The detention of immigrants without charge for up to 1 week on suspicion of supporting terrorism[159]

This act has sparked a great deal of controversy, especially those provisions that allow for intelligence gathering and sharing. Various groups, from constitutional conservatives to civil libertarian activists, were concerned that the law would encroach on civil freedoms, particularly those that protect citizens from government infringement on those freedoms guaranteed by the Constitution and the Bill of Rights.[160] However, there are others that are of the position that the act does not infringe on individuals' civil freedoms. Further, some emphasize the need to be less emotional and partisan when analyzing the provisions of the act:

USA PATRIOT Act: focuses on collecting communications information and data, conducting foreign intelligence investigations, controlling money laundering, and funding and enhancing national border security

LEARNING CHECK 14.3

The establishment of the _____ was considered the most noteworthy transformation of the U.S. government in more than 50 years. The problem of _____ arose when agencies involved in the reorganization not only acquired new responsibilities but also were to continue with their agencies' missions prior to the merge. One of the most controversial of the new government policies after 9/11 is the _____ .

Answers located at www.sagepub.com/schram

The Patriot Act headlines and sound bites that have permeated the print media and airwaves have created genuine public concern in the United States. . . . It is important for lawyers and scholars to stand back and look at the exact provisions of the Patriot Act, consider how they relate to established law, and identify where these provisions are consistent with the Constitution and case law and where they may have reached beyond the boundaries.[161]

In May 2011, President Obama approved a 4-year extension of expiring provisions of the PATRIOT Act. These three provisions included extending the government's authority to conduct "roving wiretaps," allowing the government to access personal records of terrorism suspects (i.e., the "library provision"), and providing the government power to investigate foreigners who have no known affiliation with terrorist groups (i.e., the "lone wolf" provision).[162]

CONCLUSION

An essential purpose of this chapter is for readers to obtain a greater understanding of certain types of crime that have, in recent years, received significant attention in the media as well as in criminal justice courses. Criminal activities such as terrorism and hate crimes reveal the multicultural and multinational facets of crime.

The first section of this chapter discussed hate crimes. We started this section by attempting to answer the question "What is a hate crime?" It is essential for readers to realize that an incident designated as a hate crime is a conventional offense (e.g., murder, vandalism, robbery) with an additional factor of bias. Hate crimes must be *motivated* by some form of bias, such as the victim's race, religion, disability, sexual orientation, or ethnicity/national origin. Further, various types of hate crimes are identified by this particular motivation. The next portion provided a general overview of various anti-hate-crime legislation, such as the Hate Crime Statistics Act of 1990, the Violent Crime Control and Law Enforcement Act of 1994, and the Matthew Shepard and James Byrd, Jr., Hate Crimes Prevention Act of 2009. One theoretical framework that has been applied to understanding hate crimes is routine activities theory.

The next section of this chapter presented an overview of terrorism. These types of criminal activities have received a tremendous amount of media attention and government response, especially after the September 11 attacks. Again, we started this section with the question "What is terrorism?" It is interesting to note that there is no common definition of terrorism, even among the various agencies in the U.S. government. Next, we briefly reviewed various types of terrorism,

such as state-sponsored and religious terrorism, as well as the extent of terrorist activities. The following portion of the chapter provided students with a brief historical context of modern terrorism. While many may consider terrorism a relatively "new" experience, this section illustrates that terrorism has deep historical roots. A noteworthy aspect to terrorism is the fluidity and constant flexibility of the organizational structure, as well as the financial support; this is especially evident given the major advances in technology. We concluded this section on terrorism with a few theoretical explanations, including routine activities and game theory.

The last section in this chapter began with an overview of homeland security, including its origins and definition. Next, we reviewed the organizational network by focusing on some of the agencies responsible for homeland security, such as TSA, CBP, ICE, and FEMA. With the establishment of the DHS, and the merging of these various agencies, there have been some bureaucratic problems, such as conflicting political interests and mission distortion. We concluded this section with a discussion of how counterterrorism efforts have raised some challenges for civil liberties; especially controversial is the USA PATRIOT Act of 2001.

At the beginning of this chapter, we presented the case study of John McGraham, who was brutally murdered on the streets of Los Angeles. Some would argue that this should be considered a hate crime. While the offense is a "conventional" crime, one must also consider the *motivation* for the crime. To label this a hate crime, one would argue that the offense was motivated by McGraham's status as homeless.

KEY TERMS

Campus Hate Crimes Right to Know Act of 1997

Church Arson Prevention Act of 1996

criminal terrorism

Department of Homeland Security

dissident terrorism

domestic terrorism

Federal Emergency Management Agency (FEMA)

fundraising

game theory

Hate Crime Statistics Act of 1990

hate crimes

homeland security

human rights

Matthew Shepard and James Byrd, Jr., Hate Crimes Prevention Act of 2009

mission distortion

model state legislation for hate crimes/ violence against people experiencing homelessness

money laundering

National Counterterrorism Center

religious terrorism

state-sponsored terrorism

Transportation Security Administration (TSA)

U.S. Citizenship and Immigration Services (USCIS)

U.S. Coast Guard

U.S. Customs and Border Protection (CBP)

U.S. Immigration and Customs Enforcement (ICE)

U.S. Secret Service

USA PATRIOT Act

Violent Crime Control and Law Enforcement Act of 1994

STUDENT STUDY SITE

Visit the student study site at **www.sagepub.com/schram** to access links to the video, audio, city and state rankings, author podcasts, and SAGE journal and reference articles featured in this chapter, as well as additional study tools, including eFlashcards, web quizzes, web resources, and chapter outlines.

DISCUSSION QUESTIONS

1. What are the various motivations associated with hate crimes?

2. What are some of the major legislative responses to hate crimes?

3. How would you apply routine activities theory to hate crimes?

4. What are some key features of terrorist activities?

5. What are some of the various motivations for engaging in terrorist activities?

6. What are the different organization networks associated with terrorist groups?

7. How do some terrorist groups finance their activities?

8. How would you apply routine activities theory to terrorist activities?

9. What is the purpose of homeland security?

10. What are some of the agencies that make up the Department of Homeland Security?

11. What are some of the bureaucratic problems associated with the Department of Homeland Security?

12. What are some of the controversial issues and challenges associated with counterterrorism efforts?

WEB RESOURCES

FBI's *Terrorism 2002–2005*

http://www.fbi.gov/stats-services/publications/terrorism-2002-2005/terror02_05.pdf

Hate Crime Statistics, 2011

http://www.fbi.gov/about-us/cjis/ucr/hate-crime/2011

CHAPTER 15

Drugs and Crime

INTRODUCTION

Over the past few decades, there has been an increase in public attention on drug and alcohol abuse. For instance, some of the more popular antidrug and anti-alcohol slogans include "Just say no"; "This is your brain. This is your brain on drugs. Any questions?"; "Say not to pot"; "Hugs not drugs"; "Stay alive. Don't drink and drive"; "If you choose the booze, you lose"; and "Get high on life, not on drugs." During this time, there also has been tremendous emphasis on law enforcement strategies to combat illegal drug possession and sales in the United States. This has had some significant effects on the criminal justice system—from arrest to incarceration rates.[1] For instance, in 2009, the highest arrest counts among both Part I and Part II offenses were for drug abuse violations (estimated at 1,531,251 arrests) and driving under the influence (estimated at 1,215,077).[2] In 2010, slightly more than half (51%) of all federal prisoners were serving time for drug offenses; in 2009, the most recent year for which data are available, about 18% of state prisoners were serving time for drug offenses.[3] This does not, however, include those individuals who committed a crime while under the influence of alcohol and/or drugs, or those who committed a crime to support their drug habit.

Drugs (including alcohol) and crime go hand in hand, and this chapter illustrates that relationship for students. The chapter begins with a section on the various types of drugs. Next, we review trends over the past century regarding drug use, as well as society's response. Then, we examine the primary ways drugs contribute to the increasing crime rate, with an emphasis on violent crime. The next section of this chapter presents different strategies that have been implemented to address the drug problem in the United States, including eradication, interdiction, and drug courts. The chapter concludes with recommendations for future policies regarding drugs and alcohol.

COMMONLY ABUSED DRUGS

DEPRESSANTS

With the exception of alcohol, most **depressants** are prescription drugs.[4] Depressants slow down, or "depress," the normal activity of the central nervous system (i.e., the brain and spinal cord). Thus, physicians often prescribe depressants for people who are anxious or cannot sleep.[6] Below, we briefly discuss various types of depressants that are routinely abused, including alcohol, barbiturates, and tranquillizers (including benzodiazepines).

ALCOHOL. In 2011, 51.8% of Americans age 12 and older reported using **alcohol** at least once in a 30-day period; young adults between the ages of 18 and 22 enrolled full-time in college were more likely than those not enrolled full-time to have used alcohol in the previous month, as well as to binge drink and drink heavily; and 64.3% of adults 18 years or older who were employed full-time used alcohol, compared with 54.1% of adults who were unemployed. In 2011, about 11.1% of individuals 12 years or older reported driving under the influence of alcohol at least once during the previous year. This has dropped since 2002 (from 14.2%). When breaking

LEARNING OBJECTIVES

As students read this chapter, they should consider the following questions:

- How would you distinguish between the different types of drugs?

- What are some trends pertaining to alcohol use in the United States?

- What are some key factors associated with the various trends of substance use in the United States?

- What is the difference between eradication and interdiction strategies?

- What are some key aspects of drug courts, such as how they differ from traditional criminal courts?

- What are the main features of harm reduction programs?

- What are some of the pros and cons to maintenance and decriminalization policy?

- What should be incorporated in future policies on substance use?

CASE STUDY

AMBER AND SCOTT LANDRY

In July of 2012, Amber Rose (29) and Scott Paul Landry (31) were held without bond at the Charlotte County Jail on charges of aggravated manslaughter of a child. In November of 2011, Charlotte County Sherriff's deputies were dispatched to the Landry's home. They were responding to a call that one of the Landry children was unresponsive; the infant boy was not breathing. He was transported to a hospital, where he later died. The emergency room doctor stated that the infant went into full cardiac arrest prior to his death.

Subsequently, detectives interviewed the parents. Scott stated that he was on methadone and Amber was attending a methadone clinic. The father also reported that he did not take any other medications and that the methadone was locked in a drawer at home. After the parents signed a waiver authorizing a search of their home, detectives found three empty prescription bottles for oxycodone; these were prescribed to Scott. They also found two empty prescription bottles of methadone.

Four days after the infant's death, an autopsy revealed no suspicious trauma to the body; however, the toxicology report did show that the baby had a toxic level of oxycodone in his blood, as well as a high level of oxymorphone in his urine. The medical examiner's office reported that the cause of death was a drug overdose. In a later interview, the parents stated that they were snorting the drug the night before the baby's overdose. Two other children, ages 2 and 9, were also living in the home. These children tested positive for benzodiazepines and oxycodone. The children were placed with their grandparents.

The detectives concluded that the parents' abuse of oxycodone resulted in a lack of parental supervision for the three children living in the home.[5] After reading about this incident, what questions or opinions do you think people may have about drug abuse? Would some consider that drug and alcohol abuse have negative effects that go beyond just those individuals abusing these substances? Would some maintain that substance abuse should still be considered a *victimless* crime?

> AN AUTOPSY REVEALED NO SUSPICIOUS TRAUMA TO THE BODY; HOWEVER, THE TOXICOLOGY REPORT DID SHOW THAT THE BABY HAD A TOXIC LEVEL OF OXYCODONE IN HIS BLOOD.

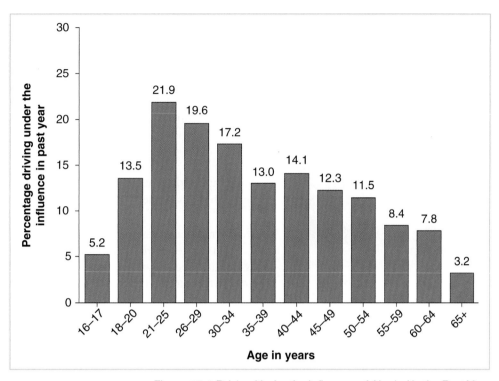

Figure 15.1 Driving Under the Influence of Alcohol in the Past Year
Among Persons Aged 16 or Older, by Age: 2011

Source: Substance Abuse and Mental Health Services Administration. (2012). *Results from the 2011 National Survey on Drug Use and Health: Volume I. Summary of national findings.* Washington, DC: U.S. Department of Health and Human Services, p. 38.

ETHANOL DOSE (OZ/HOUR)	BLOOD ETHANOL (MG/100 ML)	FUNCTION IMPAIRED	PHYSICAL STATE
1–4	up to 100	judgment fine motor coordination reaction time	happy talkative boastful
4–12	100–300	motor coordination reflexes	staggering slurred speech nausea, vomiting
12–16	300–400	voluntary responses to stimulation	hypothermia hyperthermia anesthesia
16–24	400–600	sensation movement self-protective reflexes	comatose
24–30	600–900	breathing heart function	dead

Table 15.1 Effects of Alcohol on Behavior and Physical State

Source: Kuhn, C., Swartzwelder, S., & Wilson, W. (2003). *Buzzed: The straight facts about the most used and abused drugs from alcohol to ecstasy.* New York: W. W. Norton, p. 37. Copyright © 1998 by Cynthia Kuhn, Scott Swartzwelder, and Wilkie Wilson. Used by permission of W. W. Norton & Company, Inc.

this down by age, the highest percentage (21.9%) of adults driving under the influence was between 21 and 25 years old (see Figure 15.1).[7] Table 15.1 lists the general effects of alcohol, ranging by dose.

depressants: slow down, or "depress," the normal activity of the central nervous system

alcohol: ethanol is the only alcohol that should be consumed; rapidly absorbed through the stomach and small intestine into the bloodstream

This accident was caused by a drunk driver.

In this society, alcohol is often the drug of choice. Kuhn and her colleagues argue that this is clearly evident when one critically observes how alcohol is advertised in the United States:

> We use alcohol to celebrate successes, to mourn failures and losses, and to celebrate holidays of cultural and religious significance. Implicit in these uses are the hope and promise that alcohol will amplify the good times and help us through the bad ones.[8]

They also maintain that alcohol advertising is most often targeted toward adolescents and young adults, especially young men. Figure 15.2 provides two examples of screening tests that are implemented to assess whether an individual may have an alcohol problem.

An issue related to alcohol use is **binge drinking.** According to the National Institute on Alcohol Abuse and Alcoholism, binge drinking, or heavy episodic drinking, refers to an individual who drinks so much alcohol within a 2-hour period that it results in at least a

---

Kuhn, Swartzwelder, and Wilson provided two different screening tests that are used in doctors' offices and clinics as a *first indicator* that an individual may have an alcohol problem. They did stress that a diagnosis of alcohol abuse, alcohol dependency, or alcoholism can be made only by a health professional trained specifically in addiction; sometimes it does more harm than good to confront a friend or relative with the impression that he or she may have a drinking problem; and these screening techniques rely on one critical component—the individual's responses.

The first screening test is called CAGE:

- Have you ever felt the need to **C**ut down on your drinking?
- Have you ever felt **A**nnoyed by someone criticizing your drinking?
- Have you ever felt **G**uilty about your drinking?
- Have you ever felt the need for an **E**ye-opener (a drink at the beginning of the day)?

If an individual gives two or more positive responses to these questions, there is a chance that he or she has some type of alcohol problem.

The second screening test is called TWEAK; this has been especially useful with women:

- **T**olerance: How many drinks does it take to make you high?
- **W**orried: Have close friends or relatives worried or complained about your drinking?
- **E**ye-opener: Do you sometimes take a drink in the morning to wake up?
- **A**mnesia (memory loss): Has a friend or family member ever told you things you said or did while you were drinking that you could not remember?
- **(K)** Cut: Do you sometimes feel the need to cut down on your drinking?

This test is scored differently than CAGE; however, a positive score of three or more is considered to indicate that the person has a drinking problem.

Figure 15.2 The CAGE and TWEAK Screening Tests

Source: Kuhn, C., Swartzwelder, S., & Wilson. W. (2003). *Buzzed: The straight facts about the most used and abused drugs from alcohol to ecstasy.* New York: W. W. Norton, pp. 49–50. Copyright © 1998 by Cynthia Kuhn, Scott Swartzwelder, and Wilkie Wilson. Used by permission of W. W. Norton & Company, Inc.

binge drinking: heavy episodic drinking; drinking so much alcohol within a 2-hour period that it results in at least a .08 blood alcohol concentration

.08 blood alcohol concentration.[9] According to the Substance Abuse and Mental Health Services Administration, binge drinking is defined for males as at least five drinks and for females as at least four drinks on the same occasion (i.e., at the same time or within a few hours of each other) on at least one day.[10]

One facet of binge drinking is *drinking games*. Drinking games have been known to be popular on college campuses. Binge drinking, however, does vary among student populations. For instance, African American and Asian, female, and older students are less likely to engage in binge drinking compared with white, male, and younger students.[11] Zamboanga and his colleagues defined drinking games as consisting of a set of rules and guidelines that encourage heavy alcohol use.[12] Continued involvement in such games can result in an individual becoming more intoxicated and his or her skill at the game diminishing, leading to more drinking. Further, most drinking games include those individuals who are purposely "losing" to receive the penalty of drinking.

Individuals involved in such drinking games are at a higher risk of heavy alcohol consumption and negative alcohol-related consequences. For instance, this kind of drinking could result in increased aggression and driving under the influence.[13] Also, others on campus may experience the negative effects of this type of drinking in the form of physical assaults, property damage, and unwanted sexual advances.[14]

BARBITURATES. The first **barbiturate**, barbital, was discovered in 1903 by two German scientists working at Bayer—Emil Fischer and Joseph von Mering. Barbital was marketed by Bayer under the trade name Veronal.[15] There are now about a dozen barbiturates in medical use.[16] The various types of barbiturates are often referred to "on the street" by their color; the most common types include Amytal (blue heavens), Nembutal (yellow jackets), Seconal (red birds), and Sombulex and Tuinal (rainbows, or reds and blues).[17] Barbiturates can induce a wide continuum of central nervous system depression, ranging from mild sedation to coma.[18] They can be physically and psychologically addictive. In general practice, barbiturates have essentially been replaced by benzodiazepines for treatment of anxiety and insomnia.[19]

TRANQUILIZERS (INCLUDING BENZODIAZEPINES). Kuhn and her colleagues noted that benzodiazepines are "remarkable because they are one of the closest drugs we have to a 'magic bullet' for anxiety."[20] If used properly, benzodiazepines can help individuals with anxiety without disrupting normal functions. In fact, these are among the most commonly prescribed drugs. Diazepam (Valium), alprazolam (Xanax), and estazolam (ProSom) are some types of benzodiazepines. However, this is not a "perfect" class of drug. Problems with benzodiazepines are that initial use causes sleepiness and incoordination, they can affect an individual's learning process, and they can cause amnesia.[21]

Recently, two specific types of **tranquilizers** have received a great deal of media attention and have been dubbed "date-rape drugs," or predatory drugs. The first is flunitrazepam, trade name Rohypnol. Some of the street names associated with Rohypnol are "forget-me-pill," "lunch money drug," "roofies," "ruffies," "wolfies," "pingus," and "R2." The Food and Drug Administration has never approved Rohypnol for medicinal use in the United States. It was brought to the public's attention when some individuals used it to physically and psychologically incapacitate women, for the purpose of then sexually assaulting them.[22] The second type of tranquilizer is gamma-hydroxybutyric acid (GHB). Some of the street names for GHB are "liquid ecstasy," "scoop," "easy lay," "liquid X," and "goop." GHB can come in the form of an odorless, colorless liquid or as a white powder. As with Rohypnol, offenders have used GHB as a predatory drug in the commission of sexual assaults because it renders the victim incapable of resisting, as well as causing memory problems.[23]

VIDEO

Common Drugs

AUDIO

Drug Abuse Programs

barbiturate: a type of depressant; can induce a wide continuum of central nervous system depression, ranging from mild sedation to coma

tranquilizers: a type of depressant; can help with anxiety without disrupting normal functions. Problems include sleepiness and incoordination, hampered learning process, and amnesia

NARCOTICS

The term **narcotics** has been used historically, and often inaccurately, to refer to *all* illegal drugs. More accurately, *narcotics* refers to opiates (drugs derived from the opium poppy) or opioids (synthetically produced opiates).[24] In this section, we briefly discuss morphine, heroin, and other synthetic narcotics such as oxycodone.

MORPHINE. The term **morphine** is derived from the Greek god of dreams, Morpheus, who was often depicted with a handful of opium poppies. The effect of opiate use was even depicted in the film *The Wizard of Oz*, when Dorothy and her friends are running through the field of poppies. In 1805, morphine, the major active ingredient in the opium poppy, was purified. Coupled with the invention of the hypodermic syringe in 1853, the first major wave of morphine addiction occurred during the American Civil War.[25] Morphine has a high potential for abuse. It is also one of the most effective drugs for relieving severe physical pain. Street names include "dreamer," "God's drug," "Mister Blue," "morf," and "morpho."[26]

HEROIN. Perhaps the most infamous opiate drug is **heroin**, a chemically modified form of morphine. The color of heroin can range from white to black. Highly purified heroin is a white powder, but on the other end of the continuum, it is a black, sticky substance, sometimes referred to as "black tar heroin."[27] Heroin can be snorted/sniffed, smoked, or injected. Initially, it is often sniffed or snorted. When tolerance builds, one may use the method of "skin-popping" (injecting it into the skin but not into a vein). When tolerance builds further, one may "mainline" heroin (injecting it into the bloodstream).[28] Those users who inject heroin are at risk for infectious diseases, including HIV/AIDS and hepatitis. Further, street heroin usually contains toxic contaminants or additives that can lead to serious health issues.[29]

OTHER SYNTHETIC NARCOTICS. Synthetic narcotics are produced entirely within the laboratory, as opposed to other narcotics derived from opium.[30] Examples of synthetic opiates include hydrocodone (Vicodin, Lorcet, Lortab), hydromorphone (Dilaudid), meperidine (Demerol), **oxycodone** (OxyContin, Percodan, and Percocet), propoxyphene (Darvon), and codeine.[31] OxyContin has recently been the focus of much media attention. While the promotion and marketing of OxyContin could be deemed a commercial success, the result has also been a public health concern:

> The extraordinary amount of money spent in promoting a sustained-release opioid was unprecedented. During OxyContin's first 6 years on the market, Purdue spent approximately 6 to 12 times more on promoting it than the company had spent on promoting MS Contin. . . . Although OxyContin has not been shown to be superior to other available potent opioid preparations, by 2001 it had become the most frequently prescribed brand-name opioid in the United States for treating moderate to severe pain.[32]

Prescriptions for OxyContin have practically doubled every year since its release in 1996. In 2000, physicians issued more than 6.5 million prescriptions for OxyContin.[33]

STIMULANTS

As the name implies, **stimulant** drugs create a sense of energy, alertness, talkativeness, and well-being considered pleasurable to the user. Physiological effects include increased heart rate and blood pressure, as well as dilation of the bronchioles (breathing tubes) in the lungs.[34] Two of the most common forms of stimulants in our society, and perhaps the most popular drugs in the world, are caffeine (in coffee, tea, and

narcotics: opiates (drugs derived from the opium poppy) or opioids (synthetically produced opiates); includes morphine, heroin, and oxycodone

morphine: one of the most effective drugs for relief of severe physical pain; has high potential for abuse

heroin: the most infamous opiate drug; a chemically modified form of morphine that ranges in color from white to black

oxycodone: synthetic narcotic produced entirely in the laboratory; includes OxyContin, Percodan, and Percocet

stimulant: creates a sense of energy, alertness, talkativeness, and well-being considered pleasurable to the user a number of soft drinks) and nicotine (consumed through tobacco products such as cigarettes).[35] In this section, we briefly discuss stimulants such as cocaine, amphetamine, and methamphetamine.

COCAINE. **Cocaine** appears in the leaves of various species of plants grown in Bolivia, Peru, and Colombia. In fact, Colombia produces about 90% of the cocaine powder entering the United States. Street names for cocaine include "coca," "coke," "crack," "flake," "snow," and "soda cot." It is usually distributed as a white, crystalline powder and often diluted or "cut" with various substances such as sugars and local anesthetics. Cocaine base or crack comes in small, irregular-shaped pieces, or "rocks," of an opaque whitish color. Powdered cocaine can be snorted or, after dissolving it in water, injected into the veins. Crack cocaine is smoked, either by itself or with marijuana or tobacco. Known as "speedballing," sometimes cocaine is used in combination with an opiate such as heroin.[36]

AMPHETAMINE. Like other stimulants, **amphetamine** boosts the body's functioning. A number of amphetamines are legally prescribed, in some instances to treat attention-deficit hyperactivity disorder and attention-deficit disorder. Adderall and Dexedrine are some commonly prescribed amphetamines. Street names include "bennies," "black beauties," "crank," "ice," "speed," and "uppers." The effects of amphetamines are similar to those of cocaine; however, the onset of these effects is slower and the duration longer.[37] As with cocaine, amphetamines decrease appetite. In fact, these drugs were used in the first diet pills, popular in the 1950s and 1960s.[38]

METHAMPHETAMINE. The most common form of amphetamine today is **methamphetamine.**[39] Methamphetamine can take the form of a white, odorless powder that dissolves in water; clear, "chunky" crystals (i.e., crystal meth); or small, brightly colored tablets. Street names include "meth," "poor man's cocaine," "crystal meth," "ice," "glass," and "speed." Methods of use include injecting, snorting, smoking, and oral ingestion. Some of the consequences associated with methamphetamine use are psychotic behavior and brain damage. Chronic use can result in violent behavior, anxiety, confusion, insomnia, auditory hallucinations, mood disturbances, delusions, and paranoia; brain damage due to methamphetamine use is similar to that occurring from Alzheimer's disease, stroke, and epilepsy.[40]

Methamphetamine was created in Japan in 1919 but did not become popular until the 1980s and 1990s.[41] Methamphetamine is most accessible in the Pacific region of the United States, followed by the West, Southwest, Southeast, Midwest, and Northeast regions; abuse of methamphetamine predominately occurs in the western, southwestern, and midwestern United States.[42] Another problem of the increased popularity of methamphetamine is that a major source of supply for use in the United States is clandestine laboratories in California and Mexico.[43] Methamphetamine can be made from a number of household products; thus, it is difficult to regulate the production of this drug and to prevent the dangers of such production to people and the environment.[44]

A 1970 advertisement for Obetrol methamphetamine weight-loss pills

....

cocaine: a type of stimulant that appears in the leaves of various species of plants; usually distributed as a white, crystalline powder diluted with substances such as sugars and local anesthetics

amphetamine: a type of stimulant; effects are similar to cocaine, but onset is slower and duration longer

methamphetamine: the most common form of amphetamine today, it can take the form of a white, odorless powder that dissolves in water; clear, "chunky" crystals; or small, brightly colored tablets

OTHER DRUGS

CANNABIS AND MARIJUANA. Cannabis is an extremely useful plant. For instance, hemp, a strong fiber found in the stem of this plant, can be used to make rope, cloth, and paper. The leaves and flowers can be dried into **marijuana** and used for their psychoactive and medicinal effects. The most prevalent species of cannabis are *Cannabis sativa* and *Cannabis indica*. While the cannabis plant contains hundreds of psychoactive chemicals, the most psychoactive is delta-9-tetrahydrocannabinol (THC).[45] Large quantities of marijuana are grown in countries such as Colombia, Mexico, Jamaica, and the United States. In the United States, the largest marijuana-producing states are California, Kentucky, and Hawaii.[46] Hashish and hashish oil are drugs also derived from the cannabis plant; however, they are stronger than marijuana. The main sources of hashish are the Middle East, North Africa, Pakistan, and Afghanistan.[47]

Street names for marijuana include "Aunt Mary," "BC bud," "blunts," "hash," "indo," "joint," "Mary Jane," "pot," "reefer," "skunk," and "weed." It is usually smoked as a cigarette, called a joint, or in a pipe or bong. It can also be smoked in blunts, which are cigars that have been emptied of tobacco. Sometimes other drugs are used in combination with marijuana. It has also been used in foods, as well as brewed to make tea.[48] Some of the psychoactive effects of marijuana include problems with memory and learning, distorted perception, difficulty in thinking and problem solving, and loss of coordination. Some of the physiological effects include sedation, bloodshot eyes, increased heart rate, coughing due to lung irritation, increased appetite, and decreased blood pressure.[49]

STEROIDS. Anabolic-androgenic **steroids** are synthetically produced variations of the male sex hormone testosterone.[50] Some steroids have been approved for medical and veterinary use. A legitimate use for humans is in replacement therapy for inadequate levels of hormones (e.g., delayed puberty, disease such as cancer and AIDS that results in loss of lean muscle mass). Steroids are also used in veterinary medicine for improving weight gain, increasing vigor, and enhancing coat.[51] Street names include "Arnolds," "gym candy," "pumpers," "roids," "stackers," "weight trainers," "gear," and "juice."[52] Research has revealed that abuse of steroids can lead to aggression and other negative effects.[53] While some users report "feeling good about themselves," others experience extreme mood swings and manic symptoms that could lead to violence.[54] Steroid abuse can lead to serious, and in some instances irreversible, health problems, including liver damage, jaundice, fluid retention, high blood pressure, renal failure, and severe acne.[55]

INHALANTS. Although other abused substances can be inhaled, the term **inhalants** is used to refer to various substances whose primary trait is that they are rarely taken by any delivery method other than inhalation. Inhalants are volatile substances that produce chemical vapors. These vapors are inhaled to produce a psychoactive, or mind-altering, effect. The categorization of inhalants is difficult. One classification system identified four general categories: volatile solvents, aerosols, gases, and nitrites. These categories are based on the forms in which they are often found in household, industrial, and medical products. Inhalant use includes "sniffing" or "snorting" fumes from containers; spraying aerosols directly into the nose or mouth; "bagging," which is sniffing or inhaling fumes from substances in a plastic or paper bag; "huffing," which involves stuffing an inhalant-soaked rag over the mouth; and inhaling from balloons filled with nitrous oxide. The effects of intoxication last only a few minutes; thus, abusers often prolong the high by inhaling repeatedly over the course of several hours.[56]

HALLUCINOGENS. Hallucinogens are drugs that alter one's thought processes, mood, and perceptions. The word is derived from the Latin word *alucinare*, which means "to wander in mind, talk idly, or prate."[57] There are three general categories of hallucinogens. The first category, and the most familiar, is lysergic acid diethylamide (LSD). The second major

cannabis: an extremely useful plant that contains hundreds of psychoactive chemicals, particularly delta-9-tetrahydrocannabinol (THC)

marijuana: the dried leaves or flowers of the cannabis plant

steroids: synthetically produced variations of the male sex hormone testosterone; some approved for medical and veterinary use

inhalants: volatile substances that produce chemical vapors and whose primary trait is that they are rarely taken by any other delivery method than inhalation

hallucinogens: drugs that alter one's thought processes, mood, and perceptions category is belladonna alkaloids; these have been used for thousands of years for medical and ritual purposes. The third category is dissociative anesthetics, or "horse tranquilizers," including phencyclidine (PCP) and ketamine (an anesthetic used on children and in veterinary practices).[58] Since it is so individualized, it is difficult to describe a person's experience when using a hallucinogen. However, the onset of a "trip" includes nausea, feeling jittery, and a mild increase in blood pressure, heart rate, and breathing. Subsequently, the effects include a slight distortion of sensory perception, with visual effects such as wavering images and distortion of size.[59] In some instances, these drugs can cause schizophrenia-like psychosis.[60]

LEARNING CHECK 15.1

In this society, _____ is often the drug of choice. Two types of _____ have received a great deal of media attention and have been dubbed "date-rape drugs," or predatory drugs. The color of _____ ranges from white to black. Prescriptions for _____ have practically doubled every year since its release in 1996. _____ refers to when cocaine is used in combination with an opiate such as heroin. The most common form of amphetamine today is _____. Street names for _____ include "Mary Jane," "pot," "reefer," and "weed."

Answers located at www.sagepub.com/schram

TRENDS OF DRUG USE

The history of drug use can be traced back at least 10,000 years. Anthropologists have maintained that earlier cultures learned, through a process of trial and error, that chewing, sucking, or inhaling the leaves, fruits, or roots of certain types of plants would induce physical and psychological changes. Further, some anthropologists have speculated that the discovery of grain-derived alcohol, especially beer, may have been a reason why wandering hunter-gatherer tribes of the Old Stone Age established villages. By establishing villages, these tribes could pursue agriculture to ensure a stable supply of grain.[61] As Sally Freeman notes, "drug use is woven into the history of civilization. People have used drugs for pleasure, social interaction, medicine, rebellion, self-exploration, creativity, religious ceremonies, and as commodities in economic trade."[62]

Drugs have been an integral aspect of, and woven into, American history since the arrival of the first European colonists. Interactions between the Native American and European cultures exposed each group to drugs that were new to it but familiar to the other. For instance, in the early 17th century, the British found tobacco, which was smoked by Native Americans to achieve mystical states of mind and to strengthen social agreements. For the Europeans and the British, drinking was an integral aspect of life; the colonials introduced the Native Americans to alcohol.[63] In this section, we provide a brief overview of key trends of drug use in the United States, starting with the history of opioid and cocaine addiction.

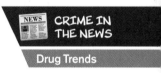

CRIME IN THE NEWS

Drug Trends

EARLY HISTORY OF COCAINE AND OPIOID ADDICTION

Around the time of the U.S. Civil War (1861–1865), opioid addiction was prevalent.[64] Soldiers were given morphine not only to ease the pain of their injuries but also to relieve the symptoms of dysentery. Upon returning home, many of the soldiers were dependent on morphine, and their addiction became known as the "soldier's disease." Some of England's most well-known literary talents were introduced to opiates through their physicians; American writer Louisa May Alcott, author of *Little Women*, used opium and morphine to address her physical ailments. Interestingly, under different pen names, she later authored thrillers that delved into topics such as drugs and violence.[65]

In 1898, the Bayer Company developed heroin, an opium derivative 10 times more powerful than morphine. It was extremely effective in relieving coughs, emphysema, asthma, and tuberculosis. As with previous opium derivatives, however, many soon realized that heroin was also highly addictive. In fact, by 1919, almost 1 million Americans were addicted to heroin or some form of opium. Physicians, pharmacists, and

Women participating in a Prohibition parade

"opportunists" were able to prescribe opioids with no restrictions. Thus, patent medicines, claiming to treat a range of ailments, were often laced with opiates, cocaine, or alcohol.[66] To address this widespread addiction and questionable practices, the government enacted the 1906 Pure Food and Drug Act, which authorized federal regulations on any medication.[67] This was followed by additional regulations when Congress passed the **Harrison Act** in 1914. This required doctors to be licensed to prescribe narcotics.[68]

Like opiates, cocaine has some therapeutic properties but is also highly addictive. Cocaine was introduced in the United States initially for medicinal use, designated as a "wonder drug." In fact, cocaine was considered by many influential physicians as a cure for addiction to morphine, opium, and alcohol.[69] Before Sigmund Freud achieved fame as the founder of psychoanalysis, he was a neurologist. In several articles for medical journals, Freud maintained that cocaine could be used for a variety of ills, such as asthma, digestive upset, and morphine addiction.[70] In 1887, however, Freud conceded that cocaine should not be used for morphine addiction. It is also essential to note that in the early 1900s, medical viewpoints concerning cocaine (as for other forms of opium) were becoming more critical of its use in the field, with the exception of its use as a local anesthetic.[71]

PROHIBITION ERA

On December 18, 1917, the U.S. Senate proposed the **Eighteenth Amendment**. Mississippi was the first state to ratify the amendment; on January 16, 1919, Nebraska was the 36th state to ratify the amendment. Thus, national **Prohibition** took effect on January 16, 1920.[72] The amendment has two operative sections:

> Section 1: After one year from the ratification of this article the manufacture, sale, or transportation of intoxicating liquors within, the importation thereof into, or the exportation thereof from the United States and all territory subject to the jurisdiction thereof for beverage purposes is hereby prohibited.

> Section 2: The Congress and the several States shall have concurrent power to enforce this article by appropriate legislation. (USCS Constitutional Amendment 18)

The passage of the amendment was influenced by such groups as the Prohibition Party, the Woman's Christian Temperance Union, and the Anti-Saloon League.[73]

During the Prohibition era, America's drinking patterns went through some changes. First, there was a significant drop in alcohol consumption among the working class; Prohibition made alcohol expensive, and many of these individuals could not afford to drink. Second, while beer and wine were difficult to manufacture and ship, distilled liquors (e.g., gin, rum, whiskey) were easy to produce and transport, which made these the more popular beverages. One of the most notable, and often cited, outcomes of Prohibition was the development of an underground system of producing and distributing alcohol.[74] While "Prohibition probably reduced per capita alcohol use and alcohol-related harm, ... these benefits eroded over time as an organized black market developed and public support ... declined."[75]

Harrison Act: passed by Congress in 1914, required doctors to have a license number to prescribe narcotics

Eighteenth Amendment: put into effect national Prohibition on January 16, 1920

Prohibition: after the passage of the Eighteenth Amendment, an era in which it was illegal to manufacture, sell, or transport intoxicating liquors within the United States

Prior to Prohibition, organized crime essentially comprised corrupt political machines, vice entrepreneurs, and, at the bottom, gangs. The onset of prohibition provided gangs an opportunity to engage in criminal activity that changed the power order, with gang leaders such as "Dutch Schultz" and Al Capone rising to the top of the organized crime "ladder."[76] On December 5, 1933, the **Twenty-First Amendment** was ratified, repealing the Eighteenth Amendment.

"REEFER MADNESS"

Although the cannabis plant has been used for various purposes since colonial times, it was not until the early 1900s that the act of smoking marijuana was considered a social problem in the United States. Further, those identified as smoking marijuana were from marginalized groups. Specifically, these individuals included Mexicans who came to America to work in the fields in the Southwest; sailors who brought back marijuana from South and Central American ports; and blacks in the South, where it was noted that as early as colonial times they smoked the hemp plant, having become familiar with the drug in Africa.[77]

Prior to the mid-1920s, there was not a great deal of public interest or concern about marijuana use. Soon thereafter, various articles appeared linking marijuana use with criminal activity.[78] For instance, in 1936, *Scientific American* reported, "Marijuana produces a wide variety of symptoms in the user, including hilarity, swooning, and sexual excitement. Combined with intoxicants, it often makes the smoker vicious, with a desire to fight and kill."[79]

Some have maintained that were it not for the zeal of Harry Anslinger, the commissioner of the new Federal Bureau of Narcotics in 1931, marijuana might be legal in the United States today. These articles, a number of which were written by Anslinger, stressed the negative effects of marijuana use. For instance, a 1927 article in the *New York Times* reported a story about a Mexican woman who went insane after eating cannabis leaves. At the Congressional hearings on the **Marihuana Tax Act** in 1937, Anslinger testified that a 21-year-old man from Florida axe-murdered his entire family because he was smoking marijuana. However, Anslinger failed to note that the authorities had attempted to institutionalize the man for insanity a year before he ever tried marijuana.[80]

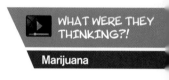

On August 2, 1937, the 75th Congress passed the 1937 Marihuana Tax Act, and it became effective October 1, 1937. While this federal law did not criminalize marijuana or its preparations, it did tax the grower, distributor, seller, and buyer. This law essentially made it impossible for a person to have any involvement with marijuana. In 1969, the U.S. Supreme Court ruled that the Marihuana Tax Act was unconstitutional. The case involved Timothy Leary, who was found with marijuana in his car while going through Customs at Laredo, Texas. The Supreme Court stated that the act violated Leary's Fifth Amendment privilege against self-incrimination.[81]

Some maintain that the Marihuana Tax Act of 1937 is one example of what one could characterize as a *racialized drug policy*. David Musto argued that the act was essentially a response to political pressure among those who feared the use of marijuana by individuals they labeled "Mexicans."[82] C. M. Goeth of Sacramento, a member of the American Coalition—a group whose goal was to "keep America American"—noted that

> marihuana, perhaps now the most insidious of our narcotics, is a direct by-product of unrestricted Mexican immigration. Easily grown, it has been asserted that it has recently been planted between rows in a California penitentiary garden. Mexican peddlers have been caught distributing sample marihuana cigarets [sic] to school children. Bills for our quota against Mexico have been blocked mysteriously in every Congress since the 1924 Quota Act. Our nation has more than enough laborers.[83]

Twenty-First Amendment: ratified on December 5, 1933, it repealed the Eighteenth Amendment

Marihuana Tax Act: effective October 1, 1937; did not criminalize marijuana or its preparations but did tax the grower, distributor, seller, and buyer

As noted previously, there was a great deal of publicity regarding the "evils" of marijuana; this media attention exaggerated marijuana's effects.

In certain regions of the United States, the fear of marijuana was more intense. Specifically, a report published in 1932 noted that the abuse of marijuana is often associated with Latin American or Spanish-speaking populations; the sale of cannabis cigarettes usually occurs in states along the Mexican border, as well as in cities in the Southwest and West.[84] Musto concluded that initially the Federal Bureau of Narcotics resisted any involvement in terms of enforcing the antimarihuana law. Pressure, most likely motivated by fear, from those in the Southwest and West regions of the country led to the implementation of federal legislation.

VIDEO

Marijuana

THE 1960S AND THE BABY BOOMERS

According to the U.S. Census, the population born between 1946 and 1964 is commonly referred to as the baby-boom generation. Due to a dramatic increase in birth rates following World War II, baby boomers now form what is considered to be one of the largest generations in U.S. history.[85] During the 1960s, these individuals were extremely influential to what has been identified as the "counterculture" of that time. Kenneth Westhues identified various characteristics of countercultures, including communistic relationships among members, sexual relationships that deviate from the nuclear family ideal, claims of superiority over the dominant society, members who look to spiritual leaders, and members who reject many of the status symbols of the larger society.[86]

The countercultural movement has also been associated with "mind-opening substances," or drugs such as LSD, mescaline, psilocybin, and other related chemicals, as well as marijuana.[87] Drugs were interwoven in various facets of this cultural movement. For instance, drug use was often referenced in music—appearing in songs by Bob Dylan, Jefferson Airplane, Jim Hendrix, The Beatles, and The Grateful Dead, just to name a few.

Art, specifically psychedelic art, was also influential at this time. Some argue that psychedelic art was inspired by the effects of such drugs as LSD and mescaline (see Figure 15.3).

THE "WAR ON DRUGS" ERA

The 1980s initiated what was designated as the **War on Drugs**:

> The drug "panic" or "crisis" of the mid-to-late 1980s illustrates the notion of the politics of social problems very nicely. Public concern about drugs, although building throughout the 1980s, *exploded* late in 1985 and early 1986—at a time, ironically, when the use of most drugs was actually *declining* [italics in original].[88]

JOURNAL ARTICLE

War on Drugs

There was extensive media coverage of drug use in the United States at this time. A well-known advertising campaign was "Just Say No." This phrase has been attributed to First Lady Nancy Reagan. During a presentation in Oakland, California, a schoolchild in the audience asked Mrs. Reagan what she and her friends should say when someone offered them drugs. The First Lady stated, "Just say no." Soon thereafter, thousands of "Just Say No" clubs had emerged in schools around the country.[89]

War on Drugs: public concern about drugs, building throughout the 1980s, exploded in late 1985 and early 1986

In the 1980s, Congress enacted mandatory minimum drug sentencing laws that resulted in lengthy prison terms for individuals convicted of nonviolent drug offenses.[90] In 1986, President Ronald Reagan stressed the need for a "nationwide crusade against drugs," such as $2 billion in federal monies to address the problem. This money included $56 million for drug testing federal employees. In September of 1986, the House of Representatives approved increased spending for education, treatment programs, and penalties against

Figure 15.3 Examples of Psychedelic Art

drug-producing countries. This was approved by the Senate in October. The Anti-Drug Abuse Act ultimately cost $1.7 billion.[91]

One particular drug often noted during this period was crack cocaine.[92] Witkin and his colleagues stated that it is amazing that crack cocaine did not become a social problem sooner. In fact, crack appeared throughout the 1970s. However, Witkin argues that crack became a craze due to mass marketing involving three groups of "sinister geniuses." The first group was the nameless kitchen chemists and drug traffickers who could set up small-scale operations. The second group comprised crime organizations, primarily in medium and large American cities; these organizations seized the local markets from smaller operators. Finally, the third group comprised gangs from both the East and West Coast; these gangs franchised crack operations.[93]

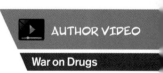

AUTHOR VIDEO

War on Drugs

During the 1990s, there was intense focus and scrutiny on women who used illegal drugs during pregnancy; this was especially evident among women who gave birth to "crack babies." Again, the media played a prominent role in perpetuating the problem of crack babies. From the media perspective, "the inhumane actions of addicted mothers often produced children who were almost beyond the pale of humanity."[94] However, some researchers have noted that after years of research, medical experts have not identified a distinctive condition, syndrome, or disorder that merits the label "crack baby."[95]

AUTHOR PODCAST

Drugs and Society

CURRENT TRENDS REGARDING DRUG USE

According to the 2011 National Survey on Drug Use and Health,

- about 22.5 million Americans aged 12 or older were current (i.e., in the past month) users of illicit drugs (i.e., marijuana/hashish, cocaine, heroin, hallucinogens, inhalants, or prescription-type psychotherapeutics used nonmedically);

- the rate of current drug users stayed about the same from 2010 (8.9%) to 2011 (8.7%);

- marijuana was the most commonly used illicit drug (with 18.1 million users);

- in 2011, there were 1.4 million cocaine users, which is similar to the number and rate for 2010;

- about 972,000 individuals have used hallucinogens, which is lower than in 2010 (1.2 million);

- nonmedical users of prescription-type psychotherapeutic drugs decreased from 6.7 million in 2010 to 6.1 million in 2011; and

- the number of individuals using methamphetamine decreased between 2006 and 2011.[96]

U.S. Attorney Sally Quillian Yates stated,

> Prescription drug abuse is our nation's fastest-growing segment of illegal drug use, causing significantly more overdose deaths than cocaine, methamphetamine, and heroin combined. Oxycodone remains one of the most widely abused prescription drugs, and it's also one of the most addictive and deadly drugs when not taken properly. The forging of prescriptions is an especially harmful situation because it completely removes the oversight of a physician from the equation.[97]

The nonmedical use of prescription drugs has become increasingly widespread in the past few years. Some maintain that this increasing use may be due to the relatively minor, if any, stigma associated with this type of drug use.[98]

The 2005 Partnership Attitude Tracking Study revealed that many youths do not perceive risks of nonmedical use of prescription drugs as comparable to risks of illegal drug use:

- Two in five teens agree that prescription medicines, even if not prescribed by a doctor, are "much safer" to use than illegal drugs.

- Almost one third of youths believe there is "nothing wrong" with using prescription medicines without a prescription "once in a while."

- About 3 out of 10 teens believe prescription pain relievers, even if not prescribed by a doctor, are not addictive.[99]

WHY DO THEY DO IT?

RYAN THOMAS HAIGHT

Ryan Thomas Haight attended Grossmont High School in La Mesa, California. He was outgoing and successful academically, and he enjoyed various athletic activities, such as skiboarding and swimming. Ryan also enjoyed using the computer.[100] On February 12, 2001, Francine Haight came home in the afternoon and noticed that her son's car had not moved. She knew then that something was wrong. She found Ryan dead in his bed. Later, one of the sheriff's deputies came out and said, "This is what we found in your son's room." It was a large bottle of Vicodin. Ryan had overdosed.

What made this situation even worse was that he had been able to purchase the Vicodin over the Internet with a debit card. This drug is strictly regulated by the DEA.[101] A physician on the Internet, whom he had never met, prescribed the drug to Ryan, and an Internet pharmacy mailed the Vicodin to his home. Ryan was only 17 years old when he purchased the drug; he was 18 when he died.[102]

Due to the growing concern over distribution of controlled substances via the Internet, the Ryan Haight Online Pharmacy Consumer Protection Act of 2008 went into effect in April 2009.[103] Some of the requirements include the following:

- *Face-to-face requirement for prescribing.* With few exceptions, a doctor must conduct at least one in-person medical evaluation of the patient.

- *Endorsement requirement.* The DEA must provide an endorsement before a pharmacy can dispense controlled substances via the Internet.

- *Enhanced penalties for Schedule III through V.* Penalties will be enhanced for unlawfully dispensing controlled substances in Schedules III through V.

- *Prohibition on advertising illegal sales.*

- *Requirement that Internet pharmacies post certain information on their websites.*

DEA Acting Administrator Michele M. Leonhart stated, "Cyber-criminals illegally peddling controlled substances over the Internet have invaded households and threatened America's youth for far too long. . . . This landmark piece of legislation will bring rogue pharmacy operators out of the shadows."[104]

The United States and New Zealand are the only countries that allow pharmaceutical companies to advertise their products directly to consumers, called direct-to-consumer advertising. Since their beginning in the 1980s, the amount of advertising among these companies has significantly increased.[105] Further, pharmaceutical companies allocate almost 2 times more funding to advertising than to research and development.[106]

Access to prescription drugs becomes even more problematic when such drugs are available through the Internet. The Drug Enforcement Administration (DEA) has noted that the Internet has become one of the fastest-growing methods of distributing controlled pharmaceuticals (see "Why Do They Do It? Ryan Thomas Haight" above for an example).

There has been growing concern over a group of drugs called **designer drugs**. Designer drugs are substances considered to be for recreational use; they are derivatives of approved drugs, so they can circumvent existing legal restrictions. The term *designer drugs*, however, has been misused and popularized by the media.[107] Unfortunately, it appears as though the only use of the term is to differentiate between synthetic drugs and drugs that appear in nature. Interestingly, the term was coined by Gary Henderson, PhD, at the University of California at Davis in the 1970s. He used the term to refer to analogues of fentanyl, a powerful synthetic opioid used in hospitals. One could use this substance only in controlled hospital settings. Henderson reported that an analogue of fentanyl, alpha-methylfentanyl, was being sold on the street as "China white"—synthetic

designer drugs:
substances considered to be for recreational use; derivatives of approved drugs that can circumvent existing legal restrictions

heroin. The problem was that prosecuting the individuals selling this substance was not possible given the limitations of the Controlled Substances Act:[108]

VIDEO ▶

Designer Drugs

The Controlled Substances Act, as it was originally enacted, contained an unforeseen but, as it turned out, major flaw. It was very specific in describing the drugs within its several schedules. Unfortunately for the drug enforcement community, underground chemists, or cookers, had become highly sophisticated. They were capable of altering the chemical structure of certain drugs, including fentanyl, so that their street products no longer fit the description of the controls.[109]

CRIME IN THE NEWS NEWS

Designer Drugs

The number of designer drugs continues to grow. Two discussed often in the media are "spice" and "bath salts." *Spice* refers to various herbal mixtures intended to produce the same experiences as marijuana. It is sold under different names, such as "K2," "fake weed," "Yucatan fire," "skunk," and "moon rocks." These "spice" mixtures have been easily accessible in head shops (i.e., stores specializing in selling drug paraphernalia), at gas stations, and on the Internet. Interestingly, the DEA has designated five chemicals often found in spice as Schedule I controlled substances; thus, it is illegal to sell, buy, or possess these chemicals. However, manufacturers of spice products continue their attempts to evade the legal restrictions by substituting different chemicals in the mixture.[110]

This herbal mixture, brand name K2 Summit, is advertised as containing rose, South American bay bean, and various other botanicals.

"Bath salts" are another emerging designer drug. The active chemicals in bath salts are mephedrone, pyrovalerone, and methylenedioxypyrovalerone. These all have stimulant properties; thus, while they are different from such drugs as amphetamine and cocaine, they have similar effects on the brain.[111] Bath salts are sold under various brand names, such as Ivory Wave, Bloom, Cloud Nine, Lunar Wave, Vanilla Sky, White Lightning, and Scarface. The National Institute on Drug Abuse noted that there have been reports of severe intoxication and dangerous health effects related to the use of bath salts. The effects can include euphoria and increased sociability and sex drive; others can experience paranoia, agitation, and hallucinations. There have also been some instances of individuals displaying psychotic and violent behaviors while on bath salts.[112]

THE DRUG-CRIME LINK

From the general public's perspective, the relationship between drugs and crime is relatively straightforward; specifically, drug use leads to criminal activity. However, the link between drugs and crime is more complex than this simple causal explanation.[113] James Inciardi maintains that "the pursuit of some simple cause-and-effect relationship may be futile."[114] The relationship between drugs and crime usually falls into one of three categories:

- *Drug-defined crimes* involve the sale and/or possession of an illegal substance.
- *Drug-related crimes* involve violent behaviors induced by the effects of a drug or illegal activity that is motivated by continued drug use.

- *Crimes associated with drug use* involve illegal activities that may have occurred while a person was under the influence of an illegal substance but those activities were not a direct result of the drug use.[115]

The time order of the drug–crime link (i.e., "Which came first?") has been the primary research focus of a number of investigators. Studies have revealed that individuals who engage in substance use, such as cocaine, heroin, or marijuana, have consistently engaged in criminal behavior prior to, or while, using illegal drugs.[116] Further, the research reveals that substance use does not necessarily precipitate an individual's involvement in criminal activity; however, substance use does influence the extent of crime, the types of crime, and the length of time an individual engages in criminal behavior.[117] In this vein, "existing data and research indicate that drug abuse and criminal activity are a part of a broader set of integrated deviant behaviors involving crime, drug use, and, often, high-risk sex."[118]

LEARNING CHECK 15.2

In 1898, the Bayer Company developed _____, an opium derivative that was 10 times more powerful than morphine. The _____ Amendment prohibited the manufacture, sale, or transportation of intoxicating liquors in the United States. Some have argued that were it not for the zeal of _____, the commissioner of the new Federal Bureau of Narcotics, marijuana might be legal in the United States today. Some researchers have noted that after years of research, medical experts have not identified a distinctive condition, syndrome, or disorder among babies born of drug-abusing mothers that merits the label _____. New Zealand and _____ are the only countries that allow pharmaceutical companies to advertise their products directly to consumers.

Answers located at www.sagepub.com/schram

Duane McBride and Clyde McCoy suggest that to enhance our understanding of the relationship between drug use and criminal behavior, one should apply an analytical framework that incorporates the following issues: (1) the historical underpinnings of current perspectives; (2) the types of drugs and criminal behavior; (3) the statistical relationship, specifically the extent and type of criminal behavior among different types of drug users, as well as the extent and type of drug use among different types of criminals; (4) the etiological nature of the relationship, such as causality and interaction; (5) the theoretical interpretations of the relationships; and (6) the policy implications of research conclusions.[119]

Benjamin Nordstrom and Charles Dackis conducted an extensive review of the literature that focuses on addiction and crime. They sought to assess whether there is support for any of the three leading hypotheses that attempt to explain the drug–crime association:

1. Drug use and criminal behavior have a common cause, which might be biological, psychological, or sociological.

2. Drug use influences criminal behavior by either disinhibiting behavior or creating the need to finance a drug habit.

3. Deviance increases the likelihood of drug use later, such as in seeking deviant, drug-using peers.[120]

For instance, they found research that examined various risk factors associated with *both* substance abuse and criminal behavior. These factors included the history of victimization, attachment to parents, a propensity for violence or aggression, and impulsivity. They also examined research that moves beyond psychological and social risk factors to explore whether meaningful life events can change the trajectory of an individual's criminal and drug-using behavior. These researchers noted that the review of the literature finds support for all the hypotheses listed above pertaining to the drug–crime association. They concluded by emphasizing that "drug users are not a monolithic group, as many drug users do not commit crimes. . . . Criminally-active drug users are also not a monolithic group."[121]

THE TRIPARTITE CONCEPTUAL FRAMEWORK

Paul Goldstein developed what has been designated the **Tripartite Conceptual Framework** of the relationship between drugs and violence.[122] This framework suggests that drugs and violence are related to each other in three ways: through psychopharmacological, economically compulsive, and systemic violence.

PSYCHOPHARMACOLOGICAL VIOLENCE. This model of drugs and violence contends that some individuals, due to either short-term or long-term use of certain drugs, may become excitable, irritable, and/or irrational. This may then result in some type of violent behavior. The most relevant drugs within this model include alcohol, stimulants, barbiturates, and PCP. There may also be instances when substance use has reverse psychopharmacological effects and subsequently offsets violent tendencies. Thus, individuals prone to violence may engage in self-medication to control their violent tendencies. Similarly, certain drugs may be used in a psychopharmacological manner because of their perceived effects. Such functional substance use includes use of tranquilizers and marijuana to control nervousness or use of barbiturates and alcohol to provide courage.

ECONOMICALLY COMPULSIVE VIOLENCE. This model maintains that some substance users engage in violent crime, such as robbery, to support their drug use. Heroin and cocaine are expensive drugs often associated with compulsive use; these substances are germane within this model. Individuals within this model are essentially motivated by economic incentives rather than impulses to act violently. Often, victims of economically compulsive drug-related violence are individuals living in the same neighborhood as the offenders. Sometimes the victims are involved in illegal activities themselves; they may be drug users, strangers coming into the neighborhood to buy drugs, or prostitutes.

SYSTEMIC VIOLENCE. This model denotes the aggressive behaviors associated with the system of drug distribution and use, such as

> disputes over territory between rival drug dealers, assaults and homicides committed within dealing hierarchies as a means of enforcing normative codes, robberies of drug dealers and the usually violent retaliation by the dealers or their bosses, elimination of informers, disputes over drugs and/or drug paraphernalia, punishment for selling adulterated or phony drugs, punishment for failing to pay one's debts, and robbery violence related to the social ecology of copping areas.[123]

Some issues pertaining to systemic violence are unresolved. For instance, while there is no question that participating in the drug business increases likelihood of engaging in violence, there is no clear time order for this association. Specifically, does the drug business make people violent *or* are violence-prone individuals drawn to the violent roles associated with the drug business?

MODERN POLICIES RELATED TO REDUCING DRUG USE

Howard Abadinsky asks the question, "To what extent does knowledge actually affect drug policy?"[124] To address this question, he emphasizes the importance of distinguishing between *scientific* knowledge and *political* knowledge:

Tripartite Conceptual Framework: suggests that drugs and violence are related to each other through psychopharmacological, economically compulsive, and systemic violence

> Scientific knowledge in the field of drug use is the body of facts and theories related to the uses of drugs. Political knowledge concerns public attitudes and organization toward drug use, including scientific knowledge. . . . Scientific knowledge can be only one of a number of factors which bear upon the symbolic and instrumental character of official public opinion.[125]

Abadinsky concludes that reducing the consumption of drugs by enhancing law enforcement efforts and providing large-scale treatment programs will not solve other sociological problems associated with drug use. These problems include the lack of educational and employment opportunities, as well as residential instability.[126] Drug abuse is not an isolated problem; rather, it is linked to other problems such as family dysfunction, child abuse and neglect, delinquency, and alcohol abuse.[127]

In this section, we review some current policies and programs that have been implemented to reduce drug use. These include interdiction, eradication, drug courts, maintenance and decriminalization, and harm reduction. When examining these policies and programs, readers should consider how these efforts address the other sociological problems linked to substance abuse.

INTERDICTION STRATEGIES

According to the *National Interdiction Command and Control Plan*, **interdiction** is a "general term used to describe the multi-step, usually sequential continuum of effort/ events focused on interrupting illicit drug trafficking."[128] The various steps in the interdiction continuum start with *cueing* (providing intelligence), followed by *detection* (initial acquisition of a contact), *sorting/classifying* (distinguishing drug-smuggling traffic from legitimate traffic), *monitoring* (tracking and/or intercept of a contact), *hand-off* (shifting primary responsibility between forces or actors), *disruption* (halting an activity, usually the transportation of contraband), *apprehension* (detention, arrest, or seizure of suspects, evidentiary items, contraband, and/or vehicles), and *prosecution* (federal activities related to the conduct of criminal proceedings).[129]

With the Anti-Drug Abuse Act of 1988, Congress established the High Intensity Drug Trafficking Areas (HIDTA) program. The program's efforts focus on reducing drug trafficking and production in the United States by facilitating cooperation with federal, state, local, and tribal law enforcement agencies, such as information and intelligence sharing and coordinated law enforcement strategies to utilize resources. There are currently 28 HIDTAs in the United States, which includes about 16% of all U.S. counties. These HIDTA-designated counties are located in 46 states and Puerto Rico, the U.S. Virgin Islands, and the District of Columbia. The HIDTA program is involved in various activities, including multiagency investigative, interdiction, and prosecution activities, as well as prevention and treatment efforts. HIDTAs are directed and guided by executive boards. These executive boards consist of both federal and nonfederal (i.e., state, local, and tribal) law enforcement leaders.[130] A key aspect of the HIDTA program is "the discretion granted to the Executive Boards to design and implement initiates that confront drug trafficking threats in each HIDTA."[131]

Ohio is designated as one of the HIDTAs; this area consists of 11 counties. This area is also linked to major drug-source regions, including Chicago, Detroit, New York City, the Southwest Border, and Canada. The Ohio HIDTA emphasizes how the numerous interstate highways are often used by drug traffickers to move illegal drugs throughout the region. For instance, Ohio has the fourth largest interstate highway system and carries the fifth largest volume of traffic in the United States. The Ohio HIDTA noted that the commercial truck traffic has increased by 90% over the past 25 years; this is expected to increase another 60% by 2020. The greatest drug threat for the Ohio HIDTA is cocaine, specifically crack cocaine. This is due to the highly addictive nature of this drug and the crime associated with its distribution and abuse.[132]

interdiction: describes the various steps implemented to interrupt illicit drug trafficking (e.g., cueing, detection, apprehension, prosecution)

COMPARATIVE CRIMINOLOGY: DRUGS

Contact With Drug-Related Problems in the Area of Residence

Since 1973, the European Commission has been involved in conducting public opinion surveys on various topics with participating member states. These surveys and studies focus on topics that affect European citizenship, such as enlargement, social situation, health, culture, technology, environment, and defense. These surveys are referred to as the "Eurobarometer."[133] One item on the 2002 *Public Safety, Exposure to Drug-Related Problems and Crime* public opinion survey asked respondents the following question:

> "Over the last 12 months, how often were you personally in contact with drug related problems in the area where you live? For example, seeing people dealing in drugs,

taking or using drugs in public spaces, or by finding syringes left by drug addicts? Was this often, from time to time, rarely or never?"[134]

Van Dijk adapted the results from this survey (see Figure 15.4). The figure is based on results from 15 European Union countries. About 19% of the respondents noted that they have been in contact with drug-related problems, either often or from time to time. This was the average percentage. One can note that countries such as the United Kingdom, the Netherlands, Portugal, Italy, and Greece were above this average. Van Dijk further noted that the United Kingdom and the Netherlands were also engaged in political debates about *incivilities* occurring in their countries. Thus, perceptions of feeling unsafe in the street were strongly associated with perceived exposure to drug problems.[135]

Source: Van Dijk, J. (2008). *The world of crime: Breaking the silence on problems of security, justice, and development across the world.* Thousand Oaks, CA: Sage, p. 108.

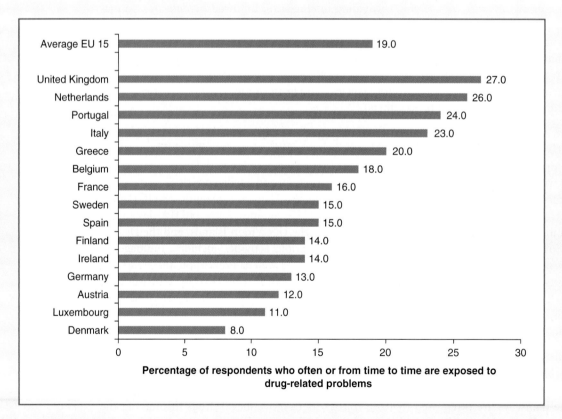

Figure 15.4 Contact With Drug-Related Problems in the Area of Residence (in %) in 15 European Union Countries (2002)

Sources: Eurobarometer, 2003, adapted.

ERADICATION STRATEGIES

There are four recognized techniques of **eradication:** mechanical destruction (i.e., slashing or uprooting), ~~bunting, chemical, and bi~~ological (including genetic).[136] Among these four techniques, mechanical and chemical destruction are the most commonly used eradication strategies.[137] Eradication efforts have focused on the opium poppy, the coca bush, and the cannabis plant.[138]

The National Drug Intelligence Center reported that worldwide production decreased by about 8% in 2007, essentially due to successful coca eradication in Colombia—the country responsible for about 55% of the annual worldwide cocaine production from 2003 to 2007. Peru is the world's second largest cocaine producing country. There was also a decline in cocaine production in this country, primarily because of increased forced and voluntary eradication. In 2007, Bolivia produced about 12% of the worldwide cocaine supply. In this country, potential pure cocaine production increased. Based on intelligence reporting, cocaine produced in Bolivia is essentially destined for Brazil and Europe.[139]

A DEA agent involved in the eradication of marijuana plants

The United States has been criticized for these eradication efforts. For instance, Colombian officials have condemned the United States for not adequately addressing the issue of consumption. During the Colombian presidential election of 1990, campaign speeches often included negative references to Marion Barry, the mayor of Washington, D.C. Federal agents videotaped the mayor in the act of smoking crack cocaine, and his misdemeanor drug conviction inflamed Colombian public opinion.[140] There are similar criticisms among citizens of Peru and Bolivia. The cultivation of coca is intertwined with factors such as culture, tradition, and poverty. These social conditions render enforcement efforts ineffective.[141] Thus, when the most profitable crops are linked to an underground economy, and there is no viable, legal crop substitute, it is difficult to prevent coca cultivation.[142]

According to the DEA Domestic Cannabis Eradication/Suppression Program, domestic cannabis eradication is increasing. The primary marijuana cultivation states include California, Hawaii, Kentucky, Oregon, Tennessee, Washington, and West Virginia. While cannabis cultivation operations are more prevalent in western states, they are increasing in eastern states. Further, indoor cannabis cultivation continues to rise. Many cultivators have either relocated or established their operations indoors to avoid law enforcement detection. Indoor cultivators can generate higher profit margins since they can produce higher potency marijuana and cultivate year-round.[143] In their assessment of cannabis cultivation in the United States, the National Drug Intelligence Center noted the following intelligence gaps:

- No reliable estimates are available regarding the amount of domestically cultivated or processed marijuana.

- The amount of cannabis cultivated and marijuana produced in the United States by large-scale drug trafficking organizations, including Asian, Caucasian, and Mexican groups, is unknown.

- The extent of indoor cannabis cultivation in the United States is largely unknown and likely underreported because of the challenges posed to law enforcement entities in locating indoor grow sites.[144]

....

eradication: four recognized techniques: mechanical destruction (i.e., slashing or uprooting), bunting, chemical, and biological (including genetic)

One example of a drug court

DRUG COURTS

By the late 1980s, offenders with substance abuse problems were clogging up the criminal justice system—from the initial arrest stage up to prisoner reentry.[145] Rigorous prosecutions and harsh sentencing policies are often costly, as well as ineffective in stopping the cycle of drug use and crime. Using prison as an approach to solving America's drug problem is expensive and ill-advised.[146] In an effort to address the increasing number of drug-using offenders clogging the criminal justice system, **drug treatment court programs** were established, especially in urban areas of the United States. The first drug court was established in 1989 in Miami, Florida. Arthur Lurigio noted that some of the basic features of drug treatment courts include expedited case processing, outpatient treatment, support services (e.g., job placement and housing), mandatory drug testing, and intensive court or probation supervision[147] (see Table 15.2 for a more detailed list of these basic features).

Drug courts consist of the collaborative efforts of justice and treatment professionals to intervene and break the cycle of substance abuse, addiction, and crime. Individuals identified as substance-abusing offenders are placed under ongoing judicial monitoring and community supervision and provided with long-term treatment services.[148] Specifically, the offender is required to participate in substance abuse treatment, drug testing, and probation supervision, as well as reporting to regularly scheduled status hearings before a judge familiar with the drug court model.[149]

BASIC FEATURES OF DRUG TREATMENT COURTS
• Prompt identification of clients and their immediate placement in treatment
• Nonadversarial court proceedings enacted by a team of judges, attorneys, and treatment providers, and designed to protect community safety as well as defendants' and offenders' due process rights
• Regular contact between clients and judges in judicial status hearings or other types of court sessions
• Intensive supervision practices that include close monitoring and frequent, random drug testing of clients
• Treatment interventions that are delivered on a continuum of care, evidence based, comprehensive, and integrated for individuals with co-occurring psychiatric disorders
• Contingencies of rewards and punishments that encourage compliance with treatment and other conditions of program participation
• Ongoing evaluations to monitor program implementation and measure the accomplishment of program objectives and goals
• Close working relationships with a wide range of community service providers and public agencies
• Interdisciplinary educational opportunities to help program staff stay current with the latest advances in offender drug treatment and case management strategies

Table 15.2 Basic Features of Drug Treatment Courts

Source: Lurigio, A. J. (2008). The first 20 years of drug treatment courts: A brief description of their history and impact. *Federal Probation, 72,* 15.

drug treatment court programs: established in an effort to address the increasing number of drug-using offenders clogging the criminal justice system

Individuals who participate in a drug court program can have their charges dismissed or reduced, address their substance abuse problem, obtain employment, and regain custody of their children. There are, however, additional rights not available to them, because other aspects of public policy continue to consider addiction from a more punitive perspective. Individuals who have completed a drug court program but are charged or convicted of a drug offense may be denied welfare benefits, access to educational loans, public housing, and voting rights.[150] Jeanne Stinchcomb argues that the

> ongoing debate over the efficacy of drug courts . . . continues to raise questions concerning the strength of their conceptual foundation, the execution of their implementation strategies, and ultimately, the future potential of their ability to maintain a prominent position on the public-policy agenda.[151]

Loreen Wolfer conducted a qualitative exploration of individuals who participated and graduated from the drug-treatment court program. When asked what changes should be implemented in the program, 13 of the 55 participants mentioned that there was a problem or weakness with how the court was conducting the urine screens. Nine of these individuals noted that more random screens should be conducted because the scheduled screens were "too predictable" and were "easy to beat." Another problem among these participants was the perceived unfairness of unequal treatment. The drug-treatment court program is specifically designed to develop a treatment plan based on individual needs. Some individuals, however, considered this as differential treatment. Comments among these participants included the words "specialized treatment" and "lack of uniformity" in treatment.[152]

MAINTENANCE AND DECRIMINALIZATION

A **maintenance** policy advocates for the accessibility of drugs through governmental regulation, such as distribution and legal age of use. A **decriminalization** policy supports the end of using criminal sanctions to address individual drug use. Often, this policy is advocated for marijuana possession.[153] Table 15.3 outlines three models of drug maintenance/decriminalization.

The pros for a maintenance/decriminalization policy are as follows:

- The resources that have been allocated for law enforcement efforts could be shifted to other areas of crime control, as well as treatment and education.

THREE MODELS OF DRUG MAINTENANCE/DECRIMINALIZATION
1. Dangerous drugs can be dispensed only through government-controlled clinics or specially licensed medical personnel and only for short-term treatment purposes; unauthorized sale or possession entails criminal penalties. Long-term maintenance is limited to the use of methadone. This is basically the approach currently used in England.
2. Dangerous drugs can be prescribed by an authorized medical practitioner for treatment or maintenance; criminal penalties are imposed for sale or possession outside medical auspices. This is the old British system.
3. Dangerous drugs can be sold and used as tobacco and alcohol products are; that is, nonprescription use by adults is permitted. This was the case in the United States before the Harrison Act.

Table 15.3 Three Models of Drug Maintenance/Decriminalization

Source: Abadinsky, H. (1997). *Drug abuse: An introduction* (3rd ed.). Chicago: Nelson-Hall, p. 325 (table only).

REFERENCE ARTICLE
Drug Courts

VIDEO
Decriminalization

maintenance: advocates for the accessibility of drugs through governmental regulation, such as distribution and legal age of use

decriminalization: a policy related to labeling theory, which proposes less harsh punishments for some minor offenses, such as the possession of small amounts of marijuana

- Due to the low cost of psychoactive substances, there would be a reduction in secondary crime (i.e., crimes committed to support an expensive drug habit).

- Criminal organizations would no longer remain viable if they continued in drug trafficking.

- The aggressive marketing strategies of traffickers would no longer be operative.

- Individuals dependent on psychoactive substances could lead more productive lives; abusers would have an opportunity to become contributing members of society.

- Individuals using heroin intravenously would not be at risk for getting AIDS or hepatitis, because each user would have his or her own hypodermic kit.

- Decriminalization would enable use of social controls that inhibit antisocial, although legal, behavior. For example, various social controls attempt to influence the behavior of smokers and drunk drivers.[154]

The cons for a maintenance/decriminalization policy are as follows:

- Drugs such as cocaine, amphetamines, and heroin that are easily available to adults could also be abused by youths, similar to cigarettes and alcohol.

- More people would be tempted to try legalized controlled substances, which could result in an increase in abuse-related problems.

- Legalizing psychoactive substances would convey some form of acceptance of their use, similar to alcohol and tobacco use.

- Making psychoactive substances legal may reduce the incentive for individuals, addicted to these substances, to enter drug treatment or pursue a drug-free lifestyle.[155]

One current policy that continues to be controversial is legalized medical marijuana. Currently, 16 states—Alaska, Arizona, California, Colorado, Delaware, Hawaii, Maine, Michigan, Montana, Nevada, New Jersey, New Mexico, Oregon, Rhode Island, Vermont, and Washington—and the District of Columbia have enacted laws to legalize medical marijuana.[156] California was the first state to pass a legal medical marijuana law, designated as the Compassionate Use Act of 1996. This allows seriously ill Californians the right to obtain and use marijuana for medical purposes. According to the act, a physician needs to determine that an individual's health would benefit from the use of marijuana in treatment for such ailments as cancer, anorexia, AIDS, chronic pain, spasticity, glaucoma, arthritis, and migraines.[157]

In November 2012, Colorado and Washington voters supported a measure that made it legal to smoke marijuana recreationally, without the required prescription or medical excuse. There are, however, questions pertaining to voter support of this law. The major issue is the conflict between the federal government and the voters of Colorado and Washington. The federal government still considers marijuana a Schedule I prohibited substance.[158] In fact, federal prosecutors have toughened their enforcement efforts in such states as California where the use of marijuana for medical purposes is allowed. Interestingly, a month later, President Obama stated that federal law enforcement agencies have "bigger fish to fry" than prosecuting marijuana users in Colorado and Washington.[159]

HARM REDUCTION

A **harm reduction** policy attempts to incorporate a public health approach to lessen the risks and harms associated with illegal drug use.[160] Harm reduction includes (1) the provision of sterile injecting equipment (i.e., needle exchange), (2) outreach and peer education efforts, and (3) substitution therapies such as methadone and supervised injection facilities. Such interventions, it is argued, assist in transforming drug use contexts that promote safe drug use as well as healthier behaviors.[161]

As noted above, one intervention associated with harm reduction is a needle exchange program. The purpose of such programs is to exchange used syringes for unused syringes among intravenous drug users to prevent the reuse of contaminated injection equipment. Needle exchange programs may offer other related materials such as bleach bottles, cotton swabs, skin ointment, condoms, and educational materials pertaining to sexually transmitted diseases and other communicable illnesses. However, "most [needle exchange programs] combine a program goal of risk reduction through needle exchange with a program goal of offering counseling and referral of participants to drug treatment programs."[162]

The legal aspects pertaining to needle exchange programs focus essentially on drug paraphernalia. Specifically, the manufacture, possession, or distribution of drug paraphernalia is illegal in 46 states and the District of Columbia.[163] Burris and his colleagues examined 49 needle exchange programs to determine how these programs operated in relation to the law. Their study revealed that nine of these programs operated without a clear legal basis; thus, participants in this program could be subject to prosecution under the paraphernalia law. Twenty-seven programs have been either directly or indirectly authorized by amendment or judicial interpretations of the laws to be exempt from prosecution. The remaining 13 programs operate under claims of legality founded on local interpretations of state public health and/or drug laws that have not been reviewed by the court.[164]

One intervention associated with harm reduction policy is a needle exchange program.

There are also ethical issues surrounding needle exchange programs. Cheryl Delgado asserts,

> The principle risk reduction accepts that a dangerous behavior like intravenous drug use is inevitable. Health officials therefore have a responsibility to the general public to reduce risks associated with the acts (drug use) they cannot prevent. Risk reduction is a more reasonable goal than attempts to eradicate illegal intravenous drug use.[165]

From this perspective, one would maintain that the reduced risk is not just to the drug user but to the community as well, with respect to limiting the spread of communicable diseases. Some, however, would argue that providing such a service may encourage intravenous drug use. Further, the time, money, and effort to implement needle exchange programs could be more productively used for treatment programs.[166]

harm reduction:
attempts to incorporate a public health approach to lessen the risks and harms associated with illegal drug use

APPLYING THEORY TO CRIME: *DRUG SELLING/TRAFFICKING AND DRUG USE*

This section applies two theoretical frameworks of crime to two of the primary offenses discussed in this chapter—drug selling/trafficking and drug use. Although readers may think the theoretical explanations for these activities are similar because both deal with illegal drugs, the most likely theories supported by research are different. This is a good example of how theories can differ, even within the same general category of criminal behavior.

Specifically, regarding drug selling/trafficking, the most logical and empirically supported theory is traditional strain theory (Desroches, 2005; Merton, 1938). Traditional strain theory places a high emphasis on individuals' innovating ways they can obtain the goals of financial success, without having to go through common conventional means (e.g., education, employment). Drug selling/trafficking can be a fast, albeit risky, way of obtaining a lot of money, without having to work hard in school or at a conventional job. Scientific studies have shown that this theory is supported as a primary reason for why individuals engage in this activity. After all, the lure of a fast payoff, given the high demand for various drugs, provides an extremely high motivation for people who have low levels of education and/or mainstream work experience.

On the other hand, drug use is not as well explained by traditional strain theory. Although Merton (1938) did identify a type of retreatist adaption to strain (i.e., escaping from reality), which would include chronic drug users, this is not a strong motivation for their behavior. Rather, other theories are likely better for explaining why some individuals become

habitual drug users. Specifically, various types of social learning theory and subcultural theory have been shown by empirical research to be highly supported as explanations of chronic drug use (Akers, 1985; Golub, Dunlap, & Benoit, 2010).

Regarding the social learning theories of drug use, differential association/reinforcement theory emphasizes the importance of peer influences in decisions to commit certain behaviors. This is likely most important in terms of drug use. After all, virtually no individuals take drugs for the first time when they are alone; rather, their initial experience in taking any drug (from alcohol to marijuana to cocaine to heroin) is almost always with other persons providing it and showing them how to ingest it, which for higher drugs (e.g., freebasing and injecting heroin) can be a complicated process. To a large extent, the initial taking of any drug is typically a social process; the person does it because a friend or group motivates him or her to "try it."

Of course, later episodes of drug use often become more solo, but the first experience is almost always peer influenced, which highly supports the social learning theories of differential association/reinforcement models of offending. The initial experience of engaging in taking illegal substances goes back to one's significant others and what they are doing and, thus, what they are exposing one to regarding drug behavior. This is supported by recent empirical studies, such as that by Golub et al. (2010), which showed that the influence of friends, peers, and intimate partners was key in engaging in drug use.

Furthermore, numerous empirical studies have shown a cultural or subcultural emphasis regarding the initial engagement in drug use. After all, it is likely that many individuals would not engage in drug use if it wasn't highly prevalent in their community or neighborhood culture. Recent studies, such as that by Golub, Johnson, and Dunlap (2005), have supported this drug subcultural effect among many individuals not only regarding their initial use but also their subsequent chronic use.

General strain theory (Agnew & Raskin White, 1992) is also a good explanation for such chronic drug use. This model places an emphasis on coping mechanisms (or lack thereof) to deal with various stressors and frustrations in our lives. When an individual has not developed healthy coping mechanisms for dealing with life stressors (e.g., exercise, watching television, religion), then he or she has a high likelihood for using drugs to self-medicate and "deal" with reality. Unfortunately, this usually leads such drug users into a downward spiral, in which the drugs create even more stressors, which in turn lead to further heavy drug use and addiction.

Ultimately, the key purpose of this section is to demonstrate that several different theories are likely explanations for various illegal behaviors regarding drugs. Furthermore, it is likely that the most fitting theories for drug selling/trafficking are somewhat different from those of chronic drug use, which reveals how important theory is for understanding certain criminal behaviors, even those within a given category of offending, such as drug activity.

Sources: Agnew, R., & Raskin White, H. (1992). An empirical test of general strain theory. *Criminology, 30,* 475–500; Desroches, F. J. (2005). *The crime that pays: Drug trafficking and organized crime in Canada.* Toronto, Ontario: Canadian Scholars' Press; Akers, R. L. (1985). Social learning theory and adolescent cigarette smoking. *Social Problems, 32,* 455–473; Golub, A., Dunlap, E., & Benoit, E. (2010). Drug use and conflict in inner-city African-American relationships in the 2000s. *Journal of Psychoactive Drugs, 42,* 327–337; Golub, A., Johnson, B. D., & Dunlap, E. (2005). Subcultural evolution and illicit drug use. *Addiction Research & Theory, 13,* 217–229; Merton, R. K. (1938). Social structure and anomie. *American Sociological Review, 3,* 672–682.

RECOMMENDATIONS FOR FUTURE POLICIES

Drug policies in the United States will never be simple; policy can often be contradictory, especially in those instances when state- and local-level policies conflict with national policy.[167] McBride and McCoy maintain that three policy implications result from the current research on the relation between drugs and crime:[168]

1. While there is no clear causal relation between drugs and crime, there is a link between substance use and levels of criminal involvement. Policy should be directed toward providing treatment services for drug users who are involved in criminal activity. Such an approach has the potential to reduce levels of crime.

2. It is essential to appreciate that the history of drug use is entangled with the differential social, political, and economic opportunities of certain marginalized groups. Policy needs to incorporate efforts to enhance educational and economic opportunities. Such efforts need to be a priority on both the local and national level.

3. Any drug policy that is implemented must never compromise an individual's civil rights. "Drug law enforcement must never be an excuse for a retreat on hard-won legal and civil rights, and drug law and policy must rest on a strong public support base.[169]

Elliott Currie argues that substance abuse is not an isolated problem limited to certain communities and groups; rather, it is intertwined with broader social problems such as family dissolution, child abuse and neglect, and alcohol abuse. If policy focuses only on treating individual substance abusers, "new" substance abusers will follow, given the broader social problems. Thus, "the best, most comprehensive programs to help addicts transform their lives will inevitably be compromised if we do not simultaneously address the powerful social forces that are destroying the communities to which they must return."[170]

STATE CRIME RANKINGS

Reported Arrests: Drug Abuse

WHY DO THEY DO IT?

PABLO ESCOBAR

In December 1993, Pablo Escobar was killed by security forces in his hometown of Medellin, Colombia. Escobar started his criminal career by selling tombstones he stole from a cemetery and sanded flat. His first arrest was in 1974 for stealing a car. He soon because known to fellow associates and enemies as intelligent, ambitious, a fast learner, having a knack for business, and possessing an unforgiving memory. He later engaged in the practice of kidnapping individuals from wealthy families and seeking ransom from their family members. However, these criminal endeavors apparently did not get him the riches he desired, so he switched to the drug business.[171] Ironically, Escobar did not enjoy taking cocaine or other hard drugs. His drug of choice was marijuana, which he was known to smoke on a consistent basis. Persons who knew him closely called him a "pothead."

In 1976, he had earned a reputation as an established drug smuggler. He also had a reputation for killing people and blowing up neighborhoods, shopping centers, and a jetliner. Escobar's innovations in the drug-smuggling business introduced new ways of transporting drugs that had not been common before, including soaking designer jeans in a liquid form of cocaine. Furthermore, he was likely the first to use submarines to carry large shipments of cocaine up the Pacific coastline, now a common practice.[172] However, he was considered by some as a type of Robin Hood. He built houses for the poor, paved roads, constructed sports stadiums, and gave employment opportunities to thousands. This is why 20,000 local citizens showed up for his funeral.

Escobar also enjoyed a luxurious lifestyle. His favorite estate was a 7,000-acre ranch in Colombia, valued at an estimated $63 million. He imported various exotic animals such as giraffes, camels, bison, llamas, cockatoos, and a kangaroo. He is known to have actually burned $2 million just to stay warm when he was "on the lam" from U.S. authorities. Later, he wanted to give the impression that he was a legitimate businessman; so he owned his own radio station and many times was accompanied by Roman Catholic priests. At the peak of Escobar's criminal activities, he and others associated with the Medellin cartel produced 60% of the cocaine in Colombia; this was about 80% of the U.S. market. In fact, *Forbes* magazine listed him as one of the world's richest people.

In 1991, after a massive manhunt, Escobar negotiated his surrender. The terms included his presiding over his drug business while incarcerated. He had cellular phones, computers, and meetings in board rooms. His living conditions were quite comfortable, with a waterbed, rugs, curtains, a stereo system, and a 60-inch television. He was soon concerned that his enemies would try to bomb the jail; officials built him a bomb shelter.

In 1992, the details of his luxurious incarceration were revealed and the government decided to transport him to a regular jail. During transport, however, he escaped. Escobar began targeting suspected traitors and rivals. When his cartel diminished, the government began to search for him, which resulted in his shooting death in December 1993.[173] In this situation, not only should one ask, "Why did he do it?" in terms of Escobar but also in terms of the government and some of the citizens of Colombia, who considered him some sort of folk hero.

WHY DO THEY DO IT?

ISRAEL KEYES

Israel Keyes is believed to have killed about a dozen people, and his victims spanned across the United States—from Vermont to Alaska. While only a few victims have been confirmed, it is strongly believed there were many more, given that numerous murder kits (caches of weapons, such as ligatures, ammunition, and silencers, and/or body disposal materials, such as garbage bags, bottles of Drano, and shovels) belonging to Keyes were found stored in Upstate New York, Washington State, Texas, and Wyoming. He admitted to killing numerous people, but we will likely never know all the details, as he slit his wrists and strangled himself while awaiting trial in the Anchorage Correctional Facility in Alaska, where he had been extradited from Texas for the death of an 18-year-old female kidnapped from a coffee stand in 2012. He was caught after he used the victim's credit card.

Although his sudden death left a lot of questions unanswered, what we do know from his initial confessions and interviews with police detectives is that he took great pleasure in murdering. Furthermore, during interrogation, Keyes, when asked his motive, replied, "Why not?" He never gave investigators a more meaningful answer. He confessed to killing at least eight individuals, but he also alluded to other killings; so the figure is estimated at around a dozen. It is believed that he had no intention of stopping, given the number of murder kits stored in states where he had not yet killed anyone at the time of his apprehension.

Like many chronic offenders, Keyes started his criminal career with theft and burglaries, which then escalated to armed robbery of banks and eventually murder. He told investigators that he enjoyed seeing coverage of his offenses in the news media, and he even seemed to get pleasure from talking about his various killings. He also claimed that he admired Ted Bundy, the notorious serial killer of several dozen women across the country in the 1970s. One key difference between Keyes and Bundy was that Bundy killed only females, whereas Keyes killed both males and females.

The point of this section is to show that while we have devoted much of this book to explaining and understanding why certain high-profile offenders committed their crimes, in Keyes's, case the answer remains relatively unknown. His notable and shocking rationale—"Why not?"—reveals that, despite all the established and well-researched theories examined in this book, in some cases there is not a clear explanation for such vicious and evil behavior. This case is meant to show that sometimes the experts simply can't understand the reasoning of chronic offenders. Yet that is what makes criminology all the more intriguing and reminds us that there is always more work to be done in attempting to understand offenders' motives and decision-making processes.

Sources: Peters, J. (2012, December 10). Was Israel Keyes the most meticulous serial killer of modern times? *Slate*. Retrieved from http://www.slate.com/blogs/crime/2012/12/10/israel_keyes_suicide_is_he_the_most_meticulous_serial_killer_of_modern_times.html; Thiessen, M. (2012, December 8). Serial killer caught in Alaska would only say "why not" when asked for motive. *NBCNews.com*. Retrieved from http://usnews.nbcnews.com/_news/2012/12/08/15775963-serial-killer-caught-in-alaska-would-only-say-why-not-when-asked-for-motive?lite.

CONCLUSION

A key purpose of this chapter is for readers to obtain a greater appreciation for the complex relationship between substance use and crime. This relation is dynamic and is influenced by factors on an individual, group, and societal level. First, a review of the various types of drugs reveals that the mere definition of "drugs" is not necessarily simple. For instance, some drugs are legal but highly addictive (e.g., nicotine); some drugs are legally prescribed for medical purposes but can be used illegally (e.g., OxyContin); and some drugs were initially deemed legal but are now considered illegal (e.g., heroin).

To further illustrate this complex link between drug use and crime, we briefly reviewed various trends of substance abuse, such as the early history of cocaine and opioid addiction, Prohibition, the "reefer madness" era, the 1960s and the baby boomers, the War on Drugs, and current patterns of substance abuse. For one to appreciate the current societal perspectives of substance use, it is essential to appreciate the historical context of such trends.[174] For instance, historically, certain drugs were legal and subsequently designated illegal (e.g., cocaine); other substances, such as alcohol, were legal, then illegal, and later deemed legal again.

The next section discussed the link between substance use and crime. While the general public's opinion may be that this relation is straightforward, it is essential for readers to appreciate that the link between drugs and crime is more complex than this simple causal explanation. We then briefly discussed the Tripartite Conceptual Framework of the relation between drugs and violence. This framework proposes that substance use and violent behavior are related in three ways: through psychopharmacological, economically compulsive, and systemic violence.

The following section reviewed modern policies that have been implemented to address the problem of substance use and criminal activity. These include interdiction and eradication strategies, drug courts, maintenance and decriminalization, and harm reduction. It is important for the reader to critically question whether such policies are effective, as well as what other policy approaches should be considered.

We started this chapter with the case study of Amber and Scott Landry, charged with aggravated manslaughter of their infant. Amber and Scott were snorting oxycodone the night before their infant son died; the infant died of an overdose. This case study illustrates the point made on numerous occasions throughout this chapter that the effects of substance abuse occur on various levels, from the individual to the family to the community and beyond.

KEY TERMS

alcohol

amphetamine

barbiturate

binge drinking

cannabis

cocaine

decriminalization

depressants

designer drugs

drug treatment court programs

Eighteenth Amendment

eradication

hallucinogens

harm reduction

Harrison Act

heroin

inhalants

interdiction

maintenance

Marihuana Tax Act

marijuana

methamphetamine

morphine

narcotics

oxycodone

Prohibition

steroids

stimulant

tranquilizers

Tripartite Conceptual Framework

Twenty-First Amendment

War on Drugs

STUDENT STUDY SITE

Visit the student study site at **www.sagepub.com/schram** to access links to the video, audio, city and state rankings, author podcasts, and SAGE journal and reference articles featured in this chapter, as well as additional study tools, including eFlashcards, web quizzes, web resources, and chapter outlines.

DISCUSSION QUESTIONS

1. What are the differences between stimulants and depressants?

2. What are the key features of the Prohibition era?

3. What are some key issues related to the 1937 Marihuana Tax Act?

4. What is meant by racialized drug policy?

5. How would you characterize the War on Drugs?

6. What is the main purpose of harm reduction programs?

7. Why were drug courts established?

8. What are the main arguments for and again maintenance and decriminalization policies?

9. What features should be eliminated from or incorporated in future policies on substance use?

WEB RESOURCES

National Institute on Drug Abuse
http://www.drugabuse.gov/

Drug Enforcement Administration
http://www.justice.gov/dea/index.shtml

Glossary

actus reus: in legal terms, whether the offender actually engaged in a given criminal act (2)

adaptations to strain: as proposed by Merton, the five ways that individuals deal with feelings of strain; see conformity, innovation, rebellion, retreatism, and ritualism (7)

add women and stir: when one uses an existing theoretical perspective based on males and "adds" women (11)

adolescence-limited offenders: a type of offender who commits crimes only during adolescence and desists in his or her 20s or adulthood (12)

adoption studies: studies that examine the criminality of adoptees as compared to the criminality of their biological and adoptive parents (5)

Age of Enlightenment: a period of the late 17th century to 18th century in which philosophers and scholars began to emphasize the rights of individuals in society (2)

aggregate studies: collection of studies, generally on a particular topic (3)

alcohol: ethanol is the only alcohol that should be consumed; rapidly absorbed through the stomach and small intestine into the bloodstream (15)

American Law Institute's Model Penal Code (ALI/MPC): one standard for the insanity defense. A key difference between the M'Naghten and the ALI/MPC tests is the M'Naghten test stipulates that the offender demonstrate *total* mental impairment; the ALI/MPC test stipulates that the offender demonstrate a lack of *substantial capacity* (6)

amphetamine: a type of stimulant; effects are similar to cocaine, but onset is slower and duration longer (15)

anomie: a concept originally proposed by Durkheim, which meant *normlessness* or the chaos that takes place when a society (e.g., economic structure) changes very rapidly (7)

atavism: belief that certain characteristics or behaviors of a person are throwbacks to an earlier stage of evolutionary development (4)

attachment theory: there are seven essential features of this theoretical perspective focusing on attachment: specificity, duration, engagement of emotion, course of development, learning, organization, and biological function (6)

autonomic nervous system: the portion of the nervous system that consists of our anxiety levels, such as the fight or flight response, as well as our involuntary motor activities (e.g., heart rate) (5)

barbiturate: a type of depressant; can induce a wide continuum of central nervous depression, ranging from mild sedation to coma (15)

binge drinking: heavy episodic drinking; drinking so much alcohol within a 2-hour period that it results in at least a .08 blood alcohol concentration (15)

bourgeoisie: a class or status Marx assigned to the dominant, oppressing owners of the means of production; believed to create and implement laws that helped retain their dominance over the working class (10)

brutalization effect: the predicted tendency of homicides to increase after an execution, particularly after high-profile executions (2)

Campus Hate Crimes Right to Know Act of 1997: amends a section of the Higher Education Act of 1965 that provides for disclosure of all criminal incidents that indicate any evidence of prejudice based on race, gender, religion, sexual orientation, ethnicity, or disability (14)

cannabis: An extremely resourceful plant that contains hundreds of psychoactive chemicals, particularly delta-9-tetrahydrocannibinol (THC) (15)

central nervous system: the portion of the nervous system that largely consists of the brain and spinal column and is responsible for our voluntary motor activities (5)

cerebrotonic: the type of temperament or personality associated with an ectomorphic (thin) body type; these people tend to be introverted and shy (4)

certainty of punishment: one of the key elements of deterrence; the assumption is that when people commit a crime, they will perceive a high likelihood of being caught and punished (2)

Cesare Lombroso: one of the earliest theorists focusing on the female offender; his book emphasized the physiological and psychological determinants of female criminality rather than socializing factors or social–structural constraints (11)

Chicago School of criminology: theoretical framework of criminal behavior that emphasizes the environmental impact of living in a high-crime neighborhood, applies ecological principles to explain how cities grow, and highlights levels of neighborhood organization to explain crime rates(8)

Child Online Protection Act: prohibits individuals from knowingly engaging in communication for commercial purposes that includes material "harmful to minors" and available to minors (13)

chivalry: pertains to behaviors and attitudes toward certain individuals that treat them as though they are on a pedestal(11)

Church Arson Prevention Act of 1996: prohibits intentional destruction of any religious real property or attempts to obstruct any person in the enjoyment of his or her free exercise of religious beliefs

classical conditioning: a learning model that assumes that animals, as well as people, learn through associations between stimuli and responses (9)

Classical School: model of crime that assumes crime occurs after a rational individual mentally weighs the potential good and bad consequences of crime and then makes a decision about whether to engage in a given behavior (2)

cocaine: a type of stimulant that appears in the leaves of various species of plants; usually distributed as a white, crystalline powder diluted with substances such as sugars and local anesthetics (15)

collective conscience: according to Durkheim, the extent to which people in a society share similarities or likenesses; the stronger the collective conscience, the less crime in that community (7)

college boy: a type of lower class male youth who has experienced the same strains and status frustration as his peers but responds to his disadvantaged situation by dedicating himself to overcoming the odds and competing in the middle-class schools despite his unlikely chances for success (7)

comparative criminology: the study of crime across various cultures to identify similarities and differences in crime patterns (1)

Computer Fraud and Abuse Act: originally designed to protect national security, financial, and commercial information; medical treatment; and interstate communication systems from malicious acts, including unauthorized access; allows victims of such crimes to bring civil suits against violators (13)

concentric circles: model proposed by Chicago School theorists that assumes that all cities grow in a natural way with the same five zones (8)

concordance rates: rates at which twin pairs either share a trait (e.g., criminality) or the lack of the trait (5)

concurrent jurisdiction: original jurisdiction for certain cases is shared by both criminal and juvenile courts; the prosecutor has discretion to file such cases in either court (1)

conflict gangs: a type of gang identified by Cloward and Ohlin that tends to develop in neighborhoods with weak stability and little or no organization; gangs are typically relatively disorganized and lack the skills and knowledge to make a profit through criminal activity (7)

conflict perspective or conflict theory: criminal behavior theories that assume most people disagree on what the law should be and that law is used as a tool by those in power to keep down other groups (1)

conformity: in strain theory, an adaptation in which an individual buys into the conventional means of success and also buys into conventional goals (7)

consensus perspective: theories that assume that virtually everyone is in agreement on the laws and therefore assume no conflict in attitudes regarding the laws and rules of society (1)

control theories: theories of criminal behavior that emphasize the assumption that humans are born selfish and that their tendencies toward aggression and offending must be controlled (9)

conventional level of morality: level of morality considered the normal adult approach used to maintain the family and social order such as the principle of the golden rule and appreciating social order (6)

Cooper v. Pate: as a result of this decision, prisoners were allowed to sue state officials in federal court, which resulted in much litigation and changed the prison conditions in the 1970s (13)

corner boy: a type of lower-class male youth who has experienced the same strains and status frustration as others but responds to his disadvantaged situation by accepting his place in society as someone who will somewhat passively make the best of life at the bottom of the social order. As the label describes, they often hang out on corners (7)

correlation or covariation: a criterion of causality that requires a change in a predictor variable (X) to be consistently associated with some change in the explanatory variable (Y) (1)

craniometry: field of study that emphasized the belief that the size of the brain or skull reflected superiority or inferiority, with larger brains and skulls being considered superior (4)

crime: here are various definitions of crime. From a legalistic approach, crime is that which violates the law. (1)

criminal gangs: a type of gang identified by Cloward and Ohlin that forms in lower-class neighborhoods with an organized structure of adult criminal behavior. Such gangs tend to be highly organized and stable (7)

criminal justice: criminal justice often refers to the various criminal justice agencies and institutions (e.g., police, courts, and corrections) that were interrelated (1)

criminal terrorism: terrorism motivated by engaging in criminal activity for profit, such as in the drug cartels in Mexico (14)

criminology: the scientific study of crime and the reasons why people engage (or don't engage) in criminal behavior (1)

cross-sectional studies: a form of research design model in which a collection of data is taken at one point in time (often in survey format) (3)

cultural/subcultural theory: perspective of criminal offending that assumes that many offenders believe in a normative system distinctly different from and often at odds with the norms accepted by conventional society (8)

cybercrime: cybercrime consists of at least three features: The act was committed using (1) a computer, (2) a "victim" computer, and (3) an intermediary network(13)

cyberstalking: when an individual engages in stalking behavior through such means as electronic mail or electronic communication (13)

cytogenetic studies: studies of crime that focus on the genetic makeups of individuals, with a specific focus on abnormalities in chromosomal makeups (5)

decriminalization: A policy related to labeling theory, which proposes less harsh punishments for some minor offenses, such as the possession of small amounts of marijuana (15)

delinquent boy: a type of lower-class male youth, identified by Cohen, who responds to strains and status frustration by joining with similar others in a group to commit crime (7)

Department of Homeland Security: a Cabinet department of the U.S. federal government, established in 2003 in response to the September 11 attacks; main responsibilities include protecting the United States from terrorist attacks and responding to terrorist attacks, man-made accidents, and natural disasters (14)

depressants: slow down, or "depress," the normal activity of the central nervous system

designer drugs: substances considered to be for recreational use; derivatives of approved drugs that can circumvent existing legal restrictions (15)

determinism: the assumption that human behavior is caused by factors outside of free will and rational decision making (4)

deterrence theory: theory of crime associated with the Classical School; proposes that individuals will make rational decisions regarding their behavior (2)

developmental theories: perspectives of criminal behavior that emphasize the evolution of individuals' criminality over time, with the individual as the unit of analysis (12)

deviance: behaviors that are not normal; includes many illegal acts, as well as activities that are not necessarily criminal but are unusual and often violate social norms (1)

differential association theory: A theory of criminal behavior that emphasizes association with significant others (peers, parents, etc.) in learning criminal behavior (9)

differential identification: a theory of criminal behavior similar to differential association theory, the major difference being that this theory takes into account associations with persons and images presented in the media (9)

differential reinforcement theory: a theory of criminal behavior that emphasizes various types of social learning, specifically classical conditioning, operant conditioning, and imitation or modeling (9)

Digital Millennium Copyright Act: criminalizes making, distributing, or using tools, such as software, to evade technological protection measures implemented by copyright owners to prevent access to copyrighted material (13)

dissident terrorism: involves terrorist activities against the government that are committed by rebellious groups (14)

dizygotic twins: twin pairs that come from two separate eggs (zygotes) and thus share only 50% of the genetic makeup that can vary (5)

domestic terrorism: unlawful use, or threatened use, of force or violence by a group or individual based in the United States to intimidate or coerce others to further political or social objectives (14)

dopamine: a neurotransmitter that is largely responsible for good feelings in the brain; it is increased by many illicit drugs (e.g., cocaine)(5)

dramatization of evil: concept proposed by Tannenbaum in relation to labeling theory; states that when relatively minor laws are broken, the community tends to dramatize it (10)

drug treatment court programs: Established in an effort to address the increasing number of drug-using offenders clogging the criminal justice system (15)

Durham: offenders are not criminally responsible, even if they are aware of their conduct, if this behavior was the "product of mental disease or defect." (6)

ectoderm: medical term for the outer layer of tissue in our bodies (4)

ectomorphic: type of body shape associated with an emphasis on the outer layer of tissue (ectoderm) during development(4)

Edwin Sutherland: coined the term *white-collar crime*; generally considered the most prominent criminologist of the 20th century (13)

ego: the only conscious domain of the psyche; according to Freud, it functions to mediate the battle between id and superego (6)

Eighteenth Amendment: Put into effect national Prohibition on January 16, 1920 (15)

Electronic Communications Privacy Act: regulates the interception of electronic communications by individuals as well as the government (13)

empirical validity: refers to the extent to which a theoretical model is supported by scientific research (1)

endoderm: medical term for the inner layer of tissue in our bodies

endomorphic: type of body shape associated with an emphasis on the inner layer of tissue (endoderm) during development (4)

Environmental Protection Agency: started in 1970, charged with protecting human health and safeguarding the natural environment (13)

eradication: Four recognized techniques: mechanical destruction (i.e., slashing or uprooting), bunting, chemical, and biological (including genetic) (15)

eugenics: the study of and policies related to the improvement of the human race via discriminatory control over reproduction (4)

experiential effect: extent to which previous experience affects individuals' perceptions of how severe criminal punishment will be when deciding whether or not to offend again (3)

extroversion: in reference to the PEN-model, traits associated with extroversion include being sociable, lively, active, assertive, sensation-seeking, carefree, dominant, surgent, and venturesome cautious) (6)

falsely accused: based on Becker's typology, when an individual has been identified as disobeying the rules but did not violate the rules (10)

family studies: studies that examine the clustering of criminality in a given family (5)

Federal Emergency Management Agency (FEMA): focuses on emergency management and recovery from a catastrophic event on a local and national level (14)

feeble-mindedness: technical, scientific term in the early 1900s meaning those who had significantly below average levels of intelligence (4)

first wave of feminism: started in the mid-1800s when women demanded the right to vote

focal concerns: primary concept of Miller's theory, which asserts that all members of the lower class focus on concepts they deem important: fate, autonomy, trouble, toughness, excitement, and smartness (8)

formal/official deterrence: deterrent effects of law enforcement, courts, and corrections(3)

frontal lobes: a region of the brain located in the frontal portion of the brain; most of the executive functions of the brain, such as problem solving, take place here (5)

fundraising: used by terrorist organizations to finance their activities (14)

game theory: assesses various scenarios by applying simulation gaming models, usually to understand why parties in competitive situations behave as they do and to advise players of the best way to play the game (14)

gender: gender usually refers to social definitions of what it means to be a *woman* or a *man* (11)

gender-specific programming: programs targeted to juvenile girls; gives females an increased sense of community that has been associated with developing and integrating a healthy identity (11)

general deterrence: punishments given to an individual meant to prevent or deter other potential offenders from engaging in such criminal activity in the future (2)

group conflict theory: Vold argued that part of human nature is that people's lives are a part, and a product, of their group associations; groups come into conflict with one another due to conflicting and competitive interests (10)

hackers: individuals who violate computer security (13)

hallucinogens: Drugs that alter one's thought processes, mood, and perceptions (15)

harm reduction: Attempts to incorporate a public health approach to lessen the risks and harms associated with illegal drug use (15)

Harrison Act: Passed by Congress in 1914, required doctors to have a license number to prescribe narcotics (15)

Hate Crime Statistics Act of 1990: as part of the Uniform Crime Report program, the attorney general was required to develop guidelines and collect data about crimes that manifest evidence of prejudice based on race, religion, sexual orientation, or ethnicity (14)

hate crimes: traditional offenses, such as murder and vandalism, with an additional factor of bias (14)

heroin: The most infamous opiate drug; a chemically modified form of morphine that ranged in color from white to black (15)

highway patrol: one type of model characterizing statewide police departments. The primary focus is to enforce the laws that govern the operation of motor vehicles on public roads and highways(1)

homeland security: a unified national effort to prevent terrorist attacks within the United States, lessen America's vulnerability to terrorism, and minimize the damage resulting from such attacks (14)

human rights: universal values and legal guarantees that protect individuals against actions or omissions, primarily by government agents, that infringe on their fundamental freedoms, entitlements, and human dignity (14)

id: a subconscious domain of the psyche, according to Freud, with which we are all born; it is responsible for our innate desires and drives (such as libido [sex drive]) and it battles the moral conscience of the superego (6)

identity theft: occurs when an individual obtains a false identity to commit identity fraud; can be used by criminals and terrorists to establish false identities and escape detection (13)

informal deterrence: factors like family, church, or friends that do not involve official aspects of criminal justice, such as police, courts, and corrections (e.g., prisons) (3)

inhalants: volatile substances that produce chemical vapors and whose primary trait is that they are rarely taken by any other delivery method than inhalation (15)

innovation: in strain theory, an adaptation to strain in which an individual buys into the conventional goals of success but does not buy into the conventional means for getting to the goals (7)

insanity: the idea of excusing offenders for their criminal actions due to a mental disease has been in existence for centuries. The term *insanity* is not a medical term; rather it is a legal term(6)

intelligence quotient (IQ): a quantified measure of intelligence (6)

interdiction: describes the various steps implemented to interrupt illicit drug trafficking (e.g., cueing, detection, apprehension, prosecution) (15)

Internet fraud: when individuals use the Internet to engage in fraud, often identity theft (13)

irresistible impulse: one standard for the insanity defense. Offenders can claim that, due to a mental disease, they were unable to control their behavior (6)

jail: jails are often designated for individuals convicted of a minor crime, and to house individuals awaiting trial (1)

Kefauver Committee: in 1950, charged with three responsibilities that focused on whether organized crime used services of interstate commerce to engage in illegal activities and identifying the persons, firms, or corporations involved in such activities (13) judicial waiver: the authority to waive juvenile court jurisdiction and transfer the case to criminal court (1)

labeling theory: theoretical perspective that assumes that criminal behavior increases because certain individuals are caught and labeled as offenders; their offending increases because they have been stigmatized (10)

learning theories: theoretical models that assume that criminal behavior of individuals is due to a process of learning from others the motivations and techniques for engaging in such behavior (9)

left realism: contends that previous criminological theories have been incomplete in that they emphasize only one part of the square of crime; attempts to provide an analysis of crime on all levels and develop a range of policy recommendations (10)

liberal feminism: one of the areas of feminist theories of crime that emphasize the assumption that differences between males and females in offending were due to the lack of female opportunities in education, employment, etc., compared with males (11)

liberation thesis: also referred to as the emancipation hypothesis; attempts to link the women's liberation movement with female crime rates (11)

life-course persistent offenders: a type of offender who starts offending early and persists through adulthood (12)

limited jurisdiction: the authority of a court to hear and decide cases within an area of the law or a geographic territory (1)

logical consistency: the extent to which concepts and propositions of a theoretical model makes sense in terms of both face value and consistency with what is readily known about crime rates and trends (1)

low self-control: a theory that proposes that individuals either develop self-control by age 10 or do not. Those who do not will manifest criminal or deviant behaviors throughout life (9)

Mafia: similar to an extended social family; members took an oath swearing, under punishment of death, to a code of silence. It started as a self-protection group, but by the 1860s expanded to criminal activities such as smuggling, cattle rustling, and extortion. (13)

Mafioso: referred to characteristics of a man such as pride, self-confidence, and a sense of "arrogant" behavior (13)

maintenance: advocates for the accessibility of drugs through governmental regulation, such as distribution and legal age of use (15)

mala in se: acts that are considered inherently evil (1)

mala prohibita: acts that are considered crimes primarily because they have been declared bad by the legal codes in that jurisdiction (1)

Marihuana Tax Act: effective October 1, 1937; did not criminalize marijuana or its preparations but did tax the grower, distributor, seller, and buyer (15)

marijuana: the dried leaves or flowers of the cannabis plant (15)

Marxist feminism: a perspective of crime that emphasizes men's ownership and control of the means of economic production; similar to critical or radical feminism but distinguished by its reliance on the concept of economic structure (11)

Matthew Shepard and James Byrd, Jr., Hate Crimes Prevention Act of 2009: makes it unlawful to willfully cause bodily injury, or attempt to do so, with a dangerous weapon when the offense is committed because of the actual or perceived race, color, religion, national origin, gender, sexual orientation, gender identity, or disability of any person (14)

mechanical societies: in Durkheim's theory, these societies were rather primitive with a simple distribution of labor (e.g., hunters & gatherers) and thus a high level of agreement regarding social norms and rules because nearly everyone is engaged in the same roles (7)

mens rea: concept regarding whether offenders actually knew what they were doing and meant to do it (2)

mental health courts: established to address the large proportion of individuals with mental illnesses involved in the criminal justice system (6)

mesoderm: medical term for the middle layer of tissue in our bodies (4)

mesomorphic: type of body shape associated with an emphasis on the middle layer of tissue (mesoderm) during development (4)

methamphetamine: The most common form of amphetamine today, it can take the form of a white, odorless powder that dissolves in water; clear, "chunky" crystals; or small, brightly colored tablets. (15)

minor physical anomalies: physical features, such as asymmetrical or low-seated ears, which are believed to indicate developmental problems (4)

mission distortion: occurred when those agencies involved in the reorganization of the Department of Homeland Security acquired new responsibilities and also were to continue with their agency's missions prior to the merge (14)

M'Naghten rule: the M'Naghten case introduced the modern concept of insanity into English Common Law. The legal standard is that "he didn't know what he was doing or didn't know it was wrong" (6)

model state legislation for hate crimes/violence against people experiencing homelessness: the National Law Center on Homelessness and Poverty and the National Coalition for the Homeless advocated for state legislation that includes homelessness in hate crimes statutes (14)

modeling/imitation: a major factor in differential reinforcement theory that proposes that much social learning takes place via imitation or modeling of behavior (9)

Moffitt's developmental theory or taxonomy: a theoretical perspective proposing that criminal behavior is caused by (1) adolescence-limited offenders and (2) life-course persistent offenders (12)

money laundering: a process whereby funds, obtained through illegal activities, are "cleansed" (14)

monozygotic twins: also referred to as identical twins, these are twin pairs that come from a single egg (zygote) and thus share 100% of their genetic makeup. (5)

morphine: one of the most effective drugs for relief of severe physical pain; has high potential for abuse (15)

multiracial feminism: an intersectional framework that includes such defining social characteristics as race, class, gender, sexuality, nationality, and age (11)

narcotics: opiates (drugs derived from the opium poppy) or opioids (synthetically produced opiates); includes morphine, heroin, and oxycodone (15)

National Counterterrorism Center: provides the Department of State with statistical information on terrorism (14)

National Crime Victimization Survey (NCVS): a primary measures of crime in the United States; collected by the DOJ and the Census Bureau, based on interviews with victims of crime (1)

natural areas: Chicago School's idea that all cities contain identifiable clusters, such as a Chinatown or Little Italy, and neighborhoods that have low or high crime rates (8)

negative reinforcement: a concept in social learning in which people are rewarded through removal of something they dislike (9)

negotiation: one of the key factors identified by Schur (i.e., labeling process); more noticeable in cases involving adults rather than juveniles (e.g., plea bargaining) (10)

Neoclassical School: assumes that aggravating and mitigating circumstances should be taken into account for purposes of sentencing and punishing an offender (2)

neuroticism: in reference to the PEN-model, neuroticism is often linked with such traits as being anxious, depressed, tense, irrational, shy, moody and emotional, and having guilty feelings and low self-esteem (6)

neurotransmitters: nervous system chemicals in the brain and body that help transmit electric signals from one neuron to another(5)

nonpartisan conflict perspective: according to Turk, the ideological position or political utilities of theories are irrelevant when assessing the validity of knowledge claims; *truth* should be independent of political ideology or personal values (10)

objectivity: refers to being "neutral," "value free," or "unbiased." Feminist scholars challenge research claims of objectivity (11)

Occupational Safety and Health Act: among other things, made it a misdemeanor to cause the death of a worker by willfully violating safety laws (13)

operant conditioning: a learning model based on the association between an action and feedback following the action (9)

organic societies: in the Durkheimian model, those societies that have a high division of labor and thus a low level of agreement about societal norms, largely because everyone has such different roles in society (7)

organized crime: sometimes defined through a typology, such as the means of obtaining the goals and the reasons for engaging in such activity: an economic objective or a political objective (13)

Otto Pollak: argued that women are more criminal in nature than has been generally perceived; suggested that criminologists should address the unknown criminality of women (11)

outlaw motorcycle gangs: the tough-guy image of these groups was perpetuated and membership increased, along with organization and sophistication. Soon, behavior of some groups was less rebellious and more openly criminal; some members refer to themselves as "one-percenters" (13)

oxycodone: synthetic narcotic produced entirely in the laboratory; includes OxyContin, Percodan, and Percocet (15) *parens patriae*: a philosophical perspective that recognizes that the state has both the right and obligation to intervene on behalf of its citizens due to some impairment or impediment such as mental incompetence, or in the case of juveniles, age and immaturity (1)

parsimony: characteristic of a good theory, meaning that it explains a certain phenomenon, such as criminal behavior, with the fewest possible propositions or concepts. (1)

partisan conflict perspective: according to Quinney, provides a theory and practice with the purpose of changing the world; associated political objective (10)

paternalism: denotes that women need to be protected for their own good. In a broader social context, paternalism implies independence for men and dependence for women (11)

pathways research: typically collects data, usually through interviews, at one point in time that provide retrospective inquiry as to an individual's life and life experiences (11)

patriarchy: a social, legal, and political climate based on male dominance and hierarchy. A key aspect to this ideology is that women's nature is biologically, not culturally, determined (11)

peacemaking criminology: incorporates three intellectual traditions: religious, feminist, and critical; contends that society should attempt reconciliation through mediation and dispute settlement (10)

PEN model: discussions of this theory emphasize that human personality can be viewed in three dimensions: psychoticism, extraversion, and neuroticism (6)

"The personal is the political": refers to the notion that the "private sphere" is as structured by power relations involving gender, sexuality, race, class, and age as the "public sphere" (11)

phenotype: an observed manifestation of the interaction of genotypical traits with the environment, such as height (5)

phrenology: the science of determining human dispositions based on distinctions (e.g., bumps) in the skull, which is believed to conform to the shape of the brain (4)

physiognomy: the study of facial and other bodily aspects to identify developmental problems, such as criminality (4)

positive reinforcement: a concept in social learning in which people are rewarded by receiving something they want (9)

Positive School: a perspective that assumes individuals have no free will to control their behavior. (4)

postconventional level of morality: when a person attempts to balance between individual rights and societal rules (6)

postmodern feminism: a perspective that says women as a group cannot be understood, even by other women, because every person's experience is unique; therefore, there is no need to measure or research such experiences (11)

power–control theory: integrated theory of crime that assumes that, in households where the mother and father have relatively similar levels of power at work, mothers will be less likely to exert control over daughters, and in households where mothers and fathers have dissimilar levels of power in the workplace, mothers will be more likely to suppress criminal activity in daughters but not in sons (11)

praxis: refers not just to consciousness raising but also to the establishment of alternative arrangements that will provide models for change, which then change consciousness (11)

preconventional level of morality: level of morality characteristic of designating what is considered "right" and "wrong" (6)

primary deviance: in labeling theory, the type of minor, infrequent offending people commit before they are caught and labeled as offenders (10)

prison: generally for those convicted of more serious crimes with longer sentences, who may be housed in a supermax, maximum, medium, or minimum security prison (1)

probation: probation is essentially an *arrangement* between the sentencing authorities and the offender requiringthe offender to comply with certain terms for a specified amount of time (1)

Prohibition: After the passage of the Eighteenth Amendment, an era in which it was illegal to manufacture, sell, or transport intoxicating liquors within the United States (15)

proletariat: in Marx's conflict theory, the oppressed group of workers exploited by the bourgeoisie; they never profit from their own efforts because the upper class owns and controls the means of production (10) psychoanalytic perspective: an individual's behavior is presumed to be due to the three aspects of his or her personality: the id, ego, and superego. Second, *anxiety, defense mechanisms,* and the *unconscious* are also key principles of the psychoanalytical perspective (6)

psychopath: refers to individuals whose antisocial behavior may be a result from a defect or abnormality within themselves rather than in their rearing or socialization (6)

psychoticism: individuals considered to have high psychoticism are associated with being aggressive, cold, egocentric, impersonal, impulsive, antisocial, unempathic, creative, and tough-minded; individuals with low psychoticism are characterized as being empathic, unselfish, altruistic, warm, peaceful, and generally more pleasant (6)

pure deviant: based on Becker's typology, an individual who disobeys the rules and is perceived as doing so (10)

qualitative: nonnumerical research methods; often compared with quantitative research methods (11)

quantitative: numerical research methods; often compared with qualitative research methods (11)

Racketeer Influenced and Corrupt Organizations (RICO) Act: provides for enhanced criminal and civil penalties for individuals engaging in activities with criminal organizations (13)

radical feminism: emphasizes the importance of personal feelings, experiences, and relationships; gender is a system of male dominance, and women's biology is the main cause of patriarchy (11)

rational choice theory: a modern, Classical School-based framework for explaining crime that includes the traditional formal deterrence aspects and other informal factors that studies show consistently and strongly influence behavior (3)

reaction formation: a Freudian defense mechanism applied to Cohen's theory of youth offending, which involves adopting attitudes or committing behaviors that are opposite of what is expected (7)

rebellion: in strain theory, an adaptation to strain in which an individual buys into the idea of conventional means and goals of success but does not buy into the current conventional means or goals (7)

relative deprivation: the perception that results when relatively poor people live in close proximity to relatively wealthy people (7)

religious terrorism: motivated by engaging in terrorist acts that are legitimized by religious dogma (14)

restorative justice: refers to the repair of justice by reaffirming a shared consensus of values involving a joint or multisided approach; emphasizes victim, community, and offender (10)

retreatism: in strain theory, an adaptation to strain in which an individual does not buy into the conventional goals of success and also does not buy into the conventional means (7)

retreatist gangs: a type of gang identified by Cloward and Ohlin that tends to attract individuals who have failed to succeed in both the conventional world and the criminal or conflict gangs of their neighborhoods (7)

retributive justice: refers to the repair of justice through a one-sided approach of imposing punishment (10)

retrospective interpretation: in labeling theory, the process by which an individual is identified as a deviant and thereafter viewed in a "new light"(10)

ritualism: in strain theory, an adaptation to strain in which an individual buys into the conventional means of success (e.g., work, school, etc.) but does not buy into the conventional goals (7)

routine activities theory (lifestyle theory): explanation of crime that assumes crime and victimization are highest in places where three factors come together in time and place: motivated offenders, suitable or attractive targets, and absence of a guardian (3)

scenario research or vignettes: studies that involve providing participants with specific hypothetical scenarios and then asking them what they would do in each situation

scope: refers to the range of criminal behavior that a theory attempts to explain (1)

second wave of feminism: developed in the 1960s when other marginalized groups were also challenging the status quo (e.g., civil rights movement, prisoners' rights movement). Feminists of this wave argued that to be fully liberated, women needed to have equal access to economic opportunities and sexual freedoms as well as civil liberties (11)

secondary deviance: in labeling theory, the more serious, frequent offending people commit after they have been caught and labeled as offenders (10)

secret deviant: based on Becker's typology, an individual who violates the rules of society but elicits no reaction from society (10) selective placement: an argument that adoptees tend to be placed in households that resemble that of their biological parents; thus, adoptees from rich biological parents are placed in rich adoptive households (5)

serotonin: a neurotransmitter that is key in information processing and most consistently linked to criminal behavior in its deficiency; low levels are linked to depression and other mental illnesses. (5)

severity of punishment: the assumption is that a given punishment must be serious enough to outweigh any potential benefits gained from a crime (2)

sex: sex differences typically refer to biological variations such as reproductive organs and hormones (11)

sex roles: research using the sex role approach has been criticized primarily because of the tendency to perceive these roles as being almost sex-linked, without incorporating a larger context for how these roles have been defined, leading to a form of biological determinism (11)

Sigmund Freud: originated psychoanalysis, founded on the perception of resistance used by individuals when therapists attempt to make them conscious of their unconscious; perceived women as anatomically inferior (11)

social bonding: a control theory that assumes that individuals are predisposed to commit crime and that conventional bonds prevent or reduce offending. This bond is made up of four constructs: attachments, commitment, involvement, and moral beliefs regarding committing crime (9)

social contract: an Enlightenment ideal or assumption that stipulates an unspecified arrangement among citizens in which they promise the state or government not to commit offenses against other citizens, and in turn, they gain protection from being violated by other citizens (2)

socialist feminism: feminist theories that moved away from economic structure (e.g., Marxism) and placed a focus on control of reproductive systems; believes that women should take control of their own bodies and reproductive functions via contraceptives (11)

sociopath: refers specifically to antisocial personalities that are due to social or familial dysfunction (6)

soft determinism: the assumption that both determinism and free will play a role in offenders' decisions to engage in criminal behavior (9)

somatotonic: type of temperament or personality associated with a mesomorphic (muscular) body type; tends to be risk taking and aggressive (4)

somatotyping: the area of study, primarily linked to William Sheldon, that links body type to risk for delinquent and criminal behavior. Also, as a methodology, it is a way of ranking body types based on three categories: *endomorphy, mesomorphy,* and *ectomorphy* (4)

specific deterrence: punishments given to an individual meant to prevent or deter that particular individual from committing crime in the future (2)

spuriousness: when other factors (often referred to as Z factors) are actually causing two variables (X and Y) to occur at the same time; it may appear as if X causes Y, when in fact they are both being caused by other Z factor(s) (1)

state police: agencies with general police powers to enforce state laws as well as to investigate major crimes, they may have intelligence units, drug trafficking units, juvenile units, and crime laboratories (1)

state-sponsored terrorism: includes terrorist acts that transpire due to the guidance of the state or government against perceived enemies (14)

status-degradation ceremony: the most dramatic way to initiate the process of giving an individual a new identity, such as a criminal trial (10)

statutory exclusion: excludes certain juvenile offenders from juvenile court jurisdiction; cases originate in criminal rather than juvenile court. (1)

stereotyping: in labeling theory, usually associated with racial prejudice and discrimination(10)

steroids: synthetically produced variations of the male sex hormone testosterone; some approved for medical and veterinary use (15)

stigmata: the physical manifestations of atavism (biological inferiority), according to Lombroso(4)

stimulant: creates a sense of energy, alertness, talkativeness, and well-being considered pleasurable to the user (15)

superego: a subconscious domain of the psyche; according to Freud, it is not part of our nature but must be developed through early social attachments (6)

swiftness of punishment: assumption is that the faster punishment occurs after a crime is committed, the more an individual will be deterred in the future (2)

symbolic interactionism: proposes that many social interactions involve symbolism, which occurs when individuals interpret each other's words or gestures and act based on the meaning of those gestures (10)

Tammany Hall: a notorious Democratic political machine in New York City from the 1790s through the 1960s, with major influence in city and state politics (13)

techniques of neutralization: a theory that suggests that individuals, especially in their teenage years and early adulthood, make excuses to alleviate guilt related to committing certain criminal acts (9)

temporal lobe: the region of the brain responsible for a variety of functions and that is located right above many primary limbic structures that govern our emotional and memory functions(5)

temporal ordering: the criterion for determining causality; requires that the predictor variable (X) precedes the explanatory variable (Y) in time(1)

testability: the extent that a theoretical model can be empirically or scientifically tested through observation and empirical research(1)

Thinking for a Change: an integrated cognitive behavioral change program that includes cognitive restructuring, social skill development, and the development of problem solving skills(6)

third wave of feminism: evolved around the late 1980s and into the 1990s; an extension of as well as a response to the shortcomings of the second wave (11)

Thornberry's interactional model: the first major perspective to emphasize reciprocal, or feedback, effects in the causal modeling of the theoretical framework (12)

traditional or conservative perspective: causes of gender inequality are due to biological sex differences, and social behavior is based on the biological sex differences; does not offer any strategies for social change since men's and women's behaviors reflect evolutionary adaptations of sex differences(11)

trajectories: paths people take in life, often due to life transitions (12)

tranquilizers: a type of depressant; can help with anxiety without disrupting normal functions. Problems include sleepiness and in coordination, hampered learning process, and amnesia. (15)

transitions: events important in altering trajectories toward or away from crime, such as marriage or employment (12)

Transportation Security Administration (TSA): provides security for all types of transportation; recruits, assesses, hires, trains, and deploys security officers for commercial airports; and provides screening of all checked luggage (14)

Tripartite Conceptual Framework: Suggests that drugs and violence are related to each other through psychopharmacological, economically compulsive, and systemic violence (15)

Twenty-First Amendment: Ratified on December 5, 1933, and repealed the Eighteenth Amendment (15)

twins separated at birth studies: studies that examine the similarities between identical twins who are separated in infancy(5)

twin studies: studies that examine the relative concordance rates for monozygotic versus dizygotic twins(5)

Uniform Crime Report (UCR): an annual report published by the FBI in the DOJ, which is meant to estimate most of the major street crimes in the United States(1)

USA PATRIOT Act: focuses on collecting communications information and data, conducting foreign intelligence investigations, controlling money laundering, and funding and enhancing national border security (14)

U.S. Citizenship and Immigration Services (USCIS): responsible for administration of immigration and naturalization adjudication functions (14)

U.S. Coast Guard: the only military organization within the Department of Homeland Security; its role includes protecting ports, maintaining border security, and coordinating intelligence with various government entities (14)

U.S. Customs and Border Protection (CBP): responsible for securing U.S. borders while also monitoring the flow of legitimate trade and travel (14)

U.S. Immigration and Customs Enforcement (ICE): focuses on identifying criminal activities and vulnerabilities that may be a threat to the country (14)

U.S. Secret Service: responsible for safeguarding the country's financial infrastructure and payment systems, as well as protecting national leaders and visiting heads of state and government (14)

utilitarianism: a philosophical concept that relates to the idea of the greatest good for the greatest number

vignettes: short, descriptive sketches(2)

Violent Crime Control and Law Enforcement Act of 1994: amended the Hate Crime Statistics Act to enhance penalties for offenses that involve a motivation bias (14) viscerotonic: the type of temperament or personality associated with an endomorphic (obese) body type; these people tend to be jolly, lazy, and happy-go-lucky (4)

War on Drugs: Public concern about drugs, building throughout the 1980s, exploded in late 1985 and early 1986 (15)

white-collar crime: criteria include (1) upper-class offender, (2) work-related violations, (3) work-related violations of blue-collar workers excluded, and (4) regular crimes committed by upper-class persons excluded(13)

W. I. Thomas: argued that there are basic biological differences between males and females (11)

Wickersham Commission: formed in 1929, the commission found that organized criminal activity flourished around bootlegging operations(13)

women's agency: the more traditional approach overlooks social locations of women's marginalization and places too much emphasis on female offenders as "active subjects" who pursue criminal opportunities. On the other end, women are denied agency and situated as mere instruments for the reproduction of determining social structures(11)

zone in transition: in the Chicago School, this zone (Zone II) was once residential but is becoming more industrial because of invading factories; tends to have the highest crime rates (8)

Notes

CHAPTER 1 NOTES

1. Henry, S., & Lanier, M. (2001). *What is crime?: Controversies over the nature of crime and what to do about it.* Lanham, MD: Rowman & Littlefield.
2. Black, H. C., Nolan, J. M., & Nolan-Haley, J. M. (1990). *Black's law dictionary* (6th ed.). St. Paul, MN: West, p. 959.
3. Ibid., p. 960.
4. Fanthorpe, L., & Fanthorpe, P. (2003). *The world's most mysterious murders.* Toronto, Ontario, Canada: Dundurn Press.
5. Tibbetts, S. G. (2012). *Criminological theory: The essentials.* Thousand Oaks, CA: Sage, pp. 3–4.
6. Adler, F., Mueller, G. O. W., & Laufer, W. S. (2007). *Criminology* (6th ed.). Boston: McGraw-Hill, p. 10.
7. Sutherland, E. H. (1934). *Principles of criminology* (2nd ed.). Philadelphia: Lippincott, p. 3.
8. Brown, S., Esbensen, F., & Geis, G. (2007). *Criminology* (6th ed.). Cincinnati, OH: LexisNexis.
9. Bernard, T. J., Paoline, E. A., & Pare, P. (2005). General systems theory and criminal justice. *Journal of Criminal Justice, 33,* 203–211, p. 205.
10. Belknap, J. (2007). *The invisible woman: Gender, crime, and justice* (3rd ed.). Belmont, CA: Thomson Wadsworth, p. 1.
11. Akers, R. L. (1997). *Criminological theories: Introduction and evaluation* (2nd ed.). Los Angeles: Roxbury.
12. Ibid., p. 139.
13. Barkan, S. E. (2012). *Criminology: A sociological understanding* (5th ed.). Boston: Prentice Hall.
14. Akers, R. L. (1997). *Criminological theories: Introduction and evaluation* (2nd ed.). Los Angeles: Roxbury, p. 140.
15. Ibid.
16. Ibid., p. 141.
17. President's Commission on Law Enforcement and Administration of Justice. (1967). *The challenge of crime in a free society.* Washington, DC: Government Printing Office, p. 7.
18. Gaines, L. K., & Miller, R. L. (2011). *Criminal justice in action* (6th ed.). Belmont, CA: Wadsworth Cengage Learning, p. 11.
19. Inciardi, J. A. (1993). *Criminal justice* (4th ed.). Fort Worth, TX: Harcourt Brace College Publishers, p. 176.
20. Gaines, L. K., & Miller, R. L. (2011). *Criminal justice in action* (6th ed.). Belmont, CA: Wadsworth Cengage Learning, p. 13.
21. Inciardi, J. A. (1993). *Criminal justice* (4th ed.). Fort Worth, TX: Harcourt Brace College Publishers, p. 181.
22. Gaines, L. K., & Miller, R. L. (2011). *Criminal justice in action* (6th ed.). Belmont, CA: Wadsworth Cengage Learning, p. 13.
23. Ibid., p. 15.
24. Ibid., p. 275.
25. Inciardi, J. A. (1993). *Criminal justice* (4th ed.). Fort Worth, TX: Harcourt Brace College Publishers, p. 313.
26. Gaines, L. K., & Miller, R. L. (2010). *Criminal justice in action* (5th ed.). Belmont, CA: Wadsworth Cengage Learning, p. 433.
27. Allen, H. E., Latessa, E. J., & Ponder, B. S. (2010). *Corrections in America: An introduction* (12th ed.). Boston: Pearson, p. 93.
28. Gaines, L. K., & Miller, R. L. (2011). *Criminal justice in action* (6th ed.). Belmont, CA: Wadsworth Cengage Learning, pp. 468–488.
29. Cromwell, P., Alarid, L. F., & del Carmen, R. V. (2005). *Community-based corrections* (6th ed.). Belmont, CA: Thomson Wadsworth.
30. Platt, A. M. (1977). *The child savers: The invention of delinquency.* Chicago: University of Chicago Press.
31. This portion of our discussion on juvenile justice is primarily based on Trojanowicz, R. C., Morash, M., & Schram, P. J. (2001). *Juvenile delinquency: Concepts and control* (6th ed.). Upper Saddle River, NJ: Prentice Hall.
32. Gardner, M. R. (1995). Punitive juvenile justice: Some observations on a recent trend. In M. L. Frost (Ed.), *The new juvenile justice.* Chicago: Nelson-Hall, pp. 103–108.
33. Rudman, C. J., Hartstone, E., Fagan, J. A., & Moore, M. (1986). Violent youth in adult court: Process and punishment. *Crime and Delinquency, 32,* 75–96.
34. Snyder, H. N., & Sickmund, M. (2006). *Juvenile offenders and victims: 2006 National report.* Washington, DC: Office of Juvenile Justice and Delinquency Prevention.
35. Ibid., p. 110.
36. Shahidullah, S. M. (2012). *Comparative criminal justice systems: Global and local perspectives.* Burlington, MA: Jones & Bartlett Learning.
37. Hardie-Bick, J., Sheptycki, J., & Wardak, A. (2005). Introduction: Transnational and comparative criminology in a global perspective. In J. Sheptycki & A. Wardak (Eds.), *Transnational and comparative criminology.* Portland, OR: Cavendish, p. 2.
38. Bennett, R. R. (2004). Comparative criminology and criminal justice research: The state of our knowledge. *Justice Quarterly, 21,* 1–21, pp. 2–3.

39. Winslow, R. W., & Zhang, S. X. (2008). *Criminology: A global perspective.* Upper Saddle River, NJ: Prentice Hall, p. 29.

40. Van Dijk, J. (2008). *The world of crime: Breaking the silence on problems of security, justice, and development across the world.* Thousand Oaks, CA: Sage, p. 3.

41. Ibid., pp. 3–13.

42. Maxim, P. S., & Whitehead, P. C. (1998). *Explaining crime* (4th ed.). Boston: Butterworth-Heinemann, p. 55.

43. Maltz, M. D. (1977). Crime statistics: A historical perspective. *Crime and Delinquency, 23,* 32–40, p. 33.

44. Federal Bureau of Investigation. (2000). *Crime in the United States, 2000.* Washington, DC: U.S. Department of Justice, p. 3.

45. Federal Bureau of Investigation. (2004). *Crime in the United States, 2004.* Washington, DC: U.S. Department of Justice, p. 6.

46. Ibid.

47. Sellin, T. (1931). The basis of a crime index. *Journal of Criminal Law and Corrections, 22,* 335–356, p. 346.

48. Federal Bureau of Investigation. (n.d.). *Crime in the United States: About the Uniform Crime Report (UCR) Program.* Retrieved from http://www.fbi.gov/about-us/cjis/ucr/crime-in-the.s/2010/crime-in-the-u.s.-2010/aboutucrmain

49. Biderman, A. D., & Reiss, A. J. (1967). On exploring the "dark figure" of crime. *Annals of the American Academy of Political and Social Science, 374,* 1–15. See also Skogan, W. G. (1977). Dimensions of the dark figure of unreported crime. *Crime and Delinquency, 23,* 41–50, p. 41.

50. Simon, D. R., & Eitzen, D. S. (1986). *Elite deviance* (2nd ed.). Boston: Allyn & Bacon, pp. 22–24.

51. Ibid., p. 23. See also Conyers, J. (1980). Corporate and white-collar crime: A view by the chairman of the house subcommittee on crime. *American Criminal Law Review, 17,* 287–300, p. 299.

52. Brownstein, H. H. (1996). *The rise and fall of a violent crime wave: Crack cocaine and the social construction of a crime problem.* Guilderland, NY: Harrow & Heston. See also Brownstein, H. H. (1991). The media and the construction of random drug violence. *Social Justice, 18,* 85–103; Brownstein, H. H. (1995). The social construction of crime problems: Insiders and the use of official statistics. *Journal of Crime and Justice, 18,* 17–30.

53. Brownstein, H. H. (1996). *The rise and fall of a violent crime wave: Crack cocaine and the social construction of a crime problem.* Guilderland, NY: Harrow & Heston, p. 27.

54. Maltz, M. D. (1999). *Bridging gaps in police crime data: A discussion paper for the BJS Fellows Program.* Washington, DC: U.S. Department of Justice, p. 16.

55. Brownstein, H. H. (1996). *The rise and fall of a violent crime wave: Crack cocaine and the social construction of a crime problem.* Guilderland, NY: Harrow & Heston, p. 22.

56. Savitz, L. D. (1978). Official police statistics and their limitations. In L. D. Savitz & N. J. Johnston (Eds.), *Crime in society* (pp. 69–81). New York: John Wiley, p. 75.

57. National Coalition for the Homeless. (2006). National advocacy groups issue report warning rise in laws criminalizing homelessness: New study finds 20 meanest cities and constructive alternatives to a "Dream Denied" [News release]. Retrieved from http://www.nationalhomeless.org/civilrights/crimpress2006.html

58. Fox, J. A., & Zawitz, M. W. (2004). *Homicide trends in the United States.* Washington, DC: Bureau of Justice Statistics. Retrieved from http://bjs.gov/

59. Riedel, M. (1990). Nationwide homicide data sets: An evaluation of the Uniform Crime Reports and the National Center for Health Statistics Data. In D. L. MacKenzie, P. J. Baunach, & R. R. Roberg (Eds.), *Measuring crime: Large-scale, long-range effects* (pp. 175–205). Albany: State University of New York Press.

60. Maltz, M. D. (1999). *Bridging gaps in police crime data: A discussion paper for the BJS Fellows Program.* Washington, DC: U.S. Department of Justice.

61. Federal Bureau of Investigation. (2004). *UCR: Uniform Crime Reporting handbook.* Washington, DC: U.S. Department of Justice, p. 104.

62. Maltz, M. D. (1999). *Bridging gaps in police crime data: A discussion paper for the BJS Fellows Program.* Washington, DC: U.S. Department of Justice, p. 31.

63. Gebo, E. (2002). A contextual exploration of siblicide. *Violence and Victims, 12,* 157–168.

64. Savolainen, J., Messner, S. F., & Kivivouri, J. (2000). Crime is part of the problem: Contexts of lethal violence in Finland and the USA. *Journal of Scandinavian Studies in Criminology and Crime Prevention, 1,* 41–55.

65. Gross, S. R., & Mauro, R. (1984). Patterns of death: An analysis of racial disparities in capital sentencing and homicide victimization. *Stanford Law Review, 37,* 27–153.

66. Bazley, T., & Mieczkowski, T. (2004). Researching workplace homicide: An assessment of the limitations of the Supplementary Homicide Reports. *Journal of Criminal Justice, 32,* 243–252.

67. Maltz, M. D. (1999). *Bridging gaps in police crime data: A discussion paper for the BJS Fellows Program.* Washington, DC: U.S. Department of Justice, p. 31.

68. Federal Bureau of Investigation. (2000). *Crime in the United States, 2000.* Washington, DC: U.S. Department of Justice.

69. Federal Bureau of Investigation. (2004). *UCR: Uniform Crime Reporting handbook.* Washington, DC: U.S. Department of Justice, p. 3.

70. Ibid., p. 3.

71. Chilton, R. (2004). Regional variations in lethal and nonlethal assaults. *Homicide Studies, 8,* 40–56.

72. Chu, L. D., & Kraus, J. F. (2004). Predicting fatal assault among the elderly using the National

Incident-Based Reporting System Crime Data. *Homicide Studies, 8,* 71–95.

73. Messner, S. F., Hugh, S., & Felson, R. B. (2004). Distinctive characteristics of assaults motivated by bias. *Criminology, 4,* 585–618.

74. Koons-Witt, B. A., & Schram, P. J. (2003). The prevalence and nature of violent offending by females. *Journal of Criminal Justice, 31,* 361–371.

75. Stolzenberg, L., & D'Alessio, S. J. (2000). Gun availability and violent crime: New evidence from the National Incident-Based Reporting System. *Social Forces, 78,* 1451–1482.

76. Campbell, A., Muncer, S., & Bibel, D. (1998). Female-female criminal assault: An evolutionary perspective. *Journal of Research in Crime and Delinquency, 35,* 413–428.

77. Federal Bureau of Investigation. (1999). *Hate crime data collection guidelines.* Washington, DC: U.S. Department of Justice, p. 1.

78. Ibid., p. 37.

79. Ibid., p. 1.

80. Federal Bureau of Investigation. (2004). *UCR: Uniform Crime Reporting handbook.* Washington, DC: U.S. Department of Justice, p. 2.

81. Ibid., p. 109.

82. Ibid., p. 110.

83. U.S. Census Bureau. (2003). *National Crime Victimization Survey: Interviewing manual for field representatives.* Washington, DC: Department of Commerce, pp. A1–A3.

84. Maxim, P. S., & Whitehead, P. C. (1998). *Explaining crime* (4th ed.). Boston: Butterworth-Heinemann, pp. 91–92.

85. U.S. Department of Justice. (2004). *The nation's two crime measures.* Washington, DC: Author.

86. Bachman, R., & Taylor, B. M. (1994). The measurement of family violence and rape by the redesigned National Crime Victimization Survey. *Justice Quarterly, 11,* 499–512.

87. Federal Bureau of Investigation. (2000). *Crime in the United States, 2000.* Washington, DC: U.S. Department of Justice, p. 460.

88. Ibid.

89. Ibid., pp. 460–461.

90. Weisberg, H. F., Krosnick, J. A., & and Bowen, B. D. (1989). *An introduction to survey research and data analysis* (2nd ed.). Glenview, IL: Scott, Foresman, pp. 14–15.

91. Johnston, L. D., O'Malley, P. M., Bachman, J. G., & Schulenberg, J. E. (2012). *Monitoring the Future: A continuing study of American youth (8th- and 10th-grade surveys).* Ann Arbor, MI: Inter-university Consortium for Political and Social Research.

92. University at Albany. (2013). Appendix 6: Monitoring the Future. In *Sourcebook of criminal justice statistics.* Retrieved from http://www.albany.edu/sourcebook/pdf/app6.pdf

93. Ibid.

94. Department of Mental Health and Human Services. (2011). *Summary of findings from the 2010 National Survey on Drug Use and Health.* Washington, DC: Author.

95. Ibid.

96. University at Albany. (2013). Appendix 7: National Household Survey on Drug Use and Health. In *Sourcebook of criminal justice statistics.* Retrieved from http://www.albany.edu/sourcebook/pdf/app7.pdf

97. Department of Mental Health and Human Services. (2011). *Summary of findings from the 2010 National Survey on Drug Use and Health.* Washington, DC: Author.

98. See, for example, Lemert, E. M. (1972). *Human deviance, social problems, and social control* (2nd ed.). Upper Saddle River, NJ: Prentice Hall.

99. Elliot, D. S., Huizinga, D., & Ageton, S. S. (1985). *Explaining delinquency and drug use.* Newbury Park, CA: Sage.

100. Elliott, D. S. (1994). Serious violent offenders: Onset, developmental course, and termination—the American Society of Criminology 1993 Presidential Address. *Criminology, 32,* 1–21; Menard, S., & Elliott, D. S. (1990). Longitudinal and cross-sectional data collection and analysis in the study of crime and delinquency. *Justice Quarterly, 7,* 11–55.

101. Ibid.

102. Cintrón, M., & McShane, M. D. (2003). National Youth Survey. In M. D. McShane & F. P. Williams (Eds.), *Encyclopedia of juvenile justice* (pp. 270–273). Thousand Oaks, CA: Sage, p. 271.

103. Snyder, H. N., & Sickmund, M. (1999). *Juvenile offenders and victims: 1999 national report.* Washington, DC: Office of Juvenile Justice and Delinquency Prevention, p. 52.

104. Egley, A., & Howell, J. C. (2012). *Highlights of the 2010 National Youth Gang Survey.* Washington, DC: Office of Juvenile Justice and Delinquency Prevention, p. 1.

105. Ibid.

106. National Youth Gang Center. (2000). *1998 National Youth Gang Survey.* Washington, DC: Office of Juvenile Justice and Delinquency Prevention.

107. Ibid.

108. Egley, A., & Howell, J. C. (2012). *Highlights of the 2010 National Youth Gang Survey.* Washington, DC: Office of Juvenile Justice and Delinquency Prevention, p. 1.

109. Anselin, L., Cohen, J., Cook, D., Gorr, W., & Tita, G. (2000). Spatial analyses of crime. In D. Duffee (Ed.), *Criminal justice 2000: Volume 4; Measurement and analysis of crime and justice* (pp. 213–262). Washington, DC: National Institute of Justice, p. 215.

110. Harries, K. (1999). *Mapping crime: Principle and practice.* Washington, DC: Office of Justice Programs, pp. 18–19.

111. Ibid., p. 1.

112. See Cohen, L. E., & Felson, M. (1979). Social change and crime rate trends: A routine activity approach.

American Sociological Review, 44, 588–605; Cornish, D. B., & Clarke, R. V. (1986). *The reasoning criminal: Rational choice perspectives on offending.* New York: Springer-Verlag.

113. Federal Bureau of Investigation. (2012). *Crime in the United States, 2011.* Washington, DC: U.S. Department of Justice. Retrieved from http://www.fbi.gov/about-us/cjis/ucr/crime-in-the-u.s/2011/crime-in-the-u.s.-2011/property-crime/motor-vehicle-theft

114. Stern, P. (n.d.). America's most stolen cars. *MSN Autos.* Retrieved from http://editorial.autos.msn.com/article.aspx?cp-documentid=434545

115. National Insurance Crime Bureau. (n.d.). *Vehicle theft fraud: Taking an age-old crime to the next level.* Retrieved from https://www.nicb.org/theft_and_fraud_awareness/fact_sheets

116. Los Angeles Police Department. (2011). Northeast community newsletter. Retrieved from http://www.lapdonline.org/northeast_community_police_station/content_basic_view/6546

117. Schriffen, J. (2012). Car thief, 11, takes police 'bait car' for joyride. *ABC News.* Retrieved from http://abcnews.go.com/blogs/headlines/2012/06/car-thief-11-takes-police-bait-car-for-joyride/

118. Federal Bureau of Investigation. (2012). *Crime in the United States, 2011.* Retrieved from http://www.fbi.gov/about-us/cjis/ucr/crime-in-the-u.s/2011/crime-in-the-u.s.-2011

119. Bureau of Justice Statistics. (2012, August 9). *Nearly 3.4 million violent crimes per year went unreported to police from 2006 to 2010* [Press release]. Retrieved from http://www.bjs.gov/content/pub/press/vnrp0610pr.cfm

120. Van Dijk, J. (2008). *The world of crime: The silence on problems of security, justice and development across the world.* Thousand Oaks, CA: Sage.

121. Ibid.; Morgan, K., Morgan, S., & Boba Santos, R. (2012). *City crime rankings 2011–2012.* Thousand Oaks, CA: CQ Press.

122. Akers, R., & Sellers, C. (2004). *Criminological theories* (4th ed.). Los Angeles: Roxbury.

123. Ibid., pp. 5–12.

124. Gottfredson, M., & Hirschi, T. (1990). *A general theory of crime.* Palo Alto, CA: Stanford University Press.

125. Lombroso, C. (1876). *The criminal man.* Milan: Hoepli.

126. See Tibbetts, S. G., & Hemmens, C. (2010). *Criminological theory: A text reader.* Thousand Oaks, CA: Sage, p. 9.

127. Akers, R. L. (1997). *Criminological theories: Introduction and evaluation* (2nd ed.). Los Angeles: Roxbury, p. 9.

128. Ibid.

129. Freeh, L. (2012). *Remarks of Louis Freeh in conjunction with announcement of publication of report regarding the Pennsylvania State University* [Press release]. Retrieved from http://progress.psu.edu/assets/content/Press_Release_07_12_12.pdf

130. Faller, K. C. (1993). *Child sexual abuse: Intervention and treatment issues.* Washington, DC: U.S. Department of Health and Human Services.

131. Ibid., p. 11.

132. Walsh, A., & Ellis, L. (2007). *Criminology: An interdisciplinary approach.* Thousand Oaks, CA: Sage, p. 135.

133. Ibid., p. 104.

134. Akers, R. L. (1997). *Criminological theories: Introduction and evaluation* (2nd ed.). Los Angeles: Roxbury, p. 11.

CHAPTER 2 NOTES

1. Death Penalty Information Center. (2009). *Gap between the murder rate of death penalty states and non-death penalty states remains large.* Retrieved from http://www.deathpenaltyinfo.org/gap-between-murder-rate-death-penalty-states-and-non-death-penalty-states-remains-large

2. Zagorin, A. (2008, May 1). D.C. Madam: Suicide before prison. *TIME U.S.* Retrieved from http://www.time.com/time/nation/article/0,8599,1736687,00.html

3. Ibid.

4. Mumola, C. J. (2005, August). *Suicide and homicide in state prisons and local jails.* Washington, DC: U.S. Department of Justice, Office of Justice Programs. Retrieved from http://bjs.gov/content/pub/pdf/shsplj.pdf

5. Brown, S. E., Esbensen, F., & Geis, G. (2004). *Criminology: Explaining crime and its context* (5th ed.). Cincinnati, OH: Anderson.

6. Associated Press. (2005, June 24). Five charged in deadly exorcism.

7. A good discussion of harsh punishment, such as quartering, can be found in Brown, S. E., Esbensen, F., & Geis, G. (2004). *Criminology: Explaining crime and its context* (5th ed.). Cincinnati, OH: Anderson.

8. Firdaus, I. (2005, June 25). Gamblers whipped in Muslim Indonesia. *Associated Press.*

9. Hobbes, T. (1958). *Leviathan.* New York: Library of Liberal Arts. (Original work published in 1651)

10. Ibid.; Montesquieu, C. (1949). *The spirit of the laws.* New York: Library of Liberal Arts. (Original work published in 1748)

11. Beccaria, C. (1963). *On crimes and punishments* (H. Paolucci, Trans.). New York: MacMillan, p. 64. (Original work published in 1764).

12. Ibid., pp. 30–31.

13. Ibid., p. 32.

14. Ibid.

15. Ibid., p. 21.

16. Ibid., p. 17.

17. Ibid., p. 99.

18. Ibid, p. 98.

19. Ibid., p. 45.

20. Ibid., p. 50.

21. For a review and analysis of the deterrent effect of capital punishment, see Stack, S. (1998). The effect of publicized executions on homicides in California. *Journal of Crime and Justice, 21,* 1–16. See also Ehrlich, I. (1975). The deterrent effect of capital punishment: A question of life and death. *American Economic Review, 65,* 397–417; Ehrlich, I. (1977). Capital punishment and deterrence. *Journal of Political Economy, 85,* 741–788; Layson, S. K. (1985). Homicide and deterrence: A reexamination of United States time-series evidence. *Southern Economic Journal, 52,* 68–89; Phillips, D. P. (1980). The deterrent effect of capital punishment: Evidence on an old controversy. *American Journal of Sociology, 86,* 139–148; Stack, S. (1987). Publicized executions and homicide, 1950–1980. *American Sociological Review, 52,* 532–540; Stack, S. (1990). Execution publicity and homicide in South Carolina. *Sociological Quarterly, 31,* 599–611; and Stack, S. (1995). The impact of publicized executions on homicide. *Criminal Justice and Behavior, 22,* 172–186.

22. Bailey, W. C. (1979). The deterrent effect of the death penalty for murder in California. *Southern California Law Review, 52,* 743–764; Bailey, W. C., & Peterson, R. D. (1989). Murder and capital punishment: A monthly time series analysis of execution publicity. *American Sociological Review, 54,* 722–743; Bowers, W. J. (1988). The effect of execution is brutalization, not deterrence. In K. Haas & J. Inciardi (Eds.), *Capital punishment: Legal and social science approaches* (pp. 49–89). Newbury Park, CA: Sage; Cochran, J. K., Chamlin, M., & Seth, M. (1994). Deterrence or brutalization? An impact assessment of Oklahoma's return to capital punishment. *Criminology, 32,* 107–134; Fox, J. A., & Radelet, M. L. (1990). Persistent flaws in econometric studies of the deterrent effect of the death penalty. *Loyola of Los Angeles Law Review, 23,* 29–44; Lester, D. (1989). The deterrent effect of execution on homicide. *Psychological Reports, 64,* 306–314. For a review, see Bailey, W. C., & Peterson, R. D. (1999). Capital punishment, homicide, and deterrence: An assessment of the evidence. In M. D. Smith & M. A. Zahn (Eds.), *Studying and preventing homicide* (pp. 223–245). Thousand Oaks, CA: Sage.

23. Cochran, J. K., & Chamlin, M. (2000). Deterrence and brutalization: The dual effects of executions. *Justice Quarterly, 17,* 685–706.

24. Beccaria, C. (1963). *On crimes and punishments* (H. Paolucci, Trans.). New York: MacMillan, pp. 46–47. (Original work published in 1764)

25. Ibid., p. 55.

26. Ibid.

27. Ibid., p. 56.

28. Ibid., p. 58.

29. Ibid.

30. Ibid., p. 43.

31. Tomislav, V., Kovandzic, J., Sloan, J., & Vieraitis, L. (2004). "Striking out" as crime reduction policy: The impact of "three strikes" laws on crime rates in U.S. cities. *Justice Quarterly, 21,* 207–240.

32. Beccaria, C. (1963). *On crimes and punishments* (H. Paolucci, Trans.). New York: MacMillan, p. 42. (Original work published in 1764)

33. Ibid., p. 93.

34. Ibid., p. 99.

35. Ibid., p. 68.

36. Vold, G., Bernard, T., & Snipes, J. (2002). *Theoretical criminology* (5th ed.). New York: Oxford University Press.

37. Federal Bureau of Investigations. (2010). *Crime in the United States, 2009.* Washington, DC: U.S. Department of Justice. Retrieved from http://www2.fbi.gov/ucr/cius2009/

38. Ibid.

39. Bureau of Justice Statistics. (2010). *Criminal victimization, 2009.* Washington, DC: U.S. Department of Justice.

40. Buzawa, E. S., & Buzawa, C. G. (2003). *Domestic violence: The criminal justice response* (3rd ed.). Thousand Oaks, CA: Sage, p. 17.

41. Sherman, L. W., & Berk, R. A. (1984). *The Minneapolis Domestic Violence Experiment.* Washington, DC: Police Foundation; Sherman, L. W., & Berk, R. A. (1984). The specific deterrent effects of arrest for domestic assault. *American Sociological Review, 49,* 261–272.

42. Mederer, H. J., & Gelles, R. J. (1989). Compassion or control: Intervention in cases of wife abuse. *Journal of Interpersonal Violence, 4,* 25–43. See also Binder, A., & Meeker, J. (1988). Experiments as reforms. *Journal of Criminal Justice, 16,* 347–358; Lembert, R. (1989). Humility is a virtue: On the publicization of policy relevant research. *Law and Society Review, 23,* 145–161.

43. Buzawa, E. S., & Buzawa, C. G. (2003). *Domestic violence: The criminal justice response* (3rd ed.). Thousand Oaks, CA: Sage, p. 97.

44. See Berk, S. F., Campbell, A., Klap, R., & Western, B. (1992). Beyesian analysis of the Colorado Springs spouse abuse experiment. *Criminal Law and Criminology, 83,* 170–200; Dunford, F. W., Huizinga, D., & Elliott, D. (1989). *The Omaha domestic violence police experiment: Final report to the National Institute of Justice and the City of Omaha.* Boulder, CO: Institute of Behavioral Science; Hirschel, J. D., Hutchison, I. W., Dean, C. W., Kelley, J. J., & Pesackis, C. E. (1991). *Charlotte Spouse Assault Replication Project: Final report.* Washington, DC: U.S. Department of Justice; Pate, A., & Hamilton, E. (1992). Formal and informal deterrents to domestic violence: The Dade County Spouse Assault Experiment. *American Sociological Review, 57,* 691–697; Sherman, L. W., Schmidt, J. D., Rogan, D. P., Smith, D. A., Gartin, P. R., Cohn, E. G., et al. (1992). The variable effects of arrest on criminal careers: The Milwaukee Domestic Violence Experiment. *Journal of Criminal Law and Criminology, 83,* 137–169.

45. Buzawa, E. S., & Buzawa, C. G. (2003). *Domestic violence: The criminal justice response* (3rd ed.). Thousand Oaks, CA: Sage, p. 104.

46. Ellis, L., Cooper, J., & Walsh, A. (2008). Criminologists' opinions about causes and theories of crime and delinquency: A follow-up. *The Criminologist, 33,* 23–26.

47. Henderson, P. (2012, October 13). California may lead prison-reform trend, ease '3 strikes.' *NBCNews.com.* Retrieved from http://www.nbcnews.com/ID/49400913/NS/POLITICS/T/CALIFORNIA-MAY-LEAD-PRISON-REFORM-TREND-EASE-STRIKES/#.UVD3rRzCaSo

48. For a review and evaluations of these programs, see Lundman, R. (1993). *Prevention and control of juvenile delinquency* (2nd ed.). Oxford, UK: Oxford University Press.

49. See Pratt, T. (2008). Rational choice theory, crime control policy, and criminological relevance. *Criminology and Public Policy, 7,* 43–52.

50. Walker, S. (2005). *Sense and nonsense about crime and drugs* (6th ed.). Belmont, CA: West/Wadsworth.

CHAPTER 3 NOTES

1. Dailey, J. (2012, August 24). Mom has son wear 'Smoked pot, got caught' sign as punishment. *WTOC 11.* Retrieved from http://www.wtoc.com/story/19373395/mother-has-son-wear-smoked-pot-got-caught-sign-as-punishment

2. Martinson, R. (1974). What works? Questions and answers about prison reform. *Public Interest, 35,* 22–54. See also Bailey, W. C. (1966). Correctional outcome: An evaluation of 100 reports. *Journal of Criminal Law, Criminology, and Police Science, 57,* 153–160.

3. Becker, G. (1968). Crime and punishment: An economic approach. *Journal of Political Economy, 76,* 169–217; Chiricos, T. G., & Waldo, G. P. (1970). Punishment and crime: An examination of some empirical evidence. *Social Problems, 18,* 200–217; Gibbs, J. P. (1968). Crime, punishment and deterrence. *Southwestern Social Science Quarterly, 48,* 515–530; Tittle, C. R. (1969). Crime rates and legal sanctions. *Social Problems, 16,* 409–423.

4. Andenaes, J. (1974). *Punishment and deterrence.* Ann Arbor: University of Michigan Press; Gibbs, J. P. (1975). *Crime, punishment and deterrence.* New York: Elsevier; Glaser, D., & Zeigler, M. S. (1974). Use of the death penalty v. outrage at murder. *Crime and Delinquency, 20,* 333–338; Tittle, C. R. (1969). Crime rates and legal sanctions. *Social Problems, 16,* 409–423; Zimring, F. E., & Hawkins, G. J. (1973). *Deterrence: The legal threat in crime control.* Chicago: University of Chicago Press.

5. Blumstein, A., Cohen, J., & Nagin, D. (Eds.). (1978). *Deterrence and incapacitation: Estimating the effects of criminal sanctions on crime rates.* Washington, DC: National Academy of Sciences.

6. Paternoster, R. (1987). The deterrent effect of the perceived certainty and severity of punishment: A review of the evidence and issues. *Justice Quarterly, 4,* 173–217; Paternoster, R., Saltzman, L. E., Waldo, G. P., & Chiricos, T. G. (1983). Perceived risk and social control: Do sanctions really deter? *Law and Society Review, 17,* 457–480.

7. Ross, H. L. (1982). *Deterring the drunk driver: Legal policy and social control.* Lexington, MA: Lexington Books; Ross, H. L. (1992). *Confronting drunk driving: Social policy for saving lives.* New Haven, CT: Yale University Press; Ross, H. L. (1994). Sobriety checkpoints, American style. *Journal of Criminal Justice, 22,* 437–444; Ross, H. L., McCleary, R., & LaFree, G. (1990). Can mandatory jail laws deter drunk driving? The Arizona case. *Journal of Criminal Law and Criminology, 81,* 156–170.

8. Ross, H. L., McCleary, R., & LaFree, G. (1990). Can mandatory jail laws deter drunk driving? The Arizona case. *Journal of Criminal Law and Criminology, 81,* 164.

9. Simpson, S., & Koper, C. S. (1992). Deterring corporate crime. *Criminology, 30,* 347–376.

10. Pogarsky, G., Kim, K., & Paternoster, R. (2005). Perceptual change in the National Youth Survey: Lessons for deterrence theory and offender decision-making. *Justice Quarterly, 22,* 1–29.

11. For a review, see Brown, S., Esbensen, F., & Geis, G. (2004). *Criminology: Explaining crime and its context* (5th ed.). Cincinnati, OH: LexisNexis, pp. 201–204; Finley, N., & Grasmick, H. (1985). Gender roles and social control. *Sociological Spectrum, 5,* 317–330; Grasmick, H., Blackwell, B. S., & Bursik, R. (1993). Changes in the sex patterning of perceived threats of sanctions. *Law and Society Review, 27,* 679–705; Grasmick, H., Bursik, R., & Kinsey, K. (1991). Shame and embarrassment as deterrents to noncompliance with the law: The case of an antilittering campaign. *Environment and Behavior, 23,* 233–251; Loewenstein, G., Nagin, D., & Paternoster, R. (1997). The effect of sexual arousal on expectations of sexual forcefulness. *Journal of Research in Crime and Delinquency, 34,* 209–228; Makkai, T., & Braithwaite, J. (1994). The dialects of corporate deterrence. *Journal of Research in Crime and Delinquency, 31,* 347–373; Nagin, D., & Paternoster, R. (1993). Enduring individual differences and rational choice theories of crime. *Law and Society Review, 27,* 467–496; Nagin, D., & Pogarsky, G. (2001). Integrating celerity, impulsivity, and extralegal sanction threats into a model of general deterrence: Theory and evidence. *Criminology, 39,* 404–430; Paternoster, R., & Simpson, S. (1996). Sanction threats and appeals to morality: Testing a rational choice model of corporate crime. *Law and Society Review, 30,* 549–583; Piquero, A., &

Pogarsky, G. (2002). Beyond Stanford and Warr's reconceptualization of deterrence: Personal and vicarious experiences, impulsivity, and offending behavior. *Journal of Research in Crime and Delinquency, 39,* 153–186; Piquero, A., & Tibbetts, S. (1996). Specifying the direct and indirect effects of low self-control and situational factors in offenders' decision making: Toward a more complete model of rational offending. *Justice Quarterly, 13,* 481–510; Richards, P., & Tittle, C. (1981). Gender and perceived chances of arrest. *Social Forces, 59,* 1182–1199. For a recent review and altered explanation of these conclusions, see Pogarsky, G. (2002). Identifying 'deterrable' offenders: Implications for research on deterrence. *Justice Quarterly, 19,* 431–452.

12. Ajzen, I., & Fishbein, M. (1977). Attitude-behavior relations: A theoretical analysis and review of empirical research. *Psychological Bulletin, 84,* 888–918; Ajzen, I., & Fishbein, M. (1980). *Understanding attitudes and predicting social behavior.* Englewood Cliffs, NJ: Prentice Hall; Fishbein, M., & Ajzen, I. (1975). *Belief, attitude, intention, and behavior.* Reading, MA: Addison-Wesley. *Psychological Bulletin, 84,* 888–918. For a recent review, see Pogarsky, G., Kim, K., & Paternoster, R. (2005). Perceptual change in the National Youth Survey: Lessons for deterrence theory and offender decision-making. *Justice Quarterly, 22,* 1–29.

13. Bachman, R., Paternoster, R., & Ward, S. (1992). The rationality of sexual offending: Testing a deterrence/rational choice conception of sexual assault. *Law and Society Review, 26,* 343–372; Grasmick, H., & Bursik, R. (1990). Conscience, significant others, and rational choice: Extending the deterrence model. *Law and Society Review, 24,* 837–861; Grasmick, H., & Green, D. (1980). Legal punishment, social disapproval and internalization as inhibitors of illegal behavior. *Journal of Criminal Law and Criminology, 71,* 325–335; Klepper, S., & Nagin, D. (1989). The deterrent effects of perceived certainty and severity of punishment revisited. *Criminology, 27,* 721–746; Loewenstein, G., Nagin, D., & Paternoster, R. (1997). The effect of sexual arousal on expectations of sexual forcefulness. *Journal of Research in Crime and Delinquency, 34,* 209–228; Nagin, D., & Paternoster, R. (1993). Enduring individual differences and rational choice theories of crime. *Law and Society Review, 27,* 467–496; Paternoster, R., & Simpson, S. (1996). Sanction threats and appeals to morality: Testing a rational choice model of corporate crime. *Law and Society Review, 30,* 549–583; Piquero, A., & Tibbetts, S. (1996). Specifying the direct and indirect effects of low self-control and situational factors in offenders' decision making: Toward a more complete model of rational offending. *Justice Quarterly, 13,* 481–510; Tibbetts, S. (1997). Gender differences in students' rational decisions to cheat. *Deviant Behavior, 18,* 393–414; Tibbetts, S. (1997). Shame and rational

choice in offending decisions. *Criminal Justice and Behavior, 24,* 234–255; Tibbetts, S., & Myers, D. (1999). Low self-control, rational choice, and student test cheating. *American Journal of Criminal Justice, 23,* 179–200.

14. Ajzen, I. (1987). From intentions to actions: A theory of planned behavior. In J. Kuhl & J. Beckmann (Eds.), *Action control: From cognition to behavior* (pp. 11–39). Berlin: Springer-Verlag; Ajzen, I., & Fishbein, M. (1969). The prediction of behavioral intentions in a choice situation. *Journal of Experimental Psychology, 5,* 400–416; Ajzen, I., & Fishbein, M. (1977). Attitude-behavior relations: A theoretical analysis and review of empirical research. *Psychological Bulletin, 84,* 888–918; Ajzen, I., & Fishbein, M. (1980). *Understanding attitudes and predicting social behavior.* Englewood Cliffs, NJ: Prentice Hall; Green, D. (1989). Measures of illegal behavior in individual behavior in individual-level deterrence research. *Journal of Research in Crime and Delinquency, 26,* 253–275.

15. Bouffard, J. A. (2002). Methodological and theoretical implications of using subject-generated consequences in tests of rational choice theory. *Justice Quarterly, 19,* 747–771.

16. Cornish, D., & Clarke, R. (1986). *The reasoning criminal: Rational choice perspectives on offending.* New York: Springer-Verlag.

17. Katz, J. (1988). *Seductions of crime.* New York: Basic Books.

18. Tibbetts, S. G., & Gibson, C. (2002). Individual propensities and rational decision-making: Recent findings and promising approaches. In A. Piquero & S. Tibbetts (Eds.), *Rational choice and criminal behavior* (pp. 3–24). New York: Routledge.

19. Grasmick, H., Blackwell, B. S., & Bursik, R. B. (1993). Changes over time in gender differences in perceived risk of sanctions. *Law and Society Review, 27,* 679–705; Grasmick, H., & Bursik, R. (1990). Conscience, significant others, and rational choice: Extending the deterrence model. *Law and Society Review, 24,* 837–861; Grasmick, H., Bursik, R., & Arneklev, B. (1993). Reduction in drunk driving as a response to increased threats of shame, embarrassment, and legal sanctions. *Criminology, 31,* 41–67; Nagin, D., & Paternoster, R. (1993). Enduring individual differences and rational choice theories of crime. *Law and Society Review, 27,* 467–496; Pogarsky, G. (2002). Identifying 'deterrable' offenders: Implications for research on deterrence. *Justice Quarterly, 19,* 431–452; Tibbetts, S. (1997). Gender differences in students' rational decisions to cheat. *Deviant Behavior, 18,* 393–414; Tibbetts, S. (1997). Shame and rational choice in offending decisions. *Criminal Justice and Behavior, 24,* 234–255; Tibbetts, S. G. (2004). Self-conscious emotions and criminal offending. *Psychological Reports, 93,* 101–131; Tibbetts, S. G., & Herz, D. (1996). Gender differences in factors of

social control and rational choice. *Deviant Behavior, 17,* 183–208; Tibbetts, S., & Myers, D. (1999). Low self-control, rational choice, and student test cheating. *American Journal of Criminal Justice, 23,* 179–200.

20. Finley, N., & Grasmick, H. (1985). Gender roles and social control. *Sociological Spectrum, 5,* 317–330; Grasmick, H., Blackwell, B. S., & Bursik, R. (1993). Changes in the sex patterning of perceived threats of sanctions. *Law and Society Review, 27,* 679–705; Pogarsky, G., Kim, K., & Paternoster, R. (2005). Perceptual change in the National Youth Survey: Lessons for deterrence theory and offender decision-making. *Justice Quarterly, 22,* 1–29; Tibbetts, S. G. (1997). Gender differences in students' rational decisions to cheat. *Deviant Behavior, 18,* 393–414; Tibbetts, S. G., & Herz, D. (1996). Gender differences in factors of social control and rational choice. *Deviant Behavior, 17,* 183–208.

21. Grasmick, H., Blackwell, B. S., & Bursik, R. (1993). Changes in the sex patterning of perceived threats of sanctions. *Law and Society Review, 27,* 679–705; Nagin, D., & Paternoster, R. (1993). Enduring individual differences and rational choice theories of crime. *Law and Society Review, 27,* 467–496; Tibbetts, S. G. (2004). Self-conscious emotions and criminal offending. *Psychological Reports, 93,* 101–131.

22. Pogarsky, G., Kim, K., & Paternoster, R. (2005). Perceptual change in the National Youth Survey: Lessons for deterrence theory and offender decision-making. *Justice Quarterly, 22,* 1–29.

23. Pogarsky, G. (2002). Identifying 'deterrable' offenders: Implications for research on deterrence. *Justice Quarterly, 19,* 431–452.

24. Federal Bureau of Investigations. (2010). *Crime in the United States, 2009.* Washington, DC: U.S. Department of Justice.

25. Insurance Institute for Highway Safety. (2013, April). *DUI/DWI laws.* Retrieved from http://www.iihs.org/laws/dui.aspx

26. Federal Bureau of Investigations. (2010). *Crime in the United States, 2009.* Washington, DC: U.S. Department of Justice.

27. Centers for Disease Control and Prevention. (2012). *Impaired driving: Get the facts.* Retrieved from http://www.cdc.gov/MotorVehicleSafety/Impaired_Driving/impaired-drv_factsheet.html

28. Fagin, M. (2010). *Statement before the Maryland Senate Judicial Proceedings Committee: Alcohol ignition interlocks.* Arlington, VA: Insurance Institute for Highway Safety, p. 1.

29. Ignition Interlock Device.org. (2010). *How the ignition interlock device works.* Retrieved from http://www.ignitioninterlockdevice.org/ignitioninterlockdevice.html

30. Fagin, M. (2010). *Statement before the Maryland Senate Judicial Proceedings Committee: Alcohol ignition interlocks.* Arlington, VA: Insurance Institute for Highway Safety, p. 1.

31. Florida Department of Highway Safety and Motor Vehicles. (2013). *Ignition interlock program.* Retrieved from http://www.flhsmv.gov/ddl/iid.html

32. Cohen, L., & Felson, M. (1979). Social change and crime rates: A routine activities approach. *American Sociological Review, 44,* 214–241.

33. Farrington, D. P., & Welsh, B. C. (2002). Improved street lighting and crime prevention. *Justice Quarterly, 19,* 313–343.

34. Sherman, L., Gartin, P. R., & Buerger, M. (1989). Hot spots of predatory crime: Routine activities and the criminology of place. *Criminology, 27,* 27–56.

35. Bernburg, J. G., & Thorlindsson, T. (2001). Routine activities in social context: A closer look at the role of opportunity in deviant behavior. *Justice Quarterly, 18,* 543–567; see also Bennett, R. (1991). Routine activity: A cross-national assessment of a criminological perspective. *Social Forces, 70,* 147–163; Hawdon, J. (1996). Deviant lifestyles: The social control of routine activities. *Youth and Society, 28,* 162–188; Massey, J. L., Krohn, M., & Bonati, L. (1989). Property crime and the routine activities of individuals. *Journal of Research in Crime and Delinquency, 26,* 378–400; Miethe, T., Stafford, M., & Long, J. (1987). Social differences in criminological victimization: A test of routine activities/lifestyles theories. *American Sociological Review, 52,* 184–194; Mustaine, E., & Tewksbury, R. (1998). Predicting risks of larceny theft victimization: A routine activity analysis using refined lifestyle measures. *Criminology, 36,* 829–857; Osgood, D., Wilson, J., O'Malley, P. M., Bachman, J., & Johnston, J. L. (1996). Routine activities and individual deviant behavior. *American Sociological Review, 61,* 635–655; Roncek, D., & Maier, P. (1991). Bars, blocks, and crimes revisited: Linking the theory of routine activities to the empiricism of hot spots. *Criminology, 29,* 725–753; Sampson, R., & Wooldredge, J. (1987). Linking the micro- and macro-level dimensions of lifestyle-routine activity and opportunity models of predatory victimization. *Journal of Quantitative Criminology, 3,* 371–393.

36. Brown, S., Esbensen, F., & Geis, G. (2004). *Criminology: Explaining crime and its context* (5th ed.). Cincinnati, OH: LexisNexis, p. 175.

37. Ibid.

38. Ibid.

39. Wilson, J. Q., & Kelling, G. (1982, March). Broken windows: The police and neighborhood safety. *Atlantic Monthly,* 29–38.

40. Shepherd, J. M. (2002). Fear of the first strike: The full deterrent effect of California's two- and three-strikes legislation. *Journal of Legal Studies, 31,* 159–201.

41. Males, M., & Macallair, D. (1999). Striking out: The failure of California's "three strikes and you're out" law. *Stanford Law and Policy Review, 11,* 65–72; Stolzenberg, L., & D'Alessio, S. J. (1997). Three strikes and you're out: The impact of California's

new mandatory sentencing law on serious crime rates. *Crime and Delinquency, 43,* 457–469.

42. Marvell, T. B., & Moody, C. E. (2001). The lethal effects of three-strikes laws. *Journal of Legal Studies, 30,* 89–106; see also Kovandzic, T., Sloan, J. J., III, & Vieraitis, L. M. (2002). Unintended consequences of politically popular sentencing policy: The homicide-promoting effects of "three strikes" in U.S. cities (1980–1999). *Criminology and Public Policy, 1,* 399–424.

43. Tibbetts, S. G. (1997). Shame and rational choice in offending decisions. *Criminal Justice and Behavior, 24,* 234–255.

CHAPTER 4 NOTES

1. Cohen, E., & Bonifield, J. (2012, March 15). California's dark legacy of forced sterilizations. *CNN Health.* Retrieved from http://www.cnn.com/2012/03/15/health/california-forced-sterilizations/index.html

2. For a good example of this perspective, see Morton, S. G. (1849). Observations on the size of the brain in various races and families of man. *Proceedings of the Academy of Natural Sciences (Philadelphia), 4,* 221–224; see also Broca, P. (1862). Sur la capacité des crânes parisiens des diverses époques. *Bulletin Societe d' Anthropologie Paris, 3,* 102–116; Morton, S. G. (1839). *Crania Americana: A comparative view of the skulls of various aboriginal nations of North and South America.* Philadelphia: John Pennington. For a review of various studies, see Rafter, N. (2005). The murderous Dutch Fiddler. *Theoretical Criminology, 9,* 65–96.

3. For example, see Bean, R. (1906). Some racial peculiarities of the Negro brain. *American Journal of Anatomy, 5,* 353–432 (showed a distinct difference in the brains across race when brains were identified by race before comparison); Mall, F. P. (1909). On several anatomical characters of the human brain, said to vary according to race and sex, with especial reference to the weight of the frontal lobe. *American Journal of Anatomy, 9,* 1–32 (showed virtually no differences among the same brains when comparisons were made without knowing the races of the brains prior to comparison); for the comparison/contrast, see discussion in Gould, S. J. (1996). *The mismeasure of man* (2nd ed.). New York: Norton.

4. See Mall, F. P. (1909). On several anatomical characters of the human brain, said to vary according to race and sex, with especial reference to the weight of the frontal lobe. *American Journal of Anatomy, 9,* 1–32; much of the discussion in this section is taken from Gould, S. J. (1996). *The mismeasure of man* (2nd ed.). New York: Norton.

5. Spitska, E. A. (1907). A study of the brains of six eminent scientists and scholars belonging to the anthropological society, together with a description of the skull of Professor E. D. Cope. *Transactions of the American Philosophical Society, 21,* 175–308.

6. Coren, S. (1993). *The left-hander syndrome.* New York: Vintage; Kalat, J. (2004). *Biological psychology* (8th ed.). New York: Wadsworth.

7. Fowler, O. S. (1842). *Fowler's practical phrenology: Giving a concise elementary view of phrenology.* New York: Author.

8. For a review, see Raine, A. (1993). *The psychopathology of crime.* San Diego, CA: Academic Press.

9. Nott, J. C., & Gliddon, G. R. (1854). *Types of mankind.* Philadelphia: Lippincott, Grambo; Nott, J. C., & Gliddon, G. R. (1868). *Indigenous races on Earth.* Philadelphia: Lippincott.

10. Lombroso, C. (1876). *L'uomo delinquente* [*The criminal man*]. Milan: Hoepli; Lombroso, C. (1878). *The criminal man* (2nd ed.). Turin: Bocca.

11. Gould, S. J. (1996). *The mismeasure of man* (2nd ed.). New York: Norton, p. 153.

12. Lombroso, C. (1876). *L'uomo delinquente* [*The criminal man*]. Milan: Hoepli, as cited and discussed in Taylor, I., Walton, P., & Young, J. (1973). *The new criminology: For a social theory of deviance.* London: Routledge, p. 41.

13. See Gould, S. J. (1996). *The mismeasure of man* (2nd ed.). New York: Norton; Taylor, I., Walton, P., & Young, J. (1973). *The new criminology: For a social theory of deviance.* London: Routledge.

14. For a review of such identifications, see Gould, S. J. (1996). *The mismeasure of man* (2nd ed.). New York: Norton.

15. Lombroso, C. (1911). *Crime: Its causes and remedies.* Boston: Little, Brown, p. 436.

16. From Waldrop, M., & Halverson, C. (1971). Minor physical anomalies and hyperactive behavior in young children. In J. Hellmuth (Ed.), *Exceptional infant: Studies in abnormalities* (pp. 343–381). New York: Brunner/Mazel, as cited in Fishbein, D. (2001). *Biobehavioral perspectives on criminology.* Belmont, CA: Wadsworth.

17. Agnew, R. (1984). Appearance and delinquency. *Criminology, 22,* 421–440.

18. Gould, S. J. (1996). *The mismeasure of man* (2nd ed.). New York: Norton.

19. Again, most of this discussion is taken from Gould, S. J. (1996). *The mismeasure of man* (2nd ed.). New York: Norton; his review is perhaps the best known in current literature.

20. Goddard, H. H. (1912). *The Kallikak family: A study of the heredity of feeble-mindedness.* New York: MacMillan.

21. Goddard, H. H. (1913). The Binet tests in relation to immigration. *Journal of Psycho-Asthenics, 18,* 105–107; quote taken from p. 106, as cited in Gould, S. J. (1996). *The mismeasure of man* (2nd ed.). New York: Norton.

22. Gould, S. J. (1996). *The mismeasure of man* (2nd ed.). New York: Norton, p. 198.

23. Goddard, H. H. (1928). Feeblemindedness: A question of definition. *Journal of Psycho-Asthenics, 33,* 219–227, as discussed in Gould, S. J. (1996). *The mismeasure of man* (2nd ed.). New York: Norton.

24. Goddard, H. H. (1928). Feeblemindedness: A question of definition. *Journal of Psycho-Asthenics, 33,* p. 224.

25. As quoted in Gould, S. J. (1996). *The mismeasure of man* (2nd ed.). New York: Norton, p. 365.

26. Hirschi, T., & Hindelang, M. (1977). Intelligence and delinquency: A revisionist review. *American Sociological Review, 42,* 571–587.

27. For a review, see Paternoster, R., & Bachman, R. (2001). *Explaining criminals and crime.* Los Angeles: Roxbury.

28. For a review, see Gibson, C. L., Piquero, A. R., & Tibbetts, S. G. (2001). The contribution of family adversity and verbal IQ to criminal behavior. *International Journal of Offender Therapy and Comparative Criminology, 45,* 574–592; see also Hirschi, T., & Hindelang, M. (1977). Intelligence and delinquency: A revisionist review. *American Sociological Review, 42,* 571–587; Moffitt, T. (1990). The neuropsychology of delinquency: A critical review of theory and research. In M. Tonry & N. Morris (Eds.), *Crime and justice: An annual review of research* (Vol. 12, pp. 99–169). Chicago: University of Chicago Press; Moffitt, T., & Henry, B. (1991). Neuropsychological studies of juvenile delinquency and juvenile violence. In J. S. Miller (Ed.), *The neuropsychology of aggression* (pp. 67–91). Boston: Kluwer; see also the conclusion in Paternoster, R., & Bachman, R. (2001). *Explaining criminals and crime.* Los Angeles: Roxbury, p. 51.

29. Herrnstein, R. J., & Murray, C. (1994). *The bell curve: Intelligence and class structure in the United States.* New York: Free Press.

30. See Brown, S., Esbensen, F., & Geis, G. (2009). *Criminology: Explaining crime and its context.* Cincinnati, OH: Anderson, p. 260.

31. Cullen, F., Gendreau, P., Jarjoura, G. R., & Wright, J. P. (1997). Crime and the bell curve: Lessons from intelligent criminology. *Crime and Delinquency, 43,* 387–411; Gould, S. J. (1996). *The mismeasure of man* (2nd ed.). New York: Norton, pp. 367–390; Hauser, R. (1995). Review of the bell curve. *Contemporary Sociology, 24,* 149–153; Hudson, J. B. (1995). Scientific racism: The politics of tests, race and genes. *Black Scholar, 25,* 1–10; Perkins, D. (1995). *Outsmarting IQ: The emerging science of learnable intelligence.* New York: Free Press; Taylor, H. (1995). Book review, "The Bell Curve." *Contemporary Sociology, 24,* 153–158.

32. Sheldon, W., Hartl, E. M., & McDermott, E. (1949). *Varieties of delinquent youth.* New York: Harper.

33. Greenberg, B. (1995, January 21). *Johnson City Press,* as cited in Brown, S., Esbensen, F., & Geis, G. (2009). *Criminology: Explaining crime and its context.* Cincinnati, OH: Anderson, p. 229.

34. Sheldon, W., Hartl, E. M., & McDermott, E. (1949). *Varieties of delinquent youth.* New York: Harper.

35. Glueck, S., & Glueck, E. (1956). *Physique and delinquency.* New York: Harper & Row; see also Cortes, J. (1972). *Delinquency and crime.* New York: Seminar Press; Hartl, E. (1982). *Physique and delinquent behavior.* New York: Academic Press. For the most recent applications, see Eysenck, H. J., & Gudjonsson, G. H. (1989). *The causes and cures of criminality.* New York: Plenum.

36. Wilson, J. Q., & Herrnstein, R. J. (1985). *Crime and human nature.* New York: McGraw-Hill.

37. Eysenck, H. J., & Gudjonsson, G. H. (1989). *The causes and cures of criminality.* New York: Plenum.

38. Cortes, J. (1972). *Delinquency and crime.* New York: Seminar Press; Glueck, S., & Glueck, E. (1956). *Physique and delinquency.* New York: Harper & Row. For a review, see Eysenck, H. J., & Gudjonsson, G. H. (1989). *The causes and cures of criminality.* New York: Plenum.

39. For a review, see Ellis, L. (2000). *Criminology: A global perspective.* Minot, ND: Pyramid Press.

40. Waldrop, M., & Halverson, C. (1971). Minor physical anomalies and hyperactive behavior in young children. In J. Hellmuth (Ed.), *Exceptional infant: Studies in abnormalities* (pp. 343–381). New York: Brunner/Mazel. See discussion in Fishbein, D. (2001). *Biobehavioral perspectives on criminology.* Belmont, CA: Wadsworth.

41. Fishbein, D. (2001). *Biobehavioral perspectives on criminology.* Belmont, CA: Wadsworth.

42. Wright, J., Tibbetts, S., & Daigle, L. (2008). *Criminals in the making: Criminality across the life course.* Thousand Oaks, CA: Sage.

43. Ibid.

CHAPTER 5 NOTES

1. Ma, K. (2011, August 26). Top 10 weirdest twin-crime stories. *TIME.* Retrieved from http://www.time.com/time/specials/packages/article/0,28804,2090549_2090540_2090537,00.html

2. Ibid.

3. Dugdale, R. L. (1910). *The Jukes: A study in crime, pauperism, disease, and heredity.* New York: Putnam; Goddard, H. H. (1912). *The Kallikak family.* New York: Macmillan.

4. For an excellent discussion of the alteration of Goddard's photographs, see Gould, S. J. (1996). *The mismeasure of man* (2nd ed.). New York: Norton.

5. See the review in Raine, A. (1993). *The psychopathology of crime.* San Diego: Academic Press; see also Christiansen, K. O. (1974). Seriousness of criminality and concordance among Danish twins. In R. Hood (Ed.), *Crime, criminology, and public policy* (pp. 63–77). New York: Free Press; Cortes, J. B. (1972). *Delinquency and crime.* New York: Seminar Press.

6. Raine, A. (1993). *The psychopathology of crime.* San Diego: Academic Press.

7. Walters, G. (1992). A meta-analysis of the gene-crime relationship. *Criminology, 30,* 595–613.

8. Hutchings, B., & Mednick, S. A. (1977). Criminality in adoptees and their adoptive and biological parents: A pilot study. In S. Mednick & K. O. Christiansen (Eds.), *Biosocial bases of criminal behavior* (pp. 127–141). New York: Gardner Press.

9. See Walters, G. (1992). A meta-analysis of the gene-crime relationship. *Criminology, 30,* 595–613; Wilson, J. Q., & Herrnstein, R. J. (1985). *Crime and human nature.* New York: Simon & Schuster.

10. Bouchard, T. J., Lykken, D. T., McGue, M., Segal, N., & Tellegen, A. (1990). Sources of human psychological differences: The Minnesota study of twins reared apart. *Science, 250,* 223–228.

11. Jacobs, P., Brunton, M., Melville, M., Brittian, R., & McClemmot, W. (1965). Aggressive behavior, mental sub-normality, and the XYY male. *Nature, 208,* 1351–1352.

12. See review in Paternoster, R., & Bachman, R. (2001). *Explaining criminals and crime.* Los Angeles: Roxbury, p. 53.

13. Walsh, A. (1995). Genetic and cytogenetic intersex anomalies: Can they help us to understand gender differences in deviant behavior? *International Journal of Offender Therapy and Comparative Criminality, 39,* 151–166.

14. Booth, A., & Osgood, D. W. (1993). The influence of testosterone on deviance in adulthood: Assessing and explaining the relationship. *Criminology, 31,* 93–117; Soler, H., Vinayak, P., & Quadagno, D. (2000). Biosocial aspects of domestic violence. *Psychoneuroendocrinology, 25,* 721–773; for a review, see Ellis, L., & Walsh, A. (2000). *Criminology: A global perspective.* Boston: Allyn & Bacon.

15. Sanchez-Martin, J. R., Fano, E., Ahedo, L., Cardas, J., Brain, P. F., & Azpiroz, A. (2000). Relating testosterone levels and free play social behavior in male and female preschool children. *Psychoneuroendocrinology, 25,* 773–783.

16. Halpern, D. (2000). *Sex differences in cognitive abilities.* Mahwah, NJ: Erlbaum.

17. Ibid.

18. Ellis, L. (2005). A theory explaining biological correlates of criminality. *European Journal of Criminality, 2,* 287–315.

19. Ibid.

20. Burr, C. (1993). Homosexuality and biology. *Atlantic Monthly, 271,* 47–65; Ellis, L. (2005). A theory explaining biological correlates of criminality. *European Journal of Criminality, 2,* 287–315; Ellis, L., & Ames, M. (1987). Neurohormonal functioning and sexual orientation: A theory of homosexuality-heterosexuality. *Psychological Bulletin, 101,* 233–258.

21. Badger, K., Simpson Craft, R., & Jensen, L. (1998). Age and gender differences in value orientation among American adolescents. *Adolescence, 33,* 591–596; Moll, J., Oliveira-Souza, J., Eslinger, P., Bramanti, B., Mourao-Miranda, J., Andreiuolo, P., et al. (2002). The neural correlates of moral sensitivity: A functional magnetic resonance imaging investigation of basic and moral emotions. *Journal of Neuroscience, 22,* 2730–2736; Reite, M., Cullum, C., Stocker, J., Teale, P., & Kozora, E. (1993). Neuropsychological test performance and MEG-based brain lateralization: Sex differences. *Brain Research Bulletin, 32,* 325–328.

22. For reviews, see Fishbein, D. (2001). *Biobehavioral perspectives in criminology.* Belmont: Wadsworth/Thomson Learning; Raine, A. (1993). *The psychopathology of crime.* San Diego: Academic Press.

23. Beaver, K. (2008). *Biosocial criminology: A primer.* Dubuque, IA: Kendall/Hunt; Raine, A. (1993). *The psychopathology of crime.* San Diego: Academic Press; Wright, J. P., Tibbetts, S. G., & Daigle, L. (2008). *Criminals in the making.* Thousand Oaks, CA: Sage.

24. Burt, S. A., & Nikolajewski, A. J. (2008). Preliminary evidence that specific candidate genes are associated with adolescent-onset antisocial behavior. *Aggressive Behavior, 34,* 1–9; for a review, see Beaver, K. (2008). *Biosocial criminology: A primer.* Dubuque, IA: Kendall/Hunt.

25. Beaver, K., Wright, J. P., DeLisi, M., Daigle, L., Swatt, M. L., & Gibson, C. (2007). Evidence of a gene x environment interaction in the creation of victimization: Results from a longitudinal sample of adolescents. *International Journal of Offender Therapy and Comparative Criminology, 51,* 620–645. For a review, see Beaver, K. (2008). *Biosocial criminology: A primer.* Dubuque, IA: Kendall/Hunt.

26. For a review, see Beaver, K. (2008). *Biosocial criminology: A primer.* Dubuque, IA: Kendall/Hunt; see also Blumensohn, R., Ratzoni, G., Weizman, A., Israeli, M., Greuner, N., Apter, A., et al. (1995). Reduction in serotonin 5HT receptor binding on platelets of delinquent adolescents. *Psychopharmacology, 118,* 354–356; Coccaro, E. F., Kavoussi, R. J., Cooper, T. B., & Hauger, R. L. (1997). Central serotonin activity and aggression. *American Journal of Psychiatry, 154,* 1430–1435; Davidson, H., Putnam, K. M., & Larson, C. L. (2000). Dysfunction in the neural circuitry of emotion regulation: A possible prelude to violence. *Science, 289,* 591–594; Dolan, M., Deakin, W. J. F., Roberts, N., & Anderson, I. (2002). Serotonergic and cognitive impairment in impulsive aggressive personality disordered offenders: Are there implications for treatment? *Psychological Medicine, 32,* 105–117; Ellis, L. (2005). A theory explaining biological correlates of criminality. *European Journal of Criminality, 2,* 287–315.

27. For a review, see Raine, A. (1993). *The psychopathology of crime.* San Diego: Academic Press, pp. 129–154; see also Tonkonogy, J. M. (1991). Violence and temporal lobe lesion: Head CT and

MRI data. *Journal of Neuropsychiatry, 3,* 189–196; Wright, P., Nobrega, J., Langevin, R., & Wortzman, G. (1990). Brain density and symmetry in pedophilic and sexually aggressive offenders. *Annals of Sex Research, 3,* 319–328.

28. Ellis, L. (2005). A theory explaining biological correlates of criminality. *European Journal of Criminality, 2,* 294; see also Fishbein, D. (2003). Neuropsychological and emotional regulatory processes in antisocial behavior. In A. Walsh & L. Ellis (Eds.), *Biosocial criminology: Challenging environmentalism's supremacy* (pp. 185–208). New York: Nova Science.

29. Anderson, B. J., Holmes, M. D., & Ostresch, E. (1999). Male and female delinquents' attachments and effects of attachments on severity of self-reported delinquency. *Criminal Justice and Behavior, 26,* 435–452.

30. Ohlson, K. (2012, Fall). The good, the bad, and the brain. *Discover: The Brain* [Special issue].

31. Ibid.

32. For a review, see Piquero, A., & Tibbetts, S. G. (2002). *Rational choice and criminal behavior: Recent research and future challenges.* New York: Routledge. See also Paternoster, R., & Simpson, S. (1996). Sanction threats and appeals to morality: Testing a rational choice model of corporate crime. *Law and Society Review, 30,* 378–399.

33. Bauer, L. O. (1997). Frontal P300 decrements, childhood conduct disorder, family history, and the prediction of relapse among abstinent cocaine abusers. *Drug and Alcohol Dependence, 44,* 1–10; Raine, A., & Venables, P. H. (1988). Enhanced P3 evoked potentials and longer P3 recovery times in psychopaths. *Psychophysiology, 25,* 30–38; for a review, see Ellis, L. (2005). A theory explaining biological correlates of criminality. *European Journal of Criminality, 2,* 287–315.

34. For a review, see Raine, A. (1993). *The psychopathology of crime.* San Diego: Academic Press, pp. 174–178; see also Hare, R. D. (1970). *Psychopathy: Theory and practice.* New York: Wiley; Venables, P. H. (1988). Psychophysiology and crime: Theory and data. In T. E. Moffitt & S. A. Mednick (Eds.), *Biological contributions to crime causation.* Dordrecht, Holland: Martinus Nijhoff; Venables, P. H., & Raine, A. (1987). Biological theory. In B. McGurk, D. Thornton, & M. Williams (Eds.), *Applying psychology to imprisonment: Theory and practice* (pp. 3–28). London: Her Majesty's Stationery Office; Volavka, J. (1987). Electroencephalogram among criminals. In S. A. Mednick, T. E. Moffitt, & S. Stack (Eds.), *The causes of crime: New biological approaches* (pp. 137–145). Cambridge, UK: Cambridge University Press.

35. For further discussion and explanation, see Raine, A. (1993). *The psychopathology of crime.* San Diego: Academic Press, pp. 174–177.

36. Boots, D. P. (2011). Neurobiological perspectives of brain vulnerability in pathways to violence over the life course. In K. Beaver & A. Walsh (Eds.), *The Ashgate research companion to biosocial theories of crime* (pp. 181–211). Burlington, VT: Ashgate.

37. Ibid., p. 197.

38. For a review, see Raine, A. (1993). *The psychopathology of crime.* San Diego: Academic Press, pp. 159–173; see also reviews and studies by Bice, T. (1993). *Cognitive and psychophysiological differences in proactive and reactive aggressive boys.* Unpublished doctoral dissertation, Department of Psychology, University of Southern California; Raine, A., & Venables, P. H. (1988). Skin conductance responsivity in psychopaths to orienting, defensive, and consonant-vowel stimuli. *Journal of Psychophysiology, 2,* 221–225; Venables, P. H. (1989). Childhood markers for adult disorders. *Journal of Child Psychology and Psychiatric and Allied Disorders, 30,* 347–364.

39. See Kindlon, D. J., Tremblay, R. E., Mezzacappa, E., Earls, F., Laurent, D., & Schaal, B. (1995). Longitudinal patterns of heart rate and fighting behavior in 9- through 12-year-old boys. *Journal of the American Academy of Child and Adolescent Psychiatry, 34,* 371–377; Mezzacappa, E., Tremblay, R. E., Kindlon, D., Saul, J. P., Arseneault, L., Seguin, J., et al. (1997). Anxiety, antisocial behavior, and heart rate regulation in adolescent males. *Journal of Psychiatry, 38,* 457–469; Rogeness, G. A., Cepeda, C., Macedo, C. A., Fischer, C., & Harris, W. R. (1990). Differences in heart rate and blood pressure in children with conduct disorder, major depression, and separation anxiety. *Psychiatry Research, 33,* 199–206.

40. Armstrong, T. (2011). The relationship between low resting heart rate and antisocial behavior: Correlation or causation? In K. Beaver & A. Walsh (Eds.), *The Ashgate research companion to biosocial theories of crime* (pp. 45–68). Burlington, VT: Ashgate.

41. For a very recent review, see Rudo-Hutt, A., Gao, Y., Glenn, A., Peskin, M., Yang, Y., & Raine, A. (2011). Biosocial interactions and correlates of crime. In K. Beaver & A. Walsh (Eds.), *The Ashgate research companion to biosocial theories of crime* (pp. 17–44). Burlington, VT: Ashgate.

42. Tibbetts, S., & Piquero, A. (1999). The influence of gender, low birth weight, and disadvantaged environment in predicting early onset of offending: A test of Moffitt's interactional hypothesis. *Criminology, 37,* 843–878.

43. Piquero, A., & Tibbetts, S. (1999). The impact of pre/perinatal disturbances and disadvantaged familial environment in predicting criminal offending. *Studies on Crime and Crime Prevention, 8,* 52–71.

44. Gibson, C., & Tibbetts, S. (1998). Interaction between maternal cigarette smoking and Apgar scores in predicting offending. *Psychological Reports, 83,* 579–586.

45. Gibson, C., & Tibbetts, S. (2000). A biosocial interaction in predicting early onset of offending. *Psychological Reports, 86,* 509–518.

46. Raine, A., Brennan, P. A., & Mednick, S. A. (1994). Birth complications combined with early maternal rejection at age 1 year predispose to violent crime at age 18 years. *Archives of General Psychiatry, 51,* 984–988; for a thorough review of recent research, see Beaver, K. (2008). *Biosocial criminology: A primer.* Dubuque, IA: Kendall/Hunt.

47. Beaver, K. (2008). *Biosocial criminology: A primer.* Dubuque, IA: Kendall/Hunt.

48. Ibid.

49. Ibid.

50. Ibid. See also Lyons, M. J., True, W. R., Eisen, S. A., Goldberg, J., Meyer, J. M., Faraone, S. V., et al. (1995). Differential heritability of adult and juvenile antisocial traits. *Archives of General Psychiatry, 52,* 906–915.

51. Beaver, K., & Walsh, A. (2011). Biosocial criminology. In K. Beaver & A. Walsh (Eds.), *The Ashgate research companion to biosocial theories of crime* (pp. 3–16). Burlington, VT: Ashgate.

52. Shoenthaler, S. J. (1991). *Improve your child's IQ and behavior.* London: BBC Books.

53. For a review, see Beaver, K. (2008). *Biosocial criminology: A primer.* Dubuque, IA: Kendall/Hunt, pp. 174–176; see also the review in Wright, J., Tibbetts, S., & Daigle, L. (2008). *Criminals in the making.* Thousand Oaks, CA: Sage.

54. For a recent review of such birth complications, see Tibbetts, S. (2011). Birth complications and the development of criminality: A biosocial perspective. In K. Beaver & A. Walsh (Eds.), *The Ashgate research companion to biosocial theories of crime* (pp. 273–290). Burlington, VT: Ashgate.

CHAPTER 6 NOTES

1. Nietzel, M. T. (1979). *Crime and its modification: A social learning perspective.* New York: Pergamon Press, p. 51.

2. Akers, R. L. (1997). *Criminological theories: Introduction and evaluation* (2nd ed.). Los Angeles: Roxbury, p. 35.

3. Freud, S. (1964). *New introductory lectures on psycho-analysis.* New York: W. W. Norton.

4. Freud, S. (1989). *An outline of psycho-analysis* (Standard ed.). New York: W. W. Norton; see also Fodor, N., Gaynor, F., & Reik, T. (1975). *Freud: Dictionary of psychoanalysis.* Westport CT: Greenwood Press, p. 90.

5. Schechter, H., & Everitt, D. (1996). *The A to Z encyclopedia of serial killers.* New York: Pocket Books, p. 92.

6. *Albert Fish confession.* (n.d.). Retrieved from http://iml.jou.ufl.edu/projects/spring03/rawlins/fishconfess.htm.

7. Schechter, H., & Everitt, D. (1996). *The A to Z encyclopedia of serial killers.* New York: Pocket Books, p. 92.

8. Ibid.

9. Coleman, J. C., Butcher, J. N., & Carson, R. C. (1984). *Abnormal psychology and modern life.* (7th ed.). Glenview, IL: Scott, Foresman, p. 62.

10. Freud, S. (1960). *The ego and the id.* New York: W. W. Norton.

11. Coleman, J. C., Butcher, J. N., & Carson, R. C. (1984). *Abnormal psychology and modern life* (7th ed.). Glenview, IL: Scott, Foresman, p. 63.

12. Ibid., p. 64.

13. Freud, S. (1964). *New introductory lectures on psycho-analysis.* New York: W. W. Norton.

14. Coleman, J. C., Butcher, J. N., & Carson, R. C. (1984). *Abnormal psychology and modern life* (7th ed.). Glenview, IL: Scott, Foresman, p. 64.

15. Fodor, N., Gaynor, F., & Reik, T. (1975). *Freud: Dictionary of psychoanalysis.* Westport, CT: Greenwood Press, pp. 29–30.

16. Aichhorn, A. (1935). *Wayward youth.* New York: World Publishing Company.

17. Ibid., p. 31.

18. Erickson, E. (1968). *Identity, youth and crisis.* New York: Norton.

19. Abrahamsen, D. (1944). *Crime and the human mind.* New York: Columbia University Press.

20. Trojanowicz, R. C., Morash, M., & Schram, P. J. (2001). *Juvenile delinquency: Concepts and control* (6th ed.). Upper Saddle River, NJ: Prentice Hall, p. 49.

21. Eysenck, H. J. (1964). *Crime and personality.* London: Routledge & Kegan Paul; see also Eysenck, H. J. (1977). *Crime and personality* (3rd ed.). London: Routledge & Kegan Paul.

22. Eysenck, H. J., & Gudjonson, G. H. (1989). *The causes and cures of criminality.* New York: Plenum Press, p. 44.

23. Ibid., pp. 44–45.

24. Rafter, N. H. (2006). H. J. Eysenck in Fagin's kitchen: The return to biological theory in 20th-century criminology. *History of the Human Sciences, 19,* 37–56.

25. Ibid., p. 43.

26. Eysenck, H. J. (1970). *Crime and personality.* (2nd ed.). London: Routledge & Kegan Paul, as cited in Rafter, N. H. (2006). H. J. Eysenck in Fagin's kitchen: The return to biological theory in 20th-century criminology. *History of the Human Sciences, 19,* p. 43.

27. Rafter, N. H. (2006). H. J. Eysenck in Fagin's kitchen: The return to biological theory in 20th-century criminology. *History of the Human Sciences, 19,* p. 43.

28. Eysenck, H. J., & Gudjonson, G. H. (1989). *The causes and cures of criminality.* New York: Plenum Press, pp. 110–111.

29. Eysenck, H. J. (1970). *Crime and personality* (2nd ed.). London: Routledge & Kegan Paul, p. 120, as cited in Rafter, N. H. (2006). H. J. Eysenck in Fagin's kitchen: The return to biological theory

in 20th-century criminology. *History of the Human Sciences, 19,* 44.

30. Eysenck, H. J., & Gudjonson, G. H. (1989). *The causes and cures of criminality.* New York: Plenum Press, p. 109.

31. Van Dam, C., De Bruyn, E. E. J., & Janssens, M. M. A. M. (2007). Personality, delinquency, and criminal recidivism. *Adolescence, 42,* 763–765.

32. See Blackburn, R. (1999). *The psychology of criminal conduct.* New York: Wiley; Farrington, D. P., Biron, L., & LeBiron, M. (1982). Personality and delinquency in London and Montreal. In J. Gunn & D. P. Farrington (Eds.), *Abnormal offenders, delinquency, and the criminal justice system* (pp. 153–201). New York: Wiley.

33. Levine, S. Z., & Jackson, C. J. (2004). Eysenck's theory of crime revisited: Factors or primary scales? *Legal and Criminological Psychology, 9,* 137.

34. Kohlberg, L. (1969). Stage and sequence: The cognitive-development approach to socialization. In D. A. Goslin (Ed.), *Handbook of socialization theory and research.* Chicago: Rand McNally; Kohlberg, L. (1976). Moral stages and moralization: The cognitive-developmental approach. In T. Lickona (Ed.), *Moral development and behavior: Theory, research, and social issues* (pp. 31–53). New York: Holt, Rinehart & Winston.

35. Kohlberg, L. (1986). A current statement on some theoretical issues. In S. Modgil & C. Modgil (Eds.), *Lawrence Kohlberg: Consensus and controversy* (pp. 485–586). Philadelphia: Falmer Press, p. 491.

36. Ibid.

37. Ibid., p. 492.

38. Damon, W. (1980). Structural-developmental theory and the study of moral development. In M. Windmiller, N. Lambert, & E. Turiel (Eds.), *Moral development and socialization* (pp. 35–68). Boston: Allyn & Bacon.

39. Ibid., p. 42.

40. Kohlberg, L. (1986). A current statement on some theoretical issues. In S. Modgil & C. Modgil (Eds.), *Lawrence Kohlberg: Consensus and controversy* (pp. 485–496). Philadelphia: Falmer Press, p. 495.

41. Damon, W. (1980). Structural-developmental theory and the study of moral development. In M. Windmiller, N. Lambert, & E. Turiel (Eds.), *Moral development and socialization* (pp. 35–68). Boston: Allyn & Bacon, p. 42.

42. Kohlberg, L. (1986). A current statement on some theoretical issues. In S. Modgil & C. Modgil (Eds.), *Lawrence Kohlberg: Consensus and controversy* (pp. 485–496). Philadelphia: Falmer Press, p. 495.

43. Gilligan, C. (1982). *In a different voice: Psychological theory and women's development.* Cambridge, MA: Harvard University Press.

44. Damon, W. (1988). *The moral child: Nurturing children's natural moral growth.* New York: Free Press, p. 96.

45. Gilligan, C. (1982). *In a different voice: Psychological theory and women's development.* Cambridge, MA: Harvard University Press.

46. Ibid., p. 18; see also Kohlberg, L. (1958). *The development of modes of thinking and choices in years 10 to 16.* Unpublished doctoral dissertation, University of Chicago; Kohlberg, L. (1981). *The philosophy of moral development.* San Francisco: Harper & Row.

47. Van der Horst, F. C. P., van der Veer, R. (2008). Loneliness in infancy: Harry Larlow, John Bowlby and issues of separation. *Integrative Psychological Behavior, 42,* 326.

48. Bretherton, I. (1992). The origins of attachment theory: John Bowlby and Mary Ainsworth. *Developmental Psychology, 28,* 759–775.

49. Bowlby, J. (1975). *Attachment and loss: Separation, anxiety and anger* (Vol. 2). New York: Basic Books, p. 60.

50. Adler, F., Mueller, G. O. W., & Laufer, W. S. (2007). *Criminology* (6th ed.). Boston: McGraw Hill, p. 88. See also Bowlby, J. (1969, 1975). *Attachment and loss: Separation, anxiety and anger* (Vols. 1 & 2). New York: Basic Books.

51. Bowlby, J. (1975). *Attachment and loss: Separation, anxiety and anger* (Vol. 2). New York: Basic Books, p. 201.

52. Bretherton, I. (1992). The origins of attachment theory: John Bowlby and Mary Ainsworth. *Developmental Psychology, 28,* 759–775.

53. Bowlby, J. (1944). Forty-four juvenile thieves: Their character and home-life. *International Journal of Psychoanalysis, 25,* 19–52.

54. Schneider, W. H. (1992). After Binet: French intelligence testing, 1900–1950. *Journal of the History of the Behavioral Sciences, 28,* 111–132.

55. Cravens, H. (1992). A scientific project locked in time: The Terman genetic studies of genius, 1920s–1950s. *American Psychologist, 47,* 183–189.

56. Ryan, P. J. (1997). Unnatural selection: Intelligence testing, eugenics, and American political cultures. *Journal of Social History, 30,* 669–685.

57. Tibbetts, S. (2012). *Criminological theory: The essentials.* Thousand Oaks, CA: Sage, p. 73.

58. Ryan, P. J. (1997). Unnatural selection: Intelligence testing, eugenics, and American political cultures. *Journal of Social History, 30,* 671.

59. Brownmiller, S. (1975). *Against our will: Men, women, and rape.* New York: Simon & Schuster. See also Clark, A. (1987). *Women silence men's violence: Sexual assault in England 1770–1845.* London: Pandora.

60. Brownmiller, S. (1975). *Against our will: Men, women, and rape.* New York: Simon & Schuster. See also Belknap, J. (2001). *The invisible woman: Gender, crime, and justice* (2nd ed.). Belmont, CA: Wadsworth, pp. 228–230; Burgess-Jackson, K. (1999). A history of rape law. In K. Burgess-Jackson (Eds.), *A most detestable crime: New philosophical essays on rape.* New York: Oxford University Press, pp. 16–17.

61. Clark, A. (1987). *Women silence men's violence: Sexual assault in England 1770–1845*. London: Pandora.
62. *State v. Sheline*, 955 S.W. 2d. 2, 44 (Tenn. 1997).
63. Burgess-Jackson, K. (1999). A history of rape law. In K. Burgess-Jackson (Eds.), *A most detestable crime: New philosophical essays on rape*. New York: Oxford University Press, p. 22.
64. Ibid., p. 24.
65. Ibid.
66. Federal Bureau of Investigation. (2012). *Crime in the United States, 2011*. Washington, DC: U.S. Department of Justice. Retrieved from http://www .fbi.gov/about-us/cjis/ucr/crime-in-the-u.s/2011/ crime-in-the-u.s.-2011/violent-crime/forcible-rape.
67. Holmes, R. M., & Holmes, S. T. (2002). *Profiling violent crimes: An investigative tool* (3rd ed.). Thousand Oaks, CA: Sage, pp. 144–145.
68. Knight, R. A., & Prentky, R. A. (1987). The developmental antecedents and adult adaptations of rapist subtypes. *Criminal Justice and Behavior, 14*, 403–426.
69. Holmes, R. M., & Holmes, S. T. (2002). *Profiling violent crimes: An investigative tool* (3rd ed.). Thousand Oaks, CA: Sage, p. 145.
70. Knight, R. A., & Prentky, R. A. (1987). The developmental antecedents and adult adaptations of rapist subtypes. *Criminal Justice and Behavior, 14*, 421.
71. Ibid., p. 411.
72. Holmes, R. M., & Holmes, S. T. (2002). *Profiling violent crimes: An investigative tool* (3rd ed.). Thousand Oaks, CA: Sage, pp. 150–151.
73. Knight, R. A., & Prentky, R. A. (1987). The developmental antecedents and adult adaptations of rapist subtypes. *Criminal Justice and Behavior, 14*, 410.
74. Ibid., p. 411.
75. Holmes, R. M., & Holmes, S. T. (2002). *Profiling violent crimes: An investigative tool* (3rd ed.). Thousand Oaks, CA: Sage, pp. 153–154.
76. Ibid., p. 672.
77. Sutherland, E. H. (1931). Mental deficiency and crime. In K. Young (Ed.), *Social attitudes* (pp. 357–375). New York: Henry Holt.
78. Van Dijk, J. (2008). *The world of crime: Breaking the silence on problems of security, justice, and development across the world*. Thousand Oaks, CA: Sage, p. 83.
79. Ibid.
80. Kangaspunta, K. (2000). Secondary analysis of integrated sources of data. In A. Alvazzi del Frate & O. Hatalak (Eds.), *Surveying crime: A global perspective*. Rome: UNICRI/ISTAT.
81. Hirschi, T., & Hindelang, M. J. (1977). Intelligence and delinquency: A revisionist review. *American Sociological Review, 42*, 571–587.
82. Hirschi, T. (1969). *Causes of delinquency*. Berkeley: University of California Press.
83. Wolfgang, M., Figlio, R. M., & Sellin, T. (1972). *Delinquency as a birth cohort*. Chicago: University of Chicago Press.
84. West, D. J. (1973). *Who becomes delinquent?* London: Heinemann.
85. Hirschi, T., & Hindelang, M. J. (1977). Intelligence and delinquency: A revisionist review. *American Sociological Review, 42*, 577.
86. Tibbetts, S. (2012). *Criminological theory: The essentials*. Thousand Oaks, CA: Sage, p. 75. See also Gibson, C. L., Piquero, A. R., & Tibbetts, S. G. (2001). The contribution of family adversity and verbal IQ to criminal behavior. *International Journal of Offender Therapy and Comparative Criminology, 45*, 574–592.
87. Herrnstein, R. J., & Murray, C. M. (1994). *The bell curve: Intelligence and class structure in American life*. New York: Free Press, p. xxiii.
88. Tibbetts, S. (2012). *Criminological theory: The essentials*. Thousand Oaks, CA: Sage, p. 76.
89. Ibid. See also Hauser, R. (1995). Review of *The Bell Curve*. *Contemporary Sociology, 24*, 149–153; Hudson, J. B. (1995). Scientific racism: The politics of tests, race, and genes. *Black Scholar, 25*, 1–10; Perkins, D. (1995). *Outsmarting IQ: The emerging science of learnable intelligence*. New York: Free Press.
90. Wilson, J. Q., & Herrnstein, R. J. (1985). *Crime and human nature*. New York: Simon & Schuster.
91. Wrightsman, L. S. (1987). *Psychology and the legal system*. Monterey, CA: Brooks/Cole, p. 347.
92. Kaplin, J. (1985, September 22). Why people go to the bad. *New York Times Book Review*, p. 7, as cited in Wrightsman, L. S. (1987). *Psychology and the legal system*. Monterey, CA: Brooks/Cole, p. 348.
93. Lilly, J. R., Cullen, F. T., & Ball, R. A. (2011). *Criminological theory: Context and consequences* (5th ed.). Thousand Oaks, CA: Sage, p. 307.
94. Gibbs, J. P. (1985). Review essay. *Criminology, 23*, 381.
95. Wilson, J. Q., & Herrnstein, R. J. (1985). *Crime and human nature*. New York: Simon & Schuster, p. 103.
96. Wrightsman, L. S. (1987). *Psychology and the legal system*. Monterey, CA: Brooks/Cole, p. 348.
97. Ibid., p. 510.
98. Wilson, J. Q., & Herrnstein, R. J. (1985). *Crime and human nature*. New York: Simon & Schuster, p. 61.
99. Lilly, J. R., Cullen, F. T., & Ball, R. A. (2011). *Criminological theory: Context and consequences* (5th ed.). Thousand Oaks, CA: Sage, p. 308.
100. Wilson, J. Q., & Herrnstein, R. J. (1985). *Crime and human nature*. New York: Simon & Schuster. See also Wrightsman, L. S. (1987). *Psychology and the legal system*. Monterey, CA: Brooks/Cole, p. 348.
101. Ibid., pp. 309–311.
102. Gibbs, J. P. (1985). Review essay. *Criminology, 23*, 382.
103. Lilly, J. R., Cullen, F. T., & Ball, R. A. (2011). *Criminological theory: Context and consequences* (5th ed.). Thousand Oaks, CA: Sage, p. 309.
104. Cleckley, H. (1982). *The mast of sanity* (Rev. ed.). St. Louis, MO: C. V. Mosby.

105. Salekin, R. T., Neumann, C. S., Liestico, A. R., & Zalot, A. (2004). Psychopathy in youth and intelligence: An investigation of Cleckley's hypothesis. *Journal of Clinical Child and Adolescent Psychology, 33,* 731.

106. Hare, R. D. (1991). *Manual for the Revised Psychopathy Checklist.* Toronto, Ontario, Canada: Multi-Health Systems.

107. Vaughn, M. G., Edens, J. F., Howard, M. O., & Smith, S. T. (2009). An investigation of primary and secondary psychopathy in a statewide sample of incarcerated youth. *Youth Violence and Juvenile Justice, 7,* 172–188.

108. Ibid., p. 173.

109. Ibid.

110. Lykken, D. T. (1996). Psychopathy, sociopathy, and crime. *Society, 34,* 31.

111. Ibid., pp. 33–34.

112. Hare, R. D. (1999). Psychopathy as a risk factor for violence. *Psychiatric Quarterly, 70,* 183–184.

113. Ibid., p. 186

114. See Hemphill, J. F., Hare, R. D., & Wong, S. (1998). Psychopathy and recidivism: A review. *Legal and Criminological Psychology, 3,* 141–172; Salekin, R. T., Rogers, R., & Sewell, K. W. (1996). A review and meta-analysis of the Psychopathy Checklist and Psychopathy Checklist–Revised: Predictive validity of dangerousness. *Clinical Psychology: Science and Practice, 3,* 203–215.

115. Hare, R. D. (1999). Psychopathy as a risk factor for violence. *Psychiatric Quarterly, 70,* 186.

116. Ibid., p. 191.

117. Teplin, L. A. (1994). Psychiatric and substance abuse disorders among male urban jail detainees. *American Journal of Public Health, 84,* 290–293.

118. James, D. J., & Glaze, L. E. (2006). *Mental health problems of prison and jail inmates* [Bureau of Justice Statistics Special Report]. Washington, DC: U.S. Department of Justice.

119. Martin, M. S., Dorken, S. K., Wambolt, A. D., & Wooten, S. E. (2012). Stopping the revolving door: A meta-analysis on the effectiveness of interventions for criminally involved individuals with major mental disorders. *Law and Human Behavior, 36,* 1–12.

120. Muskal, M., Susman, T., & Serrano, R. A. (2012). Connecticut town tries to cope with shooting massacre at elementary school. *Los Angeles Times.* Retrieved from http://www.latimes.com/news/nation/nationnow/la-na-nn-sandy-hook-connecticut-school-shooting-20121214,0,3248656.story.

121. Bengali, S., Hennessy-Fisk, M., & Murphy, K. (2012). Adam Lanza's family had kept a watchful eye on him. *Los Angeles Times.* Retrieved from http://www.latimes.com/news/nationworld/nation/la-na-shooter-profile-20121218,0,7751800.story.

122. Muskal, M. (2013). Sandy Hook violence prevention commission meets for first time. *Los Angeles Times,* para. 8. Retrieved from http://www.latimes.com/news/nation/nationnow/la-na-nn-sandy-hook-commission-20130124,0,5808576.story.

123. Rosenwald, M. S. (2013). Why do we still know so little about Adam Lanza? Because he lived in the cloud. *Washington Post.* Retrieved from http://articles.washingtonpost.com/2013–01–18/opinions/36474274_1_adam-lanza-comic-book-store-gun-violence.

124. Newman, S. S., & Ghaziuddin, M. (2008). Violent crime in Asperger syndrome: The role of psychiatric comorbidity. *Journal of Autism Development Disorder, 38,* 1848–1852.

125. Bush, J., Glick, B., & Taymans, J. (2006). *Thinking for a Change: Facilitator training.* Longmont, CO: National Institute of Corrections, U.S. Department of Justice.

126. Allen, H. E., Simonsen, C. E., & Latessa, E. J. (2004). *Corrections in America: An introduction* (10th ed.). Upper Saddle River, NJ: Prentice Hall, p. 277.

127. Bush, J., Glick, B., & Taymans, J. (1997). *Thinking for a Change: Facilitator training.* Longmont, CO: National Institute of Corrections, U.S. Department of Justice. See also Andrews, D. A., & Bonta, J. (1994). *The psychology of criminal conduct.* Cincinnati, OH: Anderson; Ross, R. R., & Fabiano, E. A. (1984). *Time to think: A cognitive model of delinquency prevention and offender rehabilitation.* Ottawa: Institute of Social Sciences and Arts.

128. Golden, L. S., Gatchel, R. J., & Cahill, M. A. (2006). Evaluating the effectiveness of the National Institute of Corrections' "Thinking for a Change" program among probationers. *Journal of Offender Rehabilitation, 43,* 55–73.

129. Wilson, R. J. (2005). Are cognitive problem-solving skills programmes really not working? A response to 'evaluating evidence for the effectiveness of the reasoning and rehabilitation programme.' *Howard Journal, 44,* 319–321.

130. Steadman, H. J., Davidson, S., & Brown, C. (2001). Law & psychiatry: Mental health courts: Their promise and unanswered questions. *Psychiatric Services, 52,* 457.

131. Council of State Governments Justice Center. (2008). *Mental health courts: A primer for policymakers and practitioners.* Washington, DC: U.S. Department of Justice, p. 3.

132. Ibid., p. 8.

133. Ibid., p. 4.

134. Allnutt, S., Samuels, A., & O'Driscoll, C. (2007). The insanity defence: From wild beasts to M'Naghten. *Australian Psychiatry, 15,* 292.

135. Perlin, M. L. (1994). *The jurisprudence of the insanity defense.* Durham, NC: Carolina Academic Press.

136. Morris, N. (n.d.). Insanity defense. *Crime File.* Washington, DC: National Institute of Justice, U.S. Department of Justice. Retrieved from https://www.ncjrs.gov/pdffiles1/Digitization/100742NCJRS.pdf

137. Ibid. See also Slodov, M. D. (1990). Criminal responsibility and the noncompliant psychiatric offender: Risking madness. *Case Western Reserve Law Review, 40,* 271–330.

138. FindLaw. (n.d.). The insanity defense among the states. Retrieved from http://criminal.findlaw.com/criminal-procedure/the-insanity-defense-among-the-states.html.

139. Wallace, H., & Roberson, C. (2008). *Principles of criminal law* (4th ed.). Boston: Pearson, p. 95.

140. Allnutt, S., Samuels, A., & O'Driscoll, C. (2007). The insanity defence: From wild beasts to M'Naghten. *Australian Psychiatry, 15,* 292–293.

141. Ibid., pp. 293–294.

142. Morris, N. (n.d.). Insanity defense. *Crime File.* Washington, DC: National Institute of Justice, U.S. Department of Justice. Retrieved from https://www.ncjrs.gov/pdffiles1/Digitization/100742NCJRS.pdf.

143. Margolick, D. (1994). Lorena Bobbitt acquitted in mutilation of husband. *New York Times.* Retrieved from http://www.nytimes.com/1994/01/22/us/lorena-bobbitt-acquitted-in-mutilation-of-husband.html?pagewanted=all&src=pm.

144. Cobun, L. S. (1984). The insanity defense: Effects of abolition unsupported by a moral consensus. *American Journal of Law and Medicine, 9,* 471–498.

145. Felthous, A. R. (2010). Psychopathic disorders and criminal responsibility in the USA. *European Archives of Psychiatry and Clinical Neuroscience, 260,* 138.

146. Wallace, H., & Roberson, C. (2008). *Principles of criminal law* (4th ed.). Boston: Pearson, p. 96.

147. Mischel, W. (1968). *Personality and assessment.* New York: Wiley.

148. Schmalleger, F. (2009). *Criminology today: An integrative introduction* (5th ed.). Upper Saddle River, NJ: Pearson/Prentice Hall, pp. 216–217.

CHAPTER 7 NOTES

1. Ellis, L., & Walsh, A. (1999). Criminologists' opinions about causes and theories of crime and delinquency. *Criminologist, 24,* 1–4; Walsh, A., & Ellis, L. (1999). Political ideology and American criminologists' explanations for criminal behavior. *Criminologist, 24,* 1, 14.

2. Much of the discussion of the development of structural theories of the 19th century is drawn from Zanden, J. W. V. (2000). *Sociology: The core* (2nd ed.). New York: McGraw-Hill, pp. 8–14.

3. Ibid., pp. 8–9.

4. For more thorough discussions of Guerry and Quetelet, see the sources from which we have drawn the information presented here: Beirne, P. (1993). *Inventing criminology.* Albany: SUNY Press; Vold, G. B., Bernard, T. J., & Snipes, J. (2002). *Theoretical criminology* (5th ed.). New York: Oxford University Press.

5. Morris, T. (1957). *The criminal area.* New York: Routledge, pp. 42–53, as cited in Vold, G. B., Bernard, T. J., & Snipes, J. (2002). *Theoretical criminology* (5th ed.). New York: Oxford University Press, p. 22.

6. U.S. Department of Justice, Bureau of Justice Statistics. (2001). *Sourcebook of criminal justice statistics, 2000* (NCJ-190251). Washington, DC: USGPO, Table 3.13, p. 194; U.S. Department of Justice, Bureau of Justice Statistics. (2001). *Sourcebook of criminal justice statistics, 2000* (NCJ-190251). Washington, DC: USGPO, Table 3.26, p. 202.

7. Beirne, P. (1993). *Inventing criminology.* Albany: SUNY Press, pp. 78–81.

8. Vold, G. B., Bernard, T. J., & Snipes, J. (2002). *Theoretical criminology* (5th ed.). New York: Oxford University Press, pp. 23–26.

9. Burton, V., & Cullen, F. (1992). The empirical status of strain theory. *Journal of Crime and Justice, 15,* 1–30; Passas, N. (1995). Continuities in the anomie tradition. In F. Adler & W. S. Laufer (Eds.), *Advances in criminological theory, Vol. 6: The legacy of anomie theory* (pp. 91–112). New Brunswick, NJ: Transaction; Passas, N. (1997). Anomie, reference groups, and relative deprivation. In N. Passas & R. Agnew (Eds.), *The future of anomie theory* (pp. 62–94). Boston: Northeastern University Press.

10. U.S. Department of Justice, Bureau of Justice Statistics. (2001). *Sourcebook of criminal justice statistics, 2000* (NCJ-190251). Washington, DC: USGPO, Table 3.124, p. 290.

11. Lee, D. S. (1993). *An empirical investigation of the economic incentives for criminal behavior.* Bachelor of Arts thesis in economics, Harvard University, Boston, as cited in Freeman, R. B. (1995). The labor market. In J. Q. Wilson & J. Petersilia (Eds.), *Crime* (pp. 103–105). San Francisco: ICS Press.

12. Beirne, P. (1993). *Inventing criminology.* Albany: SUNY Press, p. 88, as cited in Vold, G. B., Bernard, T. J., & Snipes, J. (2002). *Theoretical criminology* (5th ed.). New York: Oxford University Press, p. 25.

13. Vold, G. B., Bernard, T. J., & Snipes, J. (2002). *Theoretical criminology* (5th ed.). New York: Oxford University Press, pp. 25–26.

14. Much of this discussion of Durkheim is taken from Vold, G. B., Bernard, T. J., & Snipes, J. (2002). *Theoretical criminology* (5th ed.). New York: Oxford University Press, Chapter 6, as well as Zanden, J. W. V. (2000). *Sociology: The core* (2nd ed.). New York: McGraw-Hill, pp. 11–13.

15. Durkheim, E. (1965). *The rules of the sociological method* (G. E. G. Catlin, Ed.; S. A. Solovay & J. H. Mueller, Trans.). New York: Free Press, as cited in Vold, G. B., Bernard, T. J., & Snipes, J. (2002). *Theoretical criminology* (5th ed.). New York: Oxford University Press.

16. See discussion in Klein, M. (1995). Street gang cycles. In J. Q. Wilson & J. Petersilia (Eds.), *Crime* (pp. 217–236). San Francisco: ICS Press.

17. For more details on these issues, see E. Durkheim's works *The division of labor in society*. New York: Free Press (1893/1965); *Suicide*. New York: Free Press (1897/1951).

18. U.S. Department of Justice, Bureau of Justice Statistics. (1996). *Violent crime in the United States*. Washington, DC: Author, as illustrated in Senna, J., & Siegel, L. G. (1999). *Introduction to criminal justice* (8th ed.). Belmont, CA: West/Wadsworth.

19. Chambliss, W. J. (1976). Functional and conflict theories of crime: The heritage of Emile Durkheim and Karl Marx. In W. J. Chambliss & M. Mankoff (Eds.), *Whose law what order? A conflict approach to criminology* (pp. 1–28). New York: John Wiley, pp. 11–16.

20. For reviews of Merton's theory, see both of his original and more recent works: Merton, R. K. (1938). Social structure and anomie. *American Sociological Review, 3*, 672–682; Merton, R. K. (1968). *Social theory and social structure*. New York: Free Press; Merton, R. K. (1995). Opportunity structure: The emergence, diffusion, and differentiation as sociological concept, 1930s–1950s. In F. Adler & M. Laufer (Eds.), *Advances in criminological theory: The legacy of anomie theory* (Vol. 6, pp. 3–17). New Brunswick, NJ: Transaction Press. For reviews by others, see Akers, R. L., & Sellers, C. S. (2004). *Criminological theories: Introduction, evaluation, and application* (4th ed.). Los Angeles: Roxbury, pp. 164–168; Bernard, T. J. (1987). Testing structural strain theories. *Journal of Research in Crime and Delinquency, 24*, 262–280; Brown, S. E., Esbensen, F., & Geis, G. (2004). *Criminology: Explaining crime and its context* (5th ed.). Cincinnati, OH: Anderson, pp. 297–307; Clinard, M. B. (1964). The theoretical implications of anomie and deviant behavior. In M. B. Clinard (Ed.), *Anomie and deviant behavior* (pp. 1–56). New York: Free Press.

21. Clinard, M. B. (1964). The theoretical implications of anomie and deviant behavior. In M. B. Clinard (Ed.), *Anomie and deviant behavior* (pp. 1–56). New York: Free Press; see also the discussion in Brown, S. E., Esbensen, F., & Geis, G. (2004). *Criminology: Explaining crime and its context* (5th ed.). Cincinnati, OH: Anderson, p. 297.

22. Senna, J., & Siegel, L. J. (1999). *Introduction to criminal justice* (8th ed.). Belmont, CA: Wadsworth, p. 44.

23. Merton, R. K. (1968). *Social theory and social structure*. New York: Free Press.

24. Vold, G. B., Bernard, T. J., & Snipes, J. (2002). *Theoretical criminology* (5th ed.). New York: Oxford University Press, p. 140.

25. For examples and reviews of this research, see Akers, R. L. (1964). Socio-economic status and delinquent behavior: A retest. *Journal of Research in Crime and Delinquency, 1*, 38–46; Dunaway, G. R., Cullen, F. T., Burton, V. S., & Evans, T. D. (2000). The myth of social class and crime revisited: An examination of class and adult criminality. *Criminology, 38*, 589–632; Hindelang, M. J. (1980). *Measuring delinquency*. Beverly Hills, CA: Sage; Hindelang, M. J., Hirschi, T., & Weis, J. C. (1979). Correlates of delinquency: The illusion of discrepancy between self-report and official measures. *American Sociological Review, 44*, 995–1014; Nye, F. I. (1958). *Family relationships and delinquent behavior*. New York: Wiley; Thornberry, T., & Farnworth, M. (1982). Social correlates of criminal involvement. *American Sociological Review, 47*, 505–517; Tittle, C. R., & Villemez, W. J. (1977). Social class and criminality. *Social Forces, 56*, 474–503; Tittle, C. R., Villemez, W. J., & Smith, D. A. (1978). The myth of social class and criminality: An empirical assessment of the empirical evidence. *American Sociological Review, 43*, 643–656; for one of the most thorough reviews, see Tittle, C. R., & Meier, R. F. (1990). Specifying the SES/delinquency relationship. *Criminology, 28*, 271–299.

26. Kleck, G., & Chiricos, T. (2000). Unemployment and property crime: A target-specific assessment of opportunity and motivation as mediating factors. *Criminology, 40*, 649–680.

27. Bernard, T. J. (1987). Testing structural strain theories. *Journal of Research in Crime and Delinquency, 24*, 262–280; Messner, S. F. (1988). Merton's 'social structure and anomie': The road not taken. *Deviant Behavior, 9*, 33–53; see also discussion in Burton, V. S., & Cullen, F. T. (1992). The empirical status of strain theory. *Journal of Crime and Justice, 15*, 1–30.

28. For a review of these studies, see Land, K. C., McCall, P. L., & Cohen, L. E. (1990). Structural covariates of homicide rates: Are there any invariances across time and social space? *American Journal of Sociology, 95*, 922–963.

29. For examples and reviews of these types of studies, see Agnew, R. F., Cullen, F. T., Burton, V. S., Evans, T. D., & Dunaway, R. G. (1996). A new test of classic strain theory. *Justice Quarterly, 13*, 681–704; Burton, V., & Cullen, F. (1992). The empirical status of strain theory. *Journal of Crime and Justice, 15*, 1–30; Burton, V. S., Cullen, F. T., Evans, T. D., & Dunaway, R. G. (1994). Reconsidering strain theory: Operationalization, rival theories, and adult criminality. *Journal of Quantitative Criminology, 10*, 213–239; Farnworth, M., & Leiber, M. J. (1989). Strain theory revisited: Economic goals, educational means, and delinquency. *American Sociological Review, 54*, 263–274; Hirschi, T. (1969). *Causes of delinquency*. Berkeley: University of California Press; Liska, A. E. (1971). Aspirations, expectations, and delinquency: Stress and additive models. *Sociological Quarterly, 12*, 99–107; see also discussion of this issue in Akers, R. L., & Sellers, C. S. (2004). *Criminological theories: Introduction, evaluation, and application* (4th ed.). Los Angeles: Roxbury, pp. 173–175.

30. Farnworth, M., & Leiber, M. J. (1989). Strain theory revisited: Economic goals, educational means, and delinquency. *American Sociological Review, 54,* 263–274.

31. Agnew, R. F., Cullen, F. T., Burton, V. S., Evans, T. D., & Dunaway, R. G. (1996). A new test of classic strain theory. *Justice Quarterly, 13,* 681–704.

32. Cohen, A. (1955). *Delinquent boys: The culture of the gang.* New York: Free Press.

33. Hindelang, M. J., Hirschi, T., & Weis, J. C. (1979). Correlates of delinquency: The illusion of discrepancy between self-report and official measures. *American Sociological Review, 44,* 995–1014; Tittle, C. R., Villemez, W. J., & Smith, D. A. (1978). The myth of social class and criminality: An empirical assessment of the empirical evidence. *American Sociological Review, 43,* 643–656.

34. See Bernard, T. J. (1987). Testing structural strain theories. *Journal of Research in Crime and Delinquency, 24,* 262–280; Elliott, D., & Voss, H. (1974). *Delinquency and dropout.* Lexington, MA: D. C. Health; Jarjoura, G. R. (1993). Does dropping out of school enhance delinquent involvement? Results from a large-scale national probability sample. *Criminology, 31,* 149–172; Jarjoura, G. R. (1996). The conditional effect of social class on the dropout delinquency relationship. *Journal of Research in Crime and Delinquency, 33,* 232–255; Merton, R. K. (1995). Opportunity structure: The emergence, diffusion, and differentiation as sociological concept, 1930s–1950s. In F. Adler & M. Laufer (Eds.), *Advances in criminological theory: The legacy of anomie theory* (Vol. 6, pp. 3–17). New Brunswick, NJ: Transaction Press; Thornberry, T. P., Moore, M., & Christenson, R. L. (1985). The effect of dropping out of high school on subsequent criminal behavior. *Criminology, 23,* 3–18; see also discussion in Shoemaker, D. J. (2005). *Theories of delinquency* (5th ed.). New York: Oxford University Press.

35. Hirschi, T. (1969). *Causes of delinquency.* Berkeley: University of California Press; Liazos, A. (1978). School, alienation, and delinquency. *Crime and Delinquency, 24,* 355–370; Rogers, J. W., & Mays, G. L. (1987). *Juvenile delinquency and juvenile justice.* New York: Wiley; Tygart, C. E. (1988). Strain theory and public school vandalism: Academic tracking, school social status, and students' academic achievement. *Youth and Society, 20,* 106–118.

36. Cloward, R. A., & Ohlin, L. E. (1960). *Delinquency and opportunity: A theory of delinquent gangs.* New York: Free Press. For discussion and theoretical critique of the model, see Bernard, T. J. (1987). Testing structural strain theories. *Journal of Research in Crime and Delinquency, 24,* 262–280, and Merton, R. K. (1995). Opportunity structure: The emergence, diffusion, and differentiation as sociological concept, 1930s–1950s. In F. Adler & M. Laufer (Eds.), *Advances in criminological theory: The legacy of anomie theory* (Vol. 6, pp. 3–17). New Brunswick, NJ: Transaction Press.

37. Hirschi, T. (1969). *Causes of delinquency.* Berkeley: University of California Press; see discussion in Shoemaker, D. J. (2005). *Theories of delinquency* (5th ed.). New York: Oxford University Press, pp. 121–130; Liska, A. E. (1971). Aspirations, expectations, and delinquency: Stress and additive models. *Sociological Quarterly, 12,* 99–107; Short, J. F. (1964). Gang delinquency and anomie. In M. B. Clinard (Ed.), *Anomie and deviant behavior.* New York: Free Press, pp. 98–127; Short, J. F., Rivera, R., & Tennyson, R. A. (1965). Perceived opportunities, gang membership, and delinquency. *American Sociological Review, 30,* 56–67; Short, J. F., & Strodtbeck, F. L. (1965). *Group processes and gang delinquency.* Chicago: University of Chicago Press.

38. Short, J. F., & Strodtbeck, F. L. (1965). *Group processes and gang delinquency.* Chicago: University of Chicago Press; Spergel, I. (1964). *Racketville, Slumtown, and Haulburg.* Chicago: University of Chicago Press; Tracy, P. E., Wolfgang, M. E., & Figlio, R. M. (1990). *Delinquency careers in two birth cohorts.* New York: Plenum.

39. Empey, L. T. (1991). *American delinquency* (4th ed.). Homewood, IL: Dorsey.

40. Hindelang, M. J., Hirschi, T., & Weis, J. C. (1979). Correlates of delinquency: The illusion of discrepancy between self-report and official measures. *American Sociological Review, 44,* 995–1014; Tittle, C. R., Villemez, W. J., & Smith, D. A. (1978). The myth of social class and criminality: An empirical assessment of the empirical evidence. *American Sociological Review, 43,* 643–656.

41. For Agnew's works regarding this theory, see Agnew, R. (1985). A revised strain theory of delinquency. *Social Forces, 64,* 151–167; Agnew, R. (1992). Foundation for a general strain theory of crime and delinquency. *Criminology, 30,* 47–88; Agnew, R. (1995). Controlling delinquency: Recommendations from general strain theory. In H. Barlow (Ed.), *Crime and public policy: Putting theory to work* (pp. 43–70). Boulder, CO: Westview Press; Agnew, R. (2001). Building on the foundation of general strain theory: Specifying the types of strain most likely to lead to crime and delinquency. *Journal of Research in Crime and Delinquency, 38,* 319–361; Agnew, R., Cullen, F., Burton, V., Evans, T. D., & Dunaway, R. G. (1996). A new test of general strain theory. *Justice Quarterly, 13,* 681–704; Agnew, R., & White, H. R. (1992). An empirical test of general strain theory. *Criminology, 30,* 475–500.

42. Brezina, T., Piquero, A., & Mazerolle, P. (2001). Student anger and aggressive behavior in School: An initial test of Agnew's macro-level strain theory. *Journal of Research in Crime and Delinquency, 38,* 362–386.

43. Agnew, R., Cullen, F., Burton, V., Evans, T. D., & Dunaway, R. G. (1996). A new test of general strain theory. *Justice Quarterly, 13,* 681–704; Agnew, R., & White, H. R. (1992). An empirical test of general strain theory. *Criminology, 30,* 475–500; Baron, S. W. (2004). General strain, street youth and crime: A test of Agnew's revised theory. *Criminology, 42,* 457–484; Baron, S. W., & Hartnagel, T. F. (2002). Street youth and labor market strain. *Journal of Criminal Justice, 30,* 519–533; Brezina, T. (1996). Adapting to strain: An examination of delinquent coping responses. *Criminology, 34,* 39–60; Broidy, L. M. (2001). A test of general strain theory. *Criminology, 39,* 9–36; Hay, C. (2003). Family strain, gender, and delinquency. *Sociological Perspectives, 46,* 107–135; Hoffman, J. P., & Cerbone, F. G. (1999). Stressful life events and delinquency escalation in early adolescence. *Criminology, 37,* 343–374; Hoffman, J. P., & Miller, A. S. (1998). A latent variable analysis of general strain theory. *Journal of Quantitative Criminology, 14,* 83–110; Hoffman, J. P., & Su, S. S. (1998). Stressful life events and adolescent substance use and depression: Conditional and gender differentiated effects. *Substance Use and Misuse, 33,* 2219–2262; Jang, S. J., & Johnson, B. R. (2003). Strain, negative emotions, and deviant coping among African Americans: A test of general strain theory. *Journal of Quantitative Criminology, 19,* 79–105; Mazerolle, P. (1998). Gender, general strain, and delinquency: An empirical examination. *Justice Quarterly, 15,* 65–91; Mazerolle, P., Burton, V., Cullen, F., Evans, T. D., & Payne, G. (2000). Strain, anger, and delinquent adaptations: Specifying general strain theory. *Journal of Criminal Justice, 28,* 89–101; Mazerolle, P., & Maahs, J. (2000). General strain and delinquency: An alternative examination of conditioning influences. *Justice Quarterly, 17,* 753–778; Mazerolle, P., & Piquero, A. (1998). Linking exposure to strain with anger: An investigation of deviant adaptations. *Journal of Criminal Justice, 26,* 195–211; Mazerolle, P., Piquero, A., & Capowich, G. E. (2003). Examining the links between strain, situational and dispositional anger, and crime: Further specifying and testing general strain theory. *Youth and Society, 35,* 131–157; Paternoster, R., & Mazerolle, P. (1994). General strain theory and delinquency: A replication and extension. *Journal of Research in Crime and Delinquency, 31,* 235–263; Piquero, N. L., & Sealock, M. (2000). Generalizing general strain theory: An examination of an offending population. *Justice Quarterly, 17,* 449–484.

44. A recent review of this research can be found in Baron, S. W. (2004). General strain, street youth and crime: A test of Agnew's revised theory. *Criminology, 42,* 457–467.

45. For examples, see Hoffman, J. P., & Cerbone, F. G. (1999). Stressful life events and delinquency escalation in early adolescence. *Criminology, 37,* 343–374; Hoffman, J. P., & Su, S. S. (1998). Stressful life events and adolescent substance use and depression: Conditional and gender differentiated effects. *Substance Use and Misuse, 33,* 2219–2262; Paternoster, R., & Mazerolle, P. (1994). General strain theory and delinquency: A replication and extension. *Journal of Research in Crime and Delinquency, 31,* 235–263.

46. Baron, S. W. (2004). General strain, street youth and crime: A test of Agnew's revised theory. *Criminology, 42,* 457–467; Broidy, L. M. (2001). A test of general strain theory. *Criminology, 39,* 9–36.

47. See Brezina, T. (1996). Adapting to strain: An examination of delinquent coping responses. *Criminology, 34,* 39–60; Broidy, L. M. (2001). A test of general strain theory. *Criminology, 39,* 9–36; Mazerolle, P., & Piquero, A. (1998). Linking exposure to strain with anger: An investigation of deviant adaptations. *Journal of Criminal Justice, 26,* 195–211.

48. Mazerolle, P. (1998). Gender, general strain, and delinquency: An empirical examination. *Justice Quarterly, 15,* 65–91; Mazerolle, P., & Piquero, A. (1998). Linking exposure to strain with anger: An investigation of deviant adaptations. *Journal of Criminal Justice, 26,* 195–211; Piquero, N. L., & Sealock, M. (2000). Generalizing general strain theory: An examination of an offending population. *Justice Quarterly, 17,* 449–484.

49. Baron, S. W. (2004). General strain, street youth and crime: A test of Agnew's revised theory. *Criminology, 42,* 457–484; Mazerolle, P., Piquero, A., & Capowich, G. E. (2003). Examining the links between strain, situational and dispositional anger, and crime: Further specifying and testing general strain theory. *Youth and Society, 35,* 131–157.

50. For examples, see Baron, S. W. (2004). General strain, street youth and crime: A test of Agnew's revised theory. *Criminology, 42,* 457–484; Mazerolle, P., Burton, V., Cullen, F., Evans, T. D., & Payne, G. (2000). Strain, anger, and delinquent adaptations: Specifying general strain theory. *Journal of Criminal Justice, 28,* 89–101; see also discussion in Akers, R. L., & Sellers, C. S. (2004). *Criminological theories: Introduction, evaluation, and application* (4th ed.). Los Angeles: Roxbury, pp. 180–182; Mazerolle, P., Piquero, A., & Capowich, G. E. (2003). Examining the links between strain, situational and dispositional anger, and crime: Further specifying and testing general strain theory. *Youth and Society, 35,* 131–157.

51. Wright, J. P., Tibbetts, S. G., & Daigle, L. (2008). *Criminals in the making: Criminality across the life course.* Thousand Oaks, CA: Sage, pp. 204–207.

52. Van Voorhis, P., Braswell, M. C., & Lester, D. (2009). *Correctional counseling and rehabilitation* (8th ed.). New Providence, NJ: Anderson.

CHAPTER 8 NOTES

1. For an excellent discussion of the early history of Chicago, see Bernard, T. J. (1992). *The cycle of juvenile justice.* New York: Oxford University Press.
2. See discussion in Vold, G. B., Bernard, T. J., & Snipes, J. B. (2002). *Theoretical criminology* (5th ed.). Oxford, UK: Oxford University Press, pp. 117–122.
3. Romero, D. (2012, June 27). Gang map study shows crime happens along borders between sets in L.A. *LA Weekly.* Retrieved from http://blogs.laweekly.com/informer/2012/06/gang_maps_angeles_murder_attacks_borders_ucla_study.php?print=true. See also actual study: Brantingham, P. J., Tita, G. E., Short, M. B., & Reid, S. E. (2012). The ecology of gang territorial boundaries. *Criminology, 50*(3), 851–885. doi:10.1111/j.1745-9125.2012.00281.x.
4. These dates were taken from Famighetti, R. (2000). *The world almanac and book of facts, 2000: Millennium collector's edition.* Mahwah, NJ: Primedia Reference.
5. Park, R. E. (1936). Human ecology. *American Journal of Sociology, 42,* 32–51; Park, R. E. (1952). *Human communities.* Glencoe, IL: Free Press.
6. Burgess, E. W. (1928). The growth of the city. In R. Park, E. W. Burgess, & R. D. McKenzie (Eds.), *The city.* Chicago: University of Chicago Press.
7. See Vold, G. B., Bernard, T. J., & Snipes, J. B. (2002). *Theoretical criminology* (5th ed.). Oxford, UK: Oxford University Press, pp. 118–121.
8. Shaw, C., & McKay, H. D. (1969). *Juvenile delinquency and urban areas.* Chicago: University of Chicago Press; Shaw, C., & McKay, H. D. (1972). *Juvenile delinquency and urban areas* (Rev. ed.). Chicago: University of Chicago Press.
9. Shaw, C. (1930). *The Jackroller.* Chicago: University of Chicago Press; Shaw, C. (1931). *The natural history of a delinquent career.* Chicago: University of Chicago Press; Shaw, C. (1938). *Brothers in crime.* Chicago: University of Chicago Press.
10. Shaw, C. (1938). *Brothers in crime.* Chicago: University of Chicago Press, pp. 354–355.
11. Bursik, R. J. (1986). Ecological stability and the dynamics of delinquency. In A. J. Reiss & M. H. Tonry (Eds.), *Crime and community* (pp. 35–66). Chicago: University of Chicago Press; Bursik, R. J. (1988). Social disorganization and theories of crime and delinquency: Problems and prospects. *Criminology, 26,* 519–551; Heitgard, J. L., & Bursik, R. J. (1987). Extracommunity dynamics and the ecology of delinquency. *American Journal of Sociology, 92,* 775–787; Laub, J. (1983). Urbanism, race, and crime. *Journal of Research in Crime and Delinquency, 20,* 283–298; Sampson, R. (1985). Structural sources of variation in race-age-specific rate of offending across major U.S. cities. *Criminology, 23,* 647–673; Sampson, R. (2002). Transcending tradition: New directions in community research, Chicago style—The American Society of Criminology 2001 Sutherland Address. *Criminology, 40,* 213–230; Sampson, R., Morenoff, J. D., & Gannon-Rowley, T. (2002). Assessing 'neighborhood effects': Social processes and new directions in research. *Annual Review of Sociology, 28,* 443–478; Taylor, R., & Covington, J. (1988). Neighborhood changes in ecology and violence. *Criminology, 26,* 553–589; Wikstrom, P. O., & Loeber, R. (2000). Do disadvantaged neighborhoods cause well-adjusted children to become adolescent delinquents? *Criminology, 38,* 1109–1142.
12. Sampson, R., & Groves, W. B. (1989). Community structure and crime: Testing social disorganization theory. *American Journal of Sociology, 94,* 774–802.
13. Miller, W. B. (1962). The impact of a 'total-community' delinquency control project. *Social Problems, 10,* 168–191.
14. For a review, see Lundman, R. (1993). *Prevention and control of juvenile delinquency* (2nd ed.). New York: Oxford University Press. See also the review by Vold, G. B., Bernard, T. J., & Snipes, J. B. (2002). *Theoretical criminology* (5th ed.). Oxford, UK: Oxford University Press, pp. 125–126.
15. Schmalleger, F. (2006). *Criminology today* (4th ed.). Upper Saddle River, NJ: Prentice Hall; Vold, G. B., Bernard, T. J., & Snipes, J. B. (2002). *Theoretical criminology* (5th ed.). Oxford, UK: Oxford University Press, pp. 165–169.
16. Ferracuti, F., & Wolfgang, M. (1967). *The subculture of violence: Toward an integrated theory of criminology.* London: Tavistock.
17. As quoted in Schmalleger, F. (2006). *Criminology today* (4th ed.). Upper Saddle River, NJ: Prentice Hall, pp. 230–231.
18. Miller, W. B. (1958). Lower class culture as a generating milieu of gang delinquency. *Journal of Social Issues, 14,* 5–19.
19. Anderson, E. (1999). *Code of the streets.* New York: W. W. Norton.

CHAPTER 9 NOTES

1. Free, M. (1991). Clarifying the relationship between the broken home and juvenile delinquency: A critique of the current literature. *Deviant Behavior: An Interdisciplinary Journal, 12,* 109–167; Rankin, J. (1983). The family context of delinquency. *Social Problems, 30,* 446–497; Thornberry, T. P., Smith, C. A., Rivera, C., Huizinga, D., & Stouthamer-Loeber, M. (1999). *Family disruption and delinquency* (Juvenile Justice Bulletin). Washington, DC: Office of Juvenile Justice and Delinquency Prevention.
2. Cernkovich, S., & Giordana, P. (1987). Family relationships and delinquency. *Criminology, 25,* 295–321; Wells, L. E., & Rankin, J. H. (1988). Direct parental controls and delinquency. *Criminology, 26,* 263–285.
3. Brezina, T. (1998). Adolescent maltreatment and delinquency. *Journal of Research in Crime and*

Delinquency, 35, 71–98; Smith, C., & Thornberry, T. P. (1995). The relationship between childhood maltreatment and adolescent involvement in delinquency. *Criminology, 33,* 451–476; Widom, C. S. (1989). Child abuse, neglect, and violent criminal behavior. *Criminology, 27,* 251–271; Widom, C. S., & Ames, M. A. (1994). Criminal consequences of childhood sexual victimization. *Child Abuse and Neglect, 18,* 303–318.

4. Harlow, C. W. (1994). *Comparing federal and state prison inmates, 1991.* Washington, DC: Department of Justice; Kaufman, P., Klein, S., & Frase, M. (1999). *Dropout rates in the United States: 1997.* Washington, DC: U.S. Department of Education; Lotz, R., & Lee, L. (1999). Sociability, school experience, and delinquency. *Youth & Society, 31,* 199–223; Reed, M. D., & Rose, D. R. (1998). Doing what Simple Simon says? *Criminal Justice and Behavior, 25,* 383–393; Warr, M. (1996). Organization and instigation in delinquent groups. *Criminology, 34,* 863–864; Warr, M., & Stafford, M. (1991). The influence of delinquent peers. *Criminology, 29,* 851–866.

5. McKinley, J. (2011). Neo-Nazi father is killed; son, 10, steeped in beliefs, is accused. *New York Times.* Retrieved from http://www.nytimes.com/2011/05/11/us/11nazi.html?pagewanted=all&_r=0.

6. Willon, P. (2013). Abuse led to killing of neo-Nazi father, judge says. *Los Angeles Times.* Retrieved from http://latimesblogs.latimes.com/lanow/2013/01/abuse-led-to-killing-of-neo-nazi-father-judge-says.html.

7. Akers, R. L. (1997). *Criminological theories: Introduction and evaluation* (2nd ed.). Los Angeles: Roxbury, pp. 59–60.

8. Shaw, C. R., & McKay, H. D. (1931). *Report on the causes of crime: Social factors in juvenile delinquency, 2* (National Commission on Law Observance and Enforcement, Report No. 13). Washington, DC: U.S. Government Printing Office; Shaw, C. R., & McKay, H. D. (1942). *Juvenile delinquency in urban areas.* Chicago: University of Chicago Press.

9. Tarde, C. (1903). *The laws of imitation.* Gloucester, MA: Henry Holt; see also Tarde, G. (1972). Penal philosophy. In S. F. Sylvester (Ed.), *The heritage of modern criminology.* Cambridge, MA: Schenkman. (Original work published 1912)

10. Vine, M. S. (1960). Gabriel Tarde. In H. Mannheim (Ed.), *Pioneers in criminology* (pp. 228–240). Chicago: Quadrangle Books.

11. Sutherland, E. H. (1939). *Principles of criminology* (3rd ed.). Philadelphia: Lippincott.

12. Sutherland, E. H., & Cressey, D. R. (2006). A theory of differential association. In F. T. Cullen & R. Agnew (Eds.), *Criminological theory: Past to present* (3rd ed.). Los Angeles: Roxbury, pp. 123–124.

13. Pavlov, I. P. (1906). The scientific investigation of the psychical faculties or processes in the higher animals. *Science, 24,* 613–619; see also Pavlov, I. P. (1902). *The work of the digestive glands* (W. H. Gantt, Ed. & Trans.). London: Charles Griffin.

14. See Abraham, A. J., Ducharme, L. J., & Roman, P. M. (2009). Counselor attitudes toward pharmacotherapies for alcohol dependence. *Journal of Studies on Alcohol & Drugs, 70,* 628–635; Krishnan-Sarin, S., O'Malley, S., & Krysta, J. H. (2008). Treatment implications. *Alcohol Research & Health, 31,* 400–407.

15. Sutherland, E. H., & Cressey, D. R. (1974). *Criminology* (9th ed.). Philadelphia: Lippincott.

16. Matsueda, R. L., & Heimer, K. (1987). Race, family structure, and delinquency: A test of differential association and social control theories. *American Sociological Review, 47,* 489–504; Tittle, C. R., Burke, M. J., & Jackson, E. F. (1986). Modeling Sutherland's theory of differential association: Toward an empirical clarification. *Social Forces, 65,* 405–432.

17. Piquero, N. L., Tibbetts, S. G., & Blankenship, M. B. (2005). Examining the role of differential association and techniques of neutralization in explaining corporate crime. *Deviant Behavior, 26,* 159–188. This study also reviews other recent corporate crime studies that test differential association and other theoretical models.

18. Tittle, C. R., Burke, M. J., & Jackson, E. F. (1986). Modeling Sutherland's theory of differential association: Toward an empirical clarification. *Social Forces, 65,* 405–432.

19. Thornberry, T. (1987). Toward an interactional theory of delinquency. *Criminology, 25,* 863–887.

20. Tunnell, K. (1993). Inside the drug trade: Trafficking from the dealer's perspective. *Qualitative Sociology, 16,* 361–381.

21. Smith, D., Visher, C., & Jarjoura, G. R. (1991). Dimensions of delinquency: Exploring the correlates of participation, frequency, and persistence of delinquent behavior. *Journal of Research in Crime and Delinquency, 28,* 6–32.

22. Ploeger, M. (1997). Youth employment and delinquency: Reconsidering a problematic relationship. *Criminology, 35,* 659–675.

23. Adams, R. (1974). The adequacy of differential association theory. *Journal of Research in Crime and Delinquency, 1,* 1–8; Short, J. F. (1960). Differential association as a hypothesis: Problems of empirical testing. *Social Problems, 8,* 14–25.

24. Glaser, D. (1956). Criminality theories and behavioral images. *American Journal of Sociology, 61,* 433–444.

25. Ibid., p. 440.

26. Dawes, K. J. (1973). *Family relationships, reference others, differential identification and their joint impact on juvenile delinquency.* Ann Arbor, MI: University Microfilms.

27. Jeffery, C. R. (1965). Criminal behavior and learning theory. *Journal of Criminal Law, Criminology, and Police Science, 56,* 294–300.

28. Burgess, R., & Akers, R. (1966). A differential association-reinforcement theory of criminal behavior. *Social Problems, 14,* 131.

29. Klotter, J. C. (2004). *Criminal law* (7th ed.). Cincinnati, OH: Anderson, p. 68.

30. Ibid., p. 69.

31. Federal Bureau of Investigation. (2012). *Crime in the United States, 2011.* Washington, DC: U.S. Department of Justice, n.p.

32. Ibid., n.p.

33. Klotter, J. C. (2004). *Criminal law* (7th ed.). Cincinnati, OH: Anderson, p. 580.

34. McGee, K. P. (1995). Comment: The absence of malice? In re Christian S., the second wind of the imperfect self-defense doctrine. *Golden Gate University Law Review, 25,* 297–330.

35. World Health Organization. (2002). *World report on violence and health.* Geneva, Switzerland: Author.

36. Van Dijk, J. (2008). *The world of crime: Breaking the silence on problems of security, justice, and development across the world.* Thousand Oaks, CA: Sage.

37. Ibid.

38. Skinner, B. F. (1953). *Science and human behavior.* New York: Macmillan.

39. Van Voorhis, P., Braswell, M., & Lester, D. (2000). *Correctional counseling* (4th ed.). Cincinnati, OH: Anderson.

40. Akers, R. L. (1977). *Deviant behavior: A social learning approach* (2nd ed.). Belmont, CA: Wadsworth, p. 57.

41. Tarde, G. (1972). Penal philosophy. In S. F. Sylvester (Ed.), *The heritage of modern criminology.* Cambridge, MA: Schenkman. (Original work published 1912)

42. See Bandura, A. (1969). *Principles of behavior modification.* New York: Holt, Rinehart, & Winston; Bandura, A. (1973). *Aggression: A social learning analysis.* Englewood Cliffs, NJ: Prentice Hall; Bandura, A. (1977). *Social learning theory.* Englewood Cliffs, NJ: Prentice Hall.

43. Adams, R. (1973). Differential association and learning principles revisited. *Social Problems, 20,* 458–470.

44. Warr, M. (1991). Parents, peers, and delinquency. *Social Forces, 72,* 247–264; Warr, M., & Stafford, M. (1991). The influence of delinquent peers: What they think or what they do? *Criminology, 29,* 851–866.

45. See Akers, R., & Sellers, C. (2004). *Criminological theories* (4th ed.). Los Angeles: Roxbury, pp. 98–101.

46. See studies such as Akers, R., & La Greca, A. J. (1991). Alcohol use among the elderly: Social learning, community context, and life events. In D. J. Pittman & H. Raskin White (Eds.), *Society, culture, and drinking patterns re-examined* (pp. 242–262). New Brunswick, NJ: Rutgers Center of Alcohol Studies; Akers, R., & Lee, G. (1996). A longitudinal test of social learning theory: Adolescent smoking. *Journal of Drug Issues, 26,* 317–343; Akers, R., & Lee, G. (1999). Age, social learning, and social bonding in adolescent substance abuse. *Deviant Behavior, 19,* 1–25; Hwang, S. (2000). *Substance use in a sample of South Korean adolescents: A test of alternative theories.* Ann Arbor, MI: University Microfilms; Hwang, S., & Akers, R. (2003). Adolescent substance use in South Korea: A cross-cultural test of three theories. In R. Akers & G. F. Jensen (Eds.), *Social learning theory and the explanation of crime: A guide for the new century.* New Brunswick, NJ: Transaction.

47. Akers, R., Krohn, M. D., Lanza-Kaduce, L., & Radosevich, M. (1979). Social learning and deviant behavior: A specific test of a general theory. *American Sociological Review, 44,* 638.

48. Ibid., p. 651.

49. Akers, R., & Lee, G. (1996). A longitudinal test of social learning theory: Adolescent smoking. *Journal of Drug Issues, 26,* 317–343; Krohn, M., Skinner, W., Massey, J., & Akers, R. (1985). Social learning theory and adolescent cigarette smoking: A longitudinal study. *Social Problems, 32,* 455–471; Lawrence, R. (1991). School performance, peers and delinquency: Implications for juvenile justice. *Juvenile and Family Court Journal, 42,* 59–69; Winfree, L. T., Sellers, C., & Clason, D. (1993). Social learning and adolescent deviance abstention: Toward understanding the reasons for initiating, quitting, and avoiding drugs. *Journal of Quantitative Criminology, 9,* 101–123.

50. Pratt, T., Cullen, F., Sellers, C., Winfree, T., Madensen, T., Daigle, L., et al. (2010). The empirical status of social learning theory: A meta-analysis. *Justice Quarterly, 27*(6), 765–802.

51. Sykes, G. M., & Matza, D. (1957). Techniques of neutralization: A theory of delinquency. *American Sociological Review, 22,* 664–670.

52. Matza, D. (1964). *Delinquency and drift.* New York: John Wiley.

53. Ibid., p. 28.

54. Sykes, G. M., & Matza, D. (1957). Techniques of neutralization: A theory of delinquency. *American Sociological Review, 22,* 664–670.

55. McCorkle, L., & Korn, R. (1954). Resocialization within walls. *Annals of the American Academy of Political and Social Science, 293,* 88–98.

56. Sykes, G. M., & Matza, D. (1957). Techniques of neutralization: A theory of delinquency. *American Sociological Review, 22,* 669.

57. Piquero, N. L., Tibbetts, S. G., & Blankenship, M. B. (2005). Examining the role of differential association and techniques of neutralization in explaining corporate crime. *Deviant Behavior, 26,* 159–188.

58. Ibid., p. 164.

59. Agnew, R. (1994). The techniques of neutralization and violence. *Criminology, 32,* 563–564.

60. Minor, W. W. (1980). The neutralization of criminal offense. *Criminology, 18,* 116; Minor, W. W. (1984). Neutralization as a hardening process: Considerations in the modeling of change. *Social Forces, 62,* 995–1019. See also Austin, R. L. (1984). Commitment, neutralization, and delinquency. In T. N. Ferdinand

(Ed.), *Juvenile delinquency: Little brother grows up.* Beverly Hills, CA: Sage; Thurman, Q. C. (1984). Deviance and the neutralization of moral commitment: An empirical analysis. *Deviant Behavior, 5,* 291–304.

61. Hirschi, T. (1969). *Causes of delinquency.* Berkeley: University of California Press, p. 207. See also Hamlin, J. (1988). The misplaced concept of rational choice in neutralization theory. *Criminology, 26,* 425–438; Pogrebin, M., Poole, E., & Martinez, A. (1992). Accounts of professional misdeeds: The sexual exploitation of clients by psychotherapists. *Deviant Behavior, 13,* 229–252.

62. Lewis, M., Alessandri, S., and Sullivan, M. (1990). Expectancy, loss of control, and anger in young infants. *Developmental Psychology, 25,* 745–751; Restoin, A., Rodriguez, D., Ulmann, V., & Montagner, H. (1985). New data on the development of communication behavior in the young child with his peers. *Recherches de Psychologie Sociale, 5,* 31–56; Tremblay, R., Japel, C., Perusse, D., McDuff, P., Boivin, M., Zoccolillo, M., et al. (1999). The search for the age of 'onset' of physical aggression: Rousseau and Bandura revisited. *Criminal Behaviour and Mental Health, 9,* 8–23.

63. Tremblay, R., & LeMarquand, D. (2001). Individual risk and protective factors. In R. Loeber & D. Farrington (Eds.), *Child delinquents: Development, intervention, and service needs* (pp. 137–164). London: Sage.

64. For reviews of supporting studies, see Lewis, M. (1992). *Shame: The exposed self.* New York: Macmillan; Tangney, J. P., & Fischer, K. W. (Eds.). (1995). *Self-conscious emotions: The psychology of shame, guilt, embarrassment, and pride.* New York: Guilford Press.

65. Walsh, A., & Ellis, L. (1999). Political ideology and American criminologists' explanations for criminal behavior. *The Criminologist, 24,* 1, 14.

66. Hobbes, T. (1904). *Leviathan.* Cambridge: Cambridge University Press. (Original work published 1651)

67. Durkheim, E. (1951). *Suicide.* New York: Free Press. (Original work published 1897); Durkheim, E. (1965). *The division of labor in society.* New York: Free Press. (Original work published 1893)

68. Durkheim, E. (1951). *Suicide.* New York: Free Press. (Original work published 1897), pp. 246–247. Also, much of this discussion is adapted from Paternoster, R., & Bachman, R. (Eds.). (2001). *Explaining criminals and crime.* Los Angeles, CA: Roxbury.

69. Durkheim, E. (1951). *Suicide.* New York: Free Press. (Original work published 1897), p. 254.

70. A good discussion of Durkheim's concepts, particularly the collective conscience, can be found in Vold, G. B., Bernard, T. J., & Snipes, J. B. (1998). *Theoretical criminology* (4th ed.). New York: Oxford University Press, pp. 124–139.

71. Freud, S. (1959). The ego and the id. In J. Strachey (Ed.), *The complete psychological works of Sigmund Freud* (Vol. 19). London: Hogarth Press. (Original work published 1923)

72. Reiss, A. (1951). Delinquency as the failure of personal and social controls. *American Sociological Review, 16,* 196–207.

73. For a comprehensive review of studies of low self-control prior to year 2000, see Pratt, T., & Cullen, F. (2000). The empirical status of Gottfredson and Hirschi's general theory of crime: A meta-analysis. *Criminology, 38,* 931–964.

74. Vold, G. B., Bernard, T. J., & Snipes, J. B. (1998). *Theoretical criminology* (4th ed.). New York: Oxford University Press, pp. 202–203.

75. Toby, J. (1957). Social disorganization and stake in conformity: Complementary factors in the predatory behavior of hoodlums. *Journal of Criminal Law, Criminology, and Police Science, 48,* 12–17.

76. Hirschi, T. (1969). *Causes of delinquency.* Berkeley: University of California Press; Sampson, R., & Laub, J. (1993). *Crime in the making: Pathways and turning points in life.* Cambridge, MA: Harvard University Press.

77. Nye, F. I. (1958). *Family relationships and delinquent behavior.* New York: Wiley.

78. Seydlitz, R. (1993). Complexity in the relationships among direct and indirect parental controls and delinquency. *Youth and Society, 24,* 243–275.

79. Tittle, C. (1995). *Control balance: Toward a general theory of deviance.* Boulder, CO: Westview.

80. Reckless, W. (1967). *The crime problem* (4th ed.). New York: Appleton-Century-Crofts.

81. Ibid, p. 479.

82. Dodder, R. A., & Long, J. R. (1980). Containment theory reevaluated: An empirical explication. *Criminal Justice Review, 5,* 74–84; Lawrence, R. (1985). School performance, containment theory, and delinquent behavior. *Youth and Society, 7,* 69–95.

83. Thompson, W. E., & Dodder, R. A. (1986). Containment theory and juvenile delinquency: A reevaluation through factor analysis. *Adolescence, 21,* 365–376.

84. Akers, R. L. (2000). *Criminological theories: Introduction, evaluation, and application* (3rd ed.). Los Angeles: Roxbury, pp. 103–104.

85. Matza, D. (1964). *Delinquency and drift.* New York: John Wiley.

86. *OJJDP Statistical Briefing Book.* Arrest data for 1980–1997 from unpublished data from the Federal Bureau of Investigation, and for 1998, 1999, and 2000 from *Crime in the United States* reports. Washington, DC: U.S. Government Printing Office, 1999, 2000, and 2001, respectively.

87. "Age–arrest rate curve" is loosely based on data provided by Federal Bureau of Investigation. (1997). *Crime in the United States, 1996.* Washington, DC: U.S. Government Printing Office.

88. Vold, G. B., Bernard, T. J., & Snipes, J. B. (1998). *Theoretical criminology* (4th ed.). New York: Oxford University Press, pp. 205–207.

89. Hirschi, T. (1969). *Causes of delinquency*. Berkeley: University of California Press.

90. Ibid, p. 31, in which Hirschi cites Durkheim.

91. Ibid, p. 18.

92. Ibid, p. 22.

93. For a review, see Akers, R. L. (2000). *Criminological theories: Introduction, evaluation, and application* (3rd ed.). Los Angeles: Roxbury, pp. 105–110.

94. Ibid.

95. Elliott, D., Huizinga, D., & Ageton, S. (1985). *Explaining delinquency and drug use*. Beverly Hills, CA: Sage.

96. Walsh, A., & Ellis, L. (1999). Political ideology and American criminologists' explanations for criminal behavior. *The Criminologist, 24*, 1, 14.

97. Eisner, M. (2002). Crime, problem drinking, and drug use: Patterns of problem behavior in cross-national perspective. *Annals of the American Academy of Political and Social Science, 580*, 201–225; Vazsonyi, A., & Killias, M. (2001). Immigration and crime among youth in Switzerland. *Criminal Justice and Behavior, 28*, 329–366; Wong, D. (2001). Pathways to delinquency in Hong Kong and Guangzhou, South China. *International Journal of Adolescence and Youth, 10*, 91–115.

98. Tittle, C. (1995). *Control balance: Toward a general theory of deviance*. Boulder, CO: Westview.

99. Hickman, M., & Piquero, A. (2001). Exploring the relationships between gender, control balance, and deviance. *Deviant Behavior, 22*, 323–351; Piquero, A., & Hickman, M. (1999). An empirical test of Tittle's control balance theory. *Criminology, 37*, 319–342.

100. Hickman, M., & Piquero, A. (2001). Exploring the relationships between gender, control balance, and deviance. *Deviant Behavior, 22*, 323–351.

101. Hagan, J. (1989). *Structural criminology*. Newark, NJ: Rutgers University Press; Hagan, J., Gillis, A., & Simpson, J. (1985). The class structure of gender and delinquency: Toward a power-control theory of common delinquent behavior. *American Journal of Sociology, 90*, 1151–1178; Hagan, J., Gillis, A., & Simpson, J. (1990). Clarifying and extending power-control theory. *American Journal of Sociology, 95*, 1024–1037; Hagan, J., Simpson, J., & Gillis, A. (1987). Class in the household: A power-control theory of gender and delinquency. *American Journal of Sociology, 92*, 788–816.

102. Hagan, J., Simpson, J., & Gillis, A. (1987). Class in the household: A power-control theory of gender and delinquency. *American Journal of Sociology, 92*, 788–816; McCarthy, B., & Hagan, J. (1987). Gender, delinquency, and the Great Depression: A test of power-control theory. *Canadian Review of Sociology and Anthropology, 24*, 153–177; Morash, M., &

Chesney-Lind, M. (1991). A reformulation and partial test of the power-control theory of delinquency. *Justice Quarterly, 8*, 347–377; Singer, S., & Levine, M. (1988). Power-control theory, gender, and delinquency: A partial replication with additional evidence on the effects of peers. *Criminology, 26*, 627–647.

103. McCarthy, B., Hagan, J., & Woodward, T. (1999). In the company of women: Structure and agency in a revised power-control theory of gender and delinquency. *Criminology, 37*, 761–788.

104. Blackwell, B. S. (2000). Perceived sanction threats, gender, and crime: A test and elaboration of power-control theory. *Criminology, 38*, 439–488.

105. Ibid.; Bates, K., & Bader, C. (2003). Family structure, power-control theory, and deviance: Extending power-control theory to include alternate family forms. *Western Criminology Review, 4*, 170–190.

106. Gottfredson, M., & Hirschi, T. (1990). *A general theory of crime*. Palo Alto, CA: Stanford University Press.

107. For an excellent review of studies regarding low self-control theory, see Pratt, T., & Cullen, F. (2000). The empirical status of Gottfredson and Hirschi's general theory of crime: A meta-analysis. *Criminology, 38*, 931–964. For critiques of this theory, see Akers, R. (1991). Self-control as a general theory of crime. *Journal of Quantitative Criminology, 7*, 201–211. For a study that demonstrates the high popularity of the theory, see Walsh, A., & Ellis, L. (1999). Political ideology and American criminologists' explanations for criminal behavior. *The Criminologist, 24*, 1, 14.

108. Hay, C. (2001). Parenting, self-control, and delinquency: A test of self-control theory. *Criminology, 39*, 707–736; Hayslett-McCall, K., & Bernard, T. (2002). Attachment, masculinity, and self-control: A theory of male crime rates. *Theoretical Criminology, 6*, 15–33.

109. Piquero, A., & Tibbetts, S. (1996). Specifying the direct and indirect effects of low self-control and situational factors in offenders' decision making: Toward a more complete model of rational offending. *Justice Quarterly, 13*, 481–510.

110. Raine, A. (1993). *The psychopathology of crime*. San Diego, CA: Academic Press.

111. Walsh, A. (2002). *Biosocial criminology: Introduction and integration*. Cincinnati, OH: Anderson.

112. Fiorillo, C., Tobler, P., & Schultz, W. (2003). Discrete coding of reward probability and uncertainty by dopamine neurons. *Science, 299*, 1898–1902.

113. Grasmick, H., & Bursik, R. (1990). Conscience, significant others, and rational choice: Extending the deterrence model. *Law and Society Review, 24*, 837–861; Tibbetts, S. (1997). Shame and rational choice in offending decisions. *Criminal Justice and Behavior, 24*, 234–255.

114. Tibbetts, S., & Herz, D. (1996). Gender differences in factors of social control and rational choice. *Deviant Behavior, 17*, 183–208.

CHAPTER 10 NOTES

1. Barak, G. (2003). Revisionist history, visionary criminology, and needs-based justice. *Contemporary Justice Review, 63,* 217–225.
2. Ibid., pp. 218–219. See also Platt, T. (1974, Spring–Summer). Prospects for a radical criminology in the United States. *Crime and Social Justice, 1,* 2–6; Schwendinger, H., & Schwendinger, J. (1970). Defenders of order or guardians of human rights. *Issues in Criminology, 5,* 123–157.
3. Barak, G. (2003). Revisionist history, visionary criminology, and needs-based justice. *Contemporary Justice Review, 63,* 219.
4. Ibid.
5. Maxim, P. S., & Whitehead, P. C. (1998). *Explaining crime* (4th ed.). Boston: Butterworth-Heinemann, p. 347.
6. Greenpeace International. (2009). *Where does e-waste end up?* Retrieved from http://www.greenpeace.org/international/en/campaigns/toxics/electronics/the-e-waste-problem/where-does-e-waste-end-up/.
7. Weil, N. (2005). *Study: E-waste dumping victimizes developing nations.* Retrieved from http://www.infoworld.com/t/applications/study-e-waste-dumping-victimizes-developing-nations-867.
8. INTERPOL. (2009). *Electronic waste and organized crime: Assessing the links. Phase II report for the INTERPOL Pollution Crime Working Group,* n.p. Retrieved from http://www.google.com/url?sa=t&rct=j&q=&esrc=s&source=web&cd=2&ved=0CDQQFjAB&url=http%3A%2F%2Fwww.interpol.int%2Fcontent%2Fdownload%2F5367%2F45070%2Fversion%2F1%2Ffile%2FWastereport.pdf&ei=_83HUM_oAuqSiQLM8YDAAw&usg=AFQjCNHe6LyRv3DTXs7dBSTV_WWkASKk8Q.
9. Akers, R. L. (1973). *Deviant behavior: A social learning approach.* Belmont, CA: Wadsworth, pp. 21–22; see also Becker, H. S. (Ed.). (1964). *The other side.* New York: Free Press.
10. Cooley, C. H. (1909). *Social organization.* New York: Scribner's; Cooley, C. H. (1922). *Human nature and social order* (Rev. ed.). New York: Scribner's.
11. Cooley, C. H. (1909). *Social organization.* New York: Scribner's, p. 23.
12. Reynolds, L. T. (1994). The early interactionists: Cooley and Thomas. In N. J. Herman & L. T. Reynolds (Eds.), *Symbolic interaction: An introduction to social psychology* (pp. 30–37). New York: General Hall.
13. Ibid., p. 36.
14. Thomas, W. I., & Thomas, D. S. (1928). *The child in America.* New York: Knopf.
15. Thomas, W. I. (1923). *The unadjusted girl.* New York: Harper & Row.
16. Meltzer, B. N. (1994). Mead's social psychology. In N. J. Herman & L. T. Reynolds (Eds.), *Symbolic interaction: An introduction to social psychology* (pp. 38–54). New York: General Hall.
17. Blumer, H. (1968). *Symbolic interactionism: Perspective and method.* Berkeley: University of California Press, pp. 65–66.
18. Akers, R. L. (1997). *Criminological theories: Introduction and evaluation* (2nd ed.). Los Angeles: Roxbury, p. 101.
19. Goffman E. (1963). *Stigma: Notes on the management of spoiled identity.* Englewood Cliffs, NJ: Prentice Hall, p. 3.
20. Tannenbaum, F. (1938). *Crime and the community.* Boston: Ginn, pp. 17–18.
21. Ibid., pp. 19–20.
22. Lemert, E. M. (1951). *Social pathology: A systematic approach to the theory of sociopathic behavior.* New York: McGraw-Hill, p. 75.
23. Lemert, E. M. (1972). *Human deviance, social problems, and social control* (2nd ed.). Englewood Cliffs, NJ: Prentice Hall, p. 63.
24. Ibid., p. 48; see also Lemert, E. M. (1948). Some aspects of a general theory of sociopathic behavior. *Proceedings of Pacific Sociological Society, 16,* 23–29.
25. Lemert, E. M. (1951). *Social pathology: A systematic approach to the theory of sociopathic behavior.* New York: McGraw-Hill, p. 77.
26. Becker, H. S. (1963). *Outsiders: Studies in the sociology of deviance.* New York: Free Press, p. 15.
27. Ibid., p. 9.
28. Ibid., pp. 19–21. See also Arrigo, B. A. (2000). Social justice and critical criminology: On integrating knowledge. *Contemporary Justice Review, 3,* 7–37.
29. Schur, E. M. (1971). *Labeling deviant behavior: Its sociological implications.* New York: Harper & Row.
30. Ibid., p. 17.
31. Ibid., p. 24.
32. Schur, E. M. (1973). *Radical nonintervention: Rethinking the delinquency problem.* Englewood Cliffs, NJ: Prentice Hall, p. 120.
33. Piliavin, I., & Briar, S. (1964). Police encounters with juveniles. *American Journal of Sociology, 70,* 206–214.
34. Schur, E. M. (1973). *Radical nonintervention: Rethinking the delinquency problem.* Englewood Cliffs, NJ: Prentice Hall, pp. 120–121.
35. Ibid., p. 121.
36. Ibid., p. 122.
37. Cicourel, A. V. (1968). *The social organization of juvenile justice.* New York: Wiley, p. 132.
38. Schur, E. M. (1973). *Radical nonintervention: Rethinking the delinquency problem.* Englewood Cliffs, NJ: Prentice Hall, pp. 123–126.
39. Schrag, C. (1971). *Crime and justice: American style.* Washington, DC: Government Printing Office, pp. 89–91.
40. Wellford, W. (1975). Labelling theory and criminology: An assessment. *Social Problems, 22,* 333.
41. Broder, J. M., & Madigan, N. (2005, June 14). Michael Jackson cleared after 14-week child molesting trial. *New York Times.* Retrieved from http://

www.nytimes.com/2005/06/14/national/14jackson
.html?pagewanted=all&_r=0.

42. Horwitz, A., & Wasserman, M. (1979). The effect of social control on delinquent behavior: A longitudinal test. *Sociological Focus, 12,* 53–70; Shannon, L. W. (1988). *Criminal career continuity: Its social context.* New York: Human Sciences Press; Smith, D. A., & Paternoster, R. (1990). Formal processing and future delinquency: Deviance amplification as selection artifact. *Law & Society Review, 24,* 1109–1131; Wooldredge, J. (1988). Differentiating the effects of juvenile court sentences on eliminating recidivism. *Journal of Research in Crime and Delinquency, 25,* 264–300.

43. Matsueda, R. L. (1992). Reflected appraisals, parental labeling, and delinquency: Specifying a symbolic interactionist theory. *American Journal of Sociology, 97,* 1577–1611.

44. Adams, M. S., & Evans, D. T. (1996). Teacher disapproval, delinquent peers, and self-reported delinquency: A longitudinal test of labeling theory. *The Urban Review, 28,* 199–211.

45. Adams, M. S., Johnson, J. D., & Evans, D. T. (1998). Racial differences in informal labeling effects. *Deviant Behavior, 19,* 157–171; Albonetti, C. A., & Hepburn, J. R. (1996). Prosecutorial discretion to defer criminalization: The effects of defendant's ascribed and achieved status characteristics. *Journal of Quantitative Criminology, 12,* 63–81.

46. Rosenbaum, J. L., & Prinsky, L. (1991). The presumption of influence: Recent responses to popular music subcultures. *Crime and Delinquency, 37,* 528–535.

47. Kelley, T. M. (1983). Status offenders can be different: A comparative study of delinquent careers. *Crime and Delinquency, 29,* 365–380; Rausch, S. (1983). Court processing versus diversion of status offenders: A test of deterrence and labeling theories. *Journal of Research in Crime and Delinquency, 20,* 39–54.

48. Schwartz, R. D., & Skolnick, J. H. (1962). Two studies of legal stigma. *Social Problems, 10,* 133–142.

49. Ibid., p. 136.

50. Rosenhan, D. L. (1973). On being sane in insane places. *Science, 179,* 250–258.

51. Tittle, C. R. (1976). Labelling and crime: An empirical evaluation. In W. R. Gove (Ed.), *The labelling of deviance: Evaluating a perspective* (p. 158). New York: John Wiley.

52. Ibid.

53. Smith, D. A., & Paternoster, R. (1990). Formal processing and future delinquency: Deviance amplification as selection artifact. *Law & Society Review, 24,* 1129.

54. Gibbs, J. P. (1970). Conceptions of deviant behavior: The old and the new. In H. L. Voss (Ed.), *Society, delinquency, and delinquent behavior* (p. 217). Boston: Little, Brown.

55. Rogers, J. W., & Buffalo, M. D. (1975). Fighting back: Nine modes of adaptation to a deviant label. *Social Problems, 22,* 101–118.

56. Hagan, J. (1973). Labelling and deviance: A case study in the 'sociology of the interesting.' *Social Problems, 20,* 456.

57. Martin, R., Mutchnick, R. J., & Austin, W. T. (1990). *Criminological thought: Pioneers past and present.* New York: Macmillan, p. 361.

58. Goode, E. (1975). On behalf of labeling theory. *Social Problems, 22,* 581.

59. Wellford, C. (1975). Labelling theory and criminology: An assessment. *Social Problems, 22,* 332–345. See also Goode, E. (1975). On behalf of labeling theory. *Social Problems, 22,* 570–583; Manning, P. K. (1975). Deviance and dogma: Some comments on the labeling perspective. *British Journal of Criminology, 15,* 1–20; Meade, A. C. (1974). The labeling approach to delinquency: State of the theory as a function of method. *Social Forces, 53,* 83–91.

60. Wellford, C. F., & Triplett, R. (1993). The future of labeling theory. In F. Adler & W. Laufer (Eds.), *New directions in criminological theory* (p. 22). New Brunswick, NJ: Transaction. See also Wellford, C. F. (1997). Controlling crime and achieving justice: The American Society of Criminology 1996 Presidential Address. *Criminology, 35,* 1–11.

61. Williams, F. P., & McShane, M. D. (1999). *Criminological theory* (3rd ed.). Upper Saddle River, NJ: Prentice Hall, p. 148.

62. See Braithwaite, J. (1989). *Crime, shame and reintegration.* Cambridge, UK: Cambridge University Press; Grasmick, H. G., Bursik, R. J., & Arneklev, B. J. (1993). Reduction in drunk driving as a response to increased threats of shame, embarrassment, and legal sanctions. *Criminology, 31,* 41–67; Grasmick, H. G., Bursik, R. J., & Kinsey, K. A. (1991). Shame and embarrassment as deterrents to noncompliance with the law: The case of an antilittering campaign. *Environment and Behavior, 23,* 233–251.

63. Karp, D. R. (2000). The new debate about shame in criminal justice: An interactionist account. *Justice System Journal, 21,* 301–322.

64. Williams, F. P., & McShane, M. D. (1999). *Criminological theory* (3rd ed.). Upper Saddle River, NJ: Prentice Hall, p. 148.

65. Van de Mieroop, M. (2005). *King Hammurabi of Babylon: A biography.* Malden, MA: Blackwell.

66. Federal Bureau of Investigation. (2012). *Crime in the United States, 2011.* Washington, DC: U.S. Department of Justice, n.p. Retrieved from http://www.fbi.gov/about-us/cjis/ucr/crime-in-the-u.s/2011/crime-in-the-u.s.-2011/property-crime/larceny-theft.

67. Ibid., n.p.

68. Bureau of Justice Statistics. (n.d.). *Bureau of Justice Statistics (BJS): Property crime.* Retrieved from http://bjs.ojp.usdoj.gov/index.cfm?ty=tp&tid=32.

69. Lynch, M. J., & Groves, W. B. (1989). *A primer in radical criminology* (2nd ed). New York: Harrow & Heston, pp. 19–20.

70. Ibid., p. 20.

71. Dahrendorf, R. (1959). *Class and class conflict in industrial society*. Stanford, CA: Stanford University Press.

72. Colvin, M., & Pauly, J. (1983). A critique of criminology: Toward an integrated structural-Marxist theory of delinquency production. *American Journal of Sociology, 89*, 513–551.

73. Ibid., p. 521.

74. Ibid.

75. Vold, G. B. (1958). *Theoretical criminology*. New York: Oxford University Press.

76. Van Dijk, J. (2008). *The world of crime: The silence on problems of security, justice and development across the world*. Thousand Oaks, CA: Sage.

77. Vold, G. B., Bernard, T. J., & Snipes, J. B. (1998). *Theoretical criminology* (4th ed.). New York: Oxford University Press, pp. 4–7; see also Pelfrey, W. V. (1980). *The evolution of criminology*. Cincinnati, OH: Anderson.

78. Pelfrey, W. V. (1980). *The evolution of criminology*. Cincinnati, OH: Anderson, p. 62.

79. Vold, G. B. (1958). *Theoretical criminology*. New York: Oxford University Press, p. vii.

80. Vold, G. B., Bernard, T. J., & Snipes, J. B. (1998). *Theoretical criminology* (4th ed.). New York: Oxford University Press, p. 236.

81. Ibid., p. 237.

82. Ibid.

83. Brown, S. E., Esbensen, F., & Geis, G. (1991). *Criminology: Explaining crime and its context*. Cincinnati, OH: Anderson, p. 401.

84. Pelfrey, W. V. (1980). *The evolution of criminology*. Cincinnati, OH: Anderson, p. 64.

85. Turk, A. (1969). *Criminality and legal order*. Chicago: Rand McNally, p. 10.

86. Pelfrey, W. V. (1980). *The evolution of criminology*. Cincinnati, OH: Anderson, pp. 64–65.

87. Turk, A. (1969). *Criminality and legal order*. Chicago: Rand McNally, p. 18.

88. Ibid., pp. 36–38.

89. Vold, G. B., Bernard, T. J., & Snipes, J. B. (1998). *Theoretical criminology* (4th ed.). New York: Oxford University Press, pp. 240–241.

90. Turk, A. T. (1979). Analyzing official deviance for nonpartisan conflict analyses in criminology. *Criminology, 16*, 459.

91. Quinney, R. (1977). *Class, state, and crime*. New York: David McKay, p. 165.

92. Turk, A. T. (1979). Analyzing official deviance for nonpartisan conflict analyses in criminology. *Criminology, 16*, 464.

93. Quinney, R. (1970). *The social reality of crime*. Boston: Little, Brown, pp. 15–16.

94. Ibid., pp. 16–18.

95. Ibid., pp. 18–20.

96. Ibid., pp. 20–22.

97. Ibid., pp. 22–23.

98. Ibid., p. 23.

99. Greenberg, D. F. (Ed.). (1981). *Crime and capitalism: Readings in Marxist criminology*. Palo Alto, CA: Mayfield; Williams, F. P., & McShane, M. D. (1999). *Criminological theory* (3rd ed.). Upper Saddle River, NJ: Prentice Hall, p. 168.

100. Marx, K. (2006). *The communist manifesto*. New York: Penguin Books.

101. Marx, K. (1962). *Selected works [of] Karl Marx and Frederick Engels*. Moscow: Foreign Languages Publishing House, p. 22.

102. Williams, F. P., & McShane, M. D. (1999). *Criminological theory* (3rd ed.). Upper Saddle River, NJ: Prentice Hall, pp. 169–170.

103. Chambliss, W., & Seidman, R. (1971). *Law, order, and power*. Reading, MA: Addison-Wesley, p. 502.

104. Ibid., p. 503.

105. Ibid., p. 7.

106. Ibid., p. 113.

107. Colvin, M., & Pauly, J. (1983). A critique of criminology: Toward an integrated structural-Marxist theory of delinquency production. *American Journal of Sociology, 89*, 542.

108. Ibid., pp. 536–537.

109. Ibid., p. 538.

110. Ibid., pp. 539–542.

111. Schwendinger, H., & Schwendinger, J. (1985). *Adolescent subcultures and delinquency*. New York: Praeger.

112. Ibid., p. xiii.

113. Steven Spitzer, S. (1975). Toward a Marxian theory of deviance. *Social Problems, 22*, 641.

114. Ibid., p. 649.

115. Williams, F. P. (1980). Conflict theory and differential processing: An analysis of the research literature. In J. A. Inciardi (Ed.), *Radical criminology: The coming crises*. Beverly Hills, CA: Sage, p. 215.

116. Chambliss, W. (1964). A sociological analysis of the laws of vagrancy. *Social Problems, 12*, 67–77.

117. Becker, H. S. (1963). *Outsiders: Studies in the sociology of deviance*. New York: Free Press.

118. Robinson, A. (1999). Conflicting consensus: Public reaction to a domestic violence pro-arrest policy. *Women and Criminal Justice, 10*, 95–120.

119. Lieber, M. J., & Stairs, J. M. (1999). Race, contexts, and the use of intake diversion. *Journal of Research in Crime and Delinquency, 36*, 56–86.

120. Cureton, S. R. (2001). An empirical test of the social threat phenomenon: Using 1990 census and uniform crime reports. *Journal of Criminal Justice, 29*, 157–166; Mosher, C. (2001). Predicting drug arrest rates: Conflict and social disorganization perspectives. *Crime and Delinquency, 47*, 84–104.

121. Frazier, C. E., Bishop, D. M., & Henretta, J. C. (1992). The social context of race differentials in juvenile justice dispositions. *Sociological Quarterly, 33*, 447–458.

122. Holmes, M. D., Hosch, H. M., Daudistel, H. C., Perez, D., & Graves, J. (1996). Ethnicity, legal

resources, and felony dispositions in two Southwestern jurisdictions. *Justice Quarterly, 13,* 11–30.

123. Holmes, M. D. (2000). Minority threat and police brutality: Determinants of civil rights criminal complaints in U.S. municipalities. *Criminology, 38,* 343–367.

124. Chamlin, M. B. (1989). Conflict theory and police killings. *Deviant Behavior, 10,* 353–368.

125. Vold, G. B., Bernard, T. J., & Snipes, J. B. (1998). *Theoretical criminology* (4th ed.). New York: Oxford University Press, pp. 256–257.

126. Ibid., p. 256.

127. Federal Bureau of Investigation. (2008). *FBI 100: The Unabomber.* Retrieved from http://www.fbi.gov/news/stories/2008/april/unabomber_042408.

128. See The Unabomber manifesto. (1997). *Washington Post.* Retrieved from http://www.washingtonpost.com/wp-srv/national/longterm/unabomber/manifesto.text.htm.

129. Federal Bureau of Investigation. (2008). *FBI 100: The Unabomber.* Retrieved from http://www.fbi.gov/news/stories/2008/april/unabomber_042408.

130. Lanza-Kanduce, L., & Greenleaf, R. (1994). Police-citizen encounters: Turk on norm resistance. *Justice Quarterly, 11,* 605–624.

131. Vold, G. B., Bernard, T. J., & Snipes, J. B. (1998). *Theoretical criminology* (4th ed.). New York: Oxford University Press, p. 257.

132. Pepinsky, H. E. (1991). Peacemaking in criminology and criminal justice. In H. E. Pepinski & Quinney, R. (Eds.), *Criminology as peacemaking* (pp. 299–327). Bloomington: Indiana University Press.

133. Wheeldon, J. (2009). Finding common ground: Restorative justice and its theoretical construction(s). *Contemporary Justice Review, 12,* 93.

134. Pepinsky, H. E. (1988). Violence as unresponsiveness: Toward a new conception of crime. *Justice Quarterly, 5,* 539–563; Pepinsky, H. E. (1991). *The geometry of violence and democracy.* Bloomington: Indiana University Press; Pepinsky, H. E., & Quinney, R. (Eds.). (1991). *Criminology as peace-making.* Bloomington: University of Indiana Press; Quinney, R. (1988). Crime, suffering, service: Toward a criminology of peacemaking. *Quest, 1,* 66–75; Quinney, R. (1989). The theory and practice of peacemaking in the development of radical criminology. *Critical Criminologist, 1,* 5.

135. Wozniak, J. F. (2002). Toward a theoretical model of peacemaking criminology: An essay in honor of Richard Quinney. *Crime & Delinquency, 48,* 221.

136. Ibid., p. 214.

137. Wozniak, J. F. (2000). The voices of peacemaking criminology: Insights into a perspective with an eye toward teaching. *Contemporary Justice Review, 3,* 273–274.

138. Wozniak, J. F. (2002). Toward a theoretical model of peacemaking criminology: An essay in honor of Richard Quinney. *Crime & Delinquency, 48,* 219–220.

139. Caringella-MacDonald, S., & Humphries, D. (1991). Sexual assault, women, and the community: Organizing to prevent sexual violence. In H. E. Pepinsky & R. Quinney (Eds.), *Criminology as peacemaking* (pp. 98–113). Bloomington: Indiana University Press.

140. Rucker, L. (1991). Peacemaking in prisons: A process. In H. E. Pepinsky & R. Quinney (Eds.), *Criminology as peacemaking* (pp. 172–180). Bloomington: Indiana University Press.

141. Wenzel, M., Okimoto, T. G., Feather, N. T., & Platow, M. J. (2008). Retributive and restorative justice. *Law and Human Behavior, 32,* 375.

142. Bazemore, G., & Umbreit, M. (1999). *Balanced and restorative justice for juveniles: Framework for juvenile justice in the 21st century.* Washington, DC: Office of Juvenile Justice and Delinquency Prevention, p. 11.

143. Wheeldon, J. (2009). Finding common ground: Restorative justice and its theoretical construction(s). *Contemporary Justice Review, 12,* 93.

144. Young, J. (1992). Ten points of realism. In J. Young & R. Matthews (Eds.), *Rethinking criminology: The realist debate* (pp. 25–26). London: Sage.

145. See Dekeseredy, W. S., & Schwartz, M. D. (1991). British and U.S. left realism: A critical comparison. *International Journal of Offender Therapy and Comparative Criminology, 35,* 248–262; Lea, J. (1987). Left realism: A defense. *Contemporary Crises, 11,* 357–370.

146. Matthews, R., & Young, J. (1992). Reflections on realism. In J. Young & R. Matthews (Eds.), *Rethinking criminology: The realist debate* (pp. 19–20). London: Sage.

147. Ibid., pp. 17–19.

148. Schwartz, M., & DeKeseredy, W. (1993). *Contemporary criminology.* Belmont, CA: Wadsworth.

149. Coumarelos, C., & Weatherburn, D. (1995). Targeting intervention strategies to reduce juvenile recidivism. *Australian and New Zealand Journal of Criminology, 28,* 55–72; Levi, K. (1982). Relative redemption: Labeling in juvenile restitution. *Juvenile and Family Court Journal, 33,* 3–13.

150. Patrick, S., & March, R. (2005). Juvenile diversion: Results of a 3-year experimental study. *Criminal Justice Policy Review, 16,* 62.

151. Butts, J. A., & Buck, J. (2000). Teen courts: A focus on research. *Juvenile Justice Bulletin.* Washington, DC: Office of Juvenile Justice and Delinquency Prevention, n.p.

152. Inciardi, J. A., Pottieger, A. E., & Surrat, H. L. (1996). African Americans and the crack-crime connection. In D. D. Chitwood, J. E. Rivers, & J. A. Inciardi (Eds.), *The American pipe dream: Crack, cocaine and the inner city.* Fort Worth, TX: Harcourt Brace; Jensen, E. L., Gerber, J., & Mosher, C. (2004). Social consequences of the War on Drugs: The legacy of failed policy. *Criminal Justice Policy Review, 15,* 100–121.

CHAPTER 11 NOTES

1. Freedman, E. B. (2002). No turning back: The history of feminism and the future of women. New York: Ballantine Books, p. 7.
2. Hennessy-Fiske, M. (2012, October 12). Texas mom gets 99 years for beating, super-gluing girl's hands. Los Angeles Times. Retrieved from http://articles.latimes.com/2012/oct/12/nation/la-na-nn-mother-sentencing-hands-glued-20121012
3. Van Wormer, K. S., & Bartollas, C. (2000). Women and the criminal justice system. Boston: Allyn & Bacon, p. 5. See also Byers, M., & Crocker, D. (2012). Feminist cohorts and waves: Attitudes of junior female academics. Women's Studies International Forum, 35, 1–11.
4. Tong, R. (2009). Feminist thought (3rd ed.). Boulder, CO: Westview Press, pp. 21–22.
5. Lebedun, J. (1974). Harriet Beecher Stowe's interest in Sojourner Truth, black feminist. American Literature, 46, 359–363.
6. Boles, J. K., & Hoeveler, D. L. (2004). Historical dictionary of feminism (2nd ed.). Lanham, MD: Scarecrow Press, pp. 7–9.
7. Tong, R. (2009). Feminist thought (3rd ed.). Boulder, CO: Westview Press, p. 22; see also Hole, J., & Levine, E. (1971). Rebirth of feminism. New York: Quadrangle Books, p. 3.
8. Schnittker, J., Freese, J., & Powell, B. (2003). Who are feminists and what do they believe? The role of generations. American Sociological Review, 68, 607–622; see also Van Wormer, K. S., & Bartollas, C. (2000). Women and the criminal justice system. Boston: Allyn & Bacon.
9. Tong, R. (2009). Feminist thought (3rd ed.). Boulder, CO: Westview Press, pp. 23–24; see also Freedman, E. B. (2002). No turning back: The history of feminism and the future of women. New York: Ballantine Books, pp. 84–87.
10. Freedman, E. B. (2002). No turning back: The history of feminism and the future of women. New York: Ballantine Books, pp. 84–87.
11. Tong, R. (2009). Feminist thought (3rd ed.). Boulder, CO: Westview Press, p. 24.
12. Krolokke, C., & Sorensen, A. S. (2006). Gender communication theories and analyses: From silence to performance. Thousand Oaks, CA: Sage.
13. Byers, M., & Crocker, D. (2012). Feminist cohorts and waves: Attitudes of junior female academics. Women's Studies International Forum, 35, 1–11.
14. Tong, R. (2009). Feminist thought (3rd ed.). Boulder, CO: Westview Press, pp. 284–285.
15. Lorber, J., & Farrell, S. A. (1991). Principles of gender construction. In J. Lorber & S. A. Farrell (Eds.), The social construction of gender (pp. 7–8). Newbury Park, CA: Sage.
16. West, C., & Zimmerman, D. H. (1991). Doing gender. In J. Lorber & S. A. Farrell (Eds.), The social construction of gender (pp. 13–37). Newbury Park, CA: Sage, pp. 24–27.
17. Belknap, J. (2007). The invisible woman: Gender, crime, and justice (3rd ed.). Belmont, CA: Wadsworth, pp. 150–151; Moulds, E. F. (1980). Chivalry and paternalism: Disparities of treatment in the criminal justice system. In S. K. Datesman & F. R. Scarpitti (Eds.), Women, crime, and justice (pp. 277–299). New York: Oxford University Press, p. 279.
18. Boles, J. K., & Hoeveler, D. L. (2004). Historical dictionary of feminism. Lanham, MD: Scarecrow Press, p. 253.
19. Belknap, J. (2007). The invisible woman: Gender, crime, and justice (3rd ed.). Belmont, CA: Wadsworth, p. 10; see also Edwards, A. (1987). Male violence in feminist theory: An analysis of the changing conception of sex/gender violence and male dominance. In J. Hanmer & M. Maynard (Eds.), Women, violence, and social control (pp. 13–29). Atlantic Highlands, NJ: Humanities Press International.
20. Daly, K., & Chesney-Lind, M. (1988). Feminism and criminology. Justice Quarterly, 5, 523.
21. Ibid., pp. 536–537.
22. Boles, J. K., & Hoeveler, D. L. (2004). Historical dictionary of feminism. Lanham, MD: Scarecrow Press, p. 192.
23. Daly, K., & Chesney-Lind, M. (1988). Feminism and criminology. Justice Quarterly, 5, 537.
24. Tong, R. (2009). Feminist thought (3rd ed.). Boulder, CO: Westview Press, p. 34.
25. Ibid., p. 35.
26. Ibid., p. 43.
27. Britton, D. B. (2000). Feminism in criminology: Engendering the law. Annals of the American Academy of Political and Social Science, 571, 57–76.
28. Belknap, J. (2007). The invisible woman: Gender, crime, and justice (3rd ed.). Belmont, CA: Wadsworth, p. 13.
29. Daly, K., & Chesney-Lind, M. (1988). Feminism and criminology. Justice Quarterly, 5, 525.
30. Ibid., p. 526.
31. Boles, J. K., & Hoeveler, D. L. (2004). Historical dictionary of feminism. Lanham, MD: Scarecrow Press, pp. 270–271.
32. Daly, K., & Chesney-Lind, M. (1988). Feminism and criminology. Justice Quarterly, 5, 538.
33. Tong, R. (2009). Feminist thought (3rd ed.). Boulder, CO: Westview Press, pp. 48–51.
34. Ibid., p. 51.
35. Daly, K., & Chesney-Lind, M. (1988). Feminism and criminology. Justice Quarterly, 5, 538.
36. Tong, R. (2009). Feminist thought (3rd ed.). Boulder, CO: Westview Press, pp. 92–93; see also Ferguson, A. (1984). Sex war: The debate between radical and libertarian feminist. Signs: The Journal of Women in Culture and Society, 10, 106–112.
37. Tong, R. (2009). Feminist thought (3rd ed.). Boulder, CO: Westview Press, p. 93.

38. Ibid., p. 96.
39. Boles, J. K., & Hoeveler, D. L. (2004). Historical dictionary of feminism. Lanham, MD: Scarecrow Press, pp. 204–205.
40. Daly, K., & Chesney-Lind, M. (1988). Feminism and criminology. Justice Quarterly, 5, 537.
41. Belknap, J. (2007). The invisible woman: Gender, crime, and justice (3rd ed.). Belmont, CA: Wadsworth, p. 13; see also Hardin, S. (2004). Can men be subjects of feminist thought? In S. N. Hesse-Biber & M. L. Yaiser (Eds.), Feminist perspectives on social research (pp. 39–64). New York: Oxford University Press; Hartmann, H. I. (1987). The family as the locus of gender, class, and political struggle: The example of housework. In S. Harding (Ed.), Feminism and methodology (pp. 109–134). Bloomington, IN: Indiana University Press.
42. Stafford, F. (2008). Exactly how much housework does a husband create? University of Michigan News Service. Retrieved from http://ns.umich.edu/new/releases/6452.
43. Belknap, J. (2007). The invisible woman: Gender, crime, and justice (3rd ed.). Belmont, CA: Wadsworth, p. 538.
44. Tong, R. (2009). Feminist thought (3rd ed.). Boulder, CO: Westview Press, p. 111.
45. Ibid., p. 115.
46. Boles, J. K., & Hoeveler, D. L. (2004). Historical dictionary of feminism. Lanham, MD: Scarecrow Press, pp. 262–263.
47. Tong, R. (2009). Feminist thought (3rd ed.). Boulder, CO: Westview Press; see also Moi, T. (1985). Sexual/textual politics. London: Methuen.
48. Tong, R. (2009). Feminist thought (3rd ed.). Boulder, CO: Westview Press, p. 270.
49. Sands, R. G., & Nuccio, K. (1992). Postmodern feminist theory and social work. Social Work, 37, 492.
50. Ibid., p. 492; see also Haraway, D. (1989). Situated knowledges: The science question in feminism and privilege of partial perspective. Feminist Studies, 14, 575–599.
51. Boles, J. K., & Hoeveler, D. L. (2004). Historical dictionary of feminism. Lanham, MD: Scarecrow Press, p. 109.
52. Tong, R. (2009). Feminist thought (3rd ed.). Boulder, CO: Westview Press, pp. 237–269.
53. Boles, J. K., & Hoeveler, D. L. (2004). Historical dictionary of feminism. Lanham, MD: Scarecrow Press, p. 109.
54. Tong, R. (2009). Feminist thought (3rd ed.). Boulder, CO: Westview Press, p. 215.
55. Pomeroy, S. B. (1975). Goddesses, whores, wives, and slaves. New York: Schocken Books, p. 8.
56. Van Dijk, J. (2008). The world of crime: The silence on problems of security, justice and development across the world. Thousand Oaks, CA: Sage.
57. Kangaspunta, K. (2003). Mapping the inhuman trade: Preliminary findings of the database on trafficking in human beings. Forum on Crime and Society, 3, 81–105.
58. Van Dijk, J. (2008). The world of crime: The silence on problems of security, justice and development across the world. Thousand Oaks, CA: Sage, pp. 170–171.
59. Feinman, C. (1980). Women in the criminal justice system. New York: Praeger.
60. Young, V. D. (1986). Gender expectations and their impact on black female offenders and victims. Justice Quarterly, 3, 305–327.
61. Ibid., p. 310.
62. Ibid., p. 322.
63. Dugger, K. (1991). Social location and gender-role attitudes: A comparison of black and white women. In J. Lorber, & S. A. Farrell (Eds.), The social construction of gender (pp. 38–59). Newbury Park, CA: Sage.
64. Brownmiller, S. (1984). Femininity. New York: Fawcett Columbine.
65. West, C., & Zimmerman, D. H. (1991). Doing gender. In J. Lorber, & S. A. Farrell (Eds.), The social construction of gender (pp. 13–37). Newbury Park, CA: Sage, p. 15.
66. Carlen, P. (1982). Papa's discipline: An analysis of disciplinary modes in the Scottish women's prison. Sociological Review, 30, 97–124; Smith, B. A. (1990). The female prisoner in Ireland, 1855–1878. Federal Probation, 54, 69–81; Welter, B. (1973). The cult of true womanhood: 1820–1860. In J. E. Friedman & W. G. Shade (Eds.), Our American sisters: Women in American life and thought (pp. 96–123). Boston: Allyn & Bacon.
67. Smart, C. (1977). Criminological theory: Its ideology and implications concerning women. British Journal of Sociology, 28, 91–92.
68. Hahn, N. R. (1980). Too dumb to know better: Cacogenic family studies and the criminology of women. Criminology, 18, 3.
69. Lombroso, C. (1898). The female offender. New York: D Appleton.
70. Belknap, J. (2007). The invisible woman: Gender, crime, and justice (3rd ed.). Belmont, CA: Wadsworth, p. 33.
71. Lombroso, C. (1898). The female offender. New York: D Appleton, p. 147.
72. Ibid., p. 216.
73. See Beaman, L. G. (1998). Women's defenses: Contextualizing dilemmas of difference and power. Women and Criminal Justice, 9, 87–115; Harry, B., & Balcer, C. M. (1987). Menstruation and crime: A critical review of the literature from the clinical criminology perspective. Behavioral Sciences and the Law, 5, 307–321; Welch, M. (1997). Regulating the reproduction and morality of women: The social control of body and soul. Women and Criminal Justice, 9, 17–38.
74. Thomas, W. I. (1907). Sex and society. Boston: Little, Brown; see also Van Wormer, K. S., & Bartollas, C.

2000). Women and the criminal justice system. Boston: Allyn & Bacon, p. 27.

75. Bowker, L. H. (1978). Women, crime, and the criminal justice system. Lexington, MA: D.C. Heath, p. 44.

76. Van Wormer, K. S., & Bartollas, C. (2000). Women and the criminal justice system. Boston: Allyn & Bacon, p. 27.

77. Thomas, W. I. (1967). The unadjusted girl. New York: Harper & Row, p. 4.

78. Bowker, L. H. (1978). Women, crime, and the criminal justice system. Lexington, MA: D.C. Heath, p. 45.

79. Thomas, W. I. (1967). The unadjusted girl. New York: Harper & Row, p. 69.

80. Mann, C. R. (1984). Female crime and delinquency. University: The University of Alabama Press, p. 79.

81. Klein, D. (1980). The etiology of female crime: A review of the literature. In S. Datesman & F. R. Scarpitti (Eds.), Women, crime, and justice (pp. 70–105). New York: Oxford University Press, p. 87.

82. Freud, S. (1933). New introductory lectures on psychoanalysis. New York: Norton; see also Van Wormer, K. S., & Bartollas, C. (2000). Women and the criminal justice system. Boston: Allyn & Bacon, p. 28.

83. Klein, D. (1980). The etiology of female crime: A review of the literature. In S. Datesman & F. R. Scarpitti (Eds.), Women, crime, and justice (pp. 70–105). New York: Oxford University Press, Inc., p. 88.

84. Pollak, O. (1950). The criminality of women. Philadelphia: University of Pennsylvania Press, p. 161.

85. Ibid., p. 1.

86. Ibid., p. 5.

87. Bowker, L. H. (1978). Women, crime, and the criminal justice system. Lexington, MA: D.C. Heath, p. 48.

88. Pollak, O. (1950). The criminality of women. Philadelphia: University of Pennsylvania Press, p. 10.

89. Smart, C. (1976). Women, crime and criminology: A feminist critique. London: Routledge & Kegan Paul.

90. Klein, D. (1980). The etiology of female crime: A review of the literature. In S. Datesman & F. R. Scarpitti (Eds.), Women, crime, and justice (pp. 70–105). New York: Oxford University Press.

91. Eichler, M. (1979). The double standard: A feminist critique of feminist social science. New York: St. Martin's Press; Harding, S. (Ed.). (1987). Feminism and methodology. Bloomington: Indiana University Press; Keller, E. F. (1978). Gender and science. Psychoanalysis and Contemporary Thought: A Quarterly of Integrative and Interdisciplinary Studies, 1, 409–433; McHugh, M., Koeske, R., & Frieze, I. (1986). Issues to consider in conducting nonsexist psychological research. American Psychologist, 41, 879–890; Nielsen, J. M. (Ed.). Feminist research methods: Exemplary readings in the social sciences. Boulder, CO: Westview Press; Stanley, L., & Wise, S. (1979). Feminist research, feminist consciousness, and

experiences of sexism. Women's Studies International Quarterly, 2, 359–374; Westkott, M. (1979). Feminist criticism of the social sciences. Harvard Educational Review, 49, 422–430.

92. West, C., & Zimmerman, D. H. (1991). Doing gender. In J. Lorber & S. A. Farrell (Eds.), The social construction of gender (pp. 13–37). Newbury Park, CA: Sage, p. 24.

93. Belknap, J. (2007). The invisible woman: Gender, crime, and justice (3rd ed.). Belmont, CA: Wadsworth.

94. Smart, C. (1977). Criminological theory: Its ideology and implications concerning women. British Journal of Sociology, 28, 185.

95. Naffine, N. (1987). Female crime: The construction of women in criminology. Sydney: Allen & Unwin.

96. Daly, K. (1995). Looking back, looking forward: The promise of feminist transformation. In B. R. Price & N. J. Sokoloff (Eds.), The criminal justice system and women: Offenders, victims, and workers (pp. 443–457). New York: Mcgraw-Hill.

97. West, C., & Zimmerman, D. H. (1991). Doing gender. In J. Lorber & S. A. Farrell (Eds.), The social construction of gender (pp. 13–37). Newbury Park, CA: Sage, pp. 15–16.

98. Edwards, A. R. (1989). Sex/gender, sexism and criminal justice: Some theoretical considerations. International Journal of the Sociology of Law, 17, 165–184.

99. West, C., & Zimmerman, D. H. (1991). Doing gender. In J. Lorber & S. A. Farrell (Eds.), The social construction of gender (pp. 13–37). Newbury Park, CA: Sage, p. 18.

100. Williams, F. P., & McShane, M. D. (1999). Criminological theory (3rd ed.). Upper Saddle River, NJ: Prentice Hall, p. 252.

101. Mann, C. R. (1984). Female crime and delinquency. University: University of Alabama Press, pp. 107–108.

102. Adler, F. (1975). Sisters in crime. Prospects Heights, IL: Waveland Press, p. 30.

103. Ibid., p. 251.

104. Simon, R. (1975). Women and crime. Lexington, MA: D.C. Heath.

105. Belknap, J. (2007). The invisible woman: Gender, crime, and justice (3rd ed.). Belmont, CA: Wadsworth, p. 56.

106. Naffine, N. (1987). Female crime: The construction of women in criminology. Sydney: Allen & Unwin, p. 95.

107. Belknap, J. (2007). The invisible woman: Gender, crime, and justice (3rd ed.). Belmont, CA: Wadsworth, p. 57.

108. See Leonard, E. B. (1982). Women, crime, and society: A critique of criminology theory. New York: Longman; Radosh, P. (1990). Women and crime in the United States: A Marxian explanation.

Sociological Spectrum, 10, 105–131; Steffensmeier, D., & Steffensmeier, R. H. (1980). Trends in female delinquency. Criminology, 18, 62–85.

109. Hagan, J., Gillis, A. R., & Simpson, J. (1985). The class structure of gender and delinquency: Toward a power-control theory of common delinquent behavior. American Journal of Sociology, 90, 1151–1178; Hagan, J., Simpson, J., & Gillis, A. R. (1987). Class in the household: A power-control theory of gender and delinquency. American Journal of Sociology, 92, 788–816.

110. Hagan, J., Gillis, A. R., & Simpson, J. (1985). The class structure of gender and delinquency: Toward a power-control theory of common delinquent behavior. American Journal of Sociology, 90, 1156–1157.

111. Hagan, J. (1991). A power-control theory of gender and delinquency. In R. J. Silverman, J. A. Teevan, & V. Sacco (Eds.), Crime in Canadian society (4th ed.). Toronto: Butterworths, p. 130.

112. See Dornfeld, M., & Kruttschnitt, C. (1992). Do the stereotypes fit? Mapping gender-specific outcomes and risk factors. Criminology, 30, 397–420; Kruttschnitt, C. (1996). Contributions of quantitative methods to the study of gender and crime, or bootstrapping our way into the theoretical thicket. Journal of Quantitative Criminology, 12, 135–161; Morash, M., & Chesney-Lind, M. (1991). A re-formulation and patriarchal test of the power control theory of delinquency. Justice Quarterly, 8, 347–378.

113. Chesney-Lind, M. (1987). Girls' crime and woman's place: Toward a feminist model of female delinquency. Paper presented at the Annual Meeting of the American Society of Criminology, Montreal, Canada.

114. Harding, S. (Ed.). (1987). Feminism and methodology. Bloomington: Indiana University Press.

115. Ibid., pp. 8–9.

116. Campbell, R., & Schram, P. J. (1995). Feminist research methods: A content analysis of psychology and social science textbooks. Psychology of Women Quarterly, 19, 88.

117. Jayaratne, T. E., & Stewart, A. J. (1991). Quantitative and qualitative methods in social sciences: Current feminist issues and practical strategies. In M. M. Fonow & J. A. Cook (Eds.), Beyond methodology: Feminist scholarship as lived research (pp. 85–106). Bloomington: Indiana University Press; Stanley, L., & Wise, S. (1983). Breaking out: Feminist consciousness and feminist research. London: Routledge & Kegan Paul.

118. Denmark, F., Russo, N. F., & Frieze, I. H. (1988). Guidelines for avoiding sexism in psychological research: A report of the Ad Hoc Committee on Nonsexist Research. American Psychologist, 43, 582–585; McHugh, M. C., Koeske, R. D., & Frieze, I. H. (1986). Issues to consider in conducting nonsexist psychological research. American Psychologist, 41, 879–890.

119. MacKinnon, C. A. (1987). Feminism, Marxism, methods and the state: Toward feminist jurisprudence. In S. Harding (Ed), Feminism and methodology (pp. 135–156). Bloomington: Indiana University Press, p. 136.

120. Sherif, C. W. (1987). Bias in psychology. In S. Harding (Ed.), Feminism and methodology (pp. 37–56). Bloomington: Indiana University Press.

121. Ibid., p. 47.

122. Campbell, R., & Schram, P. J. (1995). Feminist research methods: A content analysis of psychology and social science textbooks. Psychology of Women Quarterly, 19, 88.

123. Jayaratne, T. E., & Stewart, A. J. (1991). Quantitative and qualitative methods in social sciences: Current feminist issues and practical strategies. In M. M. Fonow & J. A. Cook (Eds.), Beyond methodology: Feminist scholarship as lived research (pp. 85–106). Bloomington: Indiana University Press.

124. White, J., & Farmer, R. (1992). Research methods: How they shape views of sexual violence. Journal of Social Issues, 48, 179.

125. Burgess-Proctor, A. (2006). Intersections of race, class, gender, and crime: Future directions for feminist criminology. Feminist Criminology, 1, 30.

126. Ibid.; see also Blumstein, A., Cohen, J., Roth, J. A., & Visher, C. (1986). Introduction: Studying criminal careers. In A. Blumstein, J. Cohen, J. A. Roth, & C. Visher (Eds.), Criminal careers and "career criminals" (pp. 12–30). Washington, DC: National Academy Press; Steffensmeier, D., & Allan, E. (1996). Gender and crime: Toward a gendered theory of female offending. Annual Review of Sociology, 22, 459–487.

127. Burgess-Proctor, A. (2006). Intersections of race, class, gender, and crime: Future directions for feminist criminology. Feminist Criminology, 1, 31.

128. Klein, D. (1995). The etiology of female crime: A review of the literature. In B. R. Price & N. J. Sokoloff (Eds.), The criminal justice system and women: Offenders, victims, and workers (2nd ed., pp. 48–52). New York: McGraw-Hill.

129. Belknap, J. (2007). The invisible woman: Gender, crime, and justice (3rd ed.). Belmont, CA: Wadsworth, pp. 36–56.

130. Daly, K., & Chesney-Lind, M. (1988). Feminism and criminology. Justice Quarterly, 5, 504.

131. Ibid., p. 507.

132. Burgess-Proctor, A. (2006). Intersections of race, class, gender, and crime: Future directions for feminist criminology. Feminist Criminology, 1, 27–47.

133. Ibid., p. 43.

134. Gaarder, E., & Belknap, J. (2002). Tenuous borders: Girls transferred to adult court. Criminology, 40, 484.

135. Belknap, J. (2007). The invisible woman: Gender, crime, and justice (3rd ed.). Belmont, CA: Wadsworth, p. 70.

136. Chesney-Lind, M. (1995). Girls, delinquency, and juvenile justice: Toward a feminist theory of young women's crime. In B. F. Price & N. J. Sokoloff (Eds.), The criminal justice system and women: Offenders, victims, and workers (2nd ed., pp. 71–88). New York: McGraw-Hill.

137. Owen, B. (1998). "In the mix": Struggle and survival in a women's prison. Albany: State University of New York Press.

138. Ibid., p. 41.

139. Ibid., p. 192.

140. Sadeighi-Fassei, S., & Kendall, K. (2001). Iranian women's pathways to imprisonment. Women's Studies International Forum, 24, 701–710.

141. Gaarder, E., & Belknap, J. (2002). Tenuous borders: Girls transferred to adult court. Criminology, 40, 481–518.

142. Evans, R. D., Forsyth, C. J., & Gauthier, D. K. (2002). Gendered pathways into and experiences with crack cultures outside of the inner city. Deviant Behaviors, 23, 483–510.

143. Ullman, S. (2004). Sexual assault victimization and suicidal behavior in women: A review of the literature. Aggression and Violent Behavior, 9, 331–351.

144. Silverthorn, P., & Frick, P. J. (1999). Development pathways to antisocial behavior: The delayed-onset pathway in girls. Development and Psychopathology, 11, 101–126.

145. Zinn, M. B., & Thornton Dill, B. T. (1996). Theorizing difference from multiracial feminism. Feminist Studies, 22, 321–331.

146. Chafetz, J. S. (1997). Feminist theory and sociology: Underutilized contributions for mainstream theory. Annual Review of Sociology, 23, 97–120. See also Burgess-Proctor, A. (2006). Intersections of race, class, gender, and crime: Future directions for feminist criminology. Feminist Criminology, 1, 27–47.

147. Ginsberg, F., & Tsing, A. L. (1990). Introduction. In F. Ginsberg & A. L. Tsing (Eds.), Uncertain terms, negotiating gender in American culture (pp. 1–32). Boston: Beacon Press.

148. Martin, S. (1994). 'Outsider within' the station house: The impact of race and gender on black women police. Social Problems, 41, 383–400.

149. Zinn, M. B., & Thornton Dill, B. T. (1996). Theorizing difference from multiracial feminism. Feminist Studies, 22, 322.

150. Collins, P. H. (1999). Black feminist thought: Knowledge, consciousness and the politics of empowerment (2nd ed.). London: HarperCollins.

151. Browne, I., & Misra, J. (2003). The intersection of gender and race in the labor market. Annual Review of Sociology, 29, 487–513.

152. Burgess-Proctor, A. (2006). Intersections of race, class, gender, and crime: Future directions for feminist criminology. Feminist Criminology, 1, 36–37.

153. Ibid., p. 37.

154. See Jagger, A. M., & Struhl, P. R. (1993). Feminist frameworks: Alternative theoretical accounts of the relations between women and men (3rd ed.). New York: McGraw-Hill; Sandoval, C. (1991, Spring). U.S. Third World feminism: The theory and method of oppositional consciousness in the Postmodern World. Genders, 10, 1–24; Zinn, M. B., & Dill, B. T. (1996). Theorizing difference from multiracial feminism. Feminist Studies, 22, 321–331.

155. Gilfus, M. E. (1992). From victims to survivors to offenders: Women's routes of entry and immersion into street crime. Women and Criminal Justice, 4, 86.

156. Van de Mieroop, M. (2005). King Hammurabi of Babylon: A biography. Malden, MA: Blackwell.

157. Federal Bureau of Investigation. (2012). Crime in the United States, 2011. Washington, DC: U.S. Department of Justice, n.p.

158. Bureau of Justice Statistics. (n.d.). NCVS Victimization Analysis Tool (NVAT). Retrieved from http://www.bjs.gov/index.cfm?ty=nvat

159. Van Dijk, J. (2008). The world of crime: The silence on problems of security, justice and development across the world. Thousand Oaks, CA: Sage.

160. Maher, L. (1997). Sexed work: Gender, race and resistance in a Brooklyn drug market. Oxford, UK: Clarendon Press.

161. Ibid., p. 1.

162. Williams, F. P., & McShane, M. D. (1999). Criminological theory (3rd ed.). Upper Saddle River, NJ: Prentice Hall, p. 260.

163. Griffin, C., & Phoenix, A. (1994). The relationship between qualitative and quantitative research: Lessons from feminist psychology. Journal of Community & Applied Social Psychology, 4, 290.

164. Ibid.

165. Ibid.

166. Donovan, J. (1985). Feminist theory: The intellectual traditions of American feminism. New York: Frederick Ungar, p. 88.

167. Burgess-Proctor, A. (2006). Intersections of race, class, gender, and crime: Future directions for feminist criminology. Feminist Criminology, 1, 42. See also Andersen, M., & Collins, P. H. (2004). Race, class, and gender (5th ed.). Belmont, CA: Wadsworth; Weber, L. (2001). Understanding race, class, gender, and sexuality: A conceptual framework. Boston: McGraw-Hill.

168. Van Wormer, K. S., & Bartollas, C. (2000). Women and the criminal justice system. Boston: Allyn & Bacon.

169. Schwendinger, J. R., & Schwendinger, H. (1974). Rape myths: In legal, theoretical, and everyday practice. Crime and Social Justice, 1, 18–26.

170. Ibid., p. 21.

171. Searles, P., & Berger, R. J. (1987). The current status of rape reform legislation: An examination of state statutes. Women's Rights Law Reporter, 10, 25.

172. Ibid., pp. 25–27.

173. Bownes, D., & Albert, R. L. (1996, September). State challenge activities. OJJDP Juvenile Justice Bulletin; Kempf-Leonard, K., & Sample, L. (2000). Disparity based on sex: Is gender-specific treatment warranted? Justice Quarterly, 17, 89–128.

174. Smith, P., & Smith, W. A. (2005). Experiencing community through the eyes of young female offenders. Journal of Contemporary Criminal Justice, 21, 364–385.

175. Bond-Maupin, L., Maupin, J. R., & Leisenring, A. (2002). Girls' delinquency and the justice implications of intake workers' perspectives. Women & Criminal Justice, 13, 51–77.

176. Kakar, S., Friedemann, M., & Peck, L. (2002). Girls in detention: The results of focus group discussion interviews and official records review. Journal of Contemporary Criminal Justice, 18, 57–73; Walters, W., Dembo, R., Beaulaurier, R., Cocozza, J., La Rosa, M., Poythress, N., et al. (2005). The Miami-Dade Juvenile Assessment Center National Demonstration Project: An overview. Journal of Offender Rehabilitation, 41, 1–37.

177. Fendrich, M., Hubbell, A., & Lurigio, A. (2006). Providers' perceptions of gender-specific drug treatment. Journal of Drug Issues, 36, 667–686.

178. Van Wormer, K., & Kaplan, L. E. (2006). Results of a national survey of wardens in women's prisons: The case for gender specific treatment. Women & Therapy, 29, 133–151.

CHAPTER 12 NOTES

1. 14-year-old suspected in nearly 100 Nashville burglaries. (2012, May 18). *WSMV.com*. Retrieved from http://www.wsmv.com/story/18151966/14-year-old-suspected-in-north-nashville-burglaries.

2. Glueck, S., & Glueck, E. (1950). *Unraveling juvenile delinquency*. New York: Commonwealth Fund. See also Glueck, S., & Glueck, E. (1968). *Delinquents and nondelinquents in perspective*. Cambridge, MA: Harvard University Press.

3. Sampson, R. J., & Laub, J. H. (1993). *Crime in the making: Pathways and turning points through life*. Cambridge, MA: Harvard University Press. See also Laub, J. H., Nagin, D. S., & Sampson, R. J. (1998). Trajectories of change in criminal offending: Good marriages and the desistance process. *American Sociological Review, 63,* 225–238. For a brief discussion of how the Gluecks' work has influenced the current state of developmental theory, see Tibbetts, S. (2014). Prenatal and perinatal predictors of antisocial behavior: Review of research and interventions. In M. DeLisi & K. M. Beaver (Eds.), *Criminological theory: A life-course approach* (2nd ed., pp. 27–43). Boston: Jones & Bartlett.

4. Brame, R., Turner, M., Paternoster, R., & Bushway, S. (2012). Cumulative prevalence of arrest from ages 8 to 23 in a national sample. *Pediatrics, 129,* 21–27.

5. For an excellent review, see Piquero, A. R., Farrington, D. P., & Blumstein, A. (2003). The criminal career paradigm: Background and recent developments. In M. Tonry (Ed.), *Crime and justice: A review of research* (Vol. 30, pp. 137–183). Chicago: University of Chicago Press.

6. For more discussion, see Gibson, C. L., & Tibbetts, S. (2000). A biosocial interaction in predicting early onset of offending. *Psychological Reports, 86,* 509–518; Tibbetts, S., & Piquero, A. (1999). The influence of gender, low birth weight, and disadvantaged environment in predicting early onset of offending: A test of Moffitt's interactional hypothesis. *Criminology, 37,* 843–878.

7. DeLisi, M. (2006). Zeroing in on early onset: Results from a population of extreme career criminals. *Journal of Criminal Justice, 34,* 17–26. For a recent review, see Tibbetts, S. (2009). Perinatal and developmental determinants of early onset of offending: A biosocial approach for explaining the two peaks of early antisocial behavior. In J. Savage (Ed.), *The development of persistent criminality* (pp. 179–201). New York: Oxford University Press.

8. See numerous studies presented in Savage, J. (Ed.). (2009). *The development of persistent criminality*. New York: Oxford University Press.

9. Lincoln Police arrest man for 226th time. (2006, August 14). *KETV.com*. Retrieved from http://www.ketv.com/Lincoln-Police-Arrest-Man-For-226th-Time/-/9675214/10057612/-/6v7e1kz/-/index.html.

10. Walker, S. (2001). *Sense and nonsense about crime and drugs: A policy guide* (5th ed.). Belmont, CA: Wadsworth.

11. For a review, see Piquero, A. R., Farrington, D. P., & Blumstein, A. (2003). The criminal career paradigm: Background and recent developments. In M. Tonry (Ed.), *Crime and justice: A review of research* (Vol. 30, pp. 137–183). Chicago: University of Chicago Press.

12. Ellis, L., Cooper, J. A., & Walsh, A. (2008). Criminologists' opinions about causes and theories of crime and delinquency: A follow-up. *The Criminologist, 33,* 23–26.

13. For discussion of this ranking and past rankings, see Tibbetts, S. (2014). Prenatal and perinatal predictors of antisocial behavior: Review of research and interventions. In M. DeLisi & K. M. Beaver (Eds.), *Criminological theory: A life-course approach* (2nd ed., pp. 27–43). Boston: Jones & Bartlett.

14. Gottfredson, M., & Hirschi, T. (1990). *A general theory of crime*. Palo Alto, CA: Stanford University Press.

15. For an excellent review of studies regarding low self-control theory, see Pratt, T., & Cullen, F. (2000). The empirical status of Gottfredson and Hirschi's general theory of crime: A meta-analysis. *Criminology, 38,* 931–64. For critiques of this theory, see Akers, R. (1991). Self-control as a general theory of crime.

Journal of Quantitative Criminology, 7, 201–211. For a study that demonstrates the high popularity of the theory, see Walsh, A., & Ellis, L. (1999). Political ideology and American criminologists' explanations for criminal behavior. *The Criminologist, 24*, 1, 14.

16. Hay, C. (2001). Parenting, self-control, and delinquency: A test of self-control theory. *Criminology, 39*, 707–736; Hayslett-McCall, K., & Bernard, T. (2002). Attachment, masculinity, and self-control: A theory of male crime rates. *Theoretical Criminology, 6*, 5–33.

17. Sampson, R., & Laub, J. (1990). Crime and deviance over the life course: The salience of adult social bonds. *American Sociological Review, 55*, 609–627; Sampson, R., & Laub, J. (1993). *Crime in the making: Pathways and turning points through life.* Cambridge, MA: Harvard University Press; Sampson, R., & Laub, J. (1993). Turning points in the life course: Why change matters to the study of crime. *Criminology, 31*, 301–326.

18. Piquero, A., Brame, R., Mazzerole, P., & Haapanen, R. (2002). Crime in emerging adulthood. *Criminology, 40*, 137–170; Uggen, C. (2000). Work as a turning point in the life course of criminals: A duration model of age, employment, and recidivism. *American Sociological Review, 65*, 529–546.

19. Moffitt, T. (1993). Adolescence limited and life course persistent antisocial behavioral: A developmental taxonomy. *Psychological Review, 100*, 674–701.

20. See Tibbetts, S., & Piquero, A. (1999). The influence of gender, low birth weight, and disadvantaged environment in predicting early onset of offending: A test of Moffitt's interactional hypothesis. *Criminology, 37*, 843–878.

21. Thornberry, T. (1987). Toward an interactional theory of delinquency. *Criminology, 25*, 863–887; see also Thornberry, T., Lizotte, A., Krohn, M., Farnworth, M., & Jang, S. (1991). Testing interactional theory: An examination of reciprocal causal relationships among family, school and delinquency. *Journal of Criminal Law and Criminology, 82*, 3–35; Thornberry, T., Lizotte, A., Krohn, M., Farnworth, M., & Jang, S. J. (1994). Delinquent peers, beliefs, and delinquent behavior: A longitudinal test of interactional theory. *Criminology, 32*, 47–83.

22. Much of this discussion is taken from Bernard, T. J., & Snipes, J. B. (1996). Theoretical integration in criminology. *Crime and Justice, 20*, 314–316; and also Akers, R. L., & Sellers, C. S. (2008). *Criminological theories: Introduction, evaluation, and application* (5th ed.). New York: Oxford University Press, p. 278.

23. Thornberry, T. (1987). Toward an interactional theory of delinquency. *Criminology, 25*, 876, as quoted in Bernard, T. J., & Snipes, J. B. (1996). Theoretical integration in criminology. *Crime and Justice, 20*, 315.

24. Bernard, T. J., & Snipes, J. B. (1996). Theoretical integration in criminology. *Crime and Justice, 20*, 316.

25. Thornberry, T., Lizotte, A., Krohn, M., Farnworth, M., & Jang, S. J. (1994). Delinquent peers, beliefs, and delinquent behavior: A longitudinal test of interactional theory. *Criminology, 32*, 47–83.

26. Ibid.

27. Jang, S. J. (1999). Age-varying effects of family, school, and peers on delinquency: A multilevel modeling test of interactional theory. *Criminology, 37*, 643–685.

28. Wright, J. P., Tibbetts, S. G., & Daigle, L. (2008). *Criminals in the making: Criminality across the life course.* Thousand Oaks, CA: Sage, pp. 256–257.

29. Barnes, J. C. (2014). The impact of biosocial criminology on public policy: Where should we go from here? In M. DeLisi & K. M. Beaver (Eds.), *Criminological theory: A life-course approach* (2nd ed., pp. 83–98). Boston: Jones & Bartlett, p. 93.

30. Wright, J. P., Tibbetts, S. G., & Daigle, L. (2008). *Criminals in the making: Criminality across the life course.* Thousand Oaks, CA: Sage.

31. Wright, J. P. (2014). Prenatal insults and the development of persistent criminal behavior. In M. DeLisi & K. M. Beaver (Eds.), *Criminological theory: A life-course approach* (2nd ed., pp. 45–58). Boston: Jones & Bartlett, p. 54.

32. Wright, J. P., Tibbetts, S. G., & Daigle, L. (2008). *Criminals in the making: Criminality across the life course.* Thousand Oaks, CA: Sage.

33. Ibid.

CHAPTER 13 NOTES

1. Gerber, J. (2000). On the relationship between organized and white-collar crime: Government, business, and criminal enterprise in post-communist Russia. *European Journal of Crime, Criminal Law and Criminal Justice, 8*, 328.

2. For an excellent discussion of the origin, evolution, and recommendations regarding the definition of white-collar crime, see Geis, G. (2002). White-collar crime: What is it? In D. Shichor, L. Gaines, & R. Ball (Eds.), *Readings in white-collar crime* (pp. 7–25). Prospect Heights, IL: Waveland Press.

3. Chandler, S., & Countryman, A. (2004). 'No one is immune.' *Los Angeles Times.* Retrieved from http://www.latimes.com/business/nationworld/wire/chi-0403070362mar07,0,6283412.story.

4. Goldie, D. (2004). Martha 'not afraid' to serve 5 months. *Los Angeles Times.* Retrieved from http://www.latimes.com/business/nationworld/wire/nyc-martha0717a,0,7196681.story.

5. Ibid., p. 8.

6. A full written version of E. Sutherland's 1939 Presidential Address at the American Sociological Association Conference in Philadelphia can be found in the 1940 *American Sociological Review, 5*, 1–12.

7. Ibid., p. 4.

8. For a comprehensive review of this research, see Geis, G. (2007). *White-collar and corporate crime.* Upper Saddle River, NJ: Pearson.

9. For a review of this research prior to Sutherland's address, see Schoepfer, A., & Tibbetts, S. (2012). From early white-collar bandits and robber barons to modern-day white-collar criminals: A review of the conceptual and theoretical research. In D. Shichor, L. Gaines, & A. Schoepfer (Eds.), *Reflecting on white-collar crime and corporate crime* (pp. 63–83). Long Grove, IL: Waveland Press.

10. Josephson, M. (1934). *The robber barons: The great American capitalists.* New York: Harcourt Brace.

11. Anderson, G. W. (1905). *Consolidation of gas companies in Boston.* Boston: Public Franchise League.

12. Sutherland, E. (1940). White-collar criminality. *American Sociological Review, 5,* 12.

13. Sutherland, E. (1945). Is 'white-collar crime' crime? *American Sociological Review, 10,* 132–139.

14. Sutherland, E. (1949). *White-collar crime.* New York: Dryden.

15. Ibid., p. 9.

16. For more discussion, see Geis, G. (2002). White-collar crime: What is it? In D. Shichor, L. Gaines, & R. Ball (Eds.), *Readings in white-collar crime* (pp. 7–25). Prospect Heights, IL: Waveland Press.

17. For example, see Gottfredson, M., & Hirschi, T. (1990). *A general theory of crime.* Stanford, CA: Stanford University Press, Chapter 9.

18. Sutherland, E. (1949). The white collar criminal. In V. C. Branham & S. B. Kutash (Eds.), *Encyclopedia of criminology* (pp. 511–515). New York: Philosophical Library.

19. Ibid., p. 511; see further discussion about this entry and following discussion in Geis, G. (2002). White-collar crime: What is it? In D. Shichor, L. Gaines, & R. Ball (Eds.), *Readings in white-collar crime* (pp. 7–25). Prospect Heights, IL: Waveland Press.

20. For theoretical discussions and critiques, see Burgess, E. (1950). Comment, and concluding comment. *American Journal of Sociology, 56,* 32–34; Caldwell, R. G. (1958). A re-examination of the concept of white-collar crime. *Federal Probation, 22,* 30–36; Geis, G. (1962). Toward a delineation of white-collar offenses. *Sociological Inquiry, 32,* 160–171; Newman, D. (1958). White-collar crime: An overview and analysis. *Law and Contemporary Problems, 23,* 737–748; Quinney, R. (1964). The study of white collar crime: Toward a reorientation in theory and research. *Journal of Criminology, Criminal Law, and Police Science, 55,* 208–214; Tappan, P. W. (1947). Who is the criminal? *American Sociological Review, 12,* 96–102; for empirical studies, see Clinard, M. (1952). *The black market: A study of white collar crime.* New York: Rinehart; Cressey, D. (1953). *Other people's money: A study in the social psychology of embezzlement.* Glencoe, IL: Free Press; Hartung, F.

21. Caldwell, R. G. (1958). A re-examination of the concept of white-collar crime. *Federal Probation, 22,* 30–36; Tappan, P. W. (1947). Who is the criminal? *American Sociological Review, 12,* 96–102.

22. Sutherland, E. (1945). Is 'white-collar crime' crime? *American Sociological Review, 10,* 132–139; see discussion in Geis, G. (2002). White-collar crime: What is it? In D. Shichor, L. Gaines, & R. Ball (Eds.), *Readings in white-collar crime* (pp. 7–25). Prospect Heights, IL: Waveland Press.

23. Cressey, D. (1953). *Other people's money: A study in the social psychology of embezzlement.* Glencoe, IL: Free Press.

24. Hartung, F. (1950). White-collar offenses in the wholesale meat industry in Detroit. *American Journal of Sociology, 56,* 25–44.

25. Edelhertz, H. (1970). *The nature, impact and prosecution of white-collar crime.* Washington, DC: Law Enforcement Assistance Administration.

26. Schroeder, M. (1999). SEC aims for increased junk-bond oversight; Milken looms behind the opposition plans. *Wall Street Journal.* Retrieved from http://online.wsj.com/article/SB927209225723679025.html.

27. Eichenwald, K. (1989). Wages even Wall St. can't stomach. *New York Times,* para. 9. Retrieved from http://www.nytimes.com/1989/04/03/business/wages-even-wall-st-can-t-stomach.html.

28. Schroeder, M. (1999). SEC aims for increased junk-bond oversight; Milken looms behind the opposition plans. *Wall Street Journal.* Retrieved from http://online.wsj.com/article/SB927209225723679025.html.

29. Pfeifer, S., & Petruno, T. (2009). Michael Milken is still seeking redemption. *Los Angeles Times.* Retrieved from http://articles.latimes.com/2009/feb/03/business/fi-milken3.

30. For the purposes of this chapter, these terms will all be considered as relatively synonymous, considering that we are providing only a cursory review of the topic.

31. Smith, D. (1981). White-collar crime, organized crime, and the business establishment: Resolving a crisis in criminological theory. In P. Wickman & T. Dailey (Eds.), *White-collar and economic crime: Multidisciplinary and cross-national perspectives* (pp. 23–38). Lexington, MA: Lexington Books; Sparks, R. (1979). Crime as business and the female offender. In F. Adler & R. J. Simon (Eds.), *The criminology of deviant women* (pp. 171–179). Boston: Houghton Mifflin.

32. Clinard, M. B., & Quinney, R. (1973). *Criminal behavior systems: A typology* (2nd ed.). New York: Holt, Rinehart & Winston.

33. Newman, D. (1958). White-collar crime: An overview and analysis. *Law and Contemporary Problems,*

(1950). White-collar offenses in the wholesale meat industry in Detroit. *American Journal of Sociology, 56,* 25–44.

23, 737; for further discussion, see Geis, G. (2002). White-collar crime: What is it? In D. Shichor, L. Gaines, & R. Ball (Eds.), *Readings in white-collar crime* (pp. 7–25). Prospect Heights, IL: Waveland Press.

34. Shapiro, S. (1990). Collaring the crime, not the criminal: Liberating the concept of white-collar crime. *American Sociological Review, 55*, 346–367.

35. Gottfredson, M., & Hirschi, T. (1990). *A general theory of crime.* Stanford, CA: Stanford University Press. See also Hirschi, T., & Gottfredson, M. (1987). Causes of white-collar crime. *Criminology, 25*, 957–972.

36. Braithwaite, J. (1985). White collar crime. In R. H. Turner & J. F. Short (Eds.), *Annual review of sociology* (pp. 1–25). Palo Alto, CA: Annual Reviews.

37. See conclusion of Geis, G. (2002). White-collar crime: What is it? In D. Shichor, L. Gaines, & R. Ball (Eds.), *Readings in white-collar crime* (pp. 7–25). Prospect Heights, IL: Waveland Press.

38. Coleman, J. W. (1998). *The criminal elite: Understanding white-collar crime* (4th ed.). New York: St. Martin's Press.

39. Sutherland, E. (1945). Is 'white-collar crime' crime? *American Sociological Review, 10*, 132–139.

40. Clinard, M., & Yeager, P. (1980). *Corporate crime.* New York: Macmillan.

41. Donahue, J. (1992). The missing rap sheet: Government records on corporate abuses. *Multinational Monitor, 14*, 37–51.

42. Much of our discussion on the impact of corporate crime is drawn from Chapter 7 in Kappeler, V. E., & Potter, G. (2005). *The mythology of crime and criminal justice* (4th ed.). Long Grove, IL: Waveland; quote from pp. 148–149.

43. Keller, B. (2002). Enron for dummies. *New York Times.* Retrieved from http://www.nytimes .com/ 2002/01/26/opinion/enron-for-dummies .html?pagewanted=all&src=pm.

44. BBC News. (2002). Enron scandal at-a-glance. Retrieved from http://news.bbc.co.uk/2/hi/ business/1780075.stm.

45. Keller, B. (2002). Enron for dummies. *New York Times.* Retrieved from http://www.nytimes .com/2002/01/26/opinion/enron-for-dummies .html?pagewanted=all&src=pm.

46. Ibid., para. 10.

47. Associated Press. (2011). Enron's victims: Still angry, but coping. *Omaha.com.* Retrieved from http://www .omaha.com/article/20111203/MONEY/712039931.

48. Reiman, J. (2004). *The rich get richer and the poor get prison* (7th ed.). Boston: Allyn & Bacon; quote from p. 61.

49. Federal Bureau of Investigation. (2003). *Crime in the United States, 2002, Uniform Crime Reports.* Washington, DC: U.S. Department of Justice.

50. U.S. Congress, House of Representatives, Committee on Ways and Means. (1989). *Budget implications and current tax rules relating to troubled savings and loan institutions: Hearings before the Committee on Ways and Means, House of Representatives, 101st Congress, first session, February 22, March 9 and 15, 1989.* Washington, DC: Government Printing Office.

51. Eitzen, D. S., & Zinn, M. (2004). *Social problems* (9th ed.). Boston: Allyn & Bacon; Kappeler, V. E., & Potter, G. (2005). *The mythology of crime and criminal justice* (4th ed.). Long Grove, IL: Waveland.

52. Kappeler, V. E., & Potter, G. (2005). *The mythology of crime and criminal justice* (4th ed.). Long Grove, IL: Waveland, p. 148.

53. Barkan, S. (2001). *Criminology: A sociological understanding* (2nd ed.). Upper Saddle River, NJ: Prentice Hall, as cited and discussed in Kappeler, V. E., & Potter, G. (2005). *The mythology of crime and criminal justice* (4th ed.). Long Grove, IL: Waveland.

54. Bureau of Labor Statistics. (2003). *Number and rates of fatal occupational injuries for select occupations, 2002.* Washington, DC: U.S. Government Printing Office.

55. Federal Bureau of Investigation. (2003). *Crime in the United States, 2002, Uniform Crime Reports.* Washington, DC: U.S. Department of Justice.

56. See discussion of corporate crime over recent years in Kappeler, V. E., & Potter, G. (2005). *The mythology of crime and criminal justice* (4th ed.). Long Grove, IL: Waveland, pp. 151–157.

57. Kappeler, V. E., & Potter, G. (2005). *The mythology of crime and criminal justice* (4th ed.). Long Grove, IL: Waveland, p. 148.

58. Clinard, M., & Yeager, P. (1980). *Corporate crime.* New York: Macmillan; Mills, C. W. (1952). A diagnosis of moral uneasiness. In I. Horowitz (Ed.), *Power, politics and people* (pp. 330–339). New York: Ballantine.

59. Clinard, M., & Yeager, P. (1980). *Corporate crime.* New York: Macmillan, p. 21.

60. Kappeler, V. E., & Potter, G. (2005). *The mythology of crime and criminal justice* (4th ed.). Long Grove, IL: Waveland, pp. 164–169.

61. Some of this discussion is taken from "Environmental Protection Agency," *Wikipedia, The Free Encyclopedia,* retrieved from http://en.wikipedia. org/wiki/United_States_Environmental_Protection_ Agency.

62. Rosoff, S., Pontell, H., & Tillman, R. (2004). *Profit without honor: White-collar crime and the looting of America* (3rd ed.). Upper Saddle River, NJ: Prentice Hall.

63. Simon, D. (2002). *Elite deviance* (7th ed.). Boston: Allyn & Bacon.

64. See discussion in Kappeler, V. E., & Potter, G. (2005). *The mythology of crime and criminal justice* (4th ed.). Long Grove, IL: Waveland. See also Hagan, F. (2005). *Introduction to criminology* (5th ed.). Belmont, CA: Wadsworth.

65. Kappeler, V. E., & Potter, G. (2005). *The mythology of crime and criminal justice* (4th ed.). Long Grove, IL: Waveland.

66. Barstow, D. (2003, December 22). When workers die: U.S. rarely seeks charges for deaths in the workplace. *New York Times*. Retrieved from http://www.nytimes .com/2003/12/22/us/us-rarely-seeks-charges-for-deaths-in-workplace.html?pagewanted=all&src=pm.

67. Kappeler, V. E., & Potter, G. (2005). *The mythology of crime and criminal justice* (4th ed.). Long Grove, IL: Waveland.

68. Barstow, D. (2003, December 22). When workers die: U.S. rarely seeks charges for deaths in the workplace. *New York Times*. Retrieved from http://www.nytimes .com/2003/12/22/us/us-rarely-seeks-charges-for -deaths-in-workplace.html?pagewanted=all&src=pm.

69. Van Dijk, J. (2008). *The world of crime*. Los Angeles: Sage, pp. 182–183.

70. For more information regarding this survey, see Van Dijk, J. (2008). *The world of crime*. Los Angeles: Sage, pp. 187–189.

71. Ibid.

72. Ibid., p. 188.

73. United Nations Office on Drugs and Crime. (2005). *Corruption: Compendium of international legal instruments on corruption* (2nd ed.). Vienna: Author.

74. Schoepfer, A., & Tibbetts, S. G. (2012). From early white-collar bandits and robber barons to modern-day white-collar criminals: A review of the conceptual and theoretical research. In D. Shichor, L. Gaines, & A. Schoepfer (Eds.), *Reflecting on white-collar and corporate crime: Discerning readings* (pp. 63–83). Long Grove, IL: Waveland.

75. See Ibid., discussion of Piquero, N., Tibbetts, S., & Blankenship, M. (2005). Examining the role of differential association and techniques of neutralization in explaining corporate crime. *Deviant Behavior, 26*, 159–188.

76. Schoepfer, A., & Tibbetts, S. G. (2012). From early white-collar bandits and robber barons to modern-day white-collar criminals: A review of the conceptual and theoretical research. In D. Shichor, L. Gaines, & A. Schoepfer (Eds.), *Reflecting on white-collar and corporate crime: Discerning readings* (pp. 63–83). Long Grove, IL: Waveland, pp. 72–73.

77. Ibid., p. 71.

78. Ibid., p. 79.

79. President's Commission on Organized Crime. (1986). *Report to the president and the attorney general. The impact: Organized crime today*. Washington, DC: U.S. Government Printing Office, p. 25.

80. Maltz, M. D. (1995). On defining "organized crime": The development of a definition and a typology. In N. Passas (Ed.), *Organized crime*. Brookfield, VT: Dartmouth, pp. 19–21.

81. Abadinsky, H. (2000). *Organized crime* (6th ed.). Belmont, CA: Wadsworth/Thompson, pp. 1–4.

82. Browning, F. & Gerassi, J. (1980). *The American way of crime*. New York: G. P. Putnam, as cited in Kenney, D. J., & Finckenauer, J. O. (1995). *Organized crime in America*. Belmont, CA: Wadsworth, p. 52.

83. Kenney, D. J., & Finckenauer, J. O. (1995). *Organized crime in America*. Belmont, CA: Wadsworth, p. 69.

84. Ibid., p. 72.

85. Ryan, P. J. (1995). *Organized crime*. Santa Barbara, CA: ABC-CLIO, p. 95.

86. Lyman, M. D., & Potter, G. W. (2000). *Organized crime* (2nd ed.). Upper Saddle River, NJ: Prentice Hall, pp. 100–101; see also Kelly, R. J. (1999). United States. *Trends in Organized Crime, 5*, 85–114.

87. Hall, W. (2010). What are the policy lessons of National Alcohol Prohibition in the United States, 1920–1933? *Addiction, 105*, 1164.

88. Lyman, M. D., & Potter, G. W. (2000). *Organized crime* (2nd ed.). Upper Saddle River, NJ: Prentice Hall, pp. 108–111.

89. Reppetto, T. (2004). *American Mafia: A history of its rise to power*. New York: Henry Holt.

90. Abadinsky, H. (2000). *Organized crime* (6th ed.). Belmont, CA: Wadsworth/Thompson, pp. 297–298.

91. Ryan, P. J. (1995). *Organized crime*. Santa Barbara, CA: ABC-CLIO, p. 98.

92. Abadinsky, H. (2000). *Organized crime* (6th ed.). Belmont, CA: Wadsworth/Thompson, pp. 298–299.

93. President's Commission on Organized Crime. (1986). *Report to the president and the attorney general. The impact: Organized crime today*. Washington, DC: U.S. Government Printing Office, p. 33.

94. Ibid., p. 34.

95. Zambo, S. (2007). Digital *La Cosa Nostra*: The Computer Fraud and Abuse Act's failure to punish and deter organized crime. *New England Journal on Criminal and Civil Confinement, 33*(2), 551.

96. Roth, M. P. (2010). *Organized crime*. Upper Saddle River, NJ: Prentice Hall, pp. 570–586.

97. Ryan, P. J. (1995). *Organized crime*. Santa Barbara, CA: ABC-CLIO, p. 33.

98. Albini, J. (1971). *Mafia: Genesis of a legend*. New York: Appleton-Century-Crofts, p. 83.

99. Ryan, P. J. (1995). *Organized crime*. Santa Barbara, CA: ABC-CLIO, p. 35.

100. Hess, H. (1973). *Mafia and Mafioso: The structure of power*. Lexington, MA: D.C. Heath.

101. Ryan, P. J. (1995). *Organized crime*. Santa Barbara, CA: ABC-CLIO, p. 95.

102. Ibid., p. 37.

103. Lyman, M. D., & Potter, G. W. (2000). *Organized crime* (2nd ed.). Upper Saddle River, NJ: Prentice Hall, pp. 12–13.

104. Ibid., p. 264.

105. President's Commission on Organized Crime. (1986). *Report to the president and the attorney general. The impact: Organized crime today*. Washington, DC: U.S. Government Printing Office, p. 58.

106. Ibid., p. 61.

107. Ibid., p. 60.

108. Kenney, D. J., & Finckenauer, J. O. (1995). *Organized crime in America*. Belmont, CA: Wadsworth, p. 293.

109. Lyman, M. D., & Potter, G. W. (2000). *Organized crime* (2nd ed.). Upper Saddle River, NJ: Prentice Hall, p. 264.

110. Roth, M. P. (2010). *Organized crime.* Upper Saddle River, NJ: Prentice Hall, p. 287.

111. President's Commission on Organized Crime. (1986). *Report to the president and the attorney general. The impact: Organized crime today.* Washington, DC: U.S. Government Printing Office, p. 74.

112. Jackson, R. K., & McBride, W. D. (2000). *Understanding street gangs.* Incline Village, NV: Copperhouse.

113. Kenney, D. J., & Finckenauer, J. O. (1995). *Organized crime in America.* Belmont, CA: Wadsworth, pp. 303–304.

114. Maltz, M. (1985). Towards defining organized crime. In H. Alexander & G. Caiden (Eds.), *The politics and economics of organized crime.* Lexington, MA: D.C. Heath.

115. Kenney, D. J., & Finckenauer, J. O. (1995). *Organized crime in America.* Belmont, CA: Wadsworth, pp. 286–289.

116. Van Dijk, J. (2008). *The world of crime.* Los Angeles: Sage, p. 146.

117. Ibid., pp. 154–157.

118. Ibid., pp. 159–161.

119. Russo, G. (2006). *Supermob: How Sidney Korshak and his criminal associates became America's hidden power brokers.* New York: Bloomsbury, as cited in Roth, M. P. (2010). *Organized crime.* Upper Saddle River, NJ: Prentice Hall, p. 27.

120. Lyman, M. D., & Potter, G. W. (2000). *Organized crime* (2nd ed.). Upper Saddle River, NJ: Prentice Hall, p. 14.

121. Kefauver, E. (1951). *Special committee to investigate organized crime in interstate commerce: Third interim report.* Washington, DC: U.S. Government Printing Office, p. 20.

122. Abadinsky, H. (2000). *Organized crime* (6th ed.). Belmont, CA: Wadsworth/Thompson, p. 441.

123. Lyman, M. D., & Potter, G. W. (2000). *Organized crime* (2nd ed.). Upper Saddle River, NJ: Prentice Hall, p. 27.

124. Bell, D. (1953). Crime as an American way of life. *Antioch Reviews, 13,* 139.

125. Kelly, R. J. (2000). *Encyclopedia of organized crime in the United States: From Capone's Chicago to the new urban underworld.* Westport, CN: Greenwood Press, p. 215.

126. Abadinsky, H. (2000). *Organized crime* (6th ed.). Belmont, CA: Wadsworth/Thompson, p. 444.

127. Lyman, M. D., & Potter, G. W. (2000). *Organized crime* (2nd ed.). Upper Saddle River, NJ: Prentice Hall, pp. 14–15.

128. Task Force on Organized Crime. (1967). *Task force report: Organized crime.* Washington, DC: U.S. Government Printing Office, p. 6.

129. Roth, M. P. (2010). *Organized crime.* Upper Saddle River, NJ: Prentice Hall, p. 31.

130. Abadinsky, H. (2000). *Organized crime* (6th ed.). Belmont, CA: Wadsworth/Thompson, pp. 444–445.

131. Roth, M. P. (2010). *Organized crime.* Upper Saddle River, NJ: Prentice Hall, p. 522.

132. Abadinsky, H. (2000). *Organized crime* (6th ed.). Belmont, CA: Wadsworth/Thompson, pp. 445–448.

133. Lyman, M. D., & Potter, G. W. (2000). *Organized crime* (2nd ed.). Upper Saddle River, NJ: Prentice Hall, pp. 39–43.

134. Kenney, D. J., & Finckenauer, J. O. (1995). *Organized crime in America.* Belmont, CA: Wadsworth, p. 29; see also Reuter, P. (1987). Methodological problems of organized crime research. In H. Edelhertz (Ed.), *Major issues in organized crime control: Symposium proceedings.* Washington, DC: National Institute of Justice; Walsh, M. (1983). *An overview of organized crime.* Washington, DC: National Institute of Justice.

135. Kenney, D. J., & Finckenauer, J. O. (1995). *Organized crime in America.* Belmont, CA: Wadsworth, p. 39; see also Bell, D. (1953). Crime as an American way of life. In M. E. Wolfgang, L. Savitz, & N. Johnston (Eds.), *The sociology of crime and delinquency* (pp. 213–225). New York: John Wiley; Ianni, F. (1972). *A family business.* New York: Russell Sage; Ianni, F. (1974). *Black mafia: Ethnic succession in organized crime.* New York: Simon & Schuster.

136. Kenney, D. J., & Finckenauer, J. O. (1995). *Organized crime in America.* Belmont, CA: Wadsworth, p. 41; see also Fox, S. (1989). *Blood and power: Organized crime in 20th century America.* New York: William Morrow; Smith, D. (1980). Paragons, pariahs, and pirates: A spectrum-based theory of enterprise. *Crime and Delinquency, 26,* 358–386.

137. Reuter, P. (1987). Methodological problems of organized crime research. In H. Edelhertz (Ed.), *Major issues in organized crime control: Symposium proceedings.* Washington, DC: National Institute of Justice, as cited in Kenney, D. J., & Finckenauer, J. O. (1995). *Organized crime in America.* Belmont, CA: Wadsworth.

138. Kenney, D. J., & Finckenauer, J. O. (1995). *Organized crime in America.* Belmont, CA: Wadsworth, p. 51.

139. U.S. Department of Justice. (2001). *Online identity thief sentenced in Virginia to 14 years in prison for selling counterfeit credit cards leading to more than $3 million in losses* [Press release]. Retrieved from http://www.justice.gov/opa/pr/2011/September/11-crm-1163.html.

140. Britz, M. T. (2004). *Computer forensics and cyber crime: An introduction.* Upper Saddle River, NJ: Pearson Prentice Hall, p. 4.

141. Moore, R. (2005). *Cybercrime: Investigating high-technology computer crime.* Cincinnati, OH: Anderson, p. 2.

142. Ibid., p. 5.

143. Moitra, S. D. (2005). Developing policies for cyber-crime: Some empirical issues. *European Journal of Crime, Criminal Law and Criminal Justice, 13*, 438.

144. Ibid., pp. 445–446.

145. Wark, M. (2010). Hackers. In G. E. Higgins, *Cybercrime: An introduction to an emerging phenomenon.* Boston: McGraw-Hill, p. 129.

146. Moore, R. (2005). *Cybercrime: Investigating high-technology computer crime.* Cincinnati, OH: Anderson, p. 18–19.

147. Ibid., 24–26.

148. See also Wall, D. S. (2008). Cybercrime, media and insecurity: The shaping of public perceptions of cybercrime. *International Review of Law Computers & Technology, 22*, 45–63.

149. Gaines, L. K., & Kappeler, V. E. (2012). *Homeland security.* Boston: Prentice Hall, pp. 319–320.

150. Moore, R. (2005). *Cybercrime: Investigating high-technology computer crime.* Cincinnati, OH: Anderson, pp. 57–58.

151. Ibid., pp. 62–66.

152. Osanka, F., & Johann, S. L. (1989). *Sourcebook on pornography.* Lexington, MA: Lexington Books.

153. Taylor, R. W., Caeti, T. J., Loper, D. K., Fritsch, E. J., & Liederbach, J. (2006). *Digital crime and digital terrorism.* Upper Saddle River, NJ: Pearson Prentice Hall, p. 191.

154. Henley, J. (1996). The observer campaign to clean up the Internet: Hackers called as cybercops to drive out porn. *Observer,* as cited in Taylor, R. W., Caeti, T. J., Loper, D. K., Fritsch, E. J., & Liederbach, J. (2006). *Digital crime and digital terrorism.* Upper Saddle River, NJ: Pearson Prentice Hall.

155. Beech, R. B., Elliott, I. A., Birgden, A., & Findlater, D. (2008). The Internet and child sexual offending: A criminological review. *Aggression and Violent Behavior, 13*, 216–228.

156. Moore, R. (2005). *Cybercrime: Investigating high-technology computer crime.* Cincinnati, OH: Anderson, pp. 79–80.

157. Caeti, T. J. (2009). *Sex crimes, Part 1: Child pornography.* Law Enforcement Training Network, p. 8.

158. Ibid., p. 5.

159. Moore, R. (2005). *Cybercrime: Investigating high-technology computer crime.* Cincinnati, OH: Anderson, p. 91.

160. Lieberman, J. (2001). Name your own price . . . for hookers?!? Ebay and Priceline.com muscle in on the world's oldest business model. *PCTyrant.com,* as cited in Moore, R. (2005). *Cybercrime: Investigating high-technology computer crime.* Cincinnati, OH: Anderson, p. 92.

161. Moore, R. (2005). *Cybercrime: Investigating high-technology computer crime.* Cincinnati, OH: Anderson, pp. 93–94.

162. Ibid., p. 96.

163. Ibid., pp. 105–109.

164. Ibid., pp. 113–114.

165. Casey, E. (2004). *Digital evidence and computer crime: Forensic science, computers and the Internet* (2nd ed.). London: Elsevier, p. 601.

166. Florida Statute § 784.048.

167. Baughman, L. L. (2007). Friend request or foe? Confirming the misuse of Internet and social networking sites by domestic violence perpetrators. *Widener Law Journal, 19*, 941.

168. Casey, E. (2004). *Digital evidence and computer crime: Forensic science, computers and the Internet* (2nd ed.). London: Elsevier, p. 611.

169. Baughman, L. L. (2007). Friend request or foe? Confirming the misuse of Internet and social networking sites by domestic violence perpetrators. *Widener Law Journal, 19*, 942.

170. Casey, E. (2004). *Digital evidence and computer crime: Forensic science, computers and the Internet* (2nd ed.). London: Elsevier, p. 611.

171. Taylor, R. W., Caeti, T. J., Loper, D. K., Fritsch, E. J., & Liederbach, J. (2006). *Digital crime and digital terrorism.* Upper Saddle River, NJ: Pearson Prentice Hall, p. 280.

172. Moore, R. (2005). *Cybercrime: Investigating high-technology computer crime.* Cincinnati, OH: Anderson, p. 134.

173. Ibid., p. 135.

174. Britz, M. T. (2004). *Computer forensics and cyber crime: An introduction.* Upper Saddle River, NJ: Pearson Prentice Hall, p. 177.

175. Casey, E. (2004). *Digital evidence and computer crime: Forensic science, computers and the Internet* (2nd ed.). London: Elsevier, pp. 213–214.

176. Britz, M. T. (2004). *Computer forensics and cyber crime: An introduction.* Upper Saddle River, NJ: Pearson Prentice Hall, p. 83.

177. Casey, E. (2004). *Digital evidence and computer crime: Forensic science, computers and the Internet* (2nd ed.). London: Elsevier, pp. 62–65.

178. Moore, R. (2005). *Cybercrime: Investigating high-technology computer crime.* Cincinnati, OH: Anderson, p. 118.

179. Piquero, N. L. (2010). Intellectual property theft. In G. E. Higgins (Ed.), *Cybercrime: An introduction to an emerging phenomenon.* Boston: McGraw Hill, p. 93.

180. Gillen, M., & Garrity, B. (2000). Industry's anti-piracy efforts: 'Doomed to fail' says Forester. *Billboard, 112*, 9–11.

181. Casey, E. (2004). *Digital evidence and computer crime: Forensic science, computers and the Internet* (2nd ed.). London: Elsevier, p. 60.

182. Ibid., p. 47.

183. Taylor, R. W., Caeti, T. J., Loper, D. K., Fritsch, E. J., & Liederbach, J. (2006). *Digital crime and digital terrorism.* Upper Saddle River, NJ: Pearson Prentice Hall, p. 188.

184. Britz, M. T. (2004). *Computer forensics and cyber crime: An introduction.* Upper Saddle River, NJ: Pearson Prentice Hall, p. 87.

185. Moore, R. (2005). *Cybercrime: Investigating high-technology computer crime.* Cincinnati, OH: Anderson, p. 145.

186. Taylor, R. W., Caeti, T. J., Loper, D. K., Fritsch, E. J., & Liederbach, J. (2006). *Digital crime and digital terrorism.* Upper Saddle River, NJ: Pearson Prentice Hall.

187. Ibid., p. 38.

188. Ibid., pp. 58–59.

189. Ibid., pp. 45–46.

CHAPTER 14 NOTES

1. Deloughery, K., King, R. D., & Asal, V. (2012). Close cousins or distant relatives? The relationship between terrorism and hate crime. *Crime & Delinquency, 58,* 664. See also Green, D. P., McFalls, L. H., & Smith, J. K. (2001). Hate crime: An emergent research agenda. *Annual Review of Sociology, 27,* 479–504; Herek, G. M., Cogan, J. C., & Gillis, J. R. (2002). Victim experiences in hate crimes based on sexual orientation. *Journal of Social Issues, 58,* 319–339.

2. Green, D. P., McFalls, L. H., & Smith, J. K. (2001). Hate crime: An emergent research agenda. *Annual Review of Sociology, 27,* 483.

3. Ibid., p. 665; see also Black, D. (2004). Terrorism as social control. *Sociology of Crime, Law and Deviance, 5,* 9–18; Messner, S. F., McHugh, S., & Felson, R. B. (2004). The distinctive characteristics of assaults motivated by bias. *Criminology, 42,* 585–618.

4. Human Rights Watch. (2002). *We are not the enemy: Hate crimes against Arabs, Muslims, and those perceived to be Arab or Muslim after September 11.* Retrieved from http://www.hrw.org/reports/2002/usahate/.

5. Becerra, H. (2008, October 13). Homeless but not alone. *Los Angeles Times.* Retrieved from http://articles.latimes.com/2008/oct/13/local/me-homeless13.

6. Stateman, A. (2008, October 22). Violence against the homeless: Is it a hate crime? *Los Angeles Times.* Retrieved from http://www.time.com/time/nation/article/0,8599,1852825,00.html.

7. Federal Bureau of Investigation. (n.d.). *Hate crime: Overview.* Washington, DC: U.S. Department of Justice. Retrieved from http://www.fbi.gov/about-us/investigate/civilrights/hate_crimes/overview.

8. Federal Bureau of Investigation. (1999). *Hate crime data collection guidelines.* Washington, DC: U.S. Department of Justice.

9. Ibid., pp. 4–5.

10. Ibid., p. 4.

11. Federal Bureau of Investigation. (2012). Incidents and offenses. In *Hate crime statistics, 2011.* Washington, DC: U.S. Department of Justice, pp. 1–5.

12. Federal Bureau of Investigation. (1999). *Hate crime data collection guidelines.* Washington, DC: U.S. Department of Justice, p. 1.

13. Ibid., p. 37.

14. Ibid., p. 1; see also U.S. Department of Justice. (1994). *Violence Crime Control and Law Enforcement Act of 1994: Fact sheet.* Washington, DC: U.S. Department of Justice.

15. Hate Crime Sentencing Enhancement Act 28 U.S.C. 994.

16. National Church Arson Task Force. (n.d.). *Interim report to the president.* Retrieved from http://www.justice.gov/crt/church_arson/00000008.pdf.

17. Title 18, U.S.C., Section 247. Retrieved from http://www.fbi.gov/about-us/investigate/civilrights/federal-statutes.

18. 105th Congress, S. 1493IS. Retrieved from http://thomas.loc.gov/cgi-bin/query/z?c105:2.1493.

19. Title 18, U.S.C., Section 249.

20. U.S. Department of Justice. (n.d.). *Matthew Shepard/James Byrd, Jr., Hate Crimes Prevention Act of 2009.* Washington, DC: Author. Retrieved from http://www.justice.gov/crt/about/crm/matthewshepard.php.

21. National Coalition for the Homeless. (2012). *Hate crimes and violence against people experiencing homelessness.* Washington, DC: National Coalition for the Homeless. Retrieved from http://www.nationalhomeless.org/factsheets/hatecrimes.html.

22. National Law Center on Homelessness & Poverty (NLCHP) and National Coalition for the Homeless (NCH). (n.d.). *Model state legislation: Hate crimes/violence against homeless people.* Retrieved from http://www.nlchp.org/content/pubs/Model%20State%20Legislation.pdf.

23. Brooke, J. (1998). Gay man beaten and left for dead; 2 are charged. *New York Times.* Retrieved from http://www.nytimes.com/1998/10/10/us/gay-man-beaten-and-left-for-dead-2-are-charged.html?ref=matthewshepard.

24. Brooke, J. (1998). Gay man dies from attack, fanning outrage and debate. *New York Times.* Retrieved from http://www.nytimes.com/1998/10/10/us/gay-man-beaten-and-left-for-dead-2-are-charged.html?ref=matthewshepard.

25. Murdered for who he was [Editorial]. (1998, October 13). *New York Times.* Retrieved from http://www.nytimes.com/1998/10/13/opinion/murdered-for-who-he-was.html?ref=matthewshepard.

26. Byers, B. D., & Crider, B. W. (2002). Hate crimes against the Amish: A qualitative analysis of bias motivation using routine activities theory. *Deviant Behavior, 23,* 115–148.

27. Waldner, L. K., & Berg, J. (2008). Explaining anti-gay violence using target congruence: An application of revised routine activities theory. *Violence and Victims, 23,* 267–287.

28. Finkelhor, D., & Asdigian, N. L. (1996). Risk factors for youth victimization: Beyond a lifestyles/routine activities theory approach. *Violence and Victims, 11,* 3–19.

29. Ibid., p. 6.

30. See Craig, K. M., & Waldo, C. R. (1996). "So what's a hate crime anyway?" Young adults' perceptions of hate crimes, victims, and perpetrators. *Law and Human Behavior, 20,* 113–129; Dunbar, E., & Molina, A. (2004). Opposition to the legitimacy of hate crime laws: The role of argument acceptance, knowledge, individual differences, and peer influence. *Analysis of Social Issues and Public Policy, 4,* 91–113.

31. Plumm, K. M., Terrance, C. A., Henderson, V. R., & Ellingson, H. (2010). Victim blame in a hate crime motivated by sexual orientation. *Journal of Homosexuality, 57,* 267–286.

32. Ibid., p. 282.

33. Baker, P., Cooper, H., & Mazzetti, M. (2011). Bin Laden is dead, Obama says. *New York Times.* Retrieved from http://www.nytimes.com/2011/05/02/world/asia/osama-bin-laden-is-killed.html?pagewanted=all.

34. CNN Wire Staff. (2011). *Transcript: Obama's speech announcing the death of Osama bin Laden.* Retrieved from http://www.cnn.com/2011/WORLD/asiapcf/05/02/obama.bin.laden.transcript/index.html?iref=allsearch.

35. Gaines, L. K., & Kappeler, V. E. (2012). *Homeland security.* Boston: Prentice Hall, p. 109.

36. Schmid, A. (2004). Terrorism: The definitional problem. *Case Western Reserve Journal of International Law, 36,* 376.

37. Hoffman, B. (2009). Defining terrorism: Means, ends, and motives. In R. D. Howard, R. L. Sawyer, & N. E. Bajema (Eds.), *Terrorism and counterterrorism: Understanding the new security environment* (3rd ed.). Boston: McGraw-Hill, p. 33.

38. White, J. R. (2012). *Terrorism and homeland security* (7th ed.). Belmont, CA: Wadsworth, p. 13; see also Borum, R. (2004). *Psychology of terrorism.* Tampa: University of South Florida; Schmid, A. P., & Jongman, A. J. (2005). *Political terrorism: A new guide to actors, authors, concepts, data bases, theories, and literature.* Somerset, NJ: Transaction Books.

39. Gaines, L. K., & Kappeler, V. E. (2012). *Homeland security.* Boston: Prentice Hall, p. 123.

40. U.S. Department of State, Office of the Coordinator for Counterterrorism. (2008). *Fact sheet.* Retrieved from http://www.state.gov/s/ct/rls/fs/08/103392.htm.

41. Martin, G. (2013). *Understanding terrorism: Challenges, perspectives, and issues* (4th ed.). Thousand Oaks, CA: Sage, p. 40.

42. Gaines, L. K., & Kappeler, V. E. (2012). *Homeland security.* Boston: Prentice Hall, pp. 123–125.

43. U.S. Department of State. (2009). *Country reports on terrorism, 2008.* Retrieved from http://www.state.gov/documents/organization/122599.pdf.

44. Hoffman, B. (2006). *Inside terrorism.* New York: Columbia University Press.

45. Martin, G. (2013). *Understanding terrorism: Challenges, perspectives, and issues* (4th ed.). Thousand Oaks, CA: Sage, p. 40.

46. National Counterterrorism Center. (2010). *2009 report on terrorism.* Washington, DC: National Counterterrorism Center, p. 1.

47. Ibid., pp. 9–10.

48. Ibid., p. 13.

49. Ibid., p. 14.

50. Gaines, L. K., & Kappeler, V. E. (2012). *Homeland security.* Boston: Prentice Hall, p. 113.

51. Pratt, A. N. (2011). Terrorism's evolution: Yesterday, today, and forever. In C. C. Harmon, A. N. Pratt, & S. Gorka (Eds.), *Toward a grand strategy against terrorism.* New York: McGraw-Hill, p. 8.

52. Burgess, M. (2003). *A brief history of terrorism.* Washington, DC: Center for Defense Information.

53. Ibid.

54. Halsall, P. (1997). Maximilien Robespierre: Justification of the use of terror. *Modern History Sourcebook.* Retrieved from http://www.fordham.edu/halsall/mod/robespierre-terror.asp.

55. Burgess, M. (2003). *A brief history of terrorism.* Washington, DC: Center for Defense Information.

56. Gaines, L. K., & Kappeler, V. E. (2012). *Homeland security.* Boston: Prentice Hall, p. 113.

57. Martin, G. (2011). *Terrorism and homeland security.* Thousand Oaks, CA: Sage, p. 30.

58. Gaines, L. K., & Kappeler, V. E. (2012). *Homeland security.* Boston: Prentice Hall, p. 113.

59. Burgess, M. (2003). *A brief history of terrorism.* Washington, DC: Center for Defense Information.

60. Ibid.

61. Hoffman, B. (2006). *Inside terrorism.* New York: Columbia University Press, p. 64.

62. Gaines, L. K., & Kappeler, V. E. (2012). *Homeland security.* Boston: Prentice Hall, p. 114.

63. Burgess, M. (2003). *A brief history of terrorism.* Washington, DC: Center for Defense Information.

64. Ibid.

65. Martin, G. (2011). *Terrorism and homeland security.* Thousand Oaks, CA: Sage, p. 41.

66. Gupta, D. K. (2001). *Rule of law and terrorism.* Unpublished paper, San Diego State University, San Diego, CA.

67. Schmid, A. (2005). Links between terrorist and organized crime networks: Emerging patterns and trends. In D. Vlassis (Ed.), *Trafficking: Networks and logistics of transnational crime and international terrorism.* Proceedings of the International Conference on "Trafficking: Networks and Logistics of Transnational Crime and International Terrorism," Courmayeur Mont Blanc, Italy.

68. Van Dijk, J. (2008). *The world of crime: The silence on problems of security, justice and development across the world.* Thousand Oaks, CA: Sage, p. 282.

69. Ibid., p. 284.

70. White, J. R. (2012). *Terrorism and homeland security* (7th ed.). Belmont, CA: Wadsworth, p. 64.

71. Ibid., pp. 64–78.

72. Arquilla, J., Ronfeldt, D., & Zanini, M. (1999). Networks, netwar, and information-age terrorism. In I. O. Lesser et al. (Eds.), *Countering the new terrorism*. Santa Monica, CA: RAND, as cited in White, J. R. (2012). *Terrorism and homeland security* (7th ed.). Belmont, CA: Wadsworth.

73. Levitt, M., & Jacobson, J. (2008). The U.S. campaign to squeeze terrorists' financing. *Journal of International Affairs, 62*, 67–85.

74. Gaines, L. K., & Kappeler, V. E. (2012). *Homeland security*. Boston: Prentice Hall, pp. 301–302.

75. Kochan, N. (2005). *The washing machine*. New York: Thompson, p. 32, as cited in Olson, D. T. (2007). *Financing terror*. Washington, DC: U.S. Department of Justice.

76. Gaines, L. K., & Kappeler, V. E. (2012). *Homeland security*. Boston: Prentice Hall, pp. 301–304.

77. Roberge, I. (2007). Misguided policies in the war on terror? The case for disentangling terrorist financing from money laundering. *Politics, 27*, 196–203, as cited in Gaines, L. K., & Kappeler, V. E. (2012). *Homeland security*. Boston: Prentice Hall, p. 304.

78. Ehrenfeld, R. (2003). *Funding evil: How terrorism is financed and how to stop it*. Seattle: National Press, p. 123, as cited in Olson, D. T. (2007). *Financing terror*. Washington, DC: U.S. Department of Justice.

79. Olson, D. T. (2007). *Financing terror*. Washington, DC: U.S. Department of Justice.

80. Gaines, L. K., & Kappeler, V. E. (2012). *Homeland security*. Boston: Prentice Hall, pp. 301–312.

81. Kohlmann, E. (2006). *The role of Islamic charities in international terrorist recruitment and financing*. Copenhagen: Danish Institute for International Studies.

82. Federal Bureau of Investigation. (2008). *No cash for terror: Convictions returned in Holy Land case*. Washington, DC: U.S. Department of Justice. Retrieved from http://www.fbi.gov/news/stories/2008/november/hlf112508.

83. Cottle, S. (2006). Mediatizing the global war on terror. In A. P. Kavoori & T. Fraley (Eds.), *Media, terrorism, and theory: A reader*. Lanham, MD: Rowman & Littlefield.

84. Ross, J. I. (2007). Deconstructing the terrorism news media relationship. *Crime, Media, Culture, 3*, 215–225.

85. White, J. R. (2012). *Terrorism and homeland security* (7th ed.). Belmont, CA: Wadsworth, pp. 116–125.

86. See Anderson, B. C. (2005). *South Park conservatives: The revolt against liberal media bias*. Washington, DC: Regnery; Goldberg, B. (2003). *Bias: A CBS insider exposes how the media distort the news*. New York: Perennial Editions (HarperCollins); Slisli, F. (2000). The Western media and the Algerian crisis. *Race and Class, 41*, 43–57.

87. White, J. R. (2012). *Terrorism and homeland security* (7th ed.). Belmont, CA: Wadsworth, p. 104.

88. Federal Bureau of Investigation. (2006). *Terrorism 2002–2005*. Washington, DC: U.S. Department of Justice, p. v.

89. Federal Bureau of Investigation. (2009). *Domestic terrorism: In the post-9/11 era*. Washington, DC: U.S. Department of Justice, para. 3. Retrieved from http://www.fbi.gov/news/stories/2009/september/domterror_090709.

90. Martin, G. (2013). *Understanding terrorism: Challenges, perspectives, and issues* (4th ed.). Thousand Oaks, CA: Sage, p. 382.

91. Ibid., pp. 383–384.

92. Animal Liberation Front (ALF). (n.d.). *The ALF credo and guidelines*. Retrieved from http://www.animalliberationfront.com/ALFront/alf_credo.htm.

93. Martin, G. (2013). *Understanding terrorism: Challenges, perspectives, and issues* (4th ed.). Thousand Oaks, CA: Sage, p. 401.

94. Ibid., pp. 383–384.

95. Ibid., p. 409.

96. Ibid., p. 417.

97. Ibid., p. 418.

98. Army of God. (n.d.). Retrieved from http://www.armyofgod.com/.

99. Forst, B. (2010). Memorandum: Afterword to the State Department's country reports on terrorism for 2010—Challenges, accomplishments, and prospects. In National Counterterrorism Center. (2010). *2009 report on terrorism*. Washington, DC: Author, n.p.

100. Ibid., n.p.

101. Cohen, L., & Felson, M. (1979). Social change and crime rate trends: A routine activity approach. *American Sociological Review, 44*, 588–608.

102. Shubik, M. (1975). *The uses and methods of gaming*. New York: Elsevier, p. 6.

103. Forst, B. (2010). Memorandum: Afterword to the State Department's country reports on terrorism for 2010—Challenges, accomplishments, and prospects. In National Counterterrorism Center. (2010). *2009 report on terrorism*. Washington, DC: Author, n.p.

104. Morris, P. (1994). *Introduction to game theory*. New York: Springer-Verlag, p. vii.

105. Forst, B. (2010). Memorandum: Afterword to the State Department's country reports on terrorism for 2010—Challenges, accomplishments, and prospects. In National Counterterrorism Center. (2010). *2009 report on terrorism*. Washington, DC: Author, n.p.

106. Martin, G. (2011). *Terrorism and homeland security*. Thousand Oaks, CA: Sage, p. 270.

107. Gaines, L. K., & Kappeler, V. E. (2012). *Homeland security*. Boston: Prentice Hall, p. 2.

108. Clarke, R. (2008). *Your government failed you: Breaking the cycle of national security disasters*. New York: HarperCollins.

109. Ibid., p. 6.

110. Martin, G. (2011). *Terrorism and homeland security*. Thousand Oaks, CA: Sage, p. 267.

111. Bush, G. W. (2002). Letter from the White House. *National Strategy for Homeland Security, 2002.* Washington, DC: Office of Homeland Security, n.p.

112. White, J. R. (2012). *Terrorism and homeland security* (7th ed). Belmont, CA: Wadsworth, p. 474.

113. White House. (2002). *The Department of Homeland Security.* Washington, DC: Department of Homeland Security. Retrieved from http://www.dhs.gov/xlibrary/assets/book.pdf.

114. Office of Homeland Security. (2002). *National strategy for homeland security, 2002.* Washington, DC: Author, p. 2.

115. Ibid., as cited in Gaines, L. K., & Kappeler, V. E. (2012). *Homeland security.* Boston: Prentice Hall, p. 6.

116. Bellavita, C. (2008). Changing homeland security: What is homeland security? *Homeland Security Affairs, 4,* 1–2.

117. Ibid., p. 9.

118. Department of Homeland Security. (2011). *Creation of the Department of Homeland Security.* Washington, DC: Author. Retrieved from http://www.dhs.gov/xabout/history/gc_1297963906741.shtm.

119. Transportation Security Administration. (n.d.). *About TSA.* Washington, DC: U.S. Department of Homeland Security. Retrieved from http://www.tsa.gov/about-tsa.

120. Gaines, L. K., & Kappeler, V. E. (2012). *Homeland security.* Boston: Prentice Hall, p. 37.

121. Ibid., p. 40.

122. U.S. Customs and Border Protection. (2011). *Snapshot: A summary of CBP facts and figures.* Washington, DC: Author, p. 1.

123. Gaines, L. K., & Kappeler, V. E. (2012). *Homeland security.* Boston: Prentice Hall, p. 40.

124. Ibid., p. 43.

125. U.S. Citizenship and Immigration Services. (2010). *USCIS overview: About the U.S. Citizenship and Immigration Services (USCIS).* Washington, DC: Author. Retrieved from http://www.uscitizenship.info/us-citizenship-and-immigration-services-uscis.html.

126. U.S. Immigration and Customs Enforcement. (n.d.). *Overview.* Washington, DC: U.S. Department of Homeland Security. Retrieved from http://www.ice.gov/about/overview/.

127. Gaines, L. K., & Kappeler, V. E. (2012). *Homeland security.* Boston: Prentice Hall, p. 43.

128. Ibid.

129. U.S. Immigration and Customs Enforcement. (n.d.). *Overview.* Washington, DC: U.S. Department of Homeland Security. Retrieved from http://www.ice.gov/about/overview/.

130. Gaines, L. K., & Kappeler, V. E. (2012). *Homeland security.* Boston: Prentice Hall, p. 45; see also U.S. Secret Service. (2010). *Secret Service history.* Washington, DC: Author. Retrieved from http://www.secretservice.gov/history.shtml.

131. U.S. Secret Service. (2010). *Mission statement.* Washington, DC: Author. Retrieved from http://www.secretservice.gov/mission.shtml.

132. Federal Emergency Management Agency. (2011). *About FEMA.* Washington, DC: Author. Retrieved from http://www.fema.gov/about-fema.

133. Federal Emergency Management Agency. (2011). *FEMA strategic plan: Fiscal years 2011–2014.* Washington, DC: U.S. Department of Homeland Security, p. 1.

134. Gaines, L. K., & Kappeler, V. E. (2012). *Homeland security.* Boston: Prentice Hall, p. 48.

135. U.S. Coast Guard. (2011). *About us.* Washington, DC: Author. Retrieved from http://www.uscg.mil/top/about/.

136. Haddal, C. C. (2010). *Border security: Key agencies and their missions.* Washington, DC: Congressional Research Service, p. 4.

137. Shapiro, J. (2007). *Managing homeland security: Develop a threat-based strategy.* Washington, DC: Brookings Institution, p. 1.

138. Gaines, L. K., & Kappeler, V. E. (2012). *Homeland security.* Boston: Prentice Hall, p. 35.

139. Ibid., p. 36.

140. Federal Bureau of Investigation. (n.d.). *Terror hits home: The Oklahoma City bombing.* Washington, DC: U.S. Department of Justice. Retrieved from http://www.fbi.gov/about-us/history/famous-cases/oklahoma-city-bombing.

141. CNN. (2001). *Special forces: Timothy McVeigh.* Retrieved from http://articles.cnn.com/2001–03–29/us/profile.mcveigh_1_timothy-mcveigh-oklahoma-city-bombing-religion-basic-training-fort-bragg/2?_s=PM:US.

142. Russakoff, D., & Kovaleski, S. F. (1995). An ordinary boy's extraordinary rage. *Washington Post.* Retrieved from http://www.washingtonpost.com/wp-srv/national/longterm/oklahoma/bg/mcveigh.htm.

143. Borger, J. (2001). McVeigh faces day of reckoning. *The Guardian.* Retrieved from http://www.guardian.co.uk/world/2001/jun/11/mcveigh.usa4.

144. Ibid.

145. Office of the United Nations. (2008). *Human rights, terrorism and counter-terrorism.* Geneva, Switzerland: Author, p. 1.

146. Martin, G. (2013). *Understanding terrorism: Challenges, perspectives, and issues* (4th ed.). Thousand Oaks, CA: Sage, p. 401.

147. Hersh, S. M. (2004). Torture at Abu Ghraib. *New Yorker.* Retrieved from http://www.newyorker.com/archive/2004/05/10/040510fa_fact.

148. Ibid., para. 6.

149. Martin, G. (2013). *Understanding terrorism: Challenges, perspectives, and issues* (4th ed.). Thousand Oaks, CA: Sage, pp. 498–499.

150. Office of the United Nations. (2008). *Human rights, terrorism and counter-terrorism.* Geneva, Switzerland: Author, p. 3.

151. White, J. R. (2012). *Terrorism and homeland security* (7th ed). Belmont, CA: Wadsworth, p. 539.

152. Pew Foundation. (2005). *Pew global attitudes project.* Retrieved from http://pewglobal.org/reports/pdf/248.pdf, as cited in White, J. R. (2012). *Terrorism and homeland security* (7th ed). Belmont, CA: Wadsworth, p. 539.

153. Porteous, T. (2006). The al Qaeda myth. *TomPaine.com.* Retrieved from http://www.tompaine.com/articles/2006/04/12/the_al_qaeda_myth.php, as cited in White, J. R. (2012). *Terrorism and homeland security* (7th ed). Belmont, CA: Wadsworth, p. 539.

154. Office of the United Nations. (2008). *Human rights, terrorism and counter-terrorism.* Geneva, Switzerland: Author, p. 46.

155. Cole, D., & Dempsey, J. X. (2006). *Terrorism and the Constitution: Sacrificing civil liberties in the name of national security* (3rd ed.). New York: New Press.

156. Cohen, D. H. (2010). Post-9/11 anti-terrorism policy regarding noncitizens and the constitutional idea of equal protection under the laws. *Texas Law Review, 88,* 1339.

157. White, J. R. (2012). *Terrorism and homeland security* (7th ed.). Belmont, CA: Wadsworth, pp. 542–544.

158. Doyle, C. (2002). *CRS report for Congress: The USA PATRIOT Act: A sketch.* Washington, DC: Congressional Research Service; Executive Order 13025 of November 13, 1995, Amendment to Executive Order 13010, the President's Commission on Critical Infrastructure Protection, as cited in Gaines, L. K., & Kappeler, V. E. (2012). *Homeland security.* Boston: Prentice Hall, p. 96.

159. Martin, G. (2011). *Terrorism and homeland security.* Thousand Oaks, CA: Sage, p. 279.

160. White, J. R. (2012). *Terrorism and homeland security* (7th ed). Belmont, CA: Wadsworth, pp. 542–544.

161. Sievert, R. J. (2007). PATRIOT 2005–2007: Truth, controversy, and consequences. *Texas Review of Law & Politics, 11,* 350.

162. Mascaro, L. (2011). Patriot Act provisions extended just in time. *Los Angeles Times.* Retrieved from http://articles.latimes.com/2011/may/27/nation/la-na-patriot-act-20110527.

CHAPTER 15 NOTES

1. Lurigio, A. J. (2008). The first 20 years of drug treatment courts: A brief description of their history and impact. *Federal Probation, 72,* 13.

2. Federal Bureau of Investigation. (2012). *Crime in the United States, 2011.* Washington, DC: U.S. Department of Justice.

3. Guerino, P., Harrison, P. M., & Sabol, W. J. (2011). *Prisoners in 2010.* Washington, DC: U.S. Department of Justice. Retrieved from http://bjs.ojp.usdoj.gov/content/pub/pdf/p10.pdf.

4. Gaines, L. K. (2003). The psychopharmacology and prevalence of drugs. In L. K. Gaines & P. B. Kraska (Eds.), *Drugs, crime, and justice* (2nd ed., pp. 50–86). Prospect Heights, IL: Waveland Press, p. 57.

5. Deputies: Parents' drug abuse led to infant's death. (2012). *MyFoxTampaBay.com.* Retrieved from http://www.myfoxtampabay.com/story/19080680/deputies-parents-drug-abuse-led-to-infants-death.

6. National Institute of Drug Abuse. (2011). *What are CNS depressants.* Washington, DC: U.S. Department of Health and Human Services. Retrieved from http://www.drugabuse.gov/publications/research-reports/prescription-drugs/cns-depressants/what-are-cns-depressants.

7. Substance Abuse and Mental Health Services Administration. (2012). *Results from the 2011 National Survey on Drug Use and Health: Volume I; Summary of national findings.* Washington, DC: U.S. Department of Health and Human Services.

8. Kuhn, C., Swartzwelder, S., & Wilson, W. (2003). *Buzzed: The straight facts about the most used and abused drugs from alcohol to ecstasy.* New York: W. W. Norton, p. 198.

9. National Institute on Alcohol Abuse and Alcoholism. (n.d.). Moderate and binge drinking. Retrieved from http://www.niaaa.nih.gov/alcohol-health/overview-alcohol-consumption/moderate-binge-drinking.

10. Substance Abuse and Mental Health Services Administration. (2012). *Results from the 2011 National Survey on Drug Use and Health: Key definition for the 2011 detailed tables and national findings report.* Rockville, MD: Author, p. 4.

11. Wechsler, H., Dowdall, W., Davenport, A., & Castillo, S. (1995). Correlates of college student binge drinking. *American Journal of Public Health, 85,* 921–926.

12. Zamboanga, B. L., Schwartz, S. J., Van Tyne, K., Ham, L. S., Olthuis, J. V., Huang, S., et al. (2010). Drinking game behaviors among college students: How often and how much? *American Journal of Drug and Alcohol Abuse, 36,* 176.

13. Borsari, B. (2004). Drinking games in the college environment: A review. *Journal of Alcohol and Drug Education, 48,* 29–51.

14. Perkins, H. W. (2002). Surveying the damage: A review of research on consequences of alcohol misuse in college populations. *Journal of Studies on Alcohol, 56,* 628–634.

15. Sneader, W. (2005). *Drug discovery.* New York: John Wiley.

16. U.S. Drug Enforcement Administration. (n.d.). *Barbiturates.* Washington, DC: U.S. Department of Justice. Retrieved from http://www.justice.gov/dea_old/concern/barbiturates.html.

17. Gaines, L. K. (2003). The psychopharmacology and prevalence of drugs. In L. K. Gaines & P. B. Kraska (Eds.), *Drugs, crime, and justice* (2nd ed., pp. 50–86). Prospect Heights, IL: Waveland Press, p. 59.

18. U.S. Drug Enforcement Administration. (n.d.). *Barbiturates*. Washington, DC: U.S. Department of Justice. Retrieved from http://www.justice.gov/dea_old/concern/barbiturates.html.

19. Ainsworth, S. (2011). Barbiturates: Soldiers, saints and spies. *Practice Nurse, 41*, 32–33.

20. Kuhn, C., Swartzwelder, S., & Wilson, W. (2003). *Buzzed: The straight facts about the most used and abused drugs from alcohol to ecstasy*. New York: W. W. Norton, p. 33.

21. Ibid., p. 199.

22. Zilney, L. A. (2011). *Drugs: Policy, social costs, crime, and justice*. Boston: Prentice Hall; see also U.S. Drug Enforcement Administration. (n.d.). *Drug fact sheet*. Washington, DC: U.S. Department of Justice. Retrieved from http://www.justice.gov/dea/druginfo/all_fact_sheets.pdf.

23. U.S. Drug Enforcement Administration. (n.d.). *Drug fact sheet*. Washington, DC: U.S. Department of Justice. Retrieved from http://www.justice.gov/dea/druginfo/all_fact_sheets.pdf.

24. Gaines, L. K. (2003). The psychopharmacology and prevalence of drugs. In L. K. Gaines & P. B. Kraska (Eds.), *Drugs, crime, and justice* (2nd ed., pp. 50–86). Prospect Heights, IL: Waveland Press, p. 62.

25. Kuhn, C., Swartzwelder, S., & Wilson, W. (2003). *Buzzed: The straight facts about the most used and abused drugs from alcohol to ecstasy*. New York: W. W. Norton, p. 176.

26. U.S. Drug Enforcement Administration. (n.d.). *Drug fact sheet*. Washington, DC: U.S. Department of Justice. Retrieved from http://www.justice.gov/dea/druginfo/all_fact_sheets.pdf.

27. Kuhn, C., Swartzwelder, S., & Wilson, W. (2003). *Buzzed: The straight facts about the most used and abused drugs from alcohol to ecstasy*. New York: W. W. Norton, p. 178.

28. Neaigus, A., Atillasoy, A., Friedman, S., Andrade, X., Miller, M., Ildefonso, G., et al. (1998). Trends in the noninjected use of heroin and factors associated with the transition to injecting. In J. Inciardi & L. Harrison (Eds.), *Heroin in the age of crack-cocaine* (pp. 131–159). Thousand Oaks, CA: Sage.

29. National Institute of Drug Abuse. (n.d.). *Drug facts: Heroin*. Washington, DC: National Institutes of Health. Retrieved from http://www.drugabuse.gov/infofacts/heroin.html.

30. U.S. Drug Enforcement Administration. (n.d.). *Drug fact sheet: Narcotics*. Washington, DC: U.S. Department of Justice. Retrieved from http://www.justice.gov/dea/druginfo/drug_data_sheets/Narcotics.pdf.

31. Gaines, L. K. (2003). The psychopharmacology and prevalence of drugs. In L. K. Gaines & P. B. Kraska (Eds.), *Drugs, crime, and justice* (2nd ed., pp. 50–86). Prospect Heights, IL: Waveland Press, p. 65.

32. Van Zee, A. (2009). The promotion and marketing of OxyContin: Commercial triumph, public health tragedy. *American Journal of Public Health, 99*, 225.

33. Tough, P. (2001). The alchemy of OxyContin: From pain relief to drug addiction. *New York Times*. Retrieved from http://www.nytimes.com/2001/07/29/magazine/290XYCONTIN.html?pagewanted=all.

34. Kuhn, C., Swartzwelder, S., & Wilson, W. (2003). *Buzzed: The straight facts about the most used and abused drugs from alcohol to ecstasy*. New York: W. W. Norton, p. 211.

35. Gaines, L. K. (2003). The psychopharmacology and prevalence of drugs. In L. K. Gaines & P. B. Kraska (Eds.), *Drugs, crime, and justice* (2nd ed., pp. 50–86). Prospect Heights, IL: Waveland Press, p. 66.

36. U.S. Drug Enforcement Administration. (n.d.). *Drug fact sheet*. Washington, DC: U.S. Department of Justice. Retrieved from http://www.justice.gov/dea/druginfo/all_fact_sheets.pdf.

37. Ibid.

38. Kuhn, C., Swartzwelder, S., & Wilson, W. (2003). *Buzzed: The straight facts about the most used and abused drugs from alcohol to ecstasy*. New York: W. W. Norton, p. 219.

39. Gaines, L. K. (2003). The psychopharmacology and prevalence of drugs. In L. K. Gaines & P. B. Kraska (Eds.), *Drugs, crime, and justice* (2nd ed., pp. 50–86). Prospect Heights, IL: Waveland Press, p. 66.

40. U.S. Drug Enforcement Administration. (n.d.). *Drug fact sheet*. Washington, DC: U.S. Department of Justice. Retrieved from http://www.justice.gov/dea/druginfo/all_fact_sheets.pdf.

41. Gahlinger, P. M. (2001). *Illegal drugs: A complete guide to their history, chemistry, use and abuse*. Salt Lake City, UT: Sagebrush Press.

42. National Drug Intelligence Center. (2005). *Methamphetamine drug threat assessment*. Johnstown, PA: Author, p. 10.

43. U.S. Drug Enforcement Administration. (n.d.). *Drug fact sheet*. Washington, DC: U.S. Department of Justice. Retrieved from http://www.justice.gov/dea/druginfo/all_fact_sheets.pdf.

44. Hunt, D., Kuck, S., & Truitt, L. (2005). *Methamphetamine use: Lessons learned*. Cambridge, MA: Abt Associates, pp. iv–v.

45. Kuhn, C., Swartzwelder, S., & Wilson, W. (2003). *Buzzed: The straight facts about the most used and abused drugs from alcohol to ecstasy*. New York: W. W. Norton, p. 137.

46. Gaines, L. K. (2003). The psychopharmacology and prevalence of drugs. In L. K. Gaines & P. B. Kraska (Eds.), *Drugs, crime, and justice* (2nd ed., pp. 50–86). Prospect Heights, IL: Waveland Press, p. 75.

47. U.S. Drug Enforcement Administration. (n.d.). *Drug fact sheet*. Washington, DC: U.S. Department of Justice. Retrieved from http://www.justice.gov/dea/druginfo/all_fact_sheets.pdf.

48. Ibid.

49. Ibid.

50. National Institute on Drug Abuse. (2012). *Drug facts: Anabolic steroids.* Washington, DC: National Institutes of Health. Retrieved from http://www .drugabuse.gov/infofacts/steroids.html; see also Mosher, C. J., & Akins, S. (2007). *Drugs and drug policy: The control of consciousness alternation.* Thousand Oaks, CA: Sage.

51. Gaines, L. K. (2003). The psychopharmacology and prevalence of drugs. In L. K. Gaines & P. B. Kraska (Eds.), *Drugs, crime, and justice* (2nd ed., pp. 50–86). Prospect Heights, IL: Waveland Press, p. 81; National Institute on Drug Abuse. (2012). *Drug facts: Anabolic steroids.* Washington, DC: National Institutes of Health. Retrieved from http://www.drugabuse.gov/ infofacts/steroids.html.

52. U.S. Drug Enforcement Administration. (n.d.). *Drug fact sheet: Steroids.* Washington, DC: U.S. Department of Justice. Retrieved from http://www .justice.gov/dea/druginfo/drug_data_sheets/Steroids .pdf.

53. Pope, H. G., Kouri, E. M., & Hudson. J. I. (2000). Effects of supraphysiologic doses of testosterone on mood and aggression in normal men: A randomized controlled trial. *Archives of General Psychiatry, 57,* 133–140.

54. Pope, H. G., & Katz, D. L. (1988). Affective and psychotic symptoms associated with anabolic steroid use. *American Journal of Psychiatry, 145,* 487–490.

55. National Institute on Drug Abuse. (2012). *Drug facts: Anabolic steroids.* Washington, DC: National Institutes of Health. Retrieved from http://www .drugabuse.gov/infofacts/steroids.html.

56. National Institute on Drug Abuse. (2012). *Research report series: Inhalant abuse.* Washington, DC: National Institutes of Health. Retrieved from http:// www.drugabuse.gov/publications/research-reports/ inhalant-abuse.

57. Kuhn, C., Swartzwelder, S., & Wilson, W. (2003). *Buzzed: The straight facts about the most used and abused drugs from alcohol to ecstasy.* New York: W. W. Norton, p. 86.

58. Ibid., pp. 86–87.

59. Ibid., p. 89.

60. Mosher, C. J., & Akins, S. (2007). *Drugs and drug policy: The control of consciousness alteration.* Thousand Oaks, CA: Sage.

61. Freeman, S. (1988). *Drugs and civilization.* New York: Chelsea House, pp. 19–20.

62. Ibid., p. 20.

63. Tracey, S. W., & Acker, C. J. (Eds.). (2004). *Altering American consciousness: The history of alcohol and drug use in the United States, 1800–2000.* Amherst: University of Massachusetts Press, pp. 2–3.

64. NIDA International Program. (n.d.). Question 2: What is the history of opioid addiction in the United States? Retrieved from http://international.drugabuse.gov/ educational-opportunities/certificate-programs/meth- adone-research-web-guide/part-a/question-2-what-h.

65. Freeman, F. (1988). *Drugs and civilization.* New York: Chelsea House, pp. 64–67.

66. Ibid., p. 48.

67. NIDA International Program. (n.d.). Question 2: What is the history of opioid addiction in the United States? Retrieved from http://international. drugabuse.gov/educational-opportunities/certificate -programs/methadone-research-web-guide/part-a/ question-2-what-h.

68. Freeman, F. (1988). *Drugs and civilization.* New York: Chelsea House, pp. 48–49.

69. Ibid., pp. 49–50.

70. Flynn, J. C. (1991). *Cocaine: An in-depth look at the facts, science, history and future of the world's most addictive drug.* New York: Carol Publishing Group, pp. 24–31.

71. Ibid.

72. Vick, D. (2011). *Drugs and alcohol in the 21st century: Theory, behavior, and policy.* Sudbury, MA: Jones & Bartlett, p. 128.

73. Clark, N. H. (1965). *The drug years: Prohibition and social change in Washington.* Seattle: University of Washington Press.

74. Levine, H. G. (1984). The alcohol problem in America: From temperance to alcoholism. *British Journal of Addiction, 79,* 114.

75. Hall, W. (2010). What are the policy lessons of National Alcohol Prohibition in the United States, 1920–1933? *Addiction, 105,* 1171.

76. Abadinsky, H. (2007). *Organized crime.* Belmont, CA: Wadsworth, pp. 43–53.

77. Sloman, L. R. (1998). *Reefer madness: A history of marijuana.* New York: St. Martin's Griffin, p. 29.

78. Ray, R. (1983). *Drugs, society, and human behavior* (3rd ed.). St. Louis, MO: C. V. Mosby, p. 424.

79. Marihuana menaces youth. (1936). *Scientific American, 154,* 151.

80. Morais, R. C. (1996). Reefer madness. *Forbes, 157,* 118.

81. 395 U.S. 6; 89 S. Ct. 1532; 23 L. Ed. 2d 57.

82. Musto, D. F. (1972). The history of the Marihuana Tax Act of 1937. *Archives of General Psychiatry, 26,* 101–108.

83. Musto, D. F. (1972). The history of the Marihuana Tax Act of 1937. *Archives of General Psychiatry, 26,* 104.

84. Ibid., p. 105.

85. U.S. Census Bureau. (n.d.). *Selected charac- teristics of baby boomers 42 to 60 years old in 2006.* Retrieved from http://www.census.gov/ population/age/publications/files/2006babyboomers .pdf.

86. Westhues, K. (1972). *Society's shadow: Studies in the sociology of countercultures.* Toronto: McGraw-Hill Ryerson, pp. 15–17.

87. Miller, T. (1999). *The 60s communes: Hippies and beyond,* Syracuse, NY: Syracuse University Press.

88. Goode, E. (1999). *Drugs in American society* (5th ed.). Boston: McGraw-Hill, p. 70.

89. *Remarks at the Nancy Reagan Drug Abuse Center Benefit Dinner in Los Angeles, California.* (1989, January 4). Retrieved from http://www.reagan.utexas.edu/archives/speeches/1989/010489a.htm.

90. Chitwood, D. D., Murphy, S., & Rosenbaum. M. (2009). Reflections on the meaning of drug epidemics. *Journal of Drug Issues, 39*, 29–39.

91. Goode, E. (1999). *Drugs in American society* (5th ed.). Boston: McGraw-Hill, pp. 70–71.

92. Chitwood, D. D., Murphy, S., & Rosenbaum. M. (2009). Reflections on the meaning of drug epidemics. *Journal of Drug Issues, 39*, 29–39.

93. Witkin, G., Mukenge, M., Guttman, M., Arrarte, A., Glastris, K., Burgower, B., et al. (1991). The men who created crack. *U.S. News & World Report, 111*, 44–53.

94. Logan, E. (2004). The wrong race, committing crime, doing drugs, and maladjusted for motherhood: The nation's fury over "crack babies." In P. J. Schram & B. Koons-Witt, *Gendered (in)justice: Theory and practice in feminist criminology.* Long Grove, IL: Waveland Press, p. 247.

95. Lewis, D. C. (2004). Stop perpetuating the "crack baby" myth. *Brown University Digest of Addiction Theory and Application, 23*, 8.

96. Substance Abuse and Mental Health Services Administration. (2012). *Results from the 2011 National Survey on Drug Use and Health: Volume I; Summary of national findings.* Rockville, MD: Author. Retrieved from http://www.samhsa.gov/data/NSDUH/2k11Results/NSDUHresults2011.pdf.

97. U.S. Drug Enforcement Administration. (2011, May 12). *Feds crack down on illegal trafficking of Oxycodone* [Press release]. Retrieved from http://www.justice.gov/usao/gan/press/2011/05–12–11b.html.

98. U.S. Drug Enforcement Administration. (2008, June 24). *Online pharmacies and the problem of Internet drug abuse.* Retrieved from http://www.justice.gov/dea_old/pubs/cngrtest/ct062408.html.

99. Partnership for a Drug-Free America. (2006, May 16). *The Partnership Attitude Tracking Study (PATS): Teens in grades 7 through 12, 2005.* New York: Author.

100. RyansCause.org. (2006). About Ryan. Retrieved from http://www.ryanscause.org/section.php?id=1.

101. Mother crusades for online pharmacy regulation. (2005). *ABC10News.com.* Retrieved from http://www.10news.com/news/mother-crusades-for-online-pharmacy-regulation.

102. RyansCause.org. (2006). About Ryan. Retrieved from http://www.ryanscause.org/section.php?id=1.

103. Drug Enforcement Agency. (2009, April 31). *New rules governing Internet pharmacies go into effect next week* [News release]. Retrieved from http://www.justice.gov/dea/pubs/pressrel/pr041309.html.

104. Drug Enforcement Agency. (2008, October 1). *Congress passes Ryan Haight Online Pharmacy Consumer Protection Act* [News release]. Retrieved from http://www.justice.gov/dea/pubs/pressrel/pr100108.html.

105. Zilney, L.A. (2011). *Drugs: Policy, social costs, crime, and justice.* Boston: Prentice-Hall, p. 101.

106. Gagnon, M. A., & Lexchin, J. (2008). The cost of pushing pills: A new estimate of pharmaceutical promotion expenditures in the United States. *PloS Medicine, 5*(1). Retrieved from http://www.plosmedicine.org/article/info:doi/10.1371/journal.pmed.0050001.

107. Buchanan, J. F., & Brown, C. R. (1988). 'Designer drugs': A problem in clinical toxicology. *Medical Toxicology and Adverse Drug Experience, 3*, 1.

108. Seymour, R. B. (1997). Some so-called designer drugs are not. *Brown University Psychopharmacology Update, 8*, 1–2.

109. Ibid., p. 2.

110. National Institute on Drug Abuse. (2012). *Drug facts: Spice (synthetic marijuana).* Retrieved from http://www.drugabuse.gov/publications/drugfacts/spice-synthetic-marijuana.

111. Miller, M. C. (2011). Bath salts: A new way to get high? *Harvard Medical Health Letter, 28*, 8.

112. National Institute on Drug Abuse. (2012). *Drug facts: Synthetic cathinones ("bath salts").* Retrieved from http://www.drugabuse.gov/publications/drugfacts/synthetic-cathinones-bath-salts.

113. McBride, D. C., & McCoy, C. B. (2003). The drugs-crime relationship: An analytical framework. In L. K. Gaines & P. B. Kraska (Eds.), *Drugs, crime, and justice* (2nd ed., 87–108). Prospect Heights, IL: Waveland Press, p. 100.

114. Indiardi, J. A. (1981). Heroin addiction and street crime. In *International narcotics trafficking: Hearings before the Permanent Subcommittee on Investigations.* Washington, DC: U.S. Government Printing Office, p. 59.

115. Walker, S. (2006). *Sense and non-sense about crime and drugs: A policy guide* (6th ed.). Belmont, CA: Thomson Wadsworth.

116. McBride, D. C., & McCoy, C. B. (2003). The drugs-crime relationship: An analytical framework. In L. K. Gaines & P. B. Kraska (Eds.), *Drugs, crime, and justice* (2nd ed., 87–108). Prospect Heights, IL: Waveland Press, p. 108.

117. Zilney, K. A. (2011). *Drugs: Policy, social costs, crime, and justice.* Boston: Prentice Hall, p. 173.

118. McBride, D. C., & McCoy, C. B. (2003). The drugs-crime relationship: An analytical framework. In L. K. Gaines & P. B. Kraska (Eds.), *Drugs, crime, and justice* (2nd ed., 87–108). Prospect Heights, IL: Waveland Press, p. 108.

119. Ibid.

120. Nordstrom, B., & Dackis, C. A. (2011). Drugs and crime. *Journal of Psychiatry & Law, 39*, 666. See also Brook, J. S., Whiteman, M., Finch, S. J., & Cohen, P. (1996). Young adult drug use and delinquency: Childhood antecedents and adolescent mediators. *Journal of the Academy of Child and Adolescent Psychiatry, 35*, 1584–1592; White, H. R., Pandina, R. J., & LaGrange, R. L. (1987).

Longitudinal predictors of serious substance use and delinquency. *Criminology, 25*, 715–740.

121. Nordstrom, B., & Dackis, C. A. (2011). Drugs and crime. *Journal of Psychiatry & Law, 39*, 683.

122. Goldstein, P. J. (1989). Drugs and violent crime. In N. A. Weiner & M. E. Wolfgang (Eds.), *Pathways to criminal violence* (pp. 16–48). Newbury Park, CA: Sage.

123. Ibid., p. 30.

124. Abadinsky, H. (1997). *Drug abuse: An introduction* (3rd ed.). Chicago: Nelson-Hall, p. 308.

125. Gusfield. J. (1975). The (f)utility of knowledge? The relation of social science to public policy toward drugs. *Annals, 147*, 13.

126. Abadinsky, H. (1997). *Drug abuse: An introduction* (3rd ed.). Chicago: Nelson-Hall, p. 357.

127. Currie, E. (1993). *Reckoning: Drugs, the cities, and the American future.* New York: Hill & Wang.

128. Office of National Drug Control Policy. (2010, March 17). *National interdiction command and control plan.* Washington, DC: Author. Retrieved from http://www.whitehousedrugpolicy.gov/pdf/usic_2011_niccp.pdf.

129. Ibid., pp. 9–10.

130. Office of National Drug Control Policy. (n.d.). *High Intensity Drug Trafficking Areas (HIDTA) program.* Washington, DC: Author. Retrieved from http://www.whitehouse.gov/ondcp/high-intensity-drug-trafficking-areas-program.

131. Ibid., n.p.

132. Ohio High Intensity Drug Trafficking Area. (2009, April). *Drug market analysis 2009.* Washington, DC: National Drug Intelligence Center, U.S. Department of Justice.

133. European Commission. (2013). *Public opinion.* Retrieved from http://ec.europa.eu/public_opinion/index_en.htm.

134. Europe Opinion Research Group. (2003). *Public safety, exposure to drug-related problems and crime: Public opinion survey* (p. 62). Retrieved from http://ec.europa.eu/public_opinion/archives/ebs/ebs_181_en.pdf.

135. Van Dijk, J. (2008). *The world of crime: Breaking the silence on problems of security, justice, and development across the world.* Thousand Oaks, CA: Sage, pp. 107–109.

136. Farrell, G. (1998). A global empirical review of drug crop eradication and United Nations' crop substitution and alternative development strategies. *Journal of Drug Issues, 28*, 395–436.

137. United National Economic and Social Council. (1996). *Crops from which drugs are extracted and appropriate strategies for their reduction* (Commission on Narcotic Drugs, 39th Session document E/CN.7/1996/11), pp. 16–25.

138. Farrell, G. (1998). A global empirical review of drug crop eradication and United Nations' crop substitution and alternative development strategies. *Journal of Drug Issues, 28*, 395–436.

139. National Drug Intelligence Center. (2008, December). Cocaine. In *National drug threat assessment, 2009* (pp. 1–8). Washington, DC: Author. Retrieved from http://www.justice.gov/archive/ndic/pubs31/31379/31379p.pdf.

140. Brooke, J. (1990). Near-acquittal of Barry is outraging Colombians. *New York Times*, p. 4, as cited in Abadinsky, H. (1997). *Drug abuse: An introduction* (3rd ed.). Chicago: Nelson-Hall, p. 344.

141. Wisotsky, S. (1987). *Breaking the impasse in the war on drugs.* Westport, CT: Greenwood, p. 57, as cited in Abadinsky, H. (1997). *Drug abuse: An introduction* (3rd ed.). Chicago: Nelson-Hall, p. 344.

142. Morales, E. (1986). Coca and cocaine economy and social change in the Andes of Peru. *Economic Development and Social Change, 35*, 157, as cited in Abadinsky, H. (1997). *Drug abuse: An introduction* (3rd ed.). Chicago: Nelson-Hall, pp. 344–345.

143. National Drug Intelligence Center. (2009, July). *Domestic cannabis cultivation assessment, 2009.* Washington, DC: U.S. Department of Justice. Retrieved from http://www.justice.gov/archive/ndic/pubs37/37035/37035p.pdf.

144. Ibid., p. 29.

145. Lurigio, A. J. (2008). The first 20 years of drug treatment courts: A brief description of their history and impact. *Federal Probation, 72*, 13.

146. Hennessey, J. J. (2001). Introduction: Drug courts in operation. *Journal of Offender Rehabilitation, 33*, 1–10.

147. Lurigio, A. J. (2008). The first 20 years of drug treatment courts: A brief description of their history and impact. *Federal Probation, 72*, 13–17.

148. Huddleston, C. W., Marlow, D. B., & Casebolt, R. (2008). *A national report card on drug courts and other problem-solving court programs in the United States.* Washington, DC: National Drug Court Institute, p. 2.

149. Fox, C. L., & Huddleston, C. W. (2003, May). Drug courts in the U.S. *Issues of Democracy, 8*, 13–19.

150. Cooper, C. S. (2007). Drug courts: Just the beginning; Getting other areas of public policy in sync. *Substance Use & Misuse, 42*, 243–256.

151. Stinchcomb, J. B. (2010). Drug courts: Conceptual foundation, empirical findings, and policy implications. *Drugs: Education, Prevention and Policy, 17*, 161–162.

152. Wolfer, L. (2006). Graduates speak: A qualitative exploration of drug court graduates' views of the strengths and weaknesses of the program. *Contemporary Drug Problems, 33*, 303–320.

153. McBride, D. C., Terry-McElrath, Y., Harwood, H., Inciardi, J. A., & Leukefeld, C. (2009). Reflections on drug policy. *Journal of Drug Issues, 39*, 76.

154. Abadinsky, H. (1997). *Drug abuse: An introduction* (3rd ed.). Chicago: Nelson-Hall, pp. 319–320.

155. Ibid., pp. 320–323.

156. ProCon.org. (2013). *Medical marijuana.* Retrieved from http://medicalmarijuana.procon.org/view.resource.php?resourceID=000881.

157. California Health and Safety Code Section 11362.5.

158. Healy, J. (2012). Voters ease marijuana laws in 2 states, but legal questions remain. *New York Times.* Retrieved from http://www.nytimes.com/2012/11/08/us/politics/marijuana-laws-eased-in-colorado-and-washington.html.

159. Liptak, K. (2012). Obama: Enforcing pot laws in states that have legalized it not a top priority. *CNN Politics.* Retrieved from http://whitehouse.blogs.cnn.com/2012/12/14/obama-enforcing-pot-laws-in-states-that-have-legalized-it-not-a-top-priority/.

160. McBride, D. C., Terry-McElrath, Y., Harwood, H., Inciardi, J. A., & Leukefeld, C. (2009). Reflections on drug policy. *Journal of Drug Issues, 39,* 71.

161. Duff, C. (2010). Enabling places and enabling resources: New Directions for harm reduction research and practice. *Drug and Alcohol Review, 29,* 337.

162. Delgado, C. (2004). Evaluation of needle exchange programs. *Public Health Nursing, 21,* 171.

163. Burris, S., Finucane, D., Gallagher, H., & Grace, J. (1996). The legal strategies used in operating syringe exchange programs in the United States. *American Journal of Public Health, 86,* 1161–1166.

164. Ibid., p. 1162.

165. Delgado, C. (2004). Evaluation of needle exchange programs. *Public Health Nursing, 21,* 172.

166. Ibid.

167. McBride, D. C., Terry-McElrath, Y., Harwood, H., Inciardi, J. A., & Leukefeld, C. (2009). Reflections on drug policy. *Journal of Drug Issues, 39,* 81.

168. McBride, D. C., & McCoy, C. B. (2003). In L. K. Gaines & P. B. Kraska (Eds.), *Drugs, crime, and justice* (2nd ed.). Prospect Heights, IL: Waveland Press, pp. 114–115.

169. Ibid., p. 115.

170. Currie, E. (1993). *Reckoning: Drugs, the cities, and the American future.* New York: Hill & Wang, p. 279.

171. Penhaul, K. (2003, October 5). Drug kingpin's killer seeks Colombia office. *Boston Globe.* Retrieved from http://www.boston.com/news/nation/articles/2003/10/05/drug_kingpins_killer_seeks_colombia_office/?page=full

172. Ceaser, M. (2008, June 2). At home on Pablo Escobar's ranch. *BBC News.* Retrieved from http://news.bbc.co.uk/2/hi/americas/7390584.stm

173. McFadden, R. D. (1993). Head of Medellin cocaine cartel is killed by troops in Colombia. *New York Times.* Retrieved from http://www.nytimes.com/1993/12/03/world/head-of-medellin-cocaine-cartel-is-killed-by-troops-in-colombia.html?pagewanted=all&src=pm

174. McBride, D. C., & McCoy, C. B. (2003). In L. K. Gaines & P. B. Kraska (Eds.), *Drugs, crime, and justice* (2nd ed.). Prospect Heights, IL: Waveland Press, pp. 100–119.

Photo Credits

CHAPTER 1

Photo, chapter opener, page xxiv. © iStockphoto Veer-AYI030014-Streetlight.

Photo, page 4. © iStockphoto.com/maureenpr.

Photo, page 6. © AP Photo/BEN MARGOT.

Photo, page 8. © AP Photo/Rich Pedroncelli.

Photo, page 15. © AP Photo/Mike Derer.

Photo, page 19. iStockphoto.com/kmathews

Photo, page 20. © http://creativecommons.org/licenses/by-sa/2.5/.

Image, page 25. © BananaStock/Thinkstock

Photo, page 28. © iStockphoto.com/John Bolster

CHAPTER 2

Photo, chapter opener, page 32. © iStockphoto.com/William Mahar.

Photo, page 34. © AP Photo/Jacquelyn Martin.

Photo, page 37. NASA, JPL.

Photo, page 40. http://commons.wikimedia.org/wiki/File:Cesare_Beccaria_1738–1794.jpg.

Photo, page 41. © Comstock/Thinkstock.

Photo, page 42. ©iStockphoto.com/stephen mulcahey.

Photo, page 43. © David Owen.

Photo, page 47. © iStockphoto.com/Lisa F. Young.

Photo, page 40. © Lloyd Goldberg.

Photo, page 50. Public domain.

Photo, page 54. © Comstock/Thinkstock.

CHAPTER 3

Photo, chapter opener, page 60. © AP Photo/Joe Amon.

Photo, page 64. © Staunited (San Quentin).

Photo, page 64. © Public domain (electric chair).

Photo, page 65. © iStockphoto.com/Darren Mower.

Photo, page 67. © iStockphoto.com/enis izgi.

Photo, page 71. © Sean Murphy/Lifesize/Thinkstock.

Photo, page 72. © iStockphoto.com/Darren Mower.

Photo, page 76. © iStockphoto/monkeybusinessimages.

CHAPTER 4

Photo, chapter opener, page 85. Source: Cicely D. Fawcett and Alice Lee, "A Second Study of the Variation and Correlation of the Human Skull, With Special Reference to the Naqada Crania," Biometrika, Vol. 1, No. 4. (Aug., 1902), pp. 408–467: Plate IV: "Figure 2. Craniphor, Goniophor, and Scriber."

Photo, page 86. © iStockphoto.com/Chris Price.

Photo, page 87. Illustration (anonym): *The Physiognomist's Own Book: an introduction to physiognomy drawn from the writings of Lavater*, Philadelphia; Pittsburg 1841.

Photo, page 87. © Charles Le Brun (heads).

Photo, page 88. © Julia Margaret Cameron.

Photo, page 89. Public domain.

Photo, page 90. © Cesar Lombroso.

Photo, page 92. FBI/Wakefield Prison

Photo, page 96. National Park Service Digital Image Archives.

Photo, page 97. © Creatas/Thinkstock.

Photo, page 98. © Digital Vision/Photodisc/Thinkstock.

Photo, page 102. Public domain.

CHAPTER 5

Photo, chapter opener, page 108. © iStockphoto.com/Jon Schulte

Photo, chapter opener, page 111. Public domain

Photo, page 112. Source: Henry H. Goddard's The Kallikak Family, 1912.

Photo, page 113. © iStockphoto.com/Richard Upshur

Photo, page 115. © Hemera Technologies/PhotoObjects.Net/Thinkstock

Photo, page 117. Office of Biological and Environmental Research of the U.S. Department of Energy Office of Science. science.energy.gov/ber/.

Photo, page 122. US National Institutes of Health, National Institute on Aging.

Photo, page 123. U.S. National Library of Medicine, National Institutes of Health.

Photo, page 124. Public domain.

Photo, page 125. © AP Photo/M. SPENCER GREEN.

Photo, page 128. ©iStockphoto.com/Zurijeta.

Photo, page 130. ©iStockphoto.com/ Igor Skrbic.

Photo, page 131. © Jupiterimages/Pixland/ Thinkstock.

Photo, page 132. ©iStockphoto.com/Glenn Bo.

CHAPTER 6

Photo, chapter opener, page 136. © Ferdinand Schmutzer.

Photo, page 141. © 2012 Max Mag Theme.

Photo, page 144. © Rayes/Lifesize/Thinkstock.

Photo, page 150. Public domain.

Photo, page 157. © AP Photo/Mark R. Rummel, Times Herald.

Photo, page 158. © AP Photo/J. Scott Applewhite

Photo, page 128. ©iStockphoto.com/Zurijeta.

Photo, page 130. ©iStockphoto.com/ Igor Skrbic.

Photo, page 131. © Jupiterimages/Pixland/ Thinkstock.

Photo, page 132. ©iStockphoto.com/Glenn Bo.

CHAPTER 7

Photo, chapter opener, page 162. © BananaStock/ Thinkstock

Photo, page 164. Public domain.

Photo, page 165. © Photodisc/Thinkstock.

Photo, page 166. Library of Congress Prints and Photographs Collection.

Photo, page 168. ©iStockphoto.com/ Denis Jr. Tangney.

Photo, page 169. Public domain.

Photo, page 180. © Digital Vision/Thinkstock.

Photo, page 181. © J. Ross Baughman.

Photo, page 182. © iStockphoto.com/Catherine Yeulet.

Photo, page 183. U.S. Marshals Service photo.

Photo, page 184. © Jupiterimages/Comstock/ Thinkstock.

CHAPTER 8

Photo, chapter opener, page 194. © iStockphoto. com/Buretsu

Photo, page 197. National Archives and Records Administration (Chicago 1930s).

Photo, page 197. © Ildar Sagdejev (modern day Chicago).

Photo, page 199. © Galen Parks Smith.

Photo, page 200. © Stefan Didam (bison).

Photo, page 201. © Public domain.

Photo, page 206. © Danny Lyon, Environmental Protection Agency, Source: U.S. National Archives and Records Administration.

Photo, page 210. U.S. Marshals Service photo.

CHAPTER 9

Photo, chapter opener, page 214. © AP Photo/ RODRIGO ABD

Photo, page 216. © AP Photo/Sandy Huffaker.

Photo, page 221. © Jupiter Images/Creatas/ Thinkstock.

Photo, page 228. © iStockphoto.com/Stuart Monk.

Photo, page 229. © iStockphoto.com/Igor Skrbic.

Photo, page 235. ©iStockphoto.com/Cresta Johnson.

Photo, page 237. © Jack Hollingsworth/Photodisc/ Thinkstock.

Photo, page 242. © AP Photo/Ben Margot.

Photo, page 244. © Jupiter Images/Comstock/ Thinkstock.

Photo, page 245. © iStockphoto.com/svetikd.

Photo, page 246. © Jupiterimages/liquidlibrary/ Thinkstock.

Photo, page 249. © Florida Department of Corrections.

Photo, page 242. © AP Photo/Ben Margot.

CHAPTER 10

Photo, chapter opener, page 252. © iStockphoto .com/Luca Cepparo

Photo, page 254. © iStockphoto.com/Huguette Roe.

Photo, page 256. © Hemera Technologies/AbleStock.com/Thinkstock.

Photo, page 259. © Jupiter Images/Polka Dot/Thinkstock.

Photo, page 265. © iStockphoto.com/Antonio Ribeiro.

Photo, page 268. © iStockphoto.com/Andrew Cribb.

Photo, page 275. Federal Bureau of Investigation.

CHAPTER 11

Photo, chapter opener, page 284. © iStockphoto.com/Rich Legg.

Photo, page 287. © iStockphoto.com/Anthony Baggett.

Photo, page 295. © Brand X Pictures/Thinkstock.

Photo, page 302. Public domain.

Photo, page 306. http://www.cbsnews.com/2300–204_162–10014847–5.html.

Photo, page 317. © Florida Department of Corrections.

Photo, page 242. © AP Photo/Ben Margot.

CHAPTER 12

Photo, chapter opener, page 314. © iStockphoto.com/jabejon.

Photo, page 317. © iStockphoto.com/PIKSEL.

Photo, page 318. Lincoln Police Department.

Photo, page 317. © Florida Department of Corrections.

Photo, page 321. © ASC.

Photo, page 322. © Digital Vision/Thinkstock (wedding).

Photo, page 322. © Christopher Robbins/Digital Vision/Thinkstock (working).

Photo, page 323. United States Department of Justice.

Photo, page 324. United States Department of Justice.

Photo, page 328. United States Department of Justice.

CHAPTER 13

Photo, chapter opener, page 336. © AP Photo/David Handschuh.

Photo, page 329. United States Department of Justice.

Photo, page 341. © Erik Hester/Lifesize/Thinkstock.

Photo, page 342. © Erik Snyder/Lifesize/Thinkstock.

Photo, page 347. © Stockbyte/Thinkstock.

Photo, page 352. ©iStockphoto.com /Rich Juziak.

Photo, page 356. Thomas Nast.

Photo, page 368. Stockbyte/Thinkstock.

Photo, page 371. Jupiterimages/Comstock/Thinkstock.

CHAPTER 14

Photo, chapter opener, page 378. ©iStockphoto.com/Charles Daniel Howell.

Photo, page 381. © Bill Pugliano/Stringer/Getty Images News/Getty Images.

Photo, page 385. © Mike Stewart/Sygma/Corbis (Matthew Shepard).

Photo, page 385. © AP Photo (James Byrd, Jr.).

Photo, page 388. © AP Photo/David Guttenfelder.

Photos, pages 398–399. FBI.

Photo, page 408. © Staff Sergeant Preston Chasteen, Department of Defense.

CHAPTER 15

Photo, chapter opener, page 416. © ©iStockphoto.com/jeff reisdorfer.

Photo, page 423. Public domain.

Photo, page 426. © Comstock/Thinkstock.

Photo, page 429. ©ThinkStock.

Photo, page 432. © AP Photo/Kelley McCall.

Photo, page 437. © AP Photo/David Bundy.

Photo, page 438. © AP AP Photo/Lindsey Bauman.

Photo, page 441. © Joe Mabel.

Index

Figures, boxes, and tables are indicated by f, b, or t following the page number.

SAGE researchmethods

The essential online tool for researchers from the world's leading methods publisher

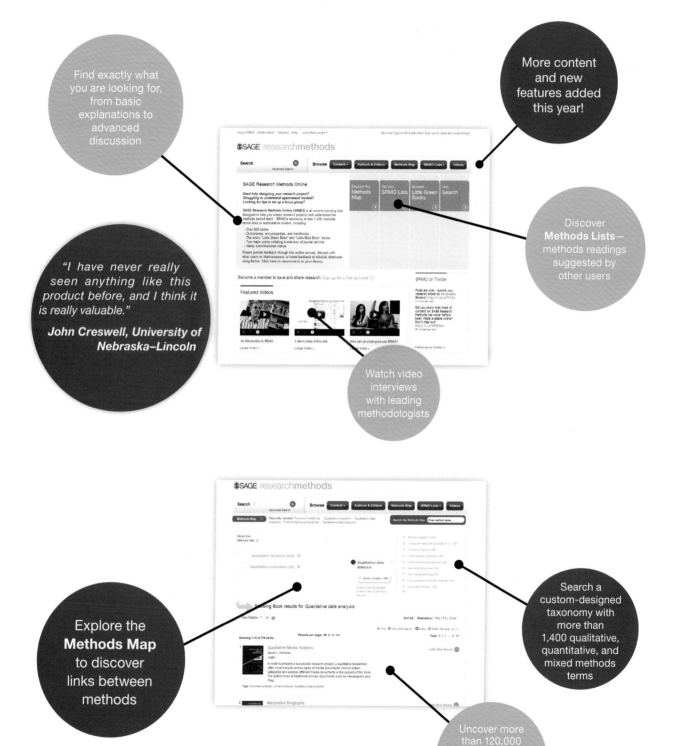

Find exactly what you are looking for, from basic explanations to advanced discussion

More content and new features added this year!

"I have never really seen anything like this product before, and I think it is really valuable."

John Creswell, University of Nebraska–Lincoln

Discover **Methods Lists**— methods readings suggested by other users

Watch video interviews with leading methodologists

Explore the **Methods Map** to discover links between methods

Search a custom-designed taxonomy with more than 1,400 qualitative, quantitative, and mixed methods terms

Uncover more than 120,000 pages of book, journal, and reference content to support your learning

Find out more at
www.sageresearchmethods.com